KAISER AND FÜHRER: A COMPARATIVE STUDY
OF PERSONALITY AND POLITICS

ROBERT G.L. WAITE

Kaiser and Führer:
A Comparative Study of
Personality and Politics

UNIVERSITY OF TORONTO PRESS
Toronto Buffalo London

© University of Toronto Press Incorporated 1998
Toronto Buffalo London
Printed in Canada

ISBN 0-8020-4185-X

Printed on acid-free paper

Canadian Cataloguing in Publication Data

Waite, Robert G.L. (Robert George Leeson), 1919–
   Kaiser and Führer : a comparative study of personality and politics

   Includes index.
   ISBN 0-8020-4185-X

   1. William II, German Emperor, 1859–1941.   2. Hitler, Adolf, 1889–1945.
   3. Germany – Politics and government – 1888–1918.   4. Germany – Politics and
   government – 1933–1945.   5. Heads of State – Germany – Biography.
   I. Title.

   DD229.W33 1998   943.08′4′092   C97-931529-8

University of Toronto Press acknowledges the financial assistance to its publishing
program of the Canada Council for the Arts and the Ontario Arts Council.

For Anne
in memoriam

Contents

PREFACE ix
ACKNOWLEDGMENTS xiii

1 Two Profiles 3

2 *Weltanschauungen*: Their Intellectual, Aesthetic, Religious, and Racial Worlds 68

3 Kaiser and Führer as Rulers in Peacetime: Theory and Practice 124

4 Kaiser and Führer as Rulers in War 203

5 Psychological Dimensions 242

6 Kaiser and Führer: The Childhood Experience 293

Reflections 346

Addendum 1: Scatology in German Life and Letters 352
Addendum 2: The *Kriegsschuldfrage* and Historical Evidence 356
Addendum 3: The Kaiser in Exile 359
Addendum 4: Historical Continuity versus Change 362
Addendum 5: Coprophilic Perversion? 365
Addendum 6: Hitler and Incest 372
Addendum 7: Dr Bloch and the Genesis of Hitler's Anti-Semitism 376
Addendum 8: Hitler and Psychiatrists 378

NOTES 380
INDEX 493

Preface

La comparaison est l'illumination réciproque.

Georges Bas-Flûte, ca. 1784

For many years I have been fascinated by the puzzling personalities of Wilhelm II and Adolf Hitler and the parts they played in shaping the history of their times; it occurred to me that it would be interesting to compare these two rulers. In doing so I have focused on their personalities; on their intellectual, aesthetic, and religious worlds – the poems and prose they wrote, the books they read, the music they enjoyed, the watercolours they painted, the sermons they preached, the racism and anti-Semitism they espoused; on their phenomenal successes and their monumental blunders as political leaders, as well as their roles in the two world wars of the twentieth century; on their psychological problems to show how these problems affected their political behaviour; and finally, on the traumatic experiences of their childhoods.

In attempting to understand the Kaiser and the Führer more fully, I have turned to psychotherapists, for I found that both men were psychologically unbalanced, and I needed all the professional help I could get in trying to fathom their bizarre and often self-defeating behaviour.

After completing his massive dual biography of Stalin and Hitler, Lord Bullock reached the melancholy conclusion, 'You can't explain people. It's one of the fallacies.'[1] Perhaps Bullock is right. We may not be able fully to *explain* the Kaiser or the Führer – or anyone else, for that matter. But we can seek to deepen our understanding of them, and for this purpose the insights of psychotherapy prove helpful.

In comparing any two people, there is a common tendency to consider only their similarities. But I have found that differences between Kaiser and Führer are equally revealing. By identifying important differences as well as striking

similarities in the personalities and performances of these two German rulers, I
hope to have provided some of the 'reciprocal illumination' that the process of
comparison offers.

Problems of Biography

L'histoire c'est un sac de ruses qu'on joue contre les morts.

Voltaire

Portraits of historical figures, no matter how carefully they are painted, will
inevitably be marred by defects and distortions. Because biographers cannot
possibly re-create a human life in full we must decide what is to be left out. And
although we may have gone through 'mountains of facts,' we may miss information that could have changed or modified our thinking. Two recently discovered poems, written by Hitler in 1915 and 1916, for example, reveal a person
capable of compassionate, even tender concern for others – an aspect of his brutal yet complex personality I had not adequately explored in my first biography.

Important sources may also have been deliberately destroyed (for example,
Eleanor Roosevelt burned revealing letters; Richard Nixon erased incriminating tapes; Oliver North shredded government documents). Published materials
may also have been abridged or bowdlerized by sympathetic editors, as were
diaries and documents dealing with the Kaiser and Hitler's memoirs and
speeches.[2] Moreover, we may unwittingly rely on sources that later prove to be
spurious. Reputable biographers of Hitler, for instance, have trusted the 'memoirs' of Josef Greiner and Brigette Dowling Hitler; both accounts are bogus.[3]

The sheer passage of time may play tricks on the dead. We of the present all
too often forget that the present, so familiar to us, once lay in some distant,
unknown future. Made wise by the passage of time, we know now what our
subjects could not possibly have known: how it would all come out. Fully
aware of the future consequences of our subjects' past decisions, we may judge
them with less charity than they deserve.

Biographers who reject the insights of psychology are prone to a different
kind of distortion. Ill-equipped to cope with psychically disturbed people,
they are likely to dismiss complex or aberrant behaviour as 'inexplicable' or
'deranged' – characterizations that do little to further our understanding. Yet
biographers who are intrigued by psychological dimensions of their subjects
must also guard against distortion. 'Psychohistorians' often become so captivated by psychologically rich material that they ignore more prosaic but no less
important evidence, and they sometimes write as if all aspects of their subjects'
careers can be explained by an analysis of their psychopathologies.

I trust that the following pages will avoid such reductionism and will not invite the conclusion that the Kaiser and the Führer were so completely patho-logical, or so irresponsible or so repellent that they could neither rule effectively nor win the confidence of their people. On the contrary, both leaders proved that they could, at times, govern with stunning effect, and both were immensely appealing to millions of Germans.

The different perspectives from which we see historical figures may produce another kind of distortion. The views of contemporaries will be different from those of later historians because contemporaries often receive distorted pictures of their political leaders. They cannot know in any detail the private lives of their rulers, and the public images they perceive may have been deliberate dis-tortions fashioned by propagandists or ministers of 'enlightenment' or by 'spin doctors.' Moreover, contemporaries are likely to indulge the very human ten-dency to believe what they prefer to believe about their heroes. Since Germans wanted to believe positive things about their Kaiser and their Führer, their images of these men were quite different and often much more favourable than those that have emerged after years of historical research.

Differences between image and reality may also give us widely divergent conceptions of what 'the dead' were once actually like. The traditional image of Otto von Bismarck, as the 'Iron Chancellor' – stolid, imperturbable master of the 'politics of realism,' the *Realpolitiker* incarnate – varies considerably from the realities discovered by historians. This man of overpowering presence actu-ally spoke in a thin, almost falsetto voice, walked with mincing steps, and was given to fits of uncontrollable weeping. This ruthless man of 'Blood and Iron' whined incessantly about real and imagined physical problems. Bismarck could not rest at night until his doctor 'like a mother with a restless child' tucked him in, murmured words of assurance, and held his hand until the great man dropped off to sleep.[4]

If biographers ignore this side of Bismarck's complex personality – or if they emphasize it too much – they will play tricks on the dead. For historic truth about Bismarck does not, as the cliché would have it, 'lie somewhere between the two extremes.' Rather, it lies in recognizing the validity of both concep-tions, for Otto von Bismarck was at once a hard-headed master of statecraft and a deeply disturbed personality.

There is a large measure of truth in Voltaire's cynical aphorism. Given the frailties of human nature, biographers – even those with the best intentions – will inevitably 'play tricks on the dead.' In the following pages I will do my best to play as few as possible on Wilhelm von Hohenzollern and Adolf Hitler.

R.G.L.W.
Williamstown and Temagami

Acknowledgments

I am delighted to have this opportunity of thanking people and institutions whose generous support through the years helped make this book possible.

For fellowships and grants in aid of research, I am indebted to the John Simon Guggenheim Foundation, the Fulbright Commission, the Social Science Research Council, the American Council of Learned Societies, and the Oakley Center for Humanities and Social Sciences of Williams College. The staffs of several archives and libraries have given me friendly professional assistance. These institutions include the Oberösterreichisches Landesarchiv of Linz, the Österreichische Nationalbibliothek in Vienna, the Bundesarchiv in Koblenz, the Bayerische Staatsbibliothek, the Bayerisches Haupstaatsarchiv, and the Institut für Zeitgeschichte in Munich, the former United States Document Center of Berlin and the Institute for Contemporary History and the Wiener Library in London, and the National Archives and the Library of Congress Manuscript Division in Washington. The Inter-Library Loan Department of Williams College has been of immense help. I also received cordial and imaginative assistance from The L.J. Verroen, the Archivist and Curator of Huis Doorn (Doorn House) in Holland, and from Henk Ooft, research librarian of the Rijksarchief in Utrecht. I am also grateful to Her Majesty Queen Elizabeth II for gracious permission to use and to quote material from family letters, those of her great, great grandparents, Queen Victoria and Prince Albert, from her great-grandaunt, Victoria, the Princess Royal (later the Empress Frederick), who was the mother of her distant cousin, Kaiser Wilhelm II. This correspondence is now held in the Royal Archives at Windsor Castle.

Friends and colleagues have given generously of their time and talent in reading my manuscript. Those who have offered valuable criticism on specific chapters include James MacGregor Burns, Edson M. Chick, Craig Clemow, Richard Q. Ford, John M. Hyde, C.J. Koepp, Elizabeth M. Kohut, William H.

Pierson Jr, E.F. Proelss, Robert F. Savadove, MD, and my former students Jeffrey and Peggy Sutton. The entire manuscript has profited from the critical reading of Oscar Collier, Harlan P. Hanson, Richard M. Hunt, Manly Johnson, Richard O. Rouse, and Heinz Just.

Special thanks are due Arlene Bouras for her careful reading and to my friend and former colleague Thomas A. Kohut, who not only drew on his comprehensive knowledge of Wilhelm II to give me the benefit of trenchant criticism, but with remarkable generosity permitted me to use his own research notes from German archives that I was unable to visit. Such notes are identified as (TAK).

I am especially grateful to Fred H. Stocking, the retired Morris Professor of Rhetoric at Williams College. He laboured mightily over several drafts to restrain my often unruly prose and offered astute suggestions about organization and sequence. His keen editorial eye, his good-humoured patience, and his generosity of spirit were simply invaluable. Without his help this book would not have been written.

Frederick William, Crown Prince of Prussia, 1884. The Kaiser's father, the future
Kaiser Friedrich III. (Photograph by Reichard & Lindner. The Royal Archives © Her
Majesty the Queen. Reproduced with permission.)

Victoria, Crown Princess of Prussia, 18 January 1883. The Kaiser's mother, the future Empress Friedrich. (Photograph by Reichard & Lindner. The Royal Archives © Her Majesty the Queen. Reproduced with permission.)

The Führer's father, Alois Hitler, ca. 1895. (Courtesy of the Library of Congress.)

The Führer's mother, Klara Pölzl Hitler, ca. 1895. (Photograph by Albert Reich, *Aus Adolf Hitlers Heimat*, Munich, 1933. Courtesy of the Library of Congress.)

The Kaiser in his first sailor suit, ca. 1862. (The Royal Archives © Her Majesty the Queen. Reproduced with permission.)

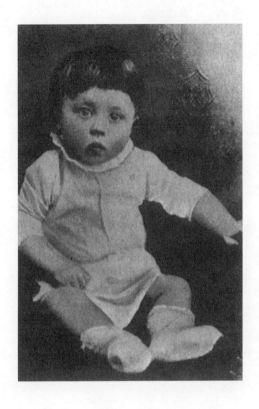

The Führer as a child, ca. 1890. (Photograph by Heinrich Hoffmann, *Hitler wie ihn Keiner kennt*, Munich [1942]. Courtesy of the Library of Congress.)

KAISER AND FÜHRER: A COMPARATIVE STUDY

1

Two Profiles

KAISER WILHELM II

The world in perplexity murmurs, who is this man that changes and multiplies himself incessantly ...?

Eca de Queiroz, 1891

Wilhelm II, last of the Hohenzollern rulers of Germany, was bequeathed a proud inheritance. His mother was the eldest daughter of Queen Victoria, his father the scion of the Hohenzollerns, the royal family of Brandenburg–Prussia, whose ancestral home had originally been in southern Germany along the upper Neckar, bordering on Lake Constance. In 1227 the ducal house had split; one branch of the Hohenzollerns remained in the south, the other – Wilhelm's ancestors – moved north, where they later converted to Protestantism, and became electors of Brandenburg in the Holy Roman Empire, then kings of Prussia, and finally German emperors of the 'Second Reich' (1871–1918).

In 1701 Elector Friedrich Hohenzollern of Brandenburg was crowned the first king of Prussia, as Friedrich I (1701–13). Among his notable successors was Friedrich Wilhelm I (1713–40), honoured by Germans as the founder of the Prussian army and the rigidly efficient bureaucracy. Upon those twin foundations he fulfiled his promises of establishing Prussia 'on a rock of bronze' and pushing a 'ramrod up the backs of my people.'[1] His army regulations of 1726 were a preview of the future: 'When one takes the oath to the flag one renounces oneself and surrenders entirely even one's life and everything to the monarch ... Through this blind obedience one receives the grace and confirmation of the title of soldier.'

The king's efforts to control the private lives of his subjects often seemed to fulfil the royal boast that 'salvation is God's affair; everything else belongs to me.'[2] He also tried to make Prussia economically self-sufficient in time of war. Oswald Spengler paid Friedrich Wilhelm no compliment in hailing him as 'the first National-Socialist.'[3]

His more famous son, Friedrich II (*der Grosse* – 'Frederick the Great,' 1740–86), one of the 'enlightened despots,' was a musician (whose compositions are still played), a political theorist, poet, and military strategist famous for his exploits in the Seven Years' War, when – with the armies of France, Austria, and Russia arrayed against him and outnumbered five to one – he outmanoeuvred and outfought all his enemies with the cunning of a wolf at bay and emerged victorious. 'Good Old Fritz,' the King of Prussia, became a pan-German hero.

Both Kaiser and Führer identified with Friedrich, and each liked to think of himself as a worthy successor. When he opened the first parliament of his reign in 1888, Wilhelm II ordered his guard of honour to dress in the eighteenth-century uniforms of Frederick the Great's army. On another occasion he garbed himself and his court in Friedrichian costume for an official portrait by Adolf von Menzel.[4] In many rooms of the Kaiser's home in exile – entrance hall, sitting-room, study, and library – his own portraits or statues were placed near pictures or busts of his illustrious ancestors. Wilhelm's library contains a complete set of the king's writings along with the hero-worshipping, ten-volume biography by Thomas Carlyle. Friedrich's picture, along with his mother's, are among the portraits in his bedroom.[5]

Adolf Hitler believed that his eyes, hands, and cranial measurements were strikingly similar to those of Friedrich. He also cherished the mistaken notion that he and the 'Philosopher King' thought very much alike, musing in his field headquarters, 'By the way, I am delighted to find in the writings of Old Fritz that his way of thinking is so similar to my own.'[6] Along with a picture of his mother, Hitler carried Frederick the Great's portrait with him as a talisman. In April 1945, with Allied armies closing in from all sides, he eagerly reread pages of the German translation of Carlyle's biography in search of a miraculous sign that he, like the beleaguered Friedrich of 1762, would suddenly be rescued by the death of an arch-enemy. Such a sign seemed to have come in the sudden death of President Franklin Roosevelt.[7]

The Kaiser's grandfather was Wilhelm I, the King of Prussia (1861–88), who, while retaining that title, also became the first ruler of the German Empire, or Second Reich (1871–1918). The Kaiser's father was Friedrich III, the 'Tragic Emperor' who died after ruling for only 99 days in 1888.

Kaiser Wilhelm II (1888–1918) was understandably proud of his predecessors, but he saw himself destined for higher things: he would be the greatest monarch of history, and *arbiter mundi* (arbiter of the world). The prospects for this brash and gifted young Hohenzollern seemed very bright indeed, for the imperial throne he ascended at the age of twenty-nine was, next perhaps to Queen Victoria's, the most stable and comfortably situated in the world. Germany was undoubtedly the strongest military and economic power on the Continent, and the new ruler could turn for counsel to his wise old chancellor and political tutor, Otto von Bismarck, the keenest political mind of the century. The new Kaiser was immensely popular. An American attending the gala coronation ceremonies observed that if Wilhelm II had not inherited the throne, and an election had taken place instead, he would have been swept into power by a landslide.

Jubilant multitudes hailed their young ruler with cries of *Hoch der Kaiser!* (Hail the Emperor!) when he promised to lead them into 'magnificent times.' Instead, he would lead them into a disastrous war and a humiliating surrender. When in 1918 he was forced to abdicate and flee to Holland, newsboys in Berlin hawking extra editions with two-inch headlines 'Kaiser Abdicates!' found they could not sell their papers: no one cared very much.

At the height of his pre-war power, the Kaiser made an impressive appearance. Of more than average height, he carried himself with a well-rehearsed regal bearing. His hair was light brown. The points of his waxed, Wilhelmian moustache bristled upward. His left arm, injured at birth, was some six inches shorter than his right, but he tried to make it less conspicuous by resting it on the pommel of his sword or hooking his thumb into his belt. His right arm was made powerful by his obsessive habit of chopping and sawing wood.[8] Wilhelm habitually wore several heavy rings and, quite often, delicate feminine bracelets on both wrists.[9]

The Kaiser's rather handsome face was dominated by remarkably light grey-blue eyes. Wilhelm thought they resembled the eyes of his heroic predecessor, Frederick the Great. Using Frederick's portrait as a model, he – like Hitler – practised piercing glances in front of a mirror, saying on one occasion, 'Those are the eyes of the victor of Rossbach!'[10] He developed a transfixing stare that was particularly disturbing because – also like Hitler – he was born with virtually no eyelashes, and his eyes were cold. They 'seemed to show absolutely no sentiment or feeling; they were like two grey mirrors on which outward things made no [inward] impression.'[11]

Also like the Führer, the Kaiser had graceful hands and was infatuated with the hands of others. A lady of the court recalled that he loved to linger and stroke women's hands and 'to kiss them many times.' Hands were for him 'objects of devotion.'[12]

The most striking characteristic of Wilhelm's personality was a fundamental dualism. Publicly he appeared as the prototype of sabre-rattlers – imperious, hyper-masculine, a decisive commander who barked orders and brooked no opposition. His closest associates, however, remembered him as a vulnerable and emotional person, constantly in search of reassurance and approval. Perhaps the most perceptive appraisal of this complex man was given by Walther Rathenau, a contemporary who found that the strutting exhibitionist was at bottom an insecure and troubled person 'in deep conflict with himself ... a being who is torn apart.'[13]

Dualities are part of the human condition. Goethe lamented, 'Alas, two souls have I within my breast,' and Freud saw our psyches as a battleground with opposing forces of Id and Superego. We are all prone to conflicting modes of conduct and desire: We want security and stability, but we welcome change and new experiences. We are people of good will and of animosity, of altruism and selfishness, of tenderness and hatred.[14]

In both the Kaiser and the Führer, duality was pushed beyond the range of normality. Both suffered from what psychoanalysts have called 'pathological splitting of the ego,'[15] or 'the divided Self.'[16] Wilhelm Hohenzollern was at once cruel and kind, generous and mean-spirited, compassionate and callous. He gloried in war and promised peace. He longed for a distant past and proclaimed himself emperor of a new age. Contemporaries observed a double image of their Kaiser. They heard him talk of reconciliation and saw him drive people into opposition. They found him both charming and boorish, considerate and callous. He trumpeted military power and gloried in his title of Supreme War Lord, yet – as we shall see – he wanted to be seen as a special emissary of Jesus Christ commissioned to bring peace to the world.[17]

Wilhelm II's vision of Germany was similarly contradictory. He wanted fundamental change, but he also wanted to keep things the same. He viewed Germany as a modernized industrial giant. He set a 'New Course' in foreign policy, and under him Germany became for the first time a naval power. At the same time he clung to ancient attitudes and institutions. He believed that his own power rested on pre-modern Prussian autocratic ideals. He expressed contempt for parliamentary democracy and sought to retain the influence of the army on society. He insisted on punctilious adherence to outmoded social forms and procedures. Theodor Fontane recognized this conflict in Wilhelm II between the old and the new: 'What I like about the Kaiser is his complete break from the old, and what I don't like about the Kaiser is this contradictory desire of his to restore the ancient.'[18]

The Kaiser's conflicting attitudes towards England – which may have been an extension of his ambivalent feelings about his English mother[19] – are illustrated with particular clarity in the very different remarks he made to members of his entourage. One day he shouted 'in blind fury' that 'one cannot have enough hatred for England.' When his daughter was made an honorary colonel, he said to her English tutor, 'She will ride at the head of the first regiment that invades England.'[20] Yet he also told his closest associate, Philipp zu Eulenburg, that England was the one place where he 'felt completely at home.'[21] President Theodore Roosevelt reported that Wilhelm had told him that 'I feel myself partly an Englishman,' and then he said with intense emphasis, '*I adore England!*'[22] On the rare occasions when the Kaiser was not in uniform, he posed either as a tweedy English country gentleman, out for a spot of grouse on the moors, or in a flashy checked suit and boater that reminded one British observer of a 'Bank Holiday tripper to Margate.'[23] In exile during the 1930s, he still spoke fluent English with an Edwardian flavour, saying that people he liked were 'ripping,' or 'topping' and describing himself as 'actually a damned topping good fellow!'[24]

The Kaiser enjoyed giving the impression that he was ruthlessly hard and merciless. In hearing reports of Belgian resistance to the unprovoked invasion of their country by German troops in August 1914, for instance, he became extremely agitated: 'Be hard! Show no mercy to this rabble! Shoot them! Burn them! Shoot them!'[25] He shocked even the German high command with his demands for bloodshed. Admiral Müller, one of his entourage, reported that on 30 August 1914 while en route to army headquarters in Plessen (Silesia), 'the Kaiser – as he has often done recently – positively revelled in blood: [He demanded] "Piles of corpses six feet high!"'[26]

This appetite for bloodshed and destruction was shown much earlier when, in 1900, during the Boxer Rebellion in China, the Kaiser wired his chancellor that 'Peking must be levelled to the ground! (*Peking muss rasiert werden!*)'[27] – an order that anticipated Hitler's famous telegram to the commandant of Paris in 1944: '*Brennt Paris?* (Is Paris burning?).' A few weeks after demanding the total destruction of Peking, the Kaiser gave his memorable 'Hun Speech,' urging his troops to behave like the 'Huns of old' and massacre their prisoners.[28]

The Kaiser's orders to massacre the enemy were not limited to the external foes of Germany; he was quite capable of giving orders to shoot his own people. He warned his soldiers that he could order them to shoot down their own parents and brothers. Both his persistent use of the first-person pronoun and his demand for unrestricted personal loyalty foreshadow Adolf Hitler. In a speech of 23 November 1891, to new recruits of the Potsdam garrison, the Kaiser's words anticipated the Führer's:

You are now my soldiers. You have given yourself to me body and soul (*ihr habt euch Mir mit Leib und Seele ergeben*). There exists for you only one enemy and that is my enemy ...

It can happen that I will order you to shoot down – God forbid – your own relatives. Your brothers, yes, even your parents, but even then you must follow my orders without a murmur.[29]

Wilhelm II also anticipated Hitler in his preoccupation with heads, skulls, and decapitation.[30] At a colonial exhibition, upon seeing photographs of an African chieftain with the skulls of his enemies stuck on poles, Wilhelm mused for a moment before commenting, 'If only I could see the Reichstag strung up like that!'[31] The Kaiser was fascinated by pictures of death. A lady-in-waiting at the court reported that in his bedroom Wilhelm had portraits hung of his grandfather, Wilhelm I, his grandmother, Queen Victoria, his father, and King Ludwig of Bavaria, all wrapped in their burial shrouds.[32]

The astonishing number of animals he killed also reveals the Kaiser's infatuation with dead bodies. Prior to one of his many 'hunts,' his gamekeepers would drive wild animals into enormous pens where the Kaiser could slaughter them by the thousands. He kept a careful account of each animal killed, boasted that he had shot his 5,000th head of game, and expressed the hope that he would 'double and treble my shooting during the next ten years.'[33] His records showed that by 1902 he had already exceeded his expectations. His hunting registry for that year recorded, 'On this day the All Highest killed his 50,000th creature: a white *Fasanenhahn* [cock-pheasant].' This historic statistic is preserved in golden letters.[34] The human slaughter in the trenches of the western front during the summer of 1916 did not dampen Wilhelm's zeal for killing. While hundreds of thousands of British, German, and French soldiers were dying in the protracted Battle of the Somme, the Kaiser withdrew to his palatial lodge in East Prussia for one of his many 'hunts.' After bagging several corralled stags, he appeared at dinner one evening proudly wearing medals he had never earned: the *Pour le Mérite* (Prussia's highest award for bravery in battle), two Iron Crosses, and the Hunter's Jubilee Badge.[35]

Yet there was also a gentler and less sanguinary Kaiser. This Wilhelm could show compassion for the wounded enemy and was haunted by the suffering of dying soldiers. In a letter to Queen Victoria of 1899 he expressed sorrow for the loss of men in the Boer War and remorse for 'those who are left behind.' His grandmother thanked him for his concern and for his generosity in giving so much money to the wives and families of the bereaved.[36] To his uncle Edward, Prince of Wales, he wrote in a Christmas letter of 21 December 1899, 'How many homes will be sad this year ... in these days of holy pleasure and peace! ...

Instead of the angel song, "Peace on Earth" and "Goodwill to Men," the new century will be greeted by the shrieks of the dying.'[37]

His ideal for the world was not of conflict but of everlasting peace. The Kaiser actually believed he had achieved it through his agreement with his cousin Tsar Nicholas II, at Björko in 1905. After signing this 'historic' pact – which was soon nullified – 'Willie' wrote euphorically to 'Dear Nicky': 'The 24th of July 1905 ... turns over a new leaf in the history of the world; which will be a chapter of Peace and Goodwill Among Great Powers ... respecting each other in friendship [and] confidence.'[38]

Wilhelm was perfectly willing to support international conferences, as long as they only *talked* about peace. His marginal comment on a report about the Hague Peace Conference of June 1899, which called for arbitration of international disputes, was pungent: 'I ... shit (*scheisse*) on all their resolutions.'[39]

The Kaiser, like the Führer, was given to gross vulgarities. He had a penchant for barnyard humour and barracks vocabulary. A member of the diplomatic corps confided to a colleague that, during one of the Kaiser's dinner parties on board his yacht, 'the chief subjects of conversation have been shitting, vomiting, pissing and fucking; pardon me for hurting your ears with these harsh words, but I cannot choose any others if I am to give you a true picture.'[40] As with Hitler, one of Wilhelm's favourite words was 'shit.' It was a preoccupation both rulers shared with the German people.[41]

Also like the Führer, the Kaiser was a prude, censoring what he considered to be indecent behaviour in others. He was so shocked, for example, by the 'moral depravity' of the new dance styles being imported from America that he forbade officers in his army and navy to dance the fox-trot; and he ordered the arrest of his young sister-in-law for daring to wear bloomers and ride a bicycle on the palace grounds. Wilhelm also severely reprimanded her husband for permitting such flagrant behaviour on the part of his wife and sentenced both culprits to a fortnight's house arrest (*Stubenarrest*).[42]

During the war, the same person who talked about shooting prisoners of war and called for piles of French bodies 'six feet high,' also showed compassion for the wounded enemy. A member of his military entourage reported, 'At lunch the Kaiser spoke very harshly of the brutality of our men, who made no effort to help badly wounded English soldiers ... He had seen to it personally that they were bandaged and carried down the line.'[43] On the issue of whether Germany should engage in unrestricted submarine warfare, the Kaiser said that if he were the captain of a U-boat, 'I would never torpedo a ship if I knew that women and children were aboard.'[44] Yet he signed orders for doing just that.

Wilhelm often spoke publicly and movingly of trust, compassion, and forgiveness. This side of the man's personality was shown most revealingly in a remarkable speech of 31 August 1907 at Münster:

During my long reign – it is now the twentieth year since my accession – I have had dealings with many people and have had to suffer much from them ... They have hurt me deeply (*haben sie mir bitter Weh getan*). And when in such moments rage seeks to overwhelm me and thoughts of retaliation arise, then I have asked myself what would be the best way to soften rage and to strengthen gentleness (*den Zorn zu mildern und die Milde zu stärken*).

The best way I have found is to say to myself all are men just like you and although they may hurt you, they too have souls from Heaven above to whence all of us want to return and in their souls too is a piece of the Creator. Whoever thinks like that will always have a milder opinion of his fellow human beings.[45]

The Kaiser was often thoughtful and kind in his personal relationships. He wrote sensitive letters of condolence. He remembered anniversaries of his relatives, friends, and employees.[46] He inquired after the health of convalescents.[47] He took time out during a visit to the front to write to a worried mother that he had seen her 'little, big boy' and that he was just fine.[48]

Wilhelm could also be mean-spirited, petty, and vindictive. He made a point of remembering past 'wrongs' done to him. In 1890 he dismissed Bismarck and gave orders that a list be made of all the people who gathered at the railroad station to bid the old chancellor farewell. When, in 1892, Bismarck's son was married in Vienna, Wilhelm used his influence to have the Habsburg court ignore the wedding. He also gave orders to the German ambassador in Vienna that members of the embassy were to decline invitations.[49]

When he wanted to, however, Wilhelm could turn on magnetic charm and captivate those who had distrusted him. The German ambassador to England reported, for example, that on the Kaiser's visit of December 1899 he was immensely successful in winning over former antagonists. Arthur Balfour remarked that his audience with Wilhelm was 'the most fascinating of his career,' and even Joseph Chamberlain, who had stridently opposed the Kaiser's foreign policy, 'spoke openly of an alliance with Germany.'[50] John Morley, a lifelong critic of royal absolutism, was also taken with the Kaiser's conviviality. His diary entry for 22 November 1907 reads in part, 'I saw much of him at Windsor, and was surprised at his gaiety, freedom, naturalness, geniality, and good humour – evidently unaffected.'[51]

A group of French actors who had performed in Berlin were enchanted by the German emperor,[52] and he was particularly skilful in impressing intellectuals. An American professor, on leave from Columbia University to lecture at the

University of Berlin, said that never in his life had he met so impressive a person or one with a 'keener mind or warmer heart.'

The Kaiser believed that his charm was irresistible. But there were many who felt otherwise. The member of the court who quoted the American professor's extravagant praise noted dryly that the Kaiser had also 'hoodwinked' a lot of other people.[53] A woman who had served as a governess for Wilhelm's children agreed that the Kaiser 'dazzled and charmed' many people but the effect was 'evanescent.'[54] A British contemporary was less flattering: 'There were at his command some gifts to which his expansive superficiality lent a flickering glamour.'[55]

Wilhelm seemed unaware of these negative reactions. He was therefore simply astonished when, after his dazzling performance during a press conference with British journalists, the newsmen had not been converted into enthusiastic proponents of German absolutism.[56] (Hitler too would express amazement that the British were not convinced of his integrity and could not understand why they refused to join him in his 'crusade' against Russia.)

The Kaiser's capacity to charm competed with his inclination to infuriate. It is remarkable how persistently he alienated the very people he most needed to cultivate if he were to establish the royal absolutism and popular monarchy he so greatly desired. At one time or another he alienated army generals, navy commanders, princes of the Empire, diplomats, journalists, members of parliament, socialists, Catholics, women, and young people. In one notable interview he managed to antagonize Britons, French, Russians, and Japanese, along with his own people.[57]

Like the Führer, the Kaiser showed remarkable courage and sang-froid in threatening situations. For instance, during a Norwegian cruise in 1889, a huge chunk of ice crashed down onto the deck, narrowly missing him. While others cried out in alarm, Wilhelm quietly watched the 'show' (Schauspiel). His conduct won the admiration of General Waldersee: 'It's clear to me that if bullets were whistling around him, he wouldn't bat an eye.'[58] During a state visit to Bremen, a mentally disturbed worker threw a piece of sharp metal at the Kaiser, cutting his cheek and narrowly missing his eye. The Kaiser calmly reassured the Lord Mayor, who offered frantic apologies, that he had not been seriously hurt. He refused anaesthesia in having a polyp removed from his throat, and his American dentist reported that the Emperor was the most courageous patient he had ever treated.[59]

It was very rare for Wilhelm to complain about his atrophied arm or express self-pity for his disability.[60] Far more striking was his courageous mastery of his handicap. One biographer has called this 'perhaps the greatest single achievement of his life.'[61] Wilhelm learned to play good amateur tennis, became an expert marksman with a rifle held in his strong right arm, and trained himself to be a superb horseman, despite his atrophied arm and an inner-ear problem that disturbed his sense of balance.

His courage in confronting difficult social or political problems was less impressive, for he had a childlike tendency to run away from them. Escape took several forms. One was simply to leave the capital and do a great deal of travelling. April and May of each year were spent on his island home on Corfu. June was reserved for yachting in Kiel or Cowes. In July and August every year, he cruised the Norwegian coast. Many weeks in September and October were spent 'hunting' and in making long excursions in his pale blue and silver private railway train. During the year August 1893 to August 1894, either on his yacht or in his railroad coach, Wilhelm II covered three-quarters of the earth's circumference.[62] The court calendar for 1910 shows that he spent 126 days travelling and that during that time he had only one meeting with Chancellor Bethmann Holweg.[63] A Berlin wag, noting the contrast among the three Kaisers who ruled in 1888 (Wilhelm I, Friedrich III, and Wilhelm II) said, 'So we have three Kaisers: first the *Greisekaiser* then the *Weisekaiser*, and now the *Reisekaiser* [aged ... wise ... travelling].' Travel became so compulsive to Wilhelm that when no trips were planned he occasionally spent the night in his railway carriage parked in a siding just five minutes from the Neues Palais. The need to keep moving was caught in his personal motto, 'I rust when I rest' (*Rast ich, so rost ich*). (Hitler felt the same way, changing only a verb: 'I rot when I rest.' He, too, had a private railway train which, surprisingly, he called '*Amerika.*')[64] Given the number of days of the year that the Kaiser was not in his office, it is surprising to hear him complaining to the Tsar that 'we poor rulers are not entitled to a holiday like other mortals.'[65]

Wilhelm also ran away from difficult or embarrassing situations by having what his wife called 'nervous collapses' and taking to his bed for several days, as he did after a disastrous interview was printed in the *Daily Telegraph*.[66] Or he escaped from reality into a world of fantasy and illusion, casting himself – as we have seen – in many imaginary roles. He busied himself in activities that served as an excuse for not facing problems. When the war was going badly, for example, the Kaiser avoided discussing the military situation with the high command by reading aloud to them long passages of Persian history and treatises on numismatics or on the eagle as a heraldic beast. He would tell an aide that he was unavailable for consultation because he was learning the language of the ancient Hittites or playing an important game of skat.[67] When the crunch came in 1918, he ran away to Holland, where he was promised immunity from extradition and possible prosecution as a war criminal.

In many respects the Kaiser's temperament and tastes remained those of a child. 'One can sense dependent childishness behind the image of mastery,' a contemporary wrote, 'a child who needs reassuring arms to protect him.'[68] Wilhelm showed little capacity for emotional growth. Like a child, he loved to dress up in uniforms and play soldier and sailor. The boyish games he continued to play after becoming Kaiser were embarrassing to anyone with a sense of propriety. At a champagne party, for instance, he ordered guests to open their mouths so that he could try to hit them with bits of cake.[69] Like a nine-year-old, he formed a special gang whose initiation rites required prospective members to tell a naughty story, for which the Kaiser punished them by spanking their backsides with the flat of his sword,[70] and one of the favourite games of the emperor of Germany was playing tag. A visitor on the Imperial yacht reported being awakened at midnight: 'I heard loud laughing and the screaming voice of the Kaiser in front of my cabin door. [His Majesty] was chasing to bed the elderly excellencies Heintze, Kessel, Scholl, et al., through the corridors of the ship.'[71] During the second Moroccan crisis of July 1911, the chief of the naval cabinet noted in his diary: 'Great silliness this morning during calisthenics. S.M. [His Majesty] had cut through [Admiral] Scholl's suspenders with a knife [so that his trousers kept falling down].'[72]

When Wilhelm was thirty-two years old, he grew a full beard like his father's in order to frighten people, saying as he banged on the table, 'With a beard like this you could thump on the table so hard that your ministers would fall down with fright and lie flat on their faces! ! ! ! ! ! !'[73]

During the First World War a military adviser was disconcerted to find that the Supreme War Lord was spending hours of his time carefully crayoning in all the green forests on the war maps. The aide commented wryly that it certainly made the maps look nice, but he wondered if a subordinate might not have spared the Kaiser all the 'Imperial effort.'[74] When the exiled monarch was eighty, during a luncheon at Doorn in August 1939, he served his guests an excellent Moselle while he himself drank an inferior Burgundy, commenting, 'I know this is not first-class, but I drink it because I was never allowed to as a little boy.' It struck his guest as 'very odd indeed' that the Kaiser should want to make up in old age for what he had been denied as a child.[75]

People who knew Wilhelm well commented on his lifelong inability to change. The Baroness von Spitzemberg, for instance, who had been a friend for many years, noted in her diary on 16 January 1907 that he simply had not matured: 'There has been no change from the impulsive youth.'[76] Wilhelm seemed unable to alter any detail of the mind-numbing sameness of his routine. His trips, his guests, his conversations remained the same. He visited the same castles, the same villages, year after year after year. One intimate noted in his diary, 'Each day passes completely routinely, one just like any other.' Another decided to stop recording the dreary days, 'It didn't pay to make any entries whatsoever, life was too dull (*stumpfsinnig*).' A general who was commanded to go on yet another of the Kaiser's annual trips to the fjords of Norway noted in a diary entry for 9 July 1907 that His Majesty kept returning to the cottage of an old sea captain: 'Every year the Emperor sits on the same chair ... and every year he has the same conversation.'[77] During the Kaiser's long exile, from 1918 to 1941, his close associate Sigurd von Ilsemann noted the same inflexibility. He was amazed to find that the turn-of-the-century portrait of his master in the memoirs of Bernhard von Bülow was the same picture he saw every day: 'Almost everything reported here is repeated now.'[78]

In the most literal sense, the Kaiser was self-centred. He took almost everything personally. For instance, when his sister converted to Orthodoxy before marrying the heir to the Greek throne, Wilhelm took it as a personal insult and banned her from his kingdom. When someone tried to calm him by suggesting that religion was a private matter, the Kaiser shouted, 'Nonsense! (*Unsinn!*).'[79] While living in exile in Holland, he asserted that the water 'still comes from my Rhine.'[80] His marginalia kept mentioning 'my' navy, 'my' army, and referred to the Berlin–Baghdad Railroad as 'my railroad ... I created it and it remains my work.'[81] All the causes of the First World War, he said, could be reduced to one: a vindictive attack on him personally. 'The Tsar of Russia and the King of England,' he told his dentist, 'when they were at the wedding of my daughter – guests at my own house, mind you, and my blood relatives – they abused my hospitality and hatched this plot against me ... Confound them! I'll show them!'[82] The Kaiser did not find it difficult to identify the real cause for Germany's defeat. Everybody had deserted him: 'I never would have believed that the navy, my own child, should so thank me. Never would I have thought it possible that my army ... would leave me in the lurch.'[83]

Wilhelm persistently felt the need to dominate and humiliate other people. To demonstrate his exalted position as the All Highest Person (*Der Allerhöchste Person*), he required that his guests remain standing while he 'conversed' with them – which is to say, delivered one of his monologues. This dreaded *Herumstehen* (standing around), as it was called, which could last for hours, was remembered bitterly in many memoirs, and was especially tiring for older people.[84]

Wilhelm would sometimes grab his guests playfully by the ear and pull them about or smack them on the rear with a tennis racket or a riding crop – knowing, of course, that they could not retaliate. On his yacht, elderly guests were required to do sit-ups, push-ups, and deep-knee bends to the point of exhaustion – while their host roared with laughter, pushed them over onto their backs, and, on one occasion at least, sat on their stomachs. The Kaiser once ordered his guests to wade a stream while stalking elk and then, on returning to the hunting lodge, gave orders that they were to come to dinner without changing.[85]

A gentle and rather shy career officer who, on the occasion of his appointment as colonial secretary, was invited to dine with His Majesty tucked his dinner napkin under his chin. The Kaiser humiliated the guest of honour and embarrassed the entire dinner party by calling for attention and then announcing, 'This is not a barber shop!'[86]

Perhaps to compensate for his own disability, Wilhelm delighted in pointing out physical abnormalities in others. He referred to the diminutive king of Italy as 'that little dwarf' and to the large-nosed king of Bulgaria as 'Fernando Nase.'[87]

There was more than a touch of sadism in the Kaiser's habit of turning his heavy, bejeweled rings inward when shaking hands with English people. A young governess who met him for the first time recalled that he regarded her 'severely with a "war-lord" kind of expression' and held out his powerful right hand. He then gave her a grip that made her want to cry out in pain. 'Ha – ha!' he said jocularly in his accented English, 'A bit of the celebrated mailed fist! What?'[88]

Among all European monarchs of the modern era, Wilhelm II was surely the most conspicuous show-off. Biographers have vied with one another to find amusing illustrations of his exhibitionism. It is said that he possessed over 250 uniforms and changed them as much as a dozen times a day – allegedly appearing once in full admiral's regalia for a performance of *Der fliegende Holländer*.[89] To dedicate a Protestant church in Jerusalem in 1898, the Kaiser entered the Holy City costumed as a crusader.[90] A Berlin photography shop in 1913 offered 267 'heroic poses' of the Kaiser, 'all different.'[91] His barber became famous for inventing a special wax that held the royal moustache with tips pointing upward so as to form the letter 'W' – Wilhelm's favourite letter. Theodore Roosevelt was surprised to see how tall the Kaiser sat behind his desk. It was because at his desks in Berlin, Corfu, and Doorn, Wilhelm sat astride English riding saddles mounted on pianolike stools that could be raised so that he could look down on visitors sitting on ordinary chairs.[92] The future Edward VIII, when Prince of Wales, was astonished when his cousin received him in his sitting-room in Potsdam mounted high on a wooden model of a horse.[93] The Kaiser sought to impress a visiting Harvard professor by feats of memory and during breakfast surprised his guest by suddenly rattling off the names, in correct order, of all the kings of Assyria.[94]

Wilhelm's grandiose ideas about his own power embarrassed and dismayed his associates, some of whom feared for his sanity. Indeed, he did give them cause for concern, saying on one occasion that 'I walk among you as your God,'[95] and claiming on a somewhat lower level that he was the arbiter of the entire world: 'My crown sends its rays through God's Grace into palaces and huts and – forgive me when I say it – Europe and the world is hushed in order to hear, "What does the German Kaiser think and say?" ... For ever and ever (*immer und ewig*) there is only one real emperor in the world and that is the German Emperor.'[96] His claims of infallibility extended to his wife's hats. He chose them for her without permitting her to try them on, and year after year he presented her with twelve hats on her birthday.[97]

Wilhelm, who had difficulty accepting criticism about anything, was particularly defensive about his speeches. Late in life he once asked an aide for critical comment. When it was given, he replied tartly, 'Well, I can say whatever I want to, whether you like it or not!'[98] Yet he was aware of his proclivity for verbal excess and worried about it – only to resume verbal bombast, regret it, and then resume once more. He confessed how often he had reason to feel remorse: 'I have often at night been kept from sleep for hours by the knowledge that in a speech delivered the previous day I had failed to observe the limitations on content and expression which I set myself in advance.'[99]

The Kaiser could speak with great effect. Lord Esher heard his address to the corps students of his alma mater, the University of Bonn, and was enormously impressed, going so far as to say that 'no man living in any country could have made so eloquent a [speech].'[100] Often, however, his undoubted rhetorical ability got out of hand. He was particularly prone to making slashing personal attacks. A favourite word was 'smash' (*zerschmettern*). He loved to smash an argument, smash an opponent. He enjoyed baiting others and then silencing discussion with a triumphant onslaught. These little conversational victories seem to have given him a feeling of power. The Kaiser – like Hitler – had an American-trained dentist who remembered one of his patient's surprising comments: '"Fix my teeth well, Davis, so that I can bite. There are lots of people I would like to bite!" He snapped his jaws together.'[101]

A typically effusive letter to his mentor in racial prejudice, Houston Stewart Chamberlain, demonstrates the Kaiser's faith in the power of aggressive words – especially spoken words:

Your powerful words strike the people and bring them to thought and battle! Attack! ... The German Michael awakes!
You wield your pen, I my slashing broadsword ...

> Your loyal & grateful friend,
> Wilhelm I.R.[102]

The slashing broadsword got him into a great deal of political difficulty, alarming foe and friend alike. A group of German academics at a dinner party were appalled at his gratuitous attack on the states of southern Germany: 'If the South Germans show signs of becoming unruly, [I will] immediately declare war on them. Prussia has so-and-so many Army Corps, they have only three or four – we'll see who would win that one!' One of the guests commented that this kind of bombast 'is really terrifying.'[103]

The Kaiser loved to talk and to listen to his own guttural and rather unpleasant voice.[104] Seemingly unable to refrain from saying whatever popped into his head, he, like the Führer, held forth on any subject under the sun or beyond it, from agronomy to astronomy, from homiletics and physics to female psychology, child-raising, musical counterpoint, military strategy, genetics, archaeology, or anything else that struck his fecund fancy. Time after time his compulsive comments alienated supporters, embarrassed his friends, and jeopardized his own plans. Chancellor von Bülow pleaded with him not to do it and reminded him how often he kept repeating the same politically damaging comments. Wilhelm turned on him with baffled indignation, 'But don't you see? I can't change!'[105]

His closest associate of many years recalled that the Kaiser's private conversations were monologues: 'He speaks without interruption. Always well, always engagingly – indeed even spellbindingly and spellbinding to himself. Once he is in full swing he is unable to desist.'[106] An editor of Wilhelm II's speeches computed that in the first twelve months of his reign he had made 'no fewer than 406 major addresses.'[107]

Volubility had begun early in life. When he was four his mother reported, 'Willie chatters all day long.'[108] Perhaps in an effort to give some direction to his spoken words, she had him read aloud to her. He did it so well that she gave him one of her very few compliments. Her positive response may have encouraged his lifelong habit of reading aloud to his entourage, inflicting upon his wife and her ladies-in-waiting all of H.S. Chamberlain's turgid tome, *Foundations of the Nineteenth Century*, and paralyzing his military advisers during the war with a history of the ancient Persian dynasties. His mother's compliment may also have inspired a belief in the magical powers of his own spoken words to solve any problem and charm his most intractable enemy.

Thus, 'he approached every problem with an open mouth'[109] and with a pen at the ready to dash off a speech, sermon, or telegram, or to add a slashing marginal comment to a state paper. His conviction that words alone could produce wondrous results was shown clearly in his reaction to the serious workers' strike of January 1918. The Kaiser was baffled by it. He could not believe it was happening because he was sure he had solved labour unrest by giving a sentimental speech at Essen – a speech, he was convinced, that had filled the workers' hearts with love and their eyes with tears. Months after the strike, he wrote on a newspaper clipping of 12 September 1918 which reported new labour demands: 'But that is pure revolution – and after I had won over the workers with my Essen speech!'

In both private and public communication he could not resist hyperbole. On a note accompanying a Christmas present to his grandmother Queen Victoria, for instance, he wrote extravagantly – and inexplicably identified himself as her nephew:

I have with your kind permission taken the liberty to venture to send you a little gift for Xmas. It is a painted photograph of myself ...

> Your devoted & respectful nephew [*sic*]
> Wilhelm, Prinze [*sic*] of Prussia[110]

When his grandmother sent him a bust of one of his many aunts, Wilhelm's response was fulsome: 'I shall always look upon it as a holy, beloved treasure ... I have placed it on a little table opposite my bed ... so that the first thing I see in awaking, and the last face ... before going to sleep, is this sweet face of Aunt Alice.'[111]

Exuberant exaggeration reached a high point when, after witnessing an experimental flight of Graf Ferdinand von Zeppelin's new invention on 8 November 1908, the Kaiser bestowed upon him the Order of the Black Eagle, proclaiming that 'what we have witnessed today has been one of the greatest moments in human culture' and declaring the count to be 'the greatest German of the twentieth century.' Since the century had barely begun, the accolade seemed somewhat premature.[112]

A correspondent of the *Times* once asked Sarah Bernhardt how she had got on with the Kaiser when he visited her after one of her performances in Berlin. She replied, 'But admirably! Are not both of us born actors?'[113] Well, not exactly, but Wilhelm had started putting on acts early in life. As a child he had tried desperately to cover up his impaired arm and to appear more purposeful and confident than he really felt.[114] As an adult he played many different roles. He did so in part because he much preferred appearances to reality. One of the most graphic portraits we have of the Kaiser as actor was sketched by the Portuguese consul general in Berlin, Eca de Queiroz, who had watched him closely for three years. In 1891 he wrote a characterization of Wilhelm at age thirty-one which shows the range of the Kaiser's histrionic talents:

As in Hamlet, there exist the germs of various men and we cannot foresee which of them will prevail or whether, when one has finally developed, he will amaze us by his greatness or by his triviality.

In this Sovereign what a variety of incarnations of Royalty! One day he is Soldier King, rigid, stiff in helmet and cuirass ... putting barrack discipline above every moral and natural law ... Suddenly he strips off the uniform and dons the working man's overalls; he is the Reform King ... eagerly convoking social congresses ... determined to go down in history embracing the proletariat as a brother whom he has set free.

Then, all unawares, he becomes King by Divine Right, haughtily resting his Gothic sceptre on the backs of his people ... subjecting the highest law to the will of the King ... convinced of his infallibility, driving [out of Germany] all who do not devoutly believe in him. Mankind is agape, when lo! he is the Courtier King ... ordering the style of headdress to be worn by ladies ...

The world smiles – and presto! he becomes the Modern King ... treating the past as bigoted ... rewarding the factory as the supreme temple, dreaming of Germany as worked entirely by electricity ...

The world in perplexity murmurs, who is this man that changes and multiplies himself incessantly?[115]

Many years later, Ilsemann, his loyal companion in exile, described one of the little dramas Wilhelm was fond of staging. On 20 January 1929 in Doorn, while celebrating his seventieth birthday, the ex-Kaiser made a theatrical entrance before a small group of guests gathered in his living-room. Attired in the full dress uniform of the commander of the First Guard Regiment, with row upon row of medals dangling from his chest, bearing sabre and revolver, and holding a field marshal's baton at salute, he felt properly equiped for his birthday party. Ilsemann describes the scene: 'Exactly as in former times, he came in with short military steps. He had donned his stern tight-lipped expression (the mask which he always put on when he left his entourage to confront strangers)' ... He started a welcoming speech in moderate voice, then suddenly changed tone and shouted at his startled guests in his best parade-ground voice: 'The first place in this house belongs to me! ... and to no one else! ... And now, gentlemen, I demand that you listen carefully, will you remain true to the oath of loyalty you have sworn, will you follow me? Yes or no? I am waiting for an answer, gentlemen!' The eyewitness continued: 'A "Yes" as at the Last Supper was heard. But it was not very loud and not really given by all those present.' The Kaiser then withdrew to his turret-study for a change of costume. He reappeared for dinner as a Death's Head Hussar.[116]

Wilhelm acted out heroic images to impress himself and to intimidate others. He also acted to please. All his life he had wanted to be liked; he hungered for the approval denied him by his mother and his tutors.[117] He therefore played up to an audience in order to win approval from individuals and groups. If he met a French actress he delighted her by reciting lines from Molière. With an Englishman, he was all for yachting, fox hunting, or a day on the moors. With an American businessman, Wilhelm would chatter about the New York Stock Exchange or about cotton plantations in the South. He would offer workers tobacco from his own pocket and joke over a glass of beer. He wanted very much to convince them all that he was, as he said, 'Really not such a bad guy! (*Ich bin doch kein böser Mensch*).'

The acting was not confined to strangers. A lady of the court, Daisy, Princess of Pless, wrote that she was fond of Wilhelm but was not sure she could trust him: 'He was ... always acting. Of course all public personages have to act a part, but the Emperor, I fear, posed to his intimates and friends, perhaps even to himself.'[118] Another contemporary was less kind, calling the Kaiser 'one of the most brilliant frauds ever wrapped in the Royal ermine.'[119]

Princess Daisy was right in saying that public personages must play different parts. Disraeli, de Gaulle, and Hitler were all actors. They immersed themselves so completely in their roles that they became convinced they really were the people they portrayed. Disraeli was the apotheosis of an exalted ancient people.[120] De Gaulle was the incarnation of French resistance, indeed of France itself. Hitler was the *Führerprinzip* in the flesh. All had the power to persuade. Wilhelm kept trying to do the same thing, but he could never quite bring it off, never quite persuade either himself or others. Like Daisy of Pless, his friends always had the uncomfortable feeling that he was putting on an act. One of them put it bluntly: 'For him *pose* was everything.'[121] That is a judicious choice of words. It reminds us of the important distinction between genuine actors – such as Charles de Gaulle and Adolf Hitler – and those who merely pose. No one ever said that Adolf Hitler was merely posing. Sarah Bernhardt did not get it quite right: Wilhelm was not a 'born actor,' but he became a consummate *poseur.*

Italy's greatest statesman of the modern era, Count Camillo Cavour (1810–61), once observed that if we did for ourselves what we do for our country, what rascals we would be! Cavour's candour had precedent. A seventeenth-century English diplomat, in a memorable *mot*, described himself as 'an honest man who is sent abroad to lie for the good of his country.'[122] The Kaiser certainly lied for what he considered to be his country's good.[123]

Like Hitler, however, Wilhelm also lied about trivial personal matters, and he did so clumsily and in ways that could easily be found out. For instance, he told a close relative that a certain Dr Renvers had never treated his sister, when the whole family knew that Renvers had indeed attended her regularly. He flatly denied having sent a telegram that he had in fact sent, as could easily be ascertained, and as he must have known.[124] Wilhelm assured his chancellor that in a famous interview with an American cleric he had never discussed German relations with England when the interview, which was available to the chancellor in foreign office files, was explicitly and almost exclusively concerned with England.[125]

There are two particularly notable examples of Wilhelm's penchant for deception: he lied about his reasons for dismissing Bismarck in 1890, and he lied about his grandmother's death in 1901. He had dismissed Otto von Bismarck essentially because he wanted 'to be his own Chancellor,' and he felt intimidated by the dominating old man.[126] He tried to convince others, however, that he had fired him because (a) he wanted to save Bismarck's life, writing to his grandmother that 'we parted in tears after a warm embrace ... I was resolved to part from him in order to keep him alive; he would infallibly [*sic*] have died of apoplexy';[127] (b) he discovered, he said, that Bismarck was about to 'shoot down the Socialists in the streets ... so I dismissed him';[128] (c) Bismarck had spoken disparagingly about the Kaiser's mother.[129] (As we shall see, few people spoke more disparagingly about the Kaiser's mother than Wilhelm himself.)

Astonishingly, he tried to deceive members of Queen Victoria's immediate family about their matriarch's death. There is no doubt that Wilhelm deeply revered his grandmother and that he was present as she lay dying in Osborne House on the Isle of Wight in January 1901. But the story he kept repeating, that Queen Victoria had 'died in my arms,' is fiction.[130]

Wilhelm's closest friend, when asked if His Majesty ever lied, replied, 'I cannot deny it ... usually whenever something embarrassed him ... in such cases he *always* lied.'[131] It seems likely that, apart from embarrassment, there was another reason for habitual dissimulation. He simply could not trust other people. Throughout his life he remained a suspicious person who was unable to establish trusting, close relationships with others. Philipp zu Eulenburg had yearned for his friendship. Wilhelm went through the motions of friendship, but deserted 'Phili' in his hour of greatest need and ordered him to return all the medals he had bestowed upon him.

The Kaiser's relationship to his first wife, the Empress Auguste ('Dona'), has been pictured – by Wilhelm as well as several biographers – as one of domestic bliss. Nevertheless, he told a member of his entourage that she 'had stabbed him in the back.'[132] When asked about his relationship with his second wife, Hermine, the Kaiser replied, 'I must dissemble with her as I do with everyone else.'[133] No one, apparently, could be trusted. Yet that was not Wilhelm's view of himself. He preferred to think that he was a trusting person who believed in the basic goodness of all people. 'Distrust,' he once said in a public speech, 'does an injustice both to others and to oneself ... We have an obligation to accept all people as good ... Following this principle, I have always accepted every person whom I had anything to do with ... one must go forward with new trust (*Vertrauen*) in humanity.'[134]

Resembling Hitler in his proclivity for denying personal distrust and deception, the Kaiser was also like the Führer in denying that he ever deceived anyone – indeed Wilhelm used almost the same words in insisting that he never lied about anything: 'Have I ever broken my word? Duplicity and intrigue are foreign to my nature. My acts should speak for themselves, but you don't hear about them, only those that are misunderstood and twisted.'[135]

If only others had been so upright and honourable towards him! Alas, they were not. Throughout his life, the Kaiser believed that they deceived him, persecuted him, betrayed, and conspired against him. In 1898, Wilhelm lamented that for years 'I have been abused, ill-treated & a butt to [sic] any bad joke.' Thirty years later, he felt the same way: 'An ocean of abuse, vilification, infamy, slanders and lies has rolled over me ... And all that quiet labour [of building peace] has been utterly & wantonly destroyed. I ... became the Archfiend, the Hun, Attila, etc. and had to undergo an ordeal of lies, slanders.'[136]

Memoirists and biographers could not be trusted to tell the truth about him. Sir Sidney Lee, the noted Shakespearean scholar and author of the official life of Edward VII, was – according to Wilhelm – a particularly venomous liar, and Wilhelm knew the reason why: 'I found out that Lee is in reality a Jew. A Mr Lazarus, [who] quietly dropped his real name and adopted that of Lee.'[137]

The Kaiser imagined that he was surrounded by diabolic schemers who seemed to befriend him, while conspiring against him. Not only had his own wife and her friends been disloyal, Bismarck, too, had betrayed his trust. 'He trampled on me,' the Kaiser wrote to Emperor Franz-Joseph, 'because I didn't give him his own way. What a dagger-thrust into my heart that was!'[138] In 1918 'the German people ... betrayed and expelled me.'[139] Only German trees and the Rhine River remained trustworthy. When Wilhelm's hostess told him upon his arrival in Holland in November 1918 that the panelling in the castle came from Germany, the ex-Kaiser replied, 'So at least my trees and my river did not desert me!'[140]

Wilhelm was convinced that his friends plotted actively against him. When he was in his mid-twenties, he thought he detected a certain coolness towards him in his grandfather, Wilhelm I, and he discovered the reason: 'Certain gentlemen of high position and great influence with Grandpapa have misrepresented [me] and a secret attempt was made to blacken me in his opinion ... They agitate against me in secret ways ... and entangle Grandpapa against me.'[141]

He was particularly suspicious of the plots he was sure his uncle Edward VII was hatching against him. When he learned that Edward planned a holiday in Paris and Biarritz, his favourite spa, and that he would travel incognito (as he often did), Wilhelm was immediately suspicious. He was sure a plot was afoot.[142]

Wilhelm's conspiracy theories made it difficult for the leaders of other countries to work with him in the interests of peace. When he received a report that a member of the British foreign office had urged a German diplomat, 'Wherever you go, pray do your best to encourage ... good relations between our two nations,' the Kaiser immediately smelled another rat. He angrily margined, 'Unbelievable effrontery! It has nothing whatever to do with us! But with the impudent British! How should Oberndorff be expected to bring them to reason?'[143]

The Kaiser believed that he was blameless for the Great War, and he wanted the world to know that. In August 1914 he had thousands of postcards sent out with his picture and the caption: 'Before God and History, I did not want this War!' The blame lay entirely with others who had plotted against him. Wilhelm's comprehensive and imaginative list was headed by the Tsar of Russia and the King of England, both of whom had personally betrayed him. He confided to a small gathering of friends his shock at discovering the real culprits: 'To think that Nickie and Georgie should have played me false! If my grandmother had been alive, she would never have allowed it.'[144]

In a particularly revealing remark, Wilhelm showed that he tried to confront his own failings and admit his mistakes, but he was not quite able to do so. The blame had to be assigned to others. Ilsemann recalled that one day in 1924, when the ex-Kaiser was reflecting on his stewardship of Germany in peace and in war and was in the midst of yet another harangue about virtue unrewarded, conspiracy and betrayal triumphant, he suddenly stopped, then continued in a barely audible voice: '"During the past years I have often thought over what I should have done at that time, and where the mistakes and deficiencies lay" ... But immediately he began to accuse others ... the nobility ... the army ... and, in the first place, Freemasonry. "Yes, even among the officers, there were Masons who committed treason."'[145] As we shall see, the Kaiser later put 'international Jewry' at the top of his list of those responsible for the war.[146]

Unable to detect his own shortcomings, Wilhelm was always conscious of the faults and foibles of others. Thus, the compulsive talker, who owned more uniforms and sported more medals than any other European monarch, poked fun at the king of Bulgaria, saying that he talked too much about himself and was 'covered with orders like a Christmas tree.'[147] The Kaiser approved Adolf Hitler's aggression, but complained that the Führer – like many other people he could mention – talked too much. Referring to Hitler's speech to the Reichstag of 7 March 1936, which announced the remilitarization of the Rhineland, the Kaiser said that Hitler 'should simply have acted and not made a speech about it.'[148]

Wilhelm took very seriously indeed his honorific British titles as 'Field Marshal' and 'Admiral of the Fleet' bestowed upon him by his uncle and his grand-mother. Since for him show was substance, he considered it proper to give the British war office detailed instructions on conducting military campaigns in the Boer War and to offer advice to the Admiralty on the construction, training, and deployment of the British navy. But when the king of Portugal, who was also an honorary admiral, inspected the British fleet lying at anchor in Vigo Bay, the Kaiser scoffed derisively, 'The fathead! It's nothing but an honorary title which gives him no rights at all!'[149]

The Kaiser's temper was volcanic. His entourage lived in terror of his sudden rages and tried at almost any cost to avoid provoking a tantrum. A close associate wrote to a friend in the foreign office, 'I feel as if I'm sitting on a powder keg' and urged him not to send discouraging news which might provoke 'further outbreaks of the royal temper ... S.M. [His Majesty] *no longer has himself under control ... I see no way out but to wait quietly and pray to God.*'[150]

Frustration of cherished plans produced especially violent reactions. He had wanted German troops, for instance, to be the first to march triumphantly into Peking after crushing the Boxer Rebellion of 1900. When he learned that Peking had already been subdued by British and Russian forces before the Germans could arrive, 'The Kaiser ... completely lost control of himself. He spoke about Russia and England, who had "betrayed" him, in the bitterest terms.'[151] When he heard that Bismarck had permitted the text of a treaty to be published, Wilhelm lost his head, summoned his aides, and 'officially ordered the arrest of Prince Bismarck on a charge of high treason.' His ministers were dumbfounded. (When the rage had spent itself, they cancelled the order.)[152] In one of his wild outbursts he yelled at a general, 'Whoever dares to say one word against me will be utterly smashed' (*zerschmettert werden*).[153]

The Kaiser simply could not understand why anyone would dare to disagree with the 'All Highest Person' who was, he insisted, 'the anointed of God.' He made sure that Article 95 of the Imperial Criminal Code dealing with *Majestätsbeleidigung (lèse majesté)* was rigorously enforced. Under that article, subjects could be arrested and charged with criminal offence for failure to rise when a toast was proposed to the Kaiser or 'for manifesting disrespectful attitudes,' or for telling jokes that poked fun at 'Siegfried Meyer' or 'S.M.' (The initials S.M. were the popular code for *Seine Majestät*, His Majesty.) In the first decade after his accession (1888–98) more than 1,000 years of imprisonment were meted out to violaters of Article 95. A contemporary student of the Imperial justice system commented that 'no section of the entire Criminal Code of the Empire [is] so frequently broken.'[154] Wilhelm's mother, greatly disturbed by her son's persecution of critics, wrote privately to the future chancellor's wife: 'These constant prosecutions and imprisonments for *Majestäts-*

beleidigung, I think it deeply to be regretted! How shocked my husband would have been! ... you must burn these lines please ... This is for *your Husband and you alone.*'[155]

The Kaiser personally went through many of the dossiers and was genuinely amazed that one particular 'criminal' should commit so heinous and inexplicable a crime as criticism of his Emperor: 'It would seem that this man hitherto has not been a criminal – son of respectful parents, himself in a respectable walk of life with a good education and yet – how do you *explain* this? This insult to the anointed of God? Strange! Strange!'[156]

Parliamentary criticism was incomprehensible to the Kaiser. When the socialist August Bebel made a less than flattering remark in the Reichstag about his government, Wilhelm, upon reading Bebel's comments, turned to an aide and 'with clouded brow and flashing eye' cried out 'in a voice trembling with passion, "All this to *me!* To *me!* What is the country coming to?"'[157]

Wilhelm was particularly shocked to discover that there was some opposition among 'his' nobility. 'I have noticed with a deeply disturbed heart,' he said in a speech at Koenigsberg, 'that even among ... the nobility who stand closest to me ... the word *opposition* has actually been uttered! Gentlemen, opposition among Prussian nobles is an absurdity *(Unding)* ... I hold this throne by the grace of God!'[158] When an adviser suggested that such speeches might further antagonize members of the nobility and that it would be politically prudent to show more self-restraint, Wilhelm did not see his point. He announced aggressively that he was not afraid of anybody. If they wanted a fight he was ready for them: 'I'll get harder and harder ... a stone will become a block of steel!'[159]

But the Kaiser's words were usually more pugnacious than his actions. His first response to criticism was bewildered belligerence; but if the critic refused to yield, the All Highest Person sometimes backed down. Once when the usually compliant chancellor, Prince Hohenlohe, stood by his guns and said with dignity, 'I am the Chancellor of the Reich and not a [minor] official,' the Kaiser was silent. He could also accept some suggestions if they were made with appropriate deference. Von Moltke, his chief of staff, for example, told him after army manoeuvres in 1904 that the morale of the generals was lowered when the Kaiser led one of the armies. There was little point in making plans, they complained, since the Kaiser's army always won. He urged the supreme warlord to observe but not to participate in manoeuvres. On this occasion, perhaps assuming that Moltke considered him an invincible commander, the Kaiser took the advice and did not botch the exercises of 1905, 1906, and 1907.[160]

One way of coping with adverse comment was to refuse to listen. The British ambassador reported that the Kaiser had the habit of cutting off any conversation that was not entirely to his liking by interrupting to say, 'I do not admit that this is so.'[161] He ordered his staff to filter his news for him. As an aide reported, 'He will only listen to what gives him pleasure ... for heaven's sake, [tell him] nothing that goes against his view of the world!'[162]

This complex man was not lacking, however, in touches of that self-irony which was totally lacking in Adolf Hitler. Wilhelm could smile, for instance, at his own volubility, once complaining that someone 'talked so much I could hardly get in a word – and with me, as you know, that doesn't happen very often!'[163] His treatment of an excessively laudatory article in a British newspaper is revealing. 'All visitors to the [German] ships confirm the statement that Wilhelm II is regarded by *those who wear his uniform with almost religious devotion.*'[164] Wilhelm's own underscoring of the article was accompanied by his wry note, 'All of them??' in the margin. He was even able to joke about the immensely popular, biting, and even scurrilous satire which compared his megalomania with that of the Roman Emperor Caligula.[165]

Yet it remained difficult for Wilhelm to admit that he personally had made a mistake. Ilsemann noted ruefully, 'I have [now] read everything the Kaiser has written ... Interesting material, but ... he proves to his own satisfaction that in all personal, political, and military affairs, His Majesty was always right. Mistakes were always the fault of others.'[166] His psychological defences were too strong to allow feelings of personal guilt to enter the fortress of his inner self. But he could feel wounded pride and embarrassment. Indeed, his sleep was disturbed by dreams in which he was mocked and ridiculed. He spent anxious nights regretting his *faux pas* – only to repeat them the next day.[167]

The Kaiser's attitude towards females would not have recommended itself to feminists. When his first child was born on 29 January 1887, his mother recorded, 'William is delighted that it is a boy and does not wish for girls who [*sic*] he considers "no use."'[168] Three years later, when he was asked if he would not like a daughter, he repeated his feeling that 'girls are useless creatures; he ... far preferred to be without.'[169] He defined the Ideal Woman in a letter to Lady Mary Montague: 'Women [should] marry, love their husbands, have lots of babies, bring them up well, cook nicely, and make their husband's home comfy for them.'[170]

When Wilhelm's wife received female visitors, they were enjoined never to talk about politics or public affairs. He read aloud to them while they listened silently and did needlework. Indeed, his second wife, Hermine, kept sewing materials handy so that her guests could embroider while the Emperor talked or read to them from his extensive collection of tedious books and monographs.

The first woman he married, Viktoria Auguste, Duchess of Schleswig-Holstein, Sonderburg-Augustenburg ('Dona') was the living embodiment of his ideal wife: a quiet woman, thoroughly trained in the domestic arts – and in all respects the opposite of his mother. Her home was her life; pleasing her husband, her mission. Queen Victoria found her 'gentle, amiable, and sweet.' The comment of a family friend was lacerating: 'I have never met *anyone* so devoid of any individual thought or agility of brain and understanding. She is just like a good, quiet soft cow that has calves & eats grass slowly & ruminates.'[171]

When Viktoria Auguste died in exile in 1921, the Kaiser was less than generous in his comments about the woman who had stood loyally at his side through triumph and disaster, had borne his children, suffered his infidelities, and listened sympathetically to his monologues and interminable readings. He confided to a companion that with her death, 'I feel free at last.'[172]

Contemporaries and most biographers have said that Wilhelm was faithful to his wife. The evidence suggests otherwise. Shortly after their marriage in 1881, Prince Wilhelm wrote a letter to a famous Viennese procuress, who supplied him with a number of high-class prostitutes and one illegitimate daughter. Another woman, one Anna Homolatsch, became pregnant by him and was paid off to keep quiet, as were 'at least three other women.'[173] If Elisabeth von Wedel's memoirs are to be believed, the Kaiser was one of her several lovers. Their affair, she insisted, took place in 1887 while she was living in the Persian embassy – the ambassador being another of her 'friends.' Wedel reprinted several sentimental letters from the Kaiser, one of which accompanied a bracelet which she refused to sell back at the behest of the court. The letters sound Wilhelmian.[174] After his accession to the throne in 1888, however, there is no evidence of any extramarital liaisons, with either mistresses or prostitutes.

The Kaiser preferred the company of men, particularly of soldiers. One hour before his wedding, Wilhelm was drilling a company of grenadiers on the parade ground. The next morning at sunrise he returned to Potsdam to be with his regiment. As a French reporter noted, 'Such zeal is, of course, most admirable, but it must have left the young wife slightly surprised.'[175] A letter to a friend sets forth his personal priorities. In commenting on a visit to Copenhagen, Wilhelm found the women lovely, particularly a beautiful redhead 'whom I especially admired.' But he added quickly and revealingly, 'What more could one want? Answer: Darkness and a military encampment!'[176] No women were invited on the annual cruises to Norway, and none were allowed in the Liebenberg Circle, the intimate gathering that met at Count Philipp zu Eulenburg's estate.

As with the Führer, the evidence of the Kaiser's homosexual inclinations is ambiguous. Eulenburg, his closest friend of many years, was a practising homosexual, as were others in the Kaiser's entourage, notably Kuno von Moltke and Friedrich Alfred Krupp. Count Eulenburg had fallen in love with Wilhelm, and, as Thomas Kohut has pointed out, that poses problems for the biographer, since

Eulenburg saw in their relationship what he wanted to see and may well have described in his extensive correspondence an intimacy that Wilhelm may not have reciprocated.[177] While it is difficult to know how the Kaiser felt about Eulenburg, there is no doubt about Eulenburg's feelings. Even in the extant letters, which were carefully selected and culled before being placed in the archives,[178] Wilhelm was to him, 'My Beloved' and the 'Darling' whom he loved 'above everyone' (that included, presumably, his wife and his eight children). When Eulenburg learned that the Kaiser had appointed his dear friend and fellow homosexual, Kuno von Moltke, to the position of *Flügeladjutant* (military aide-de-camp), he was overjoyed. 'Phili' wrote to Wilhelm how delighted he was that 'precisely *he* is to be with my hotly beloved Kaiser.'[179]

Later, the Kaiser's response to this love took an ugly turn. After Eulenburg suffered a heart attack during his long, sordid, and demeaning trial for homosexuality in 1908, and the trial was adjourned, the Kaiser was willing to let his former friend go on suffering. He wrote to one of Eulenburg's intimate friends, 'The trial must continue, even if E. [Eulenburg] remains in the fire!'[180]

Wilhelm obviously wanted to dissociate himself from his former friend and demonstrate his abhorrence of homosexuality. It is strange, however, that it had not occurred to him that as the trial wore on and the testimony became increasingly lurid, the very flames that were burning his most intimate friend would come perilously close to the Kaiser himself. Even if His Majesty were exonerated, the testimony would, at the very least, directly associate him with acknowledged homosexuals.[181] Many years later, Wilhelm insisted that Eulenburg was completely innocent and had been set up by the Kaiser's enemies and 'international Jewry' in order to defame him.[182]

It is doubtful that the Kaiser had physical sex with Eulenburg, or with any other male. He did, however, exhibit homoerotic symptoms which strongly suggest latent homosexual tendencies. His words and habits are suggestive. He said of Bülow, for instance, 'I adore him,' and reassured him that their tiffs were merely 'lovers' quarrels.'[183] He liked to pinch men's cheeks or legs, slap their buttocks, throw his arms around them, and kiss them.[184] When he learned of the death of Baron Holstein, Wilhelm called across the room to the German ambassador to Greece, 'Come quick so that I can kiss you, I've just received a telegram announcing the death of Holstein.'[185] When the first German offensive of August 1914 went well, General von Moltke was startled to find himself 'showered with kisses' by the Supreme War Lord.[186]

Members of the Liebenberg Circle knew how much their favourite guest enjoyed 'masculine' entertainment and vied with one another in inventing skits that would appeal to the Kaiser's taste for anality and the obscene. The chief of the military cabinet, Dietrich Count von Hülsen-Haeseler, had a sudden inspiration for such a skit and wrote excitedly to General Emil Graf Schlitz von Görtz:

I'll parade you like a clipped poodle! That'll be a 'hit' like nothing else. Just think: behind *shaved*, in front, long bangs out of black or white wool; in back, under a real poodle's tail, a noticeable rectal opening; and, as soon as you stand up on your hind feet, *in front* a fig leaf.

Just think how terrific [it will be] when you bark, or howl to music, shoot off a pistol or do other foolish things. It'll be simply splendid!! Nobody can make a costume as good as you can; you can model the head yourself – I already see in my mind's eye H.M. laughing like us – and I'm counting on a *succès fou*.

His Majesty did indeed find the performance hilarious, as he would on another occasion when the moose-tall Count Hülsen-Haeseler appeared dressed as a *balleteuse*, prancing about in a tutu. The laughter died, however, when the real showstopper came: the count dropped dead of a massive heart attack. The historian of Wilhelm's entourage who describes these incidents assures us that such transvestite skits, usual at Liebenberg and on the Norwegian cruises, 'never went beyond the juvenile.'[187]

The very vehemence of Wilhelm's denial of any 'feminine weaknesses,' his strident assertion of purely 'masculine' traits, and his overt conduct with male companions – the juvenile physical 'games,' the swatting of behinds, the crushing handshakes, and physical sadism disguised as 'exercise' – all bear, as Isabel Hull has suggested, the clear stamp of repressed homosexual inclinations.[188]

Here, then, was the last of the German kaisers – a man who was at once callous and considerate, charming and boorish, who rattled the sabres of war and preached goodwill to all mankind; the mighty emperor who played games of tag with his entourage, who extolled morality and delighted in bawdy skits, who trumpeted his omnipotence and pleaded for reassurance, who was able to rule an empire and unable to govern himself. This naturally gifted monarch of extraordinary promise who sought to exalt royal power was largely responsible for its demise.

THE FÜHRER, ADOLF HITLER[189]

He is like a child, kind, good, merciful. Like a cat: cunning, clever, agile. Like a lion: roaring great and gigantic. A great guy, a man! (ein Kerl, ein Mann!)

Joseph Goebbels, diary entry, 1926

He was a character out of the pages of Dostoyevsky, a man 'possessed.'

André François-Poncet, French Ambassador to Germany, 1931–8

How is it possible that he captivated me so, and for more than a decade?

Albert Speer, Hitler's architect, diary entry 20 November 1952

As Führer of the Germans, Adolf Hitler probably exercised more direct personal political power than any ruler in history. He was in very fact what Wilhelm Hohenzollern had only aspired to be: the 'All Highest Person.' Hitler created both his own political theory and a government that could not exist without him. It was he who set the standards for art, music, medicine, and poetry in Germany. His whim became national law. He dictated statutes that stipulated the religion of household servants, the colours artists could use in paintings, the way lobsters were to be cooked in restaurants, and how physics was to be taught in the universities. He decided whom Germans might marry, what they could name their children, where they were to be buried. At his command thousands of young soldiers died in hopeless battle, many with his name on their lips. On his orders millions of innocent people were tortured, maimed, and murdered. He was the arbiter of the fate of nations. Few dictators have enjoyed so much genuine support from so great a number of people.

The magic of Hitler's appeal is best remembered by an American journalist who saw the Führer enter Nuremberg one lovely September day in 1934:

Like a Roman Emperor Hitler rode into this medieval town at sundown today past solid phalanxes of wildly cheering Nazis who packed the narrow streets that once saw Hans Sachs and the Meistersinger. Tens of thousands of Swastika flags blot out the Gothic beauties of the place, the facades of the old houses, the gabled roofs ...

About ten o'clock I got caught in a mob of ten thousand hysterics who jammed the moat in front of Hitler's hotel shouting, 'We want our Führer!' I was a little shocked at the faces, especially those of the women ... They reminded me of the crazed expressions I saw once in the back country of Louisiana on the faces of some Holy Rollers who were about to hit the trail. They looked up at him as if he were a Messiah, their faces transformed.[190]

Hitler manipulated his charisma adroitly and used personal appeal with consummate artistry. As the occasion or audience demanded, he could be charming or brutal, generous or vicious. He was adored by housewives and artists, peasants and architects, professors and plumbers, children and generals. He was a ruthless opportunist with an almost perfect sense of timing, knowing instinctively the precise moment to strike. He was also a man with a faith that moved mountains. Like all dominating political leaders, Hitler combined political realism with unshakable faith in his historic destiny.

Carl Gustav Jung proclaimed him 'the incarnation of the people's soul (*Volkseele*).' Above all else, Hitler made people want to follow him. David Lloyd George, himself a notable practitioner of the political arts, stood in awe of Hitler and, after an extensive visit in Germany, proclaimed him to be one of the truly great men of the ages:

The old trust him; the young idolize him. It is not [only] the admiration accorded to a popular Leader. It is the worship of a national hero who has saved his country from utter despondency and degradation ...

He is something more. He is the George Washington of Germany – the man who won for his country independence from all her oppressors. To those who have not actually seen and sensed the way Hitler reigns over the heart and mind of Germany, this description may appear extravagant. All the same, it is the bare truth.[191]

Winston Churchill was also impressed. In 1937 he looked at Hitler's accomplishments and called them 'among the most remarkable in the whole history of the world.'[192]

Hitler's rise had indeed been one of history's great political success stories. The unknown, common soldier of the First World War, who had been a failure in all his undertakings, had come to power in 1933 in a country that despaired of solving its economic and political problems. Within five years he had given his nation new hope, and a grateful people hailed him as their Saviour (*Erlöser*), who had eliminated unemployment and had given millions of workers attractive and inexpensive vacations. He had sent the youth of the land singing as they marched down sunlit roads. He had built magnificent freeways and promised automobiles to every citizen. He had humbled the victors of Versailles and wiped out the treaty which all Germans called the Treaty of Shame. In a series of brilliant and bloodless coups, he had created a triumphant Greater Germany, proud and strong, remilitarized the Rhineland, and annexed Austria and Czechoslovakia.

If only he had died in 1939 before the onset of the Second World War, a German historian has written, he would have been remembered by his grateful countrymen as 'Adolf the Great, one of the outstanding figures in German history.'[193]

But he lived on, long enough to plunge the world into the most destructive war in human history and to set the fires of the Holocaust.

Any attempt simply to describe Adolf Hitler immediately confronts a tangle of complexities. We look at his unimpressive, even ludicrous figure and wonder how it was possible for him to hold a great nation in thrall. Physically, Hitler did not seem well cast for the role of a great historic force. He looked rather like an apprentice waiter in a second-rate Viennese cafe. Barely five feet, nine inches tall, he weighed, during his better days, about 150 pounds. He had a tendency to put on flabby weight, and his posture deteriorated through the years. His shoulders were narrow, his chest somewhat sunken with skin white, shiny, and hairless. His legs were unusually short, his knees slightly knocked and quite chubby, his feet very large. He did not appear to best advantage in the baggy riding britches and huge jackboots that he so often wore. His walk was rather mincing; he tended to drag his left foot. And he wore a Charlie Chaplin moustache.[194]

He was fascinated by his hands, which were finely structured with long, graceful fingers. In his private library there was a well-thumbed book containing pictures and drawings of the hands of famous people throughout history. Hitler liked to show his guests how closely his own hands resembled those of Frederick the Great, his historic hero. He was convinced that he could judge people's character and loyalty on the basis of their hands. On meeting someone for the first time he would stare carefully into the stranger's eyes and then closely examine the hands. When his Eagle's Nest in the Kehlstein was being built, a piece of rock shaped like a hand was found. Hitler was intrigued with it. He called it the 'Hand of Wotan' and had it mounted in a special case, as if it were a holy relic.[195]

Hitler's hair was dark brown. He parted it on the right side, his famous forelock falling over the left temple. His nose was large and coarse, his nostrils abnormally wide; his bushy moustache was cut just wide enough to help conceal them. His teeth were brownish-yellow and replete with fillings and bridges. He shielded his mouth with his hand on the rare occasions when he laughed.

The most impressive feature of his otherwise undistinguished face was his eyes. They were extraordinarily light blue in colour, with a faint touch of greenish-grey. Almost everyone who met Hitler mentioned his strangely compelling eyes. The list includes Robert Coulondre, the French ambassador, and the German dramatist Gerhart Hauptmann who, when first introduced to Hitler, stared into his famous eyes and later told friends, 'It was the greatest moment of my life!'[196] H.S. Chamberlain wrote him, 'It is as if your eyes were equipped with hands, for they grip a man and hold him fast.'[197]

Women were particularly impressed, even frightened, by Hitler's eyes. A boyhood friend recalled that when he introduced Adolf to his mother, she told him that evening, '"What eyes your friend has!" And I remember quite distinctly that there was more fear than admiration in her words.'[198] Women continued to be impressed. Nietzsche's sister found Hitler's eyes fascinating and disturbing: 'They ... searched me through and through.' And Martha Dodd, daughter of the American ambassador, wrote that the Führer's eyes were 'startling and unforgettable.'[199]

The absence of eyelashes seemed to add to their curiously hypnotic effect. Hitler knew their power and practised piercing glances in front of a mirror in order to use them when he wanted especially to impress people. At dinner or tea table Hitler enjoyed staring down a guest. Albert Speer apparently liked to play the game, too: 'Once we were seated at the round table in the tea house, Hitler began staring at me. Instead of dropping my eyes I took it as a challenge. Who knows what primitive instincts were involved in such staring duels? I had had others and always used to win them, but this time I had to muster almost inhuman strength, seemingly forever, not to yield to the ever-mounting urge to look away – until Hitler suddenly closed his eyes, and turned to the woman at his side.'[200]

Hitler's library showed his interest in the study of heads. Many of his books were devoted to the pseudo-sciences of phrenology and craniology. His own head, understandably, was of particular concern to him. An American correspondent reported that Hitler once summoned a group of medical specialists to his Munich apartment on the Prinzregentenstrasse one winter day in 1937 to examine and measure their Führer's skull. The ranking member of the group, who must have been acutely embarrassed by the whole affair, was Professor Ferdinand Sauerbruch, a surgeon of international reputation. He was obliged to watch as phrenologists and craniologists, equiped with all manner of calipers and tapes, took meticulous measurements of every conceivable portion of Hitler's head. All measurements were annotated and compared with those computed from the death masks or portraits of famous people. Hitler was as delighted as a child when his experts declared that his cranial dimensions were remarkably like those of Frederick the Great or Napoleon. He nodded benignly and said, 'Yes, yes, record it all.'[201] Posterity, however, seems to have been deprived of the notations and drawings made on that day.

Was there something about Hitler's past that made him so concerned about his head, eyes, hands, and nostrils? Why did he play that staring game?

Hitler was a person of opposites, a man who thought and spoke in disjunctive extremes. Anyone accused of crime should either be acquitted or beheaded: 'The only choice,' he said, 'is between life and death, victory or destruction, glory or ignominy ... We shall be conquering heroes or sacrificial lambs.' Or again, 'One is either a hammer or an anvil.' A person either followed him blindly or was a traitor. A leader could be either brutal and hard as steel or as soft and weak as a woman. There was no in-between.[202]

During a conversation prior to the Second World War, the constant battle within him between opposing forces of destruction and creativity was brought into sharp focus. Hitler had been meeting in his retreat overlooking the Bavarian Alps with Professor Burckhardt, the League of Nations representative in Danzig, who was trying to achieve a peaceful settlement of the Polish problem. At one moment Hitler shook with rage, crashed his fists against the table and walls, and screamed in a voice cracking with fury, 'If the slightest incident occurs, I will smash[203] the Poles without warning so that not a trace of Poland will ever be found. I'll smash them like lightning with the full power of a mechanized army.' Then he suddenly stopped, turned to look pensively out the window at the glorious Alps, and observed quietly, 'How fortunate I am when I am here. I have worked hard enough. Now I need a rest ... Oh, how gladly would I stay here and work as an artist. I am an artist, you know.' Years later, in the midst of war, Hitler mused, 'Wars come and go. What remains is only the values bestowed by culture. Hence my love of art, music, and architecture – are they not the powers which point the way for future humanity?'[204]

Albert Speer, who has been called the 'Devil's Architect,' noticed the constant conflict in Hitler between the urge to destroy and the longing to create, and observed that architecture was 'at least one pregnant clue to this strange man ... It was not his avocation; it was his obsession. And long before the end I knew that Hitler was not destroying to build, he was building to destroy.'[205] Thoughts of death and destruction kept intruding on designs for creation. In setting forth grandiose plans for magnificent stone buildings greater than the pyramids, and while proclaiming that he was 'building for eternity,' Hitler felt compelled to add a note of finality and death: 'We are the last Germany. If we should ever go down, then there will no longer be a Germany.'[206] In planning the colossal assembly hall in Nuremberg, he included sketches showing what the building would look like as a ruin.

Hitler could be a delightful and considerate dinner companion. He was also a boor, offensively gauche, insufferably rude. He did not like his guests to wear lipstick and told them that it was manufactured – variously – from sewage, human fat, or kitchen garbage. Once when women at his table in a restaurant were served suckling pig, Hitler announced loudly that '[It] looks exactly like a roast baby to me.'[207]

At social gatherings the Führer often seemed timid, ill-at-ease. He worried whether his guests would have a good time at his teas, he checked and rechecked the flowers and the seating arrangements. He fretted over which tie he should wear. Anxiously he sought reassurance that everything was just fine. While planning such an event he was heard to mutter, 'I'll show them that I know as much as they do about such matters.'

The Führer was both frugal and profligate. His eating habits – with the exception of chocolates, cake, and other sweets – were austere. At one time he developed a liking for caviar, but gave it up because it was 'sinfully expensive.' His spartan field headquarters during the war reminded his generals of a combination 'monastery and concentration camp.'

Yet Hitler was a wealthy man. The revenue he received from his portrait on German stamps and the royalties from *Mein Kampf* came to several million dollars. He had owed over half a million Reichsmarks in back taxes, but when he became chancellor, he ordered these obligations cancelled. After 1934 he paid no taxes whatsoever.[208] As his architect noted, Hitler threw away billions of marks on unnecessary and unused buildings: 'I have forgotten how many secret headquarters I ordered built for him – nine, I think, seven of which he seldom or never used.'[209]

Like the Kaiser, the Führer swung between the poles of rigidity and change. He wanted many things to remain fixed – political ideas, personal habits, wearing apparel, the members of his entourage, the same conversations about the same subjects. He prided himself on being a rigid person. Yet there was always a desire to change things and move about a great deal – to redesign and rebuild whole cities, to take sudden trips and excursions. He did not refer to his political organization as a party. That was too static. He called it his Movement (*meine Bewegung*).

Hitler was vicious and vindictive, capriciously and unpredictably cruel. He also wanted to be seen as kind and considerate. His image of himself kept swinging between the two extremes of kindliness and barbarity. Late in the night of 28–9 September 1941 he mused, 'Thank God I always avoided persecuting my enemies.' In one of his last soliloquies Hitler observed that he had 'never had the slightest desire to crush or overwhelm others.'[210] But the inclination to 'softness' and charity was immediately countered by assertions of hardness and brutality. One day at lunch, for example, he reflected, 'When I think about it, I realize that I'm extraordinarily humane.' But a few moments later he announced: 'I see no other solution but extermination [of the Jews].'

Sometimes Hitler expressed conflict over his own self-image in adjacent sentences. On the night of 25–6 September 1941, for instance, he said, 'I would prefer not to see anyone suffer, not to do harm to anyone. But then I realize that the species is in danger and ... sentiment gives way to the coldest reason.' And on the night of 1–2 February 1942, 'I was pitiless ... but in general I can say that I am full of moderation. I am certainly not a brutal man by nature.'[211]

Hitler's brutality was notorious and needs no further documentation here. His acts of genuine kindness are less well known. The future Führer's Vienna roommate, August Kubizek, recalled that Adolf 'gave as much as he possibly could to beggars and street musicians,'[212] and that as late as 1944 Hitler sent Kubizek's mother a food package and warm congratulations on her eightieth birthday: 'I never discovered how he came to know about it.'[213] Hitler paid the medical expenses of a woman who had befriended his mother in Linz. When his photographer's wife died in 1928, Hitler stood with her children at the grave comforting them and holding their hands.[214] (He must have recalled the miserable day in Leonding when, as a lad of eleven, he had stood alone by the open grave of his little brother Edmund.)[215] After the death in 1935 of Josef Popp, his landlord during his pre-war Munich years, Hitler sent anonymously a monthly stipend of 150 marks to the widow and her children. The money came from sales of *Mein Kampf*.[216] Hitler worried that his secretaries were not getting enough to eat or that they were too chilly in the cool offices he preferred: He insisted that his chauffeur eat before he himself was served. He told funny stories and romped with Wagner's grandchildren who adored their 'Uncle Wolf.' During the First World War, as we shall see, he wrote compassionate poems about wounded enemy soldiers.[217]

We do not expect Hitler to behave like that – and we really don't want to hear that he did, for we like to think that such an evil person was devoid of every humane instinct, the Devil incarnate totally unlike the rest of us decent human beings. That is a comforting caprice and one that would certainly simplify a biographer's task. But it is not that easy. We are dealing with a person of considerable complexity.

Hitler was concerned about the welfare of animals. During his Vienna days, he saved bits of dried bread to feed birds and squirrels at the Schönbrunn, where he went to read on summer evenings. Unlike the Kaiser, the Führer was violently opposed to hunting and furious with Göring when he boasted of his trophies. On one occasion Hitler yelled at him, 'If you call yourself a sportsman, why don't you face a wild animal in equal combat ... If you, Herr Master of the Chase, were to stand and kill your boar with a spear, then I should be impressed.'[218] He was particularly drawn to ravens, a bird which in German literature often appears as the omen of death. After attaining power, he gave special orders that ravens were not to be killed or molested.

The official *Reichsgesetzblatt* (registry of the Reich's laws) records a regulation that shows Hitler's solicitude about the suffering of crabs and lobsters. He had consulted biologists about the most humane way to kill them. Consequently, a Führer decree ordered that henceforth, in all German restaurants, 'Crabs, lobsters, and other crustaceans are to be killed by immersion in rapidly boiling water. When feasible, this should be done individually.' The general Law for the Protection of Animals, of which this order was a part, set forth in its preamble that the Führer's purpose was 'to awaken and strengthen compassion (*Mitgefühl*) as one of the highest moral values of the German people.'[219] Hitler's compassion for crustaceans did not always extend to human beings.

The Führer had a taste for erotic art and pornography; yet, like the Kaiser, he was a prude with unctuous concern for proper conduct. Gentlemen never removed their jackets, no matter how warm the weather. Unlike Wilhelm, however, Hitler did not tolerate dirty jokes or enjoy obscene skits. He was even shocked at Stalin for having his picture taken while smoking a cigarette and upset with Mussolini for appearing publicly in bathing trunks. 'Great statesmen,' Hitler observed in one of his more perishable political pronouncements, 'do not run around bare-chested.' (Not, one is tempted to add, if they had a chest like the Führer's.) He was terribly afraid, he said, that 'some skilful forger would set my head on a body in bathing trunks!'[220]

To limit the times a tailor touched him, Hitler would have several shirts and suits made at one fitting. These were expected to last for many years. He was embarrassed to disrobe before doctors and never allowed an X-ray to be taken of his chronically ailing stomach. He liked to have his body covered at all times. Even in the hottest weather he wore long silk underwear – as was observed for the first time in public on that sultry day of 20 July 1944, when a bomb explosion tore off part of his trousers.[221] Yet he was careful to say that he was not in the least embarrassed by nudity – it was others who were: 'The idea of nakedness torments only priests, for the education they undergo makes them perverts.'[222]

The Führer was even more concerned than the Kaiser about faeces, anality, and odours. Since he believed that his own body odours were particularly offensive, he bathed compulsively, changed his underwear twice a day, and he took huge quantities of 'Dr Köster's Anti-Gas Pills' to mitigate his propensity to flatulence. He also worried a great deal about his faeces and examined them often, as his doctors reported to American intelligence officers after the war. To alleviate chronic constipation, he frequently took enemas which he insisted upon administering himself.[223]

Surprisingly, Hitler even described himself in anal terms. During one of his wartime reveries in January 1942, when things were going badly on the eastern front, Hitler was comparing himself, once again, to Frederick the Great. But this time he noted that during the Seven Years' War, the Prussian king was outnumbered twelve to one (actually about five to one) while he, Hitler, enjoyed a numerical superiority over the Soviet army. He concluded that in comparison with 'Old Fritz' he, himself, 'looked like a shithead (*Scheisskopf*).' It was an expression Hitler often used, but never more appropriately.

Dr Henry Picker, who recorded this observation in his collection of Hitler's 'table talk,' usually bowdlerized the Führer's remarks. Albert Speer found that Picker's version of the *Tischgespräche*[224] generally coincided with his own memory of Hitler's monologues, but noted that Hitler was 'far more primitive

than he is in Picker, coarser and rougher ... He had a special fondness for scatological words like "shithead" and "crapper." '[225]

Hitler was both a brave man and a coward. As a lance corporal *Obergefreiter*
during the First World War, he had won – and deserved to win – the Iron Cross,
both first and second class, remarkable achievements for an enlisted man in the
Imperial German Army. Yet fear was one of the driving emotions of this man
who spoke so often of courage. Anyone with the stamina to read the 'Table
Conversations' in their entirety can make a catalogue of people who somehow
evoked fear and apprehension in the Führer. They included priests, hunters,
Jews, Freemasons, judges, academics, meat eaters, poets, cigarette smokers,
Americans, and skiers. He was frightened by germs, water, moonlight, and
horses – although he liked to look at statues of stallions.

The Führer kept insisting that he was never bothered by feelings of inadequacy or weakness. Max Planck remembered a remarkable interview in which
Hitler shouted that it was 'libelous' for anyone ever to accuse him of having
weak nerves. 'I tell you,' he screamed, 'I have nerves of steel!' When he said
that, Planck recalled, 'He pounded his knee, spoke ever faster, and worked himself into such a fury that there was nothing for me to do ... [but] to excuse
myself.'[226] Hitler also insisted, 'Only an insane person could say that I have an
inferiority complex ... They are absolutely crazy. *I have never had feelings of
inferiority!*'[227]

A secretary, Fräulein Schroeder, recalled that one evening during the war Hitler was whistling a classical air. When she had the temerity to suggest that he
had made a slight mistake in the melody, the Führer was furious. He showed his
vulnerability – and his lack of humour – by shouting angrily, 'I don't have it
wrong. It is the composer who made a mistake in this passage.' His press chief,
who followed him closely for ten years, recalled that if anyone corrected him on
any point of fact, in any field of knowledge, 'no matter how valid the correc-
tion, Hitler could not admit his mistake.' His personal interpreter wrote that
'throughout the time I interpreted for Hitler [1935–45] I never once heard him
make ... an admission of error even to his closest friends.'[228]

Similar statements were made about the Kaiser, and as with the Kaiser, they
need some qualification. On rare occasions Hitler did, in fact, admit a mistake.
But when he did so, like the Kaiser, he hedged his admission in a number of
ways. He would proclaim something a colossal blunder when he and his entourage knew it was trivial, or he would seem to admit an error and then
immediately conclude that someone else was to blame for it. Thus, he called
collaboration with Vichy France 'our greatest political blunder ... that too was
the work of [those] great minds in the Wilhelmstrasse!' Or else a mistake was
the result of some errant human frailty: he had been 'too soft' about Free-

masonry; he had been too lenient with the Italians, too conciliatory to the French, too kind to the Jews; he had once made the mistake of discussing politics with a woman.[229]

Throughout his life he insisted that other people were to blame for his personal failures. As a youth, when he was rejected by the Viennese Academy of Art, it was because of a Jewish conspiracy against him[230] or, his roommate recalled, 'He cursed the old-fashioned, fossilized bureacracy of the academy where there was no understanding of true artistry. He spoke of the trip-wires that were cunningly laid – I remember his very words! – for the sole purpose of ruining his career.'[231]

Years later, at the end of his career, he blamed his military failures on a number of different people: 'He talks constantly of betrayal,' an intimate reported on 23 April 1945, 'in the party leadership and in the army. The SS also lies to him now.' Soon he would add 'the betrayal of my Allies,' and, finally, the German people who were not 'worthy of me.'[232]

The pendulum kept swinging between self-doubt and grandiosity. The Führer pleaded with subordinates to reassure him of his own ability. A minor official of the German embassy in Paris, for example, recalled that on the eve of the Nazi occupation of the Rhineland in 1936 he was summoned to a conference attended by the political and military power structure of the Third Reich. The young and inexperienced official was startled when his Führer and supreme commander turned to him and asked anxiously for assurance that the invasion of the Rhineland would be successful and that the French would not resist: 'Repeatedly he asked me the curious question whether I could "guarantee" his success.'[233]

Hitler's valet recalled that before an important speech or interview, Hitler was so nervous and unsure of himself that he would rehearse passages and gestures in front of a mirror and interrupt himself by turning to his servant apprehensively, 'Does that sound right? ... Do you think I am ready to go before the audience? ... Do I look like the Führer, Linge? Do I really look like the Führer?'[234]

Fretful worries about his own image alternated with glowing assertions of indispensability, historic greatness, and immortality. Thus, to the same valet, Linge: 'My life is worth more than one or two divisions. Without me the army and Germany would collapse.' He told the Austrian chancellor, 'I have made the greatest achievement in the history of Germany, greater than any other German.' His conviction that he had mastered all human history led him, in 1919, to set forth a detailed outline for a book he planned to entitle *Die Monumentalgeschichte der Menschheit* (The Monumental History of Humanity).[235]

A speech to the commanding generals of the Wehrmacht on 23 November

1939 laid particular stress on the historic importance of his own person: 'I must in all modesty say that my own person is indispensable. Neither a military nor a civilian personality could replace me ... I am convinced of the strength of my brain and my resolution ... The fate of the Reich is dependent entirely upon me.'[236]

As the war progressed, Hitler saw himself as the personification of Germany and the single focus for all the attacks of the enemy. That he believed the entire world was marshalled against him personally was made clear in a speech of 15 February 1942: 'Today I have the honour of being this enemy because I have created a world power out of the German Reich. I am boundlessly proud that I was blessed by Providence with the permission to lead this battle.'[237]

At the very end – with his world crashing about him as he planned his suicide – Hitler still saw himself as a genius with nerves of steel. In his last political testament, he observed that during his lifetime he had made 'the most difficult decisions that ever confronted mortal man.' When a secretary, Frau Junge, asked him – as she was typing this last testament on 29 April 1945 – if National Socialism would survive his death, the Führer replied, 'The German people have shown that they are not worthy of my movement. Perhaps in a hundred years another genius will take up my ideas and National Socialism like a phoenix will rise again from the ashes.'[238]

But the pendulum kept swinging back. After making assertions of omnipotence and infallibility, Hitler worried about failure and defeat. His memoirs recalled how many times during the early days of the movement 'I had forebodings and was filled with a depressing fear.' Fear followed him after he attained power. Constantly he was obsessed by 'frightful nervous apprehension' that he was going to fail. He tried to reassure himself by protesting too much that he had absolutely no such fears, feeling it necessary to say, for example, that 'I have no fear of annihilation ... Cities will become heaps of ruins, noble monuments ... will disappear forever ... *But I am not afraid of this.*' He compressed his thinking into a familiar disjunctive, saying in 1936, 'If I win I shall be one of the greatest men in history. *If I fail* I shall be condemned, despised, and damned.'[239]

Thus, we have in Hitler, as in the Kaiser, another '*zerrissene Natur*': a man torn between opposing qualities – arrogant and vulnerable, creative and destructive, pragmatic and fanatical, brave and cowardly, rigid and malleable, pathetic and masterful, cruel and kind. (We will discuss these dualities further in Chapter 5, 'Psychological Dimensions.')

One of the striking personal characteristics of this political giant who bestrode Europe for a decade was his infantilism. There was in Hitler little capacity for mental, emotional, artistic, or sexual growth. The tastes, opinions, and lifestyle of the Chancellor and Führer were largely those of the child and adolescent of Leonding, Linz, and Vienna.

He sought to cling to his childhood by remembering it in dozens of sentimental soliloquies about his boyhood escapades. He was convinced that a magic elixir of youth really did exist, and he thought seriously of sending an expedition to India to find it. He became a vegetarian partly because he believed that a diet that (he reminded his secretaries) prolonged the lives of elephants would also add to his own.

Like a child, the Führer found oral gratification by sucking inordinate amounts of sweets and chocolates. The granddaughter of Richard Wagner remembered that as a little girl she and her sisters were fascinated by the enormous amount of sugar and chocolates Hitler consumed while visiting their mother. He told them that he ate two pounds of chocolates every single day. They waited expectantly for him to miscount the number of teaspoons of sugar he put in his tea, but he never miscalculated. Always there were seven – it was one of his favourite numbers. His valet recalled that his master was particularly drawn to chocolates in moments of tension. During an important 'Führer conference' he would leave the room, quickly devour several chocolates, then return to the meeting. In moments of agitation, the Führer of the Thousand Year Reich had the habit of sucking his little finger.[240]

The child of Leonding and the youth of Linz enjoyed going on expeditions and picnics. The adult enjoyed the same things with childlike enthusiasm. Diary entries of a close associate recorded how, in April 1926, on a motor trip to Württemberg, Hitler 'was like a youth, exuberant, singing, laughing, whistling.' On a picnic to the Königssee he was 'like a beloved, spontaneous child – enthusiastic and rapturous.'[241]

Like the Kaiser, the Führer enjoyed playing games. One of his favourites was *Biberspiel* (beaver game), which he played with his entourage on his private train or while speeding through the countryside in his open Mercedes. Anyone who saw a man with a full beard called out 'Beaver!' and counted up his triumphs. There was great excitement, his secretary assures us, when the Führer won – which he usually did. He also liked to see how fast he could dress and undress himself. His valet – who was not allowed in Hitler's bedroom – would stand just outside the door with a stopwatch and call '*Los!*' When Hitler had finished dressing he would cry '*Schluss!*' and rush out of the room to see if he had broken his record.[242]

There was nothing childish about Hitler's pre-war diplomatic coups. They were executed with a mature and masterful sense of timing and a remarkable ability to exploit the weaknesses of his victims. But his instinctive reaction to his triumphs was a childlike pleasure in the 'surprises' he played on an unsuspecting world. He chortled at his success in remilitarizing the Rhineland, in March 1936, as if he were 'enjoying a little joke of his own.' When he seized Austria in March 1938, he 'laughed joyously at our surprised faces. Another surprise packet had come off!'[243]

In March 1939, after he had intimidated the ill and elderly President Hacha of Czechoslovakia by screaming at him that he would utterly destroy the lovely city of Prague and forced him to sign away his country, Hitler ran joyously up to his secretaries and exclaimed, 'Kids, I am so happy I'd like to stand on my head!'

Informed that the Soviet–Nazi Pact had been signed in August 1939 so that he could go ahead and march into Poland, an aide recalled that the Führer turned to his entourage and chortled, ' "Won't that just make the world sit up again!" And in a mood of complete abandon ... he slapped himself delightedly on the knee and exclaimed, "That will really land them [England and France] in the soup!" '[244]

A newsreel camera recorded for history the reaction of the man who, after the fall and humiliation of France in 1940, had just been proclaimed 'The Greatest Military Commander of All Time': he giggled, slapped his thigh, and danced a little jig.

The Führer's taste in movies was juvenile. He was delighted with Joseph Goebbel's Christmas present for 1937: eighteen Mickey Mouse films.[245] Other favourites included *Snow White and the Seven Dwarfs* and *King Kong*. His favourite actress was Shirley Temple. As boy and man, he liked to read about German gods and American cowboys and Indians. He was particularly taken with the adventure stories of Karl May, a German who wrote about the American frontier – without having visited the locale – and who concocted a strange 'Western' language that his heroes spoke in a teutonized Texan drawl. The hero, Old Shatterhand, used such unlikely expletives as 'Hang it all, fellows!' 'Pshaw and damnation, Sir!' and 'Well, I shall be *bounced*!' Hitler was not alone in his admiration for May's intrepid hero. May's books sold by the thousands, and generations of German children have been captivated by Old Shatterhand's exploits; he's still going strong. Few, however, could match either the intensity or the longevity of Hitler's infatuation. As Chancellor and Führer of the Third Reich, he had a special shelf built to hold, in a place of honour, all the fruits of May's prolific pen, specially bound in vellum. Hitler read and reread the stories which served – along with the movie version of *The Grapes of Wrath* – as a main source of his knowledge about the United States. He also was convinced that Karl May knew best how to fight the Soviet army. Hitler told his entourage, 'I have ordered every officer to carry with him ... Karl May's books about fighting Indians. That's the way the Russians fight – hidden like Indians behind trees and bridges, they jump out for the kill!'[246]

Ever since he was a little boy, Adolf Hitler had been afraid to be alone at night. As an adult he insisted that someone stay up with him and talk – or, rather, hear him talk – often until dawn. He told Eva Braun, quite frankly, 'I really shudder at the thought of being alone at night.' After his guests had finally left, he sometimes summoned his dull-witted adjutant, Julius Schaub, who sat up with him until daybreak.[247]

Neither the boy nor the man had a sense of humour. The only friend of his youth said that Hitler was totally lacking in a spirit of self-irony and that 'one thing he could not do was to pass over something with a smile.' Many years later a high official of the foreign office recalled, 'I never experienced a normal bantering conversation at his table ... Concerning people, Hitler's judgments were usually bitter and derogatory. Qualities such as forbearance, humour and self-irony were completely foreign to him.'

A private secretary who was with him at the end of his life noted that Hitler liked to play tricks on people and sometimes gave a 'sort of barking gurgle when he read of some *Schadenfreude* ... [but] I must say that I never once heard him laugh out loud.' His valet of many years concurred: 'I never once heard him break out in a hearty laughter.'[248] That self-irony was not one of the Führer's strong points is suggested by his observation that 'pride is a source of strength, but pride often goes before a fall.'[249]

A secretary who had survived thousands of hours of the Führer's verbal barrages and lived to experience his final days in the Berlin bunker noted that through it all something was missing: 'Even to this day I can't define it exactly. My feeling is that in this whole deluge of words, there was lacking the humane note – the magnanimity of a cultivated human being.'[250]

The Führer was as inflexible as he was humourless. Time and again he spoke of flexibility as female weakness and obstinacy as masculine strength. He was proud of his rigidity and considered it the key to his success. In *Mein Kampf* he had insisted that his early years in Vienna were crucial to his subsequent career because 'at that time I formed an image of the world and a view of life that became the foundation for my actions ... I have had to change nothing.' Years later in his air-raid shelter, he reminisced by the hour about past political decisions and victories, which he attributed to inflexible stubbornness. He was fond, for instance, of reminding his entourage of the successful gamble he had taken in marching into the Rhineland in 1936: 'What saved us,' Hitler concluded, 'was my unshakable obstinacy and my amazing aplomb.'[251]

Inability or refusal to change was also the mark of his lifestyle and personal habits. His conversation showed a surprising number of words he had learned as a boy in rural Austria. The so-called Table Conversations in his Berlin air-raid shelter during the war found him speaking of *Dirndln, Tschapperln,* and

Bazis, of *Gigerln, Wortgegloedel,* and *Lackln.* In his more formal speeches and writings he repeated favourite words and phrases over and over. Thus, in his memoirs dictated in 1924, in his second book, dictated in 1928, and in conversations recorded in both 1934 and 1943, he spoke of 'the Holy Grail of the German blood' and referred to Jews as 'the ferment of decomposition.'[252]

As an adolescent in Vienna in 1908, Hitler promised that one day he would write a great political work about a future 'Third Reich,' and he designed the cover for the book. It was adorned with a swastika, with the author's name given as it would appear on official communication in the future: 'A. Hitler.' The actual book, written many years later, went through many editions, but Hitler could not bring himself to change any of it. A careful comparison of all the German editions of *Mein Kampf* shows that his publishers were permitted to make only minor changes to correct grammatical mistakes.[253]

Intimates all agreed that the Führer's daily routine – like the Kaiser's – was followed to the smallest detail. When taking his shepherd dog for a walk, he went through the same field every day, and each time he threw a stick it was from the same spot in the same direction. Deviation from the pattern would result in considerable agitation. He kept the same suits, raincoats, shoes, and hat year after year. He wore a necktie until it disintegrated. He listened to the same records so often that he knew their serial numbers by heart.

At Berchtesgaden and in the chancellery, the noon and evening meals had a fixed seating order made out according to his written instructions. The slightest deviation from his chart would draw down his fury. The topics discussed at meals remained constant, the same subjects coming up over and over and over again. After dinner every evening before the war there were one or two movies, some of them – like *King Kong* – repeated as many as seven times. At midnight there was the nightly gathering around a blazing fire, where the Führer – like the Kaiser – would talk on and on in monologues that were virtually programmed. His press chief of a decade described the paralyzing repetition: 'He remained perpetually in the same company, among the same faces, in the same atmosphere and, I may also say, in the same state of monotony and boredom, producing eternally the same speeches and declarations.'[254]

Hitler's last will and testament of April 1945 contains not one new idea. Line for line, and virtually word for word, his last official statement is a repetition of the program he had set forth in *Mein Kampf* and in dozens of his earlier speeches and conversations. At the end, with his Reich crashing down upon him, when an aide suggested that perhaps some things might possibly have been done differently, the Führer in baffled anguish cried out the same words the Kaiser had used: *'But don't you see, I cannot change!'*[255]

Throughout his life Hitler was inordinately concerned about food and drink.

His soliloquies were often devoted to disquisitions on healthy foods. His library contained over a dozen books on food fads and special diets. He told his dentist that he needed a special diet because noxious and unique bacteria infected his colon.[256]

Hitler may have become a vegetarian to alleviate his chronic stomach disorder, but he gave a variety of other reasons for avoiding meat. He told one doctor that he had been a vegetarian since early youth, but he told a secretary that it was only after his beloved niece – 'the only woman I could have loved' – had committed suicide in 1931 that he found the idea of eating meat repulsive. He confided to others, however, that all his life he had been plagued by excessive perspiration and had discovered as a young man that when he abstained from meat there was a great improvement: he did not sweat so much and there were fewer stains on his underwear. He also believed that a vegetable diet would prolong his life and increase his stamina. Elephants live longer than lions; horses outrun dogs, who get tired, pant, and drool repulsively. Then, too, his idol Wagner had been a vegetarian, and so Hitler said, 'I don't touch meat largely because of what Wagner says on the subject.'[257]

Only rarely did he drink wine or beer, and never – with one exception[258] – stronger spirits. As he testified at his trial for treason in 1924, 'I am almost a complete teetotaler and only take a swallow of water or beer because of the dryness of my throat.' After he became prominent, well-sweetened lemonade and weak tea were his staple drinks, supplemented with a dark beer of less than two per cent alcohol, specially brewed for him by the Holzkirchen Brewery of rural Bavaria.[259]

Hitler was a scrupulously, indeed compulsively, clean person. His boyhood friend recalled that during their Vienna days 'even more than from hunger, he suffered from a lack of cleanliness, as he was almost pathologically sensitive about anything concerning the body. At all costs, he would keep his linen and clothing clean.'

As Führer, he washed his hair every day, scrubbed his hands very often, and brushed his atrocious teeth and rinsed his mouth after every meal or snack. He shaved twice a day, never using the same blade twice and eschewing after-shave lotion. He told a British journalist that when he was poor in Vienna he had resolved that someday he would be rich enough to have two luxuries: an open fireplace in every room and a change of underwear and shirt twice a day. His well-tailored shirts were generally made of white silk.[260]

Hitler talked a great deal about dirt. People he disliked were usually described as filthy. The schoolteachers who gave him unsatisfactory grades in elementary school had 'filthy necks.' Modern artists sat on 'the dung-heap of Dadaism.' Liberals were 'dirty and false.' Jews were particularly filthy, rotten, and foul smelling: 'The smell of those caftan wearers often made me ill. Added to this were their dirty clothes ... and physical uncleanliness ... Was there any form of filth ... in which at least one Jew did not participate? When carefully cutting open such an abscess one could find a little Jew, blinded by the sudden light, like a maggot in a rotting corpse ... If the Jews were alone in this world they would suffocate in dirt and filth.'[261]

One notably unflattering metaphor revealed his private opinion of the German people. They were so much excrement, only a few of them worth recruiting for leadership positions in his party: 'We are passing a magnet over a manure heap (*Misthaufen*) and then we will see how much iron in the manure pile there is and how much will cling to our magnet.' The Jew, predictably, transformed the treasures of the world 'into dirt and dung.' Compassion and charity were to Hitler's mind 'comparable to excrement.'

Jews, he said, transformed the treasures of the world into 'filth and dung.' In talking about ridding Germany of Jews, he used the same expressions that one would use about fumigation and delousing. He wanted his Reich 'purified of Jews' (*Judenrein*) and that would be done through a process of *Entjudung* (de-Jewing). It was no accident that the lethal gas used in Hitler's death camps was Cyclon B, a form of cyanide widely used in Germany for household fumigation.

Among his other obsessions, Hitler was fascinated with wolves. As a boy he was delighted to learn that his first name came from the old German *Athalwolf* – a compound, he said, of *Athal* (noble) and *Wofa* (wolf). And 'noble wolf' he sought to remain. At the start of his political career he chose 'Herr Wolf' as his cover-name. His favourite dogs were Alsatians – in German, *Wolfshunde*. One of them, born towards the end of the war, Hitler called 'Wolf,' and he would allow no one else to touch or feed it. He named his headquarters in France *Wolfsschlucht* (Wolf's Gulch), in the Ukraine, *Werwolf* (Man-Wolf), and in East Prussia *Wolfsschanze* (Wolf's Lair). As he explained to a servant, 'I am the Wolf and this is my den.' He referred to the SS as 'my pack of wolves.' He would recall with exaltation how in the early 'battle days of the Movement' his storm troopers pounced upon the opposition 'like wolves' and were soon 'covered with blood.' In an article in his party newspaper written in 1922, Hitler used an unusual metaphor to describe how the crowds were reacting to him. They were beginning to realize, he wrote, 'that *now a wolf has been born,* destined to burst in upon the herd of seducers and deceivers of the people.'

Hitler talked his slightly backward sister Paula into changing her name to Frau Wolf. The special agent he chose to supervise purchases for his Linz library and museum was a Dr Wolfhardt (literally, 'hard wolf'). On Hitler's orders, the Volkswagen factory was to be located at 'Wolfsburg.' When he telephoned Winifred Wagner, he would say, 'Conductor Wolf calling!' The secretary he kept longer than any other (more than twenty years) was Johanna Wolf. She recalled that whereas Hitler addressed all other secretaries formally as 'Frau' or 'Fräulein,' he invariably called her 'Wölfin' (She-Wolf).

One of his favourite tunes came from a favourite movie. Often and absent-mindedly he would whistle, 'Who's afraid of the Big Bad Wolf?' – an animal, it will be recalled, who wanted to eat people up and blow their houses down.[262] Why, one wonders, this infatuation with wolves?

Just as primitive tribes attribute magical significance to blood, so did Hitler. He was sure, for example, that all of human history was explicable in its terms and, in one of his messier metaphors, asserted that 'blood is the cement of civilization.' His theory greatly simplified the historical problem of explaining the rise and fall of human cultures. Everything depended upon one factor alone: the purity or impurity of blood.

He used the word often in describing his rise to power. He promised that opponents would 'drown in a bloodbath'; he spoke of the sacred 'Blood Flag' of 9 November 1923;[263] he established a special 'Blood Order' for those who had marched on that day. He also introduced the idea of *Blutkitt* (blood cement) in training his elite SS. Hitler seems to have come across the concept in reading a book about Genghis Khan – one of his heroes – while a prisoner in Landsberg in 1924, though he may have heard that it was also practised in Egypt and in Renaissance murder societies. (Similar techniques were used by the Mau Mau in Africa and by the Devil cultists in the United States.) The idea, briefly, is this: in order to enforce absolute loyalty and obedience, organizers of terror societies force a prospective member, as part of his initiation rite, to commit an act that flagrantly violates his most sacred personal taboo. Such an atrocity, by cutting the initiate off from society and from his previous system of values, binds him irrevocably to the new organization because it is the only group that endorses the outrage he has perpetrated. In psychological terms, the traumatic act he has been obliged to commit reinforces his newly acquired superego, his new conscience.

In Hitler's Germany, medical doctors of the SS were required to perform – or to watch – 'medical experiments' such as skin grafts and abdominal surgery on the unanaesthetized bodies of Jewish or Polish 'patients.' Other initiates of the SS were required to smash the skulls of Jewish babies before the eyes of their mothers. Hitler's theory was that after his SS had participated in such activity, they would feel drawn together by bonds (*Blutkitt*) of common experience.[264]

Blood also played an important role in Hitler's private life. He thought a great deal about drinking and sucking blood. He wondered, for instance, what the blood soup of the ancient Frisians tasted like. In commenting on the history of the world as the chronic warfare of one people against another, he said, 'One creature drinks the blood of another. The death of one nourishes the other.' And he wrote that the Jew was a spider that 'sucked the people's blood out of its pores.'[265]

Hitler liked to have his own blood drawn from his body, and he enjoyed telling his secretaries what fun it was to watch leeches sucking it out. When one of the secretaries shuddered and said she didn't like the looks of those horrid creatures, he stopped her short: 'Don't say that. They're sweet little, dear little animals who have done me a geat deal of good.' He also had his quack doctor, Theodor Morell, draw his blood and save it in test tubes so that the Führer could gaze at it. Apparently Hitler wanted to get rid of his own blood. Did he think that there might be something wrong with it?

The Führer also enjoyed taunting members of his circle when he saw them eating meat. Referring to Morell's collection of his own blood, he said, 'I will have blood sausage made from my excess blood as a special culinary treat for you. Why not? You like meat so much.' He repeated this offer.[266]

Hitler had a peculiar attitude to the passage of time. He distrusted time and tried to avoid its demands. There was one clock in his office, an antique musical timepiece that once may have belonged to his family, but he never permitted it to be wound, and he never wore a wristwatch. Sometimes he carried an old-fashioned gold watch in his jacket pocket. It had a spring-cover that concealed the face. He always seemed to forget to wind it.[267]

Time was an enemy Hitler sought to defeat by saying that an idea of his or a building he designed, or anything else he approved of, would last 'for all time.' While he did not personally invent the famous sobriquet, 'the Greatest Field Commander of All Time' (*Der grösste Feldherr aller Zeiten*), he loved the sound of the phrase and grinned modestly when he heard it applied to himself. As the indefatigable German editor of his speeches and proclamations   has noted, the phrase 'of all time' is repeated in literally dozens of Hitler's speeches.[268]

The compulsive and deadly serious games that he played – such as how fast he could dress and undress – involved 'defeating' time. Hitler never really won these games. Time was constantly coming back to taunt him. Thus, he would tell his aides over and over, 'I have no time.' He had 'no time to be ill.' He had 'no time to tie his tie,' so he wore pre-tied cravats or had one tied for him by his valet.[269]

At the close of his career, Hitler blamed time for his defeat. In addition to petulance, there is a note of despair in the realization that his nemesis had defeated him in the end: 'The war came too soon,' he said in one of his last soliloquies in the bunker. '*I did not have the time* to form people according to my politics ... *we never have enough time*. Always conditions press down upon us and we ... lack time. *Time always ... works against us.*'[270]

Never enough time. Yet no ruler in all history, not even Kaiser Wilhelm II, wasted more time in pointless little trips and excursions, in hours and hours of interminable talk and twaddle. Perhaps Hitler felt that if he kept filling up the hours with words, he was in some way controlling or 'killing' time. Certainly he was destroying it for other people.

In childhood had time deceived him in some way?

Hitler had a double image of his own integrity. He considered himself an honest and completely reliable person who would, for example, abide by treaties 'blindly and faithfully.' He also saw himself as a clever dissimulator who could 'fool people' about his obligations. He confided slyly to his entourage, 'Treaties will be honoured only as long as they are useful [to me] ... Treaties exist for the purpose of being broken at the most convenient moment.'[271] In August 1939, when it was suggested to him by a Swedish emissary that the British, after long experience with his broken word, might not believe his promises with regard to Poland, Hitler was horrified at the thought. He stopped his pacing, turned in hurt surprise, and cried, 'Idiots! Have I ever in my entire life ever told a lie?'[272]

The question must be answered affirmatively. During the Blood Purge of June 1934, Hitler had ordered the murder of hundreds of people he suspected of opposing him, but two years later in a public speech he said, 'I must make here the solemn declaration: On the road of our movement, there lies not one single opponent whom we have murdered.' Repeatedly he gave his 'sacred word' to Germany and the world that he had 'no intention of threatening anyone.' He had 'no territorial demands to make in Europe.' He had no intention whatsoever of 'interfering in the internal affairs of Austria or of annexing Austria.' He swore that 'peace will never be broken by us,' and he would personally guarantee 'the inviolability' of all his neighbours' territory. 'That is not a [mere] phrase,' he said, 'that is our sacred will.'[273]

One reason he felt obliged to insist so stridently that he was an honest man may have been that he was aware of his own propensity to prevaricate. He admitted as much in a remarkably revealing comment at the beginning of a speech he gave in Berlin on 10 September 1943, when he broke a long silence after the catastrophic defeat at Stalingrad the previous winter by saying, 'Freed from the heavy burden of expectation weighing on us for a long time, I now consider that the moment has come again to address myself to the German people without having to resort to lies, either to myself or to the public.'[274]

Like the Kaiser, the Führer lied for tactical reasons, and also like him he lied gratuitously, over matters of little apparent importance. Hitler gave, to take a trivial example, many different versions of the time and occasion when he stopped smoking. He told his secretaries that as a young lad he smoked 'a long porcelain pipe ... like a chimney ... even in bed,' but he had given it up at an early age. To others, however, he confided that he had not quit smoking until years later when it occurred to him that money spent on tobacco might be better invested in food. On yet another occasion he said that he quit smoking only in 1922 because he was afraid it would impair his voice.[275]

The Führer's entourage knew how much he delighted in reading Karl May and several other novelists he recommended, yet he also told them, 'I never read a novel. That kind of reading annoys me.'[276]

Hitler's memory, like the Kaiser's, was incredibly precise. Curiously, however, he forgot – or failed to tell the truth about – generally known facts concerning his personal life. A long letter of 29 November 1921 contains patent inaccuracies about his family, describing his father, for example, as a 'postal official' when actually he had been a career customs inspector. Years later in the *Tischgespräche*, Hitler's father was made out to be a local judge.

Hitler's father and mother – and their ancestors, as far as we can tell – were born in Austria and were citizens of the Austrian or Austro-Hungarian Empire. But Hitler, on at least two occasions, tried to give a different impression. In a public speech on 22 February 1933 in Forchheim, Bavaria, he told his audience, 'I myself by my descent, my birth, and family am a Bavarian ... for the first time since the founding of the Reich the inheritance of Bismarck is in the hands of a Bavarian (*eines Bayern*).' In front of English and German diplomats who knew better, during his famous conference at Bad Godesberg in September 1938, he tried to persuade Neville Chamberlain that he could be sympathetic to England because he too was Anglo-Saxon, telling Chamberlain that since his own ancestors 'came from Lower Saxony (*Niedersachsen*)' he and the British Prime Minister could perhaps 'claim common ancestry.'[277]

Why did Hitler feel it necessary to mislead people about his ancestry?

The Führer had the ability to convince many people that each alone enjoyed his special confidence. In the end all were deceived, for Hitler could give himself in confidence and in trust to no human being. When he began to suspect that someone might be getting close to him he would reinforce his defences by deliberate dissimulation. He had to keep them all guessing.

During an interview after the war, General Halder, the perceptive and intelligent chief of the general staff, recalled the following remarkably revealing conversation with his Führer and Supreme Commander:

Hitler: You should note one thing from the start, that you will never discover my thought and intentions ...

Halder: We soldiers are accustomed to forming our ideas together.

Hitler: (smiling and with a negative wave of his hand). No. Things are done differently
in politics. You will never learn what I am thinking and those who boast most
loudly that they know my thought, to such people I lie even more.[278]

Distrust of others entered into the routines of Hitler's life. 'Always at his
desk were three [coloured] pencils,' a manservant recalled, 'one red, one green,
one blue.' The colours were used to make notes or to mark documents or letters,
not in accordance with their intrinsic importance but to remind himself of how
much he distrusted the person involved. Hitler explained the system: 'I use the
red one when I write about or to an enemy, the green one when I make notes
about friends, the blue when I have a feeling that I should be cautious [about
someone].'[279]

Mistrust became the hallmark of his government and set the tone for the society. 'The Third Reich,' an anonymous official observed, 'is a system wherein
no one trusts anyone else.' One consequence of such mistrust was, as we shall
see, governmental confusion and inefficiency.[280]

Hitler's distrust of others also had important consequences in his foreign policy. It was largely responsible for the serious misjudgment that turned his attack
on Poland into a European war, and thence a world war. He felt free to invade
Poland on 1 September 1939 because he had used his own standards of duplicity in evaluating England's intentions. He simply could not believe that Britain
would honour her treaty with the Poles. A general's private diary entry for
14 August 1939 recorded Hitler's scornful dismissal of the argument that the
invasion of Poland might precipitate a general war: 'Why should England
fight?' he scoffed. 'One does not die for an ally.'[281]

When the Führer, like the Kaiser, was besieged by doubts of his own identity
and effectiveness, it became terribly important for him to convince himself,
over and over again, that he was a man of poise and power, one who could dominate any person or group. And like the Kaiser, the Führer found that one of the
best means of such self-persuasion was *to act the part* and thus become – for the
moment – the person he wanted so much to be.

While he sometimes smiled sardonically at his own theatrics, there was an
intensity about them that was little touched by humour. He worked at his acting
and sometimes rehearsed the part he would play in meeting a stranger he
wanted to impress or control:

Hitler: What does he expect?
Hess: Authority, of course. You can speak at length. Your will is unshakable. You
give laws to the ages.
Hitler: Then I'll speak with a firm voice.

Hitler would try a few sentences. Hess would listen carefully and might comment, 'No, not like that. Quiet. No passion, commanding. It is destiny that is speaking ...' Hitler would try again with a firmer, calmer voice. After six or seven minutes he would stop, already somewhat moved by his own performance. 'Good! Now I think we have it,' he would say.[282]

Hitler's thundering tantrums were sometimes carefully staged. For he knew the shattering effect his outbursts could have on certain types of people, particularly upon the quiet and introspective. But when dignified conduct would be more effective he could be appropriately discreet.

Hitler himself recognized his talent and once referred to himself half-seriously as 'the greatest actor in Europe' (a phrase others had applied to Wilhelm von Hohenzollern). The Führer illustrated his ability in a scene involving Horace Greely Hjalmer Schacht, then minister of finance. Schacht had come into conflict with Hermann Göring over the economy and had threatened to resign. Hitler called him to his office, urged him to stay on, and pleaded with him, tears welling up in his compelling, light-blue eyes. Schacht was deeply moved and agreed once more to do his Führer's bidding. But the moment the door was closed behind the departing minister, Hitler turned to his associates and snarled, 'That fellow is always sabotaging everything!'[283]

On another occasion, 23 August 1939, when he saw an advantage in intimidating the British ambassador, Sir Neville Henderson, Hitler staged another theatrical triumph. The German secretary for foreign affairs recalled that 'only after Henderson had left the room did I realize that Hitler's performance was premeditated and acted. Hardly had the door closed on the ambassador, when Hitler slapped his thigh, gloated, and said to me, "Chamberlain will never survive this conversation. His Cabinet will fall by tonight."'[284] Late in the war, in a situation report of 24 January 1945, Hitler commented, 'I have an unpleasant task to perform today. I have to "hypnotize" Quisling.'[285]

Hitler's rages which were monumental – and for the most part genuine – were seldom caused by serious political or military defeats. When thwarted in his bid for the presidency of Germany in 1932, defeated at Stalingrad or the Battle of the Bulge, or confronted by assassination attempts, he accepted with remarkable self-control. At the end, when defeat was obvious and the decision had been made to die in Berlin, many of Hitler's entourage were in a state of hysteria. Not the Führer. A stenographer recalled that at the last military conference he was 'generally composed' and the one who 'kept his nerve best under control.'[286]

Hitler's fury was sometimes carefully staged for effect, a weapon in his armory used to frighten opponents into submission. Certainly he enjoyed his success in reducing old President Hacha of Czechoslovakia into trembling compliance by screaming threats of obliterating Prague. Foreign Minister Joachim von Ribbentrop's secretary recalled that one day in July 1938, when Hitler was lunching with Ribbentrop, it was announced unexpectedly that a British diplomat had arrived. '*Gott im Himmel!*' Hitler exclaimed in surprise, 'Don't let him in yet, I'm still in good humour.' He then proceeded, in front of his staff, to work himself up until his face darkened and his eyes flashed fire. When he felt ready, he entered the room where the Englishman was waiting. Those in the dining-room could hear the stormy interview and the fury of Hitler's voice. After some time, the Führer returned smiling. 'Gentlemen,' he said with a chuckle, 'I need some tea. He thinks I'm furious.'[287]

One of the most graphic eyewitness accounts of Hitler in a rage, however, suggests neither premeditation nor control over his own actions. A Swedish visitor in August 1939 recorded Hitler's reaction to the Swede's prediction that England would resist Nazi aggression against Poland:

Hitler ... paced up and down and declared, as if talking to himself, that [he] was invincible ... Suddenly he stopped in the middle of the room and stared straight ahead. His speech became more and more garbled, his whole behaviour gave the impression of a man who was not at all himself. Sentences tumbled after one another ...

'If there is a war,' he yelled, 'I'll build U-Boats, U-Boats, U-Boats, U-Boats!'

His voice became increasingly indistinct and gradually one could no longer understand him at all. Suddenly he collected himself, raised his voice as if addressing a vast assembly and screamed, 'I'll build airplanes, airplanes, airplanes and I'll annihilate my enemies!' ... He acted more like a demon in bad fiction than a human being. I looked at him in amazement.[288]

Throughout his life, Hitler was preoccupied with death. He was captivated by the depiction of putrefaction and death in Makart's huge canvas *Plague in Florence,* which he wanted badly for the museum he was planning for his hometown of Linz. When he finally acquired the painting in 1940, a secretary reported that he was as happy as a schoolboy. He clapped his hands as he exulted over the piles of greenish-yellow corpses. He also had filmstrips made of the execution of criminals and enjoyed watching them die. He tried to quiet his own nagging fears of death by asserting that he had the power to determine the deaths of thousands of others, saying, 'I do not play at war, I command in war ... I insist that I have the right to send the youth to their death.'[289]

Hitler hated the moon because it was dead. On a lovely, star-spangled autumnal night in 1924, while he was a prisoner at Landsberg am Lech after his abortive coup, he turned to his fellow inmate Rudolph Hess and confided, 'You know, Rudi, I hate the moon – it is something dead, and terrible, and inhuman.

And human beings are afraid of it ... It is as if in the moon a part of the terror still lives which the moon once sent down over the earth ... I hate it! That pale and ghostly fellow!'[290]

The Führer's personal concern about death had resonance in Nazi symbolism and public ceremonies. The elite SS were uniformed in black and wore the death's head insignia; the crooked cross in the flag of the Third Reich was black. The Nazis were as effective in celebrating death as they were in celebrating life. Enormously impressive ceremonies were staged at the tombs of Prussian kings, at Hindenburg's monument at the Tannenburg, at memorial services for Horst Wessel, and at the commemoration each November of the 'martyrs' of the Beer Hall Putsch. The leitmotif of death sounded sombrely at every party rally.[291]

Major political and military decisions were influenced by Hitler's fear of imminent death and his chronic concern about the passage of time. He expressed his sense of urgency when giving his reasons for running for president in 1932: 'I don't have time to wait ... I can't lose a single year. I've got to get to power shortly ... during the time remaining to me. I have *got* to. I have just *got* to.' On another occasion, 'I need ten years of lawmaking. The time is short. I have not long to live.'[292]

Hitler's decision to go to war in September 1939 was not unconnected with his fear of growing old. He wanted to wage war while he was young enough to enjoy it. In a major speech to the commanders of his armed forces on 22 August 1939, he spoke of the need for war and why it must not be delayed: 'Essentially all depends on me ... But I can be eliminated at any time by a criminal or a lunatic. No one knows how much longer I shall live. Therefore, better a conflict now.' To one of the party leaders Hitler confided, 'You see I'm getting old and need glasses. Therefore I prefer to have this war now that I am fifty rather than at sixty.'[293]

He sought to defy death by leaving imperishable memorials and monuments to his greatness. He also wanted to raise a generation of young Germans who would be immune from the fear which, despite his denials, beset their Führer. He called for 'a brutal youth ... *that shall learn to overcome the fear of death.*' But it really was not he, Hitler insisted, who was afraid of death. Once more it was somebody else, and once more it was his all-purpose scapegoat: 'The Jews fear death above everything else.'[294]

On other occasions Hitler tried to convince himself that he could cheat death through fame that would make him immortal: 'I know how to keep my hold on people after I have passed on. I shall be the Führer they will [still] look up at and go home to talk of and remember. My life shall not end in the mere form of death. It will, on the contrary, begin then.' Towards the end Hitler told his doctor, 'I have to gain immortality even if the whole German nation perishes in the process.'[295]

The thought of killing himself often crossed his mind. Among the childish games he played was a form of substitute suicide. He disliked tying his own necktie and had his valet do it for him. Hitler made a game of it – but like all his games, he took this one very seriously. He would close his eyes, hold his breath, and count slowly to ten. If Linge could finish the knot before Hitler finished counting, the Führer was greatly relieved.[296]

As with the Kaiser, decapitation was the form of death that particularly fascinated Hitler. He spoke often of severed heads. Not only did he make his famous promise – in words that the Kaiser had once used[297] – that when he came to power 'heads will roll in the sand,' but a surprising statement of years before suggests that he sometimes thought about the possibility of his own decapitation. On 24 July 1926 he promised, 'My head will not roll in the sand until I have completed my mission.'[298] When the Führer flipped a coin to determine whether he should go on a picnic, heads did not win. Heads invariably lost. When asked what he would do upon first landing in England, he replied without hesitation that he wanted most to see the place where Henry VIII chopped off the heads of his wives.

When Hitler designed a sort of promissory note for his struggling party in the mid-1920s – redeemable when he became ruler of Germany – he drew an idealized German warrior holding in his right hand a sword dripping with blood and in his left hand the severed head of a woman suspended by her long blond hair. Under the picture, in heavy Gothic type, was printed, 'Warrior of the Truth, Behead the Lie.' It is noteworthy that the Warrior is enjoined not to fight, not to pierce, but to decapitate the young lady.[299]

Hitler's definition of politics was one that does not seem to have occurred to Aristotle, Jefferson, Gladstone, or Lincoln: 'Politics is like a harlot; if you love her successfully she bites your head off.'[300]

As soon as he became chancellor, Hitler restored the use of the headsman's axe, but his preferred method of execution was strangulation. A special decree of 29 March 1933 made hanging by the neck obligatory for an exceptionally large number of criminal cases. His own fear of strangulation was further projected onto others in the grisly orders he gave for the execution of generals who had conspired against him in the plot of 20 July 1944. He ordered that each man be 'hung on a meathook and slowly strangled to death with piano wire, the pressure being periodically released to intensify death agonies.' Hitler had colour film made of the scene. He 'loved the film and had it shown over and over again; it became one of his favourite entertainments.'[301]

Even more than Wilhelm, Hitler was infatuated with the Medusa, the demigoddess whose fearsome look turned men to stone. He expressed enthusiasm for the mosaic of the Medusa head in the rotunda of the University of Munich, and one of his favourite paintings, by Franz von Stuck, was of a sinister, flashing-eyed Medusa which he had first seen in a book in Hanfstaengl's home – a painting that, as we shall see, reminded Hitler of his mother. When he designed his gigantic desk for the chancellery, three heads adorned the front panels. One was of the Medusa, with writhing snakes emerging from her hair.[302]

Freud believed that men who are fascinated with decapitation and the legend of the Medusa head are expressing castration anxiety in a disguised form. Hitler showed concern about loss of testicles in several indirect ways, but he also talked explicitly about it. He told the French ambassador, for example, that the Poles were castrating German citizens. And he tried to convince the League of Nations' representative in Danzig that the Nazi press was attempting to tone down stories of Polish atrocities: 'No one believes me about this, but I have ordered that the sensational cases, such as castration, should not be mentioned in the press. They excite public opinion too much.'[303]

As we shall see, Hitler had reason to worry about loss of testicles.

One day in the summer of 1919, a history professor of far-rightist persuasion at the University of Munich heard a recently discharged soldier harranguing a group of his colleagues. The professor was impressed: 'The men seemed spellbound ... I had the peculiar feeling that their excitement derived from him, and at the same time they, in turn, were inspiring him.'[304] This giving and receiving, this mutual nourishment between Hitler and his audience, would remain characteristic of his relationship to a crowd.

The professor recommended that Hitler be assigned to 'promoting patriotism in the ranks.' Hitler remembered the incident vividly and gloried in the power and personal satisfaction he felt in moving a crowd through the spoken word: 'Thus, I was at once offered the opportunity to speak before a large audience ... What previously I had always assumed to be true out of pure feeling without knowledge, became clear now: I was an *orator!* ... Nothing could make me happier than that.'[305]

A few days later, Hitler made one of the several 'greatest decisions of my life': he joined the tiny group of malcontents who met in a tavern and called themselves ambitiously the German Workers' Party. This was the group that Hitler would transform into one of the most effective political movements of modern history. He did it largely through the force of his personality and the power of the spoken word. His effectiveness as a demagogue is attested by nearly everyone who heard him. The Munich police reports for November 1919 describe Hitler's performances as 'masterful' and note time and again that he was received with 'tumultuous applause.' Ernst Hanfstaengl, a sophisticated

Harvard graduate (and classmate of Franklin D. Roosevelt, '04) found Hitler 'absolutely irresistible ... the master of the spoken word.' Konrad Heiden, then a university student and political opponent of Hitler who had heard him dozens of times, put his finger on a source of Hitler's effectiveness: he played the role of Man of Destiny with such conviction that he actually became the part he played. In transforming himself, he transformed his audience:

Suddenly this man, who has been awkwardly standing around ... begins to speak, filling the room with his voice, suppressing interruptions or contradictions by his domineering manner, spreading cold shivers among those present by the savagery of his declaration ...

The listener is filled with awe and feels that a new phenomenon has entered the room. This thundering demon was not there before; this is not the same timid man with the contracted shoulders. He is capable of this transformation in a personal interview [or in] facing an audience of a half million.[306]

Other opponents observed the same phenomenon: a limp, little man changed into a force of overwhelming power, the stream of speech stiffening him 'like a stream of water stiffens a hose.' Otto Strasser, whom Hitler would later condemn to death, gave one of the most graphic descriptions we have of the rhetorical skills that were to make Hitler master, first of the party, and then of Germany:

Adolf Hitler enters a hall. He sniffs the air. For a minute he gropes, feels his way, senses the atmosphere. Suddenly he bursts forth ...

His words go like an arrow to their target, he touches each private wound on the raw, liberating the mass unconscious, expressing its innermost aspirations, telling it what it most wants to hear.[307]

Hitler said that he was never so happy or fulfilled as after a successful speech that left him physically and emotionally spent.

Women of all ages were attracted to Adolf Hitler. Motherly types, such as Frau Privy Counsellor Bruckmann, and Frau Privy Counsellor Bechstein, widow of the piano manufacturer, and another woman in her sixties, a retired schoolteacher named Carola Hoffmann, would feed him his favourite tortes, cluck approval, stroke his head, and call him, 'my little Wolf' as he sat at their knees. Once, when Hitler found himself alone with Hélène Hanfstaengl, he ran to her, hid his head in her lap, and murmured, 'If only I had someone to take care of me!'

The Führer was aware of his special appeal to women and was particularly anxious to convince them that he was a man of overpowering virility. On one occasion he had invited a young woman, Pauline Kohler, to the Obersalzberg to see his books. She recalled that during the course of a dull perusal in which she was losing interest, her host sought to gain her attention by suddenly stretching out his arm in the Nazi salute. He affected a deep voice and roared:

I can hold my arm like that for two solid hours. I never feel tired when my Storm Troopers and soldiers march past and I stand at this salute.

I never move. My arm is like granite – rigid and unbending. But Göring can't stand it. He has to drop his hand after half an hour of this salute. He's flabby. But I'm hard. For two hours I can keep my arm stretched out in this salute. That is four times as long as Göring. That means I'm four times stronger than Göring. It's an amazing feat. I marvel at my own power.[308]

Hitler's dualities were particularly apparent in his attitude towards women. He idealized them; he also treated them with contempt and sought to degrade them. Hitler showed his ambivalence in the way he talked about abstract forces that controlled his life. He made these forces into contradictory female images that were sometimes generous and kind, sometimes capriciously cruel and treacherous.

All his life he felt surrounded by these unpredictable, supernatural female beings: Dame Sorrow, the Goddess of Fate, Lady Care, the Goddess of Misery. Thus, in the opening sentence of *Mein Kampf* we are told that the hero was born on the German border at Braunau because a kindly fate had designated that town as the place of his birth. But it was 'an unmerited, mean trick of Fate' that he was born 'in the period of peace between two wars.' This was the same 'inexorable hand of the Goddess of Fate' that decides the destiny of nations.

Here Hitler revealed his concern about the power of women by changing the neuter German noun *das Schicksal* to the feminine *die Göttin des Schicksals* (the Goddess of Fate). In a letter of 1914 he made another special grammatical point in order to feminize a noun. In lamenting his life spent with no other than 'Friend Care and Want,' he had to choose between a masculine or a feminine 'Friend' – he chose the feminine form: *keine andere Freundin als Sorge und Not.*

In a speech of 13 August 1920 in the Hofbräuhaus in Munich, Hitler spoke of 'the greatest goddess on earth, who oppresses man the most: the goddess called Misery' (*die Göttin der Not*). Years later, in a May Day speech in Berlin in 1927, this goddess was still preying on his mind: 'In spite of all Party dogmas and Party principles, the Goddess of Misery will come and beat on the door of a people which feel more and more the pain of want. A people slowly perishes if this need is not satisfied.'

And again – we are back to his memoirs – when he was poor, 'Poverty clasped me in her arms.' When he felt depressed, 'Dame Sorrow was my foster mother.'

To the Führer, misery was female.[309] After reading some of these statements, a distinguished psychiatrist asked, 'What had Hitler's mother done to him to make him distrust and hate women so?'[310] It is a question we shall pursue in another chapter.

Of course, the hero of Hitler's memoirs learned to bear up under all the travail and anguish – 'All this cruelty of Fate' – and even learned to accept his sufferings as 'the Wisdom of Dame Providence' because she hardened him through Nature, 'that cruel Queen of all wisdom,' until she had guided him to another turning point in his life, when, during the First World War, 'Fate graciously permitted' him to become a soldier. The war was lost because, as Hitler said in a Berlin speech of 30 January 1940, 'Providence turned *her* face from the German people.' When Hitler left the Hofbräuhaus during the night in which he made his first major political speech, he imagined that he 'walked side by side with the 'Goddess of Inexorable Revenge.' At his trial in 1924 after the failure of the Beer Hall Putsch, he was sure that 'the Goddess of History's eternal judgment will smilingly tear up the jury's verdict.'[311]

Hitler idealized women as wives and mothers and rhapsodized about the institution of marriage. As a boy in Linz he had talked to his only friend about 'pure marriage,' which alone could keep alive 'the Flame of Life.' Indeed a main reason he had planned, as a teenager, to establish one day a 'new Reich' was to accomplish two main objectives: eradicate prostitution, 'the Sin of Iniquity' (for which Jews were responsible), and preserve unsullied 'the Flame of Life.' In the new Germany of Hitler's boyhood dreams – and years later in legislative reality – early marriage would be encouraged by state loans to young couples and special bonuses for children.

When he became ruler of Germany, Hitler set aside a special day to pay homage to motherhood: on 12 August, the birthday of his own mother, fecund German mothers were awarded the Honour Cross of the Germanic Mother. There were three classes: bronze for bearing more than four children, silver for more than six, and gold for more than eight. Regulations printed in Hitler's newspapers required all members of Nazi Youth to treat mothers with the respect due to war heroes and to give the Nazi salute to wearers of the Mother's Award.[312]

He eulogized marriage in one of his nightly reveries by asking rhetorically, 'Is there a more lovely consecration of love, pray, than ... two beings [when] their love is ... magnified by the presence of children [?]'[313] But he also approved Himmler's idea of establishing SS stud farms and passed legislation legitimizing the results of their eugenic labours.

The Führer himself could not possibly marry. He gave many reasons why he must remain celibate: He had only one bride, his Motherland. His offspring might be imbeciles. The only person he could have married was his niece Geli, and she was dead. He also noted, pointedly, that an earlier Messiah had never married. At times he also urged the pragmatic political importance of preserving the image of sacrificial bachelor–patriot: 'If I married, I'd lose five million votes of German women.' Further, a wife would interfere with his mission. Perhaps he could never find a woman worthy of his genius or, conversely, insignificant enough to complement his stature, for it was one of his aphorisms that 'the greater the man, the smaller the wife should be.' But whatever the actual reasons Hitler gave, the thought of getting married and of having genital sexual relations with a woman did not appeal to him.

As a teenager in Linz, Adolf Hitler had fallen in love with a girl he called 'Stefanie,' who never knew of his existence. Although he cast her in operatic roles, wrote long romantic poems in which she was the heroine, and designed a magnificent villa for her – 'I have decided to do her house in the Renaissance style' – he could always think of many reasons why it was not possible for him actually to meet her. Extraordinary human beings like 'Stefanie' and himself, he told his friend, do not need to converse in the usual way. He knew clearly that she shared all his artistic tastes and secret thoughts. When his friend suggested that she might not really share all his interests, Adolf was furious: 'You simply don't understand because you can't understand the true meaning of extraordinary love.'[314]

The Führer's conception of Ideal Womanhood was strikingly similar to the Kaiser's:[315] 'A woman must be a cute, cuddly, naïve little thing – tender, sweet and stupid' (*Eine Frau muss ein niedliches, molliges, Tschapperl sein: weich, süss und dumm*).[316] He furiously rejected any suggestion that women should be emancipated from their traditional place in the kitchen, the church, and the nursery, asserting that 'the term "female emancipation" is a term invented by the Jewish intellect and its meaning is of the same spirit.'

On another occasion he told an aide that while he enjoyed having beautiful women near him, it was not necessary for them to be intelligent or original: 'I have enough ideas for both [of us],' he said.[317]

Apart from the contrived air of superiority he affected in their presence, there are other indications that Hitler was intimidated by females. His sister recalled that Adolf, as a very small boy, was terrified at the thought that a girl might kiss him: 'When Mother wanted him to get up in the morning, she had only to say to me, "Go and give him a kiss." As soon as he heard the word "kiss" he was out of bed in a flash because he just couldn't stand that.' Many years later, at a New Year's Eve party in 1924, a young and attractive woman manoeuvred the Führer under the mistletoe and gave him a good-natured holiday kiss. A witness recalled the consequences: 'I shall never forget the look of astonishment and horror on Hitler's face! ... Bewildered and helpless as a child, [he] stood there biting his lips in an effort to master his anger. The atmosphere, which after his arrival had shown a tendency to become formal, now became [downright] glacial.'[318]

Hitler continued to be intimidated by the thought of physical contact with women, and compared sexual intercourse to the trauma a soldier experiences in battle. In making the comparison he typically projected his own fears: it was not he who was afraid of women, but women who were afraid of all men. In his awkward prose, 'For a young woman, the revelation of her encounter with her first man can be compared to the revelation that a soldier knows when he faces war for the first time.'[319]

After he came to power Hitler was anxious not to displease his motherly – and very wealthy – patron, Frau Bechstein. On one occasion when he felt that he had done something wrong, the Führer was so fearful of a tongue-lashing that he sought out the Wagner children to run interference for him. Friedelind Wagner, the granddaughter of the Maestro, recalled that 'throughout luncheon he tried to persuade us children to soften Frau Bechstein's blows, but we were so amused at the thought of [Hitler] trembling before her that we refused to go.'[320]

One of the reasons Hitler never ordered total economic mobilization during the war was that he was afraid of women's reactions if they were deprived of beauty parlours and cosmetics. Goebbels, who urged total mobilization, recorded his disappointment with Hitler's refusal either to allow women to work in war industry or to cut down on their beauty aids. An entry in his diary of 10 May 1943, well after the catastrophic German defeat at Stalingrad, recorded Hitler's concern that 'women constitute a tremendous power and as soon as you dare to touch their beauty parlours, they are your enemies ... We must not take away their hairdryers.'[321]

He could not trust women. Like the Goddess of Fate, they were inherently hypocritical, fickle, and false. 'Women have the quality,' he said, 'that we men do not have: they kiss a friend at the same time that they are sticking them in the back with a stiletto.' He convinced himself of their inferiority and insulted them publicly. This was true of even the women closest to him. Eva Braun, for example, had given him full measure of loyalty and love. But Hitler announced in her presence that 'a highly intelligent man should [choose] a primitive and stupid woman.' He recalled on another occasion that he had once made the mistake of discussing politics with women, and some of them actually had the temerity to disagree with him: 'But I shut their mouths by saying, "You certainly will not claim that you know men as I know women." ' He concluded his observations by commenting, 'In short, gallantry forbids one to give women an opportunity of putting themselves in situations that do not suit them.'[322]

In a favourite metaphor, Hitler compared women to the masses, both of whom long to be dominated by men of passion and power. In lines notable for sadistic overtones, disdain for women and for the German people, and exaltation of brutality, he said:

Like a woman whose psychic feeling is influenced less by abstract reasoning than by undefinable sentimental longing for complementary strength, who will submit to the strong man rather than dominate the weakling, the masses love the ruler rather than the suppliant ...

Neither realizes the impudence with which they are spiritually terrorized nor the outrageous curtailment of their human liberties, for in no way does the delusion of this doctrine dawn on them. Thus they see only the inconsiderate force, the brutality ... to which they finally always submit.[323]

At another time, Hitler observed that women were like little children at a circus: immature, naïve, and susceptible to thrills. He concluded this discourse by saying, 'Someone who does not understand the intrinsically feminine character of the masses will never be an effective speaker.'[324]

The Führer was fond of quoting one of the few lines he knew from Nietzsche: 'Thou goest to women? Do not forget thy whip!' Whips, of course, are the traditional symbol and sign of sado-masochistic impulses. During the decade before he became chancellor, Hitler habitually carried heavy riding whips with which, in moments of excitement, he lashed about him, beat against his thighs, or whipped his hand as if he were a little boy being punished. The three whips he treasured most had been given to him by three motherly, older women.[325]

It seems more than coincidental that six out of the seven women who, we can be reasonably sure, had some sort of intimate relations with Adolf Hitler, committed – or seriously attempted to commit – suicide.[326] That is a statistic that gives some credence to the assertion that the Führer's sexual gratification – when not achieved through the sublimation of passionate demogogic triumphs – may have been attained by a massively sado-masochistic practice, degrading alike to himself and to his sexual partner. He is reported to have ordered young women to squat over him and urinate or defecate on his head.[327]

Hitler's sexual appeal to women was extraordinary. A hatcheck woman in the Hofbräuhaus in Munich told me in 1953 that she had always looked forward to Hitler speaking in the enormous beer hall because she received handsome tips for letting dozens of women smell the sweatband of the Führer's hat. All four of his secretaries survived the war: Johanna Wolf, Christia Schroeder, Gerda Daranowski Christian, and Gertrude Humps Junge. None ever married or remarried. Wolf and Schroeder were single; 'Traudl' Junge's husband was killed on the eastern front, Frau Christian divorced her husband in 1946. When the attractive Gerda Christian was asked why neither she nor any of her colleagues were married she replied, 'How could any of us marry after having known a man like Adolf Hitler?'[328]

Thousands of other German women felt the same way. After the war an American officer in the Army of Occupation discovered more than 8,000 'love letters to Adolf Hitler' in the ruins of the Reichschancellery.[329] Only a small fraction of the original collection, these letters had been sent by women from all walks of life. Some, written in pencil on scraps of cheap paper, were barely literate; others were elegantly written on expensive stationery. All used the familiar '*du*' form of intimate address, and all tried to articulate the fervour of their love through inventive and often untranslatable diminutives: 'My Own True Heart and Sweet little Adolfy' ... 'My own Hottest-Sweetest Lover and Mighty Führer' ... 'My Sweet-as-Sugar little Wolfie' ... 'My Very Own Hot Heart-Throb.'

Most of the letters used the conventional language of love. Others, however, were more extreme: 'You Sweetest, Dearest Most Passionate Lover, I can't find words to tell you how much I love you ... My Darling I could devour you with love and thousands of kisses so tender, so hot, so intimate (*so zärtlich, so heiss und so innig*) ... Oh, if I could only *taste* you!' Another wrote, 'So that you know how much I love you, my precious little Adolf, I tenderly kiss your Behind (*Ich küsse Dich auf Deine Buchsstaben* [a common euphemism for *Popo* or ass]) as well as your dear Front.'

Though their letters remained unanswered, the women were not deterred: 'I love you so much, My Own Dear Führer, that even though I have written ten times in vain, that will not stop me, for love hopes all things and endures all things.' One woman, who had written more than twenty unanswered letters, was convinced that her warm-hearted Beloved would not punish her for expressing her love so often. She may have been denied her wish. Gestapo files show that some of the most persistent women were labelled 'Lives Unworthy to be Lived' and sent off to 'health facilities' where they were injected with poison.

Each writer was sure that she alone was Hitler's one true love. Several pleaded with him to let them bear him a child. One woman, who saw herself as the Virgin Mary, had heard a voice in the night from heaven, saying, 'You, simple, pure and unknown German woman will bear the son of His Exalted Majesty, the Almighty Führer.' Another, who wanted to marry Hitler and bear his child, had sold her house and taken lodgings in Berlin. One of her letters enclosed two keys: one to the rooming house, the other to her bedroom. She ended her letter:

My own beloved Adolf, at the beginning of this week I sent you a package with my own hand-embroidered cushions. (The feathers came from my own comforter!)

Just think what my father and mother would say to their own Adolf and Margarete [the woman's name]. With tenderest love I kiss your prick (*Punzerl*).

May God the Almighty protect you.

Your own little Woman

Another woman suggested that if Hitler could not take the time from his busy day to sleep with her, he could send her some of his sperm so that she could fulfil her life's dream of bearing his child.

One letter, addressed 'To My Darling Husband,' told him what she was making to give the kids for their birthdays, chided him for not answering her letters or acknowledging the cookies she had sent. 'Didn't they taste good?' She signed the letter, 'Your eternally faithful, true, and loving little Wifey.'

With respect to his relationship with men, the Führer, like the Kaiser, was not an overt homosexual. It is likely, however, that he too had latent homosexual tendencies, and it is certain that he worried a great deal about them.

Hitler was concerned lest he show feminine traits – which, indeed, he very often did. The noted British diplomat and historian Sir Harold Nicolson, who was himself a practising homosexual, was particularly interested in Hitler's sexuality. He recorded in his diary a conversation with a colleague who had told him that the Führer 'is the most profoundly feminine man that he has ever met and there are moments when he becomes almost effeminate.' The American journalist William L. Shirer, who watched Hitler closely one day in September 1938, as he came out of a hotel in Bad Godesberg after meeting with Prime Minister Neville Chamberlain, wrote in his diary, 'It was a very curious walk indeed ... very ladylike. Dainty little steps.'

But a German doctor who had personal reasons for wondering about Hitler's sexual preferences reached a different conclusion: 'As a homosexual, I was fascinated by Hitler's eyes, speech, and walk. But I sensed immediately that he is not one of us.'[330]

It is true that Hitler was closely associated with Ernst Röhm and Rudolph Hess, two practising homosexuals. One cannot conclude, however, that he shared his friends' sexual tastes. Still, during the months he was with Hess in Landsberg, their relationship was very close indeed. When Hitler left the prison he fretted about his friend who still languished there, and spoke of him tenderly, using Austrian diminutives: '*Ach mein Rudi, mein Hesserl*, isn't it appalling to think that he's still there?'[331] One of Hitler's valets, Schneider, made no explicit statement about the relationship, but he did find it strange that whenever Hitler received a present he liked or drew an architectural sketch that pleased him, he would run to Hess – who was known in homosexual circles as 'Fräulein Anne' – as a little boy would run to his mother to show his prize to her.[332]

Hess's published letters[333] confirm this memory and make it clear that the months he spent in prison with Hitler were the happiest of his life. His letters to his mother and even to his fiancée are, as his biographer notes, 'breathless with young love' for Hitler. His personal adjutant described his chief as having one ambition in life: to serve and 'be the loyalist interpreter of Hitler.'[334]

In one of his letters to his fiancée Hess wrote, 'What a mixture [he is] – a mature and superior man with limitless childhood exuberance!' and in another, 'I love him! (*Ich liebe ihn!*).'[335] His infatuation with Hitler certainly impaired his literary judgment. After reading a draft of *Mein Kampf*, Hess extolled it as 'logical, lively, vivid' and reported that he was so overwhelmed by the beauty of Hitler's language (*Schönheit der Sprache*) that 'the blood hammered through my veins.'[336]

Hess's relationship to Adolf Hitler was, in several ways, like Eulenburg's to Wilhelm Hohenzollern. Both were active homosexuals who fell in love with masters who did not reciprocate their affection with equal intensity. Eulenburg, like Hess, had seen himself as his master's 'loyalist interpreter.' As the Kaiser deserted and disowned 'Philli,' so would the Führer desert 'Rudi' pronouncing him officially insane, damning him publicly as a traitor for his peace mission to Britain, which he had undertaken on Hitler's behalf but without Hitler's knowledge.

Hitler had a very special relationship with Albert Speer, the brilliant young architect and director of war production whom Hitler considered a kindred artistic spirit. Writing in the *Frankfurter Allgemeine Zeitung*, the distinguished German psychiatrist, Alexander Mischerlisch, concluded that although Hitler and Speer probably never had physical homosexual relations, there was a distinct 'homoerotic component' in their relationship which was the 'result of the needs each uniquely fulfilled for the other.' In discussing this article with his biographer, Speer said, 'Yes. Mischerlisch came closest to the truth.'

Georges Casalis, the Calvinist prison chaplain who for many months had been Speer's spiritual mentor at Spandau, agreed with the analyst. He too was convinced that 'very clearly a kind of erotic attachment' bound Hitler to Speer. He believed that the two men had been in love.

A wartime colleague of Speer's, observing the pure joy Hitler and Speer had brought to each other during their long conferences together, told Speer, 'You know what you are? You are Hitler's unhappy love.' Speer recalled his response to his friend's remark: 'You know how I felt? Happy! Dear God, I felt happy.'[337]

Hitler's need for Speer became desperate towards the end of the war when the two broke apart. Speer had told Hitler that the war was lost and refused to obey the Führer's insane 'scorched earth' orders to destroy Germany. Instead of ordering him shot for treason, Hitler only withdrew his minister's executive powers. He then told an aide to assure Speer 'that I still love him (*dass ich ihn weiter lieb habe*),' and called him to his office to plead for his support.

A memorable scene followed: If only Speer would *say* the war might possibly be won, his powers would be restored. Speer said he could not say that; the war was lost. Hitler continued to plead with him and reduced his demands, '"If you could only *believe* the war might still be won" ... Speer was silent ... "If at least you could *hope* that we aren't lost; surely you must be able to *hope*? I'd be satisfied with that."'

Emotionally drained by the power of Hitler's persuasion and his own need for Hitler, Speer found himself saying, 'My Führer, I stand unconditionally behind you!' Hitler's eyes filled with tears, he held out his hands to Speer, and reconfirmed his authority.[338]

A different kind of evidence indicates that the Führer was personally concerned about latent homosexual tendencies and struggled against them. There is a close similarity between Hitler's attempts to deny any suggestion of homosexuality and his strident efforts to prove that he could not possibly be 'tainted' by Jewish blood. In both instances he used the same defence: He denied that he was Jewish by persecuting the Jews. He denied that he had homosexual leanings by attacking homosexuals. Indeed, he made a special point of doing so.

After Hitler came to power, his government moved immediately against all types of sexual deviation and sex crimes, but the sharpest rise in prosecution was for homosexuality: the number of prosecutions increased from some 3,000 for the years 1931 through 1934 to almost 30,000 between 1936 and 1939.[339] It is also suggestive that homosexuals, along with Jews and Communists, were designated as 'enemies of the state,' and a special section of the SS was set up to root them out. But the SS itself seems to have been infected, for on 15 February 1942 Hitler found it necessary to set forth a decree punishing homosexuality within the SS with death.[340]

The Führer, like the Kaiser, also revealed fears of effeminacy by protesting so much that he had absolutely no feminine characteristics whatsoever. He was, he kept insisting, totally masculine – tough, 'hard as steel,' 'cold as ice,' ruthless, and brutal. Such excessive protestations suggest repressed homosexuality.

Here, then, was the man called Führer and Saviour of the Germans. His image was that of awesome power; but as a person he was infantile and vulnerable, beset by fears and torn by contradictions. He was the infallible dictator who anxiously sucked his little finger; who longed to create and lusted to destroy; who ordered the massacre of innocents and fretted over the death of ravens and lobsters; who exalted women and debased them; who – as we shall see – spoke the words of Jesus and hated mankind. He was, as Golo Mann asserted, 'a remarkably evil and repellent being, a monster,'[341] yet he was also capable of kindness and compassion. Certainly, ecstatic Germans looked upon him not as monster, but as Messiah and cheered him on as he conquered half a continent.

This peculiar man was one of the most compelling political personalities of history, and – along with Wilhelm II – one of its greatest enigmas.

2

Weltanschauungen: Their Intellectual, Aesthetic, Religious, and Racial Worlds

The Quality of Their Minds and Their Intellectual Interests

Consider the perverse tastelessness *(Geschmacklosigkeit)* of Wilhelm II ... Tasteless in his selection of friends and advisers, tasteless in art, in literature, in lifestyle, and in politics; tasteless in his every utterance.

Harry Graf Kessler

Hitler's mind ... was coarse, turbid, narrow, rigid, cruel. It had nothing to recommend it but its power.

Hugh Trevor-Roper

Almost all who knew the Kaiser and the Führer personally, no matter what their opinions of these rulers may have been, agreed that they were endowed with extraordinary, if unbalanced, mental powers. Wilhelm's mind was quick and retentive, and it ranged over many interests. He designed battleships, preached sermons, drew cartoons, composed music, and wrote both poetry and learned monographs on archaeology. He painted water-colours, and discussed counterpoint with Cosima Wagner. It was said that he could skim twenty or thirty pages of technical material in a few minutes and astonish experts with his understanding. The shipping magnate, Albert Ballin, and the banker, Franz von Mendelssohn, were 'simply bewitched' by Wilhelm's command of technical aspects of their professions.[1] He impressed military advisers with his memory of physical terrain and troop movements, a visiting Harvard professor with his knowledge of Persian history, and electrical engineers with his expertise on electric machinery.[2] He spoke fluent French and Dutch, wrote excellent Latin, and the language of his childhood was English.

Not everyone who knew him, however, was equally impressed with his intellect. The British ambassador to Germany noted the Kaiser's mental agility, as well as the fecundity and the range of his mind, but found it impulsive and lacking in reflective judgment, often causing him to 'jump to a conclusion without giving sufficient consideration.'[3] Princess Marie Radziwill, another unimpressed contemporary, observed that Wilhelm's much-lauded intelligence was largely a sham and the knowledge he displayed to impress others lacked solid foundation: 'He gives himself no time to grasp anything properly.'[4]

The princess did her emperor less than justice. When Wilhelm was really interested in a subject, he could indeed 'grasp it properly.' After he became 'absolutely enthralled' with an archaeological dig near his island home on Corfu, for example, he trained himself to become an archaeologist and wrote several valuable articles on the subject. Like Hitler, he was fascinated by the legend of the Medusa, and his enthusiasm was boundless when he himself unearthed a rare head of the Gorgon, one of the Medusa's repulsive sisters. Unlike Hitler, Wilhelm was capable of writing a carefully researched monograph on the subject, *Studien zur Gorgo*, which he placed with pride next to other monographs he had written.[5]

Similarly, the Kaiser's interest in naval affairs led him to extensive and disciplined studies of shipbuilding, engines, and armament. After long conversations with him, Admiral Philip Dumas, of the British navy, commented in his diary on 24 June 1906: 'To tell the truth, he amazed me with his clear knowledge.'[6] An accomplished sailor, Wilhelm competed successfully in regattas at Cowes and Kiel.

Both the Kaiser and the Führer were avid readers of newspapers. But Wilhelm's newspaper reading was largely screened for him, an aide writing, 'As far as I know, His Majesty regularly reads absolutely no unclipped newspaper with the single exception of the *Daily Graphic*.'[7] (The aide is referring to the selecting and cutting out of newspaper articles for the Kaiser that his entourage knew would please him.) He spent hours with these clippings. That he continued the habit during his long exile in Doorn is attested by bulging folders of clippings in four languages now preserved in the national archives in Utrecht.

In contrast to Hitler, Wilhelm enjoyed the company of academics and took real pleasure in historical research as well as lively intellectual debate. Among his voluminous personal papers there are full records of the scholarly society he established during his long exile in Doorn – a group that met regularly in his home to read and discuss scholarly papers on archaeology, history, and cultural anthropology.[8] The ex-Kaiser himself delivered carefully researched and lucidly written papers on many subjects ranging from a treatise on 'The Nature of Culture' and 'Pre-Historic Horse Paintings and Statues' to the origins of the swastika, arguing that the ancient Chinese monad, the Yin-Yang, through many cultural permutations, had developed into the 'swastika of the present government.' (Among the ex-Kaiser's personal effects found in Doorn House was a Nazi swastika medallion that had been attached to the radiator of his Mercedes.)

Hitler too had a remarkably retentive memory with an extraordinary, if bizarre, range of miscellaneous factual knowledge. He remembered the trademark and serial number of the bicycle he had used as wartime messenger in 1915, the names of the inns where he had stayed overnight twenty years previously, the streets down which he had been driven during past political campaigns, the age, displacement, speed, strength of armour and other data for every capital ship in the British and German navies, the names of the singers and their roles in the operas he had seen in Vienna as a youth, and the names of his army officers down to the battalion level. He had a note-perfect knowledge of the prelude to *Die Meistersinger*, and whistled it in his curious, penetrating vibrato. He is said to have memorized the entire libretto of *Lohengrin*. He knew the production figures per man-day of work in England, France, the United States, and Italy.

He played games with his knowledge, betting that a specific item in his vast but quixotic storehouse of information was correct. Almost invariably it *was*, and the Führer smiled contentedly when told that, once again, he had the right answer: 'I often asked myself,' a secretary recalled, 'how one human brain could preserve so many facts.'[9] He used his phenomenal memory to convince himself and others that he was a person of great intellectual ability, in no way inferior to those who were better educated or better trained. After impressing a naval aide with an incredible recitation of statistics on naval ordnance, he said, 'Bear in mind that my brain works about the same way as a calculating machine.'[10] It was a fairly accurate description.[11]

Hitler's data bank served as a defensive weapon to ward off displeasing arguments. When field commanders on the eastern front pointed out the strength of the enemy, Hitler would either dismiss their argument as irrelevant, because his steel-like will would overcome all problems, or overwhelm the doubter with production statistics and precise weaknesses in the armament of the enemy. He would also undercut and embarrass commanders by demanding from them information that they could not possibly be expected to remember, such as the name and rank of each of their subordinate officers or the military decorations each was entitled to wear. When field commanders admitted ignorance of such matters, Hitler would triumphantly provide the answers and announce that he was better informed about their own sectors than they were. The embarrassed commanders were thus silenced.[12]

Neither innovative nor disciplined, Hitler's mind nevertheless had a remarkable capacity to simplify, reducing ideas to effective political slogans and programs while, at the same time, creating the illusion that he was thereby achieving a higher wisdom. That was an enormous political asset. He was one of those effective political leaders whom Jacob Burckhardt called *simplificateurs terribles*.

John Kenneth Galbraith has commented on Hitler's ability to perceive the right economic policy at the right time. When he came to power at the depth of the Great Depression in 1933, he immediately instituted a well-coordinated and highly successful program of deficit spending and public works that solved the unemployment problem in Germany.[13]

One is less impressed with the quality of the Führer's mind as it ranged over a vast number of subjects in the so-called 'Table Conversations' (*Tischgespräche*),[14] the nightly disquisitions he delivered to captive audiences at field headquarters or in his Berlin air-raid shelter during the war. He considered himself particularly knowledgeable, for instance, about American history and social life: 'In the single year, 1641, fifty thousand Irish left for North America[15] ... Transplant a German in Kiev, and he remains a German, but transplant him in Miami, and you make a degenerate of him – in other words, an American ... Everything about the behaviour of American society reveals that it's half-Judaized with the other half Negrofied ... You can't imagine anything as miserable or degenerate as [American] farmers.'

In contrast to the Kaiser, who was quadra-lingual, the Führer never mastered his own language and knew no other. He nevertheless considered himself an expert on linguistics and literary criticism: 'The English language is incapable of expressing a poetic or philosophic idea ... One hour of instruction in French once a week is quite enough to master that language ... The three greatest books in the world are *Gulliver's Travels, Don Quixote*, and *Uncle Tom's Cabin* ... In no country is Shakespeare so badly acted as in England.' Hitler also had strong opinions about art: 'Anyone who paints a sky green and pastures blue ought to be sterilized.'[16]

Like the Kaiser, the Führer lectured his entourage on philosophy, theology, and biblical studies: 'It is Schopenhauer who annihilated the pragmatism of Hegel ... It is certain that Jesus was not a Jew. The Jews, by the way, regarded him as the son of a whore – of a whore and a Roman soldier ... When Paul preached in Athens in favour of the Jews, Athenians shook with laughter ...'

History and cultural anthropology were, Hitler believed, among his stronger suits: 'Russia has never suffered a famine ... To label the Bulgarians as Slavs is pure nonsense; originally they were Turkomans. The same applies to the Czechs. It is enough for a Czech to grow a moustache for anyone to see, from the way it droops, that his origin is Mongolian ... The favourite soup in Greece came from

Holstein ... Caesar's soldiers had a horror of eating meat. That is why they had magnificent teeth.' He took pride in what he believed to be his command of medical fact: 'No one in the Middle Ages suffered from high blood pressure. Their constant brawls were ample safeguard against it ... Now, thanks to the safety razor, the world's blood pressure is rising ... All half-caste families – even if they have but a minute quantity of Jewish blood in their veins – produce regularly at least one pure Jew each generation. Roosevelt affords the best possible proof of the truth of this opinion.' Hitler was also convinced that 'Any Turkish porter can move a piano by himself ... As to what gives the Mercedes-Benz its beauty ... I can claim that fatherhood.'

One of his secretaries, who had suffered through a hundred nights of Hitler's soliloquies, later reflected that 'his spate of words lacked the human note, the spiritual quality of a cultivated man ... there was [nothing] on which the human spirit had left its trace.'[17]

Although both Kaiser and Führer had phenomenal memories and commanded a remarkable amount of information – and misinformation – about an extraordinary range of subjects, they used their mental faculties for very different purposes. Wilhelm von Hohenzollern sought constantly to impress people with his dazzling personality and sparkling intellect; Adolf Hitler also enjoyed showing off, but his mental abilities were primarily devoted not to mere social bedazzlement, but to realizing his lifelong ambition of attaining power over others.

Their Reading Habits and Their Personal Libraries

Love of reading has been my salvation.

Wilhelm II, 1939

I read to confirm my ideas.

Adolf Hitler

The Kaiser's diverse library of some 5,000 volumes[18] would seem to substantiate the impression he gave contemporaries of extraordinary range and depth of knowledge. Of course it is always difficult to tell how many books in a person's library have actually been read or, if read, how much they affected the reader's thinking. Yet the Kaiser's conversations, sermons, and essays indicate a broad and discerning knowledge of good books. Certainly his library belies Count Kessler's charge of 'tastelessness.' It seems likely that Wilhelm von Hohenzollern, like many of us, kept some volumes largely for display purposes – one thinks of his beautiful leather-bound and gold-lettered edition of Schopenhauer's complete *Werke*, with uncut pages, and his grandmother Queen Victoria's presentation copy of Prince Albert's official biography, also with pages left uncut. It should be noted that the library now preserved in his exile home, 'Huis Doorn,' extensive as it is, comprises only a part of the original collection. The extant library nevertheless offers clues to Wilhelm's intellectual interests.

His library holds marked copies of literary classics in four languages, including the works of Goethe,[19] Shakespeare, Schiller, Molière, Dante, Byron, Dickens, Browning, Conrad, and Hardy. One finds many books on art and architecture – for example, the lives of Michelangelo, Leonardo, and Rembrandt; biography – for example, Lincoln, Andrew Carnegie, and Frederick the Great; on history, military and naval affairs; and several mysteries by Dorothy Sayers. Wilhelm subscribed to professional journals on architecture and city planning, including one volume entitled *Detroit: The City Beautiful*.

His interest in religion and his personal commitment to Christianity is attested by the presence of Luther's entire *Werke*, many inspirational volumes on spiritual uplift and the power of prayer, and many volumes on mysticism and mythology, notably a well-thumbed, *Norse Mythology: The Religion of Our Forefathers*, along with a study on the Cabbala.

The Kaiser's preoccupation with racism and his phobia about the 'Yellow Peril' are manifested in such titles as *Achtung! Asien marchiert!* (Beware! Asia Is on the March!). H.S. Chamberlain, as would be expected,[20] is well represented; signed copies of his books and pamphlets include *Rasse und Persönlichkeit* (Race and Personality). The Kaiser also owned Richard Wagner's scurrilous anti-Semitic diatribe on Jews in music, and a copy of *Mein Kampf*, as well as speeches of Goebbels and Göring.

Dozens of books and pamphlets disproving the 'war-guilt lie' demonstrate the Kaiser's need to reinforce his conviction that he was in no way responsible for the Great War. He owned a complete set of *Grosse Politik*, forty volumes of documents on pre-war diplomacy, with many pages marked by bits of crumbling paper.

The clues to Adolf Hitler's literary interests are confusing, and the extent of his reading is not easily determined. He liked to give the impression that he was a voracious reader who devoured 'mountains of books.' But his spoken and written words, although showing a considerable fund of miscellaneous information, do not reveal that he had read serious books of literature, history, philosophy, or science. The information – and misinformation – he cited came almost exclusively from newspapers, pamphlets, popular magazines, and translations of digests of the foreign press. His criterion for good literature was whether it supplied him with arguments to confirm his prejudices.

Hitler's adult lifestyle did not encourage serious reading. When party leader and later chancellor, his evenings at home were usually spent in watching movies and chattering until dawn. The mornings were given over to sleep, the afternoons to travel or conferences.

The few books that he indisputably did read for pleasure are not notable for their intellectual challenge. In addition to Karl May's Wild West stories, he was much taken with the adventures of a horse called Raubautz. Hitler followed him eagerly as he moved from civilian life (*Raubautz Wants to Live*) to the cavalry (*Raubautz Becomes a Soldier*). He was so fond of these boyhood novels that he kept copies of them in all his residences, and would entertain his guests by quoting long passages from memory. He also kept by his bedside a variety of statistical almanacs that supplied him with information that would impress his visitors.[21]

August Kubizek, his only companion of Linz and the first years in Vienna, despite what he wrote in his published memoirs, told the Linz archivist Franz Jetzinger that there were only two books that Hitler studied carefully and talked about repeatedly. One was a child's book on Nordic gods and heroes, the other an illustrated volume on architecture. The first contained a sketch of the swastika that impressed the future Führer: 'Hitler said at that time that the German people needed a symbol that would represent the basic concept of Germandom.'[22]

During the 'battle years' before attaining power, Hitler often borrowed books. Indeed he borrowed so many and so often from a private library belonging to a wealthy right-wing nationalist that their owner, one Friedrich Krohn, suspected that Hitler only skimmed the volumes in order to impress his patron with his industry and knowledge. At any rate, of the more than 100 books and pamphlets he borrowed from Krohn between 1919 and 1921, almost two-thirds were tawdry anti-Semitic pamphlets, including *Goethe and the Jews, Secret Laws of the Jews, Luther and the Jews, Bolshevism and Jewry, Schopenhauer and the Jews,* extracts from the *Talmud, Wagner and the Jews,* and Henry Ford's diatribe, *The International Jew: A World Problem.*

By amassing an enormous collection of books Hitler sought to give the impression of wide reading and great erudition. An intimate who prided himself on being an intellectual claimed that his Führer's personal library contained some 6,000 books.[23] He may have been right. Towards the end of the war, American soldiers found a part of Hitler's personal library hidden in a salt mine in the neighbourhood of Alt Aussee. These books, numbering about 2,000, were shipped to Washington, where they are now shelved in the Rare Books Division of the Library of Congress – shelved grotesquely adjacent to the private collections of Oliver Wendell Holmes and Thomas Jefferson.

While Hitler's library may give some indication of his reading tastes, it must be approached with caution as a key to his intellectual interests. Many of Hitler's books were probably not chosen by Hitler himself, and, with the exception of the handful of books that bear his signature or notations in pencil, there is no way of knowing whether he actually read the volumes in his library. Many of the books contain the ponderous swastika-emblazoned, oak-leaf-clustered bookplate of the Führer, but only three have his personal autograph, 'A. Hitler.'

With these caveats in mind, let us note that, despite Hitler's boast that 'I can speak several languages,'[24] there are none but German books here. Notably absent also are great works of literature. There is one slim volume dedicated to him by Heinrich Himmler of the SS, ambitiously entitled *Von Tacitus bis Nietzsche: Gedanken und Meinungen aus zwei Jahrtausenden* (From Tacitus to Nietzsche: Thoughts and Opinions from Two Millennia). There are no books on political theory. History, Hitler often said, was his favourite subject, yet we find no great historian represented and no philosopher save Fichte. With the arguable exception of Clausewitz's well-thumbed classic on war, one must agree with one of Hitler's secretaries who observed, 'His library contained not one book of humane or intellectual value.'[25]

In contrast to the Kaiser, the Führer disdained the classics as ill-suited to his political purposes. When he compared the value of Goethe and Schiller with that of Karl May, the giants of Weimar came off badly. Hitler saluted May for extolling obedience to a leader, toughness, and heroism, and those qualities, in Hitler's mind, were absolutely all the German youth needed. 'And there,' he said, 'you have the great importance of Karl May. But instead of such reading, those idiotic teachers hammered the works of Goethe and Schiller into [our] unfortunate heads.'[26] Not surprisingly, the Führer's library contains dozens of pseudo-scientific pamphlets on race and eugenics.

The Kaiser and the Führer as Writers and Poets

I should like to write ... Wars pass by. The only things that last are the works of human genius.

Adolf Hitler

The Kaiser's verbal outbursts were often impulsive and sometimes irresponsible. With the exception of his marginal notations, it was a very different matter when he wrote. In sharp contrast to Hitler's prose, Wilhelm's memoirs, letters, and monographs were carefully organized and clearly, even elegantly, written.[27]

Wilhelm's public speeches are literate, vigorous, and creative, enlivened by pungent expressions, self-coined phrases, and vivid metaphors. Adolf Hitler was capable of neither the quality of the prose nor the magnanimity of spirit expressed, for example, in the Kaiser's speech of 18 August 1899 dedicating a battlefield monument, which he had helped design, honouring a Prussian infantry regiment that had fought the French in 1870:

This bronze statue ... is a guardian and sentinel for all the dauntless soldiers of both armies who fell here, on both the French side and on the German.

For the French soldiers, too, fighting heroically for their emperor and their country, sank into a glorious grave. When our flags salute these brazen figures and droop mournfully over the last resting place of our dear comrades, may they also wave over the graves of our adversaries, whispering to them that we remember their valorous dead with melancholy respect.[28]

The Kaiser's sermons display the same vigorous eloquence.[29]

Like the Führer, the Kaiser considered himself something of a poet, and both rulers displayed a similar lack of poetic talent. Wilhelm's fascination with Norse gods inspired his ode dedicated to the Nordic god of the sea. Three verses of this long panegyric will give us the poem's essential banality, little of which is lost in translation:

Ode to Aegir

Oh, Aegir, god of fleets of might
Before whom kneeling bends Undine,
Behold, how in the morning light,
The hero troop of braves implores thee.

In setting out for cruel war,
Upon a far, far distant strand,
Through tempests, rocks and reefs and more,
Guide towards the foeman's land ...

And just as Frithjov of Ellida
Crossed in confidence thy sea,
May you be for us a leader,
We the sons of thy Army.[30]

The author was so proud of his ode that he wanted it published. He planned to donate royalties from its sale – which he assumed would be enormous – to the building fund for a memorial church to honour the memory of his grandfather, Kaiser Wilhelm I (the *Gedächtniskirche* of central Berlin). Wilhelm missed the irony noted by the editor of the Social Democratic newspaper *Vorwärts,* who suggested that the church might be more appropriately named '*Aegirkirche.*' Wilhelm saw to it that the editor was sentenced to six months in jail for *lèse majesté.*[31]

As a youth, the Führer had played with the idea of becoming a dramatist. Night after night in his walk-up room in the Stumpergasse of Vienna he stayed up long after midnight working over plays and operas under a flickering kerosene lamp. His grandiose projects required elaborate staging ranging from Hell to Heaven with forests, mountains, cataracts, and lakes in between. When his roommate suggested that he might begin his career with somewhat more modest productions, Adolf was furious. He seems not to have finished any of his projects.[32]

Letters and postcards Hitler wrote from Vienna in 1908, from Munich in 1914, and from the front during the war, show that as a young man of twenty to twenty-five he still deserved the 'unsatisfactory' mark in the German language that he had received as a schoolboy.[33] The same grammatical mistakes occur in letters dating from both his adolescent and his mature years. He continued to misspell the German forms of such common words as *theatre, deaf, namely, immediately, destiny, corruption, injustice,* and *Bismarck,* as well as *Darwinism, Bolshevism, socialism* – and even *anti-Semitism* and *pogroms.*[34] Since Hitler never finished his 'Monumental History of Humanity,' his major literary production was to remain *Mein Kampf,* a work which became a bestseller and made its author a millionaire, for reasons quite extraneous to its literary merit.

This two-volume work was begun in the summer of 1924, while Hitler was enjoying special concessions as a prisoner in 'honourable confinement' in Landsberg am Lech. There is dispute about whether Hitler actually wrote *Mein Kampf* or dictated his ideas to one of his aides who transcribed them on a typewriter.[35] Whether dictated or pecked out by Hitler on a typewriter, and from a literary viewpoint it doesn't seem to make much difference,[36] the first volume was nearly completed when he left Landsberg on 20 December 1924, and the second volume was dictated a year later.

The whole manuscript was gone over by Father Bernhard Stempfle, a Jesuit editor of an anti-Semitic newspaper who was subsequently murdered at Hitler's orders during the Blood Purge of 30 June 1934. Others who read the proofs and struggled to clarify the turbid prose included Ernst Hanfstaengl and the geopolitician Professor Karl Haushofer. The original manuscript was sent as a gift to Hitler's motherly patroness of many years, Frau Bechstein.

Fortunately for sales, the original title, 'Four and One Half Years of Battle Against Lies, Stupidity and Cowardice: Account Settled,' was changed to *Mein*

Kampf, at the suggestion of Max Amann. By the 1940s it had been translated into sixteen languages and had become one of the most widely published books in the world.[37]

According to the count of an indefatigable German literary scholar, the work contains over 164,000 errors in German grammar and syntax,[38] and not even the most conscientious and imaginative translation can rescue meaning from some of the prose.[39] Nevertheless, *Mein Kampf* performed the same role as Marx's *Das Kapital*, Mao's *Red Book*, and Louis Napoleon's *Ideés Napoléoniennes*. It was not important that these 'bibles of the movement' be either read or comprehended. Indeed their very prolixity was an advantage, for it impressed many admirers with the author's profundity and ability to solve problems that had baffled their readers.[40] Although his book was a smashing success, Hitler planned a still more important literary work that would preserve his *pensées* for posterity. 'When this war is over,' he mused in January 1942, 'I should like to write ... Wars pass by. The only things that last are the works of human genius.'[41]

Like the Kaiser, the Führer wrote poetry. Indeed his earliest extant writing was a poem which he wrote ten days after his sixteenth birthday, at a time when he was freed by the death of his tyrannical father and indulged by his permissive mother.[42] Adolf was attending school in Steyr in Lower Austria, baiting his teachers and earning low marks in German.

The poem (now in the Bundesarchiv in Koblenz) appeared under a doodle of an Austrian village church tower on a page of the guest book of a local inn. Some words are indecipherable, as indicated here with brackets and ellipses. This translation accurately reflects the poet's awkward German.[43]

On the Damberg, near Steyer, 30 April 1905
[Entry in a guest book]

People sit there in the airy house
Feasting on wines and beers
And eat and drink without a pause
[...] till they can't raise their rears.

Up the higher mountains they strut
[...] their faces so proud and daring
And then they roll down, a bouncing lot
And cannot regain their bearings.

And once they sadly at home arrive
And the hours have been forgotten

Then comes to the man [...] his wife [...]
And heals with thrashings his bottom.

(Und komen sie traurig zu Hause an
Und sind dann vergessen die Stunden
dann komt [...] sein Weib (...) Mann
Und heilt ihm mit Prügeln die Wunden.)[44]

Adolf Hitler

The last verse may be read simply as young Hitler's clumsy effort at humour, the *Schadenfreude* of reversing the usual roles, and, instead of the Austrian husbands coming home to beat up their wives, the drunken males get a thrashing from their spouses. Hitler seems to have enjoyed that scenario. Many years later, during a nocturnal soliloquy of 8–9 January 1942 at field headquarters during the war, he took inordinate pleasure in recalling at length, and in remarkable detail, how, when he was living in a private house ('Grünmarkt, No. 9, Steyr') his landlady ('whose name was Petunella something, I've forgotten her last name') would often thrash unmercifully her meek little husband ('how I despised that wet rag!').[45]

As we shall see, Adolf's father, Alois, drank at the local tavern and often returned to batter his wife and children.[46] In the adolescent poem and in adult soliloquies, Hitler clearly takes the side of the wife (his mother, Klara). The German psychiatrist who translated the poem concludes that, in his poetic fantasy, young Hitler 'acts as [his mother's] ally and delegate and makes her triumph over a husband who comes across as weak, pretentious, and ridiculous.'[47]

Two of the five extant poems Hitler wrote during the First World War reveal a very different side of this complex man. If they had been written by almost any other soldier, these sensitive and compassionate lines would have been quite unremarkable; that they are Adolf Hitler's is startling.[48] The doggerel of the first poem is not particularly noteworthy, except for the ironic twist in the last couplet.

An Idyll of Wartime

With four illustrations and text by Lance Corporal Adolf Hitler, a true incident near Arras, Autumn 1915.

Idyll of War, I

Medic Gottlieb Krause in passing by
An Arras cottage heard a woman's cry.

'I must help,' he thought, and helpful, too, were his comrades.
In midst of strife, they brought a little *Frank* into life.

[*A drawing shows a woman in bed, a newborn child in a washbasin, and a soldier pouring milk into a dish.*]

Idyll of War, II

With gentlest care Krause tended that child
Proving to all he was no savage wild.
With joy he lifted the babe for comrades to see
This man who knew nought of Delcassé or Isvolski.[49]

[*A drawing shows two German soldiers; one is holding aloft a small baby.*]

Idyll of War, III

Milk was sorely needed now,
Two other soldiers spied a cow,
Not shrapnel burst nor cannon's blast
Could stay these men from mercy's task.

[*A drawing shows a soldier, in the midst of a bombardment, milking a cow.*]

Idyll of War, IV

From soldier's flask with loving care.
Krause fed the babe life-giving fare
The mother also, from his soldier's pack
He fed with milk-softened Zwieback –
An idyll that here proves anew
Germans are Samaritans too.
And if the Frenchies don't blast them away,
Mother and child will be there today.[50]

[*A drawing shows a German soldier bidding farewell to a woman who holds a baby in swaddling clothes.*]

Once in a Thicket of the Artois Woods

This is a true happening within the woods of Artois, depicted in poem and drawing by Adolf Hitler, Flanders, 1916.

Once in a thicket of Artois' forest,

Deep in the woods on blood-soaked ground
Lay a German warrior in direst distress
Crying out in the dark and silent night.

No answer ... No echo to his call.
Will he bleed to death like a hunted beast,
Ending his life all alone?

Then suddenly from the right a heavy tread –
Fresh hope arises in the wounded's soul
And now from the left ... now from both sides
Two soldiers approach the pain-racked ground
One is German, the other French
They eye each other with hostile glare
And raise their rifles to fire.

Then asks the German warrior, 'What do you here?'
'I heard a cry for help'
'But he is your enemy!'
'Yea – but a human in need!'

In silence they lower their rifles
And with straining arms gently bear
The wounded man to the German line.
Now 'tis done, he'll be safe now.

The Frenchman turns back to the wood,
But the German stays him and grasps his hand;
With care-filled eyes, forebodingly he speaks:

'I know not what Fate hath in store –
What lies hidden in stars above.
Mayhap your bullet will end my life;
Mayhap you'll perish from one of mine.

For who can know what battle brings?
But what e'er may come, we lived one holy hour
When humans found each other ...
And now, Friend, farewell, and God go with thee.'

Adolf Hitler, springtime, 1916

[*A drawing depicts a French and a German soldier carrying a wounded German on a make-shift litter.*]

These two extraordinary poems show that as a young man, Hitler was capable of tender and compassionate feelings.

Another extant poem is an ode to motherhood. This peculiarly sombre tribute, written in 1923, testifies both to one aspect of Hitler's love for his own mother and to the limits of his poetic talent.

Be Reminded!

When your mother has grown old
And you have older grown,
When things she once did e'er so lightly
Are now a burden, heavy borne,
When her eyes so dear and trusting
No more, as once, look forward brightly,
When her weary, falt'ring feet
No longer carry her step lightly –
Then give to her a helping hand,
Accompany her with gladsome smile –

The hour nears when you a-weeping
Must go with her on her last mile!
And if she asks, so give her answer,
And if again, let words not cease,
And if once more, then stay her questions
Not harshly but with restful Peace!
And if she can't quite understand you,
Explain as if 'twere joyous task;
The hour comes, the bitter hour,
When her dear mouth no more can ask.[51]

After he came to power in 1933 the Führer was able to have this poem published in an edition of a Nazi paper devoted to extolling motherhood. It is remarkable that a grown person, indeed the chancellor of a great country, who prided himself on his literary taste should think that his own efforts warranted publication.

The quality of the verse is less interesting than its psychological undertones: particularly the attitudes it reveals about mothers, especially Hitler's own. In the last lines, for example, there are clear indications of guilt feelings over memories of attacking his mother verbally or of impatiently silencing her when she asked questions that annoyed him. There are also strong indications that he was intrigued by his mother's death; indeed, that he may even have repressed a death wish. Consider the line reading in German, *'Geleite sie mit froher Lust'* (here uncertainly translated as 'Accompany her with gladsome smile'). It is surprising to find the word *Lust* used in a poem involving a dying mother. No matter how one translates this equivocal word, the results are psychologically interesting. Is Hitler accompanying his dying mother on her 'last mile' (a) *gladly* and without reservation? Or does he do so (b) with *pleasure*, or (c) with *desire*?

In the lines where unspecified questions are to be answered 'in gentle peace' (*in sanfter Ruh*), a death image is clearly conveyed. In German usage that phrase is reserved for funeral wreaths and death announcements. Thus, Hitler seems to be saying that his mother's repeated questions will be answered not merely patiently and with gentle or soft language, but with the ultimate peace of the grave: *Rest in Peace.*

The quality of the Kaiser's and the Führer's poems may seem to be at the same low level. But the differences are revealing. As a literary critic has observed, Wilhelm's poems are 'more or less conventional, superficial literary exercises that any schoolboy could turn out, whereas at least two of Adolf's poems – for all their artistic crudity – invite psychological analysis because they are related to deep internal forces.'[52]

Their Tastes in Art and Music

Art that ignores the laws and limitations which I set forth, is no longer art.

Wilhelm II

Art is a sublime mission demanding fanaticism.

Adolf Hitler

If I were not the Kaiser, I would have liked to be an architect.

Wilhelm II

If the war had not come along, I would certainly have been an architect and ... probably one of the best architects ... in Germany.

Adolf Hitler

The Kaiser and the Führer both had strong views about art and both tried to impose their tastes on the German people.

Wilhelm's taste was xenophobic. An American newspaper reported that the director of a Berlin gallery was required to submit lists of proposed acquisitions directly to the Kaiser, giving the name and nationality of the artist as well as the subject of each painting. His Majesty crossed out the names of all artists who were not German.[53] He felt sufficiently confident in his artistic taste to announce, in a speech of 18 December 1901, that henceforth he would determine the canons of art in Germany: 'Art that ignores the laws and limitations which I set forth is no longer art.'[54] Since he believed that art must fulfil the awesome task of uplifting and ennobling the German people, it badly needed his guiding hand. 'Art can prosper,' he said, 'only under a monarchy and the protection of princes. Without their supportive hand it must atrophy.'[55] Every picture and statue, the Kaiser wrote, should 'convey a message of unquestioned loyalty, pride and assertive self-confidence.'[56] Artists who displeased the Kaiser were labelled 'enemies of the state' (Reichsfeinde).[57]

His own artistic preferences were relentlessly traditional, favouring uncomplicated renderings of historical subjects, demurely sexless female nudes, conventional landscapes, and genre scenes of happy village schoolchildren, country horse auctions, and widows weeping silently under drooping willows.[58]

Unlike Hitler's, Wilhelm's taste in art was puritanical. He vetoed the nomination of Anders Zorn for an award because he ruled that Zorn's art was not 'morally uplifting' and the artist was 'too fond of erotic scenes.'[59] He cancelled a retrospective exhibit planned to honour Max Liebermann, saying, 'It was not only [my] right but my duty to denounce the influence of Liebermann since such people [are] poisoning the soul of the German nation.'[60]

The Kaiser indulged his personal taste in heroic 'Germanic' art by commissioning and supervising the carving of thirty-two statues of the warrior kings of Prussia. These pretentious memorials to his ancestors were lined up on either side of the Siegesallee (Avenue of Victory), a broad avenue cutting through central Berlin. At its dedication in December 1901 Wilhelm set forth his own artistic ideals. 'True art,' said the Kaiser, in an address that infuriated artists throughout Germany, 'has the mission to aid in educating the masses ... however art, as is nowadays often the case, injures and sins against the German people ... Art must stretch out her hand to uplift the people, instead of pulling them down into the gutter.'[61] On this and many other occasions, the Kaiser made it very clear indeed that he, like Hitler, did not like anything 'modern.' The Führer would officially declare it 'degenerate' (entartet); the Kaiser pronounced it 'filth' (Schmutzichkeit).[62] Artists whom Wilhelm II considered Reichsfeinde were, almost invariably, modernists.

Given Wilhelm's pronouncement, it is not surprising that he fought a running battle with all those who, he said, were dragging art 'down into the gutter.' He suspected, quite rightly, that they had all been dabbling in 'French art.' To his mind that in itself was moral corruption and a form of treason. In 1889 the Kaiser prohibited German artists from exhibiting at the World's Fair in Paris, labelling the city 'the whorehouse of the world' and asserting that French-inspired art was ipso facto un-German,[63] and *that* was very bad indeed. Similarly, when German Impressionists were invited to exhibit at the St Louis World's Fair of 1904, the Kaiser saw to it that their invitations were withdrawn. He chose instead paintings that were 'uncompromisingly traditional and dull.'[64] On two other occasions the Kaiser cancelled gold medal awards to recipients selected by a jury of independent artists and gave the medals instead to artists of his own choice.[65]

Wilhelm was in constant conflict with the director of the National Gallery, the Swiss-born and widely respected art historian, Hugo von Tschudi (1851–1911). The Kaiser was furious with Tschudi for purchasing several Manets, Monets, Renoirs, and Cézannes – indeed the German National Gallery had been the first museum in Europe to purchase a Cézanne.[66] When Tschudi sought Wilhelm's permission to purchase more Impressionists from a London dealer at an extraordinarily advantageous price, the Kaiser vetoed the sale. Tschudi resigned.[67]

Progressive artists were not slow in counter-attacking. They were led by Max Liebermann (1847–1935), who had a double incentive for entering the lists against the Emperor. The Kaiser had not only insulted him and his art, but had added injury to insult by erecting the monstrous memorial statuary on the Siegesallee immediately beneath his studio windows. Liebermann was condemned to look at this pretentious caricature of 'classical' art every working day. 'All I can do about it,' he lamented to a friend, 'is to wear dark goggles, but it is a life sentence.'[68]

Liebermann and his friends formed an opposition group of those who had seceded from the Royal Academy, controlled by the Kaiser's appointees. These 'secessionists' wore their rejection from the academy like a badge of honour. They established their own galleries in Berlin and other German cities and defiantly promoted contemporary art. One of their shows in 1901 exhibited Pissarro, Renoir, Whistler, and – in special defiance of the Kaiser – Zorn. Another show in 1903 exhibited Kandinsky, Monet, and Manet, whose five paintings were hung on a 'wall of honour.'[69] All this was gall to the Kaiser. He came to despise all modern artists and was heard to mutter that their 'gutter art should be assigned to the dustbin ... If it were up to me I'd keep [them] in line with a rod.'[70]

It was not entirely up to him, however, and therein lay a crucial difference between the Kaiser and the Führer. The Kaiser could fulminate against progressive artists and bar their works from some exhibitions, but that – though a great deal – was all he could do. He could not prevent them from showing their work in independent galleries in Berlin and throughout Germany, nor could he throw them into concentration camps or threaten to castrate them if they painted the sky green or the grass blue. Moreover, as so often happened with him, Wilhelm succeeded in defeating his own purposes. His efforts at suppression and censorship served as a great boost to modern art in Germany and promoted the unity of all political parties in opposition to his arrogant censorship. The *Frankfurter Zeitung* carried a lead article under the heading 'Berlin's Autocratic Art Policies Protested from All Quarters,' and a speaker in the Reichstag was applauded when he ended an oration supporting freedom for the arts by saying that Germany did not need a governance of art with 'Wilhelm II at its head.' The speaker was immediately ruled out of order and reprimanded for mentioning the Kaiser's name. But he had won applause and had made his point.[71]

The Kaiser's own artistic creations suggest that he, like the Führer, had a modest talent. A letter from Queen Victoria of 1883 records that she was much impressed with a plate her grandson had painted 'representing part of the bombardment of Alexandria.'[72]

Wilhelm, like Hitler, also enjoyed designing tombstones and memorials. And like the Führer he preferred painting in water-colours. Copies of his water-colour, *Kampf der Panzerkreuzer* (Battle of Heavy Cruisers) of 1895, were sold at a price of 6 marks a copy and the *Illustrierte Zeitung* lavished praise and ran a picture of the Kaiser's belligerent painting, *Der deutsche Michael als Friedenshüter* (German Michael as Protector of the Peace).[73] Wilhelm expressed his racial prejudices and fear of the 'Yellow Peril' in a widely circulated poster featuring a caricature of a long-fanged Japanese menacing Europe and bearing the caption 'People of Europe, Guard Your Most Sacred Possessions!'[74]

Several of the Kaiser's pencil drawings and a few of his water-colours are preserved in Doorn House, which is now a museum owned by the Dutch government. The original water-colours of seascapes and battleships have, unaccountably, been removed,[75] but a folder of drawings contains several sketches of a Germanic Michael with flaming sword warning Europa of the rising threat from the Orient. Among a pile of paintings in the dusty attic of the Gate House, I found an arresting pencil drawing. As young Adolf Hitler in 1907 had lingered in the darkening death room to sketch his beloved mother's emaciated body, so young Prince Wilhelm in 1888 had drawn his revered grandfather in death. The dark, soft-lead drawing, now slightly smudged on yellowed paper, is labelled 'Wilhelm der Grosse.'

Like the Führer, however, the Kaiser considered his real forte to be architecture. He once confessed to a member of his entourage, 'If I were not the Emperor I would have liked to be an architect.'[76] He loved to design houses, castles, churches, and – especially – ships. As in many other areas, 'his ability was smaller than his enthusiasm.'[77] An admirer spoke of the Kaiser's 'passion for reconstruction' and recalled that he considered himself the 'enemy of ruins.' He entirely rebuilt the Hohkönigsburg castle in the Vosges Mountains and reconstructed a fortified Roman camp in the Taunus which he dedicated to 'Emperor Hadrian by his colleague, Wilhelm II.'[78] His enthusiasm for reconstruction prompted the humour magazine, *Simplicissimus,* to run a cartoon showing a callow Crown Prince driving past the Coliseum in Rome and exclaiming, '*Donnerwetter!* Now that would be something for Papa to restore!'[79]

Wilhelm spent months studying battleship designs and, finding fault with all of them, sent his own design to a noted Italian naval architect. The Italian wrote back complimenting the Kaiser on the ship's impressive size and enormous guns. He also admired the detailed appointments for everyone from captain to cabin boy. He concluded, however, that 'this wonderful ship has only one fault: if she were put on the water she would sink like a lump of lead.'[80]

The Kaiser's favourite composer, like the Führer's, was Richard Wagner, and he astonished professional musicians with his detailed knowledge of the *Ring, Parsifal,* and *Lohengrin.*[81] Like Hitler, he was drawn to Wagner because *der Meister* shared his fascination with Nordic myth. Just as the Führer had tried, as a youth, to compose a Wagnerian opera based on Germanic legend,[82] the Kaiser composed what he considered to be Wagnerian music for the paean of praise he had written to honour Aegir, Nordic god of the sea, and had his music orchestrated by the royal music director. Wilhelm conducted the piece and, on one occasion, sang the aria.[83]

The Kaiser and the Führer both saw themselves as Wagnerian heroes. Hitler would have himself painted as Lohengrin in shining armour, bearing the swastika and mounted on a prancing steed;[84] Wilhelm preferred posing as Lohengrin standing, appropriately helmeted, as the peerless knight in search of the Holy Grail of Germandom.[85] In one respect the Kaiser outdid the Führer: he had *his* superpowered Mercedes fitted with a horn that blared forth the *Donnerhallmotiv* from the *Rheingold.* Hitler never thought of doing that.

Whoever wants to understand National Socialism must first know Richard Wagner.

Adolf Hitler

To an even greater degree than the Kaiser, the Führer considered himself to be unusually gifted in musical sensitivity and artistic taste. The attributes Hitler assigned to political leaders were those that mirrored his own self-image. True statesmen, he observed, should begin their careers at the age of thirty (as he had), and they definitely must be musical. In 1925, Hitler ruled out General Ludendorff as a political leader because he had no ear for music. In 1945, when talking about possible successors, he rejected Heinrich Himmler because he was not nearly musical enough. Only musical people, he was convinced, were able to feel 'the folkic soul' (*Volksseele*); they alone find 'the sensitive word that can move men'; they alone can 'put the correct political action into effect.'[86]

Music was an obsession with the Führer. As Karl Menninger has noted, good music can help to heal destructive tendencies in deeply riven personalities. It is, Menninger writes, 'a bulwark against self-destruction.'[87] That it served as such a bulwark for Hitler is suggested by the effect that Wagner had upon young Hitler. His friend of the Vienna years recalled:

When [Adolf] listened to Wagner's music, he was a changed man; his violence left him, he became quiet, yielding and tractable. He no longer felt lonely and outlawed and misjudged by society. He was intoxicated and bewitched ... From the stale, musty prison of his back room he was transported into blissful regions of German antiquity, that ideal world which was the lofty goal for all his endeavours.[88]

Wagner remained for him the greatest source of inspiration. 'Whoever wants to understand National Socialism,' he said, 'must first know Richard Wagner.' Hitler told an American correspondent, 'For me Wagner is something Godly and his music is my religion. I go to his concerts as others go to church.'[89]

Hitler was not much interested in the classical music of balance and restraint. He disliked Bach, Handel, Haydn, and Mozart. Next to Wagner, his favourite composer was Bruckner. He wanted to make Linz a shrine for Bruckner's works, as Bayreuth was for Wagner's. At the age of nineteen he drew plans for the Linz concert hall which he solemnly consecrated to Bruckner's memory, and years later, his enthusiasm unabated, he tried to buy the manuscript of Bruckner's Third Symphony for $7,500.[90] He disliked Italian opera for two reasons: it was based upon 'trickery and deception,' and it was not German. Art and architecture were also consuming passions of Hitler's life. Shortly before swallowing a lethal dose of cyanide on the afternoon of 30 April 1945, he was heard to exclaim, 'Ah, what an artist dies in me!'[91] On several previous occasions he said that the main reason he had entered politics was to implement his artistic plans, and he repeatedly expressed regret that the war had interrupted their fulfilment: 'If the war had not come along,' he observed, 'I would certainly have become an architect and perhaps, yes, even probably, one of the best architects if not the best architect in Germany.'[92]

The water-colours and drawings Hitler produced as a youth were not good enough to gain him admission to the Vienna Academy of Art. But they sold well enough to art dealers, or to those who wanted something pleasant with which to show off their elaborate picture-frames. On the average, his paintings, which he sold largely to generous Jewish art dealers, brought the equivalent of about $10 to $15 each. He also did some water-colours during the First World War, and his careful pictures of French buildings in ruins and later of Bavarian churches suggest that he was not without talent.

Doodling was a lifetime habit of the Führer. As a boy in Linz he sketched a hated schoolmaster in the act of masturbating; he also entertained his schoolmates with drawings of gruesome severed heads. Forty years later, Baldur von Schirach recalled that after meals the Führer would sit 'drawing on one of the little cards he always had with him, mostly severed heads of men and women.'[93]

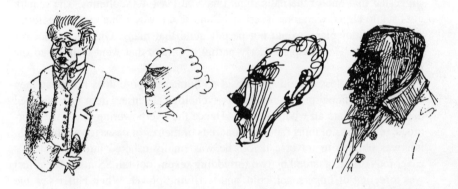

Hitler's early sketches for enormous buildings, memorials, and bridges – carefully collected by Albert Speer – became the actual working diagrams for the buildings he and Speer started to erect many years later. Indeed, so closely did Hitler supervise the execution of the public buildings in the Third Reich that they must be considered his own artistic creations.

Two obsessions dominate the architectural plans for buildings he never constructed: gargantuan size and the use of domes and columns. Hitler's Nuremberg stadium would have had a cubic volume three times the mass of the Great Pyramid of Cheops and was designed to seat 400,000 people. The meeting hall he planned for his new capital of 'Germania' was to be situated on the *Prachtallee* (Avenue of Splendour), which was to be twice the width and three times the length of the Champs Elysées. The dome of the *Kuppelhalle* would have been 825 feet in diameter, with a volume sixteen times that of St Peter's. The Arch of Triumph, originally designed by Hitler in 1925, was to stand 400 feet high. Fifty of Napoleon's 'paltry' triumphal arches in Paris would have fitted within the Führer's 'gate of glory.' A fourth massive building, the Führer's own palace, which was to be erected on the new capital's 'Adolf Hitlerplatz,' was to include a dining-hall that could seat 2,000 guests and a reception room with a volume of over 74,000 cubic feet. Memorial statues he planned would be 46 feet higher than the Statue of Liberty's 151 feet.

After early victories during the war, Hitler further expanded his plans. Speer recalled how he had first suggested to Hitler that a giant golden German eagle with a swastika in its talons might top the *Kuppelhalle*. But the Führer overruled him, having decided that this design would no longer do. It should be altered so that the eagle held a globe of the world clutched in its claws.[94]

The Führer's infatuation with columns was so well known to members of his entourage that they sometimes made cautious little jokes about it. On one occasion when Hitler was remodelling one of his own buildings, Göring jocularly suggested that one of the halls should have at least 400 columns. The remark got back to Hitler, who took it seriously, and said it was a fine idea but unfortunately his floor plans would not permit quite that many. One of his doctors observed that 'He was particularly partial to pillars that went right up to the roof.'[95]

That these colossal buildings served no human purpose does not mean they were non-functional in a political and psychological sense. Hitler had designed them to intimidate all who saw them. Hence the overpowering mass, the enormous, relentless columns flanking hundreds of metres of passageway that a visitor was obliged to traverse before he was finally ushered into the Führer's cavernous office, guarded by two forbidding seven-foot-tall SS men. The effect was a feeling of impersonal, cold, and terrifying power. When Hitler saw the gigantic proportions of his new chancellery, he smirked with satisfaction, 'Good, good! When the diplomats see that they will learn to know fear!' (*werden sie das Fürchten lernen!*). Albert Speer was right in stating, much later, that Hitler's buildings were 'the very expression of tyranny.'[96]

The Führer's preferences in painting are shown both in his private collection and in the works he allowed to be exhibited in his Reich, for he had appointed himself the arbiter of national taste. Approved paintings were displayed in the new House of German Art which he designed and dedicated in Munich in 1937 – an enormous, many-columned white mass which Müncheners dubbed the *Weisswurstpalast* (White Sausage Palace). Over its portal in block letters of bronze was emblazoned the motto that set forth the Führer's personal aesthetic theory:

Die Kunst ist eine Erhabene und zum
Fanatismus verpflichtende Mission
(Art is a sublime mission demanding fanaticism)

At first it was planned that a jury of art critics would select the paintings to be exhibited; but when Hitler learned that examples of expressionism and abstraction might be included, he shouted that no 'degenerate' art would desecrate his new gallery. The jury was dismissed and Heinrich Hoffmann, Hitler's personal photographer, and a man who has been called by a noted art historian 'abysmally ignorant' of art, was ordered to screen thousands of paintings.[97] Hitler, like the Kaiser, personally made the final selections. Like the Kaiser's, his tastes were banal, with the notable exception of Franz von Stuck (of whom, more in a minute). The paintings Hitler promoted were from the school of sentimental realism. The paintings he selected for the Museum of German Art were of sturdy peasants, pleasant landscapes, and solid buildings – all providing an illusion of stability, order, and healthy *Gemütlichkeit* in a secure and serene world of simplicity and permanence.[98]

The Führer's ideas about architecture, like his political ideas, underwent no important changes. The idealized buildings of his sketchbooks were modifications of the classical buildings he had admired in Vienna as a youth. Even when he drew plans for his monstrous halls, they remained neo-classical.[99] But he broke completely with the classical spirit of rational balance and harmony in the graceless enormity of his projections. It is very difficult to determine which of the hundreds of paintings Hitler acquired were intended for his private collection and which were to be assigned to Linz, where he had planned, as a monument to himself, a monstrous art centre with a colonnaded facade over 150 metres long. In either case, his taste ran heavily to nineteenth-century romantic landscapes and insipid scenes of peasant life – along with erotic nudes. The war did not dampen the Führer's ardour for collecting pieces for his museum. During 1943 and 1944 some 3,000 paintings were set aside. In 1944 and 1945, as the Allies moved in from the west and the Soviet armies from the east, Hitler still expended millions of marks on his collection. After the war, American soldiers found in the salt mines at Alt Aussee alone – the largest but not the only cache – 6,755 paintings and 237 packing cases of books for the Linz centre.[100]

By all odds the artist who impressed the Führer most was Franz von Stuck. Indeed, Hitler once told Ernst Hanfstaengl that the two creative artists who had the greatest impact on his life were Wagner and Stuck. He was 'absolutely enthralled by them both.'[101] On visiting Hanfstaengl's spacious, art-cluttered home on the Pienzenauerstrasse in Munich, the Führer would invariably ask for a volume containing Stuck's paintings of provocative nudes. He pored over them as his breath escaped in little gasps of pleasure. The volume that aroused such passion in Hitler contained the following pictures: *Das böse Gewissen* (Evil Conscience), a title that intrigued him; *Die Sinnlichkeit* (Sensuality), showing a voluptuous nude smiling enigmatically as a huge black snake slithers through her thighs and around her neck; *Verfolgung* (Pursuit), in which a black centaur, a favourite theme of Stuck's, chases a generously breasted blonde; and *Das Laster* (Depravity), depicting a nude lying on the floor laughing as the black python undulates between her thighs.[102]

Both Kaiser and Führer insisted that German artists were the finest in the world and asserted that Classical and Renaissance art was really 'Aryan.' Both despised contemporary art, both painted pleasant water-colours, and both thought of themselves as artists who had been forced by war and politics to abandon their careers as architects. Yet their views about art were different.

The Kaiser's commitment to art and music was not nearly as intense as the Führer's, and he was unable to force art to serve politics. Wilhelm simply enjoyed looking at beautiful pictures and felt, in a general way, that art enhanced life.

The Führer had a different view. He believed that the primary purpose of art was to serve political ends. He might have agreed with Wilhelm that it should be 'ennobling.' But to Hitler, ennoblement meant *fanaticism* – a word of the highest praise in Nazi vocabulary.[103] Thus, art, for Hitler, was another weapon in his political armoury. Along with literature, its purpose was to 'fanaticize' the masses and make them malleable.

Moreover, the Kaiser, unlike the Führer, was unable to impose his tastes on his nation. Indeed, his ill-advised statements to suppress 'modern' art actually encouraged artistic criticism, helped quicken interest in contemporary art and fill private galleries with paintings that defied royal displeasure. Hitler's ruthless policy of 'coordination' (*Gleichschaltung*) – read: coercion – forced all forms of cultural expression into one political mould and banned contemporary art from every gallery in Germany, replacing it with officially approved works of utter banality. When voices of protest and ridicule arose, Hitler simply forbade all forms of artistic criticism. Art journals were forbidden to criticize *any* painting.[104]

Personal Religious Commitments

Obey my voice and I will be thy God
And ye shall be my people.

Wilhelm II

I am doing the work of the Lord.

Adolf Hitler

Both rulers were confident that they were the special agents of Almighty God. Both delivered sermons, and both considered themselves dedicated Christians. They differed, however, radically in the kinds of salvation they sought to bring as well as in their conceptions of what constituted Christian faith.

In one of his more exalted moments, occasioned by the consecration of a new garrison church at Potsdam in May 1897, the Kaiser wrote, 'Obey my voice and I will be thy God and ye shall be my people' on the flyleaf of the altar Bible that he presented to the church that day.[105] He expressed his special relationship to God in words that would later be echoed by the Führer. In a Königsberg speech of 1910, Wilhelm said, 'Seeing myself as an instrument of the Lord, I go my way without regard for the views or opinions of the day.'[106] In a speech of 13 March 1936 Hitler would proclaim, 'Neither threats nor warnings will deter me from my path. I go the way which Providence dictates to me, with all the assurance of a sleep-walker (*traumwandlerischer Sicherheit*).'[107]

In a remarkable speech to the Reichstag of 6 May 1898 the Kaiser admonished the delegates to follow his orders because one day they would want to have a clear conscience on that awful Day of Judgment 'when you must face both God and your Kaiser.' This speech prompted a lady of the court to observe dryly that Wilhelm's posture often 'resembles too closely a fourth member of the Trinity.'[108]

In exile after the overthrow of his government and his abdication in November 1918, the Kaiser maintained his confidence in God's special guidance and continued to hand out Bibles inscribed with statements of his divinely appointed mission, prompting his hostess, Lady Bentinck, to remark ruefully, 'If he had had a sense of humour, perhaps he'd still be ruling.'[109]

Such effusions, however, reflected only one facet of Wilhelm's many-sided personality. It was more usual for him to express religious convictions that were humble and recognizably Christian. His childhood religious training had been unexceptional. His parents were committed Christians who held family prayers and insisted upon regular church attendance. They had been raised in the traditions of their country's state religions: his mother in the Church of England, his father in the Prussian Evangelical Church.[110] Wilhelm's boyhood tutor, the austere Georg Hinzpeter, was a devout but not doctrinaire Calvinist who encouraged the young prince to eschew sectarian dogma and adhere to broad moral principles, Christian love, and social concern.[111]

As a teenager Wilhelm was deeply impressed by his confirmation, a ceremony marking his first public affirmation of Christian commitment. He wrote his beloved grandmother, Queen Victoria:

The ceremony in our Friedrichskirche was very beautiful and touching, and I shall not forget it. I had to struggle to master my emotions, to read clearly & answer loudly enough that everyone might hear me ... I felt happy before the Altar & neither saw or [*sic*] heard anybody except the Clergymen & felt myself quite alone in the presence of

God. The indescribable feeling of peace & happiness filled my heart, so that your Prayers were heard & I hope you will ever continue them for

Your most dutiful, loving,
obedient & grateful Grandson,
William of Prussia[112]

Although Wilhelm continued to confirm his commitment to traditional Christian belief, he later changed his mind about the validity of the Old Testament. During his long exile following the collapse of the Second Reich, he became increasingly anti-Semitic and his growing hatred and suspicion of Jews affected his thinking about their contributions to religion. In a letter to the notorious racist, H.S. Chamberlain, Wilhelm said that he had now reached the conclusion that the whole Bible was in urgent need of reform and 'reconstruction.' The Old Testament in particular 'must be shortened and purified' (*verkürzt und gereinigt*).' He was especially disturbed by what he called 'the Jewish conception of God.'

In a revealing projection of his own prejudice onto the Jews, Wilhelm then asked rhetorically, 'Where does intolerance come from?' He answered immediately, 'From *Jewry,* from that revengeful, cursing *Jawe.* Therefore I say, *Fort mit Jawe!* (Away with Yahweh!). Christ must come in his place. Therefore first the New Testament, then, as far as it may be necessary, the Old in an abridged form ... Christ, the Son of God, the Saviour of Man, Saviour of the World!'[113]

In another letter to Chamberlain Wilhelm confided that he had reached the conclusion, later shared by Adolf Hitler, that Jesus Christ could not possibly have been Jewish. The Kaiser was emphatic: 'Jesus was a Galilean by extraction and therefore *no Jew!*' (emphasis in the original). As proof, he said that he had read a monograph that showed that 'in archives of the Caesarini family in Rome there exists a report that describes our Lord as a child of "surpassing beauty, his hair ... darkish blond."' That, Wilhelm insisted, was proof sufficient.

Throughout his reign the Kaiser took seriously his role as *Summus Episcopus* of the established church of Germany. He actively engaged in denominational disputes, assigned topics and biblical texts for pastors' sermons, and set the maximum length for a sermon at thirty minutes. He personally delivered homilies, far exceeding that time restriction, which he either wrote himself or adapted from those prepared by army or navy chaplains.[114]

Among the ex-Kaiser's voluminous personal papers, now deposited in the Dutch National Archives, there are copies of dozens of his sermons.[115] Several of them are especially revealing. In one, to his army, for example, he gave a sample prayer as the model to be followed. This notably belligerent invocation reminded God of His special obligation to the German army and warned the Almighty that if He did not cooperate, the Kaiser would keep on badgering Him.[116]

A 'Sea Sermon' of June 1905 on board the *Hohenzollern*, entitled 'The Lord of Hosts Is with Us,' reveals Wilhelm's concern about temptations of the flesh and his fits of temper:

Yes, *Gott mit uns*, those words make us strong and *steadfast to withstand temptation* [emphases are Wilhelm's] ... When flesh and blood are stirred up, call upon your God! When dark powers of rage and despair seek to overwhelm you, raise your eyes to heaven! When the flames of desire ... come over your being, remember this: God sees me! God will punish me!

The last paragraph of a sermon preached in 1906 in the New Palace, Potsdam, expressed his double standard of sexual morality. Preaching on a text from Saint Matthew's Gospel that raises the question of faith in Jesus, the Kaiser concluded: 'Therefore, German women, be not confused by the question what shall we make of Jesus. Believe in Him! Trust in Him! Be faithful to Him! ... When men are unfaithful to you, you must still remain faithful to them so that our race will not perish from the earth.'[117]

English visitors to Doorn in 1929, and again in 1939, reported that the ex-Kaiser continued to conduct daily family prayer services and to preach every Sunday to family and staff.[118] He preached often from the Gospel of Saint John. It was his favourite – as it was Adolf Hitler's.[119]

Defeat and the desolation of exile did not shake Wilhelm's faith. He gained solace and spiritual strength in prayer and daily reading of his Lutheran Bible. On 20 March 1921, in a particularly revealing sermon, the ex-Kaiser preached on John 16: 32: 'Yet I am not alone, for the Father is with me.' He noted that when we think of Christ's loneliness and suffering, we tend to think of physical pain: 'But the most bitter suffering comes from within. Particularly when our thoughts turn to our failures and defeat and death, we can be sustained by knowledge of Jesus' triumph over such pain and death ... Remember this: "*Ich bin nicht allein, der Vater ist bei mir.*" *Amen!*'[120]

In a memoir he wrote during his long exile in Holland, Wilhelm recalled that one of the most moving religious experiences of his life took place on Corfu in the chapel of the beautiful island home, Achilleion, which he had purchased from the late Empress of Austria-Hungary. At an Easter morning service, he had been overwhelmed by feelings of 'the triumph of love and faith, the victory of a God who died not only for His friends but for His enemies.'[121]

Yet one is reminded of the incongruities of the Kaiser's personality by the peculiar way he ended this chapter, entitled 'Easter on Corfu.' It closed with a drawing that is inappropriate for his theme of Christ's triumph over death: he sketched a snaky-headed Gorgon with her tongue sticking out.

Adolf Hitler was raised in a strict Roman Catholic household. His long-suffering mother, Klara Pölzl Hitler, was a daily communicant in the parish churches of the several villages of rural Austria where her restless and irascible husband had moved his family. Her difficult young son was constantly in her prayers.

Adolf's father, Alois (Schickelgruber) Hitler, had once thought briefly of becoming a priest, but entered the customs service instead. A brutal and bigoted man, Alois got into a frightful row with the village priest in Leonding and swore that he would never again set foot in church while that 'damned priest' was there. He even refused to attend the funeral services for his little son Edmund, Adolf's younger brother. Nevertheless, although Alois had stopped going to church himself, he insisted that the rest of his family attend. A neighbour assures us there would have been a dreadful 'blow-up' (Krach) if they had dared to disobey.[122]

Young Hitler received Catholic instruction in village schools. Years later the Führer recalled with relish how much fun he had had in baiting the harried priests who came to the school to give religious instruction: 'I was the eternal asker of questions. Since I was completely master of the material,' he observed with typical modesty, 'I was unassailable ... and took naughty pleasure in asking embarrassing questions.'[123] It may be that Hitler's adult study of the Bible was initiated by his lingering boyhood desire to diminish his teachers and other authoritarian figures.

While the family was living in Lambach and when Adolf was ten, he sang in the choir of the Lambach monastery, probably at his father's insistence. Hitler reported that he was immensely impressed – 'intoxicating myself' – with the splendour of Church ritual. During these impressionable years he may have acquired the sense of pageantry later revealed in the pseudo-religious ceremonies he and Goebbels would design for the Nuremberg party rallies. Young Adolf had been so taken with the power and majesty of the Catholic Church that he dreamed of becoming a monk and of rising higher in the hierarchy: 'The position of abbot appeared to me to be the highest ideal obtainable.' It was not to be. 'Herr Father' pronounced this a ridiculous idea and Adolf himself, recognizing that a career in the Church was not really 'in keeping with my temperament,'[124] decided to do something else with his life – a career decision that the world would come to regret.

Hitler's personal relationship to the Church in later years is not entirely clear. In one of his midnight soliloquies in his Berlin bunker during the war he said, 'Since my fourteenth year, I have felt liberated from the superstition that the priests used to teach.' His fourteenth year was in 1903, the year his father died. He gave a different impression, however, in October 1937 while talking to party leaders about his feelings of impending death. He said that he did not have long to live, noting that his mother and father had both died young. He must there-fore hurry to solve major problems confronting Germany, problems that only he could solve, such as *Lebensraum* and the 'Jewish question.' He then confided that 'after difficult inner struggle' he had decided to free himself from 'still existing religious ideas of childhood.' That decision, he said, had brought him a great sense of relief: 'I feel fresh as a colt in the meadow.'[125]

Neither declaration, however, apparently meant that he had severed all con-nections with the Catholic Church or with his commitment to his peculiar ver-sion of Christ's teaching. One of his most trusted private secretaries, Fräulein Christa Schroeder, who was with him to the end, affirmed that Hitler remained a member of the Catholic Church and regularly paid his Church dues. He told her that after the war he planned to break away from the Church as a symbolic act that 'would signify the end of one historic era for Germany and the beginning of a new epoch for the Third Reich.' After the war he would establish a new religion that would completely replace Christianity, but he was not yet satisfied with his plans. 'It is impossible to escape the problem of God,' he mused in a midnight monologue, 'when I have the time, I'll work out the formula.'[126]

The Führer's personal relationship both to God and to Jesus Christ directly influenced his political and racist ideology. His concept of human history was essentially eschatological and religious, one of sin and redemption. He believed that long ago a pure Germanic people had dwelt in the Garden of Eden. These pure-souled Aryans had been tempted by the Devil, appearing in the form of the Jew, 'the personification of the Devil and of all evil.' This Devil had enticed the good but naive Germans into committing 'the original sin (*Erbsünde*) of racial pollution.' To save Germany and the world from this corrosive evil, God in His mercy had sent his agent, Adolf Hitler, to perform a special mission: 'I believe today,' he wrote, 'that I am doing the work of the Almighty Creator. Yes, in fighting the Jews I am doing the work of the Lord.'[127]

Hitler's sense of divine mission was made manifest when he returned in triumph to the scenes of his youth in 1938 after absorbing Austria into his 'Greater German Reich.' Addressing the jubilant thousands gathered in the cen-tral square of Linz, soon to be renamed Adolf Hitlerplatz, he proclaimed his providential mission: 'If Divine Providence once called me from out of this city to the leadership of the Reich, then Providence must thereby have given me a mission and it could only have been the mission of bringing my dear homeland back into the Reich. I have believed in that mission, I have lived for it, fought for it. And I believe that I have now fulfilled this mission.'[128]

A few days later, speaking in the great hall of the railway station in Vienna where he had first arrived thirty years before as an expectant and frightened teenager, he again evoked the image of a boy sent forth by God to fulfil a divine mission: 'I believe that it was God's will to send forth a boy here into the Reich, to let him grow up, to lift him to become Führer of the nation in order to make it possible for him to lead his homeland back into the Reich'[129]

Adversity seemed only to strengthen his conviction that God was guiding him. After the overwhelming military defeat at Stalingrad, in January 1943, he ended his proclamation to his armies: 'We believe that we can call upon the Lord God to grant us His blessing in the coming year as in the past.'[130] His miraculous escape from the assassination attempt of 20 July 1944 confirmed Hitler's conviction that he was a special agent of the Almighty. His valet, Heinz Linge, reported that after the explosion of the bomb, the Führer was very calm; he turned quietly to Linge and said, 'That is new proof that I have been chosen by Providence from among all other men to lead Greater Germany to victory ... It is clearer than ever that the fate of Germany lies in my hands.'[131] His secretary was surprised to find that the Führer was actually elated by the event. He described it with enthusiasm and in great detail, chattering on about the rips in his new trousers, and giving orders to have them saved as a relic and sent to Eva Braun in Berchtesgaden as proof of divine dispensation.[132]

The Führer's followers recognized him as a religious figure. His acceptance as 'Redeemer' and 'Saviour' was widespread among the Nazis, but exaltation reached some sort of apogee in a speech by Robert Ley, leader of the Labour Front: 'Adolf Hitler! We are bound to Thee. In this hour we renew our solemn vows (Gelöbnisse) unto Thee. On this earth we believe only in Thee ... We believe that there is a Lord God in Heaven who sent Adolf Hitler to free Germany from hypocrites and pharisees so that Germany would have a foundation for all eternity.'[133] In Hitler's Reich children prayed to a new deity. Two graces before meals were typical:

> Führer, my Führer, sent down from the Lord,
> Protect me through life and be ever adored.
> To Thee who has saved us from our deepest woe,
> For this daily bread our thanks we owe;
> Never forsake us by day and by night,

Führer, my Führer, my Faith and my Light!
Heil, mein Führer![134]

Younger children were taught to pray:

Close your eyes and bow your heads,
Think of Adolf Hitler ever;
He gives us our daily bread [and]
From Jewish Peril doth deliver.

Although Hitler said that he did not want to be deified like Lenin,[135] and on occasion even announced that he wanted no streets named or memorials raised in his memory, he raised no objections when streets and squares and schools throughout the Reich were, in fact, named after him. Moreover, he personally drew up the plans for his own enormous black marble mausoleum which was designed to dwarf Lenin's tomb in Red Square. It was to form the centre of a gargantuan complex in Munich to be called the *Hitlerzentrum* and to endure 'until the end of time.'[136]

The Führer was fond of pointing out striking parallels between himself and Jesus Christ. Both, he insisted, were Aryans; both had been born of humble parents. He considered both to be 'Volksführer' of their people. Both had refused to marry – Hitler saying his 'only bride is Germany.'[137] 'Like Christ,' he observed on another occasion, 'I have a duty to my people.'[138] In a public speech he said that he wanted to be judged by the people, and if he were found lacking they should 'crucify me.'[139] In 1925, during a Christmas celebration in Dingolfing, Lower Bavaria, Hitler compared the first Christmas and the birth of Jesus to his own advent as the herald of a saving political faith:

At that time, too, the materialistic world was contaminated by Jews. At that time, too, salvation would come ... through a herald who was born under the most miserable circumstances.

Christ came into a rotten world and preached the faith. He, too, was at first scorned, yet from this faith has grown a world movement. We want to accomplish the same thing in the political realm ... From Germany the light will shine forth that will lead the world to salvation (*Erlösung*).[140]

Throughout his career Hitler constantly identified himself with Jesus as Saviour, even going so far as to draw a comparison between what he called his 'betrayal' by Ernst Röhm in 1934 and the betrayal of Jesus by Judas: 'Among the twelve apostles there was a Judas, and it is not surprising that our movement also has had a similar phenomenon. But in spite of Judas, Christianity was victorious and in spite of [Röhm] our movement will be victorious.'[141] The number of times Hitler quoted the words of Jesus bespeaks personal identification with Christ, as well as a careful culling of the Gospels, most notably that of Saint John, as well as Saint Paul's letters and the Revelation of John.[142]

Hitler castigated the Christian Church, showed disdain for priests and pastors, and swore that as soon as the war was over he would put an end to both Christian confessions. Yet he actually considered himself a Christian. Indeed, he believed that he was the only person who understood Christ's teachings, and that he had been chosen by God to establish a Christian kingdom on earth. That, he insisted, was the primary purpose of his Third Reich. The association in Hitler's mind between Jesus and Nazism was symbolized in the Brown House, party headquarters in Munich where a life-size statue of Jesus was placed above an enormous gold swastika.

The clearest and fullest statement of his peculiar Christian commitment can be found in the extensive private conversations he had with one of his early followers, Otto Wagener, during the years 1930 to 1933. Wagener records several of the Führer's long soliloquies which were, in effect, sermons.[143] There is an important sense in which all of Hitler's speeches were homilies. As a student of his rhetoric has noted, 'Only when we recognize Hitler's orations as sermons (*Predigten*) of a political faith, and the speaker as a secular-political Saviour (*Erlöser*) does Hitler's rhetoric become fully intelligible.'[144]

In thinking about the advent of Jesus, Hitler, like every other student of the New Testament, often reflected on the opening sentence of Saint John's Gospel: 'In the beginning was the *Logos*.' That problematic Greek term was translated by Luther (as it would be by King James's scholars) as, 'In the beginning was the *Word* (*Wort*).' But that translation bothered Hitler, who told a disciple in the 1930s, 'When I use the word "divine" 'I do not visualize a God in human form with a long white beard ... God is for me the *Logos* of John who became flesh and lived in the world ... God is force (*Trieb*) and bestows generating power (*Triebskraft*).'[145] Hitler's use of the word *Trieb* poses problems. The standard rendering as 'force,' 'power,' 'instinct,' or 'drive,' as E.F. Proelss has pointed out, does not catch the overtones of 'biological mysticism,' so important to Hitler, with which the word is freighted. Adjectives help convey the meaning: 'animating force,' 'generating power,' 'life-giving force,' or 'primal drive.'[146] Luther's translation as 'Word' was too bland for a man obsessed with power. Hitler also disagreed with Goethe's translation: 'Goethe attempted to correct [Luther's translation] with the critical sentence, "I value that word so highly that I must translate it differently: in the beginning was the Deed (*Tat*)."[147] But I say in the beginning was the germinating power! (*der Trieb*) And this power exists for all eternity! And *Trieb* was a creation of God and God Himself was this *Trieb* ... and this *Trieb* was made manifest also in us.' As we shall see, Hitler kept coming back to *Trieb*.

Hitler was also intrigued by the social teaching of Jesus and concluded that 'Christ sought to establish the socialism of the people. This, the new great [socialist] religion, will come because it is divine! It awaits the Messiah.'[148] In another homily addressed to Wagener, Hitler promised, in turgid and slightly garbled prose, a new heaven in a new earth flowing with the milk of human kindness in a Thousand Year Reich: 'A new faith is awakening, a faith in divine justice, in heavenly truth, the faith in a celestial future paradise (*überirdische paradiesische Zukunft*) in which domination, power, and enmity shall no longer reign, but equality and brotherhood, a spirit of sacrifice and a spirit of community, love and truth and the will to step before the throne of the Most High with the open heart of a faithful servant willing to serve. And they will have sufficient strength to speak for their fathers and brothers saying, "Forgive them, Father, for they know not what they do!"' Wagener reports that after making these pronouncements Hitler fell silent: 'The inner emotion had driven the blood from his cheeks. His eyes shone like lights ... I thought to myself: our thinking has been so puny.'

A few days later, in another homily, the Führer reaffirmed his purpose of fulfilling Christ's mission and inveighed against the established churches who misunderstood his intentions, bore false witness against him, and persecuted his followers: 'The struggle which those who falsely call themselves Christians directed against National Socialism is only the continuation of the criminality of the Inquisition and the witch burning with which the Jewish-Romish world exterminated whoever offered resistance to their shameful parasitism. All we really want to bring about is the fulfilment of the life mission of Christ (*die Erfüllung der Lebensaufgabe Christi*).'

In another sermon Hitler proclaimed that he would resurrect true Christian doctrine: 'National Socialism is a *Weltanschauung*; but this *Weltanschauung* is actually not new.' This revelation came to him, Hitler said, from reading the prophets and 'especially the sayings of Jesus Christ. *He* was the one who actually created this *Weltanschauung* which we call socialism.' The religious establishment of Jesus' day did not understand Jesus any more than they understood Hitler. He, too, was betrayed and denied: 'Thus the holy idea of Christian Socialism was subverted.' Hitler then became very excited. The following sentences appear in italics:

But we were the first to exhume these teachings! Through us alone, and not until us, do these teachings celebrate their resurrection!

Mary and Magdalen stand before an open tomb. For *they sought the dead!* But we have raised up the *treasures of the living Christ!* Here lies the essence of our task: we must bring these teachings again to the German people.

For who has falsified the original idea of Christian Love, the community of Fate (*Schicksalsgemeinschaft*) before God and before Socialism? *By their fruits ye shall know them.*

This sermon ended with words that sound passing strange on the lips of Adolf Hitler. After inveighing against 'the suppression of freedom of opinion, the persecution of true Christians, and the vile mass murders of the Inquisition,' he closed with a plea for Christian love and compassion: 'We must especially raise youth in the spirit of the words of Christ which we must interpret anew: "Love one another"; recognize your humanity; remember that every last one of you is a creature of God and you are all brothers.' In parting from Wagener, Hitler transfixed him with eyes that 'shone like stars' and admonished him with words his disciple could never forget: 'Cherish these thoughts. Be the Guardian of the Grail whose deepest truths can be disclosed to only a few.'

The reliability of Wagener's remarkable testimony about Hitler's early Christian convictions is confirmed indirectly by the most recent edition of Joseph Goebbels's diaries which he had never intended for publication. The diaries show that the Führer and his Minister of Enlightenment and Propaganda were in complete agreement that Nazism was to be a new version of a Christian commonwealth. Both men believed that they were fulfilling the teachings of Jesus as revealed in the Gospel according to Saint John and in the Revelation to John, books that both Hitler and Goebbels mistakenly thought were written by the same John.[149]

They found in the book of Revelation the concept of a Reich that was to last one thousand years after the forces of the Antichrist and his followers had been totally destroyed. Revelation also inspired their belief that the world was divided apocalyptically into the Powers of Light and Darkness, Good and Evil, Love and Hate, Christ/God and Antichrist/Satan. They identified Christ (and Hitler) with Goodness/Love/Truth; they identified Jews with Evil/Hatred/ Perfidy – collectively the forces of Antichrist who must be utterly destroyed. Goebbels is clear about the dichotomy and its component parts:

Christ is the genius of love, as such the diametrical counterpart of Jewry which is the incarnation of hatred. The Jew creates a non-race (*Unrasse*) among the races of the earth. He has the same function as poisoning bacilli have within the human organism.

Christ is our model as the great adversary of the Jews (*Judengegner*). He declared war against the Jews when He said, 'Thou shalt devour all peoples' (*Du sollst alle Völker fressen!'*). Therefore, the Jews determined to kill Him ... The Jew is the incarnation of lies. For the first time in history the Jew put eternal Truth on the cross.[150]

Although Hitler was intrigued by legends of Nordic gods and at the end of his life may have seen himself as the reincarnation of Wotan,[151] his primary identification was with Jesus. He had no intention of trying to establish his Reich on foundations of cultic neo-paganism, as some of his followers had wanted him to do. On the contrary, Hitler insisted that his Reich would fulfil Christian doctrine and that his hatred for Jews simply followed good Christian teachings set forth in Saint John's gospel and in official statements of the Catholic and Lutheran churches. Hitler was not entirely mistaken. In point of fact, Saint John is disturbingly anti-Semitic.[152]

As Nazi Minister of Propaganda,[153] a title inspired by the Catholic Church's *Congregatio de Propaganda Fide*, Goebbels became one of the architects of Hitler's campaign against the Jews. His ministry, too, was charged with 'the propagation of the faith,' and this required that Germany be 'purified' of all Jews. Goebbels followed the progress of genocide with satisfaction, noting in his diary on 14 February 1942, 'The Jews have earned the catastrophe that they are experiencing today. Along with the destruction of our enemy, the Jews will be destroyed.' And six months later, 'The judgment against the Jews will be fulfilled. It is indeed barbaric, but they have fully deserved it. One cannot be deterred by sentimentality in these matters. If we did not defend ourselves from them, the Jews would destroy us.'[154] Hitler, too, it will be recalled, had said that in destroying the Jews he was 'performing the work of the Lord.'

A delegation of Christian leaders came to Hitler one day and expressed alarm about Nazi treatment of Jews. The Führer replied that he was only putting into effect what the Christian Church had 'preached and practised for 2,000 years.'[155] He had a point.

Hundreds of years before Hitler, Martin Luther had indeed preached hatred and persecution of Jews. As early as 1543 Luther had demanded that Jewish synagogues and schools be set afire, that their silver and gold be taken from them, that their houses and prayer-books be seized and destroyed, that brimstone and pitch be poured over them, and that they be driven away 'like mad dogs' – a program that Adolf Hitler would put into practice in detail on a national scale beginning with the infamous *Reichskristallnacht* of 9–10 November 1938 which, by a quirk of chronology, fell on Luther's birthday.

Centuries before Luther, Catholic bishops and priests had also thundered against an imaginary 'Jewish menace.' Indeed, the anti-Semitic record of both Christian confessions is one of the most appalling in the history of religion. Published statements made by saints of the Catholic Church were later used as texts for Nazi anti-Semitic broadsides. Saint Gregory of Nyssa (d 396), for example, described Jews as 'slayers of the Lord, murderers of the prophets, haters of God, advocates of the Devil, a brood of vipers.' Saint Ambrose, Augustine's teacher, wanted synagogues burned to the ground and boasted that he personally had set fire to one of them. Saint John Chrysostom (d 406) called Jews 'lustful, rapacious, greedy, perfidious bandits.' He preached that 'it is the duty of Christians to hate the Jews,' proclaiming that Jews 'are fit for slaughter.' Saint Thomas Aquinas, the most influential theologian in the history of the Catholic Church, argued that it was morally justifiable for Jews to serve Christians as slave labourers because, as the slayers of God, they were bound to 'perpetual servitude.'

The Church practised what its Fathers preached. The Synod of Elvira in 306, for instance, forbade intermarriage and sexual relations between Christians and Jews. The Synod of Claremont in 535 decreed that Jews could not hold public office. The Third Synod of Orleans in 538 made it illegal for Jews to walk in public streets during Passion Week. The Fourth Lateran Council in 1215 decreed that Jews mark their clothing with a special badge. The Council of Oxford in 1222 forbade the construction of new synagogues. The Council of Basel in 1434 prohibited Jews from obtaining academic degrees. Hitler took special pleasure in reminding Christians of this feature of their heritage.

Both Kaiser and Führer believed that they were the special agents of God, but they saw their missions differently.

Wilhelm, in his better moments, set aside bombastic rhetoric and spoke of leading the world to peace and universal Christian harmony. Year after year, the Kaiser's New Year's greeting to relatives and friends included a prayer for such a world. Hitler's purpose was not to create a kinder and gentler world, but to conquer and reshape the world after his own brutal image. Characteristically, Hitler's New Year's card of 1926 shows a hard-jawed storm trooper pushing his bayonet deep into the stomach of the 'Jew republic.' The greeting reads, 'Forward, Comrades, into a New Year of Battle.' Despite occasional assertions of his divine power ('I walk among you as your God'), the Kaiser more often showed that he was aware of both his own limitations and the pretensions of royal power: 'Anyone who has stood on a ship's bridge at sea with only God's starry heaven overhead and has looked into his own heart,' he said in 1890, 'draws up a balance-sheet ... This is enough to cure anyone of over-estimating himself.'[156] When his first wife died during their exile, and the pastor wanted to stage an impressive royal funeral, Wilhelm told him to keep it simple and brief: 'The good [Pastor] Drander wants to make it all "royal,"' he said, 'Oh, my God, what is royalty before the majesty of death!'[157]

There was also a vast difference in the ways in which contemporary Germans responded to their rulers' assertions of divine dispensation. The Kaiser's theatrical effusions were often greeted with embarrassed silence, together with regret that he lacked a sense of humour. The Führer's assertions were believed. Germans hailed him as their Saviour and offered him their prayers.

The Kaiser and the Führer held differing views of the relationship between church and state. Wilhelm accepted the traditional Lutheran doctrine which exalted the authority of the state but recognized an area of spiritual life beyond the reach of secular authority. He did not seek to interfere in another person's 'inner realm' or to doubt that in spiritual matters the Christian believer was free. As titular head of the established church, the Kaiser regulated the length of pastors' sermons, but not their contents.

The Führer used the church, as he used every other institution, as a means for increasing his personal power and domination. In his Germany Hitler tolerated no 'spiritual freedom' or any notions about separating spiritual from secular authority. In his totalitarian Reich all belief was to be 'coordinated' (*gleichgeschaltet*) into one ideology of monolithic power. Hitler's ultimate goal was to destroy the Christian Church and create his own form of religion. The Kaiser had no such intention. He sought to preserve the traditional churches of Germany and to expand their influence for doing good.

The Kaiser believed that the hope of the world lay in spreading the gospel of Jesus. The values endorsed by Hitler were in flat contradiction to those that Jesus set forth. Christ had called blessed those who loved their enemies, who were gentle and merciful, who sought peace and hungered and thirsted after righteousness. Hitler called blessed those who were 'courageous aggressors,' 'merciless,' and 'ruthlessly brutal.' He wanted the youth of the New Germany, he said, 'to be violent, domineering, undismayed, cruel ... There must be nothing weak or gentle about them. The free, splendid beast of prey must once again flash from their eyes.'[158]

The Führer proclaimed that he was a true follower of Jesus. But his Christ was a proto-Nazi, a heroic, blond *Volksführer* who, like Hitler, had struggled against the establishment of his day, who hated the Jews, and who fought to establish a racially pure and stridently anti-Semitic nationalistic socialism in a totalitarian Reich. When he quoted Saint Paul, as he often did, in urging his followers to have that 'faith that can remove mountains,' Hitler never once completed the sentence from Paul's first letter to the church at Corinth. The omitted words are crucial: 'and if I have all faith so as to remove mountains *and have not love, I am nothing.*'[159]

The heart of the Christian gospel is love. Something very different lay at the core of Hitler's soul. After the war, Albert Speer, who knew Hitler as well as anyone, thought back over the Führer's career and said he had gradually come to understand that at the core of this man was hatred, 'pathological hatred.'[160]

Pagan Gods

While confessing to be Christians, both the Kaiser and the Führer were also impressed with the power of pagan Nordic gods. One reason for the Kaiser's annual sea voyages up the Norwegian coast was to commune with the mysterious gods who spoke to him from out the swirling mists of the echoing fiords. Like Hitler after him, Wilhelm was particularly taken with Wotan, ruler of gods and man, and ancestor of Germanic kings. There were several Wotanian characteristics that appealed to the Kaiser, largely, one suspects, because he felt they corresponded to his own. Wotan, too, was versatile. He was, variously, the god of wisdom and war, of poetry and agriculture, of wind and death. (He was never concerned, however, either with justice or with healing.) Cunning and devious, Wotan appeared in many disguises and was called the 'great deceiver.'[161] (Wilhelm never aspired to that title, though he certainly appeared in different costumes and liked to fool people.)

Like the Kaiser, and like the Führer, Wotan was riven by opposing impulses to create and to destroy. He is reputed to have discovered the creative mystery of the runes, to have invented language and inspired poetry. But he was also the god of destruction who appeared on the Wild Hunt (*Wilde Jagd*), the apotheosis of terror and desolation; Wotan unleashed Ragnarok, the final cataclysmic battle that would destroy gods and men. Also the god of war, Wotan created the Berserkers, warriors driven by frenzy to 'run berserk.'[162] Two ravens, with the unlikely names of Hugin and Munin, representing Thought and Memory, perched upon Wotan's shoulders. A horrendous wolf with blood-drooling jaws named Fenrir was chained at his feet and devoured the dead of Valhalla. Wotan would set Fenrir loose at the moment of Ragnarok.

The sheer inscrutability of Wotan also appealed to Wilhelm, for he, again like Hitler after him, was fond of boasting that no one could understand him, no one could know his thoughts or comprehend his actions, and that he was accountable to no entity on this earth.

Aegir, the Nordic god of ships and the sea, was another favourite of Wilhelm, the creator of the Imperial German Navy and self-styled 'Admiral of the Atlantic Ocean.' Aegir, like Wotan, was a god of mighty power for good and for evil. Vengeful and terrible in their fury, 'the jaws of Aegir' were said to devour ships and men lost at sea. Germanic marauders sought to appease his awful wrath by sacrificing one-tenth of all their captives to him. In some versions of the myths, he had nine daughters, one of whom was Heimdall, guardian of the gates of Valhalla. This god so intrigued the Kaiser that, as we have seen, he composed a sort of prayer to him which he called 'Ode to Aegir.'[163]

In another exalted moment when the Kaiser saw himself as *arbiter mundi*, he likened himself to Heimdall (this time appearing in his male form): 'Hohenzollern domination of the world (*Hohenzollernweltherrschaft*) now stands where once the old heroic god Heimdall stood, watching over the destiny of the earth.'[164]

The Führer's personal library contained many volumes on Nordic myths. As we have noted, his only boyhood friend reported that Adolf had two favourite books to which he returned again and again. One was on architecture, the other a popular edition entitled *Legends of Gods and Heroes: The Treasure of Germanic Mythology*.[165] Hitler was drawn to Richard Wagner in part because of the *Meister*'s vicious anti-Semitism, but primarily for his reworking of the ancient Nordic myths. Young Hitler felt in Wagner a kindred creative spirit. He became terribly excited when his roommate, a student at the Vienna Conservatory of Music, told him that among Wagner's posthumous papers, an opera based on the legend of Wieland the Smith had recently been discovered. Hitler knew the story well. Wieland, the half-god son of a giant, had been taken captive by a king who crippled him and forced him to work as the royal blacksmith. Wieland raped the king's daughter and then enticed his two sons into the smithy, where he murdered them. He fashioned beakers out of the boys' skulls and drank a toast to the spirit of revenge before rising on the iron wings he had forged and disappearing into the flaming sunset. It was a splendid story, Hitler thought, and he was determined to write an opera about it and dedicate it to Wagner. The music for his opera was to be performed on the primitive horns, drums, and whistles used by the ancient Teutons.[166]

Nordic mysteries that had enthralled the boy continued to intrigue the man. On the night of 25–26 January 1942, while German soldiers froze and bled on the Russian front, the Führer sucked chocolate-covered cherries and mused about eerie pre-creation emanations. He had come to believe, he exclaimed, that science would someday actually recapture emanations coming from Wagner's legendary world and that those vibrations would transmit the secret of the cosmos. Only he and Richard Wagner had ever really understood those mysterious messages: 'When I listen to Wagner, it seems to me that I hear rhythms of the pre-creation world (*Vorwelt*)! I imagine to myself that one day science will discover in the waves set in motion by the *Rheingold* secret, mutual relations connected with the order of the world.'[167]

Of all the Nordic gods, the Führer was drawn most powerfully to Wotan. Perhaps he felt that they had much in common. First, of course, Wotan was the supreme ruler of gods and men. He was also a worker of miracles and a trickster who appeared in many different guises. Hitler, who rather liked being called 'the greatest actor in Europe,' also appeared differently to different people. Wotan appealed to Hitler as the all-knowing creator and the source of all inspiration. But Hitler saw himself as destroyer as well as creator, and Wotan was the god of desolation and death, insatiable in his demands for human sacrifice.

The Führer's identification with Wotan was much more intimate than the Kaiser's had been. Wotan and Hitler, for example, shared the same taste in animals. Both were fond of ravens. Wotan had pet ravens; Hitler gave special orders that ravens were never to be shot.[168] In the archives of *Time-Life* there exists a snapshot of a raven perched on Hitler's right shoulder. Others in the picture seem amused, but the Führer's eyes flash in an unsmiling face.[169]

Both Wotan and Hitler identified with wolves, which, as we have seen, had a special fascination for Hitler.[170] Fenrir, symbol of chaos and destruction, crouched in fetters at Wotan's feet, eating food from his hand alone. In his last days in the Berlin bunker, Hitler permitted no one but himself to feed Blondi's pup. His secretary reported that 'he stroked the animal incessantly and kept muttering its name, "Wolf, Wolf, Wolf."'[171] At the end of time, Wotan would give the awful orders for Ragnarok, the cataclysmic battle, with 'appalling deeds of murder and incest ... the wolf Fenrir advances, his great gaping jaws filling the gap between earth and sky ... relentlessly, hideously, he devours gods and men.' In 1945 Hitler ordered his own version of Ragnarok, the final *Götterdämmerung*. In designing the enormous parade ground for his party rallies at Nuremberg, Hitler designated one of the squares *Wotanplatz*. (It has since been renamed *Platz der Opfer des Faschismus*, Victims of Fascism Square.)[172]

It seems quite possible that the Führer also visualized himself physically as Wotan, at least the Wotan portrayed by Franz von Stuck. The Municipal Gallery in the Lenbach House, Munich, holds a peculiar painting entitled *Die wilde Jagd* (The Wild Hunt) which inexplicably portrays Wotan in such a way that visitors to the gallery have actually mistaken the Nordic god for the German Führer.[173] Indeed the Wotan of this painting does bear an uncanny resemblance to Adolf Hitler: the same dark brown hair with the famous forelock over the left temple, the brooding eyes, the large-nostrilled nose, the memorable Charlie Chaplain moustache, and a blood-red cape, like the one Hitler affected at the first Nuremberg rally, swirling behind the rider. Hitler's favourite images are also pictured: decapitation, wolves, rapine, and death. A human head dangles at the tip of Wotan's sword; wolflike animals howl at the horse; hollow-eyed little creatures scream soundlessly; ravished women and corpses are left in the wake of the wildly galloping horseman. The most startling feature of this very strange painting, however, is its date. Inscribed in the lower left-hand corner are the words, 'Franz Stuck, *Mein erstes Oelgemälde*' (my first oil painting). The date is 1889, the year in which Adolf Hitler was born!

All his life the Führer was given to childlike fantasizing. In his boyhood he delivered impassioned orations to trees on lonely hills near Leonding. In his teens he envisaged himself rebuilding whole cities and establishing a new Reich. As an adult he imagined himself to be the German Saviour to whom it was proper for little children to pray. Sometimes he thought of himself as Christ, at other times he said that he was one of the immortals who would live forever among his fellow Olympian gods, confiding to his entourage on 27 February 1942, 'I shall feel that I am in my proper place if, after my death, I find myself, together with the historic company of others like me, on some sort of Olympus. I shall be among the most enlightened spirits of all time.'[174]

But at the end, as I shall suggest, Hitler may have seen himself as a different sort of deity. He did not really feel like Jesus or any of the serenely radiant company on the azure heights of Olympus. Rather, he was the frightening god of havoc and destruction of Stuck's painting. Germany had become 'no longer worthy of me, let her perish,' that is, let the ancient myth of Wotan be fulfilled. Hitler too would order the *Götterdämmerung* of his world, the greatest planned destruction in history. For in April 1945 his task was to achieve a catastrophe of a magnitude sufficient to ensure his immortality. As we recall, he told a member of his entourage, 'I have to attain immortality even if the whole German nation perishes in the process.'[175]

Both the Kaiser and the Führer were drawn to the Nordic gods, and both saw in Wotan something of an *alter ego*. But the striking differences in their interests reflect a familiar pattern: Hitler's personal commitment was far more intense, longer lasting, and it had a political resonance lacking in the Kaiser's moments of infatuation. The primitive tribalism of Nazism was in many ways an atavistic reversion to Nordic paganism.

The Supernatural and the Occult

The Kaiser and the Führer were intrigued with a spirit world quite apart from Christian or Nordic beliefs. The extent of Wilhelm's personal belief in spiritualism, however, is not at all clear. Certainly his closest friend and confidant, Count Philipp zu Eulenburg-Hertefeld, was a true believer who had a long and intimate association with spiritualists and faith-healers. Wilhelm had participated enthusiastically in seances and had personally experienced, he believed, supernatural visitations, once confiding to a friend, 'I have no hesitation in declaring that ... my spiritualist experiences have made my convictions firm as a rock.'[176] He was drawn to Eulenburg in part because of a mutual interest in the occult.[177]

It is clear that the Kaiser loved to hear and tell tales of the weird and inexplicable. Eulenburg reported in February 1902 that on a Norwegian cruise the Kaiser told fantastic stories 'with the most complete conviction and without permitting the slightest scepticism.'[178] Eulenburg says that he warned the Kaiser about repeating such stories outside his immediate entourage. While reaffirming his own belief in the spiritual world and its influence on human affairs, he had urged on Wilhelm 'the greatest caution in applying such things to politics.'[179] This was one piece of advice the Kaiser followed. He enjoyed talking about the occult to his friends, but it was not as important to him as it was to the Führer.

Wilhelm did, however, believe that the spirit of his grandfather, Wilhelm I, hovered near him. In a speech at a banquet commemorating the hundredth anniversary of his grandfather's birth, Wilhelm expressed the conviction that the old man was actually present in the room and that 'he certainly paid a visit last night to the colours.' The British ambassador, in reporting the incident, noted that the Kaiser felt so close to his dead grandfather that for the special ceremony of moving the colours, 'the Emperor actually appointed himself ... *aide-de-camp* to his late grandfather.'[180]

The Kaiser, like the Führer, was also fascinated by the magical power he detected in numbers. He worried, for example, lest certain numerical combinations produce ominous results. Sometime in 1906 or 1907 a German journalist assured a noted British colleague that war would certainly not come to Europe before the year 1914 because the Kaiser was 'haunted by the fear' that a prophecy made to his grandfather might come true. Because of that prophecy, the journalist asserted, the Kaiser would never risk war 'until 1913 is safely over.'

According to the story, the prophecy took place in 1849 when the Kaiser's grandfather, the future German Emperor, Wilhelm I, was a young man and still Crown Prince Wilhelm of Prussia. Because of his role in repressing the revolution of 1848, he was living in exile in Mainz when one day a Gypsy woman hailed him as 'Your Imperial Majesty.' When the startled young prince asked what empire she had in mind, the Gypsy replied that it was the new Germanic empire which he was going to establish in the year 1871. To humour her, the prince asked how long he would rule over this empire. 'Until 1888,' was her reply. And how long will the empire endure? 'Until a great war will come in 1913, and the empire will be overthrown. Beware of that year!' When the prince looked sceptical, she asked for a piece of paper and worked out the following numbers with dates listed both horizontally and vertically:

1849	1871	1888
1	1	1
8	8	8
4	7	8
9	1	8
1871	1888	1913

Prince Wilhelm had scoffed at the prophecy, but he kept the piece of paper, and his grandson, the future Wilhelm II, never forgot.[181]

Hitler's interest in cosmic and supernatural forces took a different turn from the Kaiser's. The Führer was not interested in dabbling in spiritualism, listening to ghost stories, or tapping tables. His was a much heavier investment, and it yielded far more terrifying returns. From the supernatural he sought, and he believed he had found, both the magical force that animates all life and the source of all evil. The supernatural also inspired Hitler's political and racial theories.

The Führer's lifelong search for the supernatural began in 1908 when he arrived in Vienna in late adolescence. He later recalled how one day, while living in the Stumpergasse, he came across the writings of an Austrian engineer named Hans Goldzier who, 'according to the name, might have been a Jew and therefore wrote under the name of Th. Neuert ... I was very much impressed by Goldzier's ideas. Goldzier believed that the ultimate creative energy behind all life was something he called *Erdelektrizität* [literally: earth-electricity] which forms and enlivens human beings.' Some people, Hitler added pointedly, have much more of this electrical force than others.[182]

As we have noticed, Hitler had sought to find the mysterious *Trieb*, the animating force of life, in Saint John's gospel. But not even his own peculiar distortion of Christianity satisfied him. In the 1930s one of Hitler's followers told him about the 'Od-Ray Theory' (*Od-Strahlentheorie*) of a certain Baron von Reichenbach. The Führer became immensely excited. According to 'Doctor' Reichenbach, each person possesses a certain number of these mysterious rays that affect everyone within a person's immediate orbit. Young people emit more emanations than others. Hitler's disciple reports that the Führer was so impressed with the idea that 'his eyes shone like a child looking at a lighted Christmas tree. "Yes! Yes!" he exclaimed, "that's why little children cry when grandmothers try to cuddle them; they don't want the old woman to take away their precious rays ... Wagener! The scales fall away from my eyes as I hear about this theory for the first time ... That is the reason for the strong cohesion of ... my Storm Troopers, it is because they all are one *Od-Gemeinschaft!* ... And that is why I like to be surrounded by young people: they give me strength."'[183]

Among the two thousand volumes recovered from Hitler's private library were many testifying to the Führer's lifetime search for the *Trieb* of life, as well as works on magic symbols, the occult, and tracts on the 'science' of anti-Semitism and racism. Representative of the latter is a well-thumbed pamphlet by one G. Lanz von Liebenfels entitled *Das Buch der Psalmen Teutsch: das Gebetbuch der Ariosophen Rassen-mystiker und Antisemiten* (The Book of German Psalms: The Prayerbook of Ariosophic Racial Mystics and Anti-Semites).

This tawdry little paperback may have caused a turning-point in Hitler's life. For when he arrived in Vienna he had been racked with doubt: 'As usual when I am in doubt,' Hitler confides in his memoirs, 'I turn to reading books and pamphlets.' The pamphlets gave him the ideas that would dominate his personal life and form the foundation of his Reich, 'a foundation so firm, I had later only to change a few details.'[184] These ideas did not come from such alleged precursors of Nazism as the philosophers Hegel, Fichte, Nietzsche, or de Lagarde. Hitler understood none of them. His inspiration came from a shallower and more poisonous source: most notably the pamphlets of 'Jörg Lanz von Liebenfels.'[185]

In 1900 Liebenfels established a secret society called 'the New Temple,' which heralded the coming of a racial 'New Order.' His society published its own periodical and purchased a ruined castle in Upper Austria at Werfenstein. In 1907 Liebenfels hoisted a swastika flag of racial purity over its tower and led his followers in incantations to Teutonic spirits. His production of occult claptrap was prodigious. Year after year dozens of tracts spewed from his pen. They included one entitled *Theo-zoology, or Tales of Sodom-Ape Men and Electronic God, with 45 Illustrations*. Another was called *Odish-Energy* (*Odische Energie*).

Most of *his* energies, however, went into writing for the New Order's official organ, *Ostara*, named after the Teutonic goddess of spring, since Liebenfels looked forward to a reawakening of Teutonic spirit and a glorious new Reich of racial purity as described in another of his pamphlets, *Die Ostara und das Reich des Blonden*.[186] Young Hitler read these pamphlets in Vienna,[187] and he applied their principles in the Third Reich. A 1907 issue of *Ostara* warned darkly about the evils of polluted blood, using pronouncements that Hitler would later plagiarize: 'The roots of all our misfortune lie in blood pollution ... Sin against the blood is the Original Sin (*Erbsünde*) of this world.' Such silly ideas and extravagant prose would be amusing if they had not been harbingers of horrors to come. In an issue of 1908, after demanding 'racial warfare as far as the castration knife,' Liebenfels wrote:

Without Thor's smashing hammerblows, we cannot prevail.
Bring sacrifices to Fruja, ye sons of the gods!

Up! Up to arms! Bring to him the *Schrättlingskinder!* [188]

Our Hymn of Power demands the extermination of sub-humanity (*Ausmerzung des Untermenschentums*). Then the higher race can arise from out the grave of racial degradation and ascend to the heights of immortality.

Thirty years after Liebenfels called for the 'sacrifice' of misshapen children, the Führer established a 'euthanasia' program that killed thousands upon thousands of malformed or retarded children – children who were, in Hitler's phrase, 'unworthy of life.' The Führer also followed his mentor's instruction for the sterilization and extermination of those whom he considered 'sub-human.'

In 1932 Liebenfels wrote jubilantly to one of the Brothers of the Order: 'Do you know what? Hitler is one of my disciples! You will still see that he – and with him all of us – will triumph. A movement is coming that will make the world tremble with its power. *Heil Dir!*'[189] Liebenfels had good reason to be satisfied. Few teachers have been taken more seriously.

Both Kaiser and Führer were fascinated with the supernatural, mysterious, and occult, but Wilhelm's passing interests did not seriously affect either his personal or his public life. By contrast, the Führer's lifelong commitment to supernatural forces was infinitely more pernicious, as we shall see in discussing his political and racial theories.

The Kaiser and the Führer as Racists

Let no German rest ... until the hateful tribe of Judah is annihilated and rooted out of German soil.

Kaiser Wilhelm II

I will exterminate the Jews.

Adolf Hitler

The Kaiser was in the habit of jotting down marginal comments on everything from state documents to private letters. These impulsive, often imprudent remarks could be peppered with explosive expressions: 'Never trust a Frenchman!' ... 'Pure nonsense!' ... 'The man is a sheephead!' ... 'They are all full of shit!' Such marginalia on the state documents in the enormous collection of pre-First World War diplomatic papers known as *Die Grosse Politik der Europäischen Kabinette* (forty volumes, fifty-four parts) would have been even more pungent if they had not been bowdlerized and carefully abridged by patriotic German editors.[190] Still, the marginal comments that have survived deletion and censorship continue to provide insight into the Kaiser's attitude towards racial and religious groups. Lydia Franke, a German scholar who has gone methodically through the Kaiser's marginalia on hundreds of state papers, has concluded that Wilhelm's attitude to race 'is one of the most consistent aspects of his thought.'[191]

In Wilhelm's opinion, race should be a determining force in international relations. Particularly important was the terrible threat of what he called the 'Yellow Peril' (*die gelbe Gefahr*). That threat, Franke tells us, became for Wilhelm an *idée fixe*, a 'fantasy that was always on his mind.'[192] He was convinced, as he noted in the margin of one document, that 'the great, final battle between the White and the Yellow races ... between Christianity and Buddhism, Western culture and Eastern half-culture' was imminent and that the 'White race' had better prepare for it.

The Kaiser drew several versions of a poster-caricature of a sinister Oriental attacking Europe. The caption reads, 'Peoples of Europe! Defend your holiest possessions!' He gave orders that all ships of the Hamburg-Amerika and the North German Lloyd lines sailing to the Far East display this poster. His chancellor tried to dissuade him, arguing that the poster was insulting to the Japanese; but the Kaiser was adamant.[193]

Wilhelm seized an opportunity to smash the Chinese in body and spirit when a European military force was organized to put down the Boxer Rebellion of 1900. He saw it as the first stage of his crusade against the 'Yellow Peril.' He could not go himself, but as the first contingent of German soldiers left Bremerhaven on 27 July 1900, he gave instructions on how they should conduct themselves when confronting Orientals. In this speech the Kaiser himself proudly referred to Germans as 'Huns,' thereby providing the epithet used effectively by Allied propagandists against the Germans in the Great War:

No quarter will be given. No prisoners to be taken. Whoever falls into your hands, let his life be forfeit! The Huns under King Etzel (Attila) a thousand years ago made a name for themselves that has remained mighty in tradition and saga to this day; may you make the name of 'German' a thing to conjure with in China for a thousand years so that never again will a Chinese dare to as much as look askance at a German. The blessings of God go with you ... Clear the path for civilization once and for all. Now you can depart. Farewell, *Kameraden*![194]

Chancellor Bernhard von Bülow (1900–9), recognizing the dangers of the 'Hun speech,' immediately sent a watered-down version to the press. But Wilhelm refused to be rescued. When he read the bowdlerized version on board his yacht, he complained, 'They have left out the best part!' Only when he read a full account in a Bremen paper, whose reporter had taken down the whole speech stenographically, including the reference to the Huns, did Wilhelm nod his head and grin with pleasure.[195]

Wilhelm made similar remarks to later contingents of departing troops, telling them, for example, that 'by nature the Chinaman is a cowardly cur ... tricky and double-faced' (speech of 2 August 1900); 'Give no quarter! Do not rest until the enemy, crushed to the earth, asks pardon on his bended knees ... Do honour to the German name, to the flag, and – do not forget it – to me' (speech of 14 August).[196] Wilhelm did not explain how his troops would honour either the German name or their Kaiser by emulating Attila's Huns.

Yet with respect to race, as in many other matters, Wilhelm was inconsistent and ambivalent. He sometimes spoke favourably of the Chinese as bulwarks between Europe and the rapacious Japanese. He also found positive things to say about Chinese civilization, once congratulating the Chinese for originating the swastika, symbol of the sun, creativity, and racial purity. (To this writer, the connecting line between the yin-yang monad and the Nazi *Hakenkreuz* remains obscure.)[197]

All Asians, as part of the 'Yellow Peril,' were suspect, but the Japanese – whom the Kaiser repeatedly referred to as 'enlarged apes' – were particularly menacing. He was convinced that they were about to land along the Chinese coast, sweep on through Russia, and attack western Europe. During the 1890s he sent hyperbolic letters to his 'cousin,' Tsar Nicholas II, warning him repeatedly of the 'Yellow Peril' and urging him to start a 'preventive' war against the Japanese while there was yet time. He assured the Tsar in a letter of 26 April 1895 that 'I will do all in my power to keep Europe quiet and also guard the rear of Russia so that nobody shall hamper your actions in the Far East!'[198]

When Russia and France negotiated a series of understandings known as the Entente Cordiale, the Kaiser was outraged, not only because he saw these agreements as aimed against him personally, as he tended to see any agreement reached by other countries, but because France and Russia were both blind to the need of all European countries to unite against Japan. In the margin of news of the pact he pencilled furiously, 'How the Yellows will rejoice at this!' He also inveighed against the blindness of Russia's Balkan policy: 'Stupid! ... they'll get involved in the Balkans until, one day, the Yellows are at the Urals!'

As tension between Japan and Russia increased by the turn of the century, the Kaiser rejoiced. Here, at last, was a chance to get those 'stupid Slavs' to fight the 'Yellows.' He was furious with Nicky for hesitating. On 14 February 1904 Wilhelm broke into his chancellor's office and shouted that Nicholas was 'as spineless as ever. He does not seem to want to fight.' When Bülow tried to calm him, the Kaiser would have none of it: 'You overlook one enormous danger ... the Yellow Peril, the greatest danger threatening the whole [white] race, Christianity and our entire culture. If the Russians run away from the Japanese now, the yellow race will be in Moscow and Posen within twenty years!'[199]

His entire diplomatic corps, the Kaiser said, were equally blind to the danger. On 11 August 1904 he warned them of the coming Armageddon:

Attention All My Diplomats!

A final battle (*Endkampf*) is coming between the Yellow and the White races when the Japanese and Chinese will mount battle against Europe. It will also be the final battle between the two religions of Christianity and Buddhism, western culture and oriental culture.

We must not forget that in the present war Japan is not fighting the Russians as Russians but because they belong to the white race! ... *I know definitely that one day we must fight to the death against Japan* ... the situation is clear and I make my preparations accordingly.[200]

Japanese victories in the Russo-Japanese War seemed proof positive that Wilhelm's direst expectations were justified. In a letter of 28 December 1907 'Willy' reminded 'Nicky' of all the warnings he had given him, including the picture he had sent of the 'Yellow Peril.' He offered further proof. The Japanese, he asserted, had sent ten thousand troops to southern Mexico in preparation for seizing the Panama Canal, then under construction: 'This is my *secret* information for you *personally* ... It is sure information and good ... The Japanese are going in for the whole of Asia preparing blows *against the white race* in general! Remember my picture, it's coming true!'[201]

Later in exile the Kaiser, for a moment at least, changed his mind about the 'Yellow Peril.' Instead of preaching a crusade against Orientals, he now wanted to ally with them against a greater menace: the 'Black nations' of France and England. In a conversation of 1923, Wilhelm showed his capacity to transform the world once again according to his own shifting visions: 'Finally I realize the future we Germans have been called upon to fulfil! ... We will be the Leader of the East against the West! I must now change my [earlier] picture of "The Peoples of Europe," for we belong now on the other side! When we have got the Germans to understand that the French and English are not whites at all but black! (*gar nicht Weisse, sondern Schwarze!*).' As John Röhl has observed in quoting these words, 'Whoever could maintain that the English and French are Negroes would have no difficulty in proclaiming that Jesus of Nazareth was ... "never a Jew."'[202]

The Kaiser changed his mind again in 1929, however, and told an English journalist that it was absolutely essential for Europe to unite against the threat of the yellow races.[203] In this mood, Wilhelm wanted to sound the tocsin again by reissuing his broadside *Die gelbe Gefahr.* He was proud of that pamphlet: 'The world should see that I can still make an intellectual contribution and that I'm not such an idiot as many people think.' His wife is reported to have commented, we must presume *sotto voce*, with a line from Goethe: *Gegen die Dummheit kämpfen die Götter selbst vergebens* (Against stupidity, the gods themselves struggle in vain).[204]

In fairness to Wilhelm, it should be noted that he was not blinded by racial prejudice to the point of failing to recognize individual personal accomplishment. After the fall of Port Arthur to the Japanese in 1905, he bestowed Prussia's highest military award, the *pour le mérite,* upon both the Russian defender of Port Arthur, General Stosser, and the victorious Japanese commander, General Noghi. When the London *Times* pointed out that the Russian had clearly not earned the award (indeed he had surrendered without a struggle) and suggested that the Kaiser might have waited for an evaluation of his conduct by German military advisers before granting so prestigious a citation, Wilhelm's comment was quintessentially Wilhelmian: 'Pfui! Such pettiness from such petty British souls!'[205]

The Kaiser wanted the world to know about the superiority of the white race and Protestant Christianity. In 1908 he gave a two-hour interview to a certain Reverend William Bayard Hale, an American pastor and newspaperman, and asked him to publish the entire interview in the *Century Magazine.*[206] Once again the Kaiser demonstrated how firmly his belief in racial superiority was fixed in his mind:

'The future' – his voice rang out – 'the future belongs – to the White race, never fear!' His shoulders squared, his eye flashed ... 'It belongs to the Anglo-Teuton, the man who came from Northern Europe ... the home of the German.

'It does not belong, the future, to the Yellow, nor to the Black, nor to the Olive-coloured. It belongs to the Fair-skinned Man and it belongs to Christianity and to Protestantism. We are the only people who can save [humanity].'[207]

Racism was heavily on the Kaiser's mind as the Great War approached. In December 1912 he excitedly informed Albert Ballin that a 'racial battle' (*Rassenkampf*) between 'Germans' and the 'increasingly insolent Slavs' might well take place – a battle that would determine 'the very existence of the Fatherland.'[208] When war did break out against the 'insolent' Russians, Wilhelm set a precedent for Hitler by ordering that the ninety thousand Russian prisoners of war captured by his armies after the battle of Tannenberg (August 1914) be deprived of all food and water so that they would starve to death.[209]

Their Mentor in Racism, Houston Stewart Chamberlain

You bring light into my darkness.

Wilhelm II

You have made imperishable contributions.

Adolf Hitler

The Kaiser's ideas about Germanic superiority were drawn, very largely, from the racist writings of the English expatriate Houston Stewart Chamberlain, an author who also confirmed Adolf Hitler's racial prejudices.

Reading Chamberlain's turgid two-volume tome *Grundlagen des neunzehnten Jahrhunderts* (Foundations of the Nineteenth Century) was hailed by Wilhelm as the single most formative intellectual experience of his life. For reasons that are not very clear, Chamberlain's ponderous tome was immensely popular at the turn of the century.[210] Chamberlain was sure that he had discovered, as he wrote, 'the most important secret of all human history: namely, that purity of race is sacred (*heilig*).'[211] (Many years later, Adolf Hitler made a similar claim, calling racism 'my Copernican discovery.')

Chamberlain's thesis was as asinine as it was pernicious: 'Beyond all question,' he wrote, 'Teutons are the greatest contributors to world civilization.' His argument cannot be sustained, even if one were to accept his remarkably elastic definition of 'Teutonic.' He would have the term embrace Dante and Shakespeare and 'all other geniuses of the Renaissance,' as well as Jesus Christ, who, Chamberlain said flatly, 'was no Jew.'[212] The magnificently creative Germanic people, he insisted, are destined to dominate the world; all other people, including Slavs, Orientals, and Jews, must bend their necks to a Teutonic yoke.

The Germans historically were great warriors, Chamberlain continued, but in their natural and endearing naïveté they had not realized that 'the greatest battle of all is a silent battle, a battle for life and death,' a struggle for racial purity. That silent, deadly battle pitted German against Jew.

Just as the youthful Adolf Hitler experienced his great spiritual awakening through reading the racist tracts of Lanz von Liebenfels in Vienna, Wilhelm was transformed, he said, by reading Chamberlain. Both the flavour of Wilhelm's prose and the extent of his indebtedness to Chamberlain are manifest in a letter of 31 December 1901. He had been stumbling in the dark, he said, seeking for the 'spiritual foundations' upon which to build the 'New Reich' of his dreams: 'Then you come along and with one magic stroke bring order into the confusion, light into the darkness. You show the goals for which we strive and work, explain those things we had sensed only dimly, and reveal the paths which must be followed for the salvation of the Germans and thus the salvation of mankind! ... What a salvation! So! Now you know, my dear Mr Chamberlain, what was going on in my mind when I felt your hand in mine.'[213]

Wilhelm was so captivated by the *Grundlagen* that he read the tome aloud every evening to the Empress and her ladies-in-waiting,[214] and in 1903 he wrote Chamberlain that he had ordered his masterpiece to be made compulsory reading in all training schools for teachers in Germany. He also distributed copies to army leaders and members of his entourage.[215]

The teacher was delighted to find so avid and appreciative a student. He wrote many long letters, often running to eighteen or twenty pages in their printed versions, urging Wilhelm to fulfil his 'holy mission' of expanding Germandom throughout the world.[216] Although Chamberlain remained an inspiration to the Kaiser throughout his exile in Holland (1918–41),[217] the feeling was no longer reciprocated.

In fairness it should be noted that on occasion Wilhelm expressed kindly feelings about 'non-Aryans.' His admonition to soldiers embarking for German Southwest Africa on 15 June 1894, for example, offers a sharp contrast to his harangues to soldiers being sent forth to smash the Boxer Rebellion in China: 'Keep constantly in mind that the people you will meet there, even if they have a different skin colour, also possess the same heart and sense of honour as we do. Treat these people gently *(Behandeln Sie diese Leute mit Milde).*'[218] The Kaiser was also active in famine relief. He sponsored committees to raise money for starving people in India, proudly reporting to his grandmother that he had raised half a million marks in a relatively short time.[219]

After Wilhelm's crusade against his native England had failed so disastrously in 1918, Chamberlain shifted his loyalty from Kaiser to Führer. For Chamberlain now recognized Adolf Hitler as the long-awaited saviour who would redeem Germany and establish a racially pure Reich. The first meeting between the prophet and his disciple took place in October 1923 when Hitler made the first of many pilgrimages to the Wagnerian shrine at Wahnfried. There he was received by Cosima Wagner, widow of the *Meister*, mistress of Bayreuth, and mother of Eva, who was the wife of Houston Stewart Chamberlain. Hitler delighted everyone. He told Frau Wagner that her husband had been the greatest influence of his life, that 'it all began' in Linz after the young Hitler first heard *Rienzi*; he flattered Wagner's son Siegfried; he absolutely captivated the grandchildren.

And then a paralyzed, aging man 'with spent eyes in the face of a child' was wheeled in. It was H.S. Chamberlain, Wagner's son-in-law. Hitler thanked the old man for his 'imperishable contributions' to racism and played to the hilt the roles he knew Chamberlain expected of him: Man of Destiny and Racial Deliverer. The next day the invalid dictated a letter extolling the Führer. Like so many others, he had been taken with Hitler's hands and eyes: 'That you bestow peace upon me is largely attributable to your eyes and the gestures of your hands. It is as if your eyes were equipped with hands, for they grip a man and hold him fast' He ended the letter, 'My faith in the Germans has never wavered for a moment, but my hope, I must own, was sunk to a low ebb. At one stroke you have transformed the state of my soul.'[220]

The Kaiser and the Jews

The best way would be gas.

Wilhelm II

In her splendid book on the Kaiser's entourage, Isabel Hull used Chamberlain's influence on Wilhelm as an example of how his associates reinforced the Kaiser's worst prejudices. As a result of reading Chamberlain, Hull asserted, he became 'saturated ... with a violent and principled anti-Semitism that he had not held before.'[221]

Actually, both before and after reading Chamberlain (ca. 1901–3), the Kaiser's attitude towards Jews was consistently ambivalent. He could hardly have been so enthusiastic about Chamberlain without sanctioning his anti-Semitism, yet the Kaiser's speeches and marginal notes, along with his actions, indicate that 'violent' is not an appropriate adjective for describing his antipathy towards Jews, at least not until 1918.[222]

Unlike Hitler, Wilhelm had not become an anti-Semite in his youth. When he was fifteen and a *Gymnasium* student in Kassel, he wrote to his mother that his 'very best friend' was a Jew named Siegfried Sommer. He invited Sommer to hang his school cap next to his and to share his sandwiches. He also reported that he often put his arm around Sommer's waist, 'as one does with a pretty girl.' Years later Wilhelm appointed Sommer to a district judgeship.[223]

Wilhelm's anti-Semitic outbursts in the 1880s seem to have been associated with his increasing estrangement from his parents. Their support of Jews, in his mind, was all a part of other pernicious 'English ideas' such as parliamentary government and liberal reform.[224] Wilhelm was furious when his mother called anti-Semites 'vicious and hateful' and when his father donned his field-marshal's uniform to attend services in a Berlin synagogue and said, 'We are ashamed of this hatred of Jews ... it oversteps all bounds of human decency.'[225]

Wilhelm's antipathy to Jews was closely involved with his curiously ambivalent attitude towards the English people. On a diplomatic dispatch he wrote, quite erroneously, that the distinguished British journalist Sir Donald Mackenzie was 'very clever and charming – a Jew, naturally,'[226] and he convinced himself that 'a bunch of loutish Anglo-Jewish doctors' were to blame for his own birth injury and had caused his father's death.[227]

The Kaiser's closest advisers insisted that he was not anti-Semitic.[228] What they probably meant was that neither they nor the Kaiser directly associated themselves with the racist anti-Semitic political movement that was becoming a pernicious force in Wilhelmian Germany. Wilhelm's closest confidant, Philipp zu Eulenburg, was also 'no friend of the Jews,' as he euphemistically put it, but he advised the Kaiser against supporting 'the anti-Semites' and urged him to dissociate himself publicly from them.[229] In this instance, Wilhelm followed his advice.

It is true that in 1913 Wilhelm told his heir, Crown Prince August Wilhelm, 'to exclude Jewish influence from the army and the administration and to restrict its power in all artistic and literary activity,' but he refused to support the Pan-German League when it demanded restrictive legislation against Jews as well as their expulsion from Germany.[230]

Wilhelm could even be quite complimentary to Jews. He sent an autographed picture of himself, along with warm greetings, to Baron Rothschild, thanking him for his support in raising money for famine relief in India.[231] He called upon Albert Ballin and Franz Mendelssohn for financial advice; and he some-times invited other Jews to the palace for social gatherings. He was highly selective, however, preferring to cultivate only wealthy 'court Jews.' During one of his outbursts against Jews, someone in his entourage had the temerity to remind him that his friends Ballin, Mendelssohn, and Rothschild were Jewish. The Kaiser closed the conversation abruptly by announcing sternly that he did not consider them to be Jews[232] – a comment anticipating Hermann Göring's cynical statement, '*Wer Jude ist, bestimme ich* (I decide who is Jewish).'

For a time, the Kaiser even supported Theodor Herzl's Zionist movement as a solution to the 'Jewish problem,' and he wrote Herzl, 'Your movement, with which I am thoroughly familiar, is based on a sound, healthy idea. There is room here [in Jerusalem] for everyone.'[233] Other letters extolled the Jewish people for their 'industry and creativity' and predicted a great future for the Jews in their historic homeland. But when his friend Abdul Hammid II, who richly deserved his title of the 'Abomination,' objected to the establishment of a Jewish state within his own realm, Wilhelm dropped his support.[234]

Two chilling comments made by Wilhelm during a visit to England in 1907 reveal a vicious aspect of his anti-Semitism. Viscount Esher reports that during a banquet in Windsor Castle, Wilhelm II 'declaimed vehemently against Jews: "There are far too many of them in my country. They want stamping out."'[235] Similarly, he told Sir Edward Grey that for the good of his country the Jews 'must be stamped out.'[236]

After Germany's defeat in 1918, the Kaiser's anti-Semitism mounted to a phobia. He insisted that the Jews were responsible for causing the war, engi-neering Germany's defeat, and writing the hateful Treaty of Versailles. Like Hitler, he became an ardent believer in the fraudulent *Protocols of the Elders of Zion*; he, too, was convinced that 'the Jews in alliance with the German prole-tariat are fomenting revolution.'[237] The Bolsheviks must be destroyed, Wilhelm shouted, along with 'the whole of international Jewry.'[238] In concluding a hand-written letter of 1919, he used the same ugly metaphors and vocabulary that Hitler would later employ, referring to Jews as 'these fungi on the German oak': 'Let no German ever forget and let them not rest until this ... hateful tribe of Judah ... is annihilated and rooted out (*vertilgt und ausgerottet*) from German soil.'[239] He also anticipated Hitler by referring to the French as that '*negroid-afrikanische Nation der Franzosen*' and insisted that Jews too had 'Afro-negroid' blood.[240]

In a Sunday morning sermon of June 1926 in Doorn, on the text, 'Why are you so frightened, O ye of little faith?,' Wilhelm II told his household congregation, 'While my generals and the brave army of the front-lines fought for victory under me, the war was lost at home because of the lies and deceptions of the Jews and the Entente.'[241] He had discovered that his closest friend, Philipp zu Eulenburg, whom he had deserted in his hour of need, had been the victim of 'international Jewry ... Eulenburg's trial [for homosexuality] was the first blow against the monarch, the beginning of the Revolution.'[242]

Wilhelm set aside his anti-Catholicism and called on Catholics to join Evangelical Christians in common battle against the 'Jewification (*Verjudung*) of Germany ... After the purification (*Bereinigung*) of Germany, we must continue the battle against the Jewification of the world by taking up arms against world Jewry (*Weltjudentum*).'[243] By the summer of 1929 he had decided that the Jews had become a 'plague' from which 'humanity must be freed one way or another ... I think the best way would be gas! (*das beste wäre Gas!*).'[244] In 1940, shortly after sending Hitler a congratulatory telegram for his glorious victory over France,[245] the Kaiser wrote exuberantly to an admirer that the fundamental cause for both world wars was 'Jewish high finance.' The real anti-Christ, he asserted, was not Adolf Hitler: 'The anti-Christ of today is – as it has been since Golgotha – Judah, Freemasonry and World Jewry and its power of gold ... [the Jews] started this war to establish the world empire of Judah ... The Jewish anti-Christ must be rooted out (*hinausgestossen*) from the entire European continent.'[246]

Nevertheless, the Kaiser recoiled when Hitler actually started to root out the 'Jewish anti-Christ' and 'purify' Germany. He was genuinely shocked when he read reports of Hitler's first major pogrom against the Jews in the infamous *Kristallnacht* of 9–10 November 1938. 'I never thought it was possible,' he confided to a visitor in Doorn, 'that the day would come when I would be ashamed to be a German.'[247] He told his entourage that 'all decent Germans' should speak out against the anti-Jewish terror perpetrated by the lawless Nazis, yet he could not bring himself to do so. He never raised a public protest.[248]

He knew about Jewish persecutions and the horror of Hitler's concentration camps through the British press and the BBC, but throughout the rest of his life the Kaiser continued to verify Edmund Burke's famous admonition: 'All that is necessary for evil to triumph is for good men to do nothing.'

Although the Kaiser and the Führer held similar views about race, there were also crucial differences. The Kaiser's antipathy towards Asian people and, in his later days, towards Jews never approached the intensity of Hitler's incandescent hatred of the Jewish people. Moreover, Wilhelm's racism never seriously affected his private life or public policy. Although anti-Semitism was certainly widespread in the Kaiser's Reich, it was not sponsored by his government. Not one governmental decree, not one piece of legislation, was directed expressly against Jewish people. It is important to remember that when the influential Pan-Germans urged him to institute a program that clearly discriminated against the Jews, the Kaiser flatly refused and called their program stupid, criminal, and childish. True, the Kaiser, like the Führer, talked about the menace of 'international Jewry,' but to his mind it did not, at least not until after his abdication, pose as serious a threat to Western civilization as the 'Yellow Peril.'

Wilhelm did believe that 'Teutons' were infinitely superior to Semites, and he even said that Germany would be better off if all the Jews were somehow 'rooted out' and 'exterminated.' But he did not mean that to be taken literally. He was surprised and alarmed when Hitler put *his* words into brutal action. Once again the Kaiser's fulminations were essentially rhetorical flourish.

Therein lay a profound difference between the two rulers. Hitler meant what he said, and he practised what he preached. As he had promised, he established a government founded on racism; he institutionalized hatred of Jews. He had said that he would kill all the Jews of Europe, and he tried his best to do just that.

A fragment of conversation as early as 1922 (now preserved in a Munich archive) reveals something of the depth and intensity of Hitler's loathing of the Jewish people, his confidence that one day he would come to power, and his assurance that when he did, he would do 'the work of the Lord' by killing every Jew in Germany. The method of murder that Hitler then envisaged also reveals his continuing personal concern about filth, stench, putrefaction, and strangulation: 'As soon as I have the power, I shall have gallows after gallows erected, for example in Munich on the Marienplatz ... Then the Jews will be hanged one after another, and they will stay hanging until they stink. They will stay hanging as long as hygienically possible. As soon as they are untied, then the next group will follow and that will continue until the last Jew in Munich is exterminated. Exactly the same procedure will be followed in other cities until Germany is cleansed of the last Jew!'[249]

Twenty years later, more efficient methods of mass murder were found.

3

Kaiser and Führer as Rulers in Peacetime: Theory and Practice

PART I: THEORIES OF GOVERNMENT

There is only one master in the Reich and that is I ... There is but one law and that is my will ... I am responsible to God alone.

Kaiser Wilhelm II

Our ideology is intolerant ... and peremptorily demands ... that public life be completely transformed to conform to its ideas.

Adolf Hitler

On a blustery, lowering January day in 1933, most Germans viewed the coming to power of Adolf Hitler with apprehension.[1] By contrast, everyone had recognized the promise of young Wilhelm von Hohenzollern and predicted a brilliant reign when he ascended the throne of Imperial Germany on a lovely June day in 1888.[2]

Never since Frederick the Great had a German prince been blessed with such varied natural gifts or been better educated for the job. Wilhelm's training had begun early in life. His austere and formidable Calvinist tutor, Dr Georg Hinzpeter, had instilled in him concern for social problems, admonishing his pupil that when he became monarch he would be obliged to fulfil his Christian obligations to the disadvantaged people of his realm.[3] At his mother's insistence he had received a classical education in a first-class *Gymnasium*, and he had learned to speak 'flawless French,'[4] the language of international relations. His mother had insisted that he read and be tested on the political and constitutional essays written by her father, Prince Consort Albert.[5] Wilhelm had studied political theory and jurisprudence at the University of Bonn; he had been tutored in government by that master of statecraft himself, Otto von Bismarck, who, before the young Kaiser dismissed him in 1890, had touted his pupil's abilities and had made a solemn promise: 'I will stand by my sovereign's side to my last breath, he who is so gifted, so conscientious and so dedicated to the welfare of the Reich.'[6] Bismarck also reinforced Wilhelm's convictions by telling him that 'the royal will is and remains the only decisive (*der allein entscheidende*) force in the State.'[7] Moreover, Wilhelm possessed an indispensable ingredient for political success: he *wanted* to succeed. He was determined to be the greatest monarch in all history. And his countrymen applauded his ambition.

Wilhelm's plan was simple: he would be 'his own chancellor'; he alone would rule Germany. He set his course early in his reign. After dismissing Bismarck in 1890 he distributed a memorandum to all his ministers telling them, 'I will smash anyone who stands in my way.'[8]

Populace and press had joined in hailing their new monarch, and the president of the Reichstag greeted Wilhelm's accession in 1888 with bubbling enthusiasm: 'Gentlemen, all that the Kaiser does must fill us with admiration and we may thank Providence for giving us, in such a time as this, such a Kaiser!'[9]

At his accession Wilhelm's appeal to the German people was so great that an American observer reported, 'If the whole country had to vote tomorrow for a leader embodying the qualities they most desired, their choice would fall unquestionably on their present ... ruler.'[10]

In many ways Wilhelm did indeed embody the qualities his countrymen 'most desired.' He seemed perfectly in tune with his times. The powerful Germany of 1888 was as flamboyant, confident, and ambitious as its brash young ruler. Walther Rathenau was right: 'Never has an epoch with greater justification appropriated the name of its monarch.'[11] It was indeed 'Wilhelmian.'

The Kaiser's Royal Absolutism

Kaiser Wilhelm's theory of royal power was endorsed by the German people and sanctioned by long tradition. Unlike the Führer, who created his own political ideology, the Kaiser largely inherited his. Like his Hohenzollern ancestors, he believed that royal absolutism was ordained by Almighty God. As an admirer commented, 'For him the "Divine Right of Kings" was no empty phrase, but a deep reality ... [It was] his firm conviction that in some mysterious way he was the Vice-Regent of Christ on Earth.'[12] He constantly reminded his subjects that the source of his power was divine and that consequently whatever pleased him had the force of law.

The young Kaiser's belief in the divine right of monarchy could draw strength from German religious and philosophic tradition. Martin Luther, and thousands of Lutheran pastors after him, preached the doctrine of the 'two realms.' In the 'inner realm' of faith and spirit the Christian believer is free; but in the 'outer realm' of secular and political life he enjoys no such personal freedom. On the contrary, he is duty-bound to obey the earthly rulers ordained by God. Resistance to rulers, 'whether they be right or wrong,' is a mortal sin. Luther's exaltation of monarchs was intensified by his distrust of the people: 'The Princes of this world are gods; the common people are Satan ... I would rather suffer a Prince doing wrong than a people doing right.'[13]

Luther never recognized anything resembling the natural rights of the citizen. Indeed the concept of 'citizen' was foreign to him. He knew only 'subjects' whose political function was simply to obey Authority (*Obrigkeit*). Thus, a common Lutheran expression of religious conviction – *Alles kommt von oben herab* (Everything comes down from above) – was transformed into an affirmation of political faith.[14]

Kaiser Wilhelm's idea that his subjects should revere the state as an instrument of God had been championed by Germany's most influential philosopher of the nineteenth century, Georg Wilhelm Friedrich Hegel (1770–1831). Hegel wrote and lectured early in the century, but his influence was greatest during the Wilhelmian years when his philosophy of the state became virtually the official creed of German academics.[15]

Hegel's writings are difficult, abstruse, and often incomprehensible to all but Hegelians, and they often disagree about his meaning. On one point, however, there is no disagreement, for Hegel is very clear indeed: the State must be revered above all earthly institutions, for it is no mere human creation; it is an inspired act of God. The Kaiser read and savoured Hegel's words: 'The State is divine will ... one should therefore revere the State as something divine upon earth (*irdischgöttliches*) ... Sacrificing one's individuality for the individuality of the state is ... *a general duty.*'[16]

Wilhelm was also attracted to Hegel's assertion that God used certain 'world historical individuals' as His special instrument to fulfil His purposes. Wilhelm II saw himself as one of those rare historic individuals.

The imperial constitution also buttressed Wilhelm's conception of royal power. Students of British history are accustomed to using the phrase 'constitutional monarchy' interchangeably with 'limited' or 'parliamentary' monarchy. The German constitution of 1871 embodied no such concept.[17] This document was not the product of a constituent assembly; it had been written by one man, Otto von Bismarck, allegedly in one afternoon. In other countries, constitutions were written to limit the powers of the Crown; the German document was designed to increase royal power. The Kaiser was the commander of all military forces and the head of the Established Church; he chose and could dismiss at his pleasure all government officials from chancellors and army generals to university professors and judges. Decisions for war and peace were in his hands.

Theoretically there was one constitutional limitation on his sweeping powers: the Kaiser was obliged to have all important royal decrees countersigned by the imperial chancellor. But this limitation was more apparent than real, for there were two royal jokers in this deck. The chancellor was responsible solely to the Kaiser and could be dismissed at the royal whim; furthermore, the chancellor could be questioned by the Reichstag, but the Kaiser could not. In countersigning all legislation the chancellor assumed responsibility to the parliament; but the Emperor was released from all such accountability. It was tacitly assumed that the Kaiser was 'inviolable and unanswerable.'[18]

Neither the Kaiser nor any officer in his army took an oath to defend the constitution. Instead, officers swore a personal oath of unqualified loyalty to the monarch as his *Kriegsherr* (Warlord). 'To all intents and purposes,' Gordon Craig has concluded, 'the army was left outside of the constitution, subject only to the king's control and serving to protect his authority against legislative encroachment.'[19]

Control over the army guaranteed Wilhelm's political power. Mirabeau's memorable *mot* of the eighteenth century gained increased validity during the Second Reich: 'Prussia is not a state that has an Army; it is an Army that has a state.' In his massive study of German militarism, Gerhard Ritter noted, 'In the West, the army was a sort of necessary evil, but here it formed the highest pride of the nation.'[20]

In a national questionnaire of 1899, Germans were asked to name 'the greatest German thinker of the century.' They chose General Helmuth von Moltke, ranking him well ahead of Hegel, Kant, Schopenhauer, and Goethe. Werner Sombart, a noted economic historian, expressed the attitude of his countrymen when he looked about him on the eve of the Great War, found militarism everywhere, pronounced it good, and reached a fulsome conclusion: 'German militarism is the most complete synthesis of Potsdam and Weimar. It is Beethoven in the trenches.'[21]

Popular support for militarism and monarchy was bolstered by hundreds of veterans' societies (*Kriegervereine*) that spread even into the smallest villages of Germany during the 1880s and 1890s.[22] Several million strong, these societies were nationalist, stridently anti-Socialist, anti-Semitic, and devoutly monarchist. Members took a 'sacred oath of loyalty' (*heiliger Treueid*) to the King-Emperor; this was the cement that bound them all together, uniting the lowliest soldier to the most senior general. Their spirit was encapsuled in a remarkable sermon preached on 26 June 1892 by a Lutheran pastor who was also a member of the Oldenburger Kriegerbund: 'Dear comrades, in this holy hour (*in heiliger Stunde*) a holy oath! But our oath ... is not laid aside when we remove the garb of honour (*Ehrenkleider*). No, it goes with us to the grave, for we are ... the special property of our Imperial Lord (*das besondere Eigentum unseres Kaiserlichen Herrn*) ... This is the ultimate satisfaction of an old soldier and his wreath of glory: Loyalty, soldierly fidelity [to the Kaiser] until life's last breath.'[23]

The priority Wilhelm himself gave to the army was expressed in his first proclamation as German emperor. He addressed it not 'to my people' but 'to my army,' reminding them, and everyone else in Germany, that 'soldiers and the Army and not parliaments forged the Reich.'

The citizens of Germany basked in the glow of imperial glory and gained a measure of pride and personal power, as they would again under Hitler, by participating vicariously in the massive power of the Reich. Heinrich Mann, who recognized how much the image of the Kaiser appealed to the middle and lower middle classes, called Wilhelm 'king of the bourgeoisie,' a title usually reserved for Louis Philippe of France. Mann recalled a scene to illustrate what he meant. The Kaiser was riding out of the Berliner Schloss with Lohengrinian helmet on head. A *Bürger* doffed his hat and called out, 'We thank thee! We thank thee!'[24] As another writer put it in a best-seller of 1897, the masses longed to be ruled by an overwhelming personality (*überlegenen Persönlichkeit*) ... a true Master.'[25]

Support for Kaiser Wilhelm also came from unexpected quarters. Given Wilhelm's strident Protestantism and his condemnation of 'Catholics, Jews, and Freemasons' as *Reichsfeinde*, one might have expected that Catholics would have been less than enthusiastic. Yet Ludwig Windthorst, the leader of the Catholic Centre Party who had defended his religion in his battle against Bismarck during the *Kulturkampf*, told an American interviewer in 1890, 'If other parties do not support the Kaiser, we shall ... The Kaiser carries the banner, we march behind him.'[26] Even pacifists hailed Wilhelm as their champion. They persuaded themselves that his promise of using German power to become *arbiter mundi*, a promise that alarmed other countries, was actually the best hope for peace, not only for Europe but for the entire world.[27]

The most respected intellectuals of Germany joined in hailing their Kaiser, endorsing his power and his plans for aggression. Max Weber's inaugural lecture as rector of the University of Freiburg in 1895 was a clarion call for power. Weber told his fellow academics that war 'is the basic condition of national life' and that they should look forward to 'heavy battles' as the only means of achieving world domination.[28] Later in Wilhelm's reign, the dean of Germany's historians, Friedrich Meinecke, joined the swelling chorus: 'We Germans ... demand a Führer for our nation, one for whom we will go through fire!'[29]

The German parliament, Wilhelm's only possible rival for political sovereignty, never served as an effective counterpoise to royal absolutism. In the crisis of August 1914 European powers waited anxiously to see if the House of Commons would cast the crucial vote that would bring Britain into the Great War; in Germany, when the Kaiser declared war on 3 August 1914, members of the Reichstag first learned about it in the newspapers.

In short, prospects for a successful reign were very bright indeed for Wilhelm II. On that day in June 1888 the man and the moment seemed to have met. Past history and present circumstance both smiled upon him. He had inherited a religious and intellectual tradition congenial to autocracy; constitutional and non-constitutional practices endorsed his claims; dominant social classes and the broad masses alike hailed him and wished him well. He had no competitor for political power, and his cocky and confident temperament reflected the flamboyant temper of the times.

Seldom has an aspiring young ruler been given such a splendid opportunity to play the starring role he had always wanted. Later in this chapter we will evaluate his performance.

Hitler's Ideology

The history of National Socialist ideology ... from beginning to end, is the history of its underestimation.[30]

Karl Dietrich Bracher

Wilhelm von Hohenzollern was 'to the purple born.' Adolf Hitler clawed and connived his way to power through flophouses, back alleys, and beer halls. Nor had he inherited a theory of government. He contrived one that was tailored to himself. Unlike royal absolutism in the totality of its claim over the lives of people, Nazism was unlike other dictatorships of the twentieth century in its commitment to racial supremacy and to the personal power of a specific Leader.

Any political theory is determined by the theorist's view of human nature. John Locke and Thomas Jefferson believed that self-government was possible because they believed that people are fundamentally decent and essentially rational. Hitler viewed mankind very differently. At bottom, people are treacherous, irrational, base, and stupid. This 'great stupid mutton-herd of our sheeplike people,' he said, are 'as stupid as they are forgetful'; they are 'weak and bestial'; 'they long to yield to a man of steel-hard will.'[31] Upon such convictions is tyranny constructed.

From Hitler's view of human nature emerged an ideology of five essential components. The first of these was a distinctive doctrine about political leadership: the *Führerprinzip*. Two portraits dominated the entrance hall of the Nazi party headquarters in Munich. One was of Hitler's personal hero, Frederick the Great; the other was of himself. The caption under his picture expressed the essence of the *Führerprinzip* and set forth his political ideal: 'Nothing happens in this Movement, except what I desire.' A respected historian concurs: 'There was and there is no National Socialism without Hitler. The two are identical ... everything else is simply a misunderstanding.'[32]

After the death of President von Hindenburg in 1934, Hitler abolished the democratic title of president and styled himself 'Führer and Chancellor of the Third Reich.' In 1939 he dropped the 'and Chancellor,' pointing out that there might conceivably be another chancellor someday, but no one else could ever be Führer. The constitutional power of the new title was set forth succinctly in an official legal journal: 'The character of the Reich is determined solely by the Führer in accord with racial principles as determined by the Führer.'[33]

Hitler's concept of leadership placed his political theory on a different plane from that of any other authoritarian system. The theory of royal absolutism was based not upon the personality of the incumbent but upon the *institution* of monarchy. The cry 'The King is Dead, long live the King!' expressed a conception impossible among the Nazis. Adolf Hitler, and only Adolf Hitler, could be the Führer. Mussolini also styled himself 'Leader' *Duce*. But Mussolini was dependent to the end for his position on the Grand Council of Fascism. It had appointed him and it would depose him. No council ever deposed Adolf Hitler. Joseph Stalin, it is certainly true, exerted enormous personal power. But he was really not supposed to, and Marxist theorists decried his regime for fostering a heretical 'cult of personality.' That is a crucial difference: Nazism was nothing without the cult of Hitler's personality.

Rudolf Hess expressed the concept in two impassioned sentences at the gigantic Nuremberg rally of 1934:

Die Partei ist Adolf Hitler, Hitler ist die Partei!
Das Volk ist Hitler! Hitler ist das deutsche Volk!

The intimate association, the emotional bonding, of Führer and *Volk* was a constant theme of Nazi writers, who insisted that Führership required a 'Followship' (*Gefolgschaft*). Neither was imaginable without the other: no Führer without Followship, no Followship without the Führer. As one Nazi enthusiast put it, 'The highest law of community is discipline expressed through the concept *"Führer–Gefolgschaft."*'[34] Hitler's ability to exploit that relationship was a key to his success as a political leader.

The *Führerprinzip* was never clearly articulated by Nazi writers. It was not possible to do so, for ultimately it was a mystery. Unable to discuss it rationally, devout Nazis resorted to mysticism and bad metaphysics. Alfred Rosenberg, for instance, assured his readers that 'the Führer is the ultimate essence of *völkisch* Being' – a concept that might as well have been rendered, 'The Führer is the Ultimate Whichness and the Whole Works.'

The Führer himself spoke only obliquely about the concept, preferring to say what he considered himself not to be: 'I am not the Head of State in the sense of being either a dictator or a monarch. I am the Führer of the German people. I could have given to myself ... other titles.' On the night of 3–4 January 1942 he told his entourage: 'There is no finer title than that of Führer ... As for the expression, "My Führer," I imagine it was born in the mouths of women.'[35]

Hitler's idea of leadership differed from that of Italian or Spanish Fascism. Mussolini as *Duce* and Franco as *Caudillo* were the leaders of the state, but the German *Führer* claimed to be a great deal more than that. Indeed, any writer in the Third Reich who attempted to limit the *Führerprinzip* to the concept of a political ruler was in danger of being called a Fascist, a pejorative term in Nazi Germany. To stress the ineffable power of the Führer as leader of a spiritual movement, Hitler and those theorists who understood him properly advanced a theory that went far beyond what was called the 'static, impersonal state.'[36]

On an even more rarefied level, the Führer was a mystical and magnetic force drawing together Volk and State. He was the *Volksgeist* made incarnate: 'The essential link which in the National Socialist theory of the state unites the people with the Führer is a mystical conception ... He is no representative to whom the people have given a mandate; he is the incarnation of the Spirit of the People (*Volkgeist*) and it is only through his interpretation that the Volk is led to a full realization of itself.'

This extraordinary statement, as Alan Bullock remarked in quoting the passage, is 'a faithful summary, not of Nazi propaganda, but of sober constitutional and legal opinion as it was expressed in the standard texbooks of the Third Reich.'[37] Hans Frank, Germany's leading judicial official, provided a summary: 'Our constitution is the will of the Führer.'[38]

As the 'incarnation of the spirit of the people,' the Führer was a myth. Like all powerful myths, he embodied in a variety of images a cluster of ideas and attitudes. These images, reappearing in poetry, painting, prayer, and song, all gloried him as Leader, Father, and Saviour.

The Führer-image was not, however, merely a myth that Hitler imposed on the people. As J.P. Stern has noted, this myth was also a creation of the masses.[39] Image-building was a reciprocal process. Hitler invented himself as the long-awaited myth/ hero, the Messiah sent from God to save his people. His followers in turn created their own image of him and yearned for it to become a reality.

Their myth involved a number of contradictory images. Hitler was imaged as a benign father-figure who loved little children, yet he was also seen as 'brutal' – a word of praise in the Nazi lexicon. Thus, the Führer was described as a man of 'brutal determination' who was, when necessary, 'brutally inconsiderate,' 'brutally tough,' and a 'brutal seeker of the truth (*brutaler Wahrheitssucher*).'[40] At other times Hitler was seen as a lonely man of simple tastes, modest in his lifestyle, whose homely virtues made him 'one of us.' But at the same time he was the remote and infallible Leader, an aloof genius carrying his crushing burdens alone and working selflessly for the welfare of his people.

The popular press substantiated and embellished the myth of a hero sent from God to lead his people to new glories. Adulation reached some sort of apogee in 1941 after victories over France and the Low Countries: 'The Führer is the highest synthesis of his race ... He embodies the universalism of Goethe, the depth of Kant, the dynamism of Hegel, the genius of Frederick II, the realism of Bismarck, as well as the tumultuous inspiration of Wagner, the perspicacity of Spengler. He embodies the inspiration of Tannenberg and the dash of *Sturm und Drang*.'[41]

There was an obvious political advantage in an ideology of such personal exaltation. But there was also a frightful risk: Hitler had condemned himself to infallibility.

The second component of Hitler's ideology was exaltation of force. The commitment was proclaimed in dozens of speeches during the 1920s. In Chemnitz, 2 April 1928: 'The first fundamental of any *Weltanschauung* is the fact that in the universe force alone is decisive. Whatever goal man has reached is due to his originality plus his brutality.' In Munich on 21 November 1927: 'Man is the most brutal creature on earth. He knows nothing but the extermination of his enemies.'[42] In trumpeting this message, Hitler gave the German people a clear picture of the kind of government they could expect from him. Seldom has a person aspiring to public office been so explicit in his purposes and so open in his promises. From the beginning, Hitler promised war, as he did in Munich as early as 1928 and 1929: 'There is no distinction between war and peace ... One is either a free lord or a slave ... The battlefield is the final test of the foreign policy of a people.' To Adolf Hitler there was something deeply personal about conflict. Exaltation of war was more than rhetorical bombast, as it had been with the Kaiser. For Hitler war was a personal necessity. Hitler needed war in a quite literal sense. He had always needed war: 'I did not establish the Wehrmacht in order not to strike,' he said, 'The decision to strike was always within me (*war immer in mir*).'[43]

Hitler's racial theory, the third component of his ideology, was the bedrock upon which all else depended. Battle and conflict were important to him, but the most decisive struggle of all history was racial; the *Führerprinzip* was crucial, but the mission of this leader was prescribed for him, namely, to establish a 'racially pure' society.

Hitler was so preposterous when he spoke about race that he was never fully believed by his sensible critics. Yet he meant precisely what he said. In dozens of appallingly sincere statements he promised the German people that he intended to build a New Order based upon racial persecution and genocide. He kept that promise.

It is a simple matter to set forth his racial theory; it is not so easy, however, to convey its importance to him as a person or to his government, where it took on the dimension of a historic force. We must listen to Hitler and take his metaphors seriously: 'The race question furnishes the key not only to world history, but also to human culture'; mixture of the blood was *the* Original Sin; 'people do not perish by lost wars, but by the loss of that force which is contained only in the pure blood.' In a messy metaphor Hitler asserted that 'blood is the cement of civilization.'[44]

Unlike other German political theorists who joined Hegel in exalting the state as 'the institutionalization of God on earth,' Hitler considered political forms of secondary importance: 'The state is a means to an end. Its end is the preservation of the blood and the promotion of the [racial] community.'

He was impatient with those who stressed the importance of either economic or political revolutions: 'There is absolutely no other revolution but a racial revolution. There is no economic, no political, no social revolution. There is only the struggle of lower races against the dominant, higher races.'

Art, too, is racial. To those who talked about the international character of art, or even of national art, Hitler replied, 'Everything you say only proves that you have no understanding of art. There is in art absolutely no such thing as modern art or ancient art ... Dutch art, Italian art ... There is absolutely only one [true] art, namely Greco-Nordic Art.'[45]

There has been only one creative race in all history: 'The Aryans, manifestly the bearers of all culture, the true representatives of all humanity ... Take away the Nordic Germans and nothing remains but the dance of apes.'[46]

As there was only one creative people, so there had to be, in Hitler's disjunctive way of thinking, one completely decadent and destructive race: the Jews. It is both symbolically and actually true that his political career began and ended with a warning against the 'Jewish Peril,' which he was convinced threatened all civilization.

In a letter dated 16 September 1919, which may have been the first piece of political writing in his career, Hitler stated his goal as 'ruthless intervention' against the Jews and their 'removal' from Europe. In this significant statement, Hitler was careful to emphasize that his commitment to anti-Semitism was not based on sentiment, but on cold intellectual analysis: 'Anti-Semitism based on purely emotional grounds will always find its ultimate expression in the form of progroms [sic]. A rational anti-Semitism, however, must lead to the systematic legal fight ... Its ultimate goal must unalterably be the elimination (*Ausmerzung*) of the Jews altogether.'[47]

At the end of his career, when he dictated his political testament to the German people, the last word of the last sentence of his last order should be noted: 'Above all else I charge the leaders of this nation ... to a scrupulous maintenance of the racial laws and to the merciless opposition to the universal poisoner of all nations, international Jewry.'[48]

Hitler meant what he said about the Jews; he had meant it all along.[49] Rarely in history has a theory of a government been so ruthlessly consistent with its practices; never have ideas been more fully implemented in action. The hell of Hitler's Germany was this: it put into practice what its Führer preached. If he sometimes adapted his ideas to fit circumstances, more often he adapted circumstances to fit his ideas.

Hitler's ideas about race determined the laws, art, education, and wage scales of the Third Reich. They determined that physics in the universities was to be taught without Einstein, psychology without Freud, and that Mendelssohn could not be heard in concert. They decided whether millions of people would live or die.

An adjunct to his racial theory was his idea of *Volksgemeinschaft*, a community of the racially pure. The word itself is freighted with menace, for by adding the adjective 'racial' (*Volks*) to 'community' (*Gemeinschaft*) Hitler was applying crude Darwinian biology to politics. In doing so, he could count on the support of the established German scientific and academic communities along with welfare associations, for they too wanted to find biological solutions to social problems – including a Final Solution to racial problems.[50] The Holocaust was inherent in the concept of *Volksgemeinschaft*.

A fourth ingredient of his ideology was the concept of *Lebensraum* (livingspace). All his life Adolf Hitler had been fascinated by space. He loved to shape and control it in colossal domed and long-columned buildings; he wanted to bind it together by superhighways and gigantic canals; he liked to travel through it in his open, super-charged Mercedes. The vast spaces of eastern Europe constantly beckoned him.

Since the Führer's personal feelings often became public policy, demand for *Lebensraum* was an integral part of Nazi ideology and a guiding principle in military planning. That Germany's destiny lay in the East and that its pursuit would mean war with Russia was a promise made as early as *Mein Kampf* and later repeated in many public and private speeches:

We terminate the endless German drive to the South and West of Europe and direct our gaze towards the land of the East. We finally terminate the colonial and trade policy of the pre-war period and proceed to the territorial policy of the future. But if we talk about new soil and territory in Europe today we can think primarily only of *Russia* and its vassal border states.[51]

The Führer's long dreams of *Lebensraum* in the East seemed about to be fulfilled during the first months of the war he had unleashed against the Soviet Union in June 1941. Again and again, in his nocturnal monologues at headquarters, Hitler talked excitedly about 'the grandeur of the open spaces' and planned how he would settle thousands of square kilometres of land. To those who asked if it would be sufficient to set his frontier at the Urals, he replied, 'For the present it is enough.'

The Führer's vision went far beyond that. He dreamed of vast spaces connected by superhighways stretching to the Crimea ('our Riviera') and the Caucasus. He saw the Danube, the river of his boyhood, as 'the river of the future.' It would be connected by an enormous system of canals from the Moselle, Rhine, and the Main to the Dniester, Dnieper, and Don to the Black Sea. The highways and canals 'will be studded along their whole length with German towns and around these towns our colonists will settle.' Germans would live grandly 'in marvelous buildings and palaces' and in 'handsome, spacious farms.'

Hitler left no doubt what would happen to the local population: 'The ridiculous hundred million Slavs' would live in 'pigpens' without vaccination or 'hygienic cleanliness.' They might be taught enough to read German road signs, but anyone who 'talks about cherishing the local inhabitant and civilizing him ... goes straight off to a concentration camp.'[52]

Two parts of his ideology, anti-Semitism and *Lebensraum* to the east, combined to form the driving force behind Hitler's invasion of Russia.[53] In his mind the Soviet Union was at once the 'spawning ground of the Jewish–Bolshevist world conspiracy' and the master of all the 'living space in the east.' He needed to solve both problems before he could establish his racially pure 'Greater Reich of the German Nation.'

Hitler's ideology becomes more comprehensible when it is seen – as Hitler intended it to be seen – as a religion, a fifth component. From the beginning of his political career, Hitler believed that the German masses hungered and thirsted after a new faith, a new religion. He would supply their need. As early as 1922, he said that he would 'give to the seeking and erring masses a new faith that will not abandon them in time of confusion – a faith upon which they can dedicate their lives.'[54]

Two years later in *Mein Kampf* he wrote, 'I consider those who establish or destroy a religion much greater than those who establish a state.'[55] Again, in the 1930s, he told his disciples that National Socialism was not a political party, and it was not 'merely a movement; *we are a religion.*'[56]

There was a very good reason why Nazi ceremonies reminded observers of religious worship. They were designed that way. The number of times religious expressions appeared in Hitler's speeches and in Nazi publications is revealing. These words occurred with particular frequency: 'resurrection,' 'eternal,' 'miracle,' 'piety,' 'dogma,' 'trinity,' 'revelation,' 'creed,' and 'faith.'[57] And the greatest of these was faith. Time and again Hitler emphasized the primacy of faith (*Glaube*) over reason, of creed (*Bekenntnis*) over cognition (*Erkenntnis*); and he stressed that the political faith he had in mind demanded 'fanatical devotion (*fanatische Hingabe*).' A speech of 1927 was typical: 'Only faith creates a state. What motivates people to go and to battle and to die is religion. Not reasoning but blind faith.'[58]

Like the Catholic Church, Hitler preached a doctrine of faith *and* works, action as well as faith: 'True and vigorous faith cannot exist in the abstract, it reaches its fulfilment only in the deed. The deed is the only true witness to faith: *faith–movement–action!* ... These are the three words that determine for us the natural path of human piety.'[59] In one of the most revealing of all his speeches, Hitler said that his personal will must become the faith of the nation.[60]

Other religions have their holy cities of Mecca or Jerusalem or Rome. As Hitler pointed out, 'We have Munich, the holy city of National Socialism ... the Bethlehem of our Movement.' For there Nazism was born, there the 'martyrs' of the Beer Hall Putsch were buried. The annual re-enactment of Hitler's march down the Rosenheimlandstrasse, over the Ludwigsbrücke, through the Isartor into the Tal, and north to the Odeonsplatz, with a long pause at the Feldherrnhalle, became 'a re-enactment of the Stations of the Cross and the Passion Play.'[61] The ceremony reached its climax when each of the SA standards was brought forward to touch the 'sacred blood flag' and be blessed by the Führer. Only he, as the high priest of the movement, could perform that rite.

German schoolchildren were encouraged to see parallels between Jesus and Hitler and to accept the Führer as their 'saviour' and 'redeemer' (*Erlöser/ Retter*). On 16 March 1934 they were given the following dictation to copy into their exercise books:

Jesus and Hitler

As Jesus freed people from sin and hell, so Hitler freed the German people from destruction. Jesus and Hitler were both persecuted, but while Jesus was crucified, Hitler was raised up to be Chancellor. Whereas youth denied Jesus and left him in the lurch, sixteen comrades died for their Führer ... Jesus strove for Heaven; Hitler strives for the German earth.[62]

The Nazis found a saviour (the Führer) and created a devil (the Jew). The idea was made graphic for little children on the roadside signs that appeared in rural Bavaria not far from traditional Christian shrines:

Wer den Jude kennt,
Kennt den Teufel.

(Who knows the Jew
Knows the Devil.)

As the symbol of his religion, Hitler chose a form of cross, the *Hakenkreuz*. The holy writ was *Mein Kampf* (My Battle), which replaced the Bible on the coffee-tables and glass-fronted bookcases in German parlours – and was probably read as infrequently. Instead of blessing young married couples with copies of the New Testament, party officials considered it appropriate to bestow *Mein Kampf* upon newly-weds. The Nazis had little sense of irony. (The copy before me as I write is inscribed, 'To the young married couple with the blessings and best wishes for a happy life in the racial community from the Bürgermeister of Gmund. *Heil Hitler!'*)

In reminiscing about the influences that had shaped his thinking, Hitler once said that he had learned a great deal from the Catholic Church, from the (bogus) 'Protocols of the Elders of Zion,' and from the Bolshevists. But, 'Above all, I have learned from the Jesuit Order.' The SS were required to study Loyola's *Spiritual Exercises* as a training manual for 'spiritual discipline.'[63] Just as the Jesuits took a special oath of obedience directly to the Pope, members of the SS swore a special oath to the Führer. They alone wore on their belt buckles the sacred runic symbols (⚡⚡) encircled by the slogan composed by the Führer: *Meine Ehre heisst Treue* (Loyalty is my honour).

Nazi holidays were designed to replace traditional Christian rites. Initiation into the Hitler Youth, for example, took the place of confirmation and served the same function in the new religion. The ceremony, performed on the Führer's birthday (20 April), also replaced Whitsun (Pentecost) in the Christian calendar, traditionally the day the Christian Church was founded. The oath-taking on the

Nazis' 'sacred occasion' is best described by a contemporary newspaper: 'Yesterday witnessed the profession of the Religion of the Blood in all its imposing reality. Yesterday saw the triumphant ... beginning of our fight to make National Socialism the only racial religion of the German people.'[64]

Other religious services were designed as substitutes for Christian rites of baptism, marriage, and burial. A serious – but unsuccessful – effort was made to replace Christmas with a Nazi Yuletide. The ceremony was concluded with a re-dedication to 'Our Führer, Adolf Hitler. *Sieg Heil.*' New words were composed for the Germans' favorite Christmas carol:

> Silent night! Holy night!
> All is calm, all is bright
> Only the Führer, steadfast in fight,
> Watches o'er Germany by day and by night
> Always caring for us.

> Silent night! Holy night!
> All is calm, all is bright,
> Adolf Hitler is Germany's wealth
> Brings us greatness, favour and health
> Oh, give us Germans all power![65]

In another version, the carol ends, 'Hitler our Führer is here! Hitler our Führer is here!' – a revision of the original words, *Christus der Retter ist da!* (Christ the Saviour is here!)

The idea of replacing Christianity with the religion of Nazism was given explicit statement in the words of another song:

New Song of the Hitler Youth .

> We are the merry Hitler Youth
> We need no so-called Christian truth
> For our Führer Adolf Hitler
> Is sufficient Intercessor.

> No priest or any other schemer
> Can stop us hailing our Redeemer
> Away with incense and sacred vessel
> We need no Christ, we have Horst Wessel!

> I am no Christian, no Catholic
> I follow the SA through thin and thick

You can take away your Church
The Swastika blesses us on earth.[66]

Hitler also expressed his religious purposes in stone and reinforced concrete. His architect, Albert Speer, in an interview after his release from prison, said that many of the buildings he helped Hitler design simply made no sense unless they were seen as religious edifices. In describing the monstrous Assembly Hall, for example, with its dome eight times the mass of St Peter's, Speer noted that basically it was a hall of worship whose purpose 'would have been unintelligible' if one were not aware of its religious significance to Hitler.[67]

At the start of his career, Hitler saw himself as a religious leader, and he did so towards its close. In his air-raid shelter in Berlin he mused about quitting politics and taking on a purely religious role: 'I'm going to become a religious figure. Soon I'll be the great chief of the Tartars. Already Arabs and Moroccans are mingling my name [with Allah] in their prayers. Among the Tartars I shall become Khan. The only thing of which I shall be incapable is to share the sheiks' mutton.'[68]

PART II: THE POLITICAL PERFORMANCE OF THE KAISER

Germany is the economically most prosperous, the best administered, and the worst governed country in Europe.

Friedrich Stampfer, ca. 1910

Rather than sketching a general survey of the political history of the Second and Third Reichs,[69] in this chapter, I shall select a few key events to illustrate the strengths and weaknesses of the Kaiser and the Führer as peacetime rulers. The role each ruler played in the two world wars that shaped the history of the twentieth century will be discussed in the next chapter.

Wilhelm II's political performance as ruler of Germany from 1888 to 1918 was erratic in the extreme. Like the little girl with a curl, when he was good he was extraordinarily good; when he was bad, he was appalling.

The Kaiser displayed impressive political skill in handling the dismissal of Bismarck and in building the Imperial German Navy. His initial plans for dealing with problems of German labour were promising, but he then reversed himself and undermined his own program. He showed sound political judgment in rejecting the idea of a royal coup, but monumental political stupidity in interviews he gave to English and American journalists. He had a prodigious talent for defeating his own political objectives by alienating the very people who could have helped him attain them.

The Kaiser and German Labour

I will become known as 'King of the Destitute.'

Wilhelm II, 1890

Wilhelm's first encounter with labour unrest and the rise of Marxian socialism put him on a collision course with his great chancellor, Otto von Bismarck. Prior to Wilhelm's accession, Bismarck had sought to solve the 'socialist problem' by a twofold attack. On the one hand, he inaugurated widespread social reforms in the 1880s that were intended 'to kill socialism with kindness.' On the other, he struck with an iron fist by authorizing legislation designed to destroy the Social Democratic party. Neither tactic was successful. Socialism continued to grow; during his administration it became the most potent political movement in Germany.

The issue was brought to a head in 'the Great Strike' of May 1889, when Germany experienced the largest work stoppage in its history. Starting in the Ruhr, the strike spread 'like a tidal wave'[70] through the Saar to Saxony and Silesia, as determined workers demanded higher wages and better work conditions. Chancellor Bismarck, who had become disillusioned with his efforts to placate workers and undermine socialism, advised Wilhelm to goad the strikers to violence and then smash them with military force.

The young Kaiser refused. Anxious to gain personal glory by achieving industrial peace, and eager to show the concern for the poor that he had learned from his boyhood tutor Georg Hinzpeter, Wilhelm resolved to show Bismarck, and everyone else, how to win the workers away from 'the twin evils of socialism and anarchism.' He set forth a program for workers in two remarkably far-sighted and sensible memoranda of 21 and 22 January 1890, 'Observations on Workers' Problems' and 'Proposals for Improving the Conditions of Workers.'[71] These memoranda should give pause to those who would dismiss Wilhelm as a political incompetent and buffoon.

The Kaiser prefaced his proposals with a wise admonition: 'When justifiable demands [of workers] are not considered, they quickly grow into extremism and immoderation and become unjustifiable under the influence of anarchists and socialists.' He then wrote the following and underlined it: '*Almost all revolutions in history can be traced back to the fact that timely reforms were denied by the government.*'

Wilhelm II's memoranda demonstrated his understanding of workers' complaints. Sunday labour should be prohibited except in emergencies. Night work
was 'unconditionally prohibited' for women and children. Women should not
work during the last three weeks of pregnancy and the first three weeks after
childbirth. Child labour should be strictly limited. The Kaiser also proposed an
international conference on labour, which he would chair, to establish fair practices among all workers of the world.[72]

He followed his own memoranda by calling a meeting of the Crown Council
on 24 January to discuss and implement his proposals. He emphasized that
workers should be encouraged to believe 'they are not being used as machines'
and that their relationship to their employees should be one of 'collegiality.'
Revolutions, he warned again, are born when governments fail to make timely
and reasonable concessions. Inaction and repression would invite the spread of
socialism. He then listed the reforms he had set forth in his memoranda of 22
and 23 January, adding that model worker communities with savings banks,
churches, schools and hospitals should be constructed. 'I want to be known,'
the Kaiser concluded broadly, as *'le roi des queux* (king of the destitute).'

Unfortunately, Wilhelm's enthusiasm on behalf of 'the lower classes' spent
itself on memoranda and speeches. He soon became embittered by the workers'
'rank ingratitude' and by their refusal to be reconciled to the 'proper position
within the social fabric' to which he had assigned them. They kept pressing
their demands and they joined the Marxist party in droves. In the Reichstag
elections of February 1890 they increased their membership by a full 87 per
cent.[73]

The Kaiser liked quick fixes and he simply could not understand why his
admirable intentions, eloquent orations, and radiant memoranda had not solved
the social problems of Germany and stopped socialism in its tracks. He became
increasingly alarmed by the 'Anarchist–Socialist Peril' that seemed rampant
throughout the world. Anarchist bombs had been thrown at government officials in Italy and France; socialist demonstrations had taken place in Prague; the
mayor of Chicago had been murdered.

Convinced that his own throne was in danger, the Kaiser now endorsed the
very proposals he had so recently condemned, by sending to the Reichstag draconian legislation that would 'wipe out socialism once and for all.' Neither the
Reichstag nor the public shared his visceral fear of 'Socialist Peril,' and the legislation was roundly defeated. Wilhelm was furious. 'We are now left,' he blus-
tered, 'with fire hoses for ordinary situations and cartridges as a final resort.'[74]

Wilhelm continued to misjudge the socialists, alternately gazing into a
clouded crystal ball to reassure the German people that socialism was merely 'a
passing fad' that would soon die out[75] and then seeing it as an imminent threat

to his crown. He was unable to perceive the political advantage of cultivating the vast majority of moderate socialists who were loyal to the monarchy so as to split them off from the few radicals who wanted to overthrow it. Instead, Wilhelm seemed bent on uniting all socialists in opposition by proclaiming contentiously that all of them were 'traitors' and 'unworthy of bearing the name of German.' Socialism, in all its forms, must be 'completely rooted out of Germany (*ausgerottet werden bis auf den letzten Stumpf*).'[76] Speeches such as these prompted the socialist leader August Bebel to remark with high irony, 'Every time the Kaiser speaks, he wins 100,000 votes for us.'[77]

After a promising start, Wilhelm abandoned his glowing expectation of solving the problems of German labour.

Dismissal of Bismarck, 1890

The Kaiser will be his own Chancellor one day.

Otto von Bismarck

Almost any monarch would have had difficulty accommodating himself to the imperious and formidable Iron Chancellor. The ambitious and self-assertive young Kaiser found him intolerable. Yet there were grave political risks in ridding himself of this paragon who was rapidly becoming a national monument. Wilhelm's decision to fire him was accelerated by a humiliating confrontation with Bismarck after stepping into one of the wily chancellor's carefully laid traps.

Wilhelm, who aspired to conduct his own diplomacy, had planned a trip to the court of Alexander III of Russia (1881–94), whom he thought he could charm into a special alliance. Bismarck, who was jealous of his reputation as the most astute diplomat in Europe and resented any intrusion onto his turf, said slyly that he possessed private information indicating that Wilhelm's visit was ill-advised. As Bismarck expected, the Kaiser demanded to see the evidence. Feigning reluctance, Bismarck handed him a personal letter from the Tsar. Wilhelm's face turned red, then white with anger, as he read what Tsar Alexander had written about him: '*C'est un garçon mal élevé et de mauvaise foi. Il est fou*' (He is a badly raised young fellow and can't be trusted. He is crazy). Wilhelm slammed out of the room, suspecting, with good reason, that his chancellor had used the Tsar's letter as bait in a trap designed to humiliate him.[78] He was determined to avenge the insult. But the way he did it was not one of the rash, ill-considered actions of which he was all too capable. This time Wilhelm waited for a propitious moment, prepared the political ground carefully, and moved decisively.

By the early spring of 1890 Wilhelm sensed that the old man was losing political influence. In this instance, the Kaiser judged public opinion aright. Germans admired Bismarck as a historic hero, but felt increasingly that the vigorous young monarch rather than the aging chancellor was more in tune with the new and stirring times. An editorial in *Die Badische Presse* of 4 October 1889 clearly reflected this attitude, praising Prince Bismarck as 'the greatest statesman of the century,' but noted that 'the youthful Reich [now] has the good fortune to have a Kaiser who wants to be his own chancellor' and concluded, 'Kaiser Wilhelm II ... with his youth and energy is "the right man in the right place" for the new Reich.'[79]

For years Bismarck's imperious ways had alienated important government officials. As he grew older and his physical sufferings increased, the old man became increasingly irascible. Anyone who disagreed with him might suffer ugly defamation of character, imprisonment on charges of high treason, and the destruction of his career. The chancellor's leading biographer has concluded that by the ferocity of his personal attacks, 'Bismarck drove a nail into his own political coffin.'[80]

The Kaiser skilfully cultivated the Prince's enlarging group of opponents. On this occasion he curried the favour of the imperial princes and wooed the Council of State 'brilliantly,' as even Holstein – who would later oppose him – admitted.[81] Wilhelm was especially solicitous with the ministers and state secretaries of Prussia, subtly reminding them of their personal grievances against Bismarck and turning on his vaunted charm while entertaining them individually at splendid dinners. His solicitude paid off. With the exception of his son Herbert, no one raised his voice or a finger to keep Bismarck in office.[82]

Having been manoeuvred into an untenable position, Prince Bismarck on 18 March 1890 reluctantly signed a letter of resignation. The Kaiser's response was masterful. 'My dear Prince!' he began, 'It is with the deepest emotion that I see from your request of 18 March that you have decided to resign from the positions you have occupied for so many years with incomparable success.' He had hoped, the Kaiser continued, to have a long relationship, but he now realized 'with troubled heart' that the great man's 'wish' was irreversible. In an effort to cut off future criticism from the man he was firing, Wilhelm expressed his hope that Bismarck's 'counsel and prowess, your faithfulness and dedication would always remain available to me and to the Fatherland.' Rehearsing again the prince's imperishable achievements for Prussia, Germany, and the Hohenzollern dynasty, he closed by promoting Bismarck to the rank of field marshal in the Prussian Army and bestowing on him the title of 'Duke of Lauenburg.' As a final touch, Wilhelm promised to send Bismarck a 'life-size portrait' of himself.[83]

Thus did the young Kaiser outmanoeuvre the old chancellor, who left Berlin, trailing a cellar of 13,000 bottles of fine wines and cognacs[84] into disgruntled retirement on his estate at Friedrichsruhe. From there he wrote self-serving memoirs and gave interviews that kept up a sustained barrage of criticism aimed directly at his successors and indirectly at the Kaiser's policies. The man who had spent his last weeks in office plotting a coup that would have gutted parliament, now with righteous indignation accused Wilhelm's government of opposing democratic processes.[85]

But the wizard's spell had been temporarily broken.[86] Wilhelm had triumphed. The way now seemed open for his own 'personal regime.'

The Kaiser and Naval Legislation

Germany's future lies on the waters.

Wilhelm II

The Kaiser's handling of the naval bills of 1898 and 1900 also demonstrated impressive political skill as he mobilized public opinion to achieve a political objective. For Wilhelm, however, a powerful navy was more than a political goal; it was a historic mission to which all else, even the army, was subordinate. His most cherished childhood memory, he later recalled, was of standing on the eastern cliffs of the Isle of Wight watching great British warships steam past majestically. At that moment he promised himself that one day he would have even bigger and faster ships.

The boy's daydreams became the man's obsession. His favourite outfit as a child had been an authentic little sailor suit given him by his grandmother; his favourite uniform as Kaiser was that of an Admiral of the Fleet in the Royal Navy, another gift from Queen Victoria. And as a child his favourite hobby had been sketching warships. In later years the Kaiser designed and painted them in water-colours,[87] and his favourite diversion was plowing through the North Sea in command of his own ship. In contrast to Hitler, who was terrified by water, Wilhelm was in his element when at sea. He revelled in storms and, on at least one occasion, had himself lashed to the mast so that he could howl defiance in the teeth of a booming gale.

Wilhelm realized that his plans for a huge navy would require broad popular support. In the summer of 1897 he made the most successful appointment of his career in choosing as state secretary of the Imperial Naval Office the extraordinarily dedicated, energetic, and imaginative Alfred Tirpitz. Together these two men plotted a political campaign to win Reichstag approval for the naval bills of 1898, 1900, and subsequent years.[88]

Their immediate objective was to achieve what the Kaiser called 'a spiritual mobilization' of the masses. On a scale previously unknown in Germany, Wilhelm's government shaped the political attitudes of the man in the street. The Kaiser seemed to be adjusting himself to the age of mass politics and forging an alliance between monarchy and popular nationalism.[89]

To gain national support, the Kaiser encouraged (although that was scarcely needed) the effusions of such patriotic societies as the Pan-German League, the Naval League (which he had helped establish), and the Society for the Expansion of Germanism Abroad. His own fervent speeches throughout the Reich stirred visions of German power expanding over the surface of the globe, visions that only a mighty navy could carry out. He personally campaigned to have branches of the Naval League established throughout Germany. So great was the enthusiasm that in land-locked Bavaria alone, the league collected 273,000 signatures supporting the navy and sent them to the Reichstag before it voted on the naval bill of 1898.[90]

Wilhelm and Tirpitz also turned to the popular press 'to educate the masses to the urgent need for a powerful Navy,' inundating the Reich with thousands of brochures and pamphlets. One typical broadside, numbering five million copies, was entitled 'Why Each One of Us Needs a Strong German Navy.' Prefabricated newspaper stories were sent out to home-town newspapers all over Germany, and patriotic professors were enlisted to beat the drums of nationalism and naval power.[91]

To arouse the population further, and to put more pressure on the Reichstag representatives before voting on the comprehensive naval bill of 1900, the Kaiser dispatched a 'torpedo fleet' up the Rhine River. These small boats, decked out in the national colours along with flags of the local states, stopped at all ports on the Rhine in Prussia, Hesse, Bavaria, and Baden. Brass bands playing *Die Wacht am Rhein, Deutschland über Alles,* and other patriotic tunes greeted them at each stop. The Kaiser had sent preparatory telegrams to his fellow sovereigns in each state and personally congratulated the rulers and officials when they cooperated in welcoming his little flotilla. 'It is no wonder,' a contemporary observed, 'that the Reichstag made record time in adopting this most important bill, which that body did on 12 June 1900.'[92]

The Kaiser's campaign for naval legislation was setting an important precedent. It has been called 'the starting point of the modern era of propaganda ... through which the masses, by comprehensive and ceaseless state intervention, are mobilized and fanaticized in support and legitimization of governmental policy.'[93]

Wilhelm was the primary force behind the *Marineschwärmerei* (naval craze or naval mania) that swept imperial Germany at the turn of the century, but, like all crazes, it was emotionally fed and sustained from below. The naval program was a smashing success because it responded to emotional needs for prestige, power, glory, and grandeur that the Kaiser shared with his people.[94]

After passing the naval bill of 1900 Wilhelm invited members of the Reichstag, including deputies of opposition parties, to an enormous banquet. Gracious and charming, he raised his glass to the president of the Reichstag, handed out autographed photographs of himself, spoke individually to deputies, and showered everyone with extravagant praise. He gloried in their roaring response: *'Hoch der Kaiser!'* For Wilhelm it was a shining hour.[95]

Wilhelm and a 'Royal Coup d'état,' 1913

It is not our practice in Germany to govern by *coups.*

Wilhelm II

Wilhelm also demonstrated political skill in responding to the threat of a military-rightist *coup d'état* in 1913. Throughout the 1880s right-wing circles in the Conservative party, along with members of the army, patriotic societies, and veterans' groups, had viewed with increasing alarm the steady growth of 'socialism–anarchism' which they perceived as a direct and ominous threat to their establishment. The idea of crushing socialism and establishing a monarchy unfettered by parliament 'was widespread and persistent' throughout the period.[96]

By the late 1880s Bismarck himself had become so alarmed by the rise of socialism and anarchism that he was prepared to overthrow his own constitutional creation of 1871. He joined the extreme right in urging the new Kaiser to approve a coup 'from above.' The plan was to take such stringent action against the socialists that they would be driven to violent reaction; the ensuing chaos would then be used to justify calling in the army to restore law and order and crush the socialists. The Reichstag would be dissolved and a new constitution written which would, in effect, establish a royal dictatorship.[97]

The moderates – if that is the word – advised Wilhelm against participating in a coup. Instead, they urged a 'successful war' to divert attention from domestic unrest and to rally the people behind their monarch against dangerous democratic tendencies.

Among Pan-German zealots, however, enthusiasm for a 'coup from above' did not abate. In 1913 they prepared a memorandum setting forth a program the Kaiser should follow including military seizure of government, the replacement of Chancellor Bethmann Hollweg with a militant nationalist of their choice, closing down opposition newspapers, and using the press to propagate their ultranationalist ideas. They also called for confiscating Jewish property and driving the Jews out of Germany. The crown prince, always a backer of far-right causes,[98] enthusiastically endorsed these plans and sent them to his father with a covering note urging him to adopt them.

Wilhelm answered his son in a blistering letter. Government by coups, the Kaiser wrote scathingly, 'might be acceptable in Latin America but is *not*, thank God, our practice in Germany.' Coups are totally unacceptable 'whether they come from above or below'; they are a threat to monarchy because they actually promote the revolution they seek to prevent. With regard to the proposals for muzzling the press, the Kaiser said that in a modern state it is stupid and dangerous to stifle the press which serves as 'an indispensable safety valve.' The Pan-Germans' plans for the Jews were 'equally childish.' It was true that Jewish influence was mounting, but to drive the Jews out of Germany would be an economic and cultural disaster: 'We would injure our own national welfare and commercial life with such a blow that it would set us back 100 years and exclude us from the ranks of cultured nations.'[99]

The Kaiser had averted a political crisis. Yet it was ominous that during the months prior to 1914, as war clouds were gathering over Europe, his advisers were seriously considering a 'successful war' as an acceptable means of coping with the perceived threat of civil unrest.

Alienation of Supporters

What the public thinks is quite immaterial to me.

Wilhelm II

At times politically skilful and circumspect, Wilhelm could also be remarkably inept. One of the besetting problems of his regime was his penchant for alienating influential people who could have helped him.

In his sensible letter to his son rejecting the proposals of the Pan-Germans, Wilhelm had pointed out the value of a free press as a safety valve for complaint. He also knew that the press was a valuable instrument for winning support for his policies, and had used it effectively to get his naval program enacted. Yet he compromised his own interests by responding to constructive editorial criticism with choleric outbursts, calling journalists 'liars' and 'traitors' and announcing, 'our stupid press ... that pig-press should shut its yap.'[100]

To rule effectively in Prussia–Germany, the Kaiser obviously needed the approval of the Junkers and the army. This he knew. Yet he seemed bent on jeopardizing their support. In 1899, for instance, when conservative agrarians opposed his scheme for an east–west canal because they feared it would benefit western industrialists, the Kaiser was furious. 'If these dogs,' he yelled, 'turn against me ... as sure as I stand here, heads will roll. This is high treason!'[101] In 1891 Wilhelm infuriated senior generals by setting forth a scheme for the complete reorganization of the imperial army without consulting the high command or his chancellor, who was then General Leo von Caprivi, a devoted monarchist. The chancellor, predictably, was offended, and when he expressed his regret at not being consulted, the Kaiser said he was 'a sensitive old fathead.'[102] He angered all military men by calling their idol, the incomparable Helmuth von Moltke, 'a pygmy.'[103] He told the chief of the great general staff that he was 'no more than a kind of amanuensis to me.'[104] During a discussion of military strategy with senior generals, the Kaiser erupted in fury and yelled, 'You old asses think that you all know better than I because you are older ... Now your stupidity is avenging itself!'[105] On at least two occasions when he lost at one of his incessant games of skat, he announced loudly that his opponents, who were generals of the army, were cheats. The insult rankled.

The Kaiser's military manoeuvres were 'fraudulent exercises designed to give Wilhelm the exhilaration of perpetual victory, a charade served up to flatter the sovereign's ego.'[106] During these exercises, he shook the confidence of the army by giving silly commands and making an ass of himself. He once placed himself at the front of a regiment of cavalry and swept gloriously across an open field against well-entrenched machine-guns and artillery. When the charge was over, the Kaiser, flushed with excitement and bursting with pride, reined in his horse, expecting high praise from his staff. He was met with stunned silence and then the dry comment of a battle-tough officer, 'All of your men are dead, Sire, except one: Your Imperial Majesty.'[107] When the general staff prepared several traps for the opposing 'enemy,' which was commanded by Wilhelm, he 'gaily rode into every one of them.' He blamed his mistakes on his military advisers; he contradicted his generals in front of staff officers. And he once ordered an elderly Prussian general to imitate the chancellor's dog by barking and jumping over a stick.[108]

The Kaiser also alienated naval commanders, people he certainly needed to cultivate if he were to carry out his ambitious plans for 'world policy.' When his appointee, the chief of the naval cabinet, suggested that together he and the Kaiser should discuss plans for wintering the fleet, Wilhelm flew into a rage: 'I'm fed up with these discussions, I give the orders and that's all there is to it ... To hell with it, I am the All-Highest Warlord, I do not "decide"; I simply command.'[109]

After dismissing Bismarck in 1890, the 'New Course' Wilhelm proposed to steer in foreign policy required the support of career diplomats. Yet the Kaiser continuously by-passed and insulted them. In foreign capitals he relied on his military attachés rather than on civilian envoys. He failed to consult with the most influential person in the Wilhelmstrasse, the Baron Friedrich von Holstein, whom he met only once personally, and perfunctorily, at a formal dinner party.[110] He told the Italian envoy that 'next to the French, the people I hate most are diplomats.'[111] When a member of the foreign office tried to dissuade the Kaiser from further alarming England with increased naval appropriations, Wilhelm roundly cursed him along with everyone else in the diplomatic corps: 'I'll tell you something, you diplomats have filled your pants. The entire Wilhelmstrasse stinks of shit'[112] – one of his favourite words.

When Graf von Metternich, the highly respected German ambassador to Great Britain, sought to tone down the naval race, the Kaiser wrote on a foreign office dispatch, 'He can kiss my ass ... I forbid him to carry on such conversations! Metternich should have a firecracker stuck up his rear. He's such a wimp!'[113]

Wilhelm took pride in his diplomatic skill in dealing with his fellow European monarchs, and on occasion he could be charmingly effective. More often, however, he could not resist saying, writing, or doing things that embarrassed or infuriated his royal colleagues. He wanted to be on especially good terms with his 'true friend and dear cousin,' Tsar Nicholas II of Russia (1895–1917), yet at a social gathering he announced, 'The Tsar is only fit to live in a countryhouse and grow turnips.'[114] He also wrote insufferably patronizing letters to 'Dearest Nicky,' which he apparently believed would be gratefully received. 'It is my duty to tell you,' Wilhelm felt compelled to write, 'that Russia misses a firm hand on the helm' and is not 'guided by a masterly mind with clear purpose, steering towards a clearly defined goal,' a leader who could 'electrify' his people by his presence[115] – which was to say, Russia needed a ruler just like Wilhelm II.

On a visit in 1903 to his Italian colleague King Victor Emmanuel III, Wilhelm referred to his diminutive host, in front of German-speaking Italians, as 'that little dwarf.' To call attention to the king's height, the Kaiser surrounded himself with an escort of giants, all over six feet six, who had been brought to Italy especially for the occasion. At a formal reception honouring him, the Kaiser announced that the Queen of Italy was 'a peasant ... the daughter of a cattle thief.'[116]

King Ferdinand of Bulgaria had an unusually large nose. At a reception, the Kaiser addressed him loudly as 'Fernando Nase,' announced that he was a hermaphrodite, and slapped him hard on his rear. When the infuriated Bulgarian king stalked out of the room, Wilhelm complained that he was a poor sport.[117]

The Kaiser could have gained politically from the support of the proud princes of the German empire. Indeed he had shown tact and conciliation to win their approval for navy appropriations. But again, what he gained with one hand he took away with the other. He had an irresistible penchant for infuriating his royal colleagues by bringing up petty matters of court etiquette in order to flaunt his rank. He challenged their little prerogatives and belittled them as 'my lackeys.' He interfered unconstitutionally, and gratuitously, in the local affairs of little principalities.[118] When the Prince Regent of Bavaria wrote him a formally correct but insufficiently obsequious letter, the Kaiser responded brusquely: 'Your letter received ... I hereby forbid you to use that tone ... in writing to me.' A Bavarian newspaper defiantly reprinted Wilhelm's insulting words under the headline, *Wir sind keine Vasallen!* (We Are Not Vassals!). The Bavarian ruler subsequently gave orders that on the Kaiser's birthday the imperial German flag was not to fly over public buildings in the kingdom of Bavaria.[119]

Wilhelm liked to call himself the 'People's Emperor' (*Volkskaiser*), who was 'filled with responsibility towards my entire people,'[120] and in fact he often voiced the sentiments of his countrymen and evoked enthusiastic response. Yet in 1892 he told his chancellor that he 'couldn't care less about popularity or the opinions of the uncomprehending rabble.' His advice to his chancellor was to ignore what the people thought: 'Only trust in my leadership and fight bravely where I point the way and we shall have no trouble in managing the rabble (*canaille*).'[121] Another government official received the following telegram in 1896: 'What the public thinks or does not think is quite immaterial.'[122] In dozens of widely quoted utterances Wilhelm jeopardized public support by seeming to hold his people in contempt, expressing his scorn in doggerel which he recited on inappropriate occasions:

Ich schau herab von meinem Tier
Auf das Gehudel unter mir.[123]

(Mounted high in my saddle,
I glance beneath me at the rabble.)

The Kaiser also encouraged resentment and opposition in a miscellaneous group of other Germans who had wished him well. He said of Chancellor Bülow that the world had not seen 'such a hypocrite and liar since Caesar Borgia.'[124] He once announced that his counselors (also hand-picked by him) were 'mere pygmies.'[125] He told the women of Germany that they had no business joining any group or association that was concerned with social or political issues: 'The primary task of a German woman does not lie ... in the attainment of presumed rights in which she should be equal to men, but rather in the quiet labour of the home and family. She should raise the young, above all, in matters of obedience and respect for their elders!' German women responded to these and similar remarks with the first demonstrations for women's rights ever held in the Fatherland.[126]

Wilhelm II also turned off thousands of young people in Germany by endorsing legislation designed to 'protect' German youth, whom the Kaiser referred to as 'saucy youngsters and babes-in-arms,' from the 'infection' of socialist ideas and from 'all activities directed against the state.' The Imperial Law of Association codified his attitude. Section 17 prohibited 'all young people under the age of 18 from joining political clubs or attending political meetings or any other public assemblies called for the purpose of discussing political matters.' Such legislation, predictably, invited hostility and contributed directly to the growth of opposition journals. The circulation, for instance, of *Die Arbeiter-Jugend* (Working Youth) jumped from 20,000 in 1908 to 108,000 in 1914. By the thousands, young adults defiantly joined the ranks of the 'traitorous' Social Democrats, which soon became the party of German youth.[127]

Why, one keeps wondering, did Wilhelm keep spurning so many potentially valuable allies? It is a question to which we must return.[128]

The Kaiser's gratuitous alienation of the German parliament must be considered one of his greatest political blunders. By cooperating with the legislature Wilhelm would not have diminished royal power; he would have broadened and strengthened its political base. To get his programs enacted, he needed the support of parliament, as he had shown so effectively during the passage of the naval bills. Yet while he continued to write a conciliatory letter to a member of the Reichstag, more often he treated deputies with contempt.

When members of the Reichstag raised the question of taxing the princes of the empire to help pay for enormous military and naval expenditures, the Kaiser was furious, calling deputies 'scoundrels' and 'a bunch of swine.'[129] On other occasions he shifted metaphors to say that they were 'mutton-heads' and 'apes who jump around in their cage.'[130]

Disastrous Newspaper Interviews, 1908

The Kaiser is completely crazy.

President Theodore Roosevelt, 1908

The worst political performances of the Kaiser's career took place during two extraordinary interviews in 1908 that produced a major political crisis. In his first interview, published in the London *Daily Telegraph* in October 1908, he had wanted to show his friendship with England; for by the turn of the century relations between the two countries had become badly strained, thanks in no small measure to the Kaiser's own inflammatory statements.

As background to the interview, it should be recalled that the British conflict with the Boers of South Africa had aroused widespread sympathy in Germany for the Boers. The Kaiser had increased tensions with England by sending a telegram to Paul Krüger, the president of the South African Republic, congratulating him on defeating a British incursion into the Transvaal. Wilhelm had hoped, he said, to prove to the English how much they needed German friendship. Instead, the very term, 'Krüger Telegram,' spread indignation through the British Isles.

The Kaiser continued to fan smouldering embers of British animosity with his exuberantly bellicose speeches. Grandly identifying himself as the 'Admiral of the Atlantic,' he proclaimed that 'Germany's future lies on the waters,' spoke of 'wrestling Neptune's trident from England,' and seizing it in his 'mailed fist.' In a speech widely quoted in the British press on the occasion of launching yet another warship, he promised to forge ahead into *Weltpolitik*: 'The ocean is indispensable for Germany's greatness. But the ocean also reminds us that there are realms far beyond. Without Germany and the German Kaiser no great decision will be made anywhere in the world.'[131]

Wilhelm simply could not understand why the English were disturbed by such statements, asking his chancellor incredulously, 'What is it that makes them all so annoyed?'[132]

The Kaiser had further increased animosity when, as an 'Admiral of the Fleet' in the British navy, he felt called upon to write letters of advice to the First Lord of the British Admiralty, assuring him of his friendship, telling him the kind of ships the British should be building, and expressing shock at the lack of discipline in the British navy.[133] When the letters were quoted in the British press, the public, along with the Admiralty, was outraged by this interference of the German Kaiser in British affairs. During 1899 and 1900 Wilhelm also sent a series of unsolicited 'Aphorisms on the War in the Transvaal' to his Uncle Edward, Prince of Wales, criticizing the British military campaigns in South Africa and telling him in detail how to improve his military tactics.[134] And then, on 28 October 1908, the *Daily Telegraph* published the contents of an incredible conversation the previous summer between the Kaiser and his host on the Isle of Wight, a certain Colonel Edward Stuart Wortley.[135]

There can be no doubt that Wilhelm's intentions were good. He wanted to prove to the sceptical British that he was their best friend in a hostile world. He was genuinely surprised to discover that his interview had precisely the opposite effect, and, further, that it had not only infuriated the British, it had also aroused the anger of Russians, French, Japanese, and his own countrymen. This performance reveals a great deal about Wilhelm's personality and the problems it posed for his political leadership.

In the interview, the Kaiser first expressed his 'warmest desire for the very best relations with England' and said he simply could not understand why the English continually misjudged him and rebuffed his overtures. 'You English are mad, mad as March hares ... you are so completely given to suspicions.' He admitted that the prevailing attitude in Germany was 'hostile, deeply hostile' to England, but that he, the Kaiser, was a staunch and true friend. Consider, for example, how he had befriended England during the Boer War:

When the struggle was at its height, the German Government was invited by the Governments of France and Russia to join with them [to save the Boers and] to humiliate England to the dust.

What was my reply? I said that ... Germany would use her armed might to *prevent* such concerted action. Posterity will one day read the exact terms of the letter – now in the archives of Windsor Castle ... Englishmen, who now insult me by doubting my word, should know what were my actions in the hour of their adversity.

Furthermore, he continued, during the darkest days of the war for Britain, he had received a letter from Queen Victoria, 'my revered grandmother ... written in sorrow and affliction,' expressing acute anxieties that were 'preying on her mind and health.' She called on him for help. Wilhelm not only reassured her, 'But I did more than that ... I worked out what I considered to be the best plan of [military] campaign ... and submitted it to my General Staff for criticism. Then I dispatched it to England, and that paper likewise is among the State Papers at Windsor Castle ... Was that, I repeat, the act of one who wished England ill? Let Englishmen be just and say!'[136] The Kaiser then talked about his navy and sought to defuse the explosive issue. Again his words did nothing to reassure the British: 'But you will say, what of the German Navy? ... My answer is clear ... Germany must have a powerful fleet to protect her ... manifold interests in even the most distant seas. She expects those interests to go on growing and she must be able to champion them manfully in any quarter of the globe. Germany looks ahead. Her horizons stretch far away.' Finally, he concluded, Englishmen should be grateful to him, because his navy's presence in the Pacific was warding off Japanese aggression throughout the Far East.

Reaction to the interview was immediate and devastating. The British were outraged. They did not like to be told that they were 'mad as March hares.'

They resented the Kaiser's characterization of Queen Victoria as a senile hysteric who, distrusting her own countrymen, felt obliged to call upon the German Kaiser for help in South Africa. Lord Roberts and his colleagues in the British army were infuriated by the suggestion that they were incapable of defeating the Boers and had been forced to rely upon military plans drawn up by the German Kaiser. Nor were Englishmen reassured to learn that Germany's naval power would soon extend to 'even the most distant seas.'

The French and Russians, in turn, were angered by the false accusation that they had invited Germany to join them in a war against England that would 'humble her into the dust.' Even if it had been true, how in the future could they make confidential agreements with the Kaiser? The Japanese did not take kindly to the suggestion that they were a threat to civilization.

The shock and dismay were greater in Germany when, on 22 November 1908, the interview was reprinted in German newspapers. The whole country had been cheering for the Boers in their gallant and uneven struggle. Germans were now appalled to learn that the Kaiser claimed to have helped the hated English defeat the beleaguered Boers. Wilhelm had reinforced the suspicion that he, like his mother, was basically Anglophile, and never a 'true German.'[137] Within a week of the publication, the executive committee of the Pan-German League released a manifesto declaring that the Kaiser lacked 'the essential qualities of a ruler' and must henceforth be excluded from all policy decisions on Germany.[138] In reporting public reaction in Germany, an American journalist wrote, 'Nothing has done him such hurt as his confessed treachery to the Boers ... He is more damaged by the past week's Conservative criticism than by fifteen years of Socialist attacks.'[139]

If the Kaiser had deliberately planned to antagonize simultaneously British, French, Russians, Japanese, and his own countrymen, it would be difficult to imagine a greater success.

On 9–10 November, for the first time in German history, the actions of a reigning monarch were openly criticized in the Reichstag. Prior to that session, it had been an unwritten law that the person of the Kaiser was not to be discussed in the Reichstag; but during those two days the sole topic of debate was Kaiser Wilhelm and his stewardship of Germany. The barrage of criticism came from left, from the middle, and even from the conservative right. A spokesman for the moderate People's party noted that the Kaiser who says he 'cannot tolerate pessimists (*Schwarzseher*) ... has created pessimists by the millions.' A Conservative member said that for the first time in his memory, 'grave disquietude' was spreading in ranks traditionally loyal to the Kaiser.[140]

Outside parliament, the reaction among supporters of the Kaiser was equally bitter. Hans Delbrück, editor of the influential *Preussische Jahrbücher*, who considered the Hohenzollern monarchy to be 'the best form of government ever designed by modern man,'[141] commented sadly that the Kaiser's performance was 'the worst defeat that Prussia has suffered since the Humiliation of Olmütz.'[142]

The Baroness Spitzemberg, always an acute observer of her countrymen and an admirer of the Kaiser, was shocked by the disrespect Wilhelm had evoked. She noted in her diary, 'He is actually laughed at, not taken seriously; feared and yet ridiculed.'[143]

Germany's popular humour magazine, *Simplicissimus*, made the same point in a different way. An issue of December 1908 carried a two-part cartoon. The first picture shows the Kaiser on New Year's Eve pouring molten lead into a dish of water, a traditional way in Germany to forecast the future; the second shows the lead forming an unmistakable configuration. The first caption reads, 'I'll just see what the future will bring me.' The second, 'Confound it! This looks just like a muzzle!'[144]

The Kaiser was oblivious to the political consequences of his interview, dismissing the criticisms as mean-spirited personal attacks by irresponsible detractors. He had actually believed that publishing the interview would be a smashing political success. Indeed he had urged Colonel Wortley to send it to a popular newspaper. Wortley had agreed and submitted the proposed text to the Kaiser, asking His Majesty to check it for accuracy. The Kaiser was delighted with the draft. He thanked his friend in an astonishing letter :

Dear Colonel Stuart Wortley,

I have carefully examined the draft ... which you kindly sent me ... It embodies correctly all the principal items of our conversation ... and deals in a most reasonable and straightforward manner with the justified complaints that I have to make ... I authorize you to make a discret [*sic*] use of the article in the manner you think best. I firmly hope that it may have the effect of bringing about a change in the tone of some English newspapers.

Thanking you most sincerely for the endeavours you have been taking in the matter, believe me, dear Colonel Stuart Wortley,

Yours very Truly,
Wilhelm, I.R.[145]

When the storm broke, Wilhelm's first reaction was to run away and hide. He took to his bed for several days with 'violent fits of weeping' and what his friends called 'a complete nervous collapse,' giving strict orders not to be disturbed for any reason whatever. Then, while attacks were mounting in the

Reichstag and the press, he escaped from the political heat of Berlin to spend several weeks on the estates of his friends, hunting and enjoying bawdy cabaret skits.[146]

The Kaiser returned, apparently recovered from his dejection, to lash out at all those who had 'abandoned' him and done him such 'rank injustice.' He blamed 'the lying press of European pan-Judaism,'[147] but his spleen was particularly vented on the Conservatives and his chancellor. He said he would never forgive the Conservatives for their 'treachery (*Verrat*)'; Chancellor Bülow had 'betrayed and deserted' him. He would 'fire the bounder.'[148]

A few weeks after the *Daily Telegraph* debacle, another bomb burst, when it was learned that the Kaiser had granted an equally explosive interview to another foreigner, this time an American clergyman and journalist, William Bayard Hale, the literary editor of the *New York Times* and an ordained pastor. Hale had been the Kaiser's guest on the royal yacht during July 1908, engaging him in long conversations about international affairs. Again Wilhelm had given his interviewer permission to publish his remarks. He also suggested that Hale show a copy of his write-up to President Theodore Roosevelt (1901–9), one of the Kaiser's warmest admirers.[149]

Roosevelt read the manuscript, slated to appear in the December 1908 issue of *The Century,* with amazement and alarm. Fearing that it would produce an international crisis, he urged Hale to withdraw it from publication. Hale did so, but the contents were leaked to *The World*, a widely circulated New York newspaper, which ran a résumé of the interview on 22 November 1908. Though slightly garbled, the story was substantially accurate and did little injustice to the sensational original.[150]

The Kaiser had changed his mind radically since the Wortley interview published three weeks earlier. He now saw England not as his friend but as the arch-enemy of Germany, and indeed of all white nations, because it had signed a treaty with Japan, the Anglo-Japanese accord of January 1902. In response to the threat of the 'Yellow Peril' the Kaiser proposed an alliance with America in order to fight the war against both England and Japan, a war which, he said, had now become 'inevitable.' Great Britain, Wilhelm told Hale, had become 'thoroughly decadent'; it was 'governed by a bunch of ninnies'; it was a 'traitor to the white man.' His uncle, King Edward VII, was not to be trusted.

Wilhelm painted his fear of the 'Yellow Peril' in lurid colours. The Japanese, he announced, 'are devils ... sowing sedition and treachery in every quarter.' Japanese expansion was a direct threat to Australia, which would welcome both an American fleet in her waters and the defeat of Japan. He predicted that 'within two years you Americans will be at war with Japan.'

Russia should be given credit for recognizing the Japanese menace by 'fighting the White Man's battle' in the Russo-Japanese War, but it was a shame that the Russians were so inept: 'Those Russians were not fit to fight this fight. What a pity ... My God, I wish my battalions could have had a chance at 'em! We'd have made short work of it!'

The Kaiser's comments about the Catholic Church and American prelates were pungent: 'The day of Catholicism,' he said, 'is past. The dawn of universal intelligence is its doom.' He warned particularly against Archbishop Ireland, who was 'a Jesuit in disguise ... the worst foe of your country.'

Again the Kaiser was disappointed that his words should be misconstrued by mean-spirited critics in England, Japan, Russia, and America. He was particularly saddened that his admirer, President Roosevelt, had deserted him by interceding to stop publication of his interview in *The Century*.

Roosevelt had indeed been one of the Kaiser's warmest admirers, but his confidence was shattered by Wilhelm's performance. After reading Hale's account, Roosevelt wrote to a friend that the Kaiser was unstable and could not be trusted. He closed with words that would prove prophetic: 'One day he could follow a sudden impulse which would endanger the peace of the world.'[151] (When he read the *Daily Telegraph* interview a few weeks later, he wrote to his son Kermit that the Kaiser 'is completely crazy.')[152]

A noted German historian looked back on Wilhelm's political blunders during the year 1908 and found them to be *the* turning point of his reign: 'The seeds of the Kaiser's abdication during the First World War were already sown in 1908. The admiral's notebooks give a new and poignant insight ... They reflect the internal collapse of the monarchic concept in Germany.'[153]

Wilhelm, however, saw in the incident no more than vindictive attacks upon his person. He soon shrugged it off. After lunching with the Kaiser the following March, Princess Radziwill wrote to a friend that she found him 'extremely gay ... [he] appeared to have jumped from despair to unconcern without having learnt the great lesson that events should have taught him. It is sad and discouraging.'[154]

To calm the tumult over the *Daily Telegraph* affair, the Kaiser had promised, once again, that henceforth he would be more discreet in his public statements. But a toast he gave on 25 August 1910, in dedicating a plaque in Königsberg Palace, shows that he was unchastened by the incident: 'Considering myself to be the instrument of the Lord, I go my way ... without consideration for the transient feelings and opinions of the day.'[155]

The Kaiser's Administrative Style

His Majesty wants every day to be his birthday.

Otto von Bismarck

When he put his mind to it, Wilhelm could apply himself diligently to the routine chores of governance, and he sometimes impressed seasoned civil servants with his mastery of administrative detail. In 1898 one old-timer expressed his admiration for 'the brilliance and clarity of the Kaiser's survey of all aspects of foreign and domestic policy.' Another official, after a meeting devoted largely to complex issues of canal transportation, was immensely impressed with the Kaiser: 'What vitality! ... what a memory! How quick and sure his understanding. In the Crown Council this morning, I was completely overwhelmed! He gave an exposé of the terribly complicated waterways question ... which no departmental minister could have equalled for precision and accuracy.'[156]

More often, however, personal whims took precedence over public obligation. Wilhelm liked to be entertained, and he found the routines of his office, except for parades and ceremonials, an unmitigated bore. Typically he instructed General Freiherr von Lynchen, chief of the military cabinet, to keep his reports short, adding, 'Don't give me dry lectures, my dear Lynchen, now and then let's have a lusty story or two.'[157]

In his diary entry for 14 February 1910, the Kaiser's court chamberlain of many years raised a pertinent question about His Majesty's working habits: 'When does the Kaiser actually work? Nine months of the year he is travelling with only the winter months at home. But even then, when does he find time ... for quiet contemplation or earnest labour? He gets up late ... has a three-course breakfast, then goes out for a drive, then a short walk with the Reichchancellor or Foreign Secretary follows. [After luncheon] another drive, then a l to 2 hour sleep. At 6:00 dinner with guests or the theatre and then conversation until 12 or 1 o'clock.'[158] Daily schedules like this prompted Bismarck to say that Wilhelm wanted every day to be his birthday.

Even matters that interested him intensely, such as the navy, were not permitted to distract him from personal diversions. In October 1904, for instance, a crisis developed over naval policy which only the Emperor could settle. Grand Admiral Tirpitz and Admiral von Senden, chief of the naval cabinet, had travelled overnight to reach the Kaiser's hunting lodge to get a decision on this urgent matter. The Kaiser was unable to see them, however, because a large stag had been sighted, and he was off on the chase. The admirals had to wait another twenty-four hours before Wilhelm could find time for them.

Travel for Wilhelm was more than a diversion; it was an escape. A member of the court computed that between August 1893 and August 1894 His Majesty covered more than three-quarters of the earth's circumference on his yacht and in his silver and pale-blue private train.[159] Shortly after the Kaiser's accession Berliners began singing a new version of the traditional, 'Hail Thou in Victor's Wreath!': *Heil dir im Sonderzug!* (Hail to Thee in Special Train!) and insisted that the I.R. after his name really stood, not for Imperator Rex, but for *Immer Reisebereit* (always ready to travel). The court calendar for 1910 shows why his excursions had important consequences for government. During the 126 days of travel in that year the Kaiser scheduled only one meeting with Chancellor Bethmann Hollweg.[160] As a worried member of his inner circle observed, the Kaiser constantly tried to avoid difficult decisions, retreating from every obstacle, 'gaily waving it aside as if it did not exist.'[161]

The Kaiser's Advisers

On whom can the Kaiser rely?

Arthur von Brauer, a staff officer

The Kaiser's choice of associates did not contribute to effective administration. His constitutional prerogative of making all major appointments in both civil and military affairs gave him an obvious opportunity to staff his government with able people, but with one or two shining exceptions, he did not do so.

Because the Kaiser could not abide criticism, could not endure 'gloomy people around me,' and needed approval 'as he needed oxygen to breathe,'[162] he chose congenial optimists who made careers out of agreeing with him. The political penalty Wilhelm paid for this constant pampering of his ego was noted by a senior staff officer of the War Office: 'On whom can the Kaiser rely when the highest military authorities only mouth whatever he says? ... The courage to speak their own minds grows steadily smaller.'[163]

Wilhelm chose not only people who would agree with him, but those he could dominate. Yet he was dependent on them. He attached himself emotionally to the old Kaiser, to Hinzpeter, to Bismarck for a time, to elderly women like Queen Victoria or Marie Dönhoff, and later to Eulenburg and Bülow. When Bülow threatened to resign in 1905, Wilhelm was desperate. He pleaded piteously for his chancellor 'not to desert me' and threatened suicide if he did: 'You cannot, you *must* not [leave me] ... that I could not survive ... The morning after your resignation takes effect, *your Kaiser will no longer be alive!* Think of my poor wife and children!'[164] During the *Daily Telegram* affair, he threw his arms around Bülow, kissed him on both cheeks, and cried, 'Help me! Save me!'[165]

The Kaiser also chose associates who reflected and apparently satisfied two conflicting needs of his own personality: 'Tough vigorous soldiers [who] represented Wilhelm's masculine role model ... and sensitive, cultured aesthetes who responded to the softer, inner Wilhelm.'[166] Neither type was helpful as a political adviser.

Members of Wilhelm's inner circle reflected their master's immaturity. Several had been chosen because of their ability to stage bawdy sexual skits or to imitate animal sounds. His Majesty valued highly a Count von Goertz, who was called upon to roar like a lion, cackle like a hen, or crow like a rooster.[167]

The Kaiser was leery of political and military advisers whose abilities were superior to his own. Fear of being overshadowed was a major reason for getting rid of Bismarck, and he made sure that every one of the successors was more tractable and less able: General Leo von Caprivi (1890–4), a military man inexperienced in politics[168]; Prince Chlodwig zu Hohenlohe-Schillingsfürst (1894–1900), Wilhelm's ancient and inoffensive 'Uncle Chlou'; the smarmy Prince von Bülow (1900–9); the obedient Bethmann Hollweg, 'a man who means well feebly'[169] (1909–17), Georg Michaelis (1917), a virtually unknown Prussian bureaucrat and pliant tool of the high command and finally, Georg von Hertling (1917–18), a kindly old professor of philosophy.

Wilhelm's desire not to be upstaged in military matters prompted his disastrous choice of Helmuth von Moltke for chief of the general staff (1906–14). Moltke's only resemblances to his famous uncle, the brilliant chief who had engineered the military victories over Austria and France that had created the Empire, were his first and last names. The 'Younger Moltke' was considered 'soft' by his fellow Prussian officers, perhaps because he carried *Faust* in his pocket, painted water-colours, and played the cello beautifully. He also fell off his horse several times during manoeuvres and was given to mysticism, fits of melancholia, and hypochondria. Moltke was a man of considerable personal and political courage, who sometimes disagreed with the Kaiser,[170] and he recognized his own limitations. When Wilhelm told him that he was to succeed the great Count Schlieffen (1891–1906), Moltke repeatedly warned the Supreme War Lord that his appointment would be a mistake. He simply was not up to the job, he would be a terrible chief of staff: 'I lack the power of rapid decision. I am too reflective, too scrupulous ... I lack that capacity which makes greatness in such born commanders as Napoleon, or our own Frederick II, or my uncle.'[171] Wilhelm ignored this assessment. Confident that this man would not outshine him, he insisted on the appointment.

During the first fortnight of the war, Moltke fulfilled his own expectations. He botched the Schlieffen Plan. He panicked and gave confused orders that led to the catastrophic defeat at the First Battle of the Marne, 5–12 September 1914. The man the Kaiser chose as Moltke's successor, the frivolously congenial flatterer, Erich von Falkenhayn (1914–16), was no improvement. Falkenhayn jettisoned the army's century-long tradition of mobile warfare and, on 15 September 1914, embarked on the fatal strategy of attrition – a decision that a noted military historian has called 'the real turning point of the war.'[172] Two fateful decisions were thus made by two of the Kaiser's appointees within the first two weeks of the war.

The Kaiser's personal role in the outbreak and conduct of the war will be discussed in the next chapter.

PART III: THE POLITICAL PERFORMANCE OF THE FÜHRER

As a human being [Hitler was] lamentable; as a political mind, one of the most tremendous phenomena in all history.

Konrad Heiden

In discussing Hitler's performance as ruler of Germany, as with the Kaiser, I will focus on a few examples of his leadership in order to illustrate his strengths and weaknesses: his first bid for political power in the Beer Hall Putsch of November 1923, his cultivation of influential groups in attaining power, and his role in the massacre of his colleagues in the Night of the Long Knives of July 1934.

Two other subjects will be discussed later: his personal role in the Holocaust and in the Second World War. Before turning to these specific topics, however, comment must be made about the Führer's general appeal to the German people, and particularly his skill in winning the endorsement of the German middle class, for without their support he would never have had the opportunity to put his theories into practice.

Hitler's Political Appeal

He played on the *Kleinbürgertum* like a skilled harpsichordist plucking the chords of middle-class sentiments.

Horace Greely Hjalmar Schacht

During the fourteen years following the collapse of Imperial Germany in 1918, Germans experienced twelve different chancellors and eight parliamentary elections with no political party ever achieving a majority. After such confusion, the German people longed for a strong leader who would be in fact what Wilhelm II had only played at being: the 'people's Kaiser.' Hitler seemed to fit the pattern of such a leader. He was a man of the people, a common soldier with a heroic record in the war; his life reflected struggle and hardship. He promised to destroy the old privileged society and establish an ethnically pure, socially harmonious 'national community' in a powerful new Reich.[173]

Hitler's was a broad appeal. His Nazi party was the first *integrative* political movement in German history. He attracted support from all levels of society: the elite of army, industry, and academia, civil servants, church leaders, farmers, pensioners, and women. It was the party of youth, yet old people gave him more electoral votes than had previously been thought.[174] His primary support, however, was rooted and grounded in the lower middle class, the *Kleinbürgertum*, the Hans and Gretl Meyers (the John and Jane Smiths) of Germany. The membership of the party and the leadership corps were drawn predominantly from this group.[175] In 1933 they accounted for more than 60 per cent of the rank and file of the party, and for 78 per cent of the district leaders (*Gauleiter*) and other party leaders.[176]

Hitler was particularly effective in appealing to the economic needs of the middle class. He exploited brilliantly the opportunity offered him by the Great Depression of 1930–3. Other political leaders were dismayed by staggering economic problems. Not Hitler. He was in his element. 'Never in my life,' he exulted during the darkest days of Germany's economic distress, 'have I been so well disposed and inwardly contented.' As a contemporary journalist commented, 'That is Hitler. The house must burn for the sake of this flame.'[177]

With sure political instinct he saw that the economic crisis had produced profound psychological shock with widespread feelings of confusion, resentment, and despair. Other politicians offered complicated economic plans. Hitler ordered party orators to 'avoid all detailed statements concerning an economic program.'[178] Where others conveyed uncertainty and complexity, Hitler, the great simplifier, promised simple solutions, projected authority and inspired confidence and hope.

By 1933 the Meyer families of Germany had been shaken by three wrenching experiences. First, the defeat and humiliation of 1918. This was followed by the catastrophic inflation of 1923, which had not only wiped out their life's savings, but also made them doubt their entire system of values. Confidence in traditional 'German virtues' of obedience, sobriety, moderation, and thrift had proven to be so much *Quatsch* (nonsense). Third was the economic collapse of 1930–3. The Great Depression, like the Great Inflation that had preceded it, had social and political consequences as disturbing as its economic effects. All three events, by contributing to the political and psychological radicalization of the middle class, contributed greatly to Hitler's success. Like the Meyers, millions of other Germans now decided, as the slogan of the times had it, that 'radicalism is trumps.'

The Reichstag elections of September 1930 demonstrated unmistakably the connection between economic crisis and political radicalization. They showed, as Chancellor Philipp Scheidemann said in an unforgettable metaphor, that the Weimar Republic was 'a candle burning at both ends.' The moderate political parties of the centre lost more than half their previous support. By 1932 these parties altogether received only 11 per cent of the total vote. The Communists gained on the left, but it was the Nazis who registered one of the most dramatic advances in the history of electoral democracy. In 1928 Hitler's party had been a minor splinter group. By 1932 it had become the largest party in Germany,[179] even though it declared openly that it intended to overthrow democracy. Never had a political movement given so clear a promise. An editorial in Goebbels's newspaper *Der Angriff* (The Attack) of 30 May 1928 answered with brutal frankness its own question, 'What Do We Want in the Reichstag?': 'We are the enemies ... of this democracy ... so why do we want to get into the Reichstag? We are going there in order to destroy the arsenal of democracy with its own weapons ... We come not as friends and not as neutrals, we come as enemies! (*wir kommen als Feinde!*) As the wolf breaks into the sheepfold, so are we coming.'

Why did so many average German citizens desert the Republic? An important part of the answer lies in the psychological condition of the German middle class described in Erich Fromm's provocative book, whose thesis is contained in its title, *Escape from Freedom*. (In the English edition, the title is *The Burden of Freedom*.) In the Kaiser's paternalistic Reich, the middle class had enjoyed security without the responsibility for making political decisions; they proudly associated themselves with the power and the glory of authoritarian institutions. With the collapse of the Empire they were suddenly given the freedom to run their own government, but freedom had brought only failure and humiliation: Their democratic leaders had been forced to sign a hated peace treaty. Their government was unable to cope with the Great Depression; it had produced only fractious political turmoil. Life in the new democracy had become so complex and problems so intractable that thousands of Hans Meyers turned to an authoritarian figure who promised solutions to problems they felt incapable of solving.

The bewilderment of the lower middle class was expressed in the title of Hans Fallada's best-seller, *Kleiner Mann – Was nun?* (Little Man – What Now?), and in Gerhart Hauptmann's plaintive cry expressing his despair with democracy: 'If only life would demand no more solutions from us!'

There was one way that the powerless 'little men' of Germany could gain power. They could get it vicariously in Hitler's system, which fostered the heartening illusion that merely by accepting him as their Führer they would win 'a kind of magical participation in the source of all power.'[180] Fromm suggested another reason for Hitler's appeal. German society in the 1930s, he argued, suffered from something akin to group sado-masochism: The 'little man' wanted to be dominated, but he also wanted to dominate others, to hate and destroy. Hitler gave him the opportunity to do both.[181] He also offered hope – the clear, shining hope of a New Order, a true *Volksgemeinschaft*, providing both the security of authority and the pride of triumphant nationalism.

It is a mark of Hitler's political genius that he called his system 'National Socialism.' For by joining these two concepts together – they form one word in German, *Nationalsozialismus* – he harnessed the two most potent political forces of the post–First World War period, two powerful steeds which, prior to Hitler, had been pulling in opposite directions. The nationalists of the right could arouse fervour for the Fatherland, but they had no positive social program for economically distraught Germany. Nationalists were not socialists. The Marxian socialists of the left, on the other hand, were not nationalists. Hitler offered the middle class a marvelous combination of nationalism *and* socialism. His was the only non-Marxist party that promised a socialistic New Order which was stirringly nationalistic. By blending socialism with nationalism, Hitler made good his early boast that he would 'take socialism away from the socialists.'[182] Hans Meyer could have his *Schnapps* and drink it too.

Like virtually every component of his ideology, the conception of national socialism was not new with Hitler. Ironically, the idea seems to have been first proposed by a Jew. In setting forth his plans for bringing together the seven tribes of Judah into one nation, Theodor Herzl had proclaimed in 1895, 'My flag is a national-socialist flag: seven stars on a field.'[183] One year later, the popular Lutheran pastor and social reformer Friedrich Naumann established a short-lived party which he called the 'National-Socialist Party of Germany,' and the next year he published an influential book with the arresting title *National-Sozial Katechismus* (Catechism of National-Socialism).[184] Hitler recognized the power of the idea and exploited it to the full.

Hitler also showed his political acumen in his use of the term 'Reich' to describe the New Order he promised. This pleasant and untranslatable little word of Celtic origin had possessed a magical appeal in Germany for many centuries. It was a revered word in the prayers of both Catholics and Protestants: '*Dein Reich komme, dein Wille geschehe, wie im Himmel so auch auf der Erde.*' As Hitler well knew, the concept also stirred memories of past political grandeur. Every schoolchild learned that long ago a great Germanic hero named Kaiser Friedrich Barbarossa had ruled over a marvelous-sounding realm whose rhythmical name they loved to recite: '*Das heilige römische Reich deutscher Nation.*' They also knew that centuries later another hero, Otto von Bismarck, and the Prussian army had smashed all Germany's enemies and established the gloriously powerful Second Reich, preserving the rolling rhetorical rhythm: *'Mitteleuropäisches Reich deutscher Nation.'* Hitler kept alive the same lilting cadence and a similar dream. His would be the *'Grossgermanisches Reich deutscher Nation.'*[185]

By his very use of the terms 'National Socialism' and 'Third Reich,' Hitler appealed to both conservative and revolutionary. His Reich would be a continuum of the past glories of the first two Reichs, while promising future glory in a new Reich of nationalistic socialism that would 'endure for a thousand years.' (During the war, however, Hitler gave orders to drop the word 'Third' – the numerical sequence seemed less attractive when he discovered that opponents of his tyranny were looking forward to a 'Fourth Reich' of democracy. Henceforth, only the word 'Reich' was to be used.)[186]

Hitler's movement, with its dynamism of rancour, allowed deep-seated feelings of anxiety and fear to find an outlet in primitive hatred and aggression. As a person who was himself consumed by hate, Hitler knew its power to move others. One reason for his political success in 1933 was the stunningly effective way he applied the axiom he had laid down a decade earlier in *Mein Kampf*: 'Hatred is more powerful than love.' He had also noted scornfully that the leaders of the Republic had done nothing whatever to cultivate 'the most valuable of all political qualities: *wrathful hatred*,' and promised that under his leadership 'hate would become a single fiery sea of flames.' He kept that promise. A Swiss diplomat, who had watched Hitler's political performances at close hand, concluded that the main energy of Hitler was the energy of hatred. 'Never,' he said, had he 'met any human capable of generating so terrific a condensation of envy, vituperation, and malice.' Thousands of Germans were drawn to Hitler, the Swiss concluded, because 'they needed to hate and this man supplied that need.'[187]

In hundreds of electrifying speeches the Führer told cheering crowds that he stood for the opposite of everything that troubled them. Democracy was a failure; he would give them authoritarian government. Class privilege and exploitation rankled; he promised egalitarian *Volksgemeinschaft*. In place of international cooperation and the League of Nations, associated with the despised Versailles Treaty, he promised revenge and triumphant German nationalism. Above all else, Hitler sensed the longing for a heroic leader, a longing as old as the Barbarossa legend and as current as the memoir of 1934 written by a high-school teacher: 'I reached the conclusion that ... a single man alone could save Germany. This opinion was shared by others, for when the cornerstone of a monument was laid in my home town, the following lines were inscribed on it: "Descendants who read these words, know ye that we eagerly await the coming of the Man whose strong hand may restore order."'[188]

Hitler was successful with the lower middle class because they recognized him as one of their own. In the phrase of a German essayist, Hitler was a 'mirror of bourgeois boobery (*Spiesserspiegel*).'[189] The Führer was *Kleinbürger* incarnate, whose taste in art and literature was banal and whose speeches where larded with hackneyed patriotic clichés, and whose very stylistic mediocrity had wide appeal. He was 'a man of the masses,' who did not so much conquer the common man as identify with him.[190]

He certainly looked the part. His very nullity was a source of his strength. The anxious and ineffective 'little men' of Germany, who longed for power and greatness, could identify with Hitler, for he was a kindred soul. As a contemporary critic put it, 'They could see greatness emerging from a creature who was smaller than you or I – that is what made Hitler an experience for millions.'[191]

Dorothy Thompson, one of the very few foreign correspondents who were permitted a personal interview with Hitler, was surprised and disappointed by the 'startling insignificance of this man who has set the world agog ... He is the very prototype of the "Little Man,"' she wrote in the spring of 1932. And when she thought of him sitting in the seat of power over a great country, 'I involuntarily smiled: Oh, Adolph! Adolph! [*sic*] You will be out of luck!'[192]

Miss Thompson was mistaken. Like so many other political pundits, she had underestimated this nondescript politician and failed to recognize the paradox that so much of his power lay precisely in his 'startling insignificance.'

But only part of his power. For while he was one of the masses, he was set apart from them by the touch of political genius. None of Hitler's political competitors showed a remotely comparable ability to combine ideology and propaganda or anything like his capacity to sense the psychic needs of his audiences. Two or three examples from hundreds of speeches show how closely he identified with the masses: He too had been a common labourer and a common soldier; he too had known hunger and privation; he too loved Germany. He was proud to be one of his people: 'When I speak to you today and thus to millions of other German workers, I have more right to do this than anyone else. I have grown out of you yourselves; once I myself stood among you, I was among you in the war for four and a half years and now I speak to you to whom I belong, with whom I feel myself to be bound ... and for whom in the final analysis I carry on the struggle ... in my youth I was a worker like you, and then I worked my way up by industry, by study, and, I can say, by starving.' And again his words flew like an arrow to their hearts: 'We are so happy to be able to live among this people and I'm proud to be permitted to be your Leader! So proud that I cannot imagine anything in this world that I would rather be. I should a thousand times rather be the last *Volksgenosse* (racial comrade) among you than be a king anywhere else.' And again: 'I am a child of the people and will remain one forever. Through the long years behind me, I have fought for the *Volk* and I will continue to fight for them ... for this people I would let myself ... be hacked to pieces.'[193]

Hitler realized that his relationship to the masses was symbiotic, that each needed the other. He expressed this mutual dependence in a remarkable aside during an election speech of 1933, when he suddenly stopped and broke forth joyously, 'Isn't it a *miracle*! A miracle that among so many millions you found *me* and I found *you*!'

There was an important difference in the way the Kaiser and the Führer cast their speeches. Wilhelm did not expect his audiences to participate. He expected the respectful applause that was his royal due. Hitler encouraged audience participation. He left spaces in his speeches for the crowds to scream, '*Sieg Heil! Ein Volk! Ein Reich! Ein Führer!*' The Führer himself sometimes joined in the frenzied chorus.

Hitler's political success in 1933, let us remind ourselves again, cannot be explained solely in terms of his political cunning. By 1933 the Hans and Gretl Meyers of Germany were fed up with their country's first experiment with democracy. In their eyes, democracy had signed the hated Versailles *Diktat*. It had also failed to solve inflation, caused unemployment, and brought nothing but political instability. Hitler was served by one simple fact: the German people did not support the Weimar Republic.[194]

After attaining power in 1933, Hitler continued to curry favour with the masses. His propaganda about establishing a Germanic 'people's community' (*Volksgemeinschaft*) had been immensely appealing, for it promised that in a Third Reich distinctions and privileges of caste and class would be ended, with positions of power and influence opened to all racial Germans. That promise was largely fulfilled for those who accepted his regime.

A certificate from an 'Adolf Hitler School,' for instance, was a passport to a successful career in party or state. Similarly, Hitler's elite SS offered attractive careers to true believers from across the entire social strata. In the upper ranks, *Gruppenführer* and *Obergruppenführer* of the SS, roughly corresponding to generals in the regular army, of thirty-five officers in 1941, one was a former electrician, one a former truckdriver, one an army general, three had been automobile mechanics, two transient labourers, one a farmer, and seventeen had been schoolteachers. An unusually high number of PhDs and other academics joined the notorious SS murder squad, *Einsatzgruppe B*.[195]

By all odds, the most popular of Hitler's programs was the 'Strength through Joy' organization (*Kraft durch Freude* or KdF), which, for the first time in German history, offered citizens subsidized vacations as well as inexpensive tickets to concerts, exhibitions, theatre performances, and the opera. Millions of citizens each year participated in *Kraft durch Freude* activities and went home chanting Hitler's praises and lauding his concern for 'the common man.'[196] The KdF also subsidized the building of a 'people's car.' (This early *Volkswagen* never actually became available for civilian use. During the war it was modified as an all-purpose military vehicle, the German equivalent of the American Jeep. The KdF excursion liners became troop ships.)

The Nazis established party clubs for all ages and interests, from 'Hitler's Maidens' to automobile clubs, from sports associations to chess clubs. One way or another, Hitler's government brought millions of Germans to Nazi ways of thinking. Where the Kaiser had talked about being a populist leader, the 'People's Emperor,' the Führer really was one.

Hitler's appeal to the Hans Meyers of Germany also had a solid economic base. He had ended inflation and brought full employment.[197] But at a price. As we shall see, Hitler's economy required war.

The Uses of Fear

I will teach them fear.

Adolf Hitler

Hitler not only wooed the masses with recreational programs, he also intimidated them. 'The masses,' he is quoted as saying, 'thrill to terror ... They *want* to fear something ... They want someone to make them shudderingly submissive.'[198] The Führer had not been in power a month before he announced publicly the opening of the first concentration camps (*Konzentrationslager*), which became known as 'KZ' – dread initials that did indeed send a thrill of terror through the German people.

Hitler knew, as did Stalin and Saddam Hussein,[199] that fear can generate wide support for a government. Under Hitler's system of unpredictable terror, individual Germans found a form of refuge from fear by publicly displaying ostentatious support for Hitler's regime. That is to say they experienced *en masse* what Anna Freud found to be true of individuals: an intimidated person may feel less frightened by 'identifying with the aggressor.'

Terror was important to the system, but it was not its mainstay, for Hitler realized that his success depended ultimately not on Gestapo and KZ but on voluntary acceptance by the masses. Goebbels, in many respects Hitler's *alter ego*, had said in 1933 that there were two ways to transform society: 'You can go on shooting the opposition with machine-guns until they acknowledge the superiority of the gunners. That is the simpler way. But you can also transform the nation by a mental revolution, and thus win over the opposition instead of annihilating them. We National Socialists have adopted the second way.'[200]

Propaganda was another of Hitler's techniques for achieving consensus and transforming the nation through a 'mental revolution.' In the contemporary world, the word 'propaganda' is used loosely and indiscriminately. One speaks of 'good propaganda for the Republican Party,' and we are assured by admen that selling cigarettes is 'just a question of which agency has the best propaganda.' That is not what Hitler meant by the word. For him, as his masterful chapter on propaganda in *Mein Kampf* shows, propaganda was another form of terror. His meaning was best expressed long ago by a French historian who, in writing of the reign of Henry VII of England, noted that Henry was successful in cowing opposition to his church policy by means of *violence faite aux âmes, c'est à dire, propagande*. Hitler's propaganda was, and was intended to be, 'violence committed against the soul.' An editorial in the official Nazi newspaper admitted as much when it wrote that the Führer's purpose was to achieve 'complete mastery over the soul and the mind of the people.'[201]

The Führer, like the Kaiser, expressed ambivalent attitudes about public opinion. Wilhelm asserted that what his people thought was a matter of total indifference to him, yet he sought popular approval to bolster his personal self-esteem. Hitler, too, spoke disparagingly of the 'mutton-headed masses,' but unlike the Kaiser, he knew that his power depended on their approval. He sent his Gestapo out to take opinion surveys and to draw up detailed reports on popular attitudes and complaints which he studied carefully. (These Gestapo reports are an invaluable source for our knowledge of public attitudes during the Third Reich.) Hitler's fear of popular opposition to his government was one of the reasons that Nazi Germany never went on a full wartime economy. The production of consumer goods in 1942, for instance, remained at 88 per cent of pre-war levels.[202] Hitler had always been apprehensive about women and fretted lest he lose their political support. When Goebbels tried to convince him of the need for total economic mobilization after the disastrous defeat at Stalingrad, Hitler replied, 'We musn't take away their hair-dryers, Goebbels – they would never forgive us for that!'

The Führer provided circuses along with bread and hair-dryers. During the drab and virtually fête-less Weimar years,[203] Germans had looked back nostalgically to the glory days of pomp and circumstance in the 'Kaiser time.' Yet Hitler's celebrations were far more popular than the Kaiser's staged parades and rigidly prescribed 'flag-nailing' ceremonies.

Hitler even outdid Wilhelm in the number of personal photographs he distributed through an innovative scheme for presenting himself to the masses. He had his court photographer, Eva Braun's employer Heinrich Hoffmann, print tens of thousands of candid snapshots of the Führer ranging from homey to heroic poses. Made into numbered cards and distributed as premiums in cigarette packages, like latter-day bubble gum baseball cards, they were avidly collected, traded, and treasured. Hitler's cards were pasted in designated, numbered spaces in a huge volume entitled *Bilder aus dem Leben des Führers,* edited by the Cigaretten Bilderdienst (Hamburg, 1936 and many subsequent years). Though personally opposed to smoking, the Führer was not averse to receiving handsome royalties from the scheme, along with the widespread publicity of unparalleled photo opportunities. But he also won mass support for a reason quite above and beyond gimmickry and tawdry propaganda.

It is one of history's greatest ironies that Hitler – Hitler of all people! – mobilized moral outrage to gain power for a regime that would descend to the lowest depth of moral depravity. As Barrington Moore has shown in a fine book, throughout history feelings of outrage have been a far more potent cause of revolutionary change than either economic exploitation or political oppression. Revolutions, he points out, are led by those who are able to articulate mass resentment and feelings of moral outrage and point the way to a better life.[204]

Hitler did precisely that. With the fervour of an evangelical preacher, the Führer railed against the 'moral depravity and corruption of the Jewish Republic,' the rankling injustice and outrage of the *Versailles-Diktat,* the dangers of the 'godless Jewish–Bolshevik conspiracy' – and from all this he promised to save the people and lead them to the promised land of a New Order, a Thousand-Year Germanic Reich of power, prosperity, and peace.

Beer Hall Putsch, November 1923: Disaster and Triumph

Hitler's actions remain inexplicable unless we assume that he did not (either consciously or unconsciously) always intend to succeed ... Hitler was ... a man bent on doing injury to himself.

James McRandle[205]

It was a superb performance ... Hitler is a true German patriot.

Ex-Kaiser Wilhelm II, Doorn, 1924

Hitler's first bid for political power in November 1923 presaged his future performance. It showed him capable of both remarkable ineptitude and extraordinary skill as a political leader.

The suggestion that Hitler harboured a self-destructive impulse seems surprising. His life can be read as a remarkable success story with the unlikely hero played by a mentally unbalanced drop-out who wandered the streets of Linz and Vienna. This derelict, who had failed in all his previous undertakings and was jailed at the start of his political career, within a decade became master of Germany and arbiter of Europe.

Biographers are justified in dwelling on Hitler's remarkable successes: his skill in pulling the party together after the disaster of the Beer Hall Putsch, his insight and perseverance during the political crisis of 1932, his brilliant diplomatic coups and smashing military victories at the start of the war.

Yet McRandle is right in suggesting that a very different pattern of behaviour is also characteristic of this complex and deeply divided personality. Throughout his life Adolf Hitler flirted with failure, talked of defeat even in moments of triumph, and repeatedly involved himself unnecessarily in situations that were fraught with danger to himself and his movement. He once confessed that somehow he felt compelled to court disaster: 'You know, I am like a wanderer who must cross an abyss on the edge of a knife. But I *must*, I just *must* cross.'[206] Hitler's leadership of the Beer Hall Putsch suggests this pattern of choosing alternatives least likely to succeed.

In 1923 he planned not merely a seizure of power in Bavaria, but a march on Berlin to overthrow the 'Weimar traitors.' Openly and explicitly promising a new German national government, he announced to cheering followers that his purpose would be fulfilled 'only when the black-white-red swastika banner floats over the Berliner Schloss.'[207]

Yet Hitler made no effort to win the support of the two military leaders whose help for such an undertaking was absolutely essential: General Hans von Seeckt, commander of the national army, and General Eric Ludendorff, prestigious leader of patriotic–racist causes. In the week preceding his attempt to seize national power, Hitler's newspaper, the *Völkischer Beobachter*, gratuitously insulted Seeckt, calling him a tool of a 'Masonic conspiracy,' and libelled his Jewish wife. Prior to the actual night of the coup, Hitler had failed even to inform General Ludendorff about his plans.

Nor had Hitler won the confidence or neutrality of local authorities who were indispensable to the success of his venture: General Otto von Lossow, the army commander for Bavaria; Colonel Hans Ritter von Seisser, commander of the Bavarian state police; Gustav von Kahr, the so-called strongman of Bavaria. Indeed both Lossow and Seisser had given Hitler unmistakable warning two days before the event that they would crush any attempt at a putsch. The next night Hitler did nothing to win favour with this powerful triumvirate when he embarrassed them publicly and held them hostage at pistol point.[208]

Preparations for a national revolution were grossly inadequate within Munich. Outside the city they were non-existent. In the north, SA Commander

Peter Heydebreck, a former *Freikorps* leader who was itching to march on Berlin, tried to get an audience with Hitler. He was rebuffed. Heydebreck wrote disgustedly, 'I was not the only man of the north who received similar cool treatment,' and went on to complain that the SA in Berlin were given no information whatever about an impending revolution.[209]

On the night of the coup (8–9 November), after arresting Lossow, Seisser, and Kahr and making an impassioned and largely irrelevant speech, Hitler sank into despondency and seemed incapable of taking effective action. He sat and brooded. He paced ineffectively up and down. He talked excitedly about minutiae, and he left the beer hall intermittently on impromptu missions of no importance. He was heard to mutter morosely, 'If it comes out all right, well and good; if not, we'll hang ourselves.'[210]

The author of a detailed monograph on the event has reached a conclusion that is not supported by his own impressive evidence: 'He [Hitler] ran everything himself.' On the contrary, nobody ran anything that night. The first eight or ten hours of any coup attempt are of crucial importance to its success. During these hours, when it was imperative for Hitler to act quickly and decisively, *'no orders at all came from the Putschist high command.'*[211]

Hitler made no effort to do the obvious: seize key buildings such as the telephone exchange, telegraph and radio stations, transport facilities, and police headquarters. He did not even try to capture Kahr's headquarters, the official centre of governmental power in Munich. Even after the government had abandoned it, Hitler gave no orders to take over the building. During the first twelve vitally important hours, the Führer had managed to occupy and secure one beer hall on the town's periphery.[212]

Astonishingly, this specialist in propaganda, this master demagogue who had promised to lead a national revolution did not even visit the propaganda headquarters that had been set up by two assistants! He chose not to deliver one of the great orations he had promised for the next day, relegating speech-making to the unpredictable Julius Streicher, pathological liar, pornographer, and fanatical Jew-baiter – scarcely the man to be the spokesman for a national revolution. Hitler had scribbled on a piece of paper, 'Streicher is responsible for the entire organization.'[213]

As Hitler dithered, and forces of the counterrevolution gathered in strength, he made no attempt to gather more troops to reinforce his rapidly depleting ranks. Several SA units in Southern Bavaria would have come quickly to Hitler's help. He did not send for them.[214] During the course of the night Hitler left the beer hall, permitting his hostages to escape and to rally the forces that would overthrow him on the morrow. The famous march on the morning of 9 November was not Hitler's idea. The order apparently came from General

Ludendorff, who was furiously impatient with Hitler's incomprehensible behaviour: 'No one knew where the march was going, and no one had known from the start.'[215]

Hitler was torn by inner conflict and contrary impulses, one part of him urging him to succeed, another pushing him towards failure.[216] Since he could not cope with the conflict, he sank into depression, then ran away to hide in Putzi Hanfstaengl's summer home on the Stauffelsee south of Munich. When he arrived, Frau Doktor Hanfstaengl reported, Hitler was despondent and 'almost incoherent.' He wanted to be left alone, and spent the day hiding in the attic under two English lap robes, one of which Hanfstaengl treasured for decades as a kind of relic he showed visitors. The Führer kept threatening suicide until Frau Hanfstaengl disarmed him and threw his pistol into a barrel of flour she was hoarding. On 11 November Hitler surrendered to the Bavarian police.[217]

Arrested, imprisoned, charged with conspiracy and treason, and threatened with deportation, Hitler's career, everyone assumed, was finished. As the American military attaché in Munich reported, 'Only a miracle could save him, but the miracle happened.'[218]

The miracle was the shrewd way Hitler used his trial for high treason in late February and March 1924. He was given every assistance by the court. The prosecuting attorney, one Herr Doktor Stengelin, sounded as if he were appearing for the defence. Stengelin called the prisoner in the dock an admirable person, a brave soldier, and a selfless patriot who had only technically broken the law because he had been encouraged by so many patriotic supporters: 'We cannot reproach him with selfishness. His actions were not prompted by personal ambition but by enthusiasm for the cause ... We cannot deny him our respect.' The judge nodded agreement.

Hitler was in command of the trial throughout. As the transcript shows, he kept interrupting and haranguing government witnesses so loudly that the judge repeatedly asked, deferentially, if he could not perhaps lower his voice.[219]

Hitler's final plea was a masterpiece of invective, serving as harbinger of orations to come. He began the most important speech of his career by defiantly accepting full responsibility for his armed attempt to overthrow the Weimar Republic: 'I alone bear the responsibility, but I am not a criminal because of that. If I stand here as a revolutionary it is a revolutionary against the [so-called] revolution. There is no such thing as high treason against the traitors of 1918.' He spoke for four hours. When the judge was later asked why the defendant was given so much liberty, he replied that he found it impossible to interrupt the swell of Hitler's oratory. Instead of accepting the role of defendant charged with treason, Hitler put the entire government of the Republic in the dock, accusing President Ebert and Chancellor Scheidemann and all their 'lackeys' of high treason against Germany.

In this pivotal speech, in which he was fighting for his political life, Hitler's thoughts turned to mothers. The only possible way he himself could have looked upon the putsch attempt as a failure would have been 'if a mother had come to me and said, "Herr Hitler, you have my son on your conscience." No mother came to me and said that.' That is to say his own mother would not have blamed him; his own conscience was clear. Indeed, at the end of the speech a mother figure, once more appearing as a benevolent goddess,[220] smiled benignly upon him. Hitler turned to the judge and said, 'You may pronounce us guilty a thousand times, but the Goddess of the Eternal Court of History will smilingly tear up the indictment of the prosecutor and the verdict of the judges and set us free!'[221]

At the close of the trial, thousands of his supporters jammed in front of the Ministry of Justice. In a preview of coming years, they kept screaming *'Heil Hitler! Heil Hitler! Heil Hitler!'* until he appeared on a balcony to accept their homage. The Kaiser, living in exile in Doorn, followed the trial closely and was impressed with Hitler's performance. In the margin of a report of the trial in a German newspaper, he wrote, 'A true patriot, he is fighting to restore Germany's honour.'[222]

Overnight the obscure Munich street agitator had become a national hero and martyr to the cause of a resurgent Germany. In the months after his luxurious stay in prison – actually in 'honorary fortress confinement'[223] – Hitler showed great political skill in reasserting himself as undisputed Führer of his scattered and distraught party, pulling it together, and leading it to power within ten years. It was a political feat rarely matched in modern history.

During the years following the collapse of his failed coup, Hitler gave impressive demonstrations of his political acumen. He converted his failure into 'one of the enduring legends of the Nazi movement.'[224] Every year on the anniversary of the putsch, celebrations were held throughout the Reich. Hitler himself returned to the Bürgerbräukeller to give inspirational orations and to lead the march of 'Old Fighters' to the Feldherrnhalle, where they honoured 'martyrs' who had died that 'holy day.' Hitler had converted fiasco into triumph.

Even more impressive was the way he changed his political strategy, showing that, unlike the Kaiser, he could profit from his mistakes. The disastrous *Daily Telegraph* affair did not deter Wilhelm II from repeating the same kind of political blunder. The failure of the Beer Hall Putsch taught Hitler that the way to power lay not in trying to overthrow the establishment by frontal attack, but by subverting it from within. He would come to power by using the Weimar

Constitution to destroy the Weimar Republic. Hitler's police state was established democratically through acts of parliament.[225]

Courting Capitalists, Christians, and Conservatives

Corruptio optimi pessima

Latin epigram [226]

Hitler was both a fanatical ideologue and a cunning political opportunist. To emphasize either his fanaticism or his opportunism to the exclusion of the other is to misunderstand the man and to misjudge his effectiveness. His skill as a political tactician was demonstrated in the adroit way he manipulated the business community, the Christian churches, and conservatives to gain their support, first in attaining power and later in consolidating his dictatorship.

Germany's business and industrial elite recognized that monarchy was defunct, and they were less than enthusiastic about democracy. Yet while they found many things appealing about Hitler's party, they had been put off by the 'socialist' part of his program. He reassured them in one of the most successful speeches of his career, on 27 January 1932 to the Industry Club in Düsseldorf, the capital of the German steel industry. He told his formally attired audience that they were indispensable to his plans for solving Germany's economic problems. He was not at all opposed to their sort of 'creative capitalism,' only to 'Jewish finance capitalism.' He would defend their interests against the menace of communism, the claims of trade unions, and the 'stultifying egalitarianism of democracy.' He put his faith, he said, in 'creative individuality,' both in politics and in economics. The industrial elite, who at first had given him a cool reception, warmed to this message and after the speech stood up and cheered – and subsequently contributed generously to Nazi coffers.

Hitler could not have come to power without the approval of the conservatives who dominated the army. Nor could he have done it without the support of the Christian Church. His technique here too was masterful.

To cultivate Christians for his political purposes, Hitler dissociated himself from those who wanted to establish a completely de-Christianized neo-pagan Nazi 'church.' He ordered racist hotheads like Himmler, Hess, Bormann, and Streicher to tone down their neo-pagan effusions and on 11 October 1928 set forth his strategy in an important speech to party leaders, who must have been surprised to learn that their movement was Christian: 'We will tolerate no one in our ranks who harbours hostile thoughts about Christianity. Our movement is actually Christian (*tatsächlich christlich*). We are filled with the desire that

Catholics and Protestants should work together with us for the good of our people in its deepest need.'[227]

The Nazis did well in the autumn elections of 1932, but Hitler was not satisfied. A statistical analysis of the vote showed that church people were still not supportive and that women in particular were turned off by Nazi belligerence, racism, and crude anti-Semitism. The Führer therefore gave orders to change the image. Henceforth Nazis were to appear as champions of public morality and family values, defenders of Christianity, and the last bulwark against atheistic communism. It worked. From 1932 on, Protestants generally – and women especially – were Hitler's most enthusiastic supporters.[228]

Hitler had gained the chancellorship on 30 January 1933 with the help of Christians, but he had not yet been granted dictatorial power. Now he needed their votes in the Reichstag to win passage of an Enabling Act that would give him power legally. His speeches became increasingly religious and moral in tone. His first radio address as chancellor, on the evening of his first day in office, was a speech that could have been made by a Catholic or Lutheran bishop. He began by asking humbly for God's guidance, vowing to lay all his labours 'before God, our conscience, and the German people. Our first and greatest task in national renewal is to preserve Christianity and the spiritual unity of our people. Only then will the very foundation of our life be defended and our nation preserved. Christianity ... is the foundation of our morality and the family, which is the nucleus of our people.' After a ringing call for world peace and disarmament, the end of social antagonism and conflict, and the reconciliation of all peoples, Hitler closed with a benediction: 'May the Almighty God hold our labour in His Grace, direct our will, bless our endeavours, and favour us with the trust of our people, for we struggle not for ourselves but for Germany.'[229]

The Führer ordered his Storm Troopers to attend church on Sundays preceding the Reichstag elections. In every town and hamlet throughout the Reich, regular parishioners were surprised to see slightly embarrassed, but freshly scrubbed, bully boys of Hitler's 'Storm Battalions' coming to church. Their deportment was impeccable.

Hitler opened his campaign for the crucial Reichstag elections with a major broadcast on 10 February from the Berlin Sports Palace. Millions of Germans heard their Führer proclaim his personal religious faith and plead for those who had opposed him in the past to join in support of his movement. He ended with a paraphrase of the Lord's Prayer: 'Grant us ... a Reich of greatness and honour and power and glory ... Amen.'[230]

Hitler chose to close his campaign in Königsberg, East Prussia, a stronghold of Lutheranism and Prussian conservatism. The staging was a virtuoso display of political skill. Once again the Führer called upon God to bless his endeavours, praying, 'Lord God, let us never, never become cowardly, let us never forget the duty we have undertaken ... We are all proud that through God's gracious help we have all become true Germans again.'[231]

Directly after his speech the national radio burst forth in the great hymn of thanksgiving, *Wir treten zum beten*. Millions of Germans, with tears in their eyes and uplifted hearts, joined in singing the great chorale of rejoicing which appears in all Catholic and Protestant hymnbooks – which was a favourite of the Kaiser's:

Wir treten zum beten vor Gott den Gerechten,
Er waltet und haltet ein strenges Gericht.
Er lässt von den Schlechten die Guten nicht knechten;
Sein Name sei gelobt, er vergisst unser nicht.

Im Streite zur Seite ist Gott uns gestanden;
Er wollte, es sollte das Recht siegreich sein.
Da ward, kaum begonnen, die Schlacht schon gewonnen;
Du Gott warst da mit uns; der Sieg er war dein.[232]

Immediately following the hymn, Germans heard over their radios the great church bells of Königsberg ringing forth in triumph.

The next day the editor of the influential periodical *Allgemeine Evangelisch-Lutherischen Kirchenzeitung* expressed the feeling of his Christian countrymen: 'Millions of German Christians listened and joined in singing, *Wir treten zum beten* ... As the Königsberg bells sounded, there rose to heaven in that hour prayers of thanksgiving and such a jubilation as never before was heard in the history of Germany.'[233]

Neither the editor nor the German public knew that church authorities had actually forbidden the ringing of bells on behalf of the Nazi party. The sound of the bells and the chorale had not come from the churches; they came from phonograph records carefully stored in the Nazi collection for just such an occasion.[234] But that did not change the popular impression that Hitler had so carefully created. German Christians on the eve of the Reichstag elections assumed that their church leaders had given their blessing to Hitler and his Nazis.

Almost from the very beginning, German Protestant leaders had been favourably inclined to Hitler. Pastors were particularly impressed by the way Hitler appealed to the young, a group that was conspicuously falling away from the established churches.[235] In the December 1930 issue of the *Christliche Welt*, a theological student reported that 'almost all theology students' in his university were National Socialists. In January 1931 the pastor of the Evangelical Church of the Holy Ghost in Berlin reported that his large confirmation class were 'all little Nazis.'[236] In March 1933 the editor of the most influential Protestant journal in Germany set forth his reason for supporting the National Socialists: they had created a new spirit in Germany. 'Hitler,' he wrote, 'has inspired the youth of Germany to hate and shun those who would poison German thinking ... he has inscribed on his banners the old virtues of Truth, Honour, and Loyalty.'[237]

The Führer found it more difficult to win Catholic approval. In the elections of 1932 the influential Catholic Centre party had urged Catholics to vote against the Nazis. Realizing that the way to win over the Centre and their adherents was to go through the hierarchy, Hitler cultivated the Holy See and the bishops, reminding them over and over that his movement was the best defence against Bolshevism, promising to support Christian education in the schools of Germany and to negotiate a concordat with the Church. Pope Pius XI (1922–39) was impressed, saying that he welcomed the appointment 'of the good Catholic Herr Hitler' to the chancellorship. 'The man pleases me,' the pontiff said.[238]

The Catholic Church had helped Hitler gain power, but he still had to win their support, along with that of the Protestants, if he were to push through parliament the Enabling Act that would make him dictator of Germany. The Führer attracted both groups, along with the military establishment, on the day he opened the new Reichstag. He had chosen the time and the place with great care.

On 21 March in 1871, in a memorable scene, Kaiser Wilhelm I and Otto von Bismarck had opened the first Reichstag of the glorious new Second Reich. On 21 March in 1933 Hitler would open the first Reichstag of his Third Reich. The date was also two days before the vote that would give him dictatorial power. The place was Potsdam, royal village of Hohenzollern kings and seat of Prussian militarism, rather than Weimar, home of Goethe and Schiller, and now stigmatized as the birthplace of the Weimar Republic. The opening ceremonies were to be held in the Garrison Church, a shrine of the Prussian–German army. The chapel had been established by King Friedrich Wilhelm I, founder of the Prussian army. Here Frederick the Great was buried. Here the young Kaiser Wilhelm II, while rededicating the faded battle flags of Prussian regiments, had felt the presence of his dead grandfather, the first Kaiser Wilhelm, moving through the church.[239]

Hitler was a master of symbolism. The Kaiser's chair in the little church had been left vacant, with the Crown Prince, Friedrich Wilhelm, standing in full uniform behind it. He was flanked by his royal brothers, August Wilhelm and Eitel Friedrich. Two guards of honour were drawn up: on one side of the church, the army, on the other, Hitler's Storm Troopers; on one side, the black and white flags of old Germany, on the other, the black, white, and red swastikas of the new. Old Germany was represented by octogenarian Field Marshal Paul von Hindenburg und Beneckendorf, Reichspräsident of the dying Weimar Republic, the hero of the Battle of Tannenberg of 1914, who had fought in the Austrian war of 1866 and the French war of 1871 that had forged the German Empire. The old man, massive and impressive in full Field Marshal's uniform with *Pickelhaube* and medal-spangled chest, saluted the Kaiser's empty chair with his baton as he slowly proceeded to his seat.

The new Reich was represented by the school drop-out and former sub-corporal, now chancellor, and soon to be officially declared Führer of Germany.[240] He appeared not as brown-shirted revolutionary, but in cutaway and striped trousers, the traditional expression of bourgeois respectability. Deferentially, he approached President Hindenburg's chair. Bending low, he placed his sweating, feminine hands between the cool, parchment palms of the old Field Marshal in an ancient gesture of feudal homage: 'The apostolic succession was complete.'[241]

Hitler began his measured and dignified address from the pulpit with a graceful tribute to President Hindenburg. Bowing to the old man, he said, '*Herr Feldmarschall*, we thank you for your guidance.' He then gave solemn assurances to both Catholics and Protestants and made a special appeal for Catholic support: 'The national government believes that in both Christian confessions lies the most important basis for the maintenance of our national being ... The national government sees in Christianity the unmovable foundation of our moral and ethical life. Christian teaching will be preserved in our educational institutions ... We place the highest value on establishing and cultivating friendly relations with the Holy See.'[242] As the speech ended, the choir softly sang *Wir treten zum beten.*

Hindenburg's brief speech, perhaps unwittingly, put his immense prestige squarely behind Hitler: 'May the old spirit memorialized in this church,' he intoned, 'continue to inspire the present.' He then called on all Germans to unite behind the new order to achieve 'a united, free, and proud Germany.'[243] Hitler beamed with pleasure.

After the ceremony all the church bells of the village and of Greater Berlin pealed forth in jubilation. This time radio listeners throughout Germany heard live bells, tolled with the approval of church authorities. That endorsement in itself testified to the change of attitude among church leaders within a few weeks' time.

The entire ceremony was filmed by the Ministry of Propaganda and distributed to every movie house in Germany – courtesy of the cinema magnate,

Alfred Hugenberg (1866–1951), a former member of the Pan-German League and supporter of the Kaiser, now patron of the Nazis.

The message of this Potsdam scene was clear: The army and the church both stood solidly behind Adolf Hitler. This was demonstrated two days after the ceremony when the Catholic Centre joined the conservative parties and the National Socialists in voting for the Enabling Act. The way was open for Hitler's dictatorship. And it was all entirely legal.

In gaining the support of the Christian Church, Hitler had shown himself to be a master tactician. Was it merely tactics? His pious talk of religious purpose, his prayers and benedictions, his assertions that his movement was 'actually Christian' – was all this mere contrivance?

To think so is to mistake the man and grossly to underestimate his political appeal. Tactics were certainly important to Hitler's success, as they are to that of any political leader. But successful rulers must be more than tacticians. Machiavelli had given the prescription for the ideal prince in a famous metaphor. Since humans are largely animal, he argued, the successful prince must 'knowingly adopt the beast,' and the beasts most helpful to him are the fox and the lion. The ideal ruler should be crafty as a fox, one of whose tricks was to appear to be a lion of conviction and lofty purpose: 'He who has known best how to employ the Fox has succeeded best. But it is necessary to know well how to disguise this characteristic and to be a great pretender and dissembler.'[244]

Hitler's use of religion for his own political purposes shows the foxlike cunning with which he responded to the desires of the masses. What they really wanted, the Führer never tired of saying, was not freedom of choice, not liberty, not reasoned analysis, but faith, authority, and mystery. Mystery because they wanted desperately to believe in miracles.

Hitler had presented himself as Germany's new Messiah, a true follower of Jesus, when in fact he was following, not the Nazarene, but the Grand Inquisitor of Dostoyevsky's story. After throwing Jesus in jail, it will be recalled, the Grand Inquisitor taunts Him, saying that He had misjudged the masses by offering them love and freedom of choice. But they wanted neither; they wanted mystery and authority:

And if it is a mystery [they want], then we too have a right to preach a mystery and to teach them it is neither the free judgement of their hearts nor love that matters, but a mystery which they must obey blindly, even against their conscience. So we have done.

We have corrected Thy work and have founded it upon *miracle, mystery, and authority.* And men rejoiced that they were again led like sheep and that the terrible gift [of freedom] which had brought them so much suffering had at last been lifted from their hearts.[245]

Hitler showed political cunning in his adroit use of prayers, hymns, biblical quotations, and church bells in wooing Christian support during the elections of 1933 and the voting for his Enabling Act. But beyond those immediate political objectives, there was a deeper reason for using Christian symbols and ceremonies. The Führer's purpose was to destroy one religion and create another. But he was shrewd enough to know that he could not accomplish his objective by directly attacking the Christian Church, at least not until after the war. His approach was subtle. He planned to destroy traditional religion through substitution. He would nullify its appeal by supplying a more satisfying alternative. The very boldness of this plan was political cunning at its best.

Yet Hitler also starred in the role of lion, the exalted Leader of principle and conviction. But he did not play the role in quite the way Machiavelli had recommended. The Florentine had wanted his ideal prince merely to *play* the lion of principle and conviction. But with Hitler it was more than an act, and consequently all the more convincing. He was committed with deadly sincerity to what he truly believed, and he made believers out of thousands upon thousands of Germans, who were absolutely convinced that the Führer was sincere. In this, the world learned to its dismay, they were correct.

One could not listen to certain of Hitler's speeches – one cannot listen to them again on tapes or see them on films – without feeling the terrifying intensity of the man's conviction that he was touched with divinity, that he had been chosen by God to lead the German *Volk*.

There is one unforgettable ten-second sequence in Leni Riefenstahl's brilliant film of the Nuremberg party rally of 1934. The Führer is addressing the massed ranks of the Hitler Youth, the group closest to his heart. Suddenly he stops, looks up to heaven, and trembles with emotion. His eyes are aflame, and his voice breaks with passion as he cries out the words from Genesis: 'Thou art flesh of my flesh! Thou art bone of my bone! Blood of my blood!' In moments like these Adolf Hitler was a man possessed, his emotions genuinely felt and compellingly expressed.

And yet the fox was also lurking behind the scenes. The carefully contrived staging of the Nuremberg rallies, part high mass, part gigantic pep rally, part revival meeting, part Wagnerian opera with effective use of light, colour, and sound. All these remind us that with Hitler there was always contrivance as well as conviction.

Any commentator on Hitler's religious beliefs must be troubled by two surprising statements. One was made to a small gathering of his supporters, the other to a disciple in private: 'Our movement is actually Christian' and 'All we really want is the fulfilment of Christ's life mission.' One can, of course, dismiss such pronouncements, along with Hitler's homilies,[246] as the purest hypocrisy. Hypocrisy, however, is seldom pure, and it is never as dangerous as misdirected sincerity. The horrors of history from Torquemada to the witch-burners of Salem, from Hitler to Pol Pot, have been committed not by hypocrites but by sincere people bent on playing God. Hitler's form of Christianity will endure as a terrifying illustration of the ancient Latin epigram, *corruptio optimi pessima*: The worst kind of corruption is the corruption of the best.

The lion in Hitler meant what he said; yet all the time the fox within him was taking another page from the Grand Inquisitor: 'Men are vicious and rebellious, but in the end they will become obedient ... They will marvel at us and be terrified of us and be proud that we are so mighty ... and they will regard us as gods. We shall tell them that we do Thy bidding and rule in Thy name. We shall deceive them.'[247]

Hitler and the Purge of 30 June to 2 July 1934

In this hour I was responsible for the fate of the Nation. Consequently I became the German peoples' supreme judge (*oberste Gerechtsherr*).

Adolf Hitler, 1934

The Nazis called it, variously, the Blood Purge, the Röhm Purge, or the Night of the Long Knives. No event in his career illustrates more starkly Hitler's political cunning and ruthless drive for personal power. He gave the orders and supervised the massacre of hundreds, perhaps thousands,[248] of loyal supporters in order to gain the favour of the military and economic establishment.

The brown-shirted SA (from *Sturmabteilungen* or storm troops) were the 'Old Fighters' (*Alte Kämpfer*) whom Hitler had praised in 1933 as 'the first soldiers of the Third Reich,' without whose help he could not have come to power. But by the early summer of 1934, when he aspired to assume the dying President Hindenburg's mantle as head of state, the SA had become a source of embarrassment.

They were a brawling, brutish, and unpredictable lot. Many of them had been *Freikorps* fighters,[249] whose moral conduct was 'a stench in the nostrils of all decent Germans.'[250] Corruption, debauchery, and perversion were rife in their ranks. The homosexual orgies of their SA commander, Ernst Röhm, were well known. His deputy in Pomerania, Edmund Heines, a former *Freikorps* leader and now police president of Breslau, had established an organization throughout the Reich for the purpose of recruiting attractive young men for his male harem.

The SA also embarrassed Hitler by taking the socialist part of his program seriously, a program Hitler had downplayed in order to cultivate the support of the industrial and financial circles he needed if he were to stabilize the economy, solve massive unemployment, and prepare Germany for war. Radical members of the SA, who called themselves 'Bolshevists of the right,' supported their blunt and outspoken chief of staff, Ernst Röhm, in calling for a 'second revolution.' Röhm had been Hitler's comrade in arms in the 1920s, the only man who called the Führer 'Adolf' and one of the very few with whom he was on familiar '*du*' terms.[251] He had no intention of staging a coup against Hitler, whom he still considered his Führer; he simply wanted to push him towards a real revolution, one that would sweep aside class privilege and establish the *Volksgemeinschaft* Hitler had promised, but conspicuously failed to deliver. Röhm's followers called themselves 'Beefsteak Nazis' (brown on the outside, red within). Not surprisingly, neither their conduct nor their economic ideas were welcomed by the traditional establishment.

Captain Röhm's military ambitions were even more alarming to the army – and hence to Hitler, for he knew he could neither succeed Field Marshal President Hindenburg as head of state nor fulfil his plans for conquest without the army's cooperation. The army had supported Hitler's accession of power in 1933 because they saw him as a convenient tool with which they would remilitarize the country and prepare it for the war of revenge they had been planning since 1918. Moreover, like the industrialists, they assumed that they could set aside 'that Bohemian corporal,' as Hindenburg had contemptuously called him, after he had served their purposes.[252]

By 1934 the army had become alarmed at the military pretensions of the SA. Since replacing Göring as SA chief of staff in 1931, Röhm had expanded the SA to a paramilitary force of nearly three million men that was developing its own aviation, motorized, intelligence-gathering, and medical units. Röhm made it clear that he wanted to replace the traditional army with his vastly expanded SA, which would become a *Volksheer,* a true people's army, with himself as commander.[253]

Field Marshal Werner von Blomberg, the minister of defence, who learned of these plans, showed them to the high command. On 21 June 1934 Blomberg informed Hitler that unless 'necessary steps were taken,' President Hindenburg would declare a state of martial law and form a new government. Realizing that the future of his regime was at stake, Hitler worked out a deal with Blomberg: In return for the army's support for his regime and his bid for the presidency, Hitler would sacrifice Röhm and the SA.[254]

To carry out the murders Hitler called upon Röhm's bitter rival, Heinrich Himmler ('my loyal Heinrich'), commander of Hitler's special elite guard, the SS (*Schutz-Staffel* or protective staff). These dreaded Black Shirts swore a special oath of fidelity to the Führer. They wore on their caps the death's head and on their belt buckles the motto Hitler had given them: *Meine Ehre heisst Treue* (Loyalty is Mine Honour). They now proved their loyalty, if not their honour, by slaughtering their former comrades. As the army and the police of Germany looked on approvingly, the SS 'committed wholesale murder from one end of the country to the other.'[255]

To the very end Röhm and the SA remained loyal to Hitler, many dying with his name on their lips, defiantly shouting '*Heil Hitler!*' as they were gunned down. It never occurred to them that they were being killed at Hitler's personal orders because in his eyes they had now become obstacles in his relentless drive to power. They assumed that they were the victims of a plot directed by Himmler, or possibly the army, to seize power from their beloved Führer.[256]

Hitler also used the occasion to settle old political and personal scores. General Kurt von Schleicher, who had plotted against Hitler during his brief chancellorship (January 1933), was murdered along with his wife. The aged Gustav von Kahr, the former 'commissar-general' of Bavaria, who had embarrassed Hitler in the putsch fiasco of 1923, was hauled out of his bed by the SS. Kahr's body was found in a woods smashed to pieces by pick axes.[257] Catholic leaders who opposed Hitler were murdered along with Father Bernard Sempel, who had performed the unhappy task of editing the first draft of *Mein Kampf*, and, who, purportedly, had knowledge of the disgusting sado-masochistic sexual relations Hitler may have had with his niece, Geli Raubal.[258] Also on the Führer's hit list were former Chancellor Heinrich Brüning and Putzi Hanfstaengl, both of whom managed to get out of Germany in time.[259]

Throughout the massacre Hitler demonstrated a capacity for ruthless and efficient action. He personally wrote the press releases, casting himself as the courageous and energetic leader who made 'brutal decisions' in order to save the country from 'morally diseased persons' who were trying to seize power. One of his dispatches sounded a particularly high note of hypocrisy: 'The Führer demands that every future leader of the SA prove himself a true leader, friend, and comrade.'[260]

Hitler delivered one of the most diabolical and politically successful speeches of his career before the Reichstag on 13 July 1924.[261] He defended the massacres as acts of heroic patriotism. 'In that hour,' said Hitler, 'I was responsible for the fate of the nation. Consequently I became the German peoples' chief judge.' He was forced to act so decisively, he said, because he had been outraged by the moral depravity of those in the SA, who had been infected by the 'Jewish–Bolshevist poisoners of humanity.' Their conduct, the Führer regretted to say, had been 'an affront to all decent Germans.' He felt personally injured because these despicable people had 'betrayed my loyalty and trust.' [!]

The Führer had more pressing political reasons for killing his comrades than his sudden concern about their 'moral turpitude, drunkenness, and unspeakable sexual licence.' He had known about their corruption and sexuality for years and had condoned it among his closest associates, most notably Röhm and Hess.[262] As late as 31 December 1933, Hitler had said that he was 'proud to count men like Ernst Röhm among my friends.'[263] Other Nazi leaders who remained in important positions of his government were not noted for moral probity. Julius Streicher was a pornographer and sadist whose lifestyle was a 'cesspool' of corruption and sexual licence.[264] Robert Ley was a *débauché* and advanced alcoholic. Joseph Goebbels and Martin Bormann were notorious womanizers. The moral standards of the Führer himself left everything to be desired.

The economic and military establishment applauded when Hitler took personal credit for 'utterly rooting out the Jewish–Bolshevist–Anarchists and every sort of n'er-do-well' who plotted to overthrow law and order and undermine the entire social structure of Germany. The army noted with satisfaction Hitler's assertion that 'there can be only one bearer of weapons in this state and that is the army.'

After giving a stark warning that 'anyone who raises his hand against this State [read Adolf Hitler] will learn that the penalty is death,' the Führer closed on a conciliatory and righteous note: 'We want to establish a state in which all Germans live together in love under a government in which all are treated with respect and whose laws reflect the morality of our people.'

As political performance the speech was a *tour de force*. Congratulatory telegrams poured in from a grateful nation. Church leaders were enthusiastic. The ex-Kaiser in Doorn also heartily approved of Hitler's actions. Dr Gürtner, the Reich minister of justice (one of Wilhelm's many appointees), declared that Hitler's 'courageous action' (arbitrary shooting with no semblance of a trial) was 'a statesmanlike performance of duty.'[265] Joseph Stalin also approved: 'Have you heard what happened in Germany?' he asked a meeting of the Politburo after the massacre. 'Some fellow, that Hitler! Knows how to treat his political opponents.'[266]

Hitler particularly welcomed the army's response. Field Marshal Blomberg told the officers of the Wehrmacht, 'The Führer, with soldierly decisiveness and exemplary courage, personally intervened to crush the traitors and mutineers. We thank him for restoring the army as the sole arms-bearers of the people.'

Hitler's most prized telegram came from Neudeck on 2 July. The mortally ill Hindenburg had nothing but praise:

Your determined action and the brave intervention of your own person have nipped treason in the bud and saved the German nation ... I hereby convey to you my deepest thanks and my sincerest appreciation.

With best greetings,
von Hindenburg[267]

As soon as the old man died a month later, on 1 August 1934, Hitler proclaimed himself head of the government and, the next day, required every member of the armed forces to swear a personal oath to him and to 'the new state *in my name*.' As Gordon Craig has noted, the commitment to do so made effective preventive action against Hitler's subsequent atrocities impossible [268] – even if anyone had wanted to intervene. At least as significant as the oath was the symbolic fact that the swastika insignia was now sewn on all the uniforms of German armed forces.

When Hitler asked the Reichstag for legislation to legalize the murders of 30 June to 2 July as 'defensive measures during the national emergency (*Staatsnotwehr*),' the measure passed without a dissenting vote. In mid-August Hitler took his achievements to the German people, asking them in a plebiscite if they approved of his leadership of the Fatherland. The response was overwhelming: 89.93 per cent voted '*Ja!*' That was probably an accurate reflection of popular opinion.

Thus, with the approval of the traditional establishment – economic, military, and religious – and the overwhelming endorsement of the German people, Hitler had achieved total political control.

Conflict among Party and Government Agencies

It is the will of the Führer.

Nazi officials

In recent years there has been a lively debate over the way the government of the Third Reich actually functioned. One group of historians, the 'personalists,' insist that there really was a *Führerstaat*, with Adolf Hitler as its absolute master calling all the shots. Their opponents, who have been called the 'structuralists,' put the term '*Führerstaat*' in quotation marks and argue that Hitler in fact was not nearly as powerful as he imagined or his propaganda proclaimed. A leading protagonist of this school, Professor Hans Mommsen, judges Hitler a weak dictator, who, because of his laziness and ineptitude, forfeited power to the party, state, or army hierarchy, which actually ran the country.[269] Moreover, according to the structuralists, far from being a monolithic state of well-oiled Germanic efficiency, the government of the Third Reich was 'a jungle of overlapping organizations,'[270] 'administrative chaos,'[271] and 'authoritarian anarchy'[272] torn by dissension, with each of the competing authorities claiming that he was carrying out 'the will of the Führer.'

We can get a clearer view of whether the Führer's power in Nazi Germany was myth or reality by looking briefly at how the government functioned in a few key areas: the economy, education, the administration of occupied territories, and, two issues of special concern to Hitler, propaganda and 'a final solution' to the Jewish question.

Economic planning in the Third Reich serves as an illustration of 'authoritarian anarchy.' In 1936, while Horace Greely Hjalmer Schacht still remained as minister of economics, Hitler named Reichsmarschall Hermann Göring the director of the Four-Year Plan designed to make Germany ready for war by 1940. At the same time, Robert Ley exerted immense influence on the economy through the many enterprises associated with his vast Labour Front. When in February 1942 Albert Speer was finally put in 'complete charge' of all armament production, he found that after two and a half years of war there were *five* 'supreme Reich authorities' with independent and conflicting powers over German war production.

Hitler's entire economy depended on the exploitation of conquered territory in central and eastern Europe. Yet as the editors of documents on the German economy have pointed out, in the occupied areas, 'competing agencies [of the party, army, and state] operated with the massive degree of inefficiency typical of the Nazi bureaucratic machine and which, in addition, was riddled with corruption.'[273]

The education of youth, crucial to the indoctrination of Nazi ideology, was theoretically a main concern of the Führer. Yet he did not provide direction. He had appointed Bernhard Rust the Reich minister of science and education. But Rust, a weak person and ineffective administrator, could not stand up to the competition from others, each of whom claimed that the Führer had made *him* responsible for the education of German youth. They included Baldur von Schirach, head of the Hitler Youth; Minister of Propaganda and Enlightenment Joseph Goebbels; Heinrich Himmler of the SS; and Alfred Rosenberg, self-styled 'philosopher' of Nazi ideology. In the whole field of education, 'There was no clear guidance from the top, since Hitler failed to provide any consistent lines of policy ... In the vacuum, individual leaders were free to seize the initiative.'[274]

Given the intensity of the Führer's lifelong interest in propaganda as the primary means of forcing the masses to do his will,[275] one would expect that he would have kept firm control over the various agencies that dispensed approved information in Nazi Germany. But he did not. Nazi propaganda agencies were marked by the same confusion, overlapping responsibilities, and rivalry that characterized other departments of his government, with Hitler seemingly unable, unwilling, or uninterested in adjudicating among warring factions. Joseph Goebbels, as minister of propaganda and enlightenment, Otto Dietrich, as chief of the Reich's press, and Joachim von Ribbentrop in charge of the 'foreign press,' each insisted that he was responsible for all Nazi propaganda, because each claimed to be carrying out 'the will of the Führer.' Since Hitler did not intervene, conflicts among all three were left unresolved.[276]

It has been suggested that Hitler deliberately encouraged administrative rivalries as part of his calculated policy to 'divide and rule.' But Hitler created entirely too much division and ruled far too little. Moreover, he permitted his satraps to concentrate such extensive power in their own hands that vast areas of German life were, in effect, withdrawn from Hitler's supervision.[277]

The Führer's Administrative Style

When, I would ask myself, did Hitler ever work?

Albert Speer[278]

The Führer's peculiar lifestyle also contributed to inefficient government. In the mornings he often slept or lingered in his bedroom until 10 or 11 o'clock (after playing his dressing game with his valet, who was not permitted to see the Führer in his nightclothes).[279] Long luncheons filled with inane chatter about trivia took much of the afternoon. Brief bursts of energy might follow in late afternoon, with motor trips or conferences. Evenings were often given over to movies, followed by monologues lasting until well after midnight.

In asking himself when Hitler ever worked, Speer was asking the same question that intimates of the Kaiser had asked about their master. The Führer, like the Kaiser, was rarely in his office and often inaccessible for important decisions. Ministers of state were obliged to wait hours, sometimes days, for admittance to his presence. Hitler refused to read documents that were more than a page long. (The Kaiser also instructed a military adjutant to 'keep it short.') Hitler's final decision was often determined by a sudden whim and could amount to nothing more than a nod of his head, a remark thrown out casually, or a wave of his hand, which was interpreted as an incontrovertible *Führerbefehl*, 'leaving it to ministers, civil servants, and party bosses to fight over exactly what he had agreed to.'[280] (With the Kaiser, the best way to get a favourable decision, an aide recalled, was to catch him when he was out of breath after winning an exciting point in a close tennis match. Then he might be expected to nod a panting approval.)

Members of Hitler's inner circle reported that the all-powerful Führer had only a marginal interest and a dim understanding of the day-to-day workings of government and that he made no effort to learn. Administration did not fit his exalted image of himself as artist, messianic leader, and creative thinker. 'A single idea of genius,' he observed, 'is worth more than a lifetime of office work.'[281] The Führer proceeded to govern by this maxim, frittering away his days until sudden inspiration or a crisis would ignite a burst of feverish activity.

Hitler also contributed to administrative conflict and confusion by his disinclination to put orders in writing.[282] His penchant for giving orders orally, allowed, for example, each of the three rivals for power over propaganda to claim that he was fulfilling the 'will of the Führer,' as given directly to him in private conversation. That Goebbels prevailed was not because his verbal mandate was superior to that of his rivals, but because he had the ability and the political clout to beat out similarly authorized competition.

The way the Nazi government actually functioned would appear to support the view that because Hitler failed to exert rigorous control over all phases of his government, he was a 'weak dictator.' But that would be a valid conclusion only if it could be shown that Hitler *wanted* a different form of governmental structure but was unable to achieve it, or that he had *wanted* to make day-to-day decisions but powerful forces prevented him from doing so. On the contrary, there is every indication that Hitler *preferred* to let his government run that way.[283]

Hitler and the Holocaust

There is not the slightest evidence that any major change in Jewish policy took place without the knowledge and approval of Adolf Hitler.

Christopher Browning[284]

In an important article in a journal specializing in studies of National Socialism, Martin Broszat, a leading German authority on the Third Reich, contended that Hitler had not planned the Holocaust in advance and that he had given no specific order, written or unwritten, for exterminating European Jews. The Führer's thinking about the 'Final Solution of the Jewish Problem' was muddled and inconsistent. Certainly he wanted to rid his Reich of Jews, but – as with so many other decisions – he vacillated and changed his mind about how to do it.

Circumstances, Broszat argued, determined the genocide. Hitler had thought of moving the Jews either to Madagascar or to Russia. It was the failure to defeat Russia (Operation Barbarossa) that decided the fate of the Jews.[285] A respected American historian accepts this conclusion: 'Without Operation Barbarossa,' Professor Arno Mayer of Princeton writes, 'there would and could have been no Jewish catastrophe, no "Final Solution."'[286]

By the late summer of 1942, this argument goes, the Jews were crowded by the millions into the eastern provinces of Hitler's 'Greater German Reich.' And since they had no place to go, they posed insurmountable problems for local authorities. Confronted by the starvation of the local inhabitants and the threat of epidemics, district leaders of the party and the SS took it upon themselves to order the massacres as the only feasible 'escape from a *cul de sac.*' Thus, the destructive process was not the result of advanced planning or any explicit order from above. Rather, it was 'incremental' and 'piecemeal,' a series of ad hoc orders given by local SS leaders in 'pragmatic response' to local conditions. Once begun, the killing process gained momentum from its own inner dynamics. As in many other areas of his government, the argument concludes, because of Adolf Hitler's default of leadership, initiative was taken by local officials.

Historians of this persuasion ask some pertinent questions: If Hitler had planned from the beginning to kill all the Jews, why had he told Mussolini in June 1940 that he wanted to ship them to Madagascar and, as late as 27 January 1942, talked about resettling them in Russia?[287] If Hitler really believed that the Jews constituted an immediate threat to Germany, why did he not give orders for a 'preventive' massacre either before his western offensive in 1940, or before he attacked Russia in 1941? If he was really determined to kill all the Jews, why, even after the Wannsee Conference of January 1942, were hundreds of thousands of Jews consigned to work in war industries?[288]

The Holocaust could not have happened without broad support from leaders of German society and from the German people at large. Army generals, of proud tradition, cooperated actively with the SS in massacring Jews – and giving orders to kill millions of Russian prisoners of war in their care.[289]

The German judiciary contributed by raising no objections to Hitler's racial legislation; thousands of civil servants and railway officials 'processed' and shipped Jews to their death.

Industry also cooperated. The huge chemical trust I.G. Farben established a factory at Auschwitz ('I.G. Auschwitz'), where it had its own punishment block complete with whipping posts, 'standing cells' where victims could neither kneel nor sit, gallows for hanging anyone guilty of 'eating bones from the garbage' or 'sabotaging work norms by warming their hands.' Company officials argued that they 'could not afford reforms,' but while their workers died of mistreatment and malnutrition, IGF was making enormous profits selling poison gas to death camps at Auschwitz, Belsen, Chelmo, Sobibor, and Treblinka. Daimler-Benz also worked Jews to death, while becoming Germany's leading armaments maker.[290]

The academic and scientific worlds made significant contributions to the Holocaust. A disproportionate number of MDs and PhDs joined the SS. German biomedical scientists actively participated in the construction of Nazi racial policy. They endorsed both Hitler's 'euthanasia' and his 'Final Solution' because they too wanted to purge the nation of 'genetically diseased elements.'[291] German public health physicians agreed with them.[292]

The German population not only contributed massive indifference. As Daniel Goldhagen has demonstrated in his important study, hundreds of thousands of average German citizens served as 'Hitler's willing executioners.' They volunteered to pull the trigger, they had their pictures taken doing so, and they proudly sent these pictures home to their loved ones.[293] What happened in the Polish village of Józefów near Lublin one day in July 1942 is typical of what happened in hundreds of other villages.

On 30 June, Reserve Police Battalion No. 101 was given orders to shoot all 1,500 Jewish women, children, and old people who remained in the village after young males had been shipped off to work camps. The Jews were to be 'shot on the spot,' individually, in face-to-face encounter. This police battalion consisted of civilian draftees from Hamburg. Predominantly, they were married men who had been workers, artisans, clerks, and schoolteachers in civilian life, who were now considered too old for active military service. The battalion commander gave his recruits an option: if anyone felt sqeamish about this 'action,' he could refuse to participate. Very few declined and those who did were not punished. All the others volunteered to shoot all the Jews of the village.[294]

Average citizens in other countries also cooperated in the genocide. Polish and Lithuanian Christians turned in thousands of Jews to the SS. In France more citizens helped the Gestapo than supported the *Maquis*. France was the only European country from which thousands of men, women, and children were 'delivered to the gas chambers by the unsolicited decision of their government.'[295] The French resistance never attempted to stop a single deportation train bound for the crematoria. Austrians contributed 75 per cent of the staff for Nazi concentration camps and 80 per cent of Eichmann's assistants. The Dutch, by celebrating the heroism of Anne Frank and dedicating a museum to her memory, helped to hide a terrible truth: the Dutch civil service cooperated so well with the Gestapo that the Nazis needed to commit only a small number of troops to round up Jews in Holland. The death rate of Jews in the Netherlands was the highest of all western countries: about 75 per cent were turned in to the Nazis and murdered.[296]

The British Foreign Office and the American State Department gave orders that kept thousands of escaping Jews away from their shores.[297]

The Jews themselves actually cooperated with the SS and collaborated in their own destruction. It must be emphasized, however, that the words 'cooperate' and 'collaborate' in this context are badly misunderstood if they suggest voluntary willingness to help the Nazis. There can be no doubt that the Jews were deceived and coerced into compliance. And yet the heart-wrenching conclusion reached by eminent Jewish students of the Holocaust must be faced: however compelling the reasons, however extreme the duress, Jews became tragic accomplices in their own extinction. Raul Hilberg, Hannah Arendt, and Isaiah Trunk have demonstrated beyond dispute that leaders of the Jewish communities in Berlin, as in Amsterdam, Antwerp, and Warsaw, cooperated with the Nazis and smoothed the way to deportation and death. With very few exceptions, Jewish elders implemented SS directives, published and endorsed duplicitous Nazi cover stories about 'resettlement,' selected those who were to die, arranged for their transportation, and collected money from them to pay for their own transportation to the death camps – thereby helping the Nazis achieve their goal of making the Final Solution 'self-financing.' The elders of the Jewish councils (*Judenräte*) discouraged resistance and ordered compliance with Nazi directives.[298] Jews followed the orders of their leaders, many displaying what Hilberg has called 'anticipatory compliance': in pathetically futile efforts to pacify the Nazis, they turned in their jewels and gold and arrived well ahead of time at the staging areas, having paid their railway fare in advance. 'They attempted to tame the Germans,' Hilberg writes, 'as one would attempt to tame a wild beast. They avoided "provocation" and complied instantly with decrees and orders.'[299]

The Nazis were pleasantly surprised by this passive cooperation from their victims. It made their job so much easier. Adolf Eichmann, the SS officer chiefly in charge of mass murders, testified during his trial in Jerusalem that the *Judenräte* were so helpful in implementing SS orders that German personnel could be released for other service. Hannah Arendt concluded bitterly that without Jewish help, the murder of millions of Jews would not have been possible: 'To a Jew, this role of the Jewish leaders in the destruction of their own people is ... the darkest chapter of the whole dark story.'[300]

An even darker role was played by the Jewish police of the ghettos, an agency which, like the Jewish councils, the Nazis created with satanic cunning to implement their orders and to demoralize and shatter the Jewish community by setting Jews against Jews. They were not entirely unsuccessful. After the war, Jewish courts of honour determined that many members of the Jewish police had actively participated in the destruction of their fellow Jews by ferreting them out of hiding places, filling their own pockets with bribes from their victims, and beating them up in the streets to curry favour with the SS. A Jew who was to die as a victim of this treachery angrily recorded in his diary: 'Every Warsaw Jew, every woman and child, can cite thousands of cases of the inhuman cruelty and violence of the Jewish Police. Those cases will never be forgotten by the survivors, and they must and shall be paid for.'[301]

It must not be forgotten that some heroic Jews fought back at hopeless odds. Their gallant resistance was most tragically demonstrated in the uprisings against their oppressors in the Warsaw Ghetto during the spring of 1943 – the only urban uprising against the Nazis anywhere in Hitler's Europe – and in the death camp of Sobibor in October 1943.[302]

Yet the overwhelming majority of the Jews of Europe, by the hundreds of thousands, did indeed go, as furious Jewish resisters charged at the time, 'like sheep to the slaughter.' Shortly before he and his family were killed, one of the heroes of the uprising in the Warsaw Ghetto despaired over 'the passivity of the Jewish masses' and asked anguished questions: 'Why are they all so quiet? Why does the father die, and the mother, and each of the children without a single protest? ... *Why?* Why did everything come so easy to the enemy? ... This will be an eternal mystery – this passivity of the Jewish populace even towards their own police.'[303] Emmanuel Ringelblum's searing questions and the mystery he was unable to solve will continue to haunt us. We cannot possibly know what terror, despair, and abandonment can do to the human soul.

Those who are convinced that Hitler's personality and ideology were of controlling importance in the Third Reich disagree with the 'structuralists.' They insist that while historical conditions were important, the genocide of European Jews was the logical consequence of the Führer's anti-Semitic phobia, and that once he had gained total power, the Holocaust was 'merely a matter of time and opportunity'[304] – an opportunity that came with the Second World War and the conquest of Poland. According to this view, Hitler meant precisely what he said; he made his intentions clear and he carried them out by giving orders for killing every European Jew.[305]

It is true that Hitler occasionally talked about resettling Jews, but in his mind there was an overriding biological reason why resettlement could never finally solve the 'Jewish Problem.' Jewishness to Hitler was a *disease*, a contagious disease which, if not totally eradicated, would infect and ultimately destroy the German people. 'Don't be misled into thinking,' he had said in 1920, 'that you can fight diseases without killing the carrier.' And in a dozen subsequent speeches he repeated the refrain that Jews are 'the poisoners of mankind,' 'an evil virus,' 'a plague-carrying vermin,' and, most often, 'a bacillus.' On 10 July 1941 Hitler confided to his entourage, 'I feel like the Robert Koch of politics. He discovered the bacillus and showed medical science new ways. I discovered the Jews as the bacillus and the ferment of social decomposition.'[306]

In the very conversation in which he suggested that the Jews might be 'sent packing' to Russia, Hitler added ominously, 'Where the Jews are concerned, I'm devoid of all sense of pity ... In no way is it enough (keineswegs genug) to drive them out of Germany. We cannot allow them to take a return trip back to our door.'[307] In January 1942 he said, 'I see no other way than extermination.'[308] This assertion was not new with Hitler; he had been promising it for years.

Two things are particularly striking about this promise: the sheer number of times Hitler used the words 'extermination' and 'annihilation' (Ausrottung and Vernichtung)[309] and his fear that people would not take him seriously. These words, he said, were no laughing matter.

Thus, on 30 January 1942 he told his audience, 'I am careful not to make hasty prophecies,' and reminded them that when he prophesied on 1 September 1939[310] that the Jews would be annihilated, 'people laughed at my prophecies.' Eight months later, being laughed at was still on his mind: 'People always laughed at me as a prophet. Of those who laughed then, innumerable numbers [sic] no longer laugh today, and those who still laugh now will perhaps no longer laugh a short time from now.'[311] Hitler wanted his promise to kill the Jews of Europe to be taken seriously.

The officers who were charged with the responsibility for carrying out extermination did not doubt that they received authorization from the Führer himself. Himmler, Heydrich, Eichmann, and Höss all affirmed that their orders had come directly from him.[312] In Hitler's Germany no one but the Führer could possibly have given the orders for genocide. The actual contents of the order, however, and the way it was given will probably remain a matter of conjecture. It was almost certainly not put in writing.

That is not surprising. Hitler disliked committing himself in writing, and it was not really necessary for him to give an explicit order – written or oral – to kill Jews en masse. By 1941 Germans were well accustomed to mass murder. The killing of 'inferior beings' had already become standard operating procedure in Hitler's Reich. The SS who manned the death camps had gained wide experience in the so-called euthanasia program; they had already executed over two million Russian Jews and hundreds of Soviet commissars on explicit orders from Adolf Hitler.[313] (The first lethal experiments with gas chambers and Cyclon B were conducted not on Jews but on Soviet prisoners of war.) The executioners knew that the Führer's dearest wish was to have the Jews utterly destroyed[314] – and the surest way to win favour with the Führer (and to gain an edge over their rivals) was to anticipate and fulfil his wishes.

It was not necessary to give Himmler and Heydrich an explicit order, written or spoken. All that was needed to start the murder machines rolling into mass production was simply a '*nod of Hitler's head.*'[315] It must be conceded that this hypothesis is probably unprovable, but on the basis of available evidence it has a higher degree of probability than the assumption of spontaneous action by local commanders acting on their own initiative and without Hitler's knowledge.

Evidence that Hitler did not personally supervise the Holocaust does not exonerate him. It simply widens the culpability by implicating many others. Ian Kershaw has quite rightly noted that by pointing their fingers at one culprit, biographers and intentionalists tend to direct attention away from all those Germans who actively abetted Hitler.[316] The road that led to Auschwitz was long, twisted, and crowded with participants. But Hitler's ideology had required its construction.

This assertion flatly denies the contention of revisionists, such as the notorious right-wing British historian, David Irving, that Hitler never intended to kill the Jews and did not even know that the Holocaust was taking place. The blame, Irving insists, lay entirely with other people, most notably over-zealous underlings such as Himmler, Heydrich, Frank, and Eichmann, who 'pulled the wool over Hitler's eyes.'[317] On the contrary, they received their orders from the Führer, and they executed these orders with enthusiasm.

That Hitler was kept fully informed is the testimony not only of SS commanders, but of others in Hitler's immediate entourage who were in a position to know. In November 1979 Alan Bullock asked Albert Speer directly if it were possible that Hitler had not known about the genocide and had not given the orders for it. Speer replied, 'It is not possible that in this important question – the Jewish question was the most important question of his life – he remained uninformed or that he had not given the order. He gave the order; that is completely certain.'[318]

Equally important is the testimony of Christa Schroeder, a private secretary who talked daily with the Führer and typed his speeches, memos, and letters: 'I can say with certainty,' she wrote, 'that Hitler was informed in complete detail by Himmler as to what was happening in the concentration camps.'[319] Fraülein Schroeder repeated that assertion years later in a private interview: 'I can tell you emphatically that Hitler knew about the genocide. He knew about it from the start.'[320]

I conclude that Hitler personally gave orders sufficient to launch the Holocaust, knew that the orders were being carried out, and took personal credit for the genocide. Late in June 1944, as the Allies were marching on Germany from east and west, Hitler boasted that he had solved the Jewish Problem: 'I have got rid of Jewry ... there can be no revolution in Germany today. The Jew is gone.'[321] During one of his last recorded conversations, on 2 April 1945, which served as his 'Political Testament,' Hitler boasted that 'National Socialism can justly claim the eternal gratitude of the world for having eliminated the Jew.'

The 'personalists' and the 'structuralists' are both right about the Holocaust: it could not have happened without Adolf Hitler, but it could have happened only because it received widespread support from the German people. Let us not imagine, however, that we have explained the Holocaust. It remains inexplicable.[322]

The personal roles that the Kaiser and the Führer each played in the two world wars of the century will be investigated in the next chapter, but at the close of this discussion of the two as political leaders, let us first consider explanations that have been given for the failure of each leader to achieve his goals and then discuss the ways that Hitler dealt with the ex-Kaiser during his exile.

Several writers have found a simple explanation for Wilhelm's failures: this Emperor had no clothes. He put on an impressive appearance that hoodwinked a lot of people, but underneath he was just too small a man for so large a job.[323]

This explanation is unsatisfying for two reasons. First, Wilhelm was not small in either talent or ambition. Indeed, in sheer native ability he was one of the most richly gifted of all German rulers. Second, he proved on occasion that he could indeed handle his job, that he could analyse a complex political problem, give it his concentrated attention, work effectively, and carry out his stated objective. His management of naval bills, for example, was masterful. He was also capable of moderation and good sense, as he showed in rejecting a 'coup from above' in 1912.

A more sophisticated and promising explanation for Wilhelm's failure as a ruler has been suggested by Thomas Kohut, a biographer trained in both historical and psychological analysis. Kohut makes a distinction between the Kaiser's political and his symbolic leadership, arguing that the psychological problems that plagued him as a political ruler actually enabled him to become an effective symbolic leader of his people. As a symbolic leader he was a resounding success because his own 'narcissistic psychopathology' was in tune with the nation he was destined to rule. Wilhelm was a deeply driven man who lacked personal integration and hungered for approval; so did Germany. Kaiser and nation served as 'mirror-images' – two mirrors reflecting each other's own ideals and aspirations.[324] Wilhelm's personal need for popular acclaim prompted the imperial processions, parades, flag ceremonies, and oratorical flourishes about national greatness that were powerful symbolic forces binding both himself and his nation together.

This interpretation makes a valuable contribution to our understanding. Yet in my view it is not at all clear that the Kaiser was either an abject failure as a political leader or a smashing success symbolically. The record on both counts is spotty. We have noted examples of impressive political leadership. And his impulse to overstate, overreact, and overplay undermined his effectiveness as a symbolic leader.

It may have been good strategy, for example, to travel throughout his Reich showing the imperial flag, parading himself as the ruler of all Germans, and bestowing gifts with imperial largesse. But he overdid it. He travelled so often and gave such extravagant gifts that, far from achieving the acclaim he expected, his excursions provoked resentment. A contemporary noted the cost to the German people of one typical trip in which Wilhelm gave away 80 diamond rings, 150 silver medals, 50 jewelled brooches, 30 gold watches, and 20 diamond-encrusted Orders of the Prussian Eagle, along with many other costly items. The critic concluded that 'His [Wilhelm's] main achievement was a joke – a very costly joke.' His excessive travelling also invited ridicule.[325]

It was probably a good idea to show the national colours in flag ceremonies and to encourage the singing of *Deutschland über Alles* and other nationalistic songs.[326] Flags are certainly important symbols of patriotism and national unity. But, again, Wilhelm could not resist pushing the idea to the point of parody. He designed an elaborate *Fahnennagelung* (flag-nailing) ceremony during which he would hammer in the first nail holding the flag to its standard. He was followed by a long line of other dignitaries in fastidiously prescribed order, each of whom hammered another nail until the flag was thoroughly attached. The list of privileged hammer-wielders included the chief of the general staff, the commander of the Mark of Brandenburg, the chief of the military cabinet, the war minister, all of the Kaiser's adjutants, and, in order of rank, every member of his entourage who had been invited to the special occasion – of which there were a great many. The Kaiser's instructions for one such *Nagelung* (2 May 1889) filled ten pages.[327]

Instead of being an asset to his reign, his excessively gaudy, elaborate, expensive, and time-consuming ceremonies frequently evoked ridicule and resentment. Even General Helmuth von Moltke, who certainly approved of oath-taking, flag ceremonies, military parades and manoeuvres, became disenchanted with this symbolic overkill. Moltke wrote in his diary on 25 August 1905, 'It makes me sick when I see all this nonsense (*Unfug*).'[328]

The Kaiser sometimes chose the wrong symbols. He sought to make his grandfather, Wilhelm I, the symbol of Imperial Germany. But Wilhelm was not a good choice for that role. The public knew that the old gentleman had wanted only to be King of Prussia, not German Emperor. Besides, Wilhelm II's excessively adulatory speeches, virtually canonizing his grandfather and calling the humble and limited old man 'Wilhelm *der Grosse*,' laid it on too thick. It would have been quite appropriate to erect a few statues and strike a medal or two in his honour. But, again, Wilhelm II overdid it. During his reign he dedicated more than four hundred statues to Wilhelm I and handed out thousands of medals – so many that instead of exalting his grandfather, Wilhelm managed to diminish the value of both the medals and the image they were designed to enhance. Wilhelm's efforts to convert a dynastic Prussian hero into a national symbol were a failure.[329]

Another weakness of the Kaiser's symbolic leadership was that symbols, for him, often became substance, and he seemed unable to tell the difference between imagery and reality. He was convinced, for instance, that his honorary rank Admiral of the Fleet actually gave him the authority to tell the British First Lord of the Admiralty how to run the Royal Navy; and, similarly, that his honorary title and uniform of Field Marshal in the British Army entitled him to tell Lord Roberts how to conduct military campaigns in South Africa. Wilhelm's problem was not that he lacked the intellectual ability to rule effectively as both political and symbolic leader. Rather, his problem was that the very psychological forces that impaired his political performance also limited his effectiveness as a symbolic leader.

The central problem of explaining Wilhelm's political failure remains: Why did so gifted a person in such favourable circumstances fail to do the job for which he seemed peculiarly well suited? We will return to that problem in Chapter 5, 'Psychological Dimensions.'

Hitler's failures were quite different. His political career was marked by spectacular success after the fiasco of the Beer Hall Putsch. Against all odds he had achieved absolute political power in Germany; he had solved unemployment and put the Germans back to work; he had built magnificent new freeways that were the envy of the world; he had created the 'Strength through Joy' program which enabled millions of families to enjoy inexpensive holidays on the Italian Riviera or on North Sea cruises; he sent his Hitler Youth singing by the thousands as they marched through the streets and forests of the Fatherland; he had rearmed Germany; he had humbled the victors of the Great War and wiped out the hated Treaty of Versailles; he had reclaimed the Rhineland; he had expanded the Reich by incorporating Austria, and – with the approval of England and France – he had brought the Sudeten Germans of Czechoslovakia 'back home to the Reich.' After years of humiliation and despair, Germany once again stood proudly defiant, the most powerful military and economic nation on the Continent. All this within five short years and without war! It is not surprising that both Lloyd George and Winston Churchill marvelled at Hitler's achievements and acclaimed him one of history's most impressive political leaders.[330]

If only war and defeat had not followed. If the Führer had only died – let us say in the early summer of 1939 – a grateful people might have hailed him as Adolf the Magnificent, incomparably the greatest ruler of their history.

But war did come, and it came because the Führer had willed it. War, he had often said, was 'always within me.' After smashing victories over Poland, the Low Countries, and France, Hitler lost his touch, and, I have suggested, reverted to his old pattern of flirting with failure. Among his self-defeating blunders was his unprovoked invasion of the Soviet Union and his unnecessary declaration of war against the United States, two powers who confronted him with the overwhelming military strength that guaranteed his defeat.

The Führer liked to boast that he was a gambler. But unlike a good poker player, he didn't know when to quit. Perhaps to prove his mastery and dispel gnawing doubts about himself, he felt driven to take on powerful enemies. He who had controlled circumstances to a remarkable degree in his rise to power and during the first years of his reign would be overwhelmed by circumstances of his own creation. Germany's military defeat was assured when confronted by the overwhelming forces Hitler had summoned forth by attacking Russia and declaring war on the United States.

Why did Hitler do that? We will return to that question.

The Führer and the Ex-Kaiser

The behaviour of Wilhelm II was unworthy of a monarch ... a mighty wielder of the bombastic word, but a coward in deed ... and as vain and as stupid into the bargain as the vainest and most stupid peacock! ... This Bigmouth ... This fourflusher (*Bramabaseur*).[331]

Adolf Hitler

What unheard of arrogance! This Bavarian corporal, this professional housepainter, puts himself on my throne!!!

Ex-Kaiser Wilhelm II

Hitler and Wilhelm II despised each other, but each sought to use the other for his own political purposes. Since Hitler held all the high cards, he easily won the game.

The Führer had no intention whatever of restoring Wilhelm to the throne. 'Monarchy,' he had said in a private conversation, 'is an absurdity.'[332] Yet noting how desperately the Kaiser and his sons longed for Hohenzollern restoration that only he could give, Hitler gained their political support by encouraging them to indulge their fantasies.

From the moment of his arrival in Holland in November 1918, Wilhelm was driven by the conviction that he would be vindicated and returned to his Imperial throne. Doorn House, after the ex-Kaiser took occupancy in mid-May 1920, soon became 'a Mecca for all arch-enemies of the Weimar Republic.'[333] Wilhelm was given new hope for restoration when on his seventieth birthday (27 January 1928) he received over three thousand telegrams and letters containing more than a hundred thousand signatures of people who expressed hope for his restoration.[334] Shortly after that event Wilhelm set forth the clearest expression of his hopes in a memorandum whose throbbing prose and many underscorings called for all right-thinking Germans to support him in forming 'a new German Reich' that would abolish parliamentary government and establish a royal dictatorship.

With total passion, with sharpest logic, with clearest sense of purpose, *we shall kindle the flames of a sweeping national revival with the single purpose of restoring the monarchy and establishing a new German Reich under me* (*ein neues Deutsches Reich unter mir*) – a Reich in which all parliamentary parties, party politics, and party organizations will be completely smashed.

Away with parliamentarism in every form! It is totally western and consequently un-German; it corrodes our inner Germanic being ... We shall strive onward until the day breaks when *the great, pure, holy Germanic movement for Kaiser and Reich* gathers its forces and smashes duplicitous parliamentarism.[335]

By late 1932, after the National Front of conservative nationalists had failed to rally the nation, the Kaiser turned to the Nazis as his best hope for restoration. Though finding Hitler personally repulsive, Wilhelm II was attracted by many aspects of his program. He was enthusiastic about Hitler's promises of overthrowing the Weimar Republic, remilitarizing Germany, and avenging the *Versailles-Diktat*. He approved of Nazi anti-Semitism, if not some of their methods. He endorsed Hitler's crusade against 'atheistic communism,' and welcomed his support of Christian churches, and he approved of Hitler's plans for expanding Germany's frontiers.

Although the socialism of the Nazi program, as well as Hitler's crudities filled him 'with deep disquietude,' the Kaiser's reservations were subsumed by his driving desire to be restored to his rightful place as ruler of Germany. Sigurd von Ilsemann, Wilhelm's confidant in exile, recorded in his diary, 'All hopes, all thinking, speaking, and writing are rooted in this single conviction.' He added that if he had told the Kaiser that all his hopes were impossible fantasies, it would have been the end of their relationship.[336]

In pursuit of his dream, the ex-Kaiser engaged in pathetic, demeaning, and inevitably hopeless efforts to win Nazi support for his cause. In May 1932 he entertained Hermann Göring in Doorn House, taking him for long walks in his woods and raising no objections when the gargantuan Nazi appeared at his formal dinner table in baggy plus-fours. When Göring complained that the Kaiser's grandson, Prince Wilhelm (the son of Crown Prince Friedrich Wilhelm) had criticized the Führer, the Kaiser promised to reprimand the young man.[337]

Wilhelm also asked Crown Prince Friedrich Wilhelm, as well as August Wilhelm ('Auwi') his fourth son, along with his enthusiastically pro-Nazi second wife, Hermine, to curry favour with the Nazi hierarchy. This trio met often with Göring and with Hitler, on each occasion eagerly broaching the question of monarchic restoration.[338]

The Führer encouraged the royal brothers and the ambitious wife to cling to their anxious hopes. He told the Crown Prince that the final constitutional settlement of the new Reich had not yet been determined, but assured them that 'if the people should decide in favour of monarchy,' the monarch would certainly be a Hohenzollern and not a Wittelsbach.[339]

These vacuous assurances filled the Hohenzollerns with euphoria. But as the months passed and it became increasingly clear, even to the Kaiser, that Hitler had no intention of restoring the monarchy, Wilhelm's enthusiasm for the Nazis cooled. He was surprised and deeply hurt that his name was not mentioned at the Nuremberg party rallies. He was outraged by Hitler's dissolution of all monarchist societies, and 'beside himself' when Hitler styled himself 'Führer' and Prussia's oldest and proudest regiments were required to wear the swastika insignia. Wilhelm poured out his fury to his faithful confidant: 'What is this title "Führer"? What's that supposed to mean? There is no such thing! What unheard of arrogance! And what is the "Hitler State"? ... Hitler is still, as before, a Bavarian corporal and a professional housepainter and this person puts himself on my throne!!!'[340]

The Kaiser removed the swastika medallion from the radiator of his Mercedes, read exposés of the Führer in the British press, and announced – quite falsely – that Hitler had never earned his Iron Cross. (The Kaiser himself had earned none of his own self-awarded medals.) When the ambitious and disloyal Crown Prince joined Hitler's Brown Shirts and the royal brothers appeared at Doorn House in their SA uniforms, the Kaiser told his sons that he considered them enemies of the House of Hohenzollern.[341]

Wilhelm II nevertheless considered Hitler's war completely justified. He agreed that it had been caused by 'international Jewry' who were 'Satan's chief weapon,'[342] and told an admirer that the war was the fulfilment of 'God's judgment against Judah-England.'[343] He personally claimed credit for the Wehrmacht's smashing early victories.[344] In 1940 he welcomed the Nazi occupation of Holland. Radiantly charming in his medal-spangled Field Marshal's uniform, Wilhelm raised his baton to salute Wehrmacht officers and entertained them at a glittering reception in Doorn House.[345]

The ex-Kaiser rejoiced in the fall of France in June 1941, and wired his personal congratulations to the Führer. Lauding the glorious victory as the fulfilment of God's will, Wilhelm concluded, 'German hearts resound with the great chorale ... *Nun danket alle Gott.*' Hitler replied with a terse telegram thanking the ex-Kaiser for his personal endorsement[346] – and made sure that both telegrams were widely publicized.

In the spring of 1941, when, after several mild heart attacks, Wilhelm saw death approaching, his animosity for the Nazis intensified. His last will and testament specified that there should be no swastika flags and no wreaths from the party hierarchy at his funeral. He also left orders that his body be interred 'provisionally' in a private ceremony on the grounds of Doorn House in the small Greek temple he had personally designed for his mausoleum. Hitler, seeing the political advantage to be gained from a national celebration of Wilhelm's last rites, envisaged a full state funeral at Potsdam. After Wilhelm's family pleaded the Kaiser's last wishes, a compromise was reached. It was agreed that he would be buried as he had wished in the gardens of Doorn House in a private ceremony, but that the party would not be excluded from the ceremony.

At the interment on 9 June 1941, Adolf Hitler was personally represented by Arthur Seyss-Inquart, the *Reichskommissar* for Holland who would be sentenced at Nuremberg for crimes against humanity. The *Reichskommissar* brought a gigantic funeral wreath with a purple ribbon, from 'The Führer.' *Reichsführer* SS Heinrich Himmler was represented by *Gruppenführer* (Lieutenant General) Hans Albin Rauter, commissioner of 'general security' for occupied Holland, who would also be indicted for crimes against humanity. *Reichsmarschall* Hermann Göring also sent a huge memorial wreath.[347] Such was the final contact between the Nazis and the last of the Hohenzollern rulers.

Just as he had used everyone else, Hitler had used the Kaiser, both living and dead, to serve his own purposes.

4

Kaiser and Führer as Rulers in War

The cause of this war lies in the interplay of Man and Circumstance

Thucydides, *History of the Great Peloponnesian War* (ca. 411 BC)

Prologue: The Legacy of Two Wars

Wilhelm II and Adolf Hitler bear heavy responsibility for unleashing the two World Wars of the twentieth century whose horrors leave us aghast at the human capacity for wanton destruction and self-annihilation.

During the first war young men by the millions, imbued with their parents' ideals of honour, sacrifice, and duty, 'gave their merry youth away for country and for God' as they pushed back and forth across a thousand miles of 'the front,' expending their lives to gain a few acres of blood-sodden mud. In the first month of war alone, France 'lost' 300,000 of her sons; all but a remnant of the British Expeditionary Force was wiped out in the First Battle of Ypres; at Verdun (*'Ils ne passeront pas!'*) French and Germans killed one another at the rate of one death every twenty seconds. By the end of four years of war, more than ten million men had been killed and twice as many maimed for life.[1] But those are only numbers. As Tolstoy reminded us long ago, a thousand deaths is a statistic; the death of one person who was loved is a tragedy.

Apart from the staggering waste of human life and natural resources, the First World War left important political legacies. It contributed directly, for example, to the rise of totalitarianism in Europe. Essential to twentieth-century totalitarianism is a habit of mind that rejects moderation and exalts totality. That habit was well developed during a war which accustomed people to think in slogans of totality. 'Total war' and 'total mobilization' were guaranteed to bring 'total victory.' When defeat and the Versailles Treaty brought disaster to Germany instead of the promised victory, Germans experienced a terrible emptiness, a vacuum that totalitarian ideology rushed to fill. The call for simple answers to complex problems was a call to which Hitler, the century's most effective *simplificateur terrible*, gave deadly response.

Totalitarianism also specializes in mass control through calculated manipulation of popular emotions. During the Great War, the ancient wisdom attributed to Thucydides was discovered anew: 'In war, reason is the first casualty.' War propaganda everywhere sacrificed truth to 'the war effort' and stressed unthinking emotional commitment to the cause: loving one's country with unquestioning devotion and hating the enemy with limitless passion. Humanity witnessed a 'mobilization of hatred' on a scale never known before.[2]

Total mobilization was economic as well as emotional. National regulation of the economy was the rule among all belligerents, but nowhere was government intervention so comprehensive as in Germany's 'War Socialism.' From a relatively free economy in 1914, 'Germany emerged in 1918 with a thoroughly militarized economy of state socialism in which government control and regulation covered all phases of economic life.'[3]

Without the First World War and its aftermath, Hitler would never have come to power and blighted Europe. The historical connection between the two world wars is direct.

The Second World War outdid its predecessor in human suffering, physical destruction, and sheer horror. On the eastern front alone, more than three times as many soldiers were killed as on all fronts in the First World War – and that does not include the millions of civilians caught up in the firestorm of war.[4]

The Second World War was the first in human history in which more civilians than combatants were killed. About seventeen million men died on the battlefield while eighteen million non-combatants perished in assorted ways: by 'conventional' bombs, new 'atomic devices,' firing squads, poison gas chambers, and calculated starvation.[5]

Hitler's War also brought a new phenomenon to Europe: the 'Displaced Person,' or, more simply, the DP. In the war's immediate aftermath, more than thirteen million homeless people wandered hungry, cold, and ill, across the shattered landscape of Europe. They were joined by another two million starving and disoriented victims released from Hitler's concentration camps and tens of thousands of slave labourers from his mines and factories.

After this war the Continent lay in waste from the Seine to the Volga, from the Elbe to the Tiber. Homes, schools, libraries, art galleries, cathedrals, and transportation systems were smashed. Barter replaced currency; rats scurried through the rubble of great cities, and throughout Germany was heard an anguished cry from the heart, *'Nie wieder Krieg!'* For in destroying Germany and leaving it desolate, Hitler had also destroyed the Germans' proclivity for war. The call from the past had been 'The Sooner the Better!'; the slogan for the future was, 'Never Again!'

The following discussion will focus on the personal roles played by Wilhelm II and Adolf Hitler in these two wars. Yet circumstances influencing their actions should not be ignored. For Thucydides' conclusion about the causes of the Great Peloponnesian War of the fifth century BC is valid for both great wars of the twentieth century: they too were due to 'the interplay of Man and Circumstance.'

PART I: THE KAISER AND THE FIRST WORLD WAR

All roads may have led to Rome but in our country all roads from Berlin led to war.

Anonymous socialist, 1914

In pre–First World War Germany, the ruling elites looked apprehensively at the growth of socialism, seeing it as an immediate threat to their way of life. This apprehension was intensified by the last pre-war elections to the Reichstag in 1912 which dealt a shattering defeat to the parties of the establishment and made the Social Democrats the largest party in Germany. One statistic seemed particularly alarming: In 1912 one out of every three Germans had voted for the Marxist party. The spectre of revolution and social upheaval seemed to loom over Germany.[6]

Alarmed by the perceived threat of 'the socialist menace,' there grew in court and military circles the temptation to think of war as a solution to domestic turmoil; a smashingly successful war would rally national support behind Crown and country and engulf Marxist socialism in a rising tide of patriotic fervour.[7]

Many Germans also believed that war expressed two of their most cherished ideals: power and moral idealism. In an immensely popular book entitled *Germany and the Next War,* which was published in 1911 and would go through six large editions within two years, Friedrich Bernhardi proclaimed that war was the litmus test of a nation's vitality and culture. 'War's moral grandeur,' he wrote, 'provides a life-giving principle.'[8,9] Other popular books bore such titles as *War as a Cultural Force* and *War as a Creative World Principle.*

An aggressive policy was not forced on Germany by the Kaiser and a small military clique. It was a policy endorsed by eminent intellectuals, clerics, journalists, and educators. Among the general population, dozens of patriotic societies insisted that it was Germany's historic destiny to impose its will on the Continent through a war of aggression.[10]

Another force bearing directly on the decision for war in 1914 was the power and influence of the German army, so exalted since the smashing victories that had created the Second Reich. Imperial Germany was a militarist state. Repetition of that familiar statement should not diminish its importance. As an anonymous contemporary put it, 'German society is an inverted pyramid standing on its apex. And that point is the spike of the army's *Pickelhaube*.'

Of specific importance to Germany's decision for war was the military establishment's carefully developed Schlieffen Plan. It became an article of faith that with this plan Germany could defeat all the enemies that she imagined were encircling her. The plan gave no thought to defensive war. It was an instrument of aggression through two peremptory strikes: first France would be quickly smashed, then the full weight of German arms would be hurled against a slowly mobilizing Russia, and the war would be over in a few months. But everything depended on this plan (it was the only one the Germans had) and everything depended on speed. But now, in the summer of 1914, the generals were afraid that Russian military reforms were greatly increasing the 'Russian Menace.' They noted anxiously that another 500,000 men were being added to the immense Russian army, and that new Russian railroad lines, financed by French loans, were being built to the German frontier. German military planners put great pressure on the Kaiser to strike before Russia was ready.

Hypernationalism was another force bearing directly on 1914. Germany had no monopoly on strident patriotism in the decade preceding the First World War. 'Jingoism' is an English word; 'chauvinism' is French. But in no country did so many people from so many walks of life support so aggressive a nationalism, urging Germany to achieve her historic destiny in a *Drang nach Osten* against Russia and a *Drang nach Westen* against France, Belgium, and England.[11]

Strident militarism and nationalism engendered an attitude that has been called 'collective megalomania' (*kollektiver Grossenwahn*): the conviction that Germany was invincible, that her matchless army could quickly accomplish grandiose war aims. A thoughtful German historian has written that the most fatal expression of German militant nationalism was found 'in the irrational exaggeration of its power, in an almost mystical faith in its own invincibility ... The conviction was expressed in army circles that Germany could take on all three Entente powers at once.'[12]

The call for war was further prompted by the widespread belief that the Fatherland was encircled by hostile enemies – that France, Russia, and England were conspiring to launch an immediate attack. In objective fact, Germany, incomparably the strongest military and industrial power on the Continent, was in no danger from attack by any of these powers.[13] But again, the more important historical fact is that the Germans who determined national policy *believed* their country was menaced by simultaneous invasions from east and west.

Sometimes the problem for historians is not to find evidence to support an assertion such as this, but to formulate assertions that do justice to the peculiarities of the evidence. One is hard-pressed, for example, to explain a curious memorandum written by the famous Count Schlieffen, who looked at Germany in the glory days of 1909 and saw nothing but impending disaster: 'Enemies on all sides! ... At the given moment the doors will be opened, the drawbridge let down, and the million-strong armies let loose, raving and destroying across the Vosges, the Meuse, the Königsau, the Niemen, the Bug, and even the Isonzo and the Tyrolean Alps. The danger seems gigantic.' Schlieffen was not reassured by massive increases of German armament. A nervous memorandum of 1912 reaffirmed his apprehensions: 'Germany's neighbors are lying in wait for their unprotected, weaker adversary who is entirely on his own.'[14]

The consequences of these fears were ominous. By 1914 the conviction had grown among Germany's military leaders that the only way to rid themselves of their nightmares was to smash encircling enemies through 'preventive war.'

Another powerful, if perplexing, emotion helped precipitate war in 1914. Many influential Germans were convinced that the Fatherland was somehow *fated* to go to war in order to fulfil its special historic destiny. The chief of the Imperial general staff joined the chorus asserting that the Great War was ordained by fate and world historic forces. 'This war,' he reflected after it broke out, 'is a *necessity* dictated by world historical development.'[15] 'Necessity' (*Notwendigkeit*) was a favourite word of the German general staff. In an important memorandum of 1913, for instance, Moltke noted that in implementing the Schlieffen Plan, 'It is not pleasant (*angenehm*) to begin the war by violating the neutrality of a neighbouring state. But it is necessary because it is our only chance for quick success.'[16]

Fatalistic acceptance of the inevitability of war, when coupled with immense military power and combined with the Kaiser's self-image of implacable toughness, produced a lethal mixture.

The Kaiser's Personality and Decisions for War

Because [my nephew's] cowardice is even greater than his vanity ... he will unleash a war not through his own initiative and not with militant *élan*, but through weakness.

Edward VII, ca. 1905

Circumstances were important to the coming of the war, but the Kaiser's role was decisive because constitutionally he, and he alone, could make the decision for war. He was 'the Supreme War Lord.'

Wilhelm enjoyed playing that role. He practised projecting an image of heroic indomitability – not a man to negotiate with or to be pushed around. His definition of the ideal man was 'a person of crystalline character, that is to say of remorseless severity (*unerbittliche Strenge*).'[17] And that is the way he fancied himself. He gave detailed instructions for a portrait to be painted in which he appeared as Mars, god of war and apotheosis of power,[18] an image consistent with his fantasy that he was a special agent of God, answerable to Him alone, sent on earth to exercise power over the entire world.

Wilhelm fed the flames of fear that the Fatherland was isolated and encircled by predatory neighbours. The French, in his view, were decadent and treacherous. Their so-called Entente Cordiale with Russian barbarians was really a diabolical plot hatched by his uncle Edward VII during his many mysterious trips to Paris ('that whorehouse of Europe'). Their plan, Wilhelm believed, was for England to join France and Russia in simultaneously attacking from the east and the west, thereby 'annihilating' Germany.

The Kaiser's feelings about England were as ambivalent as those of most Germans. Indeed, he was a shining illustration of his countrymen's tendency both to admire and to hate 'perfidious Albion.' Wilhelm liked to play the complete English country gentleman in his deerstalker hat, tweeds, and gaiters, speaking Edwardian slang; alternately, he was the quintessential Prussian officer wearing a *Pickelhaube* and barking commands in any one of a dozen regimental uniforms – one side of him 'conspiring to frustrate the other and neither completely succeeding.'[19]. Among Wilhelm's mixed emotions about his mother's homeland was raw hatred fed by jealousy. 'One cannot have enough hatred for England,' he said.[20]

The Kaiser shared the conviction that the Fatherland was somehow fated to go to war in order to fulfil its historic destiny. He told the Austrian ambassador to Berlin that it was not enough for Germany to control Europe. His nation was driven by destiny to fulfil a greater mission: to dominate 'the entire world.'[21]

Wilhelm's personal instability also had a major bearing on his decision to go to war. Psychologically, this story should probably begin with his tortured infancy and difficult childhood.[22] But for immediate purposes let us recall that Wilhelm had suffered two humiliating personal experiences that seriously affected his mental state in the years immediately preceding the War.

In the autumn of 1908 his image of poise and 'pitiless severity' had been badly tarnished by the ruinous *Daily Telegraph* newspaper interview.[23] At the same time he was undergoing another experience that further eroded his self-image of masculine assertiveness: his most trusted adviser and closest friend was indicted for homosexuality, a punishable crime in both the Second and the Third Reichs.

The trial, replete with sordid testimony, was a *cause célèbre* that dragged on month after month. The public scandal was a personal trauma for Wilhelm.[24] He felt compelled to reaffirm his masculinity, to repress fears of weakness, and to project an image of power. To make concessions, to negotiate or to compromise, was 'feminine weakness.' The Kaiser dismissed out of hand, for example, the suggestion that Germany might seek some accommodation with Russia, saying that it was 'equivalent to self-castration *(Selbstentmannung).*'[25]

This need for Wilhelm to appear decisive, tough, and thoroughly 'masculine' directly influenced his behaviour in two major crises leading to the First World War.

A Decision for War, December 1912

The German decision to fight a major war was taken not in July 1914 in response to the Sarajevo murders, or any other immediate threat, but ... earlier on 8 December 1912.

J.C.G. Röhl

Germany's resolve to launch a major European war for control of the continent was precipitated by one of the Kaiser's temper tantrums.

One Sunday morning in December 1912, Wilhelm read a dispatch from the German ambassador in London reporting a conversation with a British official who had said that England could not permit any one power to dominate the Continent. There was nothing surprising about that statement. 'Balance of power' had brought England continental wars for centuries – one thinks of the coalition Britain mounted to restrain Louis XIV and, a century later, to stop Napoleon.

Wilhelm, however, flew into a rage. He shouted, 'There is no "balance of power" in Europe except me – me and my twenty-five army corps.' He pencilled furiously on the dispatch, *'This is a declaration of war! ... a war for our very existence.'*[26] He wrote to his Austrian ally, 'The moment for Austria and Germany now seems very propitious ... we must strike while the iron is hot!! *(Wir mussen das Eisen schmieden solange es warm ist!!).'*[27]

Why such fury? Is it possible that his outrage against English 'duplicity' and 'double-dealing' was reflection of the duplicities he thought he had experienced with an English mother who assured him of her love while she was inflicting pain?[28]

Whatever the explanation, the Kaiser's rage had immediate consequence. For on that Sunday of 8 December 1912 he ordered his military advisers to meet with him at 11:00 the same morning in the Berlin palace.[29] Neither the chancellor of Germany nor the foreign secretary was invited to this war council (*Kriegsrat*).[30]

Wilhelm opened this historic conference with an impassioned speech urging preventive war against all the enemies surrounding the Fatherland. In a remarkable preview of what would actually occur in 1914, the Kaiser said that if Austria attacked Serbia, Russia could be expected to support Serbia, and France would join her Russian ally. 'And that,' he asserted, 'would make the war inevitable.' He saw England as the primary threat and assumed that the British would march with Russia and France. 'Therefore,' he concluded, 'immediate submarine warfare against English troop transports in the Scheldt and the neighbourhood of Dunkirk [must be launched] ... and mines planted in the Thames.'[31]

Wilhelm then paused and asked for comment. The reply of General Helmuth von Moltke, the chief of staff, was memorable: '*I consider war unavoidable and the sooner the better.*'[32] Admiral von Tirpitz agreed that war was inevitable, but insisted that the navy needed at least eighteen months to prepare for it. More ships must be built and, above all, the Kiel Canal must be widened and deepened so that his battleships could move readily from the North Sea into the English Channel. Reluctantly, the Kaiser agreed to a postponement.

In the months following the December 1912 meeting, the army was further expanded and by mid-June 1914, just in time for Sarajevo, the Kiel Canal was made ready to accommodate battleships. At the Kaiser's orders[33] public opinion was systematically prepared for hostilities. Stories were planted in German newspapers warning the public of the Russian menace, of English duplicity, and of the French hunger for revenge. Newspaper editors were urged to cultivate a warlike spirit in their readers. In this, the Kaiser was setting a precedent for Adolf Hitler, who in November 1938 summoned German editors and ordered them to stop talking about peace and start getting the German people ready for war.[34] In both instances the German press responded with alacrity. The *Ostpreussische Zeitung* of 12 December 1912, for instance, looked forward to a 'brisk and merry (*frisch und fröhlich*) war,' and the organ of the Federation of Young Germans, which received state subsidies, assured its youthful readers that war 'is the noblest and most sacred manifestation of human activity ... Let us therefore make fun of old women in men's trousers who are afraid of war and complain that it is horrible or ugly. No, war is beautiful.'[35]

The Kaiser showed his indebtedness to his mentor in racism, H.S. Chamberlain,[36] by insisting that war to crush 'the Russian menace' was justified on racial grounds: it would pit Germanic *Kultur* against Slavic barbarism that threatened the entire continent. He gave clear expression of his convictions in a letter of 15 December 1912 to his friend Albert Ballin, the shipping magnate: 'This is a question not only of defending ourselves against Russian aggression. This is a *question of survival* ... This is a *War of Race (Rassenkampf).*'[37]

At a dinner he hosted for Albert, King of the Belgians, in November 1913, Wilhelm reminded Albert of German strength and told his guest that 'war with France is inevitable and close at hand. There must be action.'[38] He then assured him that he did not plan to invade Belgium. Wilhelm's assurance, possibly made out of ignorance of the Schlieffen Plan, totally belied the decision long made by the army to get at France through Belgium. Wilhelm's remarks to the king prompted Moltke to observe dryly that he was more afraid of the Kaiser than of either the French or Russians.[39]

While preparing the nation for war, the Kaiser's government launched a peace campaign designed to stress Germany's desire for peace with her neighbours. For at the outbreak of hostilities, Germany wanted to appear as the innocent victim of foreign aggression.[40]

Well before the Kaiser signed his famous 'blank cheque' in July 1914, assuring Austria that Germany would support *any* action Austria might wish to take against Serbia, he had already given such specific assurance to Franz Ferdinand in November 1912, when he met personally with 'Franzi' and urged him to 'move energetically against Serbia whenever Austria feels its prestige threatened.' If he did, the Kaiser promised, Germany would support her *'even if it means a world war with the three Entente powers.'*[41] Again in December, as we have noted, he encouraged Franz Ferdinand to strike Serbia 'while the iron is hot.'

Fully anticipating a war with England, Wilhelm not only planned submarine attacks on British shipping, as well as mining the Thames, but in 1912 he also ordered preparations – as would Hitler in 1940 – for a full-scale invasion of the British Isles.[42]

Wilhelm was the key player in December 1912, as he would be in August 1914 when he changed the slogan of 1912 from 'the sooner the better' to *'now or never!'*

Decision for War: 1914

This time I won't cave in.

Wilhelm II, 6 July 1914

While making belligerent pronouncements about going to war, a more benign and pacific Wilhelm also kept trying to assert himself. In the midst of the December crisis after urging the Austrian heir-apparent to gird his loins for combat, the Kaiser assured the Austrian ambassador in Berlin that 'despite all the warlike noise, he certainly hoped that peace would be maintained.'[43] Such contradictory statements must have confused his ally. They certainly confounded the German patriots who were pressing for an immediate showdown with France. Nationalist German newspapers consequently wrote scathing editorials calling the Supreme War Lord *'Guillaume le Timide'* and asking pointedly if Germans had become 'a race of women.'[44]

To Wilhelm such accusations were intolerable, for they revived public and personal doubts about his capacity to make 'manly' decisions. From 1912 to 1914 Wilhelm's memoranda and public statements grew increasingly assertive as he joined his countrymen in what has been called 'compensatory belligerency.'[45]

The big showdown came in July 1914, after Sarajevo, when Wilhelm was confronted with the single most important decision of his career. Once again he was tortured by *Zerrissenheit*. One side of him called for war, another for peace. This Wilhelm reflected on the folly of war and asked, 'What has become of the so-called World Empires? Alexander the Great, Napoleon I, all the great war heroes have swum in blood and suppressed the people who ... rose against them and brought their empires to naught.'[46] When he read the Serbian reply to Austria's ultimatum, this Wilhelm sighed with relief and wrote in the margin: 'A brilliant achievement! ... all reason for war is gone'[47] At the same time, another Wilhelm trumpeted power and shook a mailed fist at the world as once again opposing forces in this deeply disjointed person struggled for mastery.

Two forces moved Wilhelm to war: the pressure of military and diplomatic circumstance from without, and the lifelong pressure from within to appear relentlessly tough – a pressure intensified by his desire to emulate the victorious soldier-kings of Prussia: his father, a war hero of 1866 and 1870; his grandfather, a victor over Napoleon; and his ancestral *alter ego* and military genius, Frederick the Great. Wilhelm dreamed that he could outdo all these national heroes in a truly great war. The more the Kaiser asserted his warlike manliness and tried to act out his personal ideal of 'remorseless severity,' the more he drove himself towards a military decision.

One sentence of a conversation of July 1914 with his friend, the notorious manufacturer of arms, Gustav Krupp von Bohlen und Halbach (1870–1950),[48] is particularly revealing. Apparently recalling the ridicule he had suffered from militant nationalists when he refused to fight France in 1912, Wilhelm told Krupp, *'This time I won't cave in!'* Krupp later recalled that it was 'almost pathetic' to see how the All Highest tried to convince Krupp (as well as himself) that he really was not a weakling. With deepening voice and mounting fervour, the Kaiser repeated the same idea three different ways: *'Diesmal falle ich nicht um! ... Nein, diesmal will ich nicht umfallen! ... Hören Sie: diesmal falle ich nicht um!*[49] And indeed he didn't. This conversation took place the day after Wilhelm had made the decision that led ineluctably to war.[50]

As we shall see, this decision, which may well have been the most crucial decision in German history, was made personally by the Kaiser without consultation with military or civilian advisers.

The 'July Crisis' of 1914

Now or Never!

Wilhelm II, 4 July 1914

The events of three fateful days in early July form such a revealing microcosm of Wilhelm's personal role in the crisis that the chronology should be followed with some care. The rest of July to the opening of the war at the beginning of August can be sketched more quickly.[51]

4 July: The murder of the heir to the throne of Austria-Hungary by Serb nationalists at Sarajevo on 28 June had provided Germany with the pretext it needed to launch the great war for which the German nation had been psychologically and materially preparing since December 1912. On 4 July, in the margin of a diplomatic dispatch from the German ambassador in Vienna, the Kaiser wrote in his indelible pencil: '*Now or Never!* ... the Serbs have got to be mopped up and that *right soon!*'[52]

Members of the foreign office had sometimes smiled at the Kaiser's hyperbolic marginalia. But not this time. His ringing words, 'Now or Never!' took on the force of Imperial command and became the slogan for Germany's policy. As Imanuel Geiss has written, 'On 4 July in Berlin all confusion and divergence ... were henceforth put aside. The Kaiser had decided on war.'[53]

5 July: During lunch in Frederick the Great's Neues Palais in Potsdam, the Kaiser told the Austro-Hungarian ambassador that if his government would take immediate action against Serbia, it could rely on Germany's complete support, even if Russia intervened.[54] Later that same afternoon, at 5:00, Wilhelm summoned Chancellor Bethmann Hollweg and his military advisers to the palace and informed them of his promise to Austria. To give the Kaiser's decision a semblance of constitutional legality, the chancellor, without further discussion, formally approved the Kaiser's action. Thus, the Kaiser and the Imperial chancellor jointly signed this historic 'blank cheque to Austria.'

This perfunctory meeting on 5 July gave rise to the mistaken conclusion made by both Allied statesmen at the time and later historians that a secret

'Potsdam council' had taken place during which the Kaiser and his military and civilian entourage had gathered to plot the war. No such conference took place. Indeed, what is striking about the decision for war is the *lack* of consultation. One of the most momentous decisions of world history was made by the semi-private utterance of one man over his lunch and was only belatedly endorsed, without any consultation, at a private meeting.[55]

6 July: The Kaiser stopped off at Kiel en route to his annual pleasure cruise of the Norwegian fjords. That evening he spoke with Krupp, who assured him that German industry was fully prepared for war. It was on this occasion that Wilhelm promised he would not back away from war. A determined and decisive Kaiser had 'bared his teeth,' as he liked to put it.

The Kaiser's subsequent activity during the rest of July cast him in neither a decisive nor a heroic role. On the 8th he embarked on a long Norwegian cruise. Moltke and others of the general staff also went on conspicuous holidays, 'to keep up the appearance that nothing is going on.' On 17 July, General Waldersee wrote to a close friend in the foreign office, in a letter marked 'strictly confidential': 'I am here on furlough but ready to jump (*springbereit*) at any time. Everything is all set.'[56]

On 23 July, while the Kaiser was still cruising the fjords and harkening to the voices of the Nordic gods, Austria sent its famous ultimatum to Serbia – a note that Lord Grey called 'the most formidable document that was ever addressed from one state to another.' The rulers in Berlin hoped and confidently expected the Serbs to reject the ultimatum. The Serbian reply consequently threw them into confusion by its unexpected and unwanted tone of compliance and reconciliation.

The consternation of the German army and the foreign office was then further increased by an about-face by the Kaiser. After providing the slogan, 'now or never!' and setting the course for war, Wilhelm suddenly appeared as the champion of peace and offered his services as mediator. In his marginalia to the Serbian reply he wrote, 'After receiving this, I never would have ordered mobilization!'[57] On the same day, 28 July, in a remarkable letter he ordered the foreign office to work out a plan for peace: 'With this reply every reason for war vanishes (*durch sie entfällt jeder Grund zum Kriege*) ... I am now prepared to serve as mediator for peace ... You will therefore submit to me proposals which are to be sent to Vienna.'[58]

It was a splendid statement, one that might have brought peace to Europe. But it was never implemented. Wilhelm did not press the matter and during his long absence from Berlin, the foreign office continued to push the Kaiser's previous policy of urging Austria to attack Serbia so that Germany would have an excuse for war. Bewildered by the contradictory messages coming from the

German capital, an Austrian diplomat asked a very good question: 'Who is ruling in Berlin?' Who indeed?

Constitutionally, the Kaiser ruled in Berlin. Yet this was a ruler who kept changing his mind and giving contradictory orders, and who was often absent from the capital – most notably from 7 to 21 July 1914. Second, particularly during the Kaiser's absences, the foreign office seemed to be ruling in Berlin; but they too sent out contradictory instructions, for they too were rent by uncertainty and conflicting counsels. Third, the army also ruled in Berlin. Indeed, the army was the only member of the trio that had one completely consistent and driving policy: war, 'the sooner the better.' The power and influence of the military increased in direct proportion to the intensity of the crisis and the waffling of the Kaiser.

Nevertheless, despite his maddening inconsistencies, in hard legal fact there was only one legitimate ruler in Berlin. As the army, the foreign office, and everyone else knew full well, that ruler was His Majesty Wilhelm II by the Grace of God, King and German Emperor. Any policy, any action others might wish to take, must bear his ornate signature.

Wilhelm II signed the orders for general German mobilization on 1 August 1914. But then, frightened by what he had done, he ordered the high command to halt deployment of German troops on the western front. Moltke, who had already ordered his troops to move toward Belgium, brusquely informed the Kaiser that the Schlieffen Plan could not possibly be changed: 'Our plan of deployment against France is based on our advance through Belgium. *Nothing can be changed* with regard to deployment.'[59] Wilhelm did not countermand Moltke's order.

To justify setting the Schlieffen Plan in motion, France – like Russia – must be made to appear the aggressor. The solution found by the German army, in cooperation with the foreign office and with the approval of the Kaiser, was to invent French violations of German territory – just as Hitler would invent 'Polish atrocities' and a 'Polish attack' on the German radio station at Gleiwitz in August 1939. (These 'Polish soldiers,' who were actually concentration-camp prisoners dressed in Polish uniforms, were gunned down by SS troops.)[60]

In 1914, to justify attacking France and violating Belgian neutrality, the Germans manufactured a series of border incidents and atrocities which the foreign office dutifully communicated to German embassies in London, Brussels, and Rome. It was solemnly reported, along with other fictions, that French soldiers, dressed in German uniforms (foreshades of Gleiwitz!), had been shot while attempting to blow up a German railway tunnel,[61] that French aviators had dropped bombs on Nuremberg,[62] and that French medical officers had infected German water supplies with cholera bacilli.[63] The clumsy German fabrications of 1914, as in 1939, deceived no one.

About 9:30 p.m. on the night of 4 August 1914, the German army marched into neutral Belgium – because, it was asserted, the German government had 'indisputable proof' that the French and British were about to take over the country. England declared war on Germany one minute after midnight Greenwich time.

The Great War had begun.

The Kaiser and 'War Guilt'

The Allied and Associated Governments affirm and Germany accepts the responsibility of Germany and her allies for causing ... the war.

Treaty of Versailles, Article 231

Before God and History, my conscience is clear. I did not want this war.

Wilhelm II, 1915

On the eleventh hour, of the eleventh day, of the eleventh month of 1918 a French '75' roared one last time and rocked back on its haunches. Then an eerie silence. Then, a soldier later recalled, 'a sound like the rustle of autumnal leaves blowing in the wind' swept along a thousand miles of the western front – the sound of millions of men cheering. They threw down their rifles, hugged one another, climbed out of their trenches, and ran to embrace the men they had just been trying to kill. The Great War was over! Peace had come at last.

The kind of peace imposed on Germany at Versailles, with its so-called war-guilt clause (Article 231), produced one of the most interesting psychological phenomena of recent history: the obsession of the German people with what they called the War-Guilt Question (*Kriegsschuldfrage*). For decades after the war, long after Western historians and Allied statesmen had abandoned the untenable notion of Germany's sole 'guilt,' Germans kept belabouring the issue and inveighing against the calumny. In 1925 a German bookdealer issued a catalogue of some 2,300 books and pamphlets proving that the charges against Germany were totally, absolutely false. One periodical, entitled *Die Kriegsschuldfrage,* was devoted exclusively to denying German 'guilt' and vindicating Germany by placing the blame on the Entente Powers, especially England. This magazine continued publishing until 1934. For those who preferred lighter intellectual fare, the issue was kept alive by popular gimmicks. One publisher advertised a tear-off calendar by asserting that 'this calendar shows every month in words and pictures the rape of Germany' and promising that 'the lies about "War Guilt" are refuted by daily slogans.' Another enterprising entrepreneur capitalized on the popularity of the war-guilt issue by selling strings of rosary-like beads, each devoted to a 'prayer' denying German guilt.[64] This obsessive need to deny responsibility for the war is also shown in the way the 'official documents' of pre-war diplomacy were later edited in order to demonstrate Germany's innocence. Editors of private papers and memoirs destroyed dozens of letters which, they feared, might have lent credence to the 'War-Guilt Lie.'[65]

Why this obsession with an issue long after it had been dropped by every responsible Allied statesman and historian? Perhaps concentration on the war-guilt issue was a way to relieve feelings of humiliation, shock, and disbelief after the totally unexpected defeat of 1918. It was easier and more gratifying to disprove an untenable accusation than it was to accept the humiliating fact of defeat. The myth of 'war guilt' joined the 'stab-in-the-back' legend as an important way for German patriots to preserve personal self-respect by convincing themselves that they were innocent victims of unprovoked aggression as well as heroic warriors who had been traitorously 'stabbed in the back' by socialists and Jews.[66]

Wilhelm II joined his people in protesting too much, and the very vehemence of their relentless denials of guilt and protestations of complete innocence suggests deep-seated feelings of guilt. During the war the Kaiser had sent out tens of thousands of postcards with his picture over the caption: 'Before God and History, my conscience is clear. I did not want this war.'[67] To every guest who visited him during his long exile, until the day of his death in 1941, Wilhelm protested his total innocence, insisting over and over again that the war had been started by England and the Jews. Year after year he subscribed to the *Kriegsschuldfrage* magazine, dozens of heavily underscored copies of which may still be found in an attic closet in Doorn House along with cartons of crumbling pamphlets denying the 'War-Guilt Lie.'

What, then, was the extent of the Kaiser's personal responsibility for the coming of the Great War?

Long before making the fateful decision in July 1914, Wilhelm had demonstrated a remarkable proclivity for alarming other countries and tossing matches into inflammatory material and pouring petrol on the ensuing fires. In an age of supercharged nationalism, he made flamboyantly chauvinistic speeches. At a time of burgeoning armaments and a naval rivalry with England that threatened the peace, he refused to contemplate any restriction of arms. When the World Court in the Hague sought to arbitrate international disputes and to set limits on the excesses of war, the Kaiser announced that he would defecate on their resolutions.[68] His wildly contradictory statements about Germany's intentions invited other nations to distrust him – and consequently to distrust Germany.[69]

The First World War was not inevitable, even though it might seem in retrospect that circumstances were moving Germany inexorably and with increasing velocity towards war in 1914. Wilhelm II, as he liked to remind everyone, was the 'captain of the ship.' He personally selected his crew; and he charted the course that led 'full speed ahead' into the cataclysm. He could have given orders to sail in another direction.

The Kaiser could have encouraged those Germans who actively worked for peace. Instead, he ridiculed the peace movement and did nothing to discourage inflammatory press attacks against it. He was silent when newspapers fanned the flames of war. The *Kölnische Zeitung*, for instance, spread alarmist stories – probably planted by the government – that Russia was about to attack Germany. Another newspaper spread alarm with banner headlines, '*Der kommende Krieg mit Russland!*' and urged preventive war before Russia was fully prepared.[70] Far from discouraging such agitation, Wilhelm abetted it, commenting on one report of Russian military plans, 'I have not the slightest doubt that Russia is systematically preparing for war against us and I conduct my policy accordingly.'[71]

As commander of his armies, Wilhelm could have found out that the general staff was planning to invade neutral Belgium and could have prevented it from happening. Prior to the actual invasion of Belgium on 4 August 1914, the British cabinet had been divided over direct military support for France and Belgium. A British historian has commented with high irony that it took 'the sublime genius' of the Kaiser and the German general staff to bring England into the war against Germany.[72] Wilhelm was probably sincere when he said in 1915 that he had not wanted the war. But his generals did, and Wilhelm let them have their way.

Most crucially, the Kaiser could have chosen not to give Austria unrestricted support. Without Wilhelm's personal, flat-out assurance that he would support Austria in *any action whatever* it might take against Serbia, Austria would not have started a war in the Balkans. Moreover, Wilhelm was fully aware that a Balkan war could not possibly be localized. He and his military advisers assumed that Russia would be drawn in, and that is precisely what they wanted.[73] Instead of handing the Austrians a blank cheque, the Kaiser could have told them to be satisfied with their very considerable diplomatic triumph in forcing the Serbs to accept their stringent ultimatum – an acceptance which, in Wilhelm's own words, removed all reasons for war. He could also have made it clear to the Austrians that if they went to war and Russia came to the help of Serbia, Germany would remain neutral. If Wilhelm had done either of those things, the disastrous war could have been avoided.[74]

Perhaps the most damaging evidence against Wilhelm is negative. There does not exist a single document showing that he or his advisers made any sustained effort to save the peace.[75] On the contrary, they were determined to have the war they had decided upon at the 'war council' of December 1912. In an impulsive moment, when Wilhelm had suggested that Germany should search for a peaceful solution, he was immediately rebuffed by the army and the foreign office. Instead of pressing for peace, the Kaiser chose to go hunting.

Every document authorizing the opening of hostilities bears one unmistakable signature: 'Wilhelm II, I.R.' These crucial signatures, with their grand flourishes, were not acts of bold leadership; they were symbols of acquiescence. The First World War happened because Wilhelm II lacked the will and the courage to oppose his general staff.

King Edward VII, an astute judge of character and the person who knew Wilhelm as well as anyone, saw the essential weakness of his nephew and drew up an indictment in a remarkably prescient statement made some ten years before the war began:

Through his unbelievable vanity, my nephew falls in with all the nationalistic toadies of his entourage who continually assure him that he is the greatest sovereign in the world ... But because his cowardice is even greater than his vanity, he will cower ... before pressure of the general staff. When they dare him to draw the sword, he will not have the courage to bring them to reason. Abjectly he will be dominated by them.

He will unleash war not through his own initiative, and not with militant *élan*, but through weakness.[76]

The Kaiser as 'Supreme War Lord'

If anyone in Germany imagines that I lead the Army, he is badly mistaken.

Wilhelm II, 16 August 1914

The war had provided Wilhelm with a splendid opportunity to assert leadership and rally his people behind their Kaiser.

He started out well. The first day of August 1914, the day the Kaiser declared war, was hot and humid. That afternoon thousands of jubilant Germans crowded in front of the royal palace in Potsdam, waiting expectantly to hear from their ruler. Wilhelm did not disappoint them. From the palace balcony he summoned his people to war in the most effective and best remembered speech of his career. His last line was repeated around every supper table and every *Stammtisch* in every tavern of Germany:

Jetzt kenne ich keine Parteien mehr,
Jetzt kenne ich nur noch Deutsche! [77]

(Henceforth I no longer recognize parties,
Henceforth I know only Germans!)

Wilhelm had found exactly the right words for the occasion. The crowd, massed shoulder to shoulder, was electrified. After a momentary hush, a roar like rolling thunder burst through the sultry air: '*Hoch der Kaiser! Ein Gott! Ein Reich! Ein Kaiser!*' This was no 'Shadow Kaiser' speaking. This was a commanding presence, an authentic national leader. At that moment Kaiser and people were one.[78]

Judging correctly the mood of his people, Wilhelm made the declaration of war a time for national celebration and spiritual rejoicing. He participated in an interdenominational religious service in front of the Reichstag that began impressively with the band of the Fusilier Guards playing the *Niederländische Dankgebet*. In his rich baritone, Wilhelm led the singing of the great hymn with its opening words, '*Wir treten zum beten*' ('We gather together to ask the Lord's blessing') – the same hymn Hitler would use to achieve his smashing political success in winning German Christians to his cause.[79]

The Kaiser's court preacher then blessed the war and intoned one of the Kaiser's favourite quotations: 'We Germans fear God and, apart from that, nothing else in the world!' Significantly he, like the Kaiser, cut short the quotation, omitting Bismarck's words of warning:

Wir deutschen fürchten Gott, aber sonst nichts in der Welt, und die Gottesfurcht ist es schon, die uns den Frieden lieben und pflegen lässt.

(... and it is the fear of God that enjoins us to love and nourish peace.)

The Kaiser closed the service by leading the crowd in the Lord's Prayer.

Wars tend to increase the power and prestige of the executive – one thinks of Cromwell and Lincoln during their countries' civil wars, or of Churchill and Roosevelt in the Second World War. The opposite was true of Wilhelm II. During his war he steadily diminished his own authority as he proved unable or unwilling to provide steady, consistent leadership. Nor was he able to take his own advice and allay his people's anxieties, because he could not allay his own. After hostilities opened and he was confronted not by his romanticized vision of war but by the horror of its reality, he spent sleepless nights worrying about what he had done. His moods swung wildly between depression at military setbacks and euphoria at any hint of momentary success. A few excerpts from the diary of Admiral Müller, who saw the Kaiser almost daily, convey Wilhelm's radical shifts of mood:

21 August 1914. The K[aiser] is very gloomy ... *25 August.* The Kaiser is radiant! ... *30 August.* The Kaiser ... positively revelled in blood ... *14 September.* H[is] M[ajesty] was very depressed ... *23 September.* The K is in seventh heaven ... *11 December.* The K was very depressed today ... *17 December.* The K was elated ... *23 January 1917.* H.M. very depressed ... had not slept a wink ... *19 May.* ANOTHER skat party: very gloomy ... *22 November.* Melancholy mood, K said, 'This war will never end.' *16 January 1916.* His Majesty in fine fettle; evening skat party ... *10 July.* H.M.'s mood is at lowest ebb ... *1 May.* His Majesty in jubilant mood. The K was nearly out of his mind today ... The English 'must be made to grovel.'

Müller was so disturbed by the Kaiser's constant 'state of agitation' that in 1917 he consulted the court physician, who told him that His Majesty was on the brink of 'a complete nervous breakdown.'[80] By mid-September 1918, Wilhelm himself agreed. When someone asked him if he had slept the previous night, the Kaiser replied, 'I haven't had a wink of sleep since I left Wilhelmshöhe [some two weeks before] ... I'm gradually cracking up.'[81] After a particularly bad night, Wilhelm asked his entourage to 'treat me gently,' telling them that he had nightmares in which his English and Russian relations filed past mocking and ridiculing him. 'Only the little Queen of Norway has been kind to me.'[82]

Wilhelm's psychological condition was of sufficient concern that members of the supreme command thought seriously of declaring the Kaiser 'temporarily incapable of ruling' and of making Crown Prince Friedrich Wilhelm the regent of Germany. The plan fell through largely because the Crown prince was widely recognized as an empty-headed fop. As Kiderlin-Wächter (1852–1912), the foreign secretary, whispered to a friend during a shooting party, 'Take care you don't shoot His Majesty – his successor would be far worse!'[83]

The Kaiser's title of 'Supreme War Lord' had become a 'hollow fiction' during the war,[84] largely because his behaviour made more glaring his deficiencies as a national leader shown in peacetime.[85] Wilhelm continued to make irresponsible statements and to give wildly conflicting orders. He refused to confront reality, dismissing adverse news as 'mere rumour.' He persisted in alienating the very people who could have helped him most, and he continued to blame others for his own mistakes. He tried to avoid making important decisions by saying he was much too busy to be bothered by 'trivialities.' Actually, Wilhelm II was unable to confront crucial military or political issues because he was too busy playing skat, designing new uniforms, going on extended hunting trips, or learning the language of the ancient Hittites. Indeed, one military historian has concluded, 'It would be difficult to find even one single example of the Kaiser ... making military decisions during the war.'[86]

The Kaiser was not even consulted about the army's Schlieffen Plan with its fateful decision to invade Belgium. This startling fact was revealed by General von Moltke in a conversation of 1921 with an academic named Rudolf Steiner:

'How was it,' he [Steiner] asked, 'that a War Minister could maintain in the Reichstag that the plan for invading Belgium did not exist?'

'This Minister,' I [Moltke] answered, 'did not know of my plan. But the Chancellor was informed.'

And the Kaiser? 'Never!' I answered ... He would have blabbed it to the whole world.'[87]

Wilhelm deplored the embarrassing position that he had brought upon himself. Having surrendered his power to the generals, he then petulantly complained that they never consulted him about anything. On 6 November 1914, for instance, he sought sympathy by saying, 'The general staff tells me nothing and never asks my advice. If anyone in Germany imagines that I lead the army, they are badly mistaken ... I drink tea, saw wood, and go for walks. And then I learn from time to time that this or that has been done, just as the *Herren* [of the general staff] had wanted.'[88]

The Kaiser not only gave the supreme command *carte blanche* in making military decisions, he also forfeited political leadership. When Generals Hindenburg and Ludendorff became dissatisfied with a chancellor, the Kaiser fired him and asked Hindenburg whom he would prefer in his place. Hindenburg named a nonentity whom the Kaiser immediately approved, though he had never met the man.[89] Admiral Müller reports that the Kaiser's invariable reply to those who sought urgent interviews during the war was either, 'Can't you see I'm busy?' or 'Leave me in peace!'[90]

In short, by 1917 Wilhelm II no longer ruled Germany. Through his acquiescence and indifference the monarchy had become a military dictatorship under Hindenburg and Ludendorff. The former, who has been aptly called 'The Wooden Titan,'[91] served as a front for the unstable Erich Ludendorff (1865–1937), a rabid racist and future supporter of Adolf Hitler. Ludendorff was a worshipper of Wotan and was known to have sacrificed horses to Thor, Norse god of thunder and war, on an altar he had erected on his estate.[92]

The extent of Wilhelm's abandonment of political power is epitomized in his admonition to Prince Max of Baden, who would be the last chancellor of Imperial Germany: 'Remember you have not come here to make trouble for the high command.'[93]

Towards the end, late in October 1918, with the army in retreat from the Allies' counter-offensive after the disastrous failure of Ludendorff's 'Victory Drive,' and with social unrest spreading through the cities of Germany, the Kaiser thought of making one grand, heroic gesture. He told his staff that he was determined to ride at the head of 'his' army to crush the revolutionaries in Berlin and 'restore Germany to its senses.'

The Kaiser's illusions were smashed with one brutally blunt response of the level-headed Württemberger, Wilhelm Groener, who had replaced Ludendorff as quartermaster general. Groener turned to Wilhelm, looked him in the eye, and said, 'The German army will march home in peace and order under its leaders and commanding generals, but not under the command of Your Majesty, for it no longer stands behind Your Majesty.'[94]

The Kaiser's subsequent abdication and flight can be traced in the diaries of Princess Blücher and of Count Kessler. The princess noted sadly that the abdication of 9 November 1918 was really not much of a surprise; it had already taken place in the hearts and minds of many people:

June–July 1917. The Kaiser is daily growing more and more the shadow of a monarch. And people talk openly of his abdication as a possibility very much desired ... One consequence of his blundering is that there is murmuring everywhere ...

Berlin, 23 October 1918. The aversion towards the Kaiser is increasing daily.

Berlin 9 November. Kessler noted that extra editions of newspapers announcing, 'Abdication of the Kaiser!' had few takers because the people found the Kaiser to be 'quite irrelevant'; many were heard muttering, 'Long overdue!'[95]

Berlin, Sunday Morning 10 November 1918. More dead than alive, I [Princess Blücher] will try to write down the events and impressions of last night, which I shall never forget ... I must confess that I feel shocked and surprised at the universal rejoicing manifested at the abdication of the Kaiser. They could not be more jubilant if they had won the war.[96]

On the evening of 10 November 1918, in a driving rain, Kaiser Wilhelm II crossed the German border for the last time. Letting out a sigh of relief, he jovially clapped his reluctant Dutch host, Count Godard van Bentinck, on the back, rubbed his hands briskly together, and gave an order: 'Now give me a cup of good English tea!!'[97]

PART II: HITLER AND THE SECOND WORLD WAR

Why did Germany hail the [Great] War and embrace it when it broke out? Because we recognized it as the bringer of a Third Reich ... the synthesis of Power and Spirit.

Thomas Mann, April 1915[98]

A Third Reich at peace is an unimaginable contradiction in terms.

Tim Mason, historian

The Second World War, like its predecessor, was the product of both man and circumstance: Hitler's personality coupled with the continuity of attitudes, policies, and institutions that the Kaiser's Germany had bequeathed to Hitler's generation.[99]

The German people deeply resented the Versailles Treaty and the unjust punishment that they believed it had inflicted upon them. Consequently, when Hitler promised to throw out the 'Weimar traitors' who had signed 'the treaty of shame' and to re-establish German power, he won support across the entire social spectrum as a statistical analysis of 'who voted for Hitler' has shown.[100]

The power structure that dominated Prussia and Imperial Germany was left largely intact by the so-called revolution of 1918 that established the Weimar Republic. There had been, however, no social or economic revolution. Dominant elites in industry, the army, the civil service, education, the foreign office, the judiciary, and the Church continued their commitment to an authoritarian state at home and expansion abroad. The continuity of personnel in the foreign office between the Second and Third Reichs was striking. Officials were as willing to execute Hitler's policies as they had been to endorse the Kaiser's and the Republic's.[101]

Similarly, the military establishment, which had been decisive in determining Germany's domestic and foreign policy under Wilhelm II, continued to determine policy throughout the decade preceding Hitler's accession to power.[102] The army's attitude was clearly stated in a memorandum of 11 September 1922, written by General Hans von Seeckt, the republican army's commander, to the chancellor of the republic demanding the remilitarization of Germany in defiance of the Versailles Treaty and preparation for a war to establish German domination of Central Europe: 'Our task is to prepare the German nation for battle ... It is not the duty of our leading statesmen to keep Germany out of war ... but to make sure that we come in on the right side with all possible strength.'[103]

General Seeckt's plan for Poland in 1922 foreshadowed what Hitler would do twenty years later: Germany, in alliance with Russia, would wipe Poland from the map by dividing it between the Soviet Union and Germany. The sly and taciturn general was known as 'the sphinx with a monocle,' but there was nothing enigmatic or secretive about his prose. It is crisp and clear: 'The existence of Poland is intolerable (*unerträglich*) and incompatible with Germany's vital interests. It must disappear and will do so through its own inner weakness and through Russia – with our help.'[104]

The demands of both Seeckt and Hitler for the subjugation of Poland and the conquest of German *Lebensraum* in the east had been on the agenda of the Pan-Germans in the 1890s and written into the so-called September Program of 1914, which enjoyed the support of the Kaiser, as well as leading educators, journalists, and pastors. According to this program, 'the general aim of the war' included the elimination of France as a great power and its incorporation, along with the Low Countries, into an economic system controlled by Germany, and the creation of a huge *Mitteleuropa*, embracing Poland and huge tracts of Russia, which was to be under German control, and pushed eastward 'as far as possible.'[105]

These objectives of 1914 were continued under the democratic republic, whose foreign minister, Gustav Stresemann, had won a Nobel prize for peace for cooperating with France in the Locarno Pact of December 1925. If the Nobel prize committee had known of Stresemann's plans for eastern Europe, he would have received no prize. For in a secret memorandum of the previous January Stresemann had set forth a program that pre-dated Hitler. He demanded *Anschluss* with Austria, the 'return' of Sudeten Germans to the Reich, and the 'creation of a state whose political frontiers encompass all the German people living within ... Central Europe.'[106]

Only with regard to Russia did the plans of Kaiser and Führer differ sharply. They both agreed that it was necessary to defeat Russia; but Wilhelm was thinking in terms of traditional military victory. Hitler had something very different in mind. He planned the 'systematic extinction (*Ausrottung*) of the Russian people,' and his plans had the active support of the German generals, diplomats, and industrialists.[107]

Top-secret government documents of 1925, which did not come fully to light until 1977, show that the leaders of the Weimar Republic had no intention whatever of limiting its army to the 100,000 men prescribed by the Versailles Treaty. On the contrary, in 1925 they endorsed plans for the massive rearmament that would make aggressive war possible. Specifically, the plans called for a military force of 8 armies of 102 divisions led by 252 generals with a total of 2.8 million soldiers. High officials in the government, army, and foreign office endorsed the plans and cooperated in a program of deception and camouflage that shielded them from public knowledge. The German army planned in 1925 became Hitler's army of 1939. When Hitler invaded Poland, his Wehrmacht had precisely those same numbers: 8 armies of 102 divisions 252 generals and 2.8 million men.[108]

It was not only the 'power elites' who continued to advocate massive armament and aggression. Nationalist fervour among the masses, first manifest in Wilhelm's Germany,[109] continued unabated during the Weimar Republic before reaching a fever pitch under Hitler. The veterans' group, *Stahlhelm* (Steel Helmet) – one of dozens of such associations[110] – set forth a program in 1928 that clearly anticipated the Nazis. This influential group, with a membership of several million veterans, publicly proclaimed both its hatred of democracy and its demand for aggression: 'With heart and soul we hate the present state ... because it affords us no prospect of liberating our enslaved Fatherland, of purging the German people of the war-guilt lie, of gaining living space we need in the East.' At the *Stahlhelm* national congress of 1931 a formal declaration demanding the destruction of Poland was passed with acclamation.[111]

Educators from elementary schools to universities continued to inculcate their students with visions of German power and military aggression. No pictures of democratic leaders were displayed in the classrooms of Germany during the Weimar Republic. Students looked up to portraits of Bismarck and the Prussian generals who reminded them of past military glories. Over 90 per cent of German elementary school teachers voluntarily joined the Nazi party.

Most educators agreed with Thomas Mann and the famous philosopher, Martin Heidegger, that the Nazi movement was the 'synthesis of power and spirit.' Heidegger used this phrase in his notorious address of 1933 when, as chancellor of the University of Freiburg, he welcomed the coming of the Nazis. He was echoing words that had been used by many previous German intellectuals.[112]

Influential Christian leaders also called for nationalistic expansion in 1939 as they had in 1914. Otto Dibelius, the Evangelical Bishop of Berlin, symbolized the continuity in religious attitudes. In 1914 Dibelius had renounced peace initiatives and favoured a war of German expansion. After the defeat he looked forward to a war of revenge to fulfil Germany's 'divinely ordained destiny.' He endorsed Hitler and defended Nazi persecution of the Jews. When Hitler began his war in 1939, Dibelius – along with the majority of other church leaders – urged his flock to pray that German arms would conquer the Führer's enemies and fulfil God's purposes for the Fatherland.[113]

The Catholic hierarchy, which had approved of war in 1914, continued to endorse an aggressive foreign policy. Catholic bishops throughout Germany ordered consecrated church bells to ring on Hitler's birthday and after each of the Führer's pre-war triumphs, including the absorption of Austria into the Reich (March 1938), the annexation of the Sudetenland (September 1938), and – despite Hitler's systematic murder of Polish priests – after his ruthless conquest of Poland in September 1939. Pastoral letters continued to enjoin priests to offer prayers of gratitude for 'our Führer and chancellor, the enlarger and protector of the Reich.'[114]

The period preceding Hitler had bequeathed to him acute economic problems associated with the Great Depression. Hitler's solution to these problems required war. An English historian noted the 'dreadful logic' of the Führer's program and concluded that the 'Third Reich at peace is an unimaginable contradiction in terms.'[115]

All these forces were harnessed by Hitler to fulfil his personal need for war.

Hitler's Personality and the Second World War

The resolve to strike was always within me.

Adolf Hitler

The Kaiser's responsibility for the First World War has been debated in thousands of scholarly pages. There is no such historical debate about the Führer's responsibility for the Second World War. We agree with a colleague, 'Hitler was the one person who willed, desired, lusted after war.'[116]

In 1978 Albert Speer showed an American journalist one of the first gifts Hitler had given him. It was a postcard-sized sketch of a triumphal arch, which was of the same basic design he and Speer would copy for the blueprint of the enormous victory arch of 1940. The small sketch was initialed AH and dated 1925.[117]

Hitler had looked forward to war in 1938 during the Czech crisis and felt thwarted by Neville Chamberlain and the Munich Accord. 'No son of a bitch (*Schweinehund*),' he snarled, was going to deprive him of his war next time.[118] During the year Chamberlain promised that his meeting with Hitler meant 'peace for our time.' Meanwhile, Hitler was spending more on weapons of war than Britain, France, and the United States *combined*.[119]

It is only technically true that the Second World War began with the Nazi invasion of Poland on 1 September 1939. It had really begun on 30 January 1933, the moment Adolf Hitler came to power. Just three days after becoming chancellor, Hitler ordered leaders of the armed forces to get ready for war. The notes of a participant at the conference set forth the Führer's plans: 'Conquest of new living-space in the east and its ruthless Germanization ... Hardening of the youth and strengthening the will to war by every possible means. Instilling in youth and the entire people the belief that only through war can Germany be saved ... Building up the army ... At same time psychological mobilization of our people.'[120]

Hitler kept those promises. In 1936 he put Field Marshal Hermann Göring in charge of the Four Year Plan and charged him with the responsibility for getting Germany ready for war by 1940. Hitler's secret memorandum of 1937 (of which only three copies were made)[121] sounded the same theme: (1) The German armed forces must be operational within four years. (2) The German economy must be ready for war within four years.[122] Also as he had promised, Hitler began 'the psychological mobilization' of the nation. In doing so he faced a formidable task in public persuasion. On the one hand, he had to lull Europe by promising peace. On the other, he had to arouse his own nation for war. The latter was not easy, for despite forces congenial to war and despite Nazi indoctrination, the masses of German citizens had no stomach for a repetition of the horrors of the Great War still vivid in searing memory. The masses had screamed their approval of Hitler's foreign conquests mainly because they had all been achieved without shedding a drop of German blood.

By the autumn of 1938 the time for 'peaceful conquests' was over. On 10 November Hitler summoned more than a hundred journalists to an extraordinary meeting in Munich, where he openly announced his shift in strategy and demanded their help in 'strengthening the will to war': 'For years circumstances have compelled me to talk about almost nothing but peace. But this ... can give the people the idea that [my government] really identifies itself with the determination to preserve peace at all costs ... It is now necessary gradually to re-educate the German people psychologically and to make it clear that there are things which must be achieved by force when peaceful means fail.'[123]

In striking contrast to the Kaiser, who had alarmed Europe with belligerent speeches, the Führer, while preparing for war, talked peace and assured the world that he had absolutely no plans for aggression. As Hitler well knew, such assurances fell on receptive ears, for the Great War was still very much on people's minds. Those who had fought remembered too well the stench of the trenches, hollow-eyed, frightened men waiting 'to go over the top' to meet their death on some disputed barricade, chunks of young flesh clinging to barbed wire, the endless roar of guns, the terror encapsulated in one word screamed along the front, 'Gas!' Youthful revulsion for war was symbolized by the Oxford Union's famous debate of 9 February 1933: '[Resolved] That this House will in no circumstances fight for its King and Country.' (The motion passed by 275 votes to 153.)

Hitler's speeches of the period spoke directly to those fears: 'National Socialist Germany desires peace out of its deepest ideological convictions ... I stand before my countrymen and the entire world and give them my solemn assurance that *I will make no further territorial demands on Europe*, that is a contribution to peace greater than any number of signatures under any number of pacts.'[124]

The Führer followed his placating promises with acts of aggression. His method was seen clearly in his military reoccupation of the Rhineland in March 1936 in defiance of both the Versailles and the Locarno treaties. This was one of his many 'weekend surprises.' Hitler liked to make his moves on Fridays or Saturdays, knowing that European foreign offices and military headquarters would be understaffed for the weekend, and that on Monday morning a startled world would awaken to banner headlines announcing yet another *fait accompli* with which they were ill-prepared to cope. Immediately after occupying the Rhineland, Hitler promised again that he would make no more territorial demands, specifically stating that he had no intention whatsoever of intervening in the affairs of Austria.

The Wehrmacht marched into Austria on Saturday, 12 March 1938. Hitler proclaimed to the ecstatic Austrians that his native country was now a part of the 'Greater German Reich.' Next the Führer called for an international conference to limit armaments and outlaw the use of poison gas.[125] Then he launched the Second World War.

At 045 hours on 1 September 1939 (a Friday) Stuka dive-bombers screamed and 11-inch guns from the *Schleswig-Holstein* thundered over the sleeping city of Danzig. Hitler smiled with satisfaction and was heard to muse, 'The resolve to strike was always within me (*war immer in mir*).'[126] To fulfil this personal need Hitler had militarized a nation and sent it into battle.

The Second World War was not somehow forced by circumstance upon a reluctant Hitler. On the contrary, he had manipulated circumstances to force the war on a reluctant Europe. From the start of his career, war had been in Adolf Hitler's bones and guts and psyche. It was the very *raison d'être* of his Reich. Without war the Third Reich made no sense. This was, in truth, 'Hitler's War.' The First World War, despite being popularly called 'Kaiser Bill's War,' was only in part Wilhelm's war. Part of him had not really wanted it; he certainly had not directed it.

There is another difference between the two world wars. Neither Wilhelm's ambivalent personality nor the domestic economic or political needs of his government required war. That cannot be said of the Second World War. Historians quite rightly dislike using the word 'inevitable.' But, given Hitler's pathological personality and the nature of his Reich, the Second World War was as inevitable as any event in history can be.

Hitler's responsibility for the war is so manifest that it is not necessary to debate the issues that commanded our attention in assessing the Kaiser's role in the coming of the First World War. Instead, I shall be concerned with the Führer's peculiar behaviour during the war and suggest the possibility that, while consciously seeking victory, Hitler may have been impelled by a subliminal impulse to invite disaster through self-defeating decisions.

The Führer's Military Preparation for War

Unbelievable as it may sound, Hitler did not even have a general strategic plan for the war.

General Franz von Halder

It is not difficult for any historian, serene in the knowledge of how the future turned out, to look back on a lost war and point out the diplomatic and strategic errors that led to defeat. It is also true that even the most brilliant military commander can make mistakes. Yet Hitler's blunders were too many, too costly, and too gratuitous to be explained simply as normal 'human error.'

At the very outset, there was something peculiar about Hitler's actual military plans for the great war he had promised in his memoirs, in a dozen speeches, and in several memoranda. The scholarly Franz von Halder, Chief of the army General Staff in 1939, said in an interview after the war that 'unbelievable as it may sound, he [Hitler] did not even have a general strategic plan for the war.'[127]

Moreover, Hitler failed to prepare his troops for battle. Halder noted with alarm that munitions in 1939 were in such short supply that large-scale combat was not possible: 'Supply was sufficient for only one-third of the available divisions for fourteen days. Current production was just enough to keep the same one-third active.'[128]

A massive study of Hitler's war aims and military planning has fully substantiated Halder's opinion. It concludes that although Hitler's policy presupposed a major war, he had no coordinated military or economic plans for conducting such a conflict. 'He had not raised the question of transport ... he gave staff officers absolutely no military directives. The same was true with regard to raw material ... Effective planning simply did not exist.'[129]

It has been argued that Hitler was not concerned with building up massive reserves of raw materials and foodstuffs, or with converting to a full war economy, because he would rely instead on a series of quick victories and on looting materials from each country as he conquered it. There is merit in this argument except for one fact: even after it became obvious that this policy no longer worked, he refused to order full economic mobilization. It was not until the autumn of 1944 – well after the disastrous defeat at Stalingrad and after his 'Fortress Europe' had been entered from the west and Russia was moving in from the east – when it was much too late, that Hitler began moving haltingly towards a full-scale war economy. But he never arrived.

While the British and American war industries were working around the clock on three-shift schedules, most of German industry operated on one shift. Full use of plant and equipment was never achieved. Albert Speer had finally been made minister of munitions, but he was never given full power. Even in 1944, when German armament production reached its height, Speer noted ruefully that it still lagged behind the economic mobilization of the First World War. Luxury goods were still being produced, German women still got their hair-dryers; and Hitler continued to use millions of work hours and vitally needed rolling stock to haul Jews to their deaths and art objects into hiding.[130]

These policies were self-defeating.

Decisions During the War: Dunkirk

We were all flabbergasted by Hitler's order ... It was incomprehensible ... We were stopped within sight of Dunkirk!

Generals Warlimont and Guderian

Hitler's performance as the supreme commander of all German forces in the Second World War must be given a mixed review. It is certainly true that he sometimes showed an uncanny ability to judge his enemy aright, as when he concluded that the French would stay behind their 'impregnable' Maginot Line and not attack his undermanned western front while he was invading Poland,[131] or when Hitler guessed, correctly, in 1942 that the Red Army would counterattack at Stalingrad, not near Smolensk as his generals were insisting. Indeed, a respected British military historian concluded, 'No strategist in history has been more clever in playing on the minds of his opponents – which is the supreme art of strategy.'[132] Hitler also showed a capacity for innovation in the use of armour and air power. He greatly improved German armaments, substituting, for example, much more powerful 75-mm anti-tank guns for the existing 37- and 55-mm and long 75- and 88-mm tank guns – innovations which made major contributions to the success of German armoured divisions.[133] Also at his initiative the Panther and Tiger tanks were developed.

Hitler must also be given credit for changing the Schlieffen Plan for the

Second World War. With remarkable lack of imagination, his generals, trained in the Kaiser's army, had planned to revive the old campaign plans of 1914, with the chief thrust against France coming from the right. The French high command fully expected an attack from that direction. Disdaining his generals' rigidity, Hitler abandoned the right-wing strategy and caught the French completely off guard by smashing through the 'impassable' Ardennes forest. As Alan Bullock has written, 'What the Kaiser's armies had failed to achieve after more than four years of exhausting war with the loss of over 1,800,00 German lives, Hitler's armies had accomplished in six weeks at the cost of 27,000.'[134]

All this is impressive. The Führer, it bears repeating, could act with devastating effectiveness. Yet during the war he also displayed a lifelong impulse to flirt with failure, to seize defeat from the jaws of victory.[135] After his blitzkrieg victories over Poland in September 1939 and France in May 1940, Hitler turned to confront Britain, the only power opposing him. Then something strange happened.

Hitler refused the open invitation to smash the entire British Expeditionary Force in Europe. Instead, on 15 May 1940, he suddenly gave orders to halt all tank movement on the Dunkirk salient. Several explanations for his surprising decision have been given, including one the Führer himself later suggested: He had let the British go 'in a sporting spirit, after the English manner.'[136] (This, as Eliza Doolittle might have said, was 'not bloody likely!') It has also been suggested that Hitler halted his tanks because he was afraid they might get stuck in the mud of Flanders, or he wanted to save his armour for the pending attack on France, or Göring had assured him that it was unnecessary to attack the BEF because airpower alone would defeat Britain, or he had decided that an economic blockade would force England to surrender, or some combination of any or all of these.

None of these explanations, however, impressed the German generals at the time. At headquarters, General Halder and his adjutant, Walter Warlimont, were simply 'flabbergasted by Hitler's order,' which they found 'incomprehensible.' Field officers were equally appalled. General Heinz Guderian, the brilliant commander of armoured divisions, wrote incredulously, 'We were stopped within sight of Dunkirk!' Baffled members of General Gerd von Rundstedt's staff concluded that the only possible solution to 'the riddle of Dunkirk' was that for some inexplicable reason Hitler 'wished to help the British.'[137] Certainly that is what he accomplished. In heroic scenes, 350,000 men of the British Expeditionary Force were rescued from the beaches of Dunkirk and evacuated to fight again – while Hitler's armour stood within striking distance.

It is difficult to find a convincing explanation for Hitler's decision at Dunkirk.

Decision in War: Invasion of Russia

I felt as if I had opened a door into a darkened room, with something lurking within ...
Heavy uncertainty gripped me by the throat.

Adolf Hitler, October 1941

For several weeks after the fall of France in June 1940, Hitler was unsure about what to do next. As so often in his life, when plagued by uncertainty he turned to Wagner for inspiration and guidance. Now, late in July 1940, he journeyed to the shrine at Bayreuth to attend a performance of *Die Götterdämmerung*.

Once again Wagner worked his magic. His portrayal of heroic catastrophe, the destruction of gods and men, somehow reassured the Führer and confirmed his conviction of his own historic destiny. In the darkness of the loge at the conclusion of the performance, Hitler passionately kissed the hand of Frau Winifred Wagner, and then he left Bayreuth composed, his mind made up. Within the week he issued orders to prepare for the invasion of Russia, a decision that would lead to his own *Götterdämmerung*.[138]

The following June, with the European continent in his grip, instead of consolidating his vast 'Greater German Reich' and concentrating his forces against his only remaining foe, an isolated and desperately wounded England, Hitler turned to court his nemesis. This he did at a time when Stalin was a valued ally, shipping him thousands of tons of vital war supplies, iron ore, scrap iron, and chrome, as well as oil, wheat, platinum, rubber, and timber. One of the most astonishing pictures in the annals of warfare shows Hitler's soldiers marching eastward into Russia and staring in amazement as they see Soviet freight trains travelling westward loaded with supplies for their own Wehrmacht. Hitler also had at his disposal large quantities of oil and wheat after his army had moved into Rumania in September 1940 to 'protect' Rumanian oil and wheat fields.[139]

Hitler did not invade the Union of Soviet Socialist Republics because he needed war supplies. Other reasons have been suggested: He had long planned to find *Lebensraum* for his Reich in eastern Europe. He was getting old and wanted to win his race with death. He mistrusted Stalin and – against all evidence to the contrary – was convinced that the Soviets were about to attack him. His ideology required him to destroy the 'breeding ground of Jewish-Bolshevism.' His easy victories over the Low Countries and France had given him and his generals the euphoric feeling that the Führer was a military genius and his armies invincible. Besides, no one else from the west had ever conquered Russia. Here was his chance to prove that he was indeed 'the greatest military commander of all time' – far greater than Charles XII or Napoleon, both of whom had failed to master Russia. Then, too, Hitler had always been fascinated by space: 'In my youth, I dreamed constantly of vast spaces,' he mused one night in his 'Wolf's Lair' headquarters. 'Now life has enabled me to give the dream reality ... Space lends wings to my imagination.'[140] All these reasons for Hitler's decision may have been operative for, as Freud has reminded us, human motivation is always *'überbestimmt'* – overdetermined and multiple.

Yet there are puzzling features about his decision. The reason the Führer himself gave was that he invaded Russia in order to defeat England – not, one would think, the most direct way to achieve his stated objective. The result, predictably, achieved the opposite. England was hugely relieved by the Führer's decision, for it meant that he had abandoned plans for the invasion of Britain and had enmeshed himself, instead, in a two-front war.

It is particularly remarkable that in launching his invasion, Hitler did not ask Japan, his ally in the Tripartite Pact, to help him in any way. Indeed, the Führer actually gave explicit orders that 'no hint of the Barbarossa Operation be given to the Japanese.' If Japan had been informed while its options were still open in the spring of 1941, it might well have used the opportunity Barbarossa offered to mount its own offensive against Russia. Moreover, Hitler's refusal to consult his ally offended the Japanese, who henceforth cited the incident as an example of Hitler's 'perfidy.' Norman Rich, a close student of Hitler's war aims, has concluded that if Japan had attacked Russia in the Far East while the Wehrmacht was invading from the west, Hitler would have conquered Russia. Rich can find no adequate way to account for Hitler's 'extraordinary attitude' in failing 'to do anything of any kind to secure Japanese cooperation.'[141]

Hitler's attitude continued to be extraordinary. Even as late as the winter of 1941–2, when it was clear that he would need all the help he could get if he were to defeat Russia, and all reason demanded that he seek some sort of aid from Japan, he refused to do so. As a modest return for his own declaration of war on the United States, which had enormously helped Japan, Hitler as a minimum might have asked his ally to halt U.S. shipment of supplies going to the Soviet Union via Vladivostok. He made no such request.

Something else was curious about Hitler's behaviour. The struggle against the Soviet Union, everyone knew, would be a titanic undertaking requiring enormous amounts of supplies – the mobilization of the economic power of a great industrial nation. Yet Hitler never gave the order for such mobilization. The level of consumer goods produced in the Reich in 1941 actually exceeded the level of 1940.[142] Hitler continued to insist on circuses and well-buttered bread along with his cannons.

During the war years Hitler requisitioned enormous quantities of scarce iron and steel for constructing a winter Olympic stadium at Garmisch, for his grandiose building complexes for Berlin, and for fulfiling his boyhood dream of rebuilding Linz to replace Vienna as 'Queen of the Danube.' Just prior to the invasion of Russia, Hitler actually gave orders *to reduce* the level of armament production.[143] After studying Hitler's economic preparation for Operation Barbarossa, a British historian concluded, 'It was as if he were determined to go into his last great battle with one arm in a sling.'[144] Astonishingly, on the day preceding the invasion, 21 June 1941, Hitler reversed a previous order and gave priority to the production of submarines[145] – not very useful, one would think, in besieging Moscow.

Was all this mere bravado? That is possible. Yet there are hints that Hitler was not nearly so confident of easy victory over Russia as he gave out. He kept repeating a metaphor that bespeaks premonition of misfortune. At three o'clock on the morning of the invasion, he told an aide: 'I feel as if I've opened a door into a dark, unseen room – without knowing what's lurking behind the door.' He repeated the metaphor of the darkened room to his secretaries and added apprehensively, 'One never knows what lies in hiding!' He said the same thing to Bormann and repeated it to Ribbentrop. And again, in a speech of October 1941 in which he was trying to explain to his generals the absolute necessity of invading Russia, 'At every such step a door opens and behind it some mystery *(Geheimnis)* lies in waiting ...'[146]

And why, of all the thousands of alternatives, did Hitler insist on the code name 'Barbarossa'? His military planners had called the operational plan 'Fritz' after the victorious Prussian king. But on Hitler's direct personal order the name was changed to Barbarossa.[147]

Why? It has been suggested that Hitler saw himself as Friedrich Barbarossa, another crusader with a holy mission to destroy the infidel enemy in the east. But Barbarossa had failed. In fact he was the most celebrated failure of medieval German history: he had failed in five campaigns against the Italian city-states; he had failed to fulfil his promise of unifying the Holy Roman Empire of the German Nation; he had failed to capture Jerusalem during the Third Crusade and had drowned in 1190 while bathing in the Seleph River.

Adolf Hitler knew these things about Barbarossa. Among the books he borrowed from a private library was a detailed biography of the Hohenstaufen ruler which records these facts;[148] indeed, they were common knowledge to any patriotic schoolboy who, like Adolf, was interested in German medieval history.

That Hitler would associate himself with a man who drowned is also psychologically interesting. The Führer was pathologically afraid of water and had nightmares about loss of breath, strangulation, and drowning. The words he used in announcing the invasion of Russia are worth remembering. 'The world,' he said, 'will hold its breath.' When the Führer held his breath and counted anxiously to ten while his valet tied his tie, on one level he was playing a game; on a symbolic level, however, he may have been enacting strangulation and self-destruction.[149] Months after making his fateful decision, he recalled his anxiety about giving the orders for Barbarossa. Again he expressed apprehension about ominous darkness lurking behind an opened door. Then he shifted to a metaphor of strangulation: 'The heavy uncertainty took me by the throat.'[150]

Even before the campaign had begun, Hitler feared its failure – confiding to Rudolph Hess that he saw 'my entire life work in ruins.'[151]

Throughout the course of Operation Barbarossa, as military historians have pointed out, Hitler made a series of major mistakes. To take one glaring example, in 1941 the Ukraine was seething with resentment and hatred for Stalin's regime that had murdered thousands of Ukrainian peasants, sent their sons into Siberian exile, and cheated those who remained on the despised collective farms; yet Hitler scorned any idea of cultivating mass resentment among Ukrainians. Indeed, his draconian orders turned hatred for Stalin to hatred for the Nazi invaders who had first been greeted as liberators by oppressed Ukrainians. As Alan Bullock noted, Hitler's brutal policies 'united the Russian people as Stalin could never have done, in resistance to the [German] invaders.'[152]

After reflecting on Hitler's egregious mistakes and missed opportunities, a German authority on Hitler's military leadership asked a psychologically interesting question: 'What could have been going on in the head of this man?'[153]

The question must be broadened beyond Hitler's separate tactical and strategic blunders during the campaign. The decision to wage war against the USSR was, in itself, irrational. Consider the awful and unnecessary gamble he took in attacking so cooperative an ally. If he lost the campaign, the whole war was lost; even if he 'won' and defeated the Red armies in western Russia, the war was far from over. For Hitler would have been sucked ever farther eastward, while England, aided by America, would continue to pound him from the air. The two-front war he had created would continue. And why take the risk? Why not remain at peace with his ally and co-conspirator and simply consolidate the vast empire he had attained through his own conquests and the secret protocols of the Nazi-Soviet Pact? He already held in thrall an area stretching from the English Channel to central Poland, from the Baltic to the Mediterranean. Who could deny him his 'Greater German Reich'? Surely not battered and beleaguered England, the only country then at war against him.[154]

Reason seems to have had little to do with Hitler's decision to invade Russia.

Decision in War: Declaration of War on the United States

This war with the United States is a tragedy. It is illogical and devoid of any foundation in reality.

Adolf Hitler, February 1945

Four days after the Japanese attacked Pearl Harbor on 7 December 1941, Hitler suddenly declared war on the United States, thereby assuring that America's industrial and military power would now be directed against him rather than against Japan. This decision, made without consulting either the army or the foreign office, puzzled both contemporaries and later historians.

Immediately after the war, the United States State Department sent a delegation of specialists to Germany to interrogate Nazi leaders about Hitler's decision. After extensive interviews the leader of the mission concluded in his report: 'We found the most baffling question in the whole Nazi story to be the prompt German declaration of war on the United States.'[155] Years later an American historian writing on Nazi-American relations acknowledged that he too was baffled: 'This declaration [of war] ... has never been satisfactorily explained. It was ... contrary to everything Hitler had practiced and preached.'[156] Another historian of the war agrees: 'The underlying logic of the Führer's [decision] defies analysis ... it was an irrational act ... By the declaration of war, he lost finally and irrevocably all hope of winning the war against the Soviet Union.'[157]

Since historians are uncomfortable with mysteries, several explanations have been provided. It is said that Hitler declared war on America because he held the country in contempt and was convinced, as the Kaiser had been, that the United States presented no military problem. There is some evidence to support this view. Hitler told Mussolini that American armament statistics were 'lies pure and simple.' He assured General Halder that American military power was 'one big bluff' and concluded roundly that the United States was 'incapable of conducting war.' Moreover, Hitler's racial theory led him to conclude that America 'is half-Judaized, half-Negrified' and that 'Americans have the brains of a hen.'

Yet he also flatly contradicted his own denigrations when he asserted that, because of its Aryan stock, Americans are a superior people who are 'unbelievably clever' and 'compared with old Europe, America emerges as a young, racially select people.'[158] The Führer was in awe of American industrial power, telling Hanfstaengl that the reason Germany lost the First World War was the entry of the United States. 'That must never happen again,' he said.[159] Yet he made it happen again.

It has also been argued that Hitler declared war on the United States out of loyalty to his Japanese ally and in fulfilment of his treaty obligations. But Hitler's sense of honour was not one of his more conspicuous virtues and under the Tripartite Pact of 1940 (Germany, Japan, and Italy) there was no obligation for Germany to support Japan unless the United States attacked Japan. That is not what happened at Pearl Harbor.

The Tripartite Pact remained, as one of its historians has called it, a 'hollow alliance,'[160] torn by suspicion and reciprocal distrust. Hitler had caused Japan to lose face by refusing to inform his ally about Barbarossa, and Japan attacked the United States without informing Hitler or asking for his support. Then, with absolutely no assurance of help from his Japanese ally, and fully aware that no treaty required him to do so, Hitler simply decided on his own to declare war on America.[161]

Another explanation for this decision argues that Hitler decided on war with the United States in early December 1941 because he believed that sooner or later it would attack him, and he wanted to fight at the most advantageous time. It is true that Hitler said he had always been suspicious of Roosevelt, 'that half-Jew,' who he suspected was 'quite resolved to go to war and annihilate National Socialism.'[162] But the timing of Hitler's decision didn't make sense.

In the previous week the Red Army, under Marshal Georgi Zhukov, had begun a gigantic counter-offensive using a hundred fresh divisions that Hitler had insisted did not exist. The Germans were hurled back in confusion with enormous losses in men and material. 'In Hitler's headquarters,' Domarus reported, 'there spread a feeling of total collapse (*Weltuntergangsstimmung*).' Field Marshal Wilhelm Keitel, Hitler's toady who had replaced Halder as chief of the High Command, tried to commit suicide. Hitler himself sat gloomily staring off into space. Headquarters was further depressed by a blizzard that swept the eastern front during the first fortnight of December and again proved, as in the days of Napoleon's ill-fated Grand Army, that Russia's best field commander was General Winter. The deputy chief of operations of the Wehrmacht recalled that 'temperatures of minus 30 to 35 degrees celsius were paralyzing the troops and making weapons unusable ... reports kept coming in that the danger of severe defeat was ... limitless.'[163]

In short, it was the worst possible time for the Führer to add to his troubles by declaring war on the greatest industrial power on earth.

Hitler had been delighted to learn of American military involvement in the Far East. But that had already been achieved by the Japanese attack on Pearl Harbor, 7 December 1941. All the Führer needed to do now was to keep his mouth shut and rejoice silently in his great good fortune. Shortly before he was put to death for crimes against humanity, General Alfred Jodl, chief of the army's operation staff, commented ruefully: 'We should have preferred a new and powerful ally without a new and powerful enemy.'[164]

Hitler's decision on 11 December was a godsend to President Franklin Roosevelt. John Kenneth Galbraith recalled the triumphant joy in FDR's inner circle upon hearing the surprisingly good news:

When Pearl Harbor happened, we were desperate ... The mood of the American people was obvious – they were determined that the Japanese had to be punished. We could have been forced to concentrate all our efforts on the Pacific, unable from then on to give more than purely peripheral help to Britain. It was truly astounding when Hitler declared war on us three days later. I cannot tell you our feeling of triumph. It was a totally irrational thing for him to do.[165]

Hitler's declaration of war also solved Roosevelt's political problem. At one stroke the ground was cut from under the president's opponents. For now even the most vociferous non-interventionists in Congress could hardly object to directing U.S. military efforts against Hitler. Clear evidence of how much Hitler had helped Roosevelt came on the very day Hitler declared war. When the president asked Congress on 11 December to recognize that a state of war existed between the United States and Germany, not one member of Congress voted against a resolution which, had it been taken only a day earlier, would certainly have been defeated.[166] It is possible that the United States might have been drawn into a shooting war with Hitler at some future time. We shall never know. We do know that 'the Führer's initiative gave immeasurable aid and comfort to his opponents and his victims.'[167]

Judged in either military or political terms, Hitler's decision to declare war on the United States was an unnecessary and irrational act which benefited his enemies far more than it helped him. A former dean of American diplomatic historians has bluntly concluded, 'Hitler had not only blundered, he had ruined his own cause.'[168] The Führer himself admitted that what he had done made no sense: 'War with the United States,' he said, 'was a tragedy and illogical.'[169] He was right about that.

War and the Decision for Genocide

Our greatest enemy is the Jew, the eternal Jew.

Adolf Hitler

Hitler's appetite for impossible victories against impossible odds could not be sated even by simultaneously warring against the Soviet Union and the United States. To his mind there was an enemy more worthy of his heroic mettle. The Führer would annihilate the Jews. This decision made no political or economic or military sense. As well as being unspeakably evil, it was stupendously stupid.

At a time when reason dictated that Hitler should have concentrated all national energies on defending his Reich from the Soviet armies attacking from the east and the Allies from the west, he gave the orders[170] that diverted hundreds of trains and billions of hours to the enormous logistical task of collecting, 'processing,' and disposing of the corpses of millions of innocent people who had made enormous contributions to Germany and posed no danger whatsoever either to him or to his Reich.

Like Hitler's decisions to invade Russia and to declare war on the United States, the Holocaust was an irrational act that contributed significantly to his defeat.

The Kaiser's decision for war in 1914 and the Führer's in 1939 were, in both instances, the result of the interplay between historical conditions and the personalities of the two rulers. The circumstances, however, were different, and so were the personalities.

In the Kaiser's Germany, there were pressures that produced a climate favourable to war. But Imperial Germany was not beset by those economic problems that within Hitler's Reich could find resolution only through a war of conquest.

Political conditions in Europe differed. The Führer's potential adversaries were significantly weaker than those the Kaiser had faced in 1914.[171]

The relationships of the army with the Kaiser and with the Führer differed. In 1914 the general staff had pushed a vacillating Kaiser into war, and once hostilities had broken out the generals steadily increased both their military and their political power. The Kaiser was in awe of his generals and constantly deferred to them; the Führer treated his generals with contempt and essentially ignored them. He did not inform them, let alone consult them, about his plans for the invasion of France, the Norwegian campaign, the terms of the French armistice, or his decision for war against the United States.[172] He hanged disaffected officers on meat hooks and watched coloured films of piano wire tightening around their necks.

In both wars the German army was involved in atrocities. But with the notorious exceptions of military actions in Belgium and France in 1914, the Imperial army's treatment of enemy combatants and civilians was relatively benign, certainly when compared with the conduct of Hitler's army during the Second World War, when more than three million Russian prisoners of war died in German POW camps with the knowledge and collaboration of the army. Wehrmacht generals approved the calculated starvation of their prisoners to the point of cannibalism and permitted films to be taken to prove that the Russians were 'bestial subhumans.' There was no public outcry against the films. Audiences were reported to have seen them as confirmation of German racial theories.[173] Army trucks transported Jewish corpses for burial; at Babi-Yar, west of Kiev, army heavy equipment bulldozed thousands of bodies into mass graves.[174]

Prior to both wars, the military and industrial establishment, along with the foreign office, had welcomed German rearmament and aggression. There was a marked difference, however, in popular attitudes to war. A previous generation had marched confidently, even jubilantly into battle. In 1939 their children – despite devotion to their Führer – faced another world war with forboding.[175]

The attitudes of Kaiser and Führer towards war were also strikingly different. Wilhelm had always been thrilled by the idea of warfare as a romantic abstraction and an exciting game. He loved to dress up and play soldier in any one of his 250 uniforms, have himself photographed in sixty-seven heroic poses, and painted as the very incarnation of war. He found it was also great fun to lead cavalry charges in war-games and to demonstrate his manhood in bellicose speeches.

Wilhelm was especially excited by war in far-off places. He urged the Tsar to fight the Japanese in Manchuria. He felt personally involved in the Boer War in South Africa and drew up plans for vicarious victories. The Boxer Rebellion in China stirred him deeply. The Kaiser had talked excitedly about smashing the Chinese and repeatedly exclaimed to his chancellor, 'Now it's pure joy to be alive!'[176] The stark reality of battle was a totally different matter, and Wilhelm was heartsick at the deaths and suffering. The Führer exulted in the slaughter of war. When a field commander expressed regret over the deaths of so many brave young soldiers Hitler replied, 'But that's what young people are for!'

The two rulers reacted very differently after signing the documents launching the two world wars. Wilhelm was appalled by what he had done. Distraught and sleepless, he spent anxious hours seeking solace in prayer. An aide reported that Wilhelm could 'be found in tears in corners of churches all over the Rhineland praying for hours together.' Another associate said that he had never seen the Kaiser look so disturbed and tragic: 'Here was a man whose whole world had collapsed.'[177] On 31 August 1939, after signing Order No. 1, which would send the *Wehrmacht* crashing into Poland the next morning,[178] Hitler was 'in a state of euphoria all day,' and then he had a very good night's sleep.[179]

In discussing the political leadership of Kaiser and Führer in peace and in war, we have noted how both rulers of keen intelligence acted in irrational ways that have puzzled their biographers. Why did Wilhelm persist in saying and doing things that were bound to alienate others and to defeat his own purposes? Why was his conduct of both domestic and foreign affairs so erratic? Why did Hitler hate the Jews with such relentless intensity? Why was he compelled to take unnecessary risks and persistently court disaster?

We may never find fully satisfying answers to such questions; yet since we are dealing with two pathological personalities it will be helpful to see what psychology can contribute to our understanding of their behaviour.

5

Psychological Dimensions

What this country needs is a legal guarantee of the citizen's right not to be publicly psychoanalyzed by people he has never met. Violations of this right should be made a crime. It could be called 'Freudulence.'

Russell Baker

Prologue

The late A.J.P. Taylor, for many years one of Britain's most provocative and popular historians, would have heartily agreed with Russell Baker, for Taylor gave short shrift to those who use psychological insights in an effort to deepen their understanding of history.[1] Towards the close of his illustrious career he expressed his own historical credo in a farewell lecture that packed the Sheldonian Theatre in Oxford. Disdaining concern with irrational forces, he asserted that his own interpretations had relied entirely upon 'my greatest gift as an historian: old-fashioned common sense.'[2]

Who would dispute the manifold merits of common sense? In my view, however, common sense enjoins us to acknowledge, rather than to reject, the contributions psychologists have made to our craft. To take only one example: Taylor's common sense cannot account for the sheer *senselessness* of the Holocaust. As a leading authority on Hitler's genocide has written, every attempt to explain the Holocaust 'based on normal common sense has entirely proven fatally wrong.'[3]

Nor is Taylor's common sense able to answer such a question as this: Why – though presumably they were rational human beings – did Wilhelm Hohenzollern and Adolf Hitler persist in acting in ways least likely to succeed and most likely to defeat their own political or military purposes? The simple question of motivation is the most intractable, and the most important, question a biographer can ask in trying to understand his subject. Having repeatedly confronted this question in his magnificent five-volume study of Henry James, Leon Edel explains why he found it necessary to consult psychoanalysts in preparing his biography: 'I don't know how any biographer or historian today can start discussing the motives and behavior of his subjects and ignore the great psychological discoveries of this century or ignore the unconscious.' Edel then warns all biographers that in confronting the human personality we are dealing with 'endless and continuing mysteries.'[4]

Henry James himself had given a similar warning. He began one of his short stories with a comment that might well serve as an aphorism for biographers as well as for psychoanalysts: 'Never say you know the last word about any human heart.'[5]

With these caveats in mind, let us seek help from psychoanalysis. This approach cannot be expected to provide fully satisfying answers to that simple but tantalizingly complex question: 'What were they really like?' But it can be helpful. No larger claim should be made. As in St Thomas's medieval and still pertinent distinction, psychology is a 'necessary but not sufficient explanation.'[6]

Mysteries will certainly remain.

In the following pages I will suggest that Wilhelm II closely conforms to what psychologists have identified as the 'narcissistically disturbed personality,' and that Adolf Hitler can best be understood as a 'borderline personality.' For good reasons, however, one should hesitate to attach any diagnostic label to historic figures who are quite beyond the analyst's couch.

In the first place, biographers labour under two serious handicaps. Most of us are not trained psychologists, and we lack the direct personal communication with our subjects that is indispensable to full clinical analysis.

Second, to pin psychological labels on our subjects may suggest to the unwary that the Kaiser and the Führer were exactly like every other disturbed person who has been diagnosed as 'narcissistic' or as 'borderline.' But neither of these men was just like anyone else. Each, like the rest of us, was unique.

Third, a diagnostic label may invite the erroneous conclusion that Wilhelm's or Hitler's political problems were entirely the consequence of psychological difficulties. Not so. To understand the failures and successes of their careers – let us say it again – we must also consider the special political and social conditions confronting each of them.

Fourth, in setting a diagnosis, and arguing on its behalf, comes a real temptation to be so absorbed by the argument as to ignore important facts and choose for emphasis only the evidence that supports this diagnosis. The truth of the matter is that both Kaiser and Führer sometimes acted in ways that cannot be made to fit neatly into any diagnostic category.

Moreover, even if it is granted that the Kaiser and the Führer acted in ways that do mark them clearly as 'narcissistically impaired' or 'borderline,' *what difference does it make?* What does the discussion contribute to an understanding of their careers? The answer may be 'little or none.' We must recognize that pathological behaviour in the private lives of political leaders may have no discernible effect on their political decisions. One thinks, for example, of William Ewart Gladstone's morbid masochism and self-flagellation after prolonged conferences with prostitutes, or of William Lyon Mackenzie King's table-tapping and spectral conversations with both his deceased mother and his long-dead dog. Such behaviour, although no doubt pathological, seems not to have influenced Gladstone's Irish Home Rule policy or Mackenzie King's extraordinarily long career as the most successful prime minister in Canadian history.

Certainly there are risks in proposing a diagnosis. Yet they are worth taking if the diagnosis makes us aware of recurrent *patterns of behaviour* that would otherwise have escaped our attention.

Diagnosis is a form of generalization, and the value of any generalization depends on its specificity. We gain little insight from writers who merely affirm that the Kaiser was 'neurotic' or that Hitler was 'a madman' – or from journalists who inform us that Muammar Qaddafi or Saddam Hussein or Nicolae Ceauçescu were 'weirdos' or 'off the wall.' These, too, are diagnoses, but they are not helpful because they are so amorphous, so all-encompassing that they can be used to characterize any kind of inexplicable behaviour. We need more precise and penetrating diagnoses, and we need to recognize that any diagnosis is only a starting point, a beginning of understanding.

PART I: THE KAISER

We cannot understand the past without some ability to get into the skin of others ... We need, in Aristotle's phrase, to 'reconstruct imaginatively' what a past person imagined, hoped, wished, feared.

Isaiah Berlin[7]

One day in 1912, while reading an article in a British magazine entitled, 'The Kaiser as He Is,' Wilhelm II wrote in the margin, 'This is the Kaiser as he is *not*! I should like to know what he *really* is!!'[8] So would historians who have tried to 'get into his skin' and find answers to the riddles of his baffling personality.

Several explanations have been offered. One biographer has argued that Wilhelm may have suffered brain damage at birth.[9] But that suggestion is refuted by the mental acuity of the adult Kaiser. Wilhelm was fluent in four languages, he amazed contemporaries with his prodigious memory and command of technical detail, his prose was lucid and effective, his vigorous sermons and speeches were often extemporaneous, and his scholarly articles were impressively coherent. Moreover, he was physically well coordinated; he played a good game of tennis and was a fine marksman and an accomplished horseman. Wilhelm von Hohenzollern suffered no serious brain damage at birth or at any other time.

Two popular biographers were confident that the secret to Wilhelm's problems lay in his withered left arm. His exhibitionism, bursts of temper, and aggressiveness, they argued, were merely over-compensation for the 'inferiority complex' caused by his birth defect.[10]

A German biologist rejected the withered-arm theory and asserted instead that Wilhelm's problems all stemmed from the defective genes carrying an 'insane streak' in the English royal family.[11] Wilhelm himself agreed that his difficulties stemmed from mixed blood. He told his second wife that 'the two strains of my blood made me a riddle both at home and abroad. The Germans claimed that I was too English. The English ... complained that I was too German.'[12]

Michael Balfour, author of a widely acclaimed study of the Kaiser, found a different explanation for Wilhelm's behaviour. According to Balfour, the Kaiser suffered from basic defects of character, lacking moral fibre and the will to make 'a greater effort to overcome his weaknesses.'[13]

Those who took a more charitable view concluded that the fault lay outside Wilhelm and quite beyond his control. An inscrutable and ineluctable destiny, they believed, was responsible for all his difficulties. In raising the familiar Germanic question of *Schicksal oder Schuld?* (fate or guilt?), Wilhelm Schüssler came down heavily on the side of fate and concluded, 'Everything developed ... with an iron necessity ... as if borne along by inexorable fate (*Fatum*).'[14] Sir John Wheeler-Bennett, another proponent of the destiny theory, set forth his reflections on Wilhelm II in two debatable aphorisms: 'Few were more unsuited to the throne than Wilhelm II; few were more pitiable among the playthings of Destiny.'[15] Since the workings of destiny remain obscure, let us see what psychology can offer.

Soon after Germany's defeat in 1918 and Wilhelm's flight to Holland, a cluster of psychological studies of the Kaiser appeared. The authors clearly dissociated themselves from the Kaiser, seeking to find an explanation for the national disaster in Wilhelm's mental condition. The titles of some of these books, in translation, as well as the dates of their publication, are revealing: *Periodical Mental Illness of Wilhelm II! A Character Portrait of the Real Kaiser* (1919); *The Illness of Wilhelm II* (1919); *Wilhelm II, A Political-Psychological Study* (1919); *Wilhelm II as Cripple and Psychopath: A Reckoning with the Entente and with Monarchy* (1920). Although none of the physicians writing these volumes had actually examined their subject, they concluded almost unanimously that he was a 'manic-depressive.'[16]

Recent discoveries in psychoanalysis and more detailed studies of the Kaiser's life, however, suggest a more appropriate diagnosis.

Wilhelm as a Narcissistic Personality

He is a man who is at war with himself ... a being who is torn apart (*eine zerrissene Natur*).[17]

Walther Rathenau, 1923

To call the Kaiser a 'narcissist'[18] does not tell anyone very much who has not studied the psychological literature. But knowledge of narcissistic disorders can help historians understand Wilhelm's behaviour and how it affected his political career.

The term, as used by Heinz Kohut and other 'self' psychologists, is – like Freud's Oedipus – drawn from classical Greek mythology. Narcissus, it will be recalled, was a bedazzlingly handsome young demigod who fell in love with Echo. But since Narcissus was psychically unable to reach out for her beyond himself, he turned inward to engage in that self-idealization and self-adoration that finally destroyed him – and bequeathed his name to both a lovely flower and a psychopathic condition.

Narcissistic personalities are not psychotic. That is, they are not 'crazy' or 'insane.' They do not entirely or permanently lose contact with reality. They fantasize a good deal, but they are usually aware of who they really are and conscious of what they are doing. Psychotics, by contrast, may be totally convinced they are someone else: Napoleon, Jesus, or Marco Polo. But we know they are not. When Wilhelm claimed to be the mighty ruler of the German Empire, exalted being, the 'All-Highest Person,' he was quite justified in making these assertions, for custom and constitution underwrote these beliefs. The Kaiser was *supposed* to be high and mighty.

Narcissists derive their pathology from a chronic sense of deep injury and deprivation, a continued fear of personal fragmentation and disintegration, and they exhibit several clear, clinically identifiable characteristics. Let us consider the most persistent of them,[19] and see how well or ill they apply to Wilhelm von Hohenzollern.

Most characteristically, narcissistically impaired patients have a fragile sense of self. Constantly they feel threatened by fragmentation. Like the Kaiser, they are *zerrissene Naturen*. Over and over again they tell their therapist, 'I am falling apart. I can't hold myself together.' Yet, like the Kaiser, they *do* manage, largely by means of psychological defences, to achieve a measure of cohesion – at least enough to function quite adequately.

Like Narcissus in the legend, narcissistically impaired patients have difficulty reaching out beyond themselves, and little capacity for empathy or love. Their insatiable hunger for admiration is, as a Swiss analyst noted, a 'substitute gratification' for the love that they are unable either to give or to receive.'[20]

The British analyst Anthony Storr has said that the narcissists face a 'perpetual dilemma': If they deny their need for love and affectionate understanding, they feel isolated, abandoned, and alone; but if they accept affection and become dependent on someone, they may have the terrifying feeling that they are losing their own identity and being dominated by others.[21]

So deeply unsure of themselves, narcissists may reach out and become inordinately dependent on others, and then feel abandoned and betrayed if their analyst leaves for a brief vacation. Their resentment of dependence keeps breaking through. They may accuse their doctors or their confidants of trying to 'enslave' them. They may lash out at them as unfeeling incompetents, selfish, ignorant, and totally ineffective. Then, swept by remorse, they may seek reconciliation in emotional scenes of weeping sentimentality.

The Kaiser's continual need to assert his power and self-sufficiency is a trait associated with many narcissistically impaired people, but there was a particular reason it was so acutely felt by Wilhelm. As a child he was given by his mother to understand that there was something wrong with him and that he was inferior to his physically unimpaired and more tractable younger brothers. Wilhelm spent the rest of his life trying to prove that he was in no way inferior to anyone.[22]

Like other narcissists, Wilhelm II did not like to be left alone. Constantly he wanted to be surrounded by an admiring entourage. At the same time he resented his dependence on other people. When Bülow, his usually subservient chancellor, threatened to resign over the Bjorko affair in 1905, Wilhelm was on the verge of panic: 'I am completely falling apart,' he wrote despairingly. 'The morning after you request your resignation *will find the Kaiser no longer alive!* Think of my poor wife and children.' He entreated Bülow to send him immediately a wire reading simply, 'All right!' When his chancellor agreed to stay on, Wilhelm wired him, 'I thank you from my heart! I have been born anew! (*Ich bin neugeboren!*).'[23] But when he sensed that he had become too dependent on Bülow, he fired him, frequently pointing out later the exact spot in the garden walk where 'I sent the scoundrel packing.'

Similarly, as Wilhelm's closest friend noted, 'He struggled to stave off his bondage' to Bismarck.[24] After dismissing him and accusing him of 'abandonment' and 'betrayal,' Wilhelm sought reconciliation. He named him a prince of the Empire and a Field Marshal of the Imperial German army. Wilhelm sent Bismarck flattering letters and was so relieved by the old man's positive response to his overtures that he wrote his grandmother, 'The congratulatory message I sent to Friedrichsruhe ... so touched Prince Bismarck that he immediately sent me an answer begging to be allowed to pay his respects to me tomorrow & to congratulate me on my [birthday] ... I am so thankful that this is at last possible!'[25] Wilhelm was seen hugging and holding the old gentleman cheek-to-cheek when Bismarck boarded the Kaiser's private railway car.[26]

Narcissists often compensate for chronic self-doubt by exhibitionism and swaggering assertions of self-sufficiency. They may wear flashy clothes, talk too loudly and too much at parties, try to impress guests with parlour tricks and feats of memory, tell inappropriate jokes, and generally play the buffoon. Having embarrassed themselves, they take perverse pleasure in embarrassing others. They may regret their behaviour, yet seem unable to resist repeating it. One patient asked his analyst, 'Why do I keep on making such an *ass* of myself, Doctor?' The question may well have occurred to Wilhelm II.

The Kaiser's exhibitionism and grandiosity were notorious. Like some other narcissists, he tried to shore up his image of himself by impressing others with feats of memory: to agronomists he recited statistics of hog production in all the provinces of Prussia; to a university professor he rattled off the names, in sequence, of the kings of Assyria. Wilhelm's visiting cards measured 6 × 4 inches. He told his mother in 1894, 'Europe and the entire world pricks up its ears to ask, "What does the German Kaiser say and think?" ... For all eternity there exists only one true Emperor in the world and that is the German Kaiser.'[27] His conversations were often monologues; his disparagement of others wanton.

Wilhelm was plagued by doubts about his own sufficiency, and constantly seeking reassurance. After a speech he would ask those in his entourage, 'How did that go? Don't you think I did well?'[28] Or he would inquire anxiously, 'Are you satisfied with me now? (*Sind Sie nun mit mir zufrieden?*),' or complain plaintively, 'You never praise me.'[29] There is, of course, nothing unusual about a person's wanting approval and praise – we all do. What is striking about the Kaiser is that he needed so much praise and so constantly.

The self-improvement maxims that hung on his study and bedroom walls and the character-building aphorisms he liked to repeat also suggest that Wilhelm was less than satisfied with himself. These maxims kept urging him to cultivate forbearance, restraint, and self-mastery – qualities that he apparently felt lacking in himself.[30] The self-admonitory epigrams were quoted more often than they were practised: 'He who cannot master himself, cannot master others [a paraphrase of Goethe] ... He who prevails over himself conquers all ... A monarch's incautious utterances are like a boomerang.'[31]

Wilhelm protested too much that he personally was a model of self-mastery and steadfast constancy by quoting favourite lines from Shakespeare's *Julius Caesar*:

I am constant as the Northern Star,
Of whose true-fix'd and resting quality
There is no fellow in the firmament.
The skies are painted with unnumber'd sparks ...
Yet in their number I do know but one
That unassailable holds on his rank,
Unshaked of motion: and I am he ...[32]

Although narcissists have a propensity for making confident assertions of their mastery over all situations, in practice they tend to avoid making decisions and to run away from responsibilities.

Insensitive to the feelings of others,[33] narcissistically impaired people are usually keenly sensitive to even the most trivial slights, real or imagined. One patient, whose friend was forced to cancel a dinner engagement because his father had suddenly been taken to the hospital, was enraged by his friend's 'insult' and refused to speak to him for a week.[34] Narcissists also take little interest in what others are saying and feel compelled to dominate every conversation.

Members of the Kaiser's entourage were constantly on guard lest he take umbrage at some imagined insult. One day, for instance, while walking in the garden with two adjutants, Wilhelm sat down on a bench and beckoned them to join him. Since the bench was short, an aide drew up a second bench and was startled when Wilhelm yelled at him, 'Am I such a figure of contempt that no one wants to sit next to me?'[35]

Like other narcissists, Wilhelm paid scant attention to others. One of his admirers commented on his 'almost complete inability to enter into the thought of others ... He could not listen to others.'[36]

Wilhelm's world revolved around the pole of his own needs and desires. He told his valet that he needed women 'to do things for me'; he spoke of the Rhine as 'my river.' When an old and loyal servant made a difficult pilgrimage to Doorn and expressed his gratitude, just before his death, at seeing his Emperor for the last time, Wilhelm cut him short: 'Well, now that you're here you will notice that I am a tiger who can still fight!' The old man was then summarily dismissed. Wilhelm's companion in exile commented regretfully, 'Those were the parting words of the Kaiser to this most loyal servant who, all his life, had rendered His Majesty great personal service ... The old man was deeply shaken, tears came to his eyes.'[37]

Wilhelm burnished his self-image by insisting that it was he who was really responsible for Hitler's victories, writing to his son Eitel Friedrich, 'It fills me with great satisfaction that the soldierly spirit of [my Reich] has passed to the young soldiers of the Wehrmacht whose deeds will astonish the world.'[38] He took credit for Hitler's march of triumph through Poland, the Low Countries, and France, writing in English to an American boyhood friend that the foundations of the Third Reich had been laid by the Hohenzollerns and that 'The brilliant leading generals of this war came from *My* school, they fought under *My* command in the World War as lieutenants and captains or young majors.'[39] (The underlining and capitalizations are in the original.)

Narcissists are notably lacking in humour, except for the pratfall, *Schadenfreude* variety, and they are conspicuously deficient in the leavening grace of self-irony. It is difficult for them to smile at themselves, for to do so is to be self-critical, and their sense of self is too fragile to withstand either self-criticism or criticism by others. Therapists feel encouraged when narcissistic patients begin to show signs of humour or can actually laugh at themselves. We are reminded that a member of the Kaiser's inner circle once observed that if the Kaiser only had had a sense of humour he might not have lost his throne. On rare occasions, though, Wilhelm did show a capacity to smile at himself,[40] something Hitler was never able to do.

Like other narcissists, Wilhelm had difficulty coping with criticism and could neither abide nor understand opposition. One of the features of his reign was the rigorous application of Article 95 of the Imperial German Criminal Code, which set forth punishments for 'insulting His Majesty' (*Majestätsbeleidigung*). Insults included failure to rise when a toast was proposed to the Kaiser or for expressing 'disrespectful attitudes.' A contemporary journalist reported, 'Scarcely a week elapses without a notice in the press ... of three or four trials of this nature ... No section of the entire Criminal Code is so frequently broken.'[41] The Kaiser's mother wrote in alarm to a friend, 'These constant prosecutions and imprisonments for *Majestätsbeleidigung* [are] deeply to be regretted! How shocked my husband would have been! ... You must burn these lines, please.'[42]

Wilhelm's attitude to opposition was a combination of shock, fury, and incomprehension. He simply could not understand how anyone could oppose him and was genuinely amazed that a person could commit so unnatural a crime. 'How do you *explain* this?' he asked incredulously on the dossier of a 'criminal' who had criticized one of his enactments – 'this insult to the Anointed of the Lord?? Strange! Strange!! ... All this to *me!* To *me!* What is the country coming to?'[43]

Narcissists may feel momentarily embarrassed and even ashamed of their conduct if it puts them in a bad light, but it is debatable whether they experience a sense of guilt. Some analysts believe that their defence mechanisms are so well constructed that a feeling of personal guilt or responsibility is seldom allowed to penetrate. Their chief defences are denial and the projection of blame onto others. Other analysts believe that their sense of self is so inadequately developed that they are incapable of taking responsibility for their actions.[44]

Wilhelm told a member of his inner circle that he 'often' lay awake nights chastizing himself for social *faux pas*[45] – apparently only to repeat them. He was able to fend off feelings of shame or guilt by his prodigious capacity to project responsibility onto others. As his long-time associate in exile commented, 'Always, always someone else is to blame.'

After saying that the Krüger Telegram he had sent was an 'idiocy,' Wilhelm added, quite falsely, that he had never known anything about it, that the wire was entirely the idea of Chancellor Hohenlohe,[46] an inoffensive old gentleman who was famous for his discretion.

In signing orders for general mobilization on 1 August 1914, Wilhelm protected himself in advance from future criticism and blame for failure. After putting down his pen, he turned to his generals and said, 'Gentlemen, you will rue the day when you made me do this!'[47] As we have noted, he also denied any personal responsibility for the war by placing the blame directly on 'Georgie' and 'Nicky.'[48] The war was lost, variously, because the generals refused to take his advice and had deceived him from the start,[49] or because England had 'bought out the subversive part of my people with money to rise up against their ruler,' or because Austria had deserted him, or because the youth of Germany had been 'poisoned and blinded by Jews.'[50]

Trivial causes may produce violent outbursts of anger in narcissistic patients, because a seemingly minor incident or a random comment may reactivate an unconscious memory of childhood and challenge their grandiose vision of themselves.[51]

The Kaiser's rages were so unpredictable and incomprehensible that members of his entourage sometimes feared for his sanity.[52] One of his military advisers recalled that Wilhelm was so outraged by Bismarck's criticisms that he 'completely lost control of himself. He summoned all the officers and informed us that he had officially ordered the arrest of Prince Bismarck on a charge of high treason ... We were dumbfounded.'[53] Particularly violent tantrums occurred whenever Wilhelm felt that England was trying to thwart his plans for a navy or challenge his right to dominate the Continent. At such times he would 'break forth in paroxysms of fury.'[54]

Worried about their own identity, narcissistic people tend to act out a variety of roles. One such patient told her analyst despairingly, 'I am not real! I don't know who I am ... I am not myself – whatever that is! ... I seem to be always play-acting.' Heinz Kohut suggested that such acting is probably a kind of defence, a way of giving the patient, at least for the moment, a feeling that he or she has achieved a kind of coherent identity. Ilsemann remembered that whenever the Kaiser was to meet a stranger, he 'always put on a mask.'[55] Wilhelm's friends had the feeling that he was 'always acting,' and we recall Sarah Bernhardt telling him that they were both born actors.[56]

Narcissists swing back and forth between delusion and reality. So did Wilhelm von Hohenzollern. At times during the war he could recognize the stark reality of Germany's position. When a general staff officer gave him detailed and devastating reports on the 'Black Day of the German Army' (8 August 1918), the Kaiser discussed the situation calmly, commenting quietly, and without recrimination: 'I realize that we must face the consequences. We are at the end of our capacity to continue. The war must be stopped.'[57] Again, on 17 September, after Bulgaria had sued for peace, Wilhelm saw clearly the handwriting on the wall: 'In a week we'll be without allies; then we must make peace to avoid meaningless bloodshed.'[58]

The pendulum soon swung back to delusion. On 29 October 1918, with his armies in retreat on the western front, apparently forgetting his own dire warnings about the 'Yellow Peril,' the Kaiser talked excitedly about winning the war by forming an alliance with the Japanese. His chief of the naval cabinet reported that during his last audience with the Kaiser, Wilhelm 'already envisaged Japanese divisions arriving on the Western Front via Siberia to help throw out the Americans.'[59] On 8 November, when he heard that Bavaria had withdrawn from the war, Wilhelm excitedly exclaimed that he would lead his loyal troops – even if only a battalion strong – in a march on Berlin and 'restore Germany to its senses.'[60] In exile and with the Nazis in power Wilhelm convinced himself for a long time that Hitler would restore him to his throne. This illusion was not shattered until just before his death in 1941, when his house in Doorn was surrounded by SS troops 'for his protection.' While walking in the woods in Amerongen, the ex-Kaiser met a Nazi guard and asked him where he was from. The young man, who had no idea that he was talking to the former Kaiser, responded and then asked the nice old man with the Vandyke beard and crippled arm who he was. Shaken and speechless when he realized that he had been forgotten by the youth of Germany, the ashen-faced Kaiser took to his bed for several days and never left his property again.[61]

Philipp zu Eulenburg, who knew the Kaiser better than anyone, gave a description of his friend that could serve as a textbook characterization of a narcissistic personality. Eulenburg was advising Count von Bülow, the new chancellor, on how to handle His Majesty: 'Wilhelm II takes everything personally; only personal arguments will impress him. He likes to lecture others, but will not allow himself to be taught. He cannot bear boredom ... Wilhelm II likes to shine and to do and decide everything by himself ... To get him to accept an idea, one has to pretend that the idea is his own ... Never forget that H.M. needs to be praised.'[62]

The description of Wilhelm as a narcissistically disturbed personality rejects his mother's view that he was insane. 'Willie is mad,' she once told a startled guest, 'I mean just what I say! It is literal: Willie is mad!'[63] Other contemporary observers shared his mother's opinion. As already noted, they were so appalled by the Kaiser's raging temper, his vaulting grandiosity, his irresponsible rhetoric, his childish exhibitionism, his extreme self-centredness, and his flagrant disregard for the feelings of others, that they too concluded he was 'mad.'[64]

It seems more likely, however, that the Kaiser escaped madness precisely because these patterns of behaviour were actually therapeutic. The very behaviour that alarmed his friends and got him into political trouble served to keep him from falling apart. Without his narcissism, it may be doubted that he could have held himself together to function as well as he did.

The Kaiser's flamboyant expressions of grandiosity, for instance, allowed him to indulge his need to assert power and to assuage feelings of inadequacy and fears of fragmentation. Similarly, his violent rages served as catharsis, permitting him to vent unbearable frustrations, and his projection of blame onto others helped ward off feelings of personal failure so that he could survive psychically with his ego flying.

In November 1918, when the Kaiser went into exile in Amerongen, his hostess heard him say, 'The world says I am mad; but if it knew what tremendous difficulties I have had to contend with, it would perhaps be surprised that I am at all sane.'[65] Psychologically that seems about right. Given the experiences Wilhelm II had suffered during infancy and childhood,[66] and the pressures he faced during his reign, retention of his sanity was no mean achievement.

Personal Pathology and Public Policy

He who knows not how to rule his inner self would gladly rule his fellow men according to his own arrogant conceit.

Johann Wolfgang von Goethe

In political leaders, private motives become projected and rationalized as public policy.

Harold Lasswell

A compelling reason for studying the personalities of political leaders in any country was set forth decades ago by the American political scientist Harold Lasswell. In a seminal study published in 1930, Lasswell showed how the private lives and public careers of leaders are often closely related, and that successful statesmen may make assets out of personal difficulties by displacing and rationalizing them as national policy. Put another way, leaders may find it both personally gratifying and politically profitable to 'externalize' their internal conflicts. When personal needs coincide with those of their countrymen, the externalization can be very profitable indeed.[67]

If the political leaders are pathological, the consequences for public policy can be devastating. Viewed entirely in terms of immediate public appeal, however, pathology is not always a political handicap. Indeed, it may be an asset. Pathology proved a mixed blessing to the political career of Wilhelm II, and it was one of the main ingredients of Hitler's early success, as well as a reason for his ultimate failure.

The Kaiser's Personality and Public Policy

There was a lack of cohesion in the leadership of the Reich because there was no cohesion in His Majesty himself.

Philipp zu Eulenburg[68]

This Kaiser about whom you complain is your own mirror-image (*euer Spiegelbild*).

Friedrich Naumann[69]

The Kaiser and the German people were mutually attracted to each other and mirrored each other's needs.[70] The cocky flamboyance of the youthful monarch harmonized with the confident exuberance of the newly united country. Both the young ruler and his young nation were impatiently ambitious. Both lived in a state of dynamic tension, and both exulted in their newly acquired power.

In asserting his grandiosity, sovereignty, and power, Wilhelm was driven by his own psychic needs to deny his feelings of weakness, to reinforce his fragile sense of personal autonomy, and to force others to show him respect. These personal needs were shared by the German people, who also longed to be accepted and respected.[71] The Kaiser, who seemed so much a caricature to foreigners, was said by Germans to have embodied 'the whole spiritual personality of the nation.'[72] One of the hundreds of encomiums collected in a three-volume work published in 1913, upon the silver jubilee of Wilhelm II's reign, proclaimed, 'Our Kaiser expresses the spirit of the new era, and the era is the expression of the spirit of our Kaiser.'[73] In German eyes – and certainly in his own – 'the German Kaiser became the "World Kaiser" and "saviour of Europe, the *Arbiter mundi*." '[74] Walther Rathenau was justified in saying that no epoch in European history had more appropriately adopted the name of its monarch.[75]

Wilhelm's reasons for building a huge German navy illustrate the intimate connection between personal desires and public policy. For the navy helped assuage Wilhelm's insatiable longing to win respect, especially from England, his mother's country. In a revealing comment, the Kaiser impatiently thrust aside objections that his naval plans were prohibitively expensive, asserting that, whatever the costs, 'we will nonetheless build and increase the size of the fleet; with each additional ship *England's respect will increase.*'[76] It is psychologically interesting that the battle flag the Kaiser originally designed for his new navy was so much like the British naval ensign that an aide prevailed upon him to alter his design in order to make the two flags distinguishable.[77]

The Imperial German navy may have served no practical function,[78] but it was profoundly functional to Wilhelm. Visible for all the world to see, it dramatically demonstrated that he and his navy were worthy of the power, prestige, and respect that he had sought throughout his life. It fulfilled the bold promises Wilhelm had made in his propaganda for the fleet: an enormous navy would prove that Germans, and especially their Kaiser, were 'entitled to equality' (*Gleichberechtigung*) and 'world esteem' (*Weltgeltung*).[79]

Psychology can also shed some light on one of the most perplexing political questions of the Kaiser's reign: Why did this ruler of such promise persist in jeopardizing his prospects by alienating the very people whose support he needed if he were to rule effectively? We have noted how Wilhelm, with surprising persistence, went about infuriating the leaders of the army, navy, and foreign office – his agents for implementing the New Course he had announced after firing Bismarck. He needed popular approval as the air he breathed, yet while calling himself 'the People's Emperor,' he disdained the 'rabble' and insulted members of parliament and journalists – the people who could have helped him shape public opinion and retain favour with the masses. He had a penchant for converting loyal allies into implacable opponents.

Like his mother, Wilhelm could recognize problems intellectually, but was incapable of taking his own sensible advice.[80] On one level of comprehension, for example, he realized that in the modern era a monarch needed to pay close attention to public opinion, commenting wisely that even with all his Imperial power he was not able to act in opposition to the interests and wishes of the German people and advising Nicholas II to be careful lest he alienate his subjects. Wilhelm himself, however, was unable to comprehend how much he had alienated the very people he had wished most to impress. He actually believed his catastrophic *Daily Telegraph* interview was a diplomatic triumph that would win over the British public. He thought that his letter to Colonel Wortley would have a 'calming effect' on the populace and simply could not understand why the British 'got so excited' about what he had said. The Kaiser never seemed to tire of demonstrating the validity of his own aphorism: 'A monarch's incautious utterances are like boomerangs.'

The obvious question of why the Kaiser persisted in such conduct has evoked several explanations. A Freudian psychiatrist settled the matter with a simplistic solution: 'The reason he acted that way is clear. The man was a masochist and as a masochist he *sought* punishment.'[81] Anthony Storr gave a more thoughtful response: 'There are some people who are so preoccupied with their need for loyalty and support that they keep testing others. In effect they are saying, "I'll show my worst traits and see if he still is loving, loyal, and supportive."'[82] But Wilhelm II was not testing the loyalty and love of his friends and relations; he was gratuitously alienating influential people who could have helped him become a more effective ruler.

A more helpful approach is suggested by 'self' psychology. As we have noted, Wilhelm's capacity for empathizing with others was severely limited. Intelligent and rational as he was in many areas of intellectual inquiry, he was strikingly deficient in personal relationships. Indifferent to the opinions and sensibilities of anyone but himself, the Kaiser could not sense how others might react to his comments. Moreover, his narcissistic self-glorification gave him the illusion that as the Elect of God he was set quite apart, far above and beyond criticism and human censure. Grandiose assertions of his inviolability helped repress gnawing doubts about his personal adequacy. Consequently, when Wilhelm's advisers tried to control the political damage that the Kaiser kept inflicting on himself, and urged him to be more tactful, he would have none of it, replying tersely, 'I am the Kaiser and I can say whatever I like,' or calling those who criticized his conduct 'incredibly stupid,' or yelling belligerently. 'I'm not afraid of a fight.'[83] He was unable to appreciate or care how other people reacted to his behaviour.

The Kaiser's frightening rages and moody fits of depression had the unfortunate political consequence of making his entourage leery about giving him sound advice. The insiders' game was to keep the Kaiser happy by entertaining him with jokes and skits, not disturbing him with problems, and shielding him from criticism and bad news. Princess Daisy of Pless reported that Wilhelm's chief source for information was a careful culling of the world press known to his intimates as the 'Golden Journal.' It contained only cuttings that were 'suitable' for him to see.[84] One of the Kaiser's closest advisers, Albert Ballin, was keenly aware of the problem. Late in 1918 Ballin was determined to tell Wilhelm directly that the war was lost and Germany should immediately sue for peace. But the Kaiser had just recovered from a fit of despondency: 'His Majesty was in such sunny disposition that it seemed to me quite impossible ... even to intimate, the seriousness and the frightful danger in which Germany found itself. My determination collapsed.'[85] So did that of many others, and for the same reason.

The ways Wilhelm found to alleviate his persistent feelings of inadequacy also reduced his effectiveness as a political leader. A favourite method was simply to deny that a difficult problem existed. The British ambassador, with typical understatement, noted His Majesty's 'somewhat unfortunate habit' of cutting off any conversation not entirely to his liking by saying, 'I do not admit that this is so.'[86]

Besides denial, the Kaiser avoided uncomfortable realities by surrounding himself with flattering optimists who jollied him into thinking that all was well. He ran away from difficult political problems, often spending weeks at a time on sea cruises or train trips. A distressed Princess Radziwill lamented to a friend, in a letter from Berlin dated 13 February 1912, 'Everything here lacks direction ... From morning 'til night he's on the go somewhere ... It's impossible for him to perform any real work.'[87]

Wilhelm II found excuses for avoiding serious consultations about matters of state by occupying himself busily with all manner of trivia. He spent dozens of hours, to take but one example, in fretting over which young person should marry whom, in checking the religious and family pedigrees of all candidates, in deciding who should be invited to the wedding, who should sit next to whom at the wedding breakfast, and what livery should be worn by the staff.[88]

Lacking cohesion himself, Wilhelm was never able to develop a coherent policy in either domestic or foreign affairs. Moreover, his suspicious nature would not permit him to trust others who *did* possess a sense of direction and purpose. His attitude, for example, to liberals who wanted to bring his monarchy closer to parliament and the people was one of deep suspicion. Without investigating their proposals, he summarily dismissed them, calling his critics 'enemies of the Reich' and 'sheep-heads' and telling them he would show them 'who is master in this house.'[89] Wilhelm simply could not see his opportunity to strengthen his monarchy by allying it with parliament and people, and insisted on ruling a modern state as if it were a seventeenth-century autocracy.

The most vivid illustration of the way Wilhelm's psychopathology affected public policy is in his direction of foreign affairs. In many ways German policy reflected the childlike longings of the Kaiser. As a little boy he had felt that neither his loquacious mother nor his domineering tutor had ever really listened to him, that his words were never treated with respect.[90] His longing *to be listened to* was expressed poignantly when he said that what he really wanted as Emperor was to have his voice *heard* throughout the world. It was a cry from the heart: 'I have never thought about autocracy, but I have long ago made my program of *how* I wanted to be German Kaiser, how I conceived the German Kaiser: Deep into the most distant jungles of [the uttermost] parts of the world, everyone should know the voice of the German Kaiser. *Nothing* should occur on this earth without having first heard him. His word must have its weight placed on every scale. Well – and I think I have generally held to my program. Also domestically the word of the Kaiser should be *everything!*'[91] That unspecific childlike desire to have people pay attention to him became the unspecified but emotionally intense goal of German foreign policy. As Thomas Kohut concluded in his penetrating study, 'The emotional goal that the voice of Germany, of the German Kaiser, be listened to throughout the world was perhaps the only goal that Germans could agree upon.'[92]

The inconsistencies and confusions in the Kaiser's own mind seriously affected his country's foreign policy. Apart from wanting to be listened to, and apart from proudly proclaiming that he stood for something he vaguely called 'World Policy,' it is doubtful if Wilhelm had any specific goals in mind. Certainly, his radically contradictory assertions about Germany's intentions bewildered other statesmen. After watching the careening course of the German ship of state as it steamed 'full speed ahead' in one direction and then another, it is not surprising that an Austrian diplomat wondered who was at the helm.[93]

These confusions of German policy resulted in part from Wilhelm's unresolved conflicts between romanticism and realism and between nationalism and universalism, conflicts that were reflected in his contradictory feelings about war and about Germany's relation to the rest of the world. He gloried in the romantic idea of war and had himself painted as the incarnation of the Teutonic warrior-god; yet he also saw himself as prince of peace, the heaven-sent leader of a benevolent mission to save the world. In this too the Kaiser reflected the attitude of his nation as expressed in his version of a favourite German couplet of his day:

It will be through German means
That the world will be redeemed.

This romantic vision of universal beneficence, he liked to think, could be achieved through German military power. This combination in the Kaiser of romanticism and raw power prompted a perceptive Portuguese diplomat to call Wilhelm 'the most dangerous sovereign in Europe' and to write prophetically in 1891: 'It may indeed happen that one day Europe will take to the roar of clashing armies, only because in the soul of this great dilettante the burning desire to "know war," to enjoy war, was stronger than reason, counsel, or pity for his subjects.'[94]

When other countries were unwilling to seek redemption through German *Kultur* or accept the Kaiser as the *arbiter mundi*, Wilhelm and his countrymen concluded that such misguided wilfulness was simply further proof of unreasoning hostility.[95]

Major decisions in foreign policy during the Second Reich were directly related to Wilhelm's 'personalization of politics.'[96] He deemed it appropriate, for example, to summon the nation to avenge the 'insults' that he had personally suffered and that, in his view, the country had suffered through him.

When two German Catholic priests were murdered in China in 1897, Wilhelm took it as a personal affront and swore that he would 'show the Chinese that the German Kaiser does not let himself be trifled with.'[97] Similarly, in June 1900, when he learned that 'his' envoy in Peking had been killed by the Boxers, Wilhelm considered it 'a personal insult' and dispatched an army corps to avenge his Imperial honour.[98]

Wilhelm's feeling that he was alone in a hostile world, often mentioned by members of his inner circle,[99] was shared and amplified by the nation in the decade before the First World War. The Germans, a historian of the pre-war era has written, suffered from 'group agoramania' and 'the basic German trauma' of suspicion and fear that they were isolated and encircled by hostile foes.[100] This gnawing apprehension was accompanied by the irrational conviction that the Fatherland was about to be overrun by more powerful neighbours. This national phobia is aptly summed up by Jonathan Steinberg, 'Here was Germany, the greatest power the continent of Europe had ever known, a land full of the noise and smells of industrial expansion, guarded by the world's most terrible army, augmented by the world's second most powerful high seas fleet, a society literally bursting with every conceivable expression of strength, and here were her leaders, nervously expecting [the British navy] at any moment or the hordes of invading Slavs.'[101]

The disastrous effect on foreign policy of Wilhelm's personal suspiciousness was manifested on the very eve of war. On 29 July 1914 Prince Lichnowsky, the German ambassador in London, wired his report of an urgent conversation he had just had with British Foreign Secretary Sir Edward Grey (1862–1933). Sir Edward, Lichnowsky wrote, had shown deep concern about the 'extreme gravity of the situation' and the need to reach an understanding 'before it is too late.' Grey said that if France and Germany became involved he did not see how England could stand aside. 'If war breaks out,' Grey had continued, 'it will be the greatest catastrophe that the world has ever seen.' He said that it was far from his desire to express any sort of threat and that he only wanted to convey personally to Lichnowsky England's desire to preserve the peace and to avoid 'the reproach of bad faith.'

Wilhelm dismissed Sir Edward's overture – and with it quite possibly the last opportunity for peace. His angry marginalia is redolent of distrust bordering on paranoia:

Aha! The common cheat!! (*Aha! Der gemeine Täuscher!!*) ...

The worst and most scandalous piece of English Pharisaism that I ever saw! I will *never* enter into a naval convention with such scoundrels! ... This means that they are going to attack us! ...

Mean and Mephistophelian! ... England reveals herself in her true colours at a moment when she thinks that we are caught in the toils and, so to speak, disposed of! ... England *alone*, and not we, bears the responsibility for war.[102]

The Kaiser vented more spleen and suspicion in his marginalia on a telegram of 30 July from the German ambassador in St Petersburg reporting Russian mobilization. Now everyone, including his staunch ally Austria and his long-dead uncle Edward VII, was to blame for ensnaring him and the unsuspecting Germans:

The stupidity and ineptitude of our ally is turned into a *snare* for us ... The '*encirclement*' of Germany has finally become a completed fact ... The net has been suddenly thrown over our head, and England sneeringly reaps the most brilliant success of her persistently prosecuted purely *anti-German world policy,* against which we have proved ourselves helpless, while she twists the noose of our political and economic destruction ... as we squirm *isolated* in the net ... England now reveals her true colours. The false mask of Christian peaceableness must be publicly ripped from her face.[103]

Wilhelm could not make peace in 1914 because there was no one he could trust. In his eyes all other statesmen were Pharisaical, lying hypocrites. Sir Edward Grey was a deceitful scoundrel. Nicholas II of Russia had abandoned 'monarchic principles by lining up with Serbian revolutionaries and liberal lunatics,' and all Nicky's entreaties for peace were so many 'maneouvres.' Uncle Bertie and Cousin Georgie had 'betrayed' him and their own 'Germanic race' first by allying with the Japanese and then by joining with 'Slavs and Gallos.' The world of Wilhelm's pathological imagining was a world in which serious negotiation was impossible.

In short, Wilhelm signed the documents that sent millions of Germans into battle because he could not trust any of the peacemakers; because he felt compelled to impress the army with his masculinity and prove that he would not 'cave in'; and because he wanted to fulfil his untested self-image as a heroic military commander, the very apotheosis of war, who would prove to the world – and, above all, to himself – that he could surpass the exploits of his Hohenzollern forebears Frederick the Great, Wilhelm I, and Friedrich III, whom he honoured and envied as victorious warriors.

The Kaiser gave one final demonstration of how public decisions can be shaped by the private motives of a ruler. Too fragile psychologically to confront the personal humiliation of public disgrace and the political consequences of defeat, once again, as so often in the past, he tried to solve his problems by running away from them, seeking refuge in exile.

Although neat categories are suspect in describing a human personality, Wilhelm's patterns of behaviour correspond closely to what psychologists have identified as 'narcissistically impaired personalities.' No matter what label is attached to these patterns, however, the Kaiser's inner conflicts and contradictions were intense and their effect on his conduct of domestic and foreign affairs profound.

Hitler's behaviour patterns, though similar in several respects, were significantly different from Wilhelm's and should be identified with different terminology. Whatever the label used, the consequences of the Führer's psychopathology were even more profound.

PART II: HITLER'S PATHOLOGY

I refuse to believe that what's wrong with Hitler is that I don't like him.

Bertrand Russell

My concern, as with the Kaiser, is to discover what was psychologically 'wrong' with Hitler, to identify his particular kind of pathology, and to explore the ways it affected his political performance.

It would be helpful at the outset if we knew whether the Führer had ever been examined by specialists in mental disorders and, if so, what conclusions they had reached about him. But there is no reliable evidence that Hitler was ever examined or treated by a competent psychologist or psychiatrist.[104] After the war, Hitler's doctors told American officials that to their knowledge the Führer had never received psychiatric treatment.[105] There seems no reason to question that opinion. Given the lack of evidence to the contrary, and given Hitler's dismissal of psychology as 'Jewish medicine,' as well as his strident insistence that there was absolutely nothing amiss with his mind, it is unlikely in the extreme that he would have permitted himself to be treated for mental disorder.

Any diagnosis must therefore come after the fact and without benefit of consultation with the patient. Two such attempts were made during and shortly after the Second World War. In 1943, at the request of President Roosevelt, Walter C. Langer, an American psychoanalyst, prepared a psychological report on Hitler for the Office of Strategic Services. Limited to the materials then available to him, Langer and his associates concluded broadly that Hitler was a hysterical psychopath.[106] A second and more specific diagnosis was made by the prison psychiatrist at Nuremberg, Dr Douglas Kelley, who, after extensive interviews with Nazis who had been in Hitler's immediate circle, concluded that the Führer should be classified as a 'psychoneurotic of the obsessive and hysterical type ... he also showed paranoid or persecution patterns ... In simple terms, Hitler was an abnormal and mentally ill individual.'[107]

Neurological Speculations

Before suggesting a more specific psychological diagnosis, we should first respond to the argument that Hitler's mental peculiarities were entirely the result of physical causes.

Eyewitness accounts of Hitler's physical appearance in the last months of his life have led some doctors to conclude that he suffered from a neurological disease that impaired his brain and central nervous system. Those who observed him at close range noticed how his 'left hand and the entire left side of his body shook.' A general visiting Hitler's air-raid shelter reported, 'His gait was shuffling ... his movements slow as in a slow-motion film.' A party leader was shocked to discover that his Führer was now 'old, stooped, disintegrated ... a trembling, broken man.' Another recalled that 'he was bathed in sweat, the saliva literally poured from his mouth ... I experienced the explosion of a hate-filled soul.' Another remembered seeing 'a frightful picture ... He stared dully

... His hands were pale and the fingertips bloodless ... He spoke clearly [but] he no longer concentrated well.'[108]

Relying on such descriptions, German writers have concluded that Hitler's mental and physical condition was caused by Parkinson's disease (*paralysis agitans*), an illness of uncertain origin that attacks the nervous system and may produce involuntary tremors, slowness of movement, staring and immobile facial expression, insomnia, speech impairment, sweating, hypersalivation, and excitability. Delusional paranoid trends may also develop.[109] In the spring of 1945 a neurologist, Dr Max de Crensis of Berlin, having studied reports of Hitler's behaviour and having examined photographs of him, diagnosed brain damage associated with *paralysis agitans*.[110] After the war, the director of a psychiatric clinic in Hamburg, Professor Doctor Hans Berger-Prinz, agreed, stating confidently that Hitler was never ill 'in a psychiatric sense,' he simply suffered from Parkinson's disease.[111]

Another German doctor agreed that Hitler suffered from the illness, but he believed that it was 'late Parkinsonism' originally caused by epidemic encephalitis which Hitler had contracted at the age of eleven in 1900, when he caught an infection from his brother Edmund who had died of measles. The disease lay dormant for many years, but it later broke out as fully developed Parkinsonism.[112] An American authority on epidemic encephalitis concurred with these findings, but placed the onset of the disease later, probably as a result of the epidemic of 1916. Like his German colleague, he claimed the disease caused 'moral insanity' and 'altered [Hitler's] personality in a way which led to the tragedies and horrors' of the Third Reich.[113]

Abraham Lieberman, an American specialist in Parkinson's disease, has concluded that Hitler manifestly displayed salient symptoms associated with post-encephalitic Parkinson's disease, and he stressed that the characteristic tremors of his left arm were intermittent, arguing that this validates the diagnosis, for while the disease in general is progressive, the tremors are not; they are a response to acute anxiety and stress. Thus, Hitler's left arm trembled after his arrest following the failure of the Beer Hall Putsch in 1923; it then subsided. Again tremors appeared after the disastrous defeat at Stalingrad in 1943, and again they diminished. These tremors were strong during the Allied invasion of June 1944, but absent while Hitler planned the Ardennes offensive later that year. In the spring of 1945 they returned with increased violence. Just as the Kaiser had tried to conceal his atrophied left arm, the Führer tried to hide the trembling in his by keeping it in his tunic pocket, holding it rigidly against his side, or holding it down with his right hand.[114]

Hitler displayed neither the loss of memory nor the ability to plan or formulate ideas as is associated with Parkinson's dementia. And his psychological profile certainly did not fit some of the personality traits found by recent research that shows Parkinson's patients to be 'rigidly moral ... non-impulsive ... and slow-tempered.'[115]

A second neurological explanation has been offered for Hitler's deteriorating physical and mental condition: it was caused by the malpractice of his quack doctor, Theodor Morell. In a book entitled *Hitler: Die Zerstörung einer Persönlichkeit* (Hitler: The Destruction of a Personality), a German physician insisted that, apart from certain eccentricities indulged in by all great and gifted men, Adolf Hitler was perfectly normal in all respects until he fell into the clutches of the diabolical Morell, who slowly destroyed him through bizarre and irresponsible medication.

Any responsible physician would be appalled by the drugs Morell prescribed. Over a stretch of years from 1935 to 1945 they included massive doses of vitamins and sex hormones, some 3,000 injections of simple syrup, huge daily dosages of stimulants and sedatives, thousands of 'Dr Köster's Anti-Gas Tablets' (prescribed for the Führer's chronic flatulence and containing, among other things, a mixture of belladonna and strychnine), eye drops whose chief ingredient was cocaine, and a potency pill that Morell concocted from 'pulverized bull testicles,' apparently designed to counteract the prescription of female hormones that he was also administering, and vast quantities of amphetamines. Hence, the argument goes, Germany might well have won the war and held back the communist menace had not Hitler been incapacitated by Dr Morell.[116]

Still another physical explanation for Hitler's behaviour was offered by Dr Leonard Heston, an American psychiatrist who believed that Morell's prescription of amphetamines was alone sufficient to account for the Führer's disabilities. In a careful reconstruction of Hitler's 'Medical Casebook,' together with interviews with his valet, Heinz Linge, and with Morell's assistant, Dr Rolf Makkus, Heston concluded, 'Amphetamine toxicity can account for Hitler's disorders of emotional control, thinking and mood [and that by] the late summer of 1942, Hitler seemed to be in a more or less chronic toxic state.'[117]

Heston has made a valuable contribution to a neurological explanation of Hitler's behaviour. In his exhilaration at riding his amphetamine horse, however, Heston has forced it further than it should go. There can be little doubt that amphetamines and other drugs affected Hitler's physical and mental condition, but to conclude – as Heston did – that there is 'no evidence' to warrant considering Hitler a psychopathic personality is, in my view, untenable. It is particularly surprising for a psychiatrist to state flatly that except for a few 'small quirks' he can discover 'no significant psychopathological behaviour whatever in the Führer.'[118]

Hitler's electrocardiograms, which may be found in the National Archives in

Washington, suggest yet another diagnosis. Three extant ECGs dated 14 July 1941, 11 May 1943, and 24 September 1944, show that Hitler suffered from 'rapidly progressive coronary arteriosclerosis.'[119] This medical evidence points clearly to another physiological explanation of Hitler's behaviour. Generalized arteriosclerosis can produce tremors, insomnia, slowness of motion, and confusion of thought. It can also produce personality changes. Previously stable persons may exhibit delusions of grandeur, paranoid tendencies, and moral aberrations.[120]

The most comprehensive study of Hitler's physical condition is being prepared by Fritz C. Redlich, MD, professor of psychiatry emeritus at the University of California. Redlich agrees that Adolf Hitler suffered from progressive coronary problems and Parkinson's disease and from injesting excessive amounts of amphetamines, but his basic problem, Redlich concludes, was 'giant cell arteritis – temporal arteritis,' a disease that inflames the arteries and reduces blood flow to the heart and liver. The symptoms include general malaise, headaches, and oversensitivity to light. The causes are as yet unknown.[121]

Heinrich Himmler and others in the immediate entourage favoured another explanation for Hitler's deteriorating condition. They suspected that their Führer suffered from the ravages of syphilis, which, they assumed, he had contracted either as a youth in Vienna or during a furlough in the First World War. No persuasive evidence has been found to support this hypothesis.[122]

For two reasons it is difficult to make any final neurological diagnosis of Adolf Hitler. First, precise neurological data are lacking. Most notably, although an autopsy had been performed, no brain could be found for analysis. Second, several of the suggested diseases show similar symptoms. Involuntary tremors, insomnia, temper tantrums, lack of concentration, personality changes, hallucinations, and paranoid tendencies that have been ascribed to Parkinsonism can also be found in both neurosyphilis and generalized arteriosclerosis. Moreover, many of these symptoms could have been produced by Morell's medications.

Most important, Hitler's psychological development from infancy to his death rejects the main argument made by the proponents of exclusively neurological explanations of his behaviour, namely, that physiological damage to nerves and brain was responsible for sudden and dramatic changes in Hitler's personality during the last three years of his life. *There was no such abrupt psychological transformation.* Indeed Hitler's most striking characteristic is not change, but an intensification of tendencies whose roots can clearly be traced back to his early years.[123] The condition of the Führer's memory during the last year of his life provides a striking example of continuity. Always noted for his phenomenal ability to memorize and retain factual data, he continued to amaze his entourage. He planned the entire Ardennes offensive of December 1944 in all its details, a feat that would have been quite impossible with an impaired memory.

Neurological difficulties of one form or another may well have exacerbated Hitler's mental condition, but they were not its sole cause. The theory that Adolf Hitler suffered from heart disease, giant cell arteritis, or excessive doses of amphetamines does not explain his foibles, passions, and wickedness, or why his mental aberrations took specific forms and patterns: why he hated the Jews with such unremitting fury, and why he tried to kill them all; why he destroyed the physically and mentally handicapped; why he needed aggressive war; why he was fond of wolves, ravens, and lobsters and infatuated with decapitation; why he washed his hands compulsively and was frightened by horses and the sea and repelled by the thought of sexual intercourse.

Neurological findings contribute to psychological understanding, but they cannot replace it.

Hitler as Borderline Personality

In retrospect, I am completely uncertain when and where he was ever really himself.

Albert Speer

Since Hitler's suicide in 1945, two developments have made it possible to propose a more plausible diagnosis of his mental illness. First, recovery of the Nazi archives (including Gestapo reports on the Führer) and the publication of dozens of memoirs, monographs, and special studies have provided an enormous amount of information about Hitler that was unavailable to earlier writers. Second, important advances have been made in clinical psychology.

The condition now called the 'borderline personality disorder' offers the best clues to understanding some of Hitler's behaviour. But we should not try to fit all his behaviour neatly into that description – indeed some of Hitler's behaviour simply does not fit at all.[124] The purpose of this discussion, as with the Kaiser, is to increase our understanding, not to reduce Hitler's personality to a textbook label. We should also note that 'borderline states' are among the most disputed areas of psychological diagnosis.

Robert K. Knight, MD, formerly of the Menninger Clinic, first used the term to describe patients who are on the very 'borderline' of psychosis. As described by Knight and others,[125] such patients show patterns of behaviour strikingly similar to those people who are narcissistically impaired,[126] but they differ in a number of important respects.

The behaviour of narcissistically disturbed people tends to be episodic and transitory. Borderline personalities are much more rigid; their disturbances are more intense and protracted. The narcissist usually has enough personal cohesion to avoid serious disintegration; borderlines live on the very brink of madness.[127]

Borderline personalities are humourlessly intense. They show marked paranoid tendencies. They consider themselves especially privileged persons, and they fantasize about their magical omnipotence. They believe that they have the absolute right to exploit others for their own gratification.

As we have noted, Hitler's sense of humour was largely limited to laughing at the discomfiture of others. His roommate in Vienna observed that in all their months together, he never once heard Adolf give forth a hearty, good-natured laugh. Adolf also had no sense of fun. He did not seem to enjoy any of the peculiar games he played with such intensity.[128] That borderline patients are also characterized by emotional detachment, reveals another difference between borderlines and narcissists. Borderlines, it is generally agreed, are much more difficult to treat.[129] Some psychoanalysts find that patients resist treatment because, like alcoholics (and like Adolf Hitler), they insist that there is nothing whatever the matter with them. A key reason for adamantly rejecting therapy lies in a deep-rooted fear that if the therapist ever penetrated their emotional defences, their precarious equilibrium would be totally destroyed.[130]

Narcissists, by contrast, are much more likely to realize that they are ill, to seek help and cooperate with their analysts, forming at least temporary 'therapeutic alliances' with them.[131] Wilhelm II never actually sought professional advice for his emotional problems, but – unlike Hitler – he gave clear indications that he might have been a cooperative patient. The Kaiser confided to friends that he suffered from long periods of dark depression; he also told them of his anxiety dreams and his fears that he was 'breaking apart.' Most notably, he expressed curiosity about himself and said he would like to find out what he was 'really like.'

Like the Kaiser, the Führer was surrounded by sycophants. Unlike Wilhelm and his intimate relationship with Eulenburg, however, Hitler never became emotionally close to anyone. Temperamentally and intellectually he was probably more in tune with Goebbels than with anyone else, but to the very end Hitler held himself aloof even from him. Rudolph Hess, who had known Hitler from the start of his career and had shared a prison cell with him for months, never addressed him with the familiar '*du.*' Albert Speer, with whom Hitler shared common architectural interests over many years, noted that Hitler would never permit a friendly relationship to develop between them. Unlike the Kaiser, who could confide his worries to his intimates, Hitler never really unburdened himself. 'Never in my life,' Speer recalled, 'have I met a person who so seldom revealed his feelings, and if he did, instantly locked them up again. During my time in Spandau, I talked with Hess about this peculiarity of Hitler's. Both of us agreed that there had been moments when we felt we had come close to him. But we were invariably disillusioned. If either of us ventured a slightly more personal tone, Hitler promptly put up an unbreakable wall.'[132] Hitler illustrated Speer's point when he told a general that he lied 'even more' to those who thought they knew what he was thinking.[133]

Narcissists and borderlines are both self-centred, and they both exploit other people for their own purposes. But in their relationships with others, narcissists show some reciprocity. The Kaiser, for example, enjoyed the give and take of spirited argument – as shown by the debates of the study group he established in Doorn.[134] The Führer was incapable of genuine discussion; he did not engage in repartee, he harangued his entourage.

Borderlines are reported to have unreconciled oedipal problems, which, in Hitler's case, were probably intensified by a defective testicle and by the 'primal scene trauma' in which as an infant he saw his mother beaten and raped by his drunken father.[135] Self-destructive impulses, which we have noted in Hitler, have also been reported.[136]

In their study of borderline patients stretching over twenty years, Grinka and Werble noted other characteristics – all of which were manifested in Adolf Hitler: brutality, sadism, and hatred for others. As one of their patients noted belligerently, 'I've always done things to be cruel, to hurt other people.'[137] Another patient told his therapist, 'I have so much hatred inside me ... I seem to hate everybody.'[138] Anger and raging, these therapists concluded, 'seem to constitute the main or only affect the borderline patient experiences.' These people seem incapable of love and affection.[139]

A Swiss diplomat, it will be recalled, observed that Hitler exuded hatred from every pore of his being. The Führer prided himself on his brutality. His rages were so violent that he was given the sobriquet *Der Teppichfresser* (The Carpet-eater) because it was erroneously believed that during paroxysms of anger he would thrash about on the floor, literally chewing the carpets.

Like narcissists, borderlines are conspicuous egoists. But the 'grandiose self' of the narcissist, if he or she has gained enough personal coherence and personal esteem, can be a positive, creative force – as seen in the genius of Mozart or Picasso or Wagner. The borderline's grandiosity, by contrast, is usually negative, characterized by rigid omnipotence and omniscience which, Heinz Kohut noted, may be malicious and 'non-humanly evil.'[140]

To prove their omnipotence, and to quiet deep-seated feelings of uncertainty, borderline patients often take dangerous and unnecessary risks. They are convinced that a special dispensation of fate will miraculously intervene to rescue them from any difficulty.[141]

Hitler, who saw himself as the agent of destiny and the 'instrument of the Lord,' never seemed to tire of reminding his entourage of how many risks he had taken in his career, boasting that he was a successful gambler who 'always goes for broke' (*'Ich spiele immer Vabanc'*). We have noted his tendency to challenge disaster. Even when he harboured doubts about a reckless action, the compulsion to gamble dangerously was irresistible. 'I can't help myself,' Hitler would say, likening himself to a traveller who feels compelled to walk over chasms on the edge of a knife.

Borderline personalities are also reported to have phobias about dirt, faeces, and contamination, as did Adolf Hitler. Otto Kernberg also found that many of his patients were prone to gross forms of sexual perversion involving urine and faeces: 'Bizarre forms of perversion, especially those involving ... primitive replacement of genital aims by eliminatory ones (urination, defecation), are also indicative of an underlying Borderline Personality Organization.'[142] It is reported that Hitler ordered young women to defecate or urinate on his head.[143]

According to Kernberg, the clearest identifying characteristic of borderline personalities is a 'splitting of the ego,' which is much more extreme than the dualism noted in narcissists. It often appears, Kernberg has written, as if there were in each patient 'two distinct selves ... equally strong, completely separated from each other.' This description of 'two distinct selves' corresponds closely with Albert Speer's picture of Adolf Hitler as a person who was 'cruel, unjust, cold, capricious, self-pitying and vulgar [but also] the exact opposite of almost all those things.'[144] The discerning French ambassador to Germany was struck by the same dichotomy: 'The same man who was calm, moderate and concilia-tory, good natured in appearance and sensitive ... [who] across a tea table expressed reasonable opinions on European politics, was capable of the wildest frenzies, the most savage exaltation, and the most delirious ambitions ... like some demiurge in his madness. At other times he dreamed of being the hero of eternal peace.'[145]

Hitler's own poems and letters provide dramatic illustrations of his dualities. He was ruthlessly brutal, coldly indifferent to the sufferings of others. Yet one or two of his wartime poems – as we have seen – reveal a quite different person, compassionate, even tender-hearted.[146]

Albert Speer and many others found Hitler withdrawn and aloof, a person who rebuffed those who sought to come close to him or to be his friend. Yet some of Hitler's early postcards and personal letters do show him reaching out to others. A letter of October 1923, written to a boyhood friend in stilted, awk-ward German, is particularly revealing of this aspect:

Dear Fritz!

Yesterday with endless joy I got your dear letter reminding me of the boyhood pranks we and others played together.

I was just recently in Linz and one of the things I did was to wander through all the old streets and alleys and I walked past our old hide-out (*Grabenhaus*) ... and by chance I thought of you. The news was unexpected that you are still alive and living in Graz and wrote me. I really wouldn't have expected that, since of course so many comrades meanwhile fell during the war.

As to my family, it consists mostly only of one wonderful German shepherd dog. To more than that I have not yet attained. The gang-leader of the past is still the gang-leader of today, not yet polished enough for the more tender bonds of life.

I greet you most warmly and ask you to write again.

Your old friend,
Adolf Hitler[147]

Hitler's phrase 'not yet polished enough for the tender bonds of life (*die zärtlichen Gebundenheiten des Lebens noch nicht genug zugeschliffen*)' invites speculations: Does he regret that his family consists only of a dog and that he has not attained a 'more tender bond of life'? Does the repetition of the words 'not yet' suggest he really would like to get married? Or is the expression ironic, suggesting that Hitler's interest lies in remaining the leader of a rough gang of followers rather than in trying to polish tender bonds of family life? At any rate, this letter is a far cry from the aloof, friendless, and coldly indifferent Hitler that most other testimony describes. There may be a touch of irony, even cynicism, here, but the basic tone is amiable.

In reading the compassionate war poems and the cordial letters Hitler wrote during his early manhood, one is tempted to ask, 'Is this really Hitler? Whatever happened to him that he became such a monster?' Yet statements he made during his 'monster' period, show the same deep-seated dualities. Hitler's self-image was wildly contradictory. He saw himself as both brutal and benign. He gloried in his ruthless brutality, yet *at the same time,* he imagined himself to be a kind and gentle person.

Early in his career as chancellor, Hitler told a follower that he looked forward to a Reich where 'dominion, power and enmity shall no longer reign, but equality and brotherhood ... On these foundations alone will the new world be built.' And again, 'Thank God I have never persecuted my enemies!' He also insisted with hurt surprise that never in his entire life had he ever told a lie and that 'on the road of our movement, there lies not one single opponent who we murdered.'[148]

A decade later, with the Holocaust in full swing and with thousands upon thousands of victims tortured and murdered every day on his orders, Hitler insisted, 'I have a horror of people who enjoy inflicting suffering on others' bodies and tyranny upon their souls.'[149] Near the end, in reflecting on his career in February 1945, Hitler preferred to believe that he had never had 'the slightest desire to crush and overwhelm others ... The honour of the German people remains without a blemish.'[150]

Statements such as these go beyond hypocrisy; they bespeak pathological dualities in Hitler's personality.

If a therapist calls a patient's attention to contradictions in his or her behaviour, the first reaction is often a vehement denial that any contradiction exists. If the therapist persists, the patient may become extremely anxious. Kernberg suggests that these patients cannot bear to talk about contradictions because they fear they may be deprived of one of their two 'equally strong' selves. So they try to ward off the anxiety of choice by accepting *both* contradictory images of themselves. These defences do not solve the problem, however. They make it worse.[151]

The feeling of being split apart, of suffering 'tormenting self-deception,' plagued Hitler throughout his life. A confused and contradictory sense of his identity, coupled with doubts about his masculinity, produced nagging questions about self-mastery and self-control. It was therefore important to Hitler to present himself as someone who had absolutely no such weakness, someone always under perfect control. Hence, the endless assertions about his 'iron will' and insistence that he was invariably 'cold as ice' when making decisions – over which he had actually agonized for days. He also felt compelled to master and control the lives of others. Indeed, the essence of Hitler's political system was the domination of other people.

Borderline personalities characteristically 'reinforce splitting through introjection and projection.' The good is associated with themselves, and the bad is projected onto others. Hitler claimed as his own all the attributes he considered good: Aryan toughness, iron will, masculinity, brutality, creativity, integrity. He assigned to others – most notably Jews – all traits that were bad: degeneracy, feminine softness, filth, duplicity.

This bifurcated way of looking at things produced in Hitler, as it often does in borderline personalities, a view of the world as irreconcilably split between good and bad, with the forces of evil constantly conspiring against the good. It was, he said, his divine mission to destroy Jewry – that incarnation of absolute evil – before the Jews destroyed him. This image of the world served Hitler well psychologically. It enabled him to externalize a conflict that, if left festering within, might have led to complete mental disintegration.

Hitler was strengthened psychologically by the support and approval given him by the adoring masses, who hailed him as their Saviour and greeted one another in his name. The Führer's grandiose vision of himself also received daily reinforcement from kowtowers who made a career out of parroting, 'Jawohl, mein Führer!' The Reich he established enabled him to indulge his personal need for domination and destruction and to convert his fantasies into cruel reality.

What was psychologically therapeutic for Hitler was calamitous for millions of others.

Hitler's Pathology and Public Policy

It is not Hitler's pathology that is so strange; that riddle in the end may be solved. What remains a riddle is what caused us to follow this man.

Wellfried Wiegand[152]

One part of the answer to Wiegand's second riddle lies within the first. The German people followed this man, as they had Wilhelm II, in large part because of the remarkable way his personal pathology resonated with the psychological condition of his audiences. He became one of the most compelling demagogues in history because his personal resentments coincided with the resentments of the German people. Without their approval he could never have established one of the most vicious and certainly the most popular tyranny the world has ever known.

Like Wilhelm, Hitler was the 'mirror of his age.' But additional reasons must be sought to explain why he was able to transform masses of normally staid Germans into screaming hysterics who hailed him with mindless fervour.

Hitler's uncanny ability to excite and manipulate mass emotions owed a great deal to a cunning application of Gustav Le Bon's famous psychological study of the crowd, which had appeared in a German translation as Psychologie der Massen (Leipzig, 1908).[153]

Hitler's indebtedness to Le Bon (1841–1931) is manifested throughout Mein Kampf. In his famous chapter on propaganda, Hitler lifted central ideas directly from Le Bon's earlier work. One can surmise that in 1924, having remembered reading the book in Vienna, Hitler had a friend bring him a copy to his pleasant room in the Landsberg prison where he was dictating his dissertation on political manipulation. Hitler exploited to the full Le Bon's discovery that because the crowd operates at a primitive level, it is 'easily stimulated by calls to cruel and ruthless aggression.' The Frenchman had also discovered, long before Hitler, that the effective leader should always appeal to the emotions of the crowd, never to their reason. He should stage gigantic 'theatrical meetings,' preferably at night when people are tired and receptive. 'Mass rallies always have an enormous attraction.' The effectiveness of propaganda, according to Le Bon, depends upon violence, the technique of the big lie, and constant repetition: 'When we read a hundred, a thousand, times that X's chocolates are the best ... we end by acquiring the certitude that such is the fact.' The successful leader should avoid all discussion of his power. He should 'hit upon a new formula that is as devoid as possible of precise meaning.' He should avoid written statements, but 'in his verbal program ... there cannot be too much simplicity or too much exaggeration.' Le Bon also advised the leader to establish a pseudo-religion. The masses, he wrote in words not lost on Hitler, long for a Messiah.[154]

Hitler's rhetorical skills and his twisted sexuality abetted him in stimulating and inflaming mass passions. Le Bon had compared the crowd to a woman who 'requires a master for [she is] always ready to bow before strong authority.' Hitler parroted the idea. 'The masses are like a woman,' he said, 'who will always submit to the strong man.' And again, 'Someone who does not understand the intrinsically feminine character of the masses will never be an effective speaker.'[155]

The written text of Hitler's speeches cannot possibly convey the intimacy he felt with his audience. Hanfstaengl recalled that he often felt like a *voyeur* as he watched Hitler playing a crowd, using it as a surrogate for sex. The Führer, he remembered, would begin an important speech by drawing himself up stiffly, rocking back slowly on his heels, his voice carefully modulated and deliberately low; then, after a period of gentle introductory foreplay, he would move with mounting excitement towards the climax, the tempo rhythmically increasing until both he and his audience reached a passionate finale, 'an orgasm of words.'[156]

The German journalist Joachim Fest had precisely the same reaction. Fest spoke of Hitler's 'copulation' with his audience, 'the breathless anticipation of the masses ... the little gasps for breath ... and the crescendo rising to an ecstasy of rhetorical orgasm with women sobbing in passive surrender or fainting from pure rapture.'[157]

A passage in Hitler's memoirs that throbs with passion and erotic symbolism suggests that he used the crowd as a sexual substitute to be conquered through oral aggression:

Only a storm of burning passion (*Leidenschaft*) can change a people's destiny, only a person who harbours *passion* in himself can arouse *passion* in others.

Passion alone will give to him who is chosen by her [*sic*] the words that, like beats of a hammer, are able to open the doors to the heart of the people.

He to whom *passion* is denied and whose mouth remains closed is not chosen by Heaven as the prophet of her [*sic*] will.[158]

Eva Reichmann, a distinguished British historian who attended a Nazi party rally in 1933, recalled Hitler's spontaneous exclamation after he had reached his rhetorical climax. With heaving chest and flashing eyes, he turned to his audience and cried, 'Aren't you as *enthralled* by me as I am by you? (*Bin ich nicht Euch so verfallen wie Ihr mir?*).' Ms Reichmann added, 'The erotic character, not only of the words but also the accompanying gestures was unmistakable.'[159] After a triumphant speech, Hitler would be drenched with sweat and physically drained. 'Now,' he would say, 'I feel completely fulfilled.'

Hitler's grandiose fantasies were a political asset. Realists have said that his appeal was largely an appeal to illusions – the illusion of a non-existent Jewish menace and a pure-souled Aryan race, the illusion of the infallible Führer. The realists are correct. What they fail to appreciate is the power of illusion in human affairs, especially when it acquires the force of a myth. As Georges Sorel noticed many years ago, illusions may be stronger than facts, and myths shape the lives of men and nations. 'Guided by myth,' Sorel wrote, a society 'is ready for any act of heroic aggressiveness.' The psychoanalyst Rollo May agreed, stressing the power of myth to 'give a person the ability to handle anxiety, to face death, to deal with guilt ... We don't understand the power of the thirst for myth.'[160]

Successful political leaders *do* understand, and they either create myths or shape them to serve their own purposes. Charles de Gaulle, for instance, in radio broadcasts to France in 1940, created a myth. When he said, 'I in London, you at home are united in resistance against a common foe,' there was in fact at that time no such national French resistance to the Nazis. (Indeed more Frenchmen cooperated with the Gestapo than with the Maquis.) But when the French came to believe that the factually false was symbolically true, the mythical 'Resistance' soon developed into a fact of historic force. Hitler too knew how desperately the German people, after the defeat in the Great War and their failures with democracy, wanted to believe in heroic myths. By the alchemy of his charisma and the force of his propaganda, the cherished myths of German history were Nazified and made irresistible to millions of Germans, to whom Hitler became the long-awaited Barbarossa, the Führer who would fulfil the yearnings of the centuries and create a new and mightier Reich of the German nation.

Hitler's myth-making served an important personal function. His illusion that he was the infallible Man of Destiny helped save him from complete psychological disintegration when confronted by failure, physical deterioration, and the apparent collapse of all his personal dreams. Through it all, he retained his unshakable conviction that he would yet prevail. This grandiose self-image was a political as well as a psychological asset, for he conveyed his illusions to the German people. They too were convinced that the Führer could not fail. In March 1945, as the Red Army advanced relentlessly from the east and the Allies from the west, Albert Speer found that Hitler's magic still cast its spell on the masses. He recalled with amazement that even as their world crashed about them, people believed Hitler would save them. 'The Führer,' they said, 'has something in reserve that he'll play at the last moment. Then the turning point will come. It's only a trap, his letting the enemy come so far into our country.'[161]

Yet the myth that convinced Germans that the Führer was a miracle worker who could do the impossible proved Hitler's own undoing when he himself began to believe that he really could do the impossible. Towards the end, he persistently substituted fantasy for fact. His fantasy, for instance, that Russians were subhuman degenerates, caused him to reject solid evidence. Statistics about Soviet tank production were dismissed as 'outright lies' and 'pure fantasy' because they did not fit *his* fantasized world. Hitler gave orders that were completely divorced from reality, firing generals because they could not produce victory with new armies that existed only in his imagination.

Hitler's personal phobia about Jews was also an immediate political asset that became a liability for his regime and a tragedy for millions. Thousands of Germans had responded positively to Hitler's campaign against Jews because it offered a single, simple solution to their manifold problems. Who had stabbed the Fatherland in the back during the war, causing the disastrous defeat? Who had signed the armistice? (The answer to that one was a bit trickier. It was Matthias Erzberger, and he was a Roman Catholic. Small matter. Hitler found for him a Jewish grandparent.) Who had signed the 'treaty of shame'? Who were the profiteers and exploiters who caused the inflation and the Great Depression? Who was responsible for white slavery and moral degradation? Who were the leaders of the communist menace? Conversely, who were the rapacious 'finance capitalists' and international bankers? Hitler's answer was clear and compelling: 'My enemy is Germany's enemy: always and only the Jew!'

Anti-Semitism had other political advantages. 'The Jew' served as a safe outlet for pent-up hatred and aggression when war against an external enemy was not feasible. Jews could be presented as 'outsiders' and thus provide Germans with an opportunity to defend the Fatherland from 'alien forces.' It was also reassuring, at a time when national pride had been sullied, to parade one's superiority over 'racial mongrels.'

Many Germans were attracted to Hitler's anti-Semitism because it explained the decadence they saw all about them. The late 1920s and early 1930s was not only a time of economic, social, and political confusion, it was also a decade of crisis in traditional moral values. Germans were appalled by what they considered to be the depravity of cabaret life and concupiscence in cinema, stage, art, and literature. It was comforting to be told that such depravity was entirely the result of 'Jewish influences.' In dozens of effective speeches Hitler appeared as the 'pious deacon' making articulate the outraged conscience of the petty bourgeoisie.[162]

During this same period, beliefs long cherished as eternal verities were being challenged by three of history's most influential thinkers, all of them Jews and all of whom thought and wrote in German. These Jews – Marx, Freud, and Einstein – were dangerous radicals who preached a frightening relativism that raised doubts about familiar absolutes, and they seemed bent on overthrowing sacrosanct systems of social, economic, ethical, and scientific order. All three of these epochal thinkers found popularizers who spread their ideas with disturbing effectiveness. Emotional reaction against 'subversive Jewish thinkers' increased the appeal of Hitler's demagoguery, which thundered against 'Jewish ideas' and exalted a simple 'Germanic faith.'

By attacking 'the Jew' as the enemy of everything German, Hitler fulfilled a personal psychic need and, at the same time, greatly widened his political appeal. (It should be pointed out, however, that more Germans probably supported Hitler for his anti-Communism than for his anti-Semitism. In crucial elections in 1932 and 1933 Hitler gave orders to tone down anti-Jewish propaganda.)

As soon as he came to power, the Führer's personal rancour against the Jews was 'projected and rationalized as public policy.' Anti-Semitism became the law of the land. Hitler's first decrees to 'protect Germany from the Jewish peril' prohibited Jews from participating in the civic and cultural world to which they had contributed so much for so many generations. An 'Aryan paragraph' in the Law for the Restoration of the Civil Service of 7 April 1933 dismissed all Jewish civil servants. Later legislation expanded the prohibition to include Jewish lawyers, then writers, artists, schoolteachers, university professors, and students. Subsequent legislation required all Jews to use as their first name either 'Sarah' or 'Israel.' Jews of all ages were then required to make themselves conspicuous by wearing a large yellow badge, the Star of David, with the word *'Jude'* printed across it. At the onset of war in 1939, Jews were forbidden to drive motor vehicles or to attend cultural events.

Two specific legal clauses document Hitler's obsession with the fear of 'bad blood' from tainted ancestors. The Law for the Prevention of Progeny Suffering from Hereditary Disease (*Gesetz zu Verhütung erkrankten Nachwuchses*) provided death or sterilization for those with 'hereditary diseases' ranging from schizophrenia to congenital blindness or deafness. Women could be sterilized for colour-blindness, since, as an SS official pointed out, 'We must not have soldiers who are colour-blind. And that is transmitted only through women.' Jews, according to the Führer, were by definition 'carriers of hereditary disease.'[163]

Hitler's personal fear of 'Jewish blood' produced the Nuremberg Racial Laws of September 1935, whose wording he personally supervised. Officially entitled *Gesetz zum Schutze des deutschen Blutes und der deutschen Ehre* (Law for the Protection of German Blood and German Honour), this legislation made it a criminal offence for an 'Aryan German' to have sexual intercourse with a Jewess, and specifically forbade 'Aryan women' under the age of forty from working as domestics in Jewish households – as Adolf Hitler believed his own grandmother had done.

No amount of restrictive civil legislation and no Führer decree could provide a truly satisfactory solution to the 'Jewish Problem.' In Hitler's warped mind, the threat of the Jews was biological. He was desperately afraid that the Jews, whom he suspected of poisoning his own blood, would also poison that of the German *Volk*. The 'final solution' was inherent in the very statement of the problem: Germany could be safe only after every Jew had perished. In all the discussion of the Holocaust it must not be forgotten that its precipitating cause was rooted in the Führer's psychopathology. Since he never knew whether his own grandfather was Jewish, Hitler felt compelled to prove beyond the shadow of any doubt that he personally could not possibly have been 'corrupted' by Jewish blood. To convince himself that such a threat to his own identity and to his life's work was an utter impossibility, Hitler became history's greatest scourge of the Jews. In effect he was saying, 'I'll show you that I cannot possibly be part Jewish. I'll *prove* it. See? I am the killer of Jews.' When he screamed that he would 'annihilate the Jews down to the third generation,' was he not saying that he would obliterate the degree of blood relationship that he was trying so desperately to prove could not possibly be his own?[164]

Hitler reaped additional political benefits from his personal difficulties in achieving psychological cohesion. A man who had closely observed Hitler's face on many occasions concluded that no photograph could possibly capture the person hidden behind the image. That face, he said, 'always amazed me because of the multiplicity of expressions it contained ... A photographer ... could show only one aspect, thereby giving a false impression of the duplicity or multiplicity of being which lay behind it.'[165]

Without knowing it, this observer was accurately describing one salient characteristic of a borderline personality: a person who does not 'add up,' who lacks an integrated self, who is characterized by 'identity diffusion.' As a result, as Otto Kernberg has written, the borderline personality displays a 'chameleon-like quality.' He constantly plays different roles; he 'acts as if he were someone else.'[166]

Hitler was indeed a 'multiplicity of being,' and it was therefore terribly important to convince himself, over and over again, that he was an integrated person of poise and power. One of the best ways to convince himself was *to act the part* and thus become, at least for the moment, the dominating personality he wanted so much to be. Hitler's inner confusion may help account for two peculiar facts about his early career: For years he refused to pose for pictures, and he persisted in using a false name.

Aspiring young politicians do not usually go to extraordinary lengths to conceal their identities or to hide themselves from the public eye. But for several years after he had made his 'momentous' decision in 1919 to enter politics, Hitler refused to have his picture taken, I am suggesting, because he was too unsure of his own image to have it 'set' by a photograph. As late as 1922, a picture of Hitler was so rare that an American news agency offered a German photographer $100 for one. (At that time the going rate for a photograph of German President Friedrich Ebert was $5.) The agency's surprise over the discrepancy was no doubt increased when it learned that the asking price in Germany for a good snapshot of Hitler was $30,000! Posed photographs were simply not available.[167]

During these years Hitler also preferred not to use his real name. He asked people to call him 'Herr Wolf' and styled himself the 'nameless fighter' of the western front. It was only after he gained control over the party, and established himself as Führer, that the nameless and faceless period was over. Then he became the most photographed political leader in the world – but he never got over his need to create other images.

Hitler's ability to play a variety of roles with intensity and conviction was a distinct political asset. He appeared as a very different person to each of an extraordinary range of people, and he impressed almost all of them.[168] To the sophisticated French ambassador Hitler appeared as 'a well-balanced man, filled with experience and wisdom.' An intellectual found him 'charming ... a person of "common sense" in the English sense.' The famous British historian Arnold J. Toynbee came away from an interview 'convinced of his sincerity in desiring peace.' We recall that David Lloyd George called him 'a man of genius, the George Washington of his country,' and that, writing before the war, Winston Churchill listed Hitler as one of the truly great men of all history.[169] Hitler impressed the elegantly precise foreign secretary Anthony Eden, who noted Hitler's 'smart, almost elegant appearance' and found his command of diplomatic detail 'masterful.'[170]

The early diaries of Joseph Goebbels, never intended for publication, show the psychological insight and consummate artistry with which Hitler wooed and won this bright and brittle young man who was to become the 'Evil Genius' of his 'ministry of propaganda and enlightenment.' For Hitler responded brilliantly to Goebbels's psychological needs. He saw that young Goebbels needed, above all, someone who could dominate him: Hitler appeared 'as my master ... my father.' Contrarily, Goebbels also wanted to feel protective and paternal: Hitler appeared to him as 'a child, good, kind, warm-hearted.' Goebbels craved affection and attention: Hitler praised him, embraced him, and sent him flowers. Goebbels needed to hate: Hitler showed him 'how to hate with passion.' Goebbels needed flattery: Hitler sometimes praised him and deferred to his judgment. Goebbels longed for a saviour and found one in Hitler: 'The Führer is the Christ!' Goebbels admired cunning: Hitler appeared as 'a cat, sly, clever, shrewd.' Goebbels admired the masterful strength and confidence that he himself lacked: Hitler seemed to him 'a lion, roaring, immense ... a great guy! A Man! (*ein Kerl! ein Mann!*).'[171]

The Führer played a very different role in winning Albert Speer, the cultivated engineer who became Hitler's architect and minister of armaments and who, by 1944, had become largely responsible for Germany's entire war economy. Speer recalled how in 1931, while a student at the University of Berlin, he had been captivated by Hitler. To him Hitler appeared as a man of moderation, whose voice was controlled and well modulated, exuding quiet confidence and South German charm: 'Here it seemed to me was hope. Here were new ideas and new understanding.' In looking back from his prison cell in Spandau after the war, where he was serving time as a war criminal, Speer wondered how he had been so deceived: '[Today] I find it incomprehensible that [Hitler] impressed me so profoundly. What had done it?' And again, 'How was it possible that he captivated me so, and for more than a decade?'[172]

Hitler was an actor. Whether acting or not, the sheer *power* of his personality was overwhelming. The cynical Hermann Göring was never cynical about Hitler. He confided to the British ambassador, 'Every time I face him my heart falls into my trousers.' Later, even after Hitler had turned against him, calling him a traitor and drumming him out of the party, Göring was close to despair when he heard of his leader's death. His wife recalled that he broke down and cried, 'He's dead, Emmy! Now I shall never be able to tell him that I was true to him to the end!'[173] Admiral Dönitz, commander in chief of the German navy, felt psychically drained by his Führer's commanding presence: 'I personally went very seldom to his headquarters,' he testified, 'for I ... always had the feeling that I had to disengage myself from his power of suggestion.'[174]

In the last days of the war Speer, who realized that Germany's position was hopeless and that his Führer's orders for total destruction were maniacal, could not bring himself, even then, to stand against the compelling power of the man: 'Face to face, his magnetic power over me was too great up to the very last day ... without reflection ... my lips spoke the words, "*Mein Führer,* I stand unreservedly behind you!" ... I realized that I had lost all urge to continue my opposition. Once more Hitler had succeeded in paralyzing me psychically.'[175]

Professor Percy Schramm, who had known Hitler for years and attended many military briefings, also felt the psychic force of Hitler's presence: 'It is almost impossible to convey to those who never experienced it the personal impact of Hitler. Such could be its strength that it sometimes seemed a kind of psychological force radiating from him like a magnetic field. It could be so intense as to be almost physically tangible.'[176]

Hitler was certainly an actor, but he was not, like the Kaiser, 'only putting on an act.' With Wilhelm, the play was always the thing, and he demanded to be its star. 'He measured success,' a biographer has written, 'by flamboyance of his display, not by substantive achievement.'[177]

By contrast, Hitler was more than a flamboyant performer craving personal attention. Using his histrionic skills with deliberate cunning, Hitler remained a man of faith and conviction, a genuine fanatic with a sense of mission. His spectacular performances were always a means to an end – his means of bending the masses to his indomitable will. Unlike the Kaiser, the Führer knew exactly what he wanted, and he knew how to get it. Hitler played his roles with both calculation *and* conviction.

He used his skills as an actor in the service of his fanatical faith. He also used them to serve a psychic need – his need to *be* the myth-person he was portraying, to *be* the man of decision, the man of destiny. Psychologically, it was imperative to convince himself that the role he was playing was no mere act; it was the truth. More important for history, he compelled others to believe it was true.

Hitler may not have actually possessed the personal strength and purposefulness he projected, but he gave the illusion of possessing them. That was sufficient. He moved people because he was able – in Konrad Heiden's phrase – to 'act out greatness,' to change himself from a hesitant and unsure little man to a person of towering historic force who paralysed opposition and commanded millions to do his will. Thus, the 'acting out,' which was for him a psychic necessity, became his greatest single political asset.

Hitler's paranoid distrust of others, so typical of borderline personalities, had important consequences in his foreign policy. It was largely responsible for the serious misjudgment that turned his attack on Poland into a European war, and thence a world war. On 1 September 1939, he felt free to invade Poland because he had used his own standards of duplicity in evaluating England's intentions. He simply could not believe that Britain would honour her treaty with the Poles. A general's personal diary entry for 14 August 1939 recorded Hitler's scornful dismissal of the argument that the invasion of Poland might precipitate a general war: 'Why should England fight?' he scoffed, 'One does not die for an ally.'[178]

Belief in himself produced rigid, obdurate consistency – another hallmark of the borderline personality. For Adolf Hitler this rigidity was both a political asset and a liability. There can be no doubt that Hitler's iron will and stubbornness stood him in good stead during the Rhineland crisis of 1936, when he was saved by what he called 'my unshakable obstinacy and amazing aplomb.' Military historians also agree that his rigidity and stubborn refusal to retreat during the first setback of the Russian campaign in the winter of 1941 helped bring him out of an immediate crisis. But at Stalingrad and the final battle for Berlin, the Führer's obstinacy meant military disaster and the needless sacrifice of hundreds of thousands of lives.

Hitler's personal problems influenced military performance in another way. As Norbert Bromberg has noted, 'He was caught in a psychological trap.' Doubts about his masculinity and power could not be quieted even by astonishing successes. He was driven to keep on proving his omnipotence.[179] Stupendous successes were never enough. Hitler was condemned to stay on the offensive. In his mind, to assume a defensive posture or to retreat was to be feminine and to confess weakness. A military historian has shown the strategic consequence of this fixation: 'He could not bring himself to retreat for any reason, thus the fateful errors he made in his war leadership.'[180]

Even after smashing victories had been won, he could not stop from further attacks. 'Wherever our success ends,' he said in a revealing statement, 'it will always be only the point of departure for a new struggle.'[181]

The very word 'capitulation' (*Kapitulation*) threw Hitler into a frenzy. In an interview after the war, former State Secretary Otto Meissner said he realized for the first time that Hitler was mentally unbalanced when it was suggested in March 1945 that Germany really ought to sue for peace. Hitler's reaction was violent: 'He paced the room. His voice was out of control. He shouted and cried. He spoke without coherence. He yelled repeatedly, "*Ich kapituliere nie ... Ich kapituliere nie!*"[182] Hitler would 'never surrender as a woman surrenders to a man' – for that would reveal feminine qualities. Nor could he ever yield again, as he had been forced to yield to the will of his father who had humiliated him as a child: 'There is one word I never recognized ... capitulation. That word I do not know and I will never know as Führer of the German people and as your Supreme Commander. That word is, I repeat, capitulation, which is *the surrender of the will to another person*. Never! Never! Never!'[183]

And so it continued to the end. Because Adolf Hitler personally could not surrender, the country had to perish. It was less painful to see Germany utterly destroyed than for him to capitulate.

Psychological Speculations

In the most important part of its business, history is ... an imaginative guess.

George Macaulay Trevelyan

In reading hundreds of pages of Hitler's reminiscences, soliloquies, and speeches, I have been surprised to discover that this ruthless man repeatedly expressed concern about 'unworthiness,' 'guilt,' and 'a troubled conscience.'

As though responding to some need to dispel doubts about his own worthiness, Hitler asserted, 'I carry my heavy burdens with dutiful thanks to Providence which has deemed me worthy (*würdig*).'[184] He reassured himself that 'the Great Judge of all time ... will always give victory to those who are the most worthy.'[185] A movie star who spent the night with Hitler recalled her embarrassment when the Führer grovelled on the floor, condemning himself as 'unworthy.'[186]

It was important for Hitler to dispel any suggestion that he was troubled by a 'guilty conscience.' He therefore sought to denigrate the very existence of conscience by associating it either with Jews and animals or with morality – for which he felt only contempt.

Conscience is a Jewish invention. It is a blemish like circumcision.

I am freeing men from ... the *dirty and degrading* form of chimera [a foul-mouthed female monster] called *conscience and morality.*

We must distrust *conscience* ... Only when the time comes when the race is no longer overshadowed by *consciousness of its own guilt* will it find internal peace.

Dogs, according to the Führer, have guilty consciences.[187]

His remarks about conscience often reveal a basic contradiction. Although insisting that he had rid himself of this contemptible 'chimera,' some form of conscience still weighed on his mind: 'We must be ruthless ... *we must regain our clear conscience* as to ruthlessness ... Only thus shall we purge our people.'[188]

Hitler despised conscience as a 'Jewish invention,' yet he seems to have had qualms of conscience about something. *But what?* Unlike the Kaiser, the Führer's uneasy conscience did not stem from remorse over the sins and transgressions he had committed against God or man. Hitler gloried in brutality, despised compassion, and extolled hatred as a virtue. He felt no remorse about the calculated murder of millions of Slavs and Jews or the squandered lives of young German soldiers ('Isn't that what they're for?'). Atrocities did not trouble the conscience of the Führer or make him feel 'unworthy.' What did?

We cannot be sure. The evidence is only strong enough to permit speculation. George Macaulay Trevelyan once said, 'In the most important part of its business, history is ... an imaginative guess.'[189] Thus, taking our cue let us hazard the following guesses. Perhaps Hitler felt unworthy of being the Führer of a racially pure Reich because he himself was 'guilty of having Jewish blood,' as the barbarous expression ran in Nazi Germany.[190] Perhaps feelings of unworthiness were engendered by a sexual perversion that was disgusting and degrading to himself as well as to his sexual partner.[191] Hitler's feelings about his mother were confused and deeply contradictory. He kept protesting that he loved her, yet he had reasons for resentment. Were they intense enough to produce hatred and feelings of guilt?[192] Is it possible that Hitler felt unworthy and guilt-ridden because of memories, or fantasies, of incestuous relations with his own mother?[193] These are guesses. Although the real reasons for Hitler's feelings of guilt and unworthiness may never be known, it may be informative to explore some of the psychological defences he constructed in trying to fend them off.

He masked hatred and resentment by excessive insistence on undying love for his 'sainted mother.' He hid voyeurism and perverse sexual interests behind ostentatiously prudish behaviour. Projecting the image of moral rectitude, he denied himself alcohol and tobacco. He forbade musicians to play saxophones because he considered them 'sinful and depraved.' He censored women for wearing lipstick, and lashed out against all forms of sexual deviation.

Hitler also sought to obliterate thoughts of unworthiness by casting himself in the role of religious leader. He could not possibly be unworthy or guilt-ridden because he, the founder of a new religion who spoke the words of Jesus, had been especially selected by Almighty God to lead the German people. He also found it reassuring to insist that it was those other people who were unworthy and deserving of punishment.

Hitler's habit of keeping scrupulously clean, his excessive concern about flatulence and other body odours, his compulsion to wash his hair, scrub his hands, and to purge himself with enemas and blood-letting are familiar indications of an unconscious desire to wash away guilt feelings.

The Führer's preoccupation with personal purification was extended to the German people. They too, in his phrase, must undergo 'internal cleansing (*innere Reinigung*).' This could be done, he said, only through the elimination of 'less worthy elements (*minderwertigen Elemente*).' In 1929, at the conclusion of an early Nuremberg rally, Hitler declared that if 800,000 of the weakest and 'less worthy' of a million children born in one year were destroyed, the result would benefit the German racial stock.[194]

Ten years later, in the summer of 1939, in making plans for conquering living space for his Greater German Reich, Hitler called a conference of Nazi health officials to discuss ways of ridding Germany of 'unworthy elements.' He explained to the doctors that, as 'the father of the people,' he bore the responsibility for the racial purity of the German family. In the course of his remarks, with which the attending physicians heartily concurred, Hitler kept repeating the phrases 'internal cleansing of less worthy elements (*inneren Reinigung von minderwertigen Elemente*)' and 'the obliteration of lives not worthy of being lived.' The last phrase is equally ugly in German: '*Die Vernichtung lebensunwerten Leben.*'[195]

By the spring of 1945 Hitler had expanded his definition of unworthiness. The entire German people, he now concluded, had proven guilty and unworthy. Thus, he cried out, 'Germany is not worthy of me (*meiner nicht würdig*); let her perish.'[196] A German historian of Hitler's mass murders noticed the direct connection between his fixation on personal purification and genocide: 'If a biography of Hitler is undertaken from a psychoanalytic approach, his compulsions about hygiene and cleanliness would be its most important point of departure.'[197]

It is also possible that in addition to punishing others for unworthiness, Hitler may have sought relief from his own guilty feelings through self-punishment. If so, this would help illuminate a curious pattern we have detected in Hitler's career: an impulse to put himself at disadvantage and to flirt with failure.

Although he had handicapped himself by dropping out of *Realschule*, young Hitler was given a marvellous opportunity to join the artistic world he longed to enter. A friend of his mother had connections with Alfred Roller, an established artist who was director of scenery for the Imperial Opera in Vienna. Roller offered to help the young man, suggesting that he might serve an apprenticeship by painting backdrops for the opera. This promising position would have combined Adolf's two great loves: painting and Richard Wagner. It would also have enabled him to move in the 'artistic circles' he so greatly admired. Surprisingly, Hitler failed to take advantage of this opportunity. He did not even communicate with Professor Roller when he arrived in Vienna in February 1908, and he never mentioned the matter to his roommate.[198]

Perhaps feeling that he was destined for much higher things than mere apprenticeship to an artist, Hitler tried to enrol in the Viennese Academy of Art, but failed the entrance examination. He was given a rare second chance, yet refused to apply himself. He may have taken a few art lessons from a man named Panholzer in Vienna. But there is no basis for Werner Maser's contention that, after failing his first examination, Hitler 'now did what he had failed to do in school: worked industriously, effectively, and purposefully.'[199] On the contrary, his roommate during these months reported that Adolf did no serious painting at all. He went to the opera 'almost every night.' He spent hours walking around the Ring criticizing the buildings. He designed grandiose villas for himself and monuments to his own memory. He set forth elaborate schemes for equipping, clothing, and scheduling a 'national travelling orchestra.' He pored over dozens of racist and pseudo-scientific pamphlets. He wrote sketches for dramas and operas. He talked by the hour about life, sex, and politics. Indeed, Hitler did almost everything but apply himself purposefully to his art. He was not even admitted to the entrance examination when he reapplied in October 1908.[200]

As we have noted, Hitler's first try for political power in the Beer Hall Putsch of 1923 suggests a pattern of choosing alternatives least likely to succeed. One historian of the event commented on Hitler's 'elementary errors of judgment.' Another called Hitler's behaviour 'unfathomable.' A third found his actions so patently self-defeating that he concluded that Hitler could not have wanted to succeed.[201]

Hitler's conduct during the Second World War sometimes followed a similar pattern. Without provocation or declaration of war – and without ordering a winter issue for his army – he invaded the USSR. Then, with his troops bogged down in blizzards before Moscow and with the eastern front threatening to collapse, the Führer flabbergasted his own army commanders – and obliged both Roosevelt and Churchill – by suddenly declaring war on the United States. Throughout the time that the titanic two-front war was raging, Hitler refused to order full mobilization of the German economy. He also insisted on diverting millions of work-hours and vitally needed rolling stock to transporting millions of innocent people to their deaths.

Hitler's counter-productive behaviour may have been the result of deep internal divisions, typical of borderline personalities. His divided psyche, it can be argued, gave conflicting orders: to strive for victory; to cultivate defeat. That, however, seems unlikely.

'Self' psychology suggests a more plausible explanation for Hitler's apparently irrational behaviour. What appears irrational to us may have seemed totally appropriate to Adolf Hitler, whose feelings of grandiose omnipotence placed him far above the restrictions placed on lesser mortals, for he was convinced that destiny was guiding him unerringly ('with all the assurance of a sleepwalker') to ultimate triumph. In this view, Hitler's egregious mistakes were not so much self-punitive as they were self-delusionary, prompted by his conviction that as the darling of destiny he was destined for triumph, no matter what obstacles were placed in his path. The late Elizabeth Kohut suggested, for instance, that Hitler's refusal in Vienna to accept apprenticeship under an established artist may have been an early manifestation of his narcissistic grandiosity. That is, he scorned the offer as far beneath his artistic genius. His self-defeating conduct after his rejection by the art academy shows him indulging in more illusions of grandeur. Swaggering indifference was his way of pulling himself together psychologically and covering up feelings of inadequacy, a sense of failure, and fears of fragmentation.[202]

Easy victories in the Low Countries and France further convinced Hitler of his infallibility. His megalomania grew with each triumph. According to this interpretation, his ill-advised decision at Dunkirk, his invasion of Russia, and his 'incomprehensible' declaration of war on the United States were all prompted, not by an unconscious desire to fail but by the grandiose conviction that he ('the greatest military commander of all time') would be victorious, whatever the odds. He could take on Russia and the United States – or anyone else – at the same time. His grandiosity was contagious. Members of his high command stifled their professional doubts because they had come to believe that Hitler really could work miracles. 'In the end,' an English military historian has written, 'it was as if collective madness had seized them [all].'[203]

This interpretation could cite as its text Longfellow's paraphrase of Publius Syrus (ca. 42 BC), 'Whom the gods would destroy, they first make mad.'

The Führer preserved his grandiose self-image to the end. As the Red Army fought through the streets of Berlin in late April 1945, and others in the air-raid shelter grew increasingly hysterical, Hitler remained serenely confident. Convinced that as long as his magic presence remained in Berlin the city could not fall, he awaited miraculous deliverance. He may even have viewed his own suicide as the final victory and capstone of his exalted career, his peculiar way to triumph through physical destruction.

The act of suicide has fascinated psychologists for years. Some of their findings may help us gain further understanding of Hitler's life as well as his death.[204]

On one level, suicide may be seen as a masochistic act, the ultimate resolution of an unconscious desire for self-punishment. Hitler displayed this tendency every time he indulged his masochistic sexual practice or played his suicide games or planned his own memorials. To the pathological masochist, suicide may appear, however, not as defeat but as a twisted sort of triumph. Indeed, after years of clinical experience with masochism, Theodor Reik concluded that the essence of the masochistic patient's attitude towards life can be summed up in three words: *Victory through Defeat.* Other people may view such a person's suicide as a clear admission of failure, but the persons themselves may feel vindicated and triumphant.[205]

Suicide may also gratify feelings of hostility and aggression. By taking one's life, one inflicts punishment on survivors – parents or spouse or lover or anyone else who is deemed to have abandoned the sufferer.[206] Certainly Hitler felt that he had been abandoned by everyone. As his country lay in the rubble he had done so much to create, the Führer's thoughts turned inward: 'Nothing is spared me,' he lamented on 26 April 1945. 'No allegiances are kept, no honour lived up to ... no betrayal I have not experienced ... Nothing remains. Every wrong has already been done to me!'[207]

Karl Menninger discussed one facet of suicide that reflects an important aspect of Hitler's personality. Menninger found a connection in suicide between fear of examination and feelings of omnipotence. People who consider themselves unique, and who, like Hitler, refuse to be examined physically or to have their beliefs questioned, may find in suicide a confirmation of their grandiose omnipotence. 'To kill oneself instead of being executed or slain by fate,' Menninger wrote, 'is to retain for oneself the illusion of being omnipotent since one is, even by the act of suicide, master of life and death.' In this way, paradoxically, the obsessive drive for a triumphant life may be fulfilled through death.[208]

All his life Hitler was given to grandiose, infantile fantasizing. As a boy in Leonding playing the Austrian version of cops-and-robbers (*Räuber und Gendarm*), Adolf told his playmates that no one could 'kill' him because he was 'special.'[209] As an adolescent in Linz, he delivered impassioned orations to lonely trees on windswept hills. As a young man in Vienna, Hitler rebuilt entire cities and set forth detailed plans for the 'Third Reich of the German Nation.'[210] As an adult, he thought of himself as Christ or as one of the immortal Olympian gods.[211]

But at the end, Hitler may have fancied himself a different kind of deity. Neither Jesus nor one of the serene and radiant company on the azure heights of Olympus, he now appeared as a darkly brooding Teutonic god enthroned in Valhalla, the shadowed hall of the heroic dead. Especially as he cut himself off from the outside world in his air-raid shelter, he may have reverted to his childhood fantasy that he was Wotan, dread ruler of the universe.[212]

In ordering the *Götterdämmerung* for his world, perhaps Adolf Hitler envisaged himself as Teutonic god fulfilling ancient myth. We know that one of his most precious boyhood possessions, a treasure 'with which he never parted,' was a book of German mythology.[213] We know also of Hitler's lifelong infatuation with the ancient legends as recast by Richard Wagner. These myths foretold the inevitable destruction of the world in a colossal holocaust, with gods and men consumed by flames. Hitler knew well Wagner's conception of Wotan as 'rising to the tragic height of willing his own destruction.' He may have reinforced this image by recalling another boyhood hero of Nordic legend who, though vanquished, laughed in splendid defiance as his foes cut his heart from his living flesh.[214]

It seems likely that at the end of his own life Hitler would have been drawn yet again to Wagner, his ever-present refuge and strength in time of trouble, the fellow artist and creative genius who had inspired his Reich and of whom he had said that whoever wished to understand National Socialism must first understand Richard Wagner. 'It all began,' Hitler had also said, 'with Wagner.' Thus, too, it would end.

For his own death scene let us imagine that Hitler cast himself as Wotan-Siegfried, a commanding Wagnerian hero who would rise above death by defying it, with his faithful Brünhilde – Eva Braun Hitler – at his side. Together they soar into a final duet, *Lachend lass' uns verderben, lachend zu Grunde geh'n!* (Laughing let us perish; 'mid laughter face our doom!) Hero and heroine embrace, defiantly confronting death. Together their bodies are consumed by flames.[215]

Such fantasies were consistent both with Hitler's personality and with recent psychological studies of self-destruction which conclude that suicide is sometimes a 'magical act, actuated to achieve irrational, delusional ends.'[216]

For people given to grandiose fantasies, death through suicide is not defeat, nor is it merely an escape from intolerable reality. Rather, it is a way for them to 'acquire power, qualities, and advantages' never possessed in life, and to triumph in the end. Confronted by terrifying feelings of failure and impotence, they bring up their ultimate weapon.

By choosing to destroy their own lives, they believe that they have become masters of life itself. Through non-being, they advance to a superior order of being. They achieve 'a kind of cosmic identification.' That is, they equate the universe with themselves. By taking their own lives, they are, *at the same time*, committing 'vicarious matricide, patricide ... even genocide.'[217] For such a person feels, as did Hitler, that no one, 'no one in the entire nation is worthy of me. Let them perish.'

So it may have been with Hitler. Encircled by a host of enemies and scoffers, who dared to doubt his power and who boasted that they would destroy him, he would show them that he was still omnipotent. Little did they know that he could rise far above time and space and the travail of mortal life.

Hitler would prove his dominion over them all by a miraculous leap into a new dimension of power. He who had created the Reich would destroy a world and gain immortality. Let there be darkness. Through one single, crashing act of oblivion this psychopathic god would proclaim that his was the power and the glory forever.[218]

Limitations of the Psychological Dimension

... essential but not sufficient.

Biographers have good reason to be envious of the kind of personal knowledge psychotherapists can gain of their patients: they know them personally, they conduct private consultations over an extended period, they possess a quality and quantity of information as well as an intimacy with their subjects that is denied to us biographers. Their patients are alive; our subjects are dead.

I find experience and counsel of psychotherapists enormously helpful in trying to understand the baffling behaviour of both Kaiser and Führer. In my view, however, there are dimensions of human experience that do not yield to psychological analysis. Psychology, for example, helps me understand how Wilhelm's narcissistic self-glorification, psychic defences, and fantasies of restoration to power enabled him to weather the shocks of humiliation, defeat, and exile. Yet the ex-Kaiser himself said that, above everything else, it was daily prayer and his Christian faith that sustained him – and personal religious faith, as Anthony Burgess has remarked, can *ultimately* no more yield to psychoanalysis than music can yield to mathematics.[219]

Psychological insights help deepen my awareness of broad, underlying reasons for the dualities that plagued both Wilhelm von Hohenzollern and Adolf Hitler. But without having the opportunity to know either man personally, psychoanalysts are unable to give me answers to some of my specific questions. Why, for example, did the same Kaiser who could be considerate and kind, also enjoy the humiliation of old men or the pain of young women? Why did he ridicule rather than empathize with others who, like himself, were physically handicapped? Similarly, psychological studies of 'borderline personalities' give me a better understanding of Adolf Hitler's behaviour, but again, the therapists I have consulted were unable, in the retrospect of fifty years, to give specific reasons why the Führer showed solicitude for lobsters (why lobsters?) and for a French woman in childbirth, yet gloried in the systematic massacre of the innocents.

Neither can retrospective psychological reconstruction explain the sheer *intensity* of Hitler's hatred. Although 'psychic injury' had manifestly been done to him – as it has been done to millions of other human beings – what was it that drove Adolf Hitler to commit such unspeakable evil? We cannot fully explain it, but we can recognize consuming hatred as a driving force behind his atrocities.

Nor can psychological analysis fully account for another quality that characterized this extraordinary man: his internal strength – the tough, resilient fibre that set Hitler apart from hundreds of other pathological personalities. It enabled him to overcome moments of self-doubt and to retain until the very end his unshakable confidence in himself and in his destiny. This quality may come down finally to an act of will, and that too is a dimension of the man that resists psychological or historical analysis. Again, however, our inability to explain it does not reduce its importance. Will was the dominating power of Hitler's life, it made him a historic force.

Nor is psychological understanding in itself able to account for Hitler's political success. Psychology is, as Thomas Aquinas said of reason, 'essential to our enlightenment, but not sufficient.' Hitler could never have come to power or won such widespread public acclaim without the benefit of uniquely congenial historic circumstances. Monarchy had failed, and democracy was not solving the nation's problems; a proud people who had been humiliated by military defeat and betrayed by the 'treaty of shame' were consumed by feelings of hatred and hunger for revenge. So was Adolf Hitler. Germans found him 'one of us' – a leader who, like them, had also known humiliation, defeat, and abuse, who renewed their sense of pride and power, and provided an opportunity to mobilize their hatred. This hate-filled man spoke their language: 'I demand of you,' Hitler shouted in a speech of 10 April 1923, 'pride, will-power, defiance – *hatred, and again, hatred!*' The masses roared approval.

Psychology has not been able to solve what has been called the 'ultimate mystery' of Hitler: the overwhelming personal magnetism of the man. One of his generals reported that when he was in the presence of his Führer, 'I was drained of any will of my own.' Reichsmarshal Hermann Göring confessed, 'Every time I stand before the Führer my heart drops into the seat of my pants.' Speer, as we have seen, was determined to oppose Hitler, but melted in his presence and blurted out, 'My Führer, I stand unconditionally behind you.' Secretaries who saw Hitler daily, and recalled how they had suffered through the banality of his interminable midnight musings, were nevertheless charmed by his personality. Having known Adolf Hitler, one of them declared, 'We could never have married another man.'

After the war, the BBC set up a panel of experts to probe the nature of Hitler's personal appeal by putting questions to Albert Speer, the man who knew Hitler better than anyone else. The American statesman and lawyer George Bell spoke for a multitude when he said that he was baffled by the talk of Hitler's charisma, charm, and magnetism. Bell said that after reading what the man had written, seeing him in motion pictures, and listening to his speeches, it was 'totally incomprehensible' to him how anyone could possibly find a particular charm in the man. Turning to Speer he asked, 'How do you explain it? This is the ultimate mystery.'

Speer had often asked himself the same question: 'How was it possible that he captivated me so, and for more than a decade?'[220] Now, in his response to George Bell's question, as in a dozen other interviews, Speer groped unsuccessfully for words to explain the mystery. Like everyone else, he spoke of Hitler's 'hypnotic power' and 'magnetism.' When asked to explain *that*, he kept falling back on the untranslatable concept of *hörig*, saying that Hitler held him in *Hörigkeit*.[221] It is an interesting word and particularly interesting that Speer should use it so often. It comes from the middle high German '*hoerec*' or bondage (a *Hoerigerbauer* was a serf). The word covers a range of feeling including 'belonging to,' 'submissive dependence,' and 'helpless passivity.' It also means sexual dependency or bondage to the point of sexual slavery.

Speer had been asked to explain a force; he had described only its effect. He could not solve the mystery of Hitler's personal appeal, nor can we. We can only affirm its importance. The history of Germany from 1933 to 1945 cannot be understood without recognizing the man's mesmerizing personal power.

Finally, psychotherapists have not been able to help me very much in understanding the most striking characteristic I found in Adolf Hitler: he was evil. This word poses serious problems for psychologists because it involves personal moral judgment. As one psychotherapist put it to me, 'Sure, I might agree with you personally that Hitler was evil, but as a professional psychotherapist I am not in the business of making moral judgments.' For good reason. In treating their patients, therapists must avoid becoming judgmental or emotionally involved. They take professional pride in remaining dispassionate and 'value free.' I could not find the word 'evil' listed in the index of standard psychiatric lexicons.[222]

Evil is, however, a part of the human condition. Evil is present in the Unabomber and in anyone who rapes a four-year-old girl. Evil was manifested in the perpetrators of Auschwitz and My Lai, in the racial cleansers of Bosnia–Herzogovina, and in the Devil-worshippers of every age. *How can such evil be explained?*

In trying to find an answer to that question, Erich Fromm broke with orthodox therapists by openly using the word and identifying its psychological components. After devoting the last decades of his life to the psychological study of the Nazis, Fromm concluded that Hitler, Himmler, Eichmann, and their ilk were evil and that they suffered from a specific pathological condition Fromm called '*malignant* narcissism.'[223] His professional colleagues recognize the term 'narcissism,' but reject the word 'malignant' ('rebellious against God ... disposed to do harm') as a moral judgment lying outside the bounds of psychological analysis. It is not surprising that orthodox therapists do not cite Fromm or that his books on evil have gone out of print.

Scott Peck, an experienced American psychiatrist who is also a devout Christian, has agreed with Fromm that some of his patients suffer from 'malevolent narcissism,' and he has described their psychological symptoms.[224] But this, says Peck, is not the main thing wrong with his patients. He goes beyond Fromm in describing the underlying problem of these people. In doing so he uses a vocabulary foreign to his professional colleagues and sets forth concepts they reject: Peck assserts that his patients are possessed by evil. They are in the thrall of the Devil. He believes in Satan and in the existence of good and evil. God is the essence of good, Satan the essence of evil. God manifests Himself in the spirit and behaviour of people like Mother Theresa; Satan is active in the spirit and behaviour of people like Hitler.

Peck experiences great difficulty in treating patients who are possessed by evil. In some cases they can be helped by a combination of skilful and prolonged psychological counselling combined with religious exorcism that requires the best efforts of trained psychologists and religious counsellors.[225] Above all, Peck and his associates believe that healing can take place only through the grace of God and the faith that love is stronger than hate, that good can overcome evil. Peck freely admits that he does not fully understand how evil operates in human beings, but he believes that his unorthodox approach is legitimate and that he is making discoveries that are helpful in improving the psychological well-being of many seriously troubled patients.

It is not given to humans – whatever our psychological or religious convictions – to understand one another completely. Ultimately, we remain a mystery. All we can hope for is deeper understanding.

Although we will never find complete answers to many questions about the personalities of the Kaiser and the Führer, a close look at their tortured childhoods can illumine their adult behaviour.

6

Kaiser and Führer: The Childhood Experience

The Child is father of the Man.

Wordsworth

The behaviour of these two men invites us to explore Wordsworth's aphorism. The clinical experience of a respected psychotherapist reinforces the poet's insight and makes a biographer's exploration obligatory: 'No reputable therapist would make a diagnosis of a patient – or even think he knew the patient very well – before finding out a great deal about his life history, particularly his childhood.'[1]

On the face of it, no similarities would seem to exist between the childhood experiences of the Kaiser and of the Führer. Wilhelm von Hohenzollern, the first son of a future king, was born into luxury, position, and power. His future was ordained, his education the best that loving and privileged parents could provide. Adolf Hitler was born into obscurity and made his own way towards an uncertain future. Wilhelm became ruler of Germany through no effort on his part; Hitler became Führer through his own efforts and his extraordinary ability to bend fortuitous circumstances to his own purposes.

These differences are indeed striking. Yet the physical and psychological experiences of their childhoods show remarkable similarities.

The Kaiser's Father, Friedrich III

Friedrich III (1831–88) was the son of the first Hohenzollern German Emperor (Wilhelm I) and the father of the last (Wilhelm II).

'Fritz,' as he was called by the family, was a gentle and well-meaning man of imposing physical appearance. Strikingly handsome with a full beard of burnished gold, he was tall, powerfully built, and carried himself regally. He rode among other princes of Europe in the great procession to Westminster Abbey, on the occasion of Queen Victoria's Golden Jubilee in 1887, and was the star of the show. A heroic figure on his magnificent, prancing chestnut steed, clad in white uniform with gleaming silver cuirass, helmet topped by a spread eagle, and his golden beard shining in the afternoon sun, he drew sustained cheers from English crowds. The London press vied in their accolades, calling him 'a new Charlemagne,' 'Siegfried,' and 'Barbarossa.'[2] As we shall see, he preferred Barbarossa.

Friedrich was raised in the proud tradition of the Prussian army, and he did honour to that tradition by serving impressively in the smashing victories over Denmark (1864), Austria (1866), and France (1870–71) that forged German unity on the anvil of war. Although no military genius, he was an effective field commander who was respected by his troops and long remembered for improving their rations and visiting the wounded in field hospitals.

A general of the old school, who watched Fritz commanding troops at the battle of Wörth against Austria, wrote that the young Crown prince had become the 'idol (*Abgott*) of his army.' A British military attaché, Sir Beacham Walker, who had also seen him in action paid equally high tribute: 'In battle his poise was unshakable; in victory he was consistently humane. What more can I say about the most noble man my eyes have ever seen?'[3] A British historian agreed, calling Friedrich Wilhelm quite simply 'a knight *sans peur et sans reproche.*'[4]

Fritz was not only a military hero; German liberals adopted him as their champion. When he succeeded his reactionary, aged father to the Imperial throne in 1888, reformers dreamed that he and his brilliant English wife would usher in a brave new world of enlightened constitutional government.

Prince Albert was much impressed with the handsome Prussian prince and encouraged him to court and marry his favourite daughter, Victoria, the Princess Royal. Together the three dreamed that one day the Prince would become the enlightened ruler of a united, liberal, and thoroughly Christian German Empire. In January 1857 Friedrich Wilhelm and Victoria were married. After a brief honeymoon in Windsor Castle, they embarked for Prussia in a snowstorm on 2 February. Fritz was 26; his bride, 17.

When he ascended the throne some thirty years later, in 1888, the new Kaiser dropped the Wilhelm from his name and styled himself Friedrich III. He liked to think of himself as a successor of two previous Friedrichs illustrious in German history. First, the name recalled Friedrich II, 'the great,' the warrior king of Prussia and the first enlightened monarch; he too had been called 'Fritz.' The name also recalled a similarly red-bearded Kaiser named Friedrich: Friedrich

Barbarossa, Holy Roman Emperor of the German Nation. According to German rómantic legend, Barbarossa had not died in 1190 while on the Third Crusade, but was still alive, sleeping in a cave in the Kyffhäuser Highlands, his beard growing around a huge round marble (oak, in some versions) table. When it had completed the circle, Friedrich Barbarossa would arise, shake the sleep of centuries from his eyes and lead a united Germany into a glorious future.

The new Friedrich fancied himself as a reincarnation of Barbarossa. In the first days of his reign he copied the following verse in his diary:

To the New Kaiser

> Kaiser Friedrich Barbarossa,
> Our Great and Noble Kaiser,
> Once again he has arisen
> From the depth of the Kyffhäuser.[5]

It was not to be. At his accession Friedrich III was already dying of cancer. The reign of the 'Tragic Emperor' would last exactly ninety-nine days. Even if he had not been stricken, it is doubtful that he possessed the mental acumen, political ambition, and personal confidence to put through a program of constitutional change that would have transformed Germany from an authoritarian state into a parliamentary democracy.[6]

Friedrich's prospects for successful leadership of Germany were also diminished by his marriage. For brilliantly gifted as Victoria certainly was, she was no political asset. Germans believed that their uncomplicated and well-meaning ruler was completely under the thumb of his foreign wife. Indeed, instead of calling their new Kaiser '*Friedrich der Dritte*' (the Third), Berliners dubbed him '*Friedrich der Britte*' (the Briton).[7] Many Germans were convinced that this woman wanted to impose some sort of English government on their new Fatherland. They were not entirely mistaken.

Victoria knew what the Germans thought of her and was undeterred. Yes, she did influence her husband, and she would continue to do so. Yes, she did plan to transform Germany, for she knew what was best for the Germans. To her mother, Queen Victoria, she wrote,

It is very disagreeable to me to be thought meddling and intriguing ... [But] I am very ambitious for the country and for Fritz and the children and so I am determined to brave all the [criticism] ...

I know what a responsibility I take on myself in taking advantage of my husband's reliance on my judgement ... and in giving my advice as positively as I can ...

I shall go on with might and main trying to assist Fritz in pursuing the only road I consider right and safe.[8]

Fritz recognized his wife's superior qualities and confessed his dependence upon her. Even though he called her comfortably 'my little pet' and 'my little wifey' (*mein liebes Frauchen*), he was rather intimidated by Victoria. After telling her how well suited they were for each other he wrote, 'Nevertheless, I am sometimes afraid [because] I do not know how such a gifted, excellent being like my little pet could put up with such an inferior being as her little hubby (*Männeken*).'[9]

Friedrich III did possess many sterling qualities, however inadequate he may have been as a political leader. His letters and diaries reveal an honest, loving, and upright person, a man in whom there was no guile. His own ideals and values were set forth clearly in his diary, where he expressed his hopes and prayers for his son on the lad's birthday. Crown Prince Friedrich was writing in army headquarters in Versailles on 27 January 1871, just after the glorious Prussian victory over France and the triumphant proclamation of his father as Wilhelm I, Emperor of a united Germany. On that great day, Fritz thought about his father's advancing years (he was already 74) and the successions to come – his own and, particularly, that of his young son and future Emperor. (Interestingly, the father made a mistake about his son's age.)

Headquarters, Versailles, 27 January [1871]

Today is Wilhelm's 13th birthday [actually his 12th]. May he grow up a good, upright, true and trusty man. One who delights in all that is good & beautiful, a thorough German who will one day learn to advance further in the paths laid down by his grandfather & father for the good governance of our noble Fatherland, working without fear or favour for the true good of his country.

Thank God there is between us, his parents, a simple, natural, cordial relation, to preserve which is our constant endeavour, that he may always look upon us as his true, his best friends. It is truly a disquieting thought to realize how many hopes are even now set on this boy's head and how great a responsibility to the Fatherland we have to bear in the conduct of his education, while outside considerations of family & rank, court life in Berlin and many other things make his upbringing so much harder.

God grant we may guard him suitably against whatever is base, petty, trivial and by good guidance train him for the difficult office he is to fill![10]

The little boy's earliest memories of his father were quite vague because the Crown prince was away on army duty so much of the time, in contrast to his mother's constant supervision of his daily life. What he did remember about his father, however, was pleasant. 'My father's goodness of heart amounted to tenderness,' Wilhelm later recalled. 'He had the most genuine sympathy with any and every form of suffering.'[11]

Evidence from his infancy supports the Kaiser's memory of a warm relationship with his father. Overjoyed at his son's birth, Fritz wrote to his mother-in-law, Queen Victoria, on 12 March 1859, 'I cannot recount in words what joy I experience in this little one.'[12]

Wilhelm's mother noted the strong attraction between father and his little son with twinges of jealousy, writing to her mother, 'Fritz adores the child and certainly the baby returns the affection for he is never happy til [sic] Fritz has got him on his arm and he never wishes to come to me[13] ... Baby ... is particularly fond of Fritz – laughs and gurgles at him at the other end of the room ... I do not think he cares much about me.'[14]

The Kaiser also remembered happy times with his father during his boyhood years. Fritz tried to make up for his many absences from his son by taking him on long walks. Together they visited castles and churches and looked at picture books of military history. The seven-year-old swelled with pride when he saw his father being hailed as conquering hero after the victory over Austria in 1866, and again, five years later, at the mammoth victory parade in Berlin in 1871 celebrating the victory over France and the proclamation of the Second Reich.[15]

Even while still admiring his father as a military hero, young Wilhelm became increasingly alienated from him. He considered his father's acquiescence to his mother as a sign of weakness, and he had nothing but disdain for the political ideas of both parents. Indeed 'Willy,' as his parents called him, was quite capable of displaying lively contempt for his father. Once when Friedrich reprimanded his 21-year-old son for failing to inquire about his ailing mother's health, Wilhelm turned furiously on his father and imperiously declared that he did not want to hear such language from him again. Friedrich retreated in wounded silence. An English observer of this embarrassing scene commented that both parents were deeply hurt by the incident: 'The father at the lack of respect, the mother at the lack of love.'[16]

Wilhelm subsequently told Bismarck's son, who dutifully reported it to the Iron Chancellor, that he actually got on fairly well with his 'faint-hearted' father and could have easily dominated him, had he not had to contend with 'that vicious shrew' (jene Hetzerin), his mother.[17]

The Kaiser's Mother, Victoria

Wilhelm's mother, the Princess Royal of England and future 'Empress Frederick' of Germany, was the eldest daughter of Queen Victoria and Prince Albert.

By all accounts, 'Vicky,' as she was called within the family circle, was a complex woman of remarkable talent and a wide range of interests. She was a gifted linguist, fluent in four languages, and an accomplished painter and sculptor. Her reading included treatises on constitutional law and political theory and monographs on physics and biology. She was a skilled landscape gardener and had detailed knowledge of plants and soils. Vicky must have been the only member of European royalty to have read carefully the first edition of *Das Kapital.* She shocked contemporaries by her 'progressive ideas,' which included serving as wet-nurse to a lady in her court.[18]

Vicky could be absolutely charming. The Pope, who granted her a private audience in November 1862, later acknowledged that in the course of his long life he 'had never been more favourably impressed by anyone.'[19] A member of the British embassy in Berlin, who sat next to the princess at a dinner party, wrote, '[I] fell immediately under the charm of one of the most cultivated women I have ever met.'[20] He noted, however, her disconcerting habit of 'always being right,' and he was inclined to endorse Lord Granville's observation that she was 'very clever but not wise.' Victoria felt compelled to educate everybody, and her conversations tended to be monologues. A veteran Berlin correspondent of the *New York Tribune,* for example, was first diverted and then annoyed during a social evening when the princess lectured him for more than an hour on conditions in America, a country she had never visited. The journalist concluded that Princess Victoria was a gifted young lady who 'knew what was best for those about her.' For instance, she announced to the gathering that Germany must become completely transformed into a true parliamentary democracy and that only English upholsterers could be trusted to carry out her plans for refurbishing Frederick the Great's 'New Palace' near Potsdam.[21]

Always pronounced with assurance, Vicky's judgments were sometimes penetrating, sometimes preposterous. She insisted, for example, that 'there is not a more democratic institution in the world' than the Prussian army.[22] She seemed to go out of her way to alienate the very people she should have tried to cultivate, as when she informed Bismarck that two or three Birmingham businessmen owned more silver plate than all his Prussian nobility. Bismarck did not forget that remark.

Honest to a fault and incapable of duplicity herself, Vicky was outraged to find it in others. Hers was a direct and frontal attack on all issues. She could suffer neither fools nor opposition: 'I enjoy a pitched battle exceedingly,'[23] she wrote on one occasion, and on another, 'I am perpetually in a pugilistic frame of mind ... knocking somebody down would be an intense relief, and so *very* good for those who would be knocked down.'[24]

She put up a confident and assertive front, but her private letters reveal a terribly homesick and uncertain girl who was confronted by problems that would have staggered a wiser and more experienced person. When only a teenager, Vicky had left the comfort and security of the English court to marry and live in the cold and hostile atmosphere of Potsdam-Berlin. Victoria's defence against hostility was disdain. Nothing in Berlin, including the food and the weather, was as good, she often remarked, as in England. Her distaste for her new countrymen was reciprocated. Prussians called her 'that Englishwoman' and spat out the word as an epithet. The bride of the future King of Prussia and German Emperor, she would soon give birth, in lonely agony, to his heir, the future Kaiser Wilhelm II. The weight of her responsibilities was further increased by her intense conviction that she must raise her son Wilhelm to become the ideal progressive ruler, a paragon of princes who would fulfil the vaulting aspirations of her father, Prince Albert, the most powerful formative influence on her young life.

Albert, Prince Consort to Queen Victoria, was a man of extraordinary talents and wide-ranging interests. He really did understand the Schleswig-Holstein Question.[25] He composed music and won Mendelssohn's praise as an organist. He planned the details and administered the logistical and organizational morass of the Great Exhibition of 1851. He mastered metallurgy and built an operative toy cannon for the little battlefield he laid out for his children at Osborne House on the Isle of Wight. He was a serious collector of art, an expert cabinet-maker, and graceful dancer. His contributions to the political development of his adopted land were inestimable, and he probably did as much as any other person in the nineteenth century to guide England in the direction of parliamentary democracy. As Charles Greville concluded, 'The Queen is not clever, and everything is done by the Prince who is in all intents and purposes King ... His knowledge and information are astonishing, and there is not a department of Government regarding all the details of management of which he is not better informed and more capable than the Minister at the head of it.'[26]

For all his gifts and accomplishments, however, Prince Albert was a 'curiously ungracious personality,'[27] who could be insensitive and cruel. He flogged and publicly humiliated his son Edward. He found females 'unavoidable inconveniences' and scoffed at their 'pretensions.' Women were required to rise whenever he entered a room. Old counsellors were obliged to stand throughout lengthy consultations. He was stingy: guests were restricted to two candles in their bedrooms and expected to provide their own matches, and the newly installed water-closets were supplied with neatly cut squares of newspapers. When talking, Albert never looked a person in the eye. His own mother acknowledged that he was 'contemptuous of mankind,'[28] and his elephantine humour tended towards *Schadenfreude*.[29]

Yet he was respected. One sophisticated and rather cynical commentator on

300 Kaiser and Führer

the personalities of the court said that he had known many people and much of the world but never had he seen 'so pure a character as the Prince.'[30] Albert, be it noted, was one of those rare individuals who *was* a hero to his valet. The man who had served him day in and day out for many years declared that Albert was 'the best man I ever met in my life.'[31]

Certainly Vicky, his *Lieblingskind*, saw him that way. The relationship between father and daughter was so intimate that a careful student of the family thought it was 'not quite natural.'[32] In trying to reconstruct Vicky's feelings for her father, one hesitates merely to say that Albert was her 'beloved father' or that she 'idealized him.' These commonplace expressions do not convey the intensity of her idealization and devotion. One of Princess Victoria's closest friends believed that 'the passionate love she bore the Prince Consort had been the most powerful feeling that she was ever to know in her life. It surpassed even the deep affection she had for her husband.'[33] Queen Victoria noted the intensity of the love and said frankly that she would not be completely unhappy when Vicky left for Prussia to live with her own husband.[34]

The thought of parting from her father to take up life with Fritz was a mixed joy. Certainly she loved her handsome young husband, but, she wrote, 'I think it will kill me to leave dear Papa.'[35] During the honeymoon her father was constantly on her mind. 'Dearest Papa,' one letter reads, 'I *must* write to you on this first day of my married life and tell you from my heart how happy I am and how thankful to Heaven and to you ... Believe that there are not many hearts which [throb? the word is unclear] with the deep, tender and devoted affection like that of your dutiful daughter Victoria.'[36]

From the honeymoon yacht she wrote her father, 'The Pain of parting from you yesterday was greater than I can describe. I thought my heart was going to break when you shut the cabin door and were gone ... I miss you so dreadfully, dear Papa, more than I can say.' She assured him that next to her nuptial bed, 'your dear picture stood near me all night.'[37] On Christmas Day 1858 Vicky wrote a twelve-page love letter to her father that did not once mention her husband. A portion follows:

Dearest Papa,

This is my first Xmas spent away from you ... I will not describe all that I think and feel it wd. take too much room and time. I will only say my heart yearns after you dearest, dearest Papa and how constantly I think of you ...

> Good-bye dearest, beloved Papa
> ever your most dutiful, and afte.
> daughter
> Victoria[38]

Vicky had trouble distinguishing between her love for her father and her love for her husband, regarding the two feelings in competition with each other – feelings so intense they suggest incestuous passion for her father. By loving Fritz she felt unfaithful to Albert. Two years after her marriage she actually apologized to her father for being so happily married to her husband: 'I ... trust you will not be angry and think it ungrateful if I say that they have been the happiest years of my life and that I do not think one knows what real happiness is before marriage. You can not take it ill as I have only inherited this feeling from Mama and am only saying what I am sure she says a hundred times to you.'[39]

Prince Albert's death the following year was a blow from which Vicky never recovered. Throughout the rest of her life she kept dreaming and thinking of him. We can give only a very small sampling of her efforts to describe the extent of her loss. The first letter written after hearing of her father's sudden death is smeared by tears:

Berlin, December 16, 1861

My beloved Mama!
    Oh that I live to write to you on such an occasion. *Why has the Earth not swallowed me up* ... Why do I not die and go to him?[40]

The same day she wrote a seventeen-page letter, edged in black, to her favourite brother: 'Oh Bertie, we have lost *all* we have ... Papa was my idol. I looked up to him as ... the most perfect of human beings, to the one I reverenced most on earth.'[41] After her father's death Victoria dreamed of him 'almost every night.'[42] Early in January 1862 she wrote a thirty-page letter (albeit with wide margins) thanking her mother for sending her the casting of her father's dead hands, which she had requested and which she personally would carve in marble: 'The Casts of the dear precious hands arrived the day before yesterday – it was a *dread moment* when I first saw them. I thought my heart would break. I felt quite faint! They were the one thing that brought home to me the dreadful reality – those *dear hands*. I was so happy to kiss, so happy to hold ... Oh how dreadful to see them only in the cold plaster and to think I shall never kiss them again. It was an agony I cannot describe ... Oh beloved Papa, *how* I do love him!'[43] She made her husband promise to have her buried wearing a locket of her father's hair.[44]

Many years later, on the anniversary of her own wedding and long widowed by the death of Fritz, she did not think back to her husband and their wedding day but to her father and her love for him. Vicky wrote to her daughter Sophie:

'Tomorrow the great day. I feel very low and sad and miss Papa cruelly ... One sweet moment I can look back on! But never can I forget ... the dreadful moment of saying good-bye to my adored father ... How I worshipped him!'[45]

Princess Victoria's letters over the years support her friend's impression that Fritz could never replace her father as the man closest to her heart.

Vicky as Her Father's Delegate

Prince Albert treated his gifted and adoring daughter as an extension of himself. Both had quick, retentive minds and more than a little intellectual arrogance. They shared common interests in art, music, and science. They laughed at the same jokes, and they wrote in remarkably similar hand – a clear and controlled script that makes their biographers grateful (as Queen Victoria's scrawl has made them despair).

Above all, Albert saw his daughter as his junior partner in a magnificent enterprise. Together they would bring a new, golden era to the entire world – at least to the two countries that would dominate the world at the close of the nineteenth century: liberal England with her enlightened empire, and a powerful, liberalized Prussia which would, Albert was convinced, form the nucleus for a unified Germany. Albert had encouraged his daughter's marriage to the man who one day would become the German Emperor. He recognized that Fritz was neither especially bright nor politically ambitious. So much the better. Vicky possessed the brains and the ambition. She would mould the future Emperor's mind and shape his political thinking. She would be for Fritz what he, Prince Albert, was for Queen Victoria: mentor, goad, and guide – the *de facto* ruler of a mighty empire.

Vicky dedicated herself to what she called 'my mission in life': to carry out the will of her father. It was to her a 'sacred trust,' like carrying out the will of God. Indeed, in her mind the two deities were sometimes interchangeable. 'In doing Papa's will,' she wrote to her mother in 1861, 'I shall be doing God's will.'[46] After Vicky arrived in Berlin, her first letters dated 10–13 February 1858 sound the refrain that would be repeated until her father's untimely death: 'If you knew dear Papa *how much* I have been thinking of you lately – of you more than anybody and how dreadfully I miss you to whom I should like to come for advice ... and in fact for everything ... till now I have only been able to prove my deep love and gratitude in words, and now I am glad to have an opportunity of doing so by deeds.'[47]

Like virtually every letter Victoria wrote to her father, this one was signed 'your dutiful daughter.' Dutiful was usually underlined. This extraordinary dependence on her father's advice and approval was stated succinctly in a letter to her mother on 20 August 1861: 'Really there is not a thing I hear or see or do that my first thought is not "what would dear Papa say, what would he think"!'[48]

When she became pregnant, father and daughter were overjoyed. 'The dream of my life,' Victoria later wrote, 'was to have a son who should be something of what our beloved Papa was, a real grandson of his in soul and intellect.'[49] After the heir was born, Victoria's first letter was to Albert. Weakened by the ordeal of her delivery, she instructed a lady-in-waiting to write, 'I am to say that ... the Princess is beyond measure happy and that she only hopes that *her son may grow up to be like her beloved Papa.*'[50]

Two years later, in December 1861 when her father suddenly died, the bottom dropped out of Vicky's young life. How, she asked in tortured anguish, was she to fulfil her father's mission without his guidance? 'The unerring judgement on which I built with so much security and so much confidence for now and the future is gone! Where shall I look for advice? I am only 21 ... I try to think only what he wd. want us to think and to do and say and I shall do so all my life.'[51]

If anything, Albert's death served to increase his daughter's determination to carry out his political plans for Germany, for she found that renewed dedication was the only way she could hold her life together and give it meaning.

The Kaiser's Infancy: His Mother's Delegate

Prince Albert's death shifted a heavy burden onto the little shoulders of the infant Wilhelm, for Princess Victoria saw her son as the delegate who was commissioned to fulfil her father's lofty expectations: This child would one day be the Emperor of a united Germany, the champion of liberalism, the crusader for Christian virtue, and the saviour of Europe. She phrased her expectations in exactly the language Prince Albert had used: 'I hope to instil all that is most Christian therefore most liberal into his mind ... I have a passionate wish to see the ideal of a free and truly cultivated state become a reality ... One must have a cause to which to devote oneself and for which to live.'[52]

Almost every day of his young life Wilhelm was reminded of his obligation to become like his sainted grandfather. His mother kept telling him what a perfect man his grandfather had been. His maternal grandmother sounded the same refrain. Queen Victoria sent him portraits and mementos of the man whose garishly tinted photograph would, for the rest of her long life, lie beside her on his pillow in their double bed in Osborne House. 'Little Willy' responded by writing dutiful letters to 'my darling Beloved Grandmama' thanking her profusely for all the reminders and, most recently, for the picture of 'dearest Grandpapa.' But between the lines of the beautifully written script we find hints that the boy was getting a little fed up with having Grandfather Albert thrown at him 'almost every day.' A letter of 2 September 1874 also shows that he was becoming adept at winging it: 'The splendid portrait of my beloved Grandpapa will never leave my room as long as I live. I know you did not send it only as a valuable present ... you want me to bear in mind that I may follow as much as I can the example set ... I will use my utmost endeavours and do my best worthy [sic] ... I hear him held up as a bright example almost every day by Papa as well as Mama.'[53]

It seems likely that these constant reminders as a boy that he was the special instrument for fulfilling Prince Albert's plans contributed to his notion as an adult that he was someone very special, the emissary of a Higher Power. An associate of his mature years tells us how often the Kaiser expressed his conviction that he was 'the chosen instrument of God for whom Heaven had special designs ... as an instrument of God he was directly inspired by Him and thus could make no mistake ... God Himself would surely see to it that His instrument should fulfil its appointed task.'[54]

As he grew older Wilhelm rebelled against his mother. A part of the conflict stemmed from Vicky's conviction that her son was subverting the lofty political and moral principles set forth by her 'godlike' father. In her eyes, when Wilhelm betrayed that trust, he was also betraying his mother, for he was making it impossible for her to fulfil her sacred oath that through her son she would carry out the will of her peerless father. As she wrote in bitter letters to her mother, Queen Victoria,

The dream of my life was to have a son who should be something of what our beloved Papa was ... a real grandson of his soul and intellect ... William is, alas, completely blind ... the whole order of his ideas is radically wrong. Oh dear, to think that Fritz's son and dear Papa's grandson should ... misconceive the principles on which alone it is possible to get on ... His dear father and I are in no way responsible for his extraordinary ideas. We were for [Papa's] ideas of constitutional liberty, for quiet, steady progress ... for individualism and the development of culture not for Imperialism, Caesarism, State Socialism, etc.[55]

During her pregnancy Vicky had had a premonition that all would not go well with the delivery. She was right. Wilhelm's birth was a horrendous experience for both mother and son. Labour had lasted from midnight 26 January 1859 until 2:45 on the afternoon of 27 January, ten hours after the womb waters had broken. Chloroform was administered for 'several hours' to relieve Vicky's excruciating pain. The uterus was surgically extended to permit a breech delivery (*Steissgeburt*). To preserve royal decorum, the obstetrician was obliged to manoeuvre underneath the princess's voluminous flannel nightgown. The baby appeared to be dead at birth, but energetic slapping and dousing in ice water brought him around. It was later discovered that during the struggle the infant had suffered irreparable nerve and muscular damage to his left arm.[56]

The physical and psychological consequences of history's most famous 'withered' arm have been discussed at excessive length by the Kaiser's biographers, who have tended to overdo its importance. Many political leaders have lived with physical handicaps that did not impede their careers. Indeed, some leaders have gained strength from physical and emotional handicaps by refusing to buckle under: one thinks of Winston Churchill's severe childhood eczema and speech handicap or of Franklin Roosevelt's crippling polio. Far more important than the misshapen arm itself was Wilhelm's mother's attitude towards it, which she relentlessly communicated to her son. To her, the deformed arm was repugnant and unacceptable.

Victoria tended to judge people by their physical appearance. She described the daughter of a German nobleman as 'very tall but *so ugly*!!!' (the adjective is underlined three times, and there are three exclamation marks). She noted that another girl was 'nicely brought up but [has] an ugly figure.' The physical appearance of her second son, Henry, distressed her greatly. Indeed, the only comment she made in a letter about the boy on his tenth birthday was that 'his poor ugly face will look worse than ever – and he has grown if possible much plainer still since last year.' She also worried about her teenaged daughter Charlotte's failure to develop breasts, expressing her concern in appropriate Victorian euphemisms: 'She has not an atom of a figure or waist and shows no sign of her health beginning to change ... [she] is in everything ... like a child of ten!'[57]

The thought that her son, whom she had delegated to fulfil her own 'mission in life,' was physically deformed was something Victoria could not tolerate. Her son must be worthy of her father and something must be done to make him so. She would see to it that the arm was cured – that he was made as physically attractive as Papa, 'that godlike man.'

In dozens of letters to her father and mother Vicky documents her worry and repulsion over that 'wretched,' 'hateful' arm. What follows is a sampling: 'He can move all his fingers, clench his hand and open it and extend his fingers, but very feebly, the hand itself is about half the size of the other and that is what frightens me. Altogether I cannot tell you how it *worries me*. I am ready to cry whenever I think of it ... [when] I see the other children clapping their hands and then see his poor little arm hanging uselessly by his side ... it distresses me so much ...'[58] The idea of his remaining a cripple haunts me.'[59] ... It continues to be a great grief.'[60]

Ever since he was a baby, Wilhelm's conscientious mother had tried everything she could think of to cure his infirmity. She personally supervised the treatments, many of them frustrating and painful, and watched anxiously over him for signs of improvement.

When Willy was six months old, his good arm was strapped to his body in an effort to force him to use the deformed arm. Vicky tried to assure her mother (and herself) that 'he doesn't seem to mind in the least ... [he is] as happy and content as possible. [Dr] Wegener pricks his hand with a pin and pinches his arm to see whether he feels it. I think he feels just a little but not much.'[61]

At seven months Willy was given *'animalische Bäder,'* in which the child's arm was held in the warm entrails of freshly killed rabbits in the hope that their warmth would stimulate circulation. Vicky reported that the baby greatly enjoyed the sensation, but 'please do not tell the brothers and sisters.'[62]

When Wilhelm was two years old, his physical problems were exacerbated by acute inflammation in one of his eyes, probably caused by a corneal ulcer. The pain was excruciating and for several weeks the little boy was kept in a darkened room with the windows shut. The weather that May and early June 1861 was stiflingly hot and humid.[63]

Mother and infant son were having a difficult time coping with the 'terrible twos.' Child psychologists tell us that this is probably the most critical year of a child's development, for this is the time when infants undergo the daunting task of establishing their own individuality, their sense of selfhood. Young children are riven by conflicting needs. They still want their mother's love and approval, but they are also taking the first steps towards 'identity formation' and asserting their independence. During this formative period, as the psychologist Margaret Mahler has written, it is very important for infants to feel that their mother *accepts them as they are.* If a child develops the feeling that his mother thinks there is something wrong with him, that he is not acceptable as he is, there may develop a 'serious deficit in self-esteem' that may cause trouble in the future.[64]

Instead of assuring her son that he was acceptable, Wilhelm's mother made it clear that there was something very wrong with him. His reactions were often extreme. Victoria reported to her mother that Willy was becoming impossible to handle. He was 'very violent.'[65] He was 'very wild and unmanageable.'[66] Another letter admits that Willy was driving his mother to distraction and making her cross: 'He is dreadfully difficult to keep in order ... He has every imaginable trick which makes me quite hot before people. One is when he sees ladies standing, running up their gowns to get under them and another is spitting on the floor; when he goes driving he throws his caps, gloves and jacket out of the carriage ... Baby sister is my pet ... she is so gentle and hardly ever cries.'[67] It seems not to have occurred to Princess Victoria that when her son ran under the skirts of other women one of the things he may have been looking for was a new mother.

It was precisely during this critical period of his infancy, when Wilhelm was two years old, that Prince Albert died and his mother's world crashed down upon her. Victoria was inconsolable. She thought she would go mad with grief. She went into seclusion and withdrew almost completely from her infant son, who must have been bewildered and frightened by her loud lamentations and sudden neglect. Then she returned to him with renewed determination and redoubled effort. The death of her father made it all the more imperative that her son and heir be given the rigorous training necessary for him to fulfil the destiny she and her father had set for him. For that awesome task, Vicky needed help and advice.

As a conscientious young mother who was widely read in many areas, and who sought expert opinion on such matters as horticulture and animal husbandry, Vicky turned for advice to manuals on child care. The standard works on child raising at this time were written by the celebrated Daniel Moritz Schreber (1801–61), whose immensely influential books and pamphlets had swept the child-raising field and made his name a household word in Germany.[68] For three decades, from 1832 to 1861, new books and pamphlets poured from his pen. The titles are suggestive: *How to Attain Health, through Cold Water Methods*; *The Peculiarities of the Child's Organism*; *Harmful Body Positions and Habits of Children, Including a Statement of Counteracting Measures* – a book that seems particularly to have impressed Wilhelm's mother. One title, alone, *Aertzliche Zimmergymnastik* (Medical Indoor Gymnastics), had gone through twenty-six editions by 1899.

Schreber's theories were simple, his methods draconian. He gave detailed instructions because, as he said, he expected them to be applied 'with unyielding severity (*unnachsichtlicher Strenge*).' That was a favourite expression.[69] The main lesson he preached came through very clearly: the purpose of child training was to *master* the child. 'The most important condition,' he wrote in italics, '*is the unconditional obedience of the child (unbedingten Gehorsam des Kindes*).'[70] Disobedience and 'wilfulness' must be crushed. Parental control should be so complete that one piercing, admonishing look would be sufficient to bring the child to heel. The final goal is reached, said Schreber, when there exists 'a wonderful relationship where the child is nearly always ruled merely by parental glances.'[71]

Nail biting and thumb sucking were clear indications of moral depravity. Cold-water baths were, in Schreber's view, of inestimable value in inculcating discipline. They should be started when the infant was three months old for the purpose of physically toughening the child from its earliest days. Crying and whimpering were not to be tolerated and 'must be dealt with positively.' The infant should first be severely admonished. It is sometimes effective, he advised, to bang suddenly on the crib to startle the child into silence. If all this failed, he recommended 'intermittently repeated corporal admonishments. It is essential that this treatment be continued until its purpose is obtained.'[72] In his first year of life, the child must learn what Schreber called 'the art of renunciation.' The infant is placed in his mother's lap while she is eating candy or fruit; when the baby reaches for it, it is taken away. The child is to be fed three times a day at set intervals; he must eat everything set before him.[73]

Dr Schreber was obsessively concerned about correct posture. He developed mechanical straps and devices to hold children in the most upright possible position at all times: sitting, walking, or sleeping. Children must sit on both buttocks at the same time (*gleichzeitig*) and at rigorous attention. As an aid to posture, Schreber developed a widely used, if not popular, device called the *Schrebischer Geradehalter* which held the child in a rigid position (Illustration A). Hands must never rest obscenely in the child's lap.

Another harness held children flat on their backs while sleeping (Illustration B).

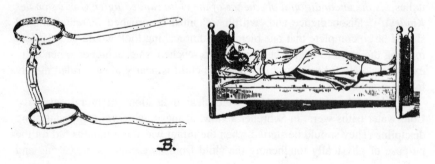

One device straightened the shoulders. Another, the 'head holder,' connected the child's hair by means of a clamp and leather strap to a button secured to his underwear at the base of his spine. If the child slouched forward, a tug of his hair jerked him back to the correct position (Illustration C).

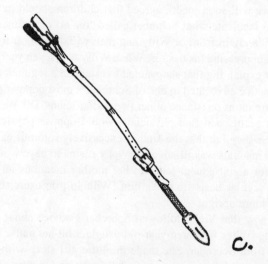

C.

Schreber was particularly worried about 'the destructive evil' of masturbation and displays of passion of any kind. From the very start of life, he warned darkly, 'the beginnings of passion must be curbed by rigorous discipline including corporal punishment at the earliest age ... because the ignoble parts of the child's crude nature must be weakened through great strictness.'[74] After being punished the child must be compelled 'to stretch out its hand to the executor of the punishment.' This, to ensure that the child harbours no feelings of 'spite and bitterness.'[75] Schreber also believed it important that children be reminded of their faults and the reasons for their punishments. Every household, he said, should have a blackboard to record by the day, week, and month a careful inventory of the child's misbehaviour which the family would evaluate at regular intervals.

Schreber practised what he preached on his own two sons, both of whom he named after himself. One, Daniel Gustav Schreber, committed suicide at the age of thirty-eight. The other, Daniel Paul Schreber, was made famous as the person diagnosed by Sigmund Freud in his early study of paranoia. He spent twenty-seven years of his life in asylums for the insane.

Kaiser Wilhelm II's childhood training corresponded with Schreber's recommendations in many particulars. The infant Wilhelm was given cold-water baths. Vicky, like Schreber, was excessively concerned with posture, and therefore Willy was required to undergo rigorous exercises to make him stand straight. A special harness, of the type Schreber prescribed, was devised to force his head into the 'correct' position. Princess Victoria made it a practice to ignore the crying of her infants. She and Wilhelm's tutor, a dedicated Schreberian (whom we will soon meet), agreed that children should never be praised. Vicky tried to inculcate what Schreber called 'the art of renunciation' by dangling fruit or candy in front of Willy and then withdrawing it to teach him the discipline of suppressing his desires. When Willy was seven years old she wrote to her mother explaining that she wanted to establish a regimen of 'home gymnastics,' a practice advocated in one of Schreber's most popular pamphlets. She ran into the strenuous resistance of her two pediatricians, Drs Wegener and Langenbeck.[76] It seems odd that physicians would oppose physical exercise for children unless they felt that the kind of excessively rigorous exertion set forth in Schreber's manuals was ill-advised. Vicky seems to have won at least a partial victory, for a subsequent letter to her mother mentions an army sergeant coming on a regular basis 'to make him [Wilhelm] do exercises to make him hold himself more upright.'

We also know that Vicky followed Schreber's advice about thumb sucking and nail biting. When her three-year-old daughter bit her nails, Vicky's remedy was straight from Schreber. She made the little girl sleep with her hands tied together and forced her to wear gloves during the day to cure her of this pernicious habit.[77] Princess Victoria's practice of supervising Willy's 'animal baths,' using the warm entrails of recently killed rabbits in an effort to stimulate his arm, also coincided with Dr Schreber's theory about the 'life-giving properties' that can be drawn from 'animal warmth.'[78]

In a letter to her mother dated 21 April 1863, Vicky drew a sketch of a Schreberian harness with straps and pulleys that was used to crank her four-year-old son's neck into a proper position. Although she hated to have her little boy undergo such treatment, she was convinced that she was acting in the child's best interest. Wilhelm simply must not appear to be deformed. The crooked neck must be straightened, and it might be possible to do so with a machine rather than by a disfiguring operation. She described the device, drew a picture of it, and emphasized how much she personally suffered when her son was strapped into it:

The machine consists of a belt round the waist to which is affixed an iron bar or rod which passes up the back to which a thing looking very much like a bridle of a horse is attached. The head is strapped into this and then turned as required with a screw which moves the iron ... so as to stretch the muscles of the right side of the neck; the object is to prevent his head from being drawn down to the right side ...

I cannot tell you what I suffered when I saw him in that machine the day before yesterday – it was all I could do to prevent myself from crying. To see one's child treated like one deformed – it is really very hard ... of course all that is necessary for his good and must be submitted to. We forbid anybody seeing him with it on. He is to wear it for an hour every day and towards the end of May, Langenbeck will decide whether or not to cut the neck ...

Of course we should be obliged that no one should *see* him with this machine on – neither servants nor brothers and sisters that it should not be talked about ... all this torments me very much.

It seems so cruel to torment the poor child, still it would be no kindness to save him inconvenience now at the expense of causing him much greater pain hereafter.[79]

The machine tormented Vicky as well as her little boy. She tried to reassure her mother (as well as herself) that 'William is very good about it as it does not hurt him.' But in the same letter she admitted that it is 'a great piece of work to make him wear it – as he flies into such violent passions when he does not wish to do a thing.'[80] A month later the boy was still wearing the contraption and still resenting it. His mother was sympathetic: 'Poor Willie is so tormented with all the machines and things that it makes him cross and difficult to manage – poor child really is sorely tried.'[81] Neither the harness nor the exercises could straighten his head. Two painful operations, cutting tendons in his neck, were finally successful.

Meanwhile, the arm remained a problem even though Vicky had been trying a new treatment since as early as 1860, when she had convinced herself that the newly discovered electrical currents ('galvanistic impulses') would stimulate the inert arm into vitality. Painful and problematical as the therapy might be, she was sure that it would work. Both of her pediatricians were opposed to the treatment, arguing that it was dangerous, since no one knew what effect electrical currents might have on the brain and nervous system. Over the physicians' objections and the screams of her child, she persisted undaunted in supervising the electric treatments. It was for his own good; she took full responsibility:

About the electricity I have no one to bear me out as Wegener is most possitive [sic] and said there are cases of grown-up people – men – patients of his who could not stand electricity being applied every day ... and that with a child he *could not* allow it every day. What am I to do? I feel so convinced that electricity is the only thing that does the child no harm.

I had a grand skirmish with Wegener this morning about the arm; he and Langenbeck will not hear of Willie's being electrified every day; *they consider it decidedly damaging* and say it will do more harm than good. All my arguments were not of the slightest use;

at last with a great deal of difficulty we made a compromise. Wegener promised that he would electrify every day for a fortnight and made me promise that if *he* thought it injured Willie's health I would have it stopped and only done once every two days. This is the only way I could make him do it at all.'[82]

We do not know the amount of electric current that was used in the treatments. It is possible that it was only a harmless charge used as a mild stimulant. There are two reasons, however, for thinking that the amount may have been considerably more than that: The pediatricians were opposed because they considered the treatments 'decidedly damaging.' Wilhelm himself – the person after all, who was subjected to the treatment – remembered them as excruciatingly painful and of no benefit.

As late as 26 November 1865, when Wilhelm was six, he was still getting 'electrical stimulations.' Apparently Vicky had enlisted an English physician named Clark as an ally to support her claims that 'galvanistic treatment' was beneficial. At any rate, in the Additional Manuscripts in the Royal Archives there is a letter from Dr Clark, presumably written at Victoria's request, urging Dr Wegener to allow Princess Victoria to continue the treatments.[83] Thus, it would seem that the boy underwent 'electrifications' for about six years, from 1860 to about 1866 – from the ages of one to seven.

As with the 'animal baths,' the neck-strengthening exercises, and the Schreberian harness, Wilhelm's mother had the best interests of her son in view. That much seems certain. It is also certain, however, that her son suffered physical pain from the treatments, resented them, and held his mother responsible. Decades later in Doorn, the exiled Kaiser expressed bitterness over the futility of the so-called 'treatments' he had endured for his withered arm. 'I was treated in all sorts of ways,' he told an admirer, 'the only result was that I was made to suffer great torture.'[84] In his memoirs he recalled the amateurish efforts to cure his arm and how they had no result, 'save excruciating pain.'[85] In 1939 he told John Wheeler-Bennett that the chief thing he remembered about his early childhood was that it was a time of suffering and pain.[86]

The animosity that Wilhelm felt as an adult for his mother became so intense that it could inspire a sudden outburst of hatred even in front of strangers. The Russian minister for foreign affairs, who had never previously met the Kaiser, recalled his first encounter which he found 'painful' and 'astonishing.' Wilhelm had drawn him aside during a reception and for more than an hour had unburdened himself about the miseries of his childhood. He whispered to the embarrassed Russian diplomat that his mother 'had never loved me' and that 'mutual estrangement between us [had] increased with every passing year.'[87]

Wilhelm's childhood hostility was later intensified by what he considered to be his mother's unforgivable negligence during his father's fatal illness, which lasted from the spring of 1887 to the spring of 1888. Wilhelm accused his mother of insisting on calling in a British doctor, Morell Mackenzie, who had failed to identify Friedrich's mortal illness as cancer of the throat and advised against an operation that, Wilhelm was convinced, might have saved his father's life.

The entire incident must be seen as a tragedy of errors and well-intentioned mistakes. It was not Vicky who took the initiative in summoning Dr Mackenzie. German specialists who had been impressed with Mackenzie's monograph on laryngology recommended that he be brought in.

German doctors had diagnosed cancer and advised an immediate operation. Dr Mackenzie insisted there was no evidence of cancer, hence no need for an operation. Wilhelm and the German doctors later failed to point out that Mackenzie had made his recommendation only after consulting with Rudolph Virchow, the most respected pathologist in Europe. Unaccountably, Virchow had assured Mackenzie that after taking biopsy specimens three times he could find no trace of cancer.[88] Thus, the German doctors who had based their opinion on surmise were proven correct, and Mackenzie, whose opinion was based on scientific analysis, turned out to be mistaken.[89]

Crown Princess Victoria rejoiced at the news that the British doctor brought her, for it confirmed what she wanted so desperately to believe: it was not cancer and 'that dear throat' did not need to be cut by German scalpels. Through the months that followed, while the cancer grew, Vicky kept insisting that Fritz was getting better all the time, that all he needed was to get away from the 'dreadful Berlin weather' which was adversely affecting the 'chronic catarrh' that made his voice so husky.[90]

Throughout the bitter controversy over the opposing diagnoses, Vicky supported Mackenzie against Wilhelm and the German doctors. These doctors, she said bitterly, had botched the delivery of her first-born son and crippled him for life. Never again, she wrote her mother, 'would I have a German doctor near me if I could help it.'[91] All Fritz needed was 'a change of air.' Consequently, she fought 'tooth and nail' to keep him in the milder climates of first the Isle of Wight and then of San Remo, Italy, through the autumn and winter months and into the spring of 1888, as Mackenzie kept assuring her that her husband would 'be better in a few months.'[92] Victoria and her husband would not leave Italy until summoned to Berlin by the death of Kaiser Wilhelm I on 9 March 1888.

Wilhelm was outraged by his mother's stubborn refusal to admit that his father had cancer and by her refusal to permit an operation which, he was absolutely convinced, would save his father's life.[93] Animosity between mother and son reached the point that Princess Victoria refused to drink a toast to her son on his birthday (27 January 1888). For his part, Wilhelm accused his mother of prolonging his father's suffering and endangering the very existence of the German Empire. He poured out his wrath in a letter to his closest friend: 'That our family escutcheon should be sullied and the Empire brought to the edge of disaster through an English princess who is my mother! That is the most frightful possible thing! Father is suffering horribly ... the poor man!'[94]

Throughout this time, vicious and irresponsible rumours were spread about the conduct of 'that English woman' during her husband's fatal illness. It was said, for instance, that she was leading a bohemian life in Italy and wanted Friedrich to die so that she could marry her lover. Victoria's gallant efforts to keep up a good front by smiling in the face of the tragedy that was ripping her apart was seen as the rankest hypocrisy. Baron Holstein, who helped spread scurrilous falsehoods, recorded in his diary in September 1887, 'She always despised her husband. She will greet his death as the moment of deliverance ... I cannot bear to see that everlasting smile on her face.'[95]

When Wilhelm II was proclaimed German Kaiser, upon the death of his father on 15 June 1888, his first official act was directed against his mother. He ordered a thorough search of the royal palace for 'state papers.' The new Kaiser himself, in the red dress uniform of the Leibgarde-Husaren with sabre in hand, stormed through his mother's residence and directed the search of his parents' private quarters. Soldiers with live ammunition were ordered to prevent Her Majesty and any 'state papers' from leaving the palace. Servants were not even allowed to wire Berlin for mourning crepe. When the Kaiserin Friedrich, as Victoria had been styled since the coronation of her husband, attempted to collect roses in her garden to place on her husband's bier, an officer of the guard ordered her back into the palace.[96] Many years later in Doorn the exiled Wilhelm defended his actions: 'The measures taken were severe, but necessary. The object of isolating the [*Neues*] *palais* was to prevent State or secret documents being conveyed to England by my mother ... that even those measures were insufficient is shown by the fact that important State papers did reach England and were published there to the detriment of the German Reich.'[97]

By 'important State papers' the ex-Kaiser was referring to his mother's private correspondence which, he suspected quite rightly, had mentioned him. (To Wilhelm, state papers were any that involved his person.) Vicky had managed to thwart her son. Shortly before her death in 1901, she summoned the British ambassador, Sir Frederick Ponsonby, to the palace and implored him to 'perform a great service.' He must smuggle her letters into England; above all, Wilhelm 'must not know of it.' Ponsonby ordered two huge crates packed with her letters, sealed, and sent to London as British diplomatic papers.[98] Thousands of these letters now reside in the Royal Archives, Windsor Castle.

Two of the Kaiser's closest associates during his later years remembered the continued animosity Wilhelm felt for his mother. Prince zu Eulenburg wrote that as long as he knew him he was aware that towards his mother 'the Kaiser felt a grievous hurt (*schweres Leid*); whether or not it was justified in actual fact or only existed in his fantasy ... he suffered from it.' Eulenburg tried repeatedly to soften the animosity, but never succeeded. 'There was only one sad moment of peace between them,' he wrote, 'when the poor Empress, wasted by ravages of cancer, died with her hands in those of her son.'[99]

Through all the years of his Dutch exile (1918–41), Wilhelm's aide-de-camp and confidant kept a detailed diary dutifully recording his master's conversations. In two volumes of memoirs there is recorded only one reference to his mother made by the Kaiser, and he did not initiate that one. Someone had asked if he planned to read the newly published volume of his mother's letters. He brusquely dismissed the idea, saying that they would probably disturb him too much.

It is easier to document the depth of Wilhelm's antagonism than to explain it. Surely the conflict between mother and son had many causes, and one would be ill-advised to seek a simple explanation. One reason for the rift may have been that mother and son were too much alike: Both were mentally agile, impulsive, quick to anger, stubborn, and dogmatic; both were convinced that their views on any issue were correct. Neither of them expressed opinions – they made pronouncements. Perhaps a British observer was right: 'Each of them resented in the other what was common to them both.'[100] But the very intensity of Wilhelm's antagonism suggests something deeper than adult rivalry, something firmly rooted in resentments reaching back into infancy. We need to return to Wilhelm's early childhood.

The physical pain he suffered must have made an important contribution. Heinz Kohut, Margaret Mahler, William Niederland, and other psychoanalysts have shown that infants do not think of pain as coming from within their own bodies. They believe that it comes from outside themselves, that it is inflicted upon them by others – most notably by their mothers. We know that Wilhelm's conscientious mother hovered over him, supervising every aspect of his training, and all the futile efforts to 'cure' his withered arm, boasting to her own mother: 'I watch over him myself, over every detail, even the minutest.'[101] Indeed she did. So much so that Queen Victoria, herself a conscientious mother, felt that her daughter's supervision of Willy was entirely too much of a good thing: 'I am sure you watch over your dear Boy with the greatest care,' she wrote, 'but I often think too great care. Too much constant watching leads to the very dangers hereafter which one wishes to avoid.'[102]

Little Willy could not help but associate his mother with the 'pain and torture' of his childhood. He knew it was his mother, and not the doctors, who insisted on continuing the painful and mysterious electrical 'stimulations,' and he deeply resented it. In addition to screaming and kicking the machine, he expressed his childish resentment in one searing question which he asked his mother over and over again: *When was she going to die so that he could get a new mother?* Vicky herself, with typical directness and with monumental naïveté, reports, 'Master Willy said to me this morning in French, "When I am grown up you will be dead. Is that not so?" Very civil was it not? He is continually occupied with when I shall die and who will be his Mama.'[103]

Princess Victoria never entirely gave up hope that Wilhelm's arm might improve, but even to her it became increasingly clear that it would never be normal and that her heir was deformed for life. He would never be able to fulfil her dream of having a son who was physically, intellectually, and morally worthy of her dear father. She persisted in making the invidious comparison. In 1865, when Wilhelm was six, she emphasized the contrast between her deformed and 'backward' son and dearest Papa who was 'perfect' in both mind and body.[104]

Meanwhile, when Willy was five years old, someone appeared who really did seem worthy of Prince Albert. In 1864 his little brother Sigismund, fondly called 'Siggy' (also 'Sigy' or 'Siggie'), was born. Victoria was ecstatic. Here was a son who was everything poor Willy was not. So beautiful, so intelligent, 'so like Papa.' Then tragedy struck. When Siggy was two years old he contracted 'brain fever' (meningitis). His young mother watched in helpless horror as her darling burned up with fever, went into convulsions, and died in her arms. Vicky collapsed and then withdrew in deepest mourning. She tried to express her loss in tear-stained letters to her mother:

... none know but God how I suffer. Oh *how* I loved that little thing from the 1st moment of its birth it was more to me than its brothers and sisters, it was so fair, so loving, so bright and merry. How proud I was of my little one ...

Oh to see it suffer so cruelly to see it die and hear its last piteous cry was an agony I cannot describe. It haunts me night and day.

The last few months my little Siggie had proven so *wonderfully* forward and intelligent and was so clever, *much* more than either of the others and I thought he was going to be like dear Papa.[105]

If Willy had harboured feelings of jealousy or the wishes of death that older brothers may feel for sibling rivals, he must have been profoundly shaken when such wishes were fulfilled and he experienced the consequences: the depth of his mother's sorrow, her withdrawal from him, and the eerie silence and gloom that hung like a pall over the household. His mother herself described the atmosphere: 'Little Sigie's loss has cast a gloom over this house and over my whole existence which will never wear off. "My dear, dear little boy," I keep on saying all day.'[106] Willy heard her repeating these words and knew that she was not referring to him.

On the anniversary of her father's death, Victoria took Wilhelm, aged seven, to the cemetery where Sigismund was buried. He watched as his mother prayed and wept over the little grave, and told him yet again about his 'dear, dear Grandfather's' death. The incident must have reinforced in his mind how much his mother associated his idealized grandfather with his dead little brother. Victoria describes the visit in a letter of 12 December 1866 which shows how vividly Siggy and Dearest Papa were joined in her mind. She thought of them existing 'side by side' (even though Prince Albert was actually buried in Windsor Park): 'These lines will reach [you] on the 14th – the 5th anniversary of the day which has left its burning mark forever ... Darling beloved Papa ... We shall pass the day at Potsdam beside our little grave for by the side of Darling Papa dwells the image of our little child. Through our tears we thank God that ... [the two] beloved beings are at rest.'[107]

Victoria took an interest in phrenology and believed that little Siggy's forehead had been very like the perfection of her father's noble brow: 'I do not believe that phrenology pushed to an extreme is to be relied on but I am convinced that the rudiments of it seldom go wrong and I find them continually confirmed. Not one of my children had so beautifully shaped a forehead as my Sigie's ... I had fondly hoped that child would have grown up a pattern likeness of dearest Papa and now my hopes are buried in his little grave.'[108]

Determined that Willy should never forget the perfection of his little brother, she composed poems extolling Siggie's virtues, poems that Wilhelm was required to commit to memory and recite before his father's military retinue. She also painted Sigismund in oil from memory, a portrait that still hangs in her former bedroom in Friedrichshof.[109] She had carved her father's likeness in marble; she now carved little Sigismund and displayed it in an unusual way, one that must have been particularly disturbing to Willy.

A decade after Siggy's death, an Englishwoman who was visiting Princess Victoria in the royal palace in Berlin recorded a remarkable experience. One evening at twilight, Vicky invited her to see a 'special' room in the palace and led her to the nursery. There, in a crib, was a curly-haired child, who held a rattle in his chubby little fist. 'That's my Siggie!' Vicky whispered. The distraught mother had carved the child in marble.[110] Wilhelm knew that this room had special meaning to his mother because of its contents and because it was preserved exactly as it had been the day Siggy died.[111]

Victoria thought of yet another way to honour Sigismund. When Wilhelm was fifteen, he was the featured attraction in an important religious ceremony that was also a state occasion. The heir to the Prussian throne was confirmed by the Established Church of which, one day, he would be the titular head. It was a big day for the adolescent. In the presence of Emperor Wilhelm I, his parents, church leaders, and other dignitaries, he made a personal statement of his religious faith. He then responded to difficult theological questions. His quick intelligence served him well, his responses were impressive, and the teenager was justifiably pleased with his performance. But he noticed that for this rather festive occasion his mother had chosen to wear black – reminding him once more she was still mourning for Sigismund, her *Lieblingssohn*.

Wilhelm noticed something else that was even more disturbing. As he knelt to take his first communion, he saw that the altar was covered with a heavy satin cloth embroidered with a large golden 'S.' It was the pall his mother had sewn many years before to cover his little brother's coffin. Vicky found this use of the pall quite appropriate for Wilhelm's confirmation. She wrote to her mother: 'The "pall" which once covered my darling Sigie's coffin ... covered the communion table. It was all of white satin with S and crosses of gold in the corners ... William behaved very well ... I thought of your absence and darling Papa, dear bright angel ... I was in black.'[112] The Kaiser later recalled that throughout his youth he had been required to go with his mother to kneel at the tomb of his little brother in the chapel of the Friedenskirche.[113]

Let us return to Wilhelm's early childhood. His sixth and seventh years had been particularly difficult for him. He had experienced the death of the paragonic little rival for his mother's attention, seen the paroxysms of her grief, and experienced her withdrawal from him. The time she spent in carving the statue of his little brother and in kneeling in prayer before it in the mysterious death room did little to diminish doubts about his mother's love for him. Then, at just this time of special emotional need, a new shock came. Vicky decided that he needed a different kind of nanny. Apparently feeling that the warm and motherly Englishwoman, Mrs Hobbes, was too soft and permissive, she replaced her with Fraülein Dobbeneck, a formidable and humourless martinette of Schreberian vigour. The Kaiser well remembered this 'Dokka' as a forbidding figure, 'a great gaunt dame of firm character.' Nor did he forget that 'her method by no means excluded the use of the palm.'[114]

Vicky fully supported the stern Prussian nurse, but felt that Willy and his younger brother Henry required even more systematic discipline, for problems with both boys were driving her to distraction. Neither of them was at all like her memory of the angelic Siggie. A worried letter of 10 December 1866 complains of Henry's stubbornness and emotional outbursts: 'I defy *anyone* to get the better of him, as he can keep it up for hours.'[115] With both boys she used Schreber's methods for attaining mastery over weeping children: 'I avoid them as much as possible ... the best way I find is to ignore [the crying] and take not the least notice of it.'[116]

At her wit's end, she took the advice of a friend, and when Willy was seven years old she hired as his tutor one Georg Hinzpeter who remained Wilhelm's mentor through his boyhood and into his adolescent years. Hinzpeter was a rigid, joyless Calvinist of firm principles and inflexible will who followed precisely Dr Schreber's methods of child-raising and education. This choice of tutor for the lonely and sensitive boy struck one of Vicky's friends as a 'great mistake ... He was the last man for his task.'[117]

The Kaiser's own opinion of Hinzpeter was ambivalent. On the one hand, he credited him with teaching the virtues of 'diligence and hard work'[118] – qualities one does not normally associate with Wilhelm von Hohenzollern. Until Hinzpeter's death in 1908, the Kaiser sought his old tutor's advice, even consulting him on the selection of new Imperial chancellors.[119] But he also remembered Hinzpeter as a forbidding person who had terrified him as a child and intensified his feelings of fear and abandonment.[120] His mother was delighted with the new tutor. She wrote in relief to her mother, 'I have no need [now] of acting the policeman.' She had found someone who would 'counter their [Wilhelm's and Henry's] defects better than I can and counter the damage done by impetuous persons, be they ever so well-meaning.'[121]

Hinzpeter himself gives a vivid illustration of how he overcame the young prince's inability to ride a horse. The boy had a very bad sense of balance, possibly because, in addition to his atrophied arm, he suffered chronic trouble with his inner ear. Wilhelm told Hinzpeter he could never learn to ride. Hinzpeter decided otherwise. This weakness, like all others, would be overcome with 'energy, discipline and ruthlessness.' Hinzpeter's iron will would prevail. Not only would the lad learn to ride; he would ride bareback and without saddle or stirrups. What followed were, in the Kaiser's memory, 'atrocious hours.' But let Hinzpeter describe how teacher mastered pupil. The process, which cost Hinzpeter, he said, 'unspeakable self-control to watch,' illustrates his method:

When the prince was eight and a half years old, a lackey still had to lead his pony by the rein, because his balance was so bad that his unsteadiness caused intolerable anxiety to himself and others. So long as this lasted, he could not learn to ride: it had to be overcome, no matter at what cost ... Therefore the tutor, using a moral authority over his pupil that now had become absolute, set the weeping prince on his horse, without stirrups and compelled him to go through the various paces.

He fell off continually, every time, despite his prayers and tears, he was lifted up and set upon its back again. After weeks of torture, the difficult task was accomplished: he had got his balance. These morning exercises ... were a nightmare to everyone: worse for the torturer than for the tortured. Such ... a weakness could, however, only be overcome by unusual energy and ruthlessness.[122]

It is not without interest that he thought in terms of 'the torturer and the tortured.'

In retrospect the Kaiser decided that the torment he had suffered under Hinzpeter's tutelage was not really his tutor's fault. He blamed his mother, telling an admirer that Hinzpeter was really a good fellow, 'The torments he inflicted on me, especially in this pony riding, must be attributed to my mother ... I was worried and afraid. When there was nobody near I wept.'[123]

Another childhood experience remained vivid in the Kaiser's memory. At the age of ten Willy was commissioned a lieutenant in the Second Pomeranian Regiment of the Imperial German army and decorated with the Order of the Black Eagle, one of Prussia's highest awards and the first of many medals of honour he would do nothing to earn. The commission would officially end Prince Wilhelm's childhood. He was now forbidden to play with his beloved toy soldiers or go to the Berlin Amusement Park or attend the Zirkus Renz.[124]

The high moment of his commissioning came when, wearing with glowing pride a proper officer's uniform, he marched in review before his grandfather, the King of Prussia and Supreme War Lord, whom he adored throughout his life. Willy thought he had done well, but his mother had dashed his boyish enthusiasm. As he reported to 'Dearest Grandmother,' Queen Victoria, in careful Spencerian script: 'I marched before the King. He told me that I marched well, but Mama said I did it very badly.'[125] Vicky thought that her son had done worse than that. She ridiculed his performance in a letter to her mother: 'Poor little Willie in his uniform looks like some unfortunate little monkey dressed up standing on the top of an organ.'[126] Wilhelm's adult defence against memories of these early attacks on his self-esteem took the form, as we have seen, of grandiose claims of omnipotence, usually made while wearing multi-medalled military uniforms.

During Wilhelm's adolescence, another rival for his parents' affection appeared, his younger brother Waldemar.[127] His mother and father both adored this handsome, charming, and intelligent little boy and saw in him everything they had hoped Willy might have been: 'a true grandson of beloved Papa.'

Again tragedy struck. When 'Waldy' was eleven years old, his horrified mother watched as this, 'the most promising of my boys,' died the slow strangulation death of diphtheria. He was buried in his mother's nightgown with his father's handkerchief over his handsome face. Vicky's anguished letters to her mother attempt to convey the depth of her grief, attest to her preference for Waldy over Wilhelm, and express her conviction that he, and not Wilhelm, would have been a worthy successor of her idealized father. On the day of his death, 27 March 1879, she wrote, 'My beloved darling, my *sweet* Waldy the dearest, nicest most promising of my boys *is gone* ... He had such a fine, straightforward, noble, honest, courageous nature, was so much more gifted than his brothers ... never gave me a moment's anxiety, so *true* and so sincere ... He was Papa's own grandson.'[128] Years later, in 1885, at the time of her open break with Wilhelm, Victoria recalled again how she had always preferred his little brothers Siggy and Waldy: 'Willy behaves so badly to us ... It nearly drives me mad! Of course his wife abets all he does ... I often sit down in my room and have a good cry. My 2 own pet boys are in their graves. How Waldy loved me and now he is gone!!'[129]

Victoria's mourning for her two *Lieblingskinder* was intensified because she associated them so closely with Prince Albert of sacred memory. She had seen them as his agents who might one day help fulfil her dreams for a better world. In their deaths she re-lived the terrible days she had suffered in the death of the person she had loved and revered 'more than any man on earth.' We are also reminded that the sorrow of a mourner involves sorrow for the self. Victoria felt the loss of her sons so intensely because their deaths diminished her own chances of fulfilling her personal mission of carrying out her dead father's mandate.

The deaths of his younger brothers had a very different effect on Wilhelm. He, like Adolf Hitler, was a survivor. In his studies of psychological reactions to death, Robert Jay Lifton has noted that the 'survival priority,' manifested by those who live while others are dying about them, forces the question, 'Why have I been selected to go on living?' The child may then develop the feeling that his life is somehow specially controlled by destiny and hence is not entirely his own. In young Wilhelm's case, as we shall see with young Adolf, the mother's fretful solicitude for him as her chosen agent and her compulsive concern for his health, would surely have reinforced his idea that he was a privileged and destined person.[130]

This picture of the relationship between young Wilhelm von Hohenzollern and his mother may help us understand aspects of his subsequent career. But who can say with any confidence exactly how childhood experiences shape future lives? When he was in his eighties, Leo Tolstoy said that the journey he had taken from the age of five to the present was not particularly interesting or difficult; but that the journey from his birth to the age of five had been incredibly complex. One of the few things we know about the first years of human life is the central role played by the mother, hence our concern with Princess Victoria.

By stressing the mistakes she made in raising her son, we may have portrayed Vicky in too harsh a light. Surely it should be said that she must have done something right, or Wilhelm would have been even less stable than he was. He certainly had good reason for feeling antagonistic towards his mother, but he must also have gained a measure of security in sensing her deep concern about his welfare. Emil Ludwig was mistaken when he wrote that Victoria turned away from her child in disgust and that 'instead of compassion, cherished in her heart a secret grudge against a misshapen son.'[131]

Far from neglecting her son and showing no compassion, she was conscientious and compassionate to a fault. She sought advice from her mother and from accepted authorities on child-raising; and she tried desperately to cure her little boy's arm, using everything from traditional compresses and 'animal baths' to the latest electrical impulses. Her unpublished letters, not available to Emil Ludwig, reveal neither secret grudges harboured against her son nor lack of compassion. On the contrary, they show constant, anguished concern for his welfare and sympathy for his suffering.[132]

Unlike most aristocratic mothers of her day, Vicky had wanted to breast-feed her baby; but her mother-in-law, Princess Augusta, was disgusted and furious at such an idea and ordered the baby given over to a wet-nurse.[133] We have also seen that Victoria was distressed at the way the neck harness and electric shocks tormented her child. When he underwent an operation to straighten his neck, she suffered for him and was 'terribly anxious.' When a second operation was needed, she was again 'anxious for him, but I see that it is necessary. The former operation having done so much good.'[134] She thanked her mother for writing tender letters to Willy, saying that because of his disability her child needed more love and compassion than other children.[135] Queen Victoria responded to her request and said that she doubted any child could be more loved than Willy – even admitting to her daughter with remarkable candour that 'I never cared for you half as much as you seem to about Baby.'[136]

It is true that Princess Victoria said some very harsh things about her son, particularly in later years, calling him 'stupid,' 'clumsy,' and 'loutish.' But not when he was a little boy. Typical of many letters are those of 10 December 1866 and 4 January 1867, which say in part, 'Willy is a dear, interesting and charming boy, clever, amusing and engaging. It is impossible not to spoil him a little ... Naturally he also has his faults, is inclined to be selfish, domineering and proud ... But he is really a companion to me.'[137]

She loved her son and worried constantly that he might not love her, repeatedly telling her mother that Willy much preferred his father.[138] When open conflict broke out between mother and son, Vicky tried to reassure herself that it was not serious, that the 'bond of love' between them was strong and growing. But she kept worrying about it.[139]

The painful treatments she administered or supervised were done out of concern for her son's welfare. The problem was that her little boy could not be expected to give credit to his mother for good intentions; all he knew was that she kept hurting him. It does not increase our understanding to conclude either that Wilhelm's mother was unintentionally cruel to him or that she was excessively compassionate. There is strong evidence to support both contentions. That point needs emphasis: to Willy his mother seemed to be *both* cruel and kind. The little boy received confusing emotional messages from his well-meaning mother. She gave hugs and kisses, then head-harnesses and electric shocks; solicitous attention, then neglect while she grieved so long and so demonstratively over the deaths of his younger brothers. Victoria was both conscientious and neglectful, and both to excess.

The contradictions the Kaiser experienced in childhood seem likely to have contributed to the conflicts and instability we have noted in his adult behaviour: his mercurial shifts in mood and sudden changes of policy that disturbed his friends, disconcerted his allies, and alarmed his foes. His childhood experience may have also contributed to a deeper conflict: between instability and rigidity, between rapid shifts of attitude and restless travelling, in conflict with his incapacity to change in any fundamental way. We recall his anxious cry, 'But don't you see, I can't change!!' We also recall his insistence on punctilious conformity to court etiquette and that one of his besetting problems as a ruler was his inability to adapt to changing political circumstances.

The contradictory signals Vicky gave to her son may also have had a bearing on Wilhelm's lifelong habit of play-acting. D.W. Winnicott, the late British analyst, noticed that his patients who had had mothers who were both 'good and bad in a tantalizingly irregular manner' tended to have children who were so muddled about themselves that they were unable, in Winnicott's term, to identify their 'true self.'[140] They often became little actors experimenting with different roles (playing the 'false self') in efforts to achieve momentary feelings of spurious identity. Yet confusion about their 'true self' remained, and they persisted in playing different roles throughout their lives.[141]

The prolonged pain young Willy suffered as a result of his mother's fruitless efforts to cure his crooked neck and atrophied arm was made more psychologically damaging by the childish notion that it was his own mother who had given him the useless arm and was to blame for all his anguish.[142] Moreover, his mother's attitude towards the arm was deeply distressing to him. She let it be known that it was repulsive to her. Yet the arm was a part of him. Did her revulsion at his arm include him?

Vicky's own emotional problems also affected Willy's development. Like other narcissistically impaired mothers, she was unable to respond adequately to her son's emotional needs because she was so preoccupied with her own. She treated Willy as an extension of herself and tried to use him as her instrument for fulfilling her own psychic needs and frustrated ambitions. Wilhelm's childhood problems were further complicated by Vicky's morbid attachment to his dead brothers, on whom she lavished the approval denied to him. She idealized Siggy and Waldy as 'perfect in body and mind' and the 'true heirs' of her revered father, claiming that if they had only lived, all her own ambitions would have been fulfilled.

Many years later, when he was an old man in Doorn, the ex-Kaiser told a visitor that as a child he had never been praised. Not by his mother nor his governess nor by his tutor. Not once. Whether that is literally true is of minor importance; Wilhelm believed it to be true. Throughout the rest of his life he felt an aching need for the approval and praise that he had been denied as a child.

In sum, Wilhelm's childhood experience did not bode well for a psychologically stable maturity.

The Führer's Childhood

I and the public know what all schoolchildren learn:
Those to whom evil is done, do evil in return.

W.H. Auden

Anyone who tries to reconstruct Adolf Hitler's childhood must contend with problems that the biographer of the young Kaiser is spared. For written evidence about Wilhelm's early years abounds. We have, for instance, literally thousands of his mother's letters,[143] as well as his father's diary and letters, affidavits from his pediatricians, his own memoirs, and accounts of interviews about his childhood that are revealing, sometimes to the point of embarrassment.

In contrast to the voluble and literate Victoria, Hitler's mother has left not one letter, not one statement written in her own hand. Indeed, whether this daughter of an impoverished Austrian farmer was even literate may be questioned.[144] Hitler's father left no diary, and as far as we know he wrote no personal letters – certainly none about his son.

The evidence we have for Hitler's early life consists of scattered bits of mosaic that must be assembled carefully, with many pieces still missing. Most of the evidence is secondhand, such as the records of interviews conducted by journalists, archivists, and members of the Gestapo in the 1930s[145] or by the American OSS during the Second World War.[146] These agencies conducted interviews with neighbours, friends, and relations who knew the Hitler family in the several villages of lower Austria where Adolf spent his childhood.

We also have Hitler's own memories of his early childhood as they come to us through comments he made to his secretaries, his entourage, or visitors. There is also the first chapter of *Mein Kampf.* These memoirs, however, point up a second difficulty: the evidence is not only sparse, it is suspect. Few prominent people have made such a determined effort to conceal their early life and to mislead their questioners. When German newspaper reporters in 1930 tried to get information about the family of the rising political phenomenon, Hitler cut them off, saying, 'These people will never find out who I am.'[147] He lied about his ancestors when he told Neville Chamberlain that they had come from Lower Saxony, rather than Austria. He sought to mislead people by saying that his father was a judge or a postal official, when they knew that he had been a customs officer. He was furious when the party put up a plaque on a house where he had lived as a child. He gave orders to obliterate his grandparents' graves, and he never had gravestones erected for his own mother and father.[148]

Mein Kampf tries not to reveal very much about the author's parents or his attitude towards them. The mother and father portrayed in those pages are concealed by a veil of stereotype: a tender-loving-understanding mother who dedicated her life to fulfilling the triune 'KKK' of church–children–kitchen (*Kirche–Kinder–Küche*); a father who is predictably stern but respected – worthy of that *Ehrfurcht* (literally 'honour/fear') due to all nineteenth-century Austrian fathers.

Wilhelm II talked openly and often to friends and total strangers about his relationship to his mother. By contrast, when Hitler described his feelings for his parents, he hid behind platitudes: 'I loved my mother; I respected my father.' Both of these assertions are rather less than true. Thus, on first reading, Hitler's memoirs do not seem very helpful. But some passages, if studied carefully, are inadvertently revealing – certainly more so than Hitler consciously intended. A leading German biographer rightly noted, 'The image he had of himself was more that of a monument than a man. From the start he endeavoured to hide behind it.'[149] The genealogy of the Kaiser can easily and accurately be traced through many generations on both sides of the family. It is set forth authoritatively in the *Almanach de Gotha.* Hitler's genealogy, by contrast, is so confused and uncertain that he could never prove to the satisfaction of his own racial laws that his own paternal grandfather was not a Jew.

The Führer's Mother: Klara Pölzl Hitler

Unhappiness was the lot of the young woman who was to become the Führer's mother. All her life Klara Pölzl was pushed about to suit the convenience of others. She was the seventh of eleven children in a peasant family of Lower Austria who lived in grinding poverty. When she was fourteen or fifteen she was sent out to earn her keep in the moderately affluent home of a relative, Alois (Schickelgruber) Hitler, the man who would become the Führer's father. Then she was sent into exile for four years at the insistence of her employer's wife, Franciska ('Fannie') Matzelberger Hitler, who was justifiably suspicious of her husband's advances to the young and not unpretty servant. When Fannie was stricken with tuberculosis, Klara was summoned back to care for the invalid and her two small children – and to accommodate her employer's sexual desires. Alois forced her to have sex with him while Fannie was still alive.

After Fannie's death, when Klara was four months pregnant with the child of her employer-relative-seducer, she was married to Alois.[150] The wedding took place in 1885 on a bleak January morning in a parish church in Braunau, Austria, where Alois was stationed as a customs official. The conspicuously pregnant bride was twenty-three, the groom forty-seven. She later recalled to a friend, 'We were married at six in the morning, and by seven my husband was already on duty again.' After the wedding, she continued to call him 'Uncle Alois'; he called her 'Niece.'[151]

Klara began her married life caring for Fannie's children, Alois Jr, aged two, and Angela, three. In a few months there was added the care of her own son, Gustav, then a second child, Ida, then promptly a third, Otto, who died after a few days. More tragedy struck when her two surviving children contracted diphtheria. Day after day, like Victoria and her son Waldemar, Klara watched in despair as the heavy, greenish-grey membrane enveloped her children's throats and slowly strangled them.[152] Little Gustav died in December 1887; Ida the next month. Three of her children had died within a space of five weeks.

Klara had been unable to care adequately for her dying first two children because she was about to give birth to her third, who soon died while she was pregnant with the future Führer, her fourth child and only surviving son. He was born at half-past six on Easter Day, 20 April 1889 – a fact that the Führer considered an omen. The day was overcast, with the temperature 67 degrees Fahrenheit and the humidity 89 per cent. The birth certificate recorded his name as Adolfus.

Adolf was a sickly baby and must have aroused in his mother fears that he, like all her other children, would die. Her energies, already taxed by four pregnancies in rapid succession, had been further drained by fruitless efforts to save her children from death, and then by having to move the household, at her husband's orders, soon after Adolf's birth. Small wonder that neighbours remembered her as an exhausted and depressed person who never lingered for conversation but hurried home to care for her children and her house.

She got no comfort or companionship from her husband. Even one of his closest friends admitted that Alois was very hard on his wife. He 'hardly ever spoke a word to her at home,' demanded an orderly and spotlessly clean house, and beat her when she did not follow his orders quickly enough.[153]

Denied affection and understanding from her husband, Klara turned for consolation to her one surviving boy. Little Adolf was her means of proving that she really was a devoted, loving mother despite all her self-doubts and feelings of guilt, indeed because of them. By loving Adolf so demonstrably, Klara could numb her sense of shame and guilt – shame of her inadequacy as a mother who bore children who died; guilt as a devout Catholic for having yielded to her 'uncle's' sexual demands at the very time his wife was dying in the same house. Constant expressions of love for her little boy could also assuage the fear of God's punishment that she felt had been visited upon her by the deaths of her first three babies. As a German psychiatrist has written, 'No wonder that Klara not only overfed Adolf, but anxiously hovered over him, desperately needing him as living proof of her being a good, giving, non-destructive mother whom God still loved.'[154]

Throughout his boyhood and adolescence, Klara continued to treat her 'Dolfie' as special, indulging all his wishes. His older half-brother, Alois Jr, complained that their mother 'pampered [Adolf] from early morning until late at night.' He expected his sister Paula to pick up after him and was excused from any unpleasant chores. Klara kept telling the other children 'endless stories about how wonderful [Adolf] was and about what a great painter he would be some day.'[155]

Hitler liked to talk about his childhood as a time when 'Dame Poverty' clasped him in her 'icy arms.' Actually, he had never known economic privation as a boy. In comparison with the families of his playmates of Braunau, Passau, and Leonding, the Hitler family was comfortably situated. Moreover, as the son of an official in the royal and Imperial civil service, he could bask in the prestige and status of his father's position. When his father died, his mother received a widow's pension of half her husband's salary and additional benefits for each child.

In June 1905, Frau Senior Customs Inspector Widow Klara Hitler sold her house in Leonding for a substantial price to one Herr Hölzl and moved to a pleasant and spacious flat on the Humboldtstrasse in Linz, where she would be close to her married stepdaughter Angela and Adolf could enjoy the opportunities of the provincial capital.

As Hitler noted in *Mein Kampf*, life picked up after his father's death when he was twelve. For now Adolf, his 'mother's darling,' could sleep until noon in a 'soft, downy bed.' His doting mother drew on her comfortable pension and the profits from the sale of her house in Leonding to indulge Adolf's every wish. Glorying in the life of leisure, as critic and patron of the arts, he rarely missed a performance of the Linz Opera. He dressed immaculately in white shirts (which he changed twice a day), a flowing cravat and stickpin, a broad-brimmed black hat set at a confident angle, and well-cut suits that were the envy of the young men of the town. In winter, for the opera, he donned a silk-lined black overcoat and affected black kid gloves, an ivory-handled walking stick, and a top hat.[156] His mother paid for a few piano lessons in Munich. In 1906 she also financed a trip to Vienna, where he spent a fortnight attending the opera and writing critical comments about the architecture of the Ring. (He was not at all pleased with the interior of the Imperial Opera.)

The Führer's Father: Alois (Schickelgruber) Hitler

In his carefully brushed and burnished-buttoned uniform of the Imperial customs service, Alois Hitler presented himself as the personification of the dedicated civil servant: a very pillar of the Austro-Hungarian Empire, a man of substance who provided his family with economic security and social status.

In his home, however, he was an arbitrary and ferocious man of violent temper who launched thunderbolts of terror, pain, and punishment. Neighbours reported that his children were never allowed to speak without being told to, and were not permitted to use the familiar '*du*' in talking to their father, who was to be addressed as 'Herr Vater.' Neighbours also recalled that he often beat his dog until it wet on the floor. Old Joseph Mayrhofer, a farmer who was for many years mayor of Leonding, had been a close friend of Alois and, after his death, was appointed Adolf's guardian. Yet in 1948, when he was eighty but still alert and clear-minded, Mayrhofer admitted that Alois Hitler was a tyrant. With deliberate understatement, he averred that his children 'were not treated with kid gloves' and that 'the wife had nothing to smile about.' Indeed, she had not. In another interview Mayrhofer allowed, 'Alois was damned rough (*Saugrob*) with her.' Klara was terrified of her husband.[157]

Adolf's sister Paula later told an American interviewer that her father whipped all his children but that Adolf was the favourite target of his rages. He was singled out for 'sound thrashings every day.'[158] Another member of the family testified that when Adolf was caught while trying to run away from home at the age of eleven, Alois beat him so violently with his dog whip that 'he was afraid that he had killed him.'[159]

The beatings were burned into Adolf's mind. Years later the Führer told his secretaries how he survived them. He said that even as a young boy he had been fond of Karl May stories about Indians who proved their courage by refusing to cry out under torture. One day, as his father thrashed him yet again with a cane and his frightened mother stood weeping outside the door, Adolf counted the blows without a murmur and proudly reported to her, 'My father gave me 230 blows!'[160]

Herr Vater also knew how to punish his son in other ways. After a particularly savage beating, Adolf again tried to run away by squeezing through his bedroom window. It was too tight a fit, so he removed his clothes. When he heard his father coming up the stairs after him, the terrified boy wrapped himself in a bedsheet and stood trembling as his father entered the room. This time Alois did not whip him. He roared with scornful laughter and yelled for his wife to come up and take a look at the stupid 'toga boy.' He enjoyed taunting him with the name. As an adult, Adolf told Ernst Hanfstaengl's wife that the humiliation of that moment hurt far worse than a whipping and it had taken 'a long time to get over.'[161] The memory seems to have lingered longer with the Führer than a similar memory of childhood humiliation had lasted with the Kaiser: the memory of when, as a lad of ten, he had paraded proudly in his new uniform past his grandfather only to be ridiculed by his mother.

In studying a group of fifty-five patients diagnosed as borderlines, Harvard psychiatrists found that more than 95 per cent of them had witnessed acts of extreme violence in their home and had suffered physical and emotional abuse as children. Several had seen their fathers batter their mothers. The traumatic incidents usually occurred, as did Adolf Hitler's, at an early age. This study concluded that 'a strong association [exists] between a diagnosis of borderline personality disorder and a history of abuse in childhood.'[162]

A Jewish Grandfather?

Apart from the whippings and verbal abuse, there was another compelling reason for Hitler's growing hatred of his father. From early childhood, Adolf had heard rumours in the village that his father, who was illegitimate and had changed his name from Schickelgruber to Hitler, was part Jewish. The suspicion that his own father had 'infected' him with Jewish blood tormented Adolf throughout his life; but when he became Führer of the racist, anti-Semitic Nazi party, the idea was absolutely intolerable.

Indeed, it was so terrifying that one day towards the end of 1930 Hitler summoned his private lawyer, Hans Frank, for urgent consultation. According to Frank, Hitler told him that he was about to be blackmailed by a relative who claimed that he could prove that the Führer himself was actually 'part Jewish' because of a Jewish grandfather. Hitler was so alarmed by this direct threat to his political career that he ordered his lawyer to investigate. Frank did so and reported back that Hitler's grandmother had become pregnant while working as a domestic in Graz 'in the home of a Jewish family by the name of Frankenberger.' From the day her baby, Hitler's father, Alois, was born until the boy was fourteen, Frankenberger paid money for the support of the child. According to Frank, when Hitler was confronted with this report, he said that the story of a Graz Jew being his own grandfather was a complete lie. He knew it was a lie because his grandmother herself had told him so. She had accepted the money from the Jew, she had said, only because she was so poor.[163]

Despite Hans Frank's well-deserved reputation as the 'Butcher of Poland,' there are reasons for believing his story. He wrote his memoirs as a condemned man who had converted to Catholicism. He wrote, in part, to expiate his sins by telling the truth. He had no apparent reason to misrepresent Hitler on this issue or to invent the story. That Hitler should have lied when he said his grandmother had assured him that his grandfather was not a Jew was not unusual. (Hitler's grandmother, Maria Anna Schickelgruber, had died more than thirty-five years before he was born.) Hitler often lied about his ancestors. What is noteworthy, however, is that he made no attempt over many years to deny that his grandmother had received money from a Jew. The evidence Hans Frank produced must have been quite impressive; at least it was good enough to force the Führer to face the staggering possibility that a Jew had been very much involved with his own grandmother.

But the written evidence has never surfaced. Frank said it consisted of correspondence between Maria Anna Schickelgruber and Frankenberger and that these letters had been 'for some time' in the possession of a woman who was related to Hitler through marriage. Frank did not say that he had actually seen the letters, and they have not been found. Further, there is nothing to corroborate Frank's statement that Hitler's paternal grandmother had worked in the household of a family named Frankenberger – if, indeed, such a family ever existed in Graz.[164]

We do not know, and we probably never will know, whether Hitler's paternal grandfather was Jewish. But the answer to that question is not nearly as important as Hitler's *belief* that he himself may have been 'poisoned' by Jewish blood. That fear constituted psychic reality for Hitler. It haunted him throughout his life. It helped shape his personality and determine public policy, a policy that destroyed millions of Jews.

Hitler expressed his apprehension in many ways. Over and over again, in public speeches and private conversations, he stressed the dangers of 'blood poisoning' through miscegenation with Jews. He could not get the idea out of his mind: 'The loss of purity of the blood destroys inner happiness forever ... never again can its consequence be removed from body and mind.' He felt the need to atone for bad blood. Unable to bring himself to admit directly his own family's 'guilt,' he used the defence of universalizing the 'sin' by claiming *all* Germans were involved. More than that: he became convinced that poisoning of the blood was the 'Original Sin' of all humanity. He told an intimate, 'All of us are suffering from the ailment of corrupted blood.' And he asked anxiously, 'How can we purify ourselves and make atonement?'

Hitler's habit from childhood of having his own blood sucked out by leeches and later by the syringes of Dr Morell reveals an obsession with the idea. He thought there was something the matter with his blood. He wanted to get rid of it.

It was a common misapprehension among Nazi racists that 'Jewishness' could be measured cranially. Hitler's interest in phrenology and the meticulous charting of his own head suggests that he was trying to prove to himself that his genes were not Jewish.[165] Hitler also had the whacky idea that Jews could be identified by the shape and contour of their ears. In August 1939, when he dispatched Joachim von Ribbentrop to Moscow to negotiate the Hitler–Stalin Pact, which allowed Hitler to unleash the war, he sent along his court photographer, Heinrich Hoffmann, who was charged with the responsibility of getting clear pictures of Stalin's ears, to ascertain whether they were 'Jewish ears.' Hitler, who greatly admired Stalin – as Stalin admired him[166] – was relieved to learn that the ears were unmistakably 'non-Jewish.'[167]

Hitler also kept brooding over the story that his own grandmother had been seduced by a Jewish employer. One of the most important state papers, the infamous Nuremberg Racial Laws of 1935, which he called the Law for the Protection of the Blood (*Blutschutzgesetz*), documents this concern. Hitler personally checked the wording of these laws and gave strict orders that not one word should be changed. Paragraph 3 makes a special point of emphasizing the following stricture: 'Jews cannot employ female household servants of German or related blood who are under 45 years of age.' Hitler's own grandmother, according to Frank's report, had been no older than forty-one when she became pregnant while working, according to Hitler's suspicions, in a Jewish household. In one of his nocturnal monologues, of February 1942, the thought was still on his mind. He told his entourage about 'a country girl who had a place in Nuremberg in the household of Herr Hirsch' and had been raped by her employer.[168]

Although Hitler did not like to talk about his family background, he showed a remarkable interest in his own genealogy. Indeed, he was so obsessed with it that he ordered his own Gestapo to investigate, presumably to prove that his grandfather could not possibly have been Jewish.[169] But the investigators could give him no such assurance. Gestapo agents were no more successful than later historians in identifying Hitler's paternal grandfather. The Führer was never relieved of his suspicions.

There is further evidence that Hitler worried about his own 'Jewishness.' Apart from ears, the two physical characteristics that he associated with Jews – body odour and large noses – were things that bothered him about himself. His obsessive concern with personal cleanliness and his abhorrence of perfume and aftershave lotion were so great, one suspects, because he was afraid that either body odour or the use of perfume to cover it up might make people think that he was a Jew. When one of his colleagues asked why Jews 'always remain strangers in the nation,' Hitler had a ready (and misinformed) answer: 'Jews [have] a different smell.' He expressed publicly his repugnance for both body odour and perfume in a speech of 29 November 1939: 'Racial instinct protected the people; the odour of that race deterred Gentiles from marrying Jews. At present in these days of perfume, where any dandy can assume the same odour as anyone else, the feeling for these finer distinctions between peoples is being lost. The Jew counts on that.'[170]

Contemporaries commenting on Hitler's physical characteristics agreed that his least attractive feature was his grossly shaped nose and his unusually large nostrils – hence the bushy little moustache just wide enough to help conceal them. With this in mind, it is worth noting Hitler's peculiar (and ignorant) observation about the Jewish people: they have, he said, one characteristic that is 'permanently common to all Jews from the ghetto of Warsaw to the bazaars of Morocco: the offensive nose, the *cruel, vicious nostrils.*'[171]

If he did have Jewish blood, his father was responsible. But didn't his beloved mother share part of the blame?

Hitler's Ambivalent View of His Mother

My mother was a saint.

Adolf Hitler

Hitler never tired of saying how much he loved his mother. Indeed, some of the neighbours believed his love 'verged on the pathological.'[172] Hitler prided himself in being as 'hard as steel' and 'cold as ice,' a man who showed no emotion in adversity. He confessed, however, to having wept twice in his life: once when he stood at the grave of his mother in December 1907 and again at the death of his Motherland in 1918.

On the late afternoon his mother died during Christmas Week of 1907, a neighbour reported, Adolf sat in the twilight, staring at her corpse. He lingered in the death room a long time, carefully drawing a picture of her cancer-ravaged corpse.

Given this adoration of his mother, it is startling to hear his comment on first seeing a copy of Franz Stuck's chilling painting of Medusa with the terrifying eyes that turned men to stone and impotence. Hitler exclaimed, 'Those eyes! Hanfstaengl, those eyes! They are the eyes of my mother!' (*Jene Augen! Jene Augen, Hanfstaengl! Sie sind die Augen meiner Mutter!*). What could have happened in Hitler's childhood to make the adult shudder at his mother's memory? W.H. Auden's question needs answering: What evil had she done to him that required such 'evil in return'?

Psychopathologists give us a clue. They tell us that mother-love of the intensity Adolf Hitler professed is not unalloyed with mistrust and even hatred. But the hatred is usually camouflaged by excessive declarations of devotion and love. Hitler's ambivalence about his mother, and, by extension, his feelings about all women, were expressed indirectly in the way he looked upon the feminine forces that governed his life. As we have seen, he made these forces into contradictory female images that were sometimes generous and kind and sometimes capriciously cruel and treacherous.[173]

Karl Menninger, writing during the Third Reich, observed that no one trained in psychoanalysis could look upon the intensity of Hitler's massive hatred and cruelty 'without wondering what Hitler's mother did to him that he now repays to millions of helpless ones.' Menninger emphasized anew the importance of the mother in conveying attitudes to her child: 'We must remind ourselves again and again' that it is the mother who is 'chiefly responsible for the personality of [her] sons.' The experience of a son who has been 'wounded by a woman is one which breeds in him an eternal distrust of that woman and all other women.'[174] How was Hitler so wounded in infancy by his beloved mother? Again the evidence is fragmentary and again we must respond with conjecture. We know that Klara Hitler was a solicitous mother who worried excessively about her son's physical well-being. She fretted about her son's feeding and toilet-training; she cajoled him to eat more food, to move his bowels regularly and on schedule, and to control his bladder. She also worried about an anatomical defect she detected in her son: one of his testicles was missing. One can speculate that she periodically felt the little boy's scrotum, checking anxiously to see if the testis had descended. Such solicitous concern would have heightened Adolf's infantile sexual feelings and increased the difficulty of a healthy mother–son relationship. Further, his mother's examination of his scrotum would have reminded him how inferior he was to his powerful and impressively 'hung' father, whom he envied, feared, and hated.[175]

Since the matter is of some importance to Hitler's psychological development from infancy onward, let us pause here and come to grips with the rather ticklish question of the Führer's left testicle. It can now be affirmed that the British Tommies had been quite right in the first line of their version of the *Colonel Bogey March*, although manifestly mistaken in the last:

> Hitler has only got one ball,
> Göring has two, but very small;
> Himmler is very sim'lar,
> And Goebbels has no balls at all.

Ribald speculation yielded to medical evidence only after the Second World War, when the Soviet government released the report of the autopsy performed by Red Army pathologists on Adolf Hitler's body, the partially burned remains of which were found in May 1945 in a shallow grave near a cement mixer outside the Führer's air-raid shelter in Berlin. The relevant medical findings are clear: 'The left testicle could not be found either in the scrotum or on the spermatic cord inside the inguinal canal, or in the small pelvis.'[176]

A missing or undescended testicle is not in itself pathogenic; it is only so when, as with young Hitler, it occurs 'within the matrix of a disturbed parent–child relationship.' Peter Blos, an American child psychoanalyst, wrote a detailed study of emotionally disturbed boys suffering from cryptorchism, the absence of a testicle. Their behaviour showed remarkable similarities to what we know of young Hitler. In all cases examined, the mother was ostentatiously loved, but also hated as the parent responsible for the patient's defect.[177]

Although there is no direct evidence of the way Klara responded to her son's malformation, it seems likely that she would have sought advice from her aunts, who were experienced farm women. There is no evidence that she consulted a physician. Her aunts probably assured her that little Adolf's condition was not at all unusual; she need not worry, it was only a matter of time until the testicle would 'come down by itself.' Thus, the anxious mother, we are guessing, repeatedly reassured herself and her little boy that everything would be all right; surely the left testicle would appear in due time.

Hitler's childhood anxiety about time, and his impatience with waiting, were extended into a lifelong concern. As we have seen, he never trusted time. He developed a preference for watches whose faces were covered and clocks that were left unwound. Time had always worked against him, he said. In one of the last 'table conversations' of which we have a record, that of 15 February 1945, he put it at the top of the list of those forces that had betrayed him and caused his defeat: 'Time – and *it's always time*, you notice – [that is] against us.'[178]

His mother's worried reassurances would have served to increase her son's apprehension. Her reminders would have further confused his ambivalent feelings about her. He did indeed love his mother, as he so often insisted. But she had done an evil thing to him, which he could not forget or forgive. She had given him a defect at birth that would mar him for life. Is this why he once said that his mother reminded him of the Medusa, a glance of whose awful eyes turned men to stone and rendered them impotent?

There was something else that she had done to him, something very strange that he did not understand but bitterly resented. During the first three years of Adolf's life, his father was away from home – on business and philandering pleasure – for extended periods. In his absence, the little boy drew very close to his mother, who sometimes took him to bed with her 'for company.'[179] It seems likely that the closer little Adolf was drawn to his mother, the more anxiety he felt about his father; and the more he feared his father, the more he clung to his mother. We may speculate that real or fantasied incestuous relations sharpened his hatred of his father as a rival, as well as his fear of paternal vengeance.

Then one night, when he was about three years old, Adolf saw – or imagined he saw – a scene of horror: his inebriated father attacked his mother and did something terrible and strange to her. Once again we are confronted with the question if little Adolf 'actually experienced' this event or 'merely imagined' it. Once again it must be emphasized that psychologically *it does not make much difference.*[180] We shall never know for sure whether young Adolf actually saw the scene of sexual assault. But in his fantasy he did, and it was for him a 'primal scene trauma.' Parenthetically, it may be said that in this instance his fantasy probably coincided with reality.

The most reliable, and indeed the only, source for the incident is Hitler himself. Although he does not describe it directly, in his memoirs he has quite unintentionally given us an eyewitness account of what seems to have been his own harrowing experience. An arresting passage in *Mein Kampf*, which ostensibly describes what happened to the little son of a 'worker,' is, in all probability, a thinly disguised memory of his own childhood.[181] (For purposes of later discussion, certain key phrases in the passage have been italicized and numbered.)

Let us imagine the following: In a basement apartment of two stuffy rooms lives a worker's family ... Among the (1) *five children there is a boy, let us say, of three.* This is the age at which a child becomes conscious of his first impressions. (2) *In gifted people (bei Begabten),* traces of these early memories are found even in old age. The (3) *smallness and overcrowding of the rooms* do not create favourable conditions. Quarreling and nagging often arise because of this. In such circumstances people do not live with one another, but (4) *push down on top of one another (drücken aufeinander)* ... But when the parents fight almost daily, their brutality leaves nothing to the imagination; then the results of such (5) *visual education* must slowly but inevitably become apparent in the little ones ... especially when the mutual differences express themselves (6) *in the form of brutal attacks on the part of the father towards the mother or to assaults due to drunkenness.* The poor little boy (7) *at the age of six,* senses things which would (8) *make even a grown-up shudder.* (9) *Morally infected* ... the young 'citizen' wanders off to elementary school ... The three-year-old has now become a (10) *youth of fifteen* who despises all authority ... Now he loiters about and God only knows when he comes home; (11) for a change *he may even beat the poor creature that was once his mother.*[182]

These phrases reinforce the idea that the passage is autobiographical. Let us look at them:

1 *five children.* For several years as a young boy, Adolf was one of five children, along with Paula and Edmund and his stepbrother and stepsister, Alois Jr and Angela.

2 *in gifted people.* Hitler liked to think of himself in this way.

3 *smallness and overcrowding of the rooms.* This is a not inaccurate description of the close quarters in the inns and a mill where the Hitlers lived during Adolf's early childhood.

4 *push down on top of one another.* This suggests the sexual act.

5 *visual education.* Once again, the importance to Hitler of the eyes; here, emphasis on what he has visualized.

6 *brutal attacks ... due to drunkenness.* These phrases and images are repeated several times in the chapter.

7 *at the age of six.* This was a particularly important time for Adolf because when he was six his rival, Edmund, was conceived.

8 *make even a grown-up shudder.* Why should the adult Hitler *shudder* at the thought of sexual intercourse? What kind of attacks was he imagining? Were they the kind of sado-masochistic sexual deviation in which Hitler himself may later have indulged?[183]

9 *Morally infected.* Is Hitler associating sexual intercourse with infection and corruption?

10 *youth of fifteen.* The school drop-out who despises authority loiters about etc. – an accurate description of Adolf's own lifestyle after the death of his father.

11 *teenager who beats his mother.* What caused Hitler to imagine such a scene? Was this fact or fantasy?

Of course it is not always traumatic for a child to see parents having sex. If it were, thousands upon thousands of Eskimos, Bedouins, and Sioux Indians would, presumably, be a great deal more neurotic than they appear to be. The experience is traumatic only if it reinforces other deeply disturbing childhood experiences.

One other passage in *Mein Kampf* calls for comment. In the midst of describing other dreadful incidents involving drunken husbands attacking passive wives, Hitler stops to make a revealing statement: *I witnessed all this personally in hundreds of scenes ... with both disgust and indignation.*'[184] We must ask where and when young Adolf had ever personally witnessed such intimate and, to him, disgusting scenes. Certainly he had never seen them outside his own home. Never as a child had he visited the homes of 'workers.' He never showed any interest in observing the workings of a child's mind at three or as it developed to the age of six and on to fifteen. Then how could he have viewed these things himself 'hundreds' of times?

It is possible that it may never have actually happened, that it was all 'only a fantasy.' But it seems much more likely – given the specific details and turns of phrase in his description – that Hitler had indeed witnessed such a terrifying scene at least once and had relived it 'hundreds of times' in his imagination.[185]

The beatings he suffered from his father, as well as his father's attacks on his mother, justified his hatred of the old man. They must also have increased his ambivalent feelings for his mother. She did not resist Alois's sexual advances, and she did not stop him from thrashing the boy 'every day.' In his later recollections Hitler was not very successful in justifying his mother's acquiescence to the beatings: 'My poor mother was always afraid for me,' [but was unable to protect me]. 'I knew that my mother stood anxiously outside the door' [but was unable or unwilling to stop the torture].[186]

Another experience of childhood gave young Hitler further reason for feeling that his mother was weak and ineffective and that she had deserted him when he needed her. This involves Adolf's younger brother, Edmund, who was born when Adolf was six and died when he was eleven. During the five years of Edmund's life, the two brothers had grown close to each other. Then suddenly Edmund was dead.

The strange story of his little brother's funeral reinforced Adolf's belief that his mother could not be trusted; she abandoned her children in their direst need. Neighbours of the Hitlers still alive in the village of Leonding in the 1950s shook their heads in incredulity as they recalled that, when Edmund Hitler died of complications following measles in February or March 1900 and was buried in the parish graveyard, neither his mother nor his father attended the funeral. They spent the day in Linz. Not even old Josef Mayrhofer, the usually outspoken village mayor and friend of Alois Hitler, could explain the curious behaviour of the parents. He refused to talk about it.

One neighbor suggested an explanation but admitted that it was not very per-suasive. He recalled that the anticlerical Alois had no liking for the village priest. It is therefore quite possible that he could have become so furious with the priest that he thumped the tavern *Stammtisch* and swore, in one of his fits of rage, that he would be damned if he would ever hear that priest pray over his dead son. And so the stubborn old man refused to go to the funeral.

Perhaps. But how to explain Klara's absence? She was a devoted mother and a devout Catholic. Even if she were not, it is strange that a mother would stay away from her own son's funeral. The most likely explanation is that Alois flatly forbade her to go into 'that priest's church,' and thus embarrass him pub-licly, and that he ordered her, on the day of the funeral, to go with him to Linz. Klara did not dare to disobey.[187]

Abandoned by his mother, Adolf stood and watched in a driving snowstorm as his little brother was lowered into a grave for which the parents never sup-plied a marker.

It seems likely that this experience increased Adolf's resentment against his ineffective mother. Consciously, he continued to displace his resentments and hatred onto his father and to blame Alois for everything. For, as Karl Men-ninger has noted, stern fathers serve to justify a son's feelings of antagonism and aggression. 'But, if we penetrate the many layers of hatred, we come even-tually to the deepest hurt of all – "my mother failed me." '[188]

Hitler may have learned a basic tenet of his political creed from this and other incidents associated with his compliant mother and brutal father: *meekness fails; brutality wins out*. The picture he had of his mother, and, by extension, of all women, was projected onto the masses. Like his mother, they were weak and subservient and longed to be dominated by a man of power and brutality.[189]

Edmund's death must have had yet another effect: to remind Adolf how many of his brothers and sisters had died – Gustav in 1887, Ida and Otto in 1888, and now Edmund in 1900. To his childish mind the most natural explana-tion for his own survival was that he had been allowed to go on living because he was under the special protection of Providence. Hitler's lifelong conviction that because he held a special mandate from God, he would not suffer the death of mere mortals, as proven by his miraculous escapes from death in battle on the western front and by his surviving several assassination attempts, may well have received its first confirmation when he was a lad of eleven.

Adolf as His Mother's 'Bound Delegate'

Helm Stierlin, a leading German psychiatrist, has suggested that Klara Hitler recruited Adolf as her 'bound delegate.'[190] He contends that through Adolf,

Klara could fulfil her own failed hopes for a meaningful and assertive life. Through Adolf's defiance of authority Klara would achieve a sense of assertion, self-realization, and achievement that she had been forced to repress out of fear of her husband's raging: 'She recruited [Adolf] to defeat ... her exploiting and disloyal husband even though, and probably because, she overtly remained to the end Alois's submissive maid.'[191]

While Klara was still alive, Adolf had already formulated grandiose plans for overthrowing the Austrian government, rebuilding whole cities, and establishing a 'New Reich.'[192] Through her son's defiant exploits and grandiose plans, the meek and submissive Klara gained a measure of vicarious excitement, effectiveness, and power that she had always felt lacking in her own life. That is why, Stierlin suggests, Klara Hitler not only acquiesced in Adolf's rebellious conduct, but actually encouraged it because she saw her son as her avenger and deliverer from the oppressive and arbitrary husband who dominated her life.

Another distinguished analyst agrees with Stierlin and suggests an additional way that Adolf became his mother's 'bound delegate.' In Adolf's mind, the blue-eyed, blonde Klara became the symbol for Germany. His mission was to save his mother (Germany) from his father (the hated part-Jewish Austrian). The liberation of Germany and the destruction of the Jewish people meant the complete annihilation of his hated father.[193]

This interpretation of Klara Hitler's attitude to her son is necessarily speculative. We can say with confidence that Victoria recruited Wilhelm to serve as her father's and her own delegate because she set forth in writing the details of the mission Wilhelm was commissioned to perform. We have no such direct evidence for Klara. We can never know what she had in mind for Adolf. She never wrote a word about it, indeed she left no extant word about anything.

Stierlin admits that hard evidence is inadequate and that his interpretation rests almost entirely on his own clinical work: 'I rely here on my experience with many subdued, self-effacing parents particularly home-bound mothers seen over months and years of family therapy, who covertly encouraged their children to do what they themselves never dared to do – e.g. be reckless, provocative or defiant – and to achieve what they themselves were never able to achieve – e.g., become famous, powerful, important.'[194]

Historical evidence to support this interesting theory is fragmentary at best, but it is worth noting. We know that Klara was indeed a self-effacing woman, dominated by a brutal husband; that she favoured Adolf as her *Lieblingssohn*; that she told her other children that Adolf was special and would be famous one day; and that she told a neighbour how she put all her hopes in her Dolphie.

There is also clear evidence to support the idea that Hitler identified his mother with Germany and that he associated his despised father with decadent, racially suspect Austria. Rather than use the more usual word, 'Fatherland,' in referring to Germany Hitler preferred 'Motherland.' Indeed, the word appears on the first page of *Mein Kampf*. One particularly revealing passage adds further credence to the psychiatrists' speculations. Passion for the Motherland pulsates through Hitler's prose as he reminisces about his 'escape' from Austria to Germany in 1913:

> The longing grew stronger to go there [Germany] where, since my early youth, I had been drawn by secret wishes and secret love ... But finally I wanted to share the joy of being allowed to work in that place where the most ardent wish of my heart (*brennendster Herzenswunsch*) was bound to be fulfilled ... There are many even today who are unable to understand the intensity of such a longing ... I appeal to all those who, severed from the Motherland ... now in painful emotion (*in schmerzlicher Ergriffenheit*) long for the hour that will permit them to return to the bosom of their faithful Mother (*an das Herz der treuen Mutter*).[195]

Hitler's mother, like the Kaiser's, died of cancer. The association between his mother's cancer and the 'Jewish cancer' that Hitler relentlessly insisted was destroying the German Motherland was made clear during the war. When speaking about the annihilation of the Jews, the specific language he used was appropriate to his mother's operation of January 1907. Hitler said that, like a surgeon, he was 'removing, extirpating, *excising the Jewish cancer from the national flesh.*'[196]

Childhood Origins of Hitler's Anti-Semitism

There is no need to rehearse here the historic consequences of Adolf Hitler's personal anti-Semitism. We do need to notice, however, that such intense and obsessive hatred had its genesis in his childhood experience.

A British historian of anti-Semitism has argued persuasively that for centuries Jews have been the target of resentments felt against fathers. He notes that the Jewish religion was the parent religion, the religion of the Father, out of which came Christianity, the religion of the Son. Jews rejected the religion of the Son and, according to some Christians, murdered that Son.[197]

For centuries Christians have accused Jews of committing 'ritual murders.' Medieval woodcuts, for example, show evil father-figures castrating and killing little Christian boys.[198] The enormously influential and completely bogus 'Protocols of the Elders of Zion' (read avidly by both Wilhelm II and Adolf Hitler) purveyed the myth of an international Jewish conspiracy to conquer the world through duplicity and stealth. This spurious document was purportedly written by father-figures.

But Adolf Hitler's hatred of the Jews did not depend on some unconscious desire to kill an abstract father-figure or upon his reading of fraudulent anti-Semitic pamphlets – though they were a staple of his intellectual diet. The main ingredient of his poisonous hatred was the awful suspicion that his own father was 'half-Jewish.' Moreover, hatred for the father who battered him was intensified after he saw, in fact or in fancy, this evil man rape his mother and infect her children with 'Jewish blood.'

A psychotherapist has suggested an additional reason for the intensity of Hitler's hatred for Jews: They served as a safe target for long repressed hatred of his father. Adolf's mother, despite her husband's brutalities, would permit absolutely no criticism of the man she continued to honour both before and after his death. Such a high degree of respect (*Ehrfurcht*) blocked young Adolf from expressing openly the burning hatred he felt for his father. 'Under these circumstances of blockage,' Richard Ford has written, 'a child must repress his hatred and discover some object which he can hate with safety.'[199] Hitler found that object in the Jews.

It was not until his later teens that Hitler began to articulate the hatred that he had felt since early childhood. Adolescence, as Erik Erikson has written, is a time when young people need both 'to repudiate and to affirm,' and often to hunger for an ideology, a total commitment to an overarching faith that will answer all personal problems. Hitler found that commitment in anti-Semitism and racist German nationalism, an ideology that was uncompromising, vivid, complete.[200]

For Hitler anti-Semitism became the ground of his being and the core of his political thinking. It allowed him to repudiate and to affirm, to destroy and to create. It demanded that he destroy the 'Jewish peril' and create a racially pure Motherland.

Hatred for Jews was thus deeply satisfying for personal as well as for ideological reasons. Hitler embraced anti-Semitism at a highly vulnerable time. Just before his mother died, when Adolf was eighteen, he had experienced one of the most shattering events of his life: his cherished ambition to become a famous artist was smashed when he was twice rejected by the Viennese Academy of Art. He soon discovered, he said, the real reason for rejection: four out of the seven members of the jury were Jewish. Outraged by the conspiracy against him, young Hitler wrote a furious letter to the director of the academy ending with a threat that would not prove idle: 'For this, the Jews will pay.'[201]

The timing of Klara's death was important; so were the causes and conditions. She died of breast cancer in December 1907 while being attended by Doctor Eduard Bloch, a Jewish physician. After the funeral, Hitler returned to

Vienna. It was during this period, in early 1908 when Hitler was nineteen, that
he became a 'fanatical anti-Semite.' Other writers have set different dates for
what he called his 'enlightenment,' but there seems no reason to dispute Hitler's
own testimony: during the Vienna period (1908–13) he formulated his childhood fear and hatred of Jews into a cohesive doctrine. Recalling those years,
Hitler later wrote, 'This was the time in which the greatest change I was ever to
experience took place in me. From a feeble cosmopolite I had turned into a
fanatical anti-Semite.' Here in Vienna he had made his 'Copernican discovery'
that race was 'the key' to world history.[202]

Further evidence pointing to the importance of the year 1908 comes in an
ungrammatical letter now in the so-called *Gestapo Berichte* in the former party
archives. Hitler wrote that 'Within less than a year' after his mother's death he
had become a 'fanatical anti-Semite' (the adjective was for Hitler a term of
approbation). Years later he confirmed the date when he told Neville Chamberlain that he had begun his racist thinking during his 'nineteenth year,' that is, in
1908.[203]

The close association between Hitler's fanatical anti-Semitism and the death
of his mother at the hands of a Jewish physician seems clear. It is, of course,
possible that the connection is purely coincidental. Appeals to coincidence are
not very satisfying, however, when there is the strong possibility of a causal
connection.[204]

Hitler's experience in 1918 and the defeat of Germany served to intensify his
hatred for Jews and to reinforce his identification of Klara Hitler with the Motherland. On 15 October 1918, when he was twenty-nine, Lance Corporal Adolf
Hitler, one of the very few common soldiers to win the Iron Cross both first and
second class, was gassed during the third battle of Ypres on the western front.
Records from the military hospital of Pasewalk near Berlin where he was evacuated simply attest that he was gassed (*Gasskrank*); but Hitler, hence all official
biographies, insisted that he was *blinded* by mustard gas. That he had exaggerated the extent of his injury seems clear not only from the army records but also
from two other facts: First, within a month after his discharge he was accepted
for re-enlistment, at a time when, after the Armistice, there was considerable
competition for the few places available in the small republican army permitted
by the Treaty of Versailles. Second, though in need of money, Hitler never
applied for a disabled veteran's pension. It seems apparent that he feared that
army hospital records would not support his claim.[205]

It also seems likely that Hitler's blindness was psychosomatic in origin, a
form of hysteria produced by the trauma of Germany's defeat. Certainly, news
of the Armistice was shattering for Hitler, and there is no reason for doubting
the sincerity and intensity of his reaction to the event: 'Everything began to go

black again before my eyes. Stumbling, I groped my way back to the ward, threw myself on my bed, and buried my burning head in the covers and pillows. I had not cried since the day I had stood at the grave of my Mother.'[206]

Klara's death was on his mind. Something else may have reminded him, unconsciously, of his mother. As a little child, had he shut his eyes to avoid seeing her being ravished by his half-Jewish father? Was he now blinded because he could not bear to see his Motherland defeated and raped, as he was convinced, by traitorous Jews?

That, admittedly, is speculation. All we know is that something clicked in the Pasewalk Hospital. It was there, at the turn of the year 1918–19, that Hitler reached what he called 'the most decisive decision of my life.' For he finally knew who he was and what he must do. He had been sent by destiny to be the leader of Germany. He must answer the 'voices' which he said he heard, like Joan of Arc, clearly calling him as he lay in his hospital bed, to rescue his Motherland from the evil Jews who had violated and humiliated her. He ends his chapter: 'With the Jews there can be no bargaining. There can only be the hard either/or ... I had resolved to become a politician.'[207]

Years later Hitler would remind his followers that when he started his mission to the German people he was thirty years old, exactly the age at which an earlier Messiah began His ministry.

Two Childhoods Compared

Every trauma of childhood is manifested, in some
form, in the adult.

Erik Erikson

I disagree with the astonishing conclusions reached by two historians who have written about the childhood experiences of the Kaiser and of the Führer. Lamar Cecil has concluded that 'Willy's infancy was unremarkable.' Leonard Heston has used the same word in writing about Adolf: 'His childhood was unremarkable.'[208] On the contrary, I believe that both German rulers suffered painful psychic and physical injuries during their infancies and that these traumas seriously affected their adult lives. Since the Führer's psychopathology was more acute, and certainly more destructive, than the Kaiser's, his childhood wounds were, presumably, deeper and festered longer.

As a little boy Wilhelm was confused by his mother's contradictory behaviour: She showered him with love and attention, then ignored him for days as she mourned extravagantly the deaths of his younger brothers. She kissed him tenderly and then hurt him with mechanical harnesses and electric shock treatments in her futile efforts to cure his crooked neck and crippled arm. Unlike young Hitler, who was a maliciously battered child suffering physical and psychological torture at the hands of a sadistic father, young Willy von Hohenzollern suffered pain inflicted by a conscientious and well-meaning young mother who loved him deeply and believed that she was acting in his best interests. Yet both children suffered grievously at the hands of their parents.

The family atmospheres of the two households were strikingly different. As a child the Kaiser must have experienced the warmth and affection that his mother and father felt for each other and for all their children. Wilhelm certainly resented the pain he endured, and blamed his mother for it, yet he also knew that both his parents cared deeply for his welfare. When he felt that he could not find comfort at home from his mother or his absent father, he could always find warmth and understanding from his two favourite grandparents.

The future Führer experienced no such family warmth and harmony. He remembered only the fear and tension that crackled and ricocheted through his childhood home, the sudden furies and slashing whips of his father, and the weepy ineffectiveness of his terrified mother. For young Adolf Hitler there was no sympathetic and kindly grandparent to whom he could turn. He learned early on that he could trust no one but himself.

Along with pain, young Wilhelm experienced tenderness and love. As we have said, the animosity he felt for his mother developed in early childhood and lasted throughout his life. But that resentment was always mitigated by a grudging respect for her and the belief, as he later acknowledged, that she had always *meant* well. A psychiatrist's observation that 'she meant well' only in order to satisfy her *own* inner needs and that her 'good intentions' served herself rather than her son, does Vicky less than justice. Moreover, it does not negate the point that Wilhelm believed his mother had meant well towards him.

There was no such mitigating influence in Hitler's hatred for his sadistic father. He learned to hate as a child, and he remained hate-filled. True, the Führer always expressed extravagant love and devotion for his 'saintly mother.' As we have suggested, however, the excessive quality of his protestations of mother-love may have masked feelings of resentment for Klara's inability to intervene and stop his savage beatings as well as for inflicting him with a physical defect and tainted blood.

As we have noted, the Kaiser often spoke of Christian virtues of compassion, forgiveness, and love, and occasionally tried very hard to practise them. These concepts, we also saw, had no meaning for Hitler except as words of contempt. His childhood had taught him a very different credo, one that he would set forth in *Mein Kampf*: 'Hatred is a more enduring emotion than love.'

The mothers of both future rulers made their sons feel that they were very special people, charged as 'delegates' to carry out the lofty plans their mothers had set for them. Like Napoleon, Wilhelm and Adolf became convinced that they had been born for greatness.

Both boys had been 'survivors' who had experienced the deaths of younger brothers. In each case survival reinforced feelings of special selection, the convictions that they had been especially chosen by destiny for historic purposes.

Both men suffered physical defects at birth that marred them for life, defects that had aroused their mothers' sympathetic solicitude. The solicitude or 'treatment' received from both well-intentioned mothers, however, served in each case, but in differing ways, to exacerbate rather than to relieve anxieties about their disabilities.

During childhood and adolescence both rulers developed attitudes that would have political resonance in the future. Young Wilhelm learned to scorn the political liberalism of his parents and his maternal grandfather, Prince Albert of England. He embraced instead the authoritarian political ideas of his paternal grandfather, the soldier-king and future Emperor, Wilhelm I. Like that of his idol, young Wilhelm's political thinking amounted to the affirmation, as an article of faith, that he had been ordained by God to govern his people righteously as a monarch by divine right, in the ancient traditions of King Solomon and his own Hohenzollern ancestors.

Adolf Hitler had nothing but contempt for monarchy, but like the Kaiser, he believed that he was a special person who was divinely ordained to rule the German people. As a child he had learned to hate his father and to abominate the 'incestuous cesspool' of his illegitimate father's beloved Austria-Hungary. He would utterly smash his father's loathsome little country and incorporate it into a vastly expanded Greater Reich of the German Nation. And he would wipe out every trace of Jewish blood from his racially purified Motherland.

The poet was right. These children became the fathers of these men.

Reflections

Si monumentum requiris, circumspice.[1]

Sir Christopher Wren

In writing this book I have tried to be fair-minded. I am not, however, morally neutral, for I believe that if we intend to interpret the past as well as merely to record it, we cannot avoid making moral judgments. How can any historian remain morally indifferent to the way the United States Army massacred American Indians and Vietnamese civilians? Are we to withhold personal judgment about Allied decisions, during the last stages of the war, to fire-bomb the lovely baroque cities of Dresden and Würzburg, whose military importance was negligible? Are we to remain 'completely objective' about Auschwitz? In my view, to assume such a stance is to abjure informed judgment and, in so doing, to abandon our responsibility as historians.

I have long been struck by the vacuity of the often-quoted French maxim, '*Tout comprendre c'est tout pardonner,*' when applied to Adolf Hitler. Of course we want to understand. Understanding, however, does not oblige us to forgive, nor does it absolve us from the obligation to judge. Moreover, 'to understand all' is quite beyond our reach. On this earth we, like Saint Paul, 'see through a glass darkly.' The best we can hope for is to understand more fully.

Before starting research on this book, I already knew in a general way that, despite obvious differences in family background and education, Kaiser and Führer displayed certain broad similarities, but I was surprised to discover the number of specific ways the two men were alike. Both had experienced painful childhoods; both suffered self-doubt and proclaimed their omnipotence; both imagined themselves to be honest men incapable of dissimulation, yet both lied about matters trivial and consequential; both demeaned women and worried about their own sexuality; both were self-centred exhibitionists who numbed their entourage with interminable soliloquies; both were racists and anti-Semites; both painted quite good water-colours, wrote poetry, and preached sermons; both claimed to be true followers of Jesus. They were also alike in the childish games they played and in their incapacity to grow emotionally. Neither of them could change his basic ideas or little routines of life, each crying out as if in one voice, 'But don't you see, I cannot change!' Both were indicted as war criminals. For each of them, his exalted position as ruler of a mighty nation served the therapeutic function of enabling him to avoid psychic disintegration by indulging his need for grandiosity and power. With both men the price paid for this personal mode of therapy was millions of human lives.

Yet within their similarities I also found that the Führer went far beyond the Kaiser in the bitterness of his childhood experience, in the depth of his pathology, in the baseness of his cruelty, in the viciousness of his anti-Semitism, and in the totality of his control over the lives of his people. 'It is your souls we want,' he told the youth of Germany.[2] These differences helped identify what is for me the single overriding difference between the two men: Adolf Hitler was fundamentally an evil person and the Kaiser, for all his faults, was not.

Differences in personalities shaped their politics – to a much greater extent with Hitler than with Wilhelm. We have seen how the Kaiser's eratic temperament seriously affected Germany's foreign policy, yet his foibles did not alter the political structure and ethos of Imperial Germany, for Wilhelm II was fundamentally a conservative who sought to preserve and strengthen the paternalistic government he had inherited from his ancestors. Hitler's purpose was radically different. He sought nothing less than the transformation of the state and the entire German ethos.[3] His 'New Order' was to be achieved through wars of annihilation, it was dedicated to the proposition that the character of a person and a nation was determined by race, that it was the destiny of superior racial beings to utterly destroy 'inferior people' whose lives were 'unworthy of being lived.' The new morality Hitler demanded reflected his personal values. He told the youth of Germany that they must be 'ruthlessly brutal ... violent, domineering, cruel,'[4] This Reich was created in Hitler's own image. In my view, it was the basic evil of the system that led ineluctably to its destruction.

Lucky breaks,[5] diabolical cunning, and terror had enabled Hitler to succeed for a season, but in the end the gods would not be mocked. The Führer's 'Greater German Reich' could not endure because it was built on the treacherous sands of duplicity, deceit, and degradation.

As I wrote this book, I kept remembering a prescient essay written in 1951 by George Kennan, one of the truly wise men of our century, in which he predicted that moral rot from within would destroy Stalin's dictatorship. What he wrote about Stalin's system of government is completely applicable to Hitler's:

Those who begin by clothing a personal lust for power and revenge with the staggering deceits and oversimplifications of totalitarianism end by [defeating themselves] ...

There can be no genuine stability in any system which is based on the evil and weakness in man's nature – which attempts to live by man's degradation, feeding like a vulture on his anxieties, his capacity for hatred, his susceptibility to error, and his vulnerability to psychological manipulation. Such a system can represent no more than the particular frustrations and bitterness of the generation of men who created it, and the cold terror of those who have been weak or unwise enough to become its agents ... It cannot long endure.[6]

Like other historians, I am interested in the relationship between continuity and change in the turbulent ebb and flow of history. The argument on each side is ancient. Heraclitus of Ephesus, about 640 BC, concluded, 'Everything is in flux. Nothing remains the same ... You cannot step into the same river twice.' An old French proverb argues for continuity: '*Plus ça change, plus c'est la même chose.*'

This debate has been particularly spirited among German historians who argue whether there was a direct connection between Wilhelm's Second Reich and Hitler's Third. I will comment on that argument in an addendum,[7] but for the moment let me note an irony: both rulers saw themselves as the champions of continuity – the Kaiser as preserver of the royal absolutism he had inherited from his Prussian ancestors, Hitler as the Führer of a new Reich that would last 'a thousand years.' Yet both rulers were the agents of change. Kaiser Wilhelm II, who had sought to exalt and perpetuate monarchy, brought monarchy to disrepute and ruin through his arrogance, indolence, and folly. Adolf Hitler was more responsible than anyone else for producing the most profound change in the whole of German history, one very different from the transformation he had planned.

There was a vast contrast in the way German citizens looked back at their former rulers, their recent wars, and the new democracies that replaced the old governments. In 1918 so thoroughly had the Kaiser discredited himself in the eyes of his people that they viewed his abdication with indifference. They did not, however, blame him either for the war or for German defeat. They believed they had fought a righteous war, that they had rallied to defend the Fatherland from encircling enemies. The war had been lost, it was widely believed, because Germany had been 'stabbed in the back' by traitorous republicans and Jews. Patriots refused to accept the peace treaty. They continued to endorse war, and thousands of them looked forward to future victory. They had no enthusiasm for the new democracy they felt had been foisted upon them. In 1945, Germans knew full well that the war had been caused and unspeakable horrors had been committed by the man they had once hailed as Saviour and now cursed as Moloch. A shocked nation looked at the ruins all about them and vowed never to go to war again. The horror of Hitler's tyranny has inspired the German people to build a government and a society that are the most free, stable, and humane that country has ever known.

In contrast to the Kaiser's shade, which has long been laid to rest, the Führer's ghost still walks abroad in Germany, goading racist hotheads to fulfil the prophecy Hitler made just before his suicide in April 1945: 'Like a phoenix, National Socialism will rise again from the ashes.' This same ghost has had the salutary effect of warning the German people, as nothing else can, that a vigilant and successful democracy is the best defense against tyranny. The power of this warning has been demonstrated in the way citizens have repudiated neo-Nazi extremism.

On 8 November 1992, the eve of both the anniversary of Hitler's first bid for power in 1923 and the infamous *Reichskristallnacht* of 1938, more than 300,000 German citizens of all ages and stations of life gathered in Berlin to protest neo-Nazi violence against foreigners. In addressing the crowd, Richard von Weizsäcker, president of the republic, showed that he had read well both the realities of the present and the lessons of the past: 'We must never forget why the first German republic failed: not because there were too many Nazis too early, but because there were too few democrats for too long. We cannot allow that to happen again.'[8]

That Germans have taken this lesson to heart was shown vividly on 7 December 1992 in Munich, the city that had once prided itself as 'the birthplace of Nazism,' when more than 300,000 citizens gathered to denounce intolerance and neo-Nazi violence. That Sunday evening, summoned by the pealing of church bells from all the churches of Munich, citizens holding candles and lanterns began gathering by the thousands, forming a *Lichterkette* (chain of lights) that stretched nearly nine miles – along much of the route Hitler and his henchmen had trod during the Beer Hall Putsch – through the centre of the old city. When the silent vigil had ended, they sang hymns, exchanged greetings, and departed for their homes. The crowd had been at least three times larger than its organizers had hoped for.[9]

On 30 January 1933 thousands of jubilant Nazis had celebrated what they called Hitler's *Machtergreifung* (seizure of power) with victorious torchlight parades. As they marched they had roared their songs into the cold night air: *Die Strassen frei ... Heute gehört uns Deutschland/ Morgen die ganze Welt!*

(Make clear the streets ... Today Germany is ours / Tomorrow the whole world!).'

Sixty years later, on Saturday, 30 January 1993, bearing candles instead of torches, Germans by the hundreds of thousands gathered in silent vigils to take their stand against neo-Nazi terror. On their own volition, in Bonn, Munich, Hanover, Dresden, Augsburg, Bremen, Leipzig, Düsseldorf, Kiel, Magdeburg, and Potsdam, they came from houses, factories, cabarets, sports clubs, churches, universities, flop-houses, and executive offices. One of the organizers of the gigantic Berlin demonstration, Martin Bucholz, a cabaret performer, said, 'On this day of the Nazi torchlight parades we have consciously chosen lighted candles to show our repudiation of that flaming madness.' The candles spelled out in enormous letters two words, '*NIE WIEDER* (never again).'[10]

The Weimar Republic had never witnessed such demonstrations or received such support.

In the end I come back to the interplay between personality and politics. The Führer's Reich was evil to the core primarily because its founder was evil and because his consummate political ability, combined with fortuitous circumstances, enabled him to construct a government that fulfilled and fortified his pathological obsessions about racism and personal power. Wilhelm II was unreliable, prejudiced, sometimes vindictive and deceitful, often petty, mean, and infuriating; but he was not a wicked person. The Kaiser's actions, as distinct from the excesses of his oratory, were usually restrained by Christian convictions, respect for traditions, and common human decency. The Führer was unencumbered by any such restraints.

The moral chasm separating the two men was shown in Wilhelm's spontaneous reaction to Hitler's first vicious pogrom against the Jewish people during *Kristallnacht*. Reading about it in exile, the ex-Kaiser said that it made him ashamed to be a German.

Throughout his long reign Kaiser Wilhelm II had tried, however ineffectively, to rule for the good of all his people. He sought to enlighten and uplift. In contrast, the Führer with diabolical cunning cultivated the basest instincts of human beings, nurtured their capacity for brutality, suspicion, hatred, and aggression, and exploited their vulnerability to psychological manipulation. When he inspired hope with promises of glorious national fulfilment, it was to further his own deadly purposes.

In a homily warning his followers about false prophets, Adolf Hitler quoted the Sermon on the Mount, saying, 'By their fruits ye shall know them.'[11] We shall indeed.

Sir Christopher Wren, the architect of St Paul's Cathedral and dozens of graceful London churches, advised those who sought his monument to 'look around you.' After the Führer's suicide the German people looked about them and saw his memorial: pulverized cities, smashed churches, two tons of human hair, enormous piles of stinking corpses, smaller piles of gold teeth and children's toys. The Kaiser had left no such reminders of his reign.

Wilhelm II's Reich is a fading historic memory. Hitler's Reich will endure in infamy. It will remain, in a newly coined German word, a *Mahnungsdenkmal* (Monument of Admonition).

Addendum 1: Scatology in German Life and Letters

Alan Dundes, professor of anthropology at Columbia University and one of the world's leading folklorists, contends that preoccupation with scatology is the single most distinguishing national characteristic of the German people. One may well question such a sweeping assertion, yet evidence for a national fascination with faeces, shared by both Kaiser and Führer, is certainly not lacking.

The title of Dundes's book, *Life Is Like a Chicken-Coop Ladder*,[1] is as surprising as his thesis. It was inspired by an old German proverb that has been quoted, in slightly different variations, by many generations in different parts of Germany. Here are a few examples:

> Das Leben ist wie eine Hühnerleiter –
> Beschissen von oben bis unten.
> (Life is like a chicken [coop] ladder,
> Shitty from top to bottom.)

> Das Leben ist eine Hühnerleiter,
> Mann kommt vor lauter Dreck nicht weiter.
> (Life is a chicken [coop] ladder,
> A person can't get ahead because of all the crap.)

> Was ist das Leben? Eine Hühnerleiter;
> Eine Sprosse ist stets beschissener wie die andere.
> (What is life? A chicken [coop] ladder,
> One rung always shittier than the last.)[2]

As Dundes has noted, references to defecation have appeared in the literature of many other cultures – one thinks of Rabelais in France,[3] Mark Twain in the United States,[4] Chaucer,[5] Swift,[6] and Joyce[7] in English letters – but, Dundes argues, it is only in Germany that it has become an enduring part of the culture. Specialists in other cultures whom I have consulted tend to agree with him.[8]

Since the sixteenth century little boys in Germany have been addressed affectionately as *Du kleiner Hosenscheisser* (You little pants-shitter). In contemporary Hamburg dialect, infants are quite often referred to affectionately as *Min' lütten Scheitbüde* (My little shitter). One popular child's riddle runs, 'Wie kommt Kuhscheisse auf das Dach? (How did the cowshit get on the roof?)' Answer: '*Hat sich Kuh auf Schwanz geschissen und dann auf das Dach geschmissen!* (The cow shat on its tail and then threw it on the roof!).'

A stock figure in German folklore is the little boy sitting on a pot shitting ducats; he is known endearingly as *Der kleine Dukatenscheisser* (the little ducats-shitter). It is even more striking that in German sweetshops one can still purchase brown-coloured confections called *Dukatenscheisser*. As Dundes noted, 'It is not clear how many cultures would relish the idea of eating this little figure who is depicted in the act of defecation.'[9] In America one can buy biscuits called lady fingers; a popular German tea-time confection takes a different form and a quite different name. Two spherical chocolate eclairs, the smaller atop the other, are known as *Nonnenfürzchen* (little nuns' farts). One can also indulge a yen for a stick of licorice by asking the confectioner for a 'bear's turd' *(Bärendreck)*. Germans seem inclined to reverse the usual order: instead of food becoming faeces, faeces become food.[10]

Etymologically, pumpernickel bread derives from a seventeenth-century compound of *'pumpern'* (to fart) and *'Nickel'* (the Devil, also Nicklaus and Old Nick). The implication seems to be that the crude bread is so difficult to digest it makes even the Devil flatulent.[11]

Wilhelm's ancestor King Friedrich Wilhelm I (1713–40), the parsimonious founder of the Prussian army, contributed a memorable couplet to the anal tradition. In a marginal note denying a request for money, he reminded the petitioner that he had a 100,000-man army to feed and that not even the king of Prussia could shit gold:

Eure Bitte kann ich nicht gewähren,
I' habe hunderttausend Männer zu ernähren.
Geld kann ich nicht scheissen,
Friedrich Wilhelm, König in Preussen.

Martin Luther believed that the most effective way to stop the Devil from pestering him was through anal attack. He was wont to fart in the Devil's face and, on one occasion, yelled at him, 'I have shit in [my] pants and you can hang them around your neck and wipe your mouth with it.' His historic inspiration that the way to salvation lay through faith came to him, Luther often recalled, while sitting on the privy. 'I am like ripe shit,' he once said at the dinner table during a melancholy moment, 'and the world is a gigantic ass-hole. We will probably let go of each other soon.'[12]

The crude expression inviting someone to kiss one's buttocks becomes even cruder in German. The concept was given classical formulation by Johann Wolfgang von Goethe when, in *Götz von Berlichingen* (1771), the noble hero gives a memorable response to an invitation to surrender: 'Tell your captain I have as always dutiful respect for His Imperial Majesty. Tell him, however, that *er kann mich im Arsch lecken*' (Act III, Scene 17).[13] Literally, 'He can lick me in the ass.' The expression is so well known in Germany it is often abbreviated to l.m.i.A.[14]

More than a hundred years before Goethe, reverberating scatological notes were sounded by the enormously popular writer Hans Jakob Christoffel von Grimmelshausen (1621[?]–76), whose picaresque stories and novels went through dozens of editions and sold thousands of copies through subsequent centuries. His novella, *Die Landstörizen Courage* (The Vagabond, Courage) (1670) inspired Bertold Brecht's *Mother Courage and Her Children* (1939) and Jerzy Kosinski's *Painted Bird* (1970). His most famous work, *The Adventurous Life of Simplicius Simplicissimus* (1669) became Germany's first best-selling novel, and, centuries later, gave its name to the humour magazine, *Simplicissimus*. Grimmelshausen graphically describes scenes of pillage, whoring, torture, and death during the Thirty Years War – scenes that the author himself had witnessed as a boy. (Kosinski would witness similar scenes three hundred years later and describe them in equally graphic detail.) Simplicius Simplicissimus becomes successively soldier, jester, courtier, robber, pilgrim, hermit, and prophet who contributed importantly to the Führer legend.

Simplicius tells of peasants, each of whom was ordered to lick out the arses of ten soldiers (p. 40). He talks with doctors who diagnosed maladies by eating their patients' excrement (p. 251). As courtier he distinguishes himself by his capacity to produce prodigious farts (pp. 70–5). As jester he regales the court with stories of ladies shitting in public (p. 80) and women so beautiful that their 'hair was the colour of a little baby's shit' (p. 100).[15]

In the modern period, major German writers who have used faeces as an important theme in their work include Thomas Mann, Franz Kafka, Wilhelm Busch, Gottfried Benn, Heinrich Böll, and Günter Grass. After describing Wilhelm Busch's graphic scatological cartoons, Peter Gay comments, 'Busch's anality was not disreputable or even disrespectful. It was only very German.'[16]

In contrast to those of other cultures, dirty jokes in Germany run heavily to excrement and anality rather than to sex,[17] as does German advertising.

In the United States, Charmin toilet paper is touted as being 'squeezably soft.' An advertisement for German toilet paper shows buttocks outlined in soft white against a blue background with the caption: 'Velvety soft Servus turns a dissatisfied butt into a satisfied face.' American women are invited to soften their skin by a lovely fingered lady who is stroking her cheek with Oil of Olay. In contrast, a full-page coloured advertisement for a German product, Creme 2, shows a woman's hand rubbing lotion into her bare buttocks. No explanation is given for choosing this part of her anatomy. The caption simply reads: 'Firm skin is beautiful. Creme 2.' An advertisement for a savings account entices customers by showing a donkey defecating five-mark coins. Most surprising is the advertisement for an eight-volume scholarly work on common German expressions which promises to analyse 120,000 sayings and provide 1,200 illustrations (Hans Küpper, ed., *Illustriertes Lexikon der deutschen Umgangssprach*). From this vast anthology, the entry chosen for illustration in a glossy brochure is the word '*Arsch*' (ass); a coloured photograph illustrates clearly the 'common' German saying, 'at the ass of the world.' Apparently the publishers chose this entry, rather than any one of 119,999 other expressions, because they knew that in Germany scatology sells.[18]

As a final illustration of the genre, it may be noted that when an American or Englishman criticizes someone for making too much of a trivial matter, he might say that the person is 'making a mountain out of a molehill.' A German might say either that he is 'making an elephant out of a gnat' or '*Er macht aus einem Furz einen Donnerschlag*' (He is making a thunderclap out of a fart).

We have noted that one of Hitler's female admirers offered, as a sign of her true love, to kiss the Führer's ass (*Popo*).

All this would seem to give credence to Professor Dundes's extraordinary contention about the German people, but it scarcely warrants his claim that their fascination with faeces amounts to *the* distinguishing national characteristic. My only point here is to show that in their personal preoccupation with scatology, Kaiser and Führer reflected a national tradition.

Addendum 2: The *Kriegsschuldfrage* and Historical Evidence

Shortly after the Great War, the new republican government established a special department within the foreign office called the *Kriegsschuldfragereferat* (office of war-guilt review).[1] This office was charged with the responsibility for distributing materials designed to refute the 'war-guilt lie' and prove that Germany was not 'guilty' for the war.

Its most important contribution to this effort was to authorize and supervise the publication of documents from the Imperial foreign office entitled *Die Grosse Politik der Europäischen Kabinette, 1871–1914* (40 volumes, 54 parts). This vast collection was hailed everywhere by historians who relied upon these documents in writing their books on pre-war diplomacy. On the basis of these 'official' documents, Sidney B. Fay of Harvard and many other noted historians reached the conclusion that the Germans were justified in denying responsibility for the war. It was not discovered until the 1950s that the documents published in *Grosse Politik* had been carefully selected, abridged, and bowdlerized by patriotic German editors, one of whom admitted in a private letter that the primary purpose of publishing the documents was 'to serve ... as much as possible, the interests of our [German] foreign policy. In my personal opinion, it is not in the interests of our foreign policy that our position should needlessly be compromised (*blossgestellt*).' This letter was written by Dr Friedrich Thimme, the editor largely responsible for selecting and editing the German documents in the collection. The British historian who found the letter concluded, quite rightly, that this startling statement raises serious doubts about the reliability of the entire collection.[2]

In addition to supervising the publication of *Grosse Politik*, the office of war-guilt review sponsored and underwrote the periodical called *Kriegsschuldfrage*, whose editor, an employee of the foreign office, received a salary equivalent to that of a ministerial counsellor.[3]

The office also hired a stable of writers, none of them professional historians, to work as propagandists. They were paid monthly salaries to write articles denying Germany's 'war guilt' that were sent to magazines and newspapers with mass circulations. These writers were paid to review publications dealing with war guilt and to attack and ridicule 'unfriendly' ones. The office also subsidized the translation and dissemination of articles and books that took a 'friendly' attitude to Germany's role in pre-war diplomacy. Hundreds of copies of approved books were delivered to local libraries and sent to German embassies throughout the world.

The *Kriegsschuldfragereferat* put pressure on publishing houses to discourage the publication of works that did not follow the official governmental position. One glaring example of their censorship was their treatment of Hermann Kantorowicz's book which, long before Albertini, Fischer, and Geiss, had contended that Germany was primarily responsible for causing the Great War. Kantorowicz's book, entitled *Gutachten zur Kriegsschuldfrage, 1914* (Appraisals of the War-Guilt Question, 1914), was submitted for publication in 1927. Three successive governments of Germany (Weimar, Hitler, Bonn) prevented its publication until, forty years after it had been written, the Bonn government reluctantly finally gave its permission.[4] The office also did its best to raise doubts about the reliability of Albertini's magisterial study of the causes of the First World War.[5] Similarly suppressed was the collection of documents edited by Karl Kautsky, *Die Deutschen Dokumente zum Kriegsausbruch, 1914*, which contained important documents that were unacceptable to the editors of *Grosse Politik*.

One consequence of government censorship and repression was the enormous excitement occasioned by the appearance in the 1960s of Fritz Fischer's books about aggressive German war aims and responsibility for the war that utilized Albertini, Kantorowicz, and Kautsky's studies of state papers.

For decades, German editors and publishers continued to cooperate with the *Kriegsschuldfragereferat*. Passages found in private diaries and letters that they considered unsympathetic to Germany were destroyed or seriously abridged. Two examples are particularly deplorable: (1) the destruction of revealing letters Wilhelm II wrote to his confidante and aunt, the Grand Duchess of Baden; (2) the deletion or distortion of many entries in the pre-war diaries of Chancellor Bethmann Hollweg's private secretary, confidant, and collaborator, Kurt Riezler.[6]

For many years the Bonn government continued this policy of censorship and repression. In 1961, for instance, when Fritz Fischer was scheduled for a lecture tour of the United States after publishing his *Griff nach der Weltmacht* (Grasp for World Power), the West German government announced that 'unfortunately, the funds have been withdrawn.' Fischer's trip was then financed by the American Council of Learned Societies. As noted, Kantorowicz's valuable volume was published only after historians had put heavy pressure on the reluctant Bonn government, which was still trying to suppress uncomfortable evidence about the causes of the First World War.[7]

It should be pointed out that all belligerents edited and slanted their 'official' documents to put their governments in the best possible light – none, however, as flagrantly as the Germans.[8]

Addendum 3: The Kaiser in Exile

The Kaiser's host in Holland was Godard Bentinck Graaf van Oldenburg–Bentinck, the head of a distinguished Anglo-Dutch-German family. The Dutch government, which had remained neutral during the Great War, offered Wilhelm sanctuary with the proviso that he not leave Holland or engage in political activity. At Queen Wilhelmina's personal urging, Count Bentinck had reluctantly agreed to invite the Kaiser to stay in his chateau in Amerongen, provided the Dutch government pay for the food and fuel consumed by the Kaiser and his entourage. (He had arrived with a retinue of seventy-nine people.) The count and countess had understood that their guest would stay for three days. Wilhelm remained for eighteen months. Finally, on 15 May 1920, he moved into a newly renovated former castle that had previously been owned by Audrey Hepburn's grandmother. It was complete with moat, drawbridge, and some 160 acres of woodland and pasture. Wilhelm renamed the handsome estate 'Huis Doorn (Doorn House).' Once he had settled in, fifty boxcar-loads of uniforms, *objets d'art*, personal effects, and housewares – including a tea set for two hundred – arrived.

Article 227 of the Versailles Treaty had arraigned the Kaiser as a war criminal, and Lloyd George urged his extradition to England for a trial to be held in Hampton Court. The Dutch government refused extradition. On 5 January 1919 U.S. Senator Luke Lea of Tennessee failed in a hare-brained scheme to kidnap the Kaiser and deliver him to the U.S. Army on the Rhine as a belated 'Christmas present.' Agitation against Wilhelm II gradually subsided, and he spent his remaining years in peace, much loved as the 'old gentleman' by the villagers of Doorn, whom he invited to his house at Christmas and on other festive occasions.

Wilhelm's routine varied little over the years. The day started with household prayers, led by the ex-Kaiser in Dutch, a language he had quickly mastered. On

Sundays he usually preached the sermon. After breakfasting with his wife and attending to his correspondence, he spent the rest of the morning working in his fine rose garden or cutting down and sawing up trees. His life total, according to household records, was more than 30,000 trees – many of them, presumably, saplings. He cut off splinters that he autographed for his guests. After lunch and a long nap, he walked through his estate or the village swinging the walking stick that had belonged to Frederick the Great. He was also seen riding through the Dutch countryside at high speed in one of his Mercedes, which was mounted with a horn that blared a Wagnerian aria and was adorned, for a time, with a Swastika medallion. Evenings were often spent entertaining guests at dinner, and keeping meticulous records of their names, social ranks, dates of birth, as well as the menus served and the amount of wine each consumed. After the early departure of his guests, he read aloud to his wife while she sat behind him knitting or embroidering. Several hours each day were spent at his desk, where, mounted on his English riding saddle, he wrote in careful longhand his memoirs, sermons, or scholarly articles on archaeology.

The exiled Kaiser kept in close contact with the outside world through prodigious reading of the foreign press. His archives contain thousands of clippings from dozens of newspapers, including those of Boston and New Delhi, New York and Warsaw, London, Johannesburg, and Istanbul. He seemed to have been particularly interested in Hitler's trial after the failure of the Beer Hall Putsch.[1] He saved clippings covering Lindberg's flight, the Spanish Civil War, Gandhi's movement, and Japan's invasion of China. He followed with special care the military campaigns of the Second World War, the Wehrmacht supplying him with daily briefings on the progress of the western campaign, the number of RAF planes shot down, the number of bombs dropped on London, and the tonnage of Allied shipping sunk by U-boats. The last briefing received at Doorn House was dated 4 June 1941,[2] the day Wilhelm II died.

The Kaiser's first wife, the Empress Auguste Victoria ('Dona'), died in April 1921 and was buried in the Antique Temple in Potsdam. The affection with which she was held by the German people was attested by the 200,000 people who were said to have lined the streets for her funeral procession. Wilhelm was not permitted to attend the services. A year later he married Hermine, a German princess of a lesser house and an admirer of Adolf Hitler. She was younger than the Kaiser's two oldest sons. After his father's death, Crown Prince Wilhelm banned Hermine from Doorn House. She died in Germany and was buried in Potsdam next to Dona. The two women had heartily disliked each other.

After several mild heart attacks, Kaiser Wilhelm II died in bed at the age of eighty-two. As we have noted, he was buried on the grounds of Doorn House in the simple mausoleum he had personally designed. To prevent the Crown prince from selling the house and its contents and giving the proceeds to the Nazis, the Dutch government purchased the entire property and converted Huis Doorn into a well-maintained national museum.[3]

Addendum 4: Historical Continuity versus Change

A confident assertion of the continuities in German history and the direct connection between the Second and Third Reichs was made by a famous journalist in an immensely popular book on the rise of Hitler's Germany. 'Nazism,' William Shirer concluded, 'was but a logical continuation of German history ... From 1871 to 1933 and indeed until Hitler's end in 1945, the course of German history ... was to run, with the exception of the interim of the Weimar Republic, in a straight line and with utter logic.'[1]

Professional German historians were quick to lambaste Shirer's book as simplistic and ill-informed about German history. These critics were stunned, however, when Fritz Fischer, one of Germany's most influential historians, also came down clearly on the side of continuity. His conclusion was remarkably similar to Shirer's: 'The ongoing structures and enduring aims of Germany,' he wrote, 'did not substantially change from 1871 until the collapse of Hitler's Reich in 1945. The single most striking feature of modern German history is *continuum*: the Prussian–German Empire, born in 1866–71, was not destroyed until 1945.'[2] Not, be it well noted, with the abdication of the Kaiser, the revolution of 1918, and the Weimar Republic. To Fischer and his followers, the end of the First World War and the Versailles settlement merely marked a twenty-year armistice. In their view, Hitler's war of 1939 sought to fulfil the 'enduring aims' of the Kaiser and the German power elite. In short, German policy in 1914, like Hitler's in 1939, deliberately aimed at world domination.[3]

Fischer's opponents, both within Germany and without, were not slow in picking up the intellectual gauntlet. Gerhard Ritter, in a bitterly defensive essay published in the staid and prestigious *Historische Zeitschrift*, vehemently denied Fischer's double thesis that Germany deliberately plotted a war of aggression in 1914, indeed in 1912, and that there was essential continuity of war aims between the governments of the Kaiser and of the Führer. The First

World War, Ritter insists, was purely defensive; Fischer is guilty of 'constructing spurious arguments in order to read into Germany policy ... motives for
imperialistic power and conquest.'[4]

Wolfgang Mommsen agrees that Wilhelm II did not personally plan war in
1912 or 1914. His argument parallels the position his brother Hans Mommsen
takes on Hitler's responsibility for the Holocaust: the Kaiser, like Hitler after
him, did not initiate the events and was thus not immediately responsible for
them; rather, Wilhelm II was pushed into the war, as Hitler was pushed into the
Holocaust, by circumstances that neither ruler was strong enough to control.[5]

Fischer's opponents admit that there may be certain similarities between the
social structures and some of the war aims of the two governments, but the
salient point to emphasize, they assert, is not continuity but change. The barbarous ethos, tone, and purpose of Hitler's state was a world apart from that of the
Kaiser's civilized Germany. Moreover, these historians argue, there was an
important difference in war aims. Wilhelm may have wanted to exert power and
influence on the Continent, but he did not intend to enslave it and massacre millions of its citizens.

In sum, they contend that all resemblance between the well-meaning but confused and ineffective Wilhelm Hohenzollern and the criminal fanatic, Adolf
Hitler, in personality, as in power and purpose, is entirely superficial and the
tendency of the 'Fischerites' to see German history as a 'tortured prologue' to
Hitler's Reich is to be deplored.[6]

I agree that there were important differences between Wilhelm von Hohenzollern and Adolf Hitler and between their two Reichs. Yet this assertion does
not weaken the conclusions, first, that the historically formative forces of German history between 1871 and 1945 were those of continuity, and, second, that
those forces together contributed significantly to the advent of Hitler.

In educational and social institutions, in bureaucracy and judiciary, in the
church as in the foreign office and the army, the structures, the authoritarian
spirit, and often the personnel of the Second Reich continued during the
Weimar Republic and into the Third Reich.

Hitler profited greatly from this continuity as well as from long-standing
national habits of discipline, obedience, and deference to the 'authorities.' He
was also helped by pernicious traditions of aggressive militarism, as well as a
persistent siren call through the centuries for a powerful leader, a new Barbarossa, and for German domination of central Europe.

Hitler's racist cause was helped by the fact that for centuries obsessive hatred
and fear of Jews had been expressed by Germany's most influential religious
and secular leaders.[7] As Elisabeth Fehrenbach has observed, 'The ominous continuity in German history can hardly be overlooked.'[8]

Indeed, it should not be; but neither should it be exaggerated. For continuities, in themselves, do not account for Hitler. He came to power because he had the ability to exploit fortuitous circumstances. He was also just plain lucky – that he had not been deported to Austria after trying to overthrow the German government in 1923, that his opponents were political mediocrities, that by 1933 millions of Germans had already decided, in Friedrich Meinecke's words, that 'democracy is a coat that does not fit our nation.' Hitler himself had created none of these circumstances, but he knew how to take advantage of them.

When he incorporated the most malevolent tendencies of the past into his barbarous ideology, Hitler both continued traditions and broke with them. If German history is marred by destructive impulses, it has also been blessed by magnificent achievements of the human spirit. The Kaiser's Reich, despite a degree of official censorship and incidents of repression, remained essentially a *Rechtsstaat*, a government that preserved respect for law. Diverse opinions were expressed in a full range of newspapers and periodicals. There was a free, and freely elected – if not very effective – parliament, comprehensive welfare legislation, and a high degree of personal liberty. Wilhelmian Germany was a time of political stagnation and cultural renaissance. Creative ideas and solid achievement enhanced every field of human endeavour: in philosophy, theology, and the social studies, in science and medicine, as well as in literature, the theatre, music, art, and architecture.[9]

In vast contrast, where Wilhelmian Germany nurtured creativity, Nazi Germany crushed it. The Führer's Reich made a mockery of law, burned books, trashed parliamentary government, stifled literary and artistic innovation, 'coordinated' culture into one drab maleficence, brutalized its citizens, and drove creative spirits out of the country.

Addendum 5: Coprophilic Perversion?

The question of Hitler's sexual perversion is a matter of concern to those interested in the psychological dimensions of his life. It is also a matter of dispute. Several contemporary observers who knew him insisted that there was no perversion. Many historians are persuaded of neither its existence nor its importance.

To my knowledge, the first published statement that Hitler may have had a coprophilic perversion was made in an article appearing in 1971[1] and drawing on a psychological investigation of Hitler prepared for the OSS during 1943 by Dr Walter C. Langer and other American psychoanalysts and clinical psychologists.[2] This wartime report, subsequently published in 1972, reached the following conclusion about Hitler's sexual preference: 'It is an extreme form of masochism in which [he] derives sexual gratification from ... having a woman urinate or defecate on him.'[3]

Historians were not slow in responding. Hugh Trevor-Roper, then Regius Professor of History at Oxford University, found the assertion of Hitler's perversion outrageous, irrelevant, and totally unsubstantiated. Without investigating the matter, he concluded with conspicuous confidence, 'There is not a shred of evidence on any of these matters.'[4]

Biographers dealing with an emotionally disturbed subject are obliged to use two dissimilar types of evidence: first the familiar kind that is often regarded, as 'solid,' objective, and factual. This sort of historical data is important and should be evaluated carefully. But another category of evidence, psychological data, may also prove valuable if handled with caution.

With regard to Hitler's alleged perversion, the traditional kind of evidence is fragmentary and not in itself convincing. It comes largely from a former intimate of Hitler's, Otto Strasser, who told OSS officials during an interview in Montreal on 13 May 1943 that he had learned about Hitler's perversion from

Geli Raubal herself. Concerning the nature of her relationship with her famous uncle, she had told him 'after much urging' that 'Hitler made her undress ... He would lie down on the floor. Then she would have to squat over his face where he could examine her at close range and this made him very excited. When the excitement reached its peak, he demanded that she urinate on him and that gave him his sexual pleasure. Geli said the whole performance was extremely disgusting to her and ... it gave her no gratification.'[5]

One might well raise questions about the reliability of Otto Strasser's testimony on this or, indeed, anything else. In particular, one might well wonder whether Geli would be likely to confide in him about such an intimate and embarrassing matter. Langer and his associates, however, reported that other informants, whose names are not mentioned, gave collaborating testimony about Hitler's perversion.[6]

Long before Langer and his colleagues drew up their report, a Catholic priest provided evidence in support of their findings. This priest, Father Bernhard Stempfle, had befriended Hitler and helped edit *Mein Kampf* for publication. He asserted that in 1929 Hitler had written Geli a shockingly compromising letter that explicitly mentioned his masochistic and coprophilic inclinations. Geli no doubt would have been repelled by the letter, but she never received it. It fell into the hands of Hitler's landlady's son, a man named Rudolph. Hitler was saved from embarrassment, and perhaps from political disaster, by a remarkable person, a gnomelike eccentric named J.F.M. Rehse. For years this indefatigable little man, who was a close friend and confidant of Father Stempfle, had collected political memorabilia. His untidy room was packed to the ceiling with cartons containing copies of official decrees, pictures, political pamphlets, and thousands upon thousands of newspaper clippings. Hitler sent the party treasurer, Franz X. Schwarz, to Rehse and asked him to buy Hitler's incriminating letter using the excuse that it was needed for a collection of party-related material. Rehse, however, seeing an opportunity to profit from Hitler's embarrassment, demanded that the Nazi leader assume financial responsibility for his beloved collection. Hitler yielded to this extortion and found the money to underwrite the so-called Rehse Collection, which may still be seen in the archives of the Nazi party (now largely on microfilm in the National Archives, Washington, D.C., and in the Hoover Institution, Palo Alto, California).

Father Stempfle apparently delivered the compromising letter to Schwarz, who gave it to Hitler. As a result of his service, Schwarz became one of the more influential though publicly obscure figures within the Nazi party. Hitler testified to his confidence in Schwarz when he made him the executor of his personal will of 2 May 1938. Father Stempfle paid heavily for his knowledge of Hitler's perversion. During the Blood Purge of 1934, when Hitler settled many accounts with people who were in a position to embarrass him politically, Father Stempfle was found dead in Herlaching Forest near Munich, with three bullets fired through his heart.[7]

We have noted one statistic that seems to support the existence of a repulsive perversion: of the seven women who apparently had intimate relations with Hitler, six committed suicide or attempted to do so.[8] The thought of women committing suicide was often on Hitler's mind. On 1 February 1943, for instance, no fewer than three times in the course of a conference with his generals, he interjected stories of women who had killed themselves. As the editor of the conference notes, 'In addition to these published passages, another mention is made in an omitted part of the record: "Such a beautiful woman, she was really first class ... she shot herself." '[9]

It is difficult to know what to make of this evidence. Is it possible that this preoccupation with female suicide was the expression of some vestigual, submerged twinge of remorse over his own responsibility for the deaths of lovely young women? Or did Hitler like to dwell on their deaths simply as further proof of his omnipotence – so masterful, so overpowering was he that he caused women to take their own lives? These conjectures are based on scattered shreds of evidence, insufficient in themselves to support a conclusion that Hitler had a sado-masochistic, coprophilic perversion. A different kind of evidence, however, gives support to the assertion: Hitler displayed behaviour patterns that are consistent with this kind of perversion, a perversion that is fully reported in the literature.[10]

Specialists in these matters have shown, first, that sado-masochistic traits are a prerequisite for such a perversion. Indeed, Phyllis Greenacre concluded that they 'are characteristic of *all* perversions.'[11] Hitler's sadism scarcely requires more documentation. What is not widely known is that from adolescence he suffered moods of deep depression and self-loathing that are consistent with masochistic inclinations. As his worried friend of his Vienna days noted, Adolf would 'torment himself' and wallow 'deeper and deeper in self-criticism ... and self-accusation,' until finally, after his mother's funeral, he lacerated himself with the most awful punishment he could devise: He said that he would 'give up Stefanie!' – that is, he would give up his fantasies about his One Great Love.[12]

As we noted in discussing latent homosexuality, Hitler stereotyped male and female differences. This tendency is another characteristic of sado-masochism. In private conversation and in public speeches Hitler revealed how constantly his mind swung between masochism (weak, submissive females) and sadism (brutal, masterful males). He would speak, typically, of the necessity to exalt 'the victory of *the better and the stronger* and to demand the submission of *the worse and weaker.*'[13]

Sado-masochistic impulses were manifested in Hitler's behaviour with women. The whip that he carried for years is a traditional symbol of sado-masochism. He plied his whips vigorously in scenes involving women who were as young as Klara had been when she married Alois. Heinrich Hoffmann's daughter, for example, told an older friend that when she was a 15-year-old girl in pigtails and flannel nightgown, Hitler, who was visiting their home, asked for a good-night kiss. When she demurred, he beat his own hand viciously with his whip.[14] On another occasion, apparently to impress the 16-year-old Mimi Reiter with his masculinity, he whipped his own dog so savagely that she was shocked by his brutality.

One June evening in 1923, while staying at Pension Moritz in Berchtesgaden, Hitler was much taken with Frau Büchner, the proprietor's wife who was a striking, six-foot-tall, blonde Brünhilde. He tried to attract her attention by striding up and down in front of her as he swung his whip and beat it against his thigh. The more she ignored him, the more aroused he became. Almost beside himself, he spoke commandingly about the decadence and moral depravity of the Jews. As he lashed about him with his whip, he shouted, 'I am like Jesus Christ when He came to His Father's temple and found it taken over by Jewish moneychangers. I can well imagine how He felt when He seized a whip and scourged them.' This story was told by Dietrich Eckart, one of Hitler's admirers.[15]

Hitler used his whip to lash out at others, but he also whipped himself. His private pilot recalled that in moments of high excitement the Führer would beat his boots or thighs with his whip.[16] Even after he had stopped carrying it, he told one of his valets that he considered the whip his personal symbol of power.[17]

The German film star Renate Mueller reported that when she was invited to spend the night in the chancellery, the Führer first described in great detail medieval and Gestapo techniques of torturing prisoners. Then, after they were undressed, he 'lay on the floor ... condemned himself as unworthy, heaped all kinds of accusations on his own head, and just grovelled around in an agonizing manner.' She finally acceded to his wishes to kick him. 'This excited him greatly; he became more and more excited.'[18]

Hitler's sado-masochist tendencies, I am suggesting, are consistent with a coprophilic perversion, which manifests both masochism and sadism. By having young women defecate or urinate on his head, Hitler would have degraded both himself and the woman.

Hitler's special interest in faeces, filth, and urine also coincides with such a perversion. Sexual pleasure can be stimulated by the rectal mucous membrane and by the retention or expulsion of the faeces. We know that Hitler enjoyed giving himself enemas and that his public and private speeches, as well as his memoirs, are replete with references to faeces, filth, and manure. People he disliked were often described as filthy. The schoolteachers, for example, who gave him low grades had '*filthy* necks and uncared-for beards'; modern artists sit on 'the *dung-heap* of literary Dadaism'; democrats are '*dirty* and false ... I say to them, "Out with you, cowardly wretches! Step back, you are *soiling* the steps [of the Reichstag]."' Jews to Hitler were particularly filthy:

The *smell* of these caftan wearers often made me ill. Added to this were their *dirty* clothes ... and physical *filthiness* ... Was there any form of *filth* ... in which at least one Jew did not participate? When carefully cutting open such a malignant growth one could find a little Jew, blinded by the sudden light, like a *maggot in a rotting corpse* ...

If the Jews were alone in this world they would suffocate in *dirt and filth*. When [the Jew] turns the treasures over in his hand they are transformed into *dirt and dung*.[19]

One of the Führer's most vivid memories of childhood, one that he repeated over and over again, illustrates his preoccupation with faeces. He recalled that as a teenager he got drunk on new wine, defecated, and wiped himself with a school certificate that he had intended to show proudly to his mother. He was overwhelmed with embarrassment and shame both at that moment and many years later, confessing, 'I am still humiliated, even now.'[20] That he kept repeating the humiliating story indicates a fixation on faeces that is consistent with the sado-masochistic perversion.

The Führer apparently enjoyed the reaction he got from women when he talked about filth and urine. His secretaries were appropriately shocked, for example, when he told them that their lipstick was made either from Parisian *Abwasser* or the urine of French prostitutes.[21] Perhaps to compensate for this fascination with faeces and filth, Hitler practised, as we have noted, the most punctilious personal cleanliness.

Hitler enjoyed talking about sex in general, but he was particularly interested in deviant behaviour. August Kupizek, his friend of Linz and Vienna, reported in a private letter that Adolf chattered 'by the hour' about 'depraved [sexual] customs.'[22]

He employed the same psychological defences against perversion that he used to defend against fantasies of incest, feelings of latent homosexuality, and fear of his own Jewishness: denial, projection, and punishment. Using a particularly revealing turn of phrase, he accused Jewish journalists of 'splashing filth in the face of humanity.'[23] In a soliloquy of 22 May 1942, Hitler made a special point of lashing out against sexual deviants. Expressing moral outrage, he castigated them as threats to 'public decency,' who should all be handed over to the Gestapo: 'Experience shows that unnatural offenders generally turn into homicidal maniacs; they must be rendered harmless however young they may be ... I have therefore always been in favour of the strongest possible punishment of these antisocial elements.'[24]

Other aspects of Hitler's personality fit what is known about the psychopathology of gross sexual perversion. His infantilism, for example, is consistent with Freud's assertion that 'perverted sexuality is nothing else but infantile sexuality, magnified and separated into component parts.' Infantilism is particularly manifest, we are told, when, as with Hitler, the perversion involves reversion to the 'anal stage.'[25] Hitler's childhood memories of a 'primal scene' experience and his monorchism also qualify as prerequisites for adult perversion as set forth by the child analyst Phyllis Greenacre, who writes, 'If I were to attempt a formula describing the development of perversion, the primary cause would lie in a disturbed mother–child relationship ... especially [one] involving the genitals. This becomes most significant ... when castration anxiety is extraordinarily acute.'[26]

Psychoanalysts have shown that the mothers of boys who become sexual perverts tend to be overly stringent about toilet training. As we have noted, Klara Hitler had a reputation in Leonding and Linz for having 'the cleanest house in town' and for keeping her children 'absolutely spotless.' In one case of perversion described by a noted analyst, the patient showed a close identification with his mother when he expressed a desire 'to have his sweetheart urinate in his presence while he encouraged her in a friendly way. He was playing the role of his mother who used to put him on the chamberpot and watch over him when he was a baby.'[27]

Adolf Hitler met all three of the criteria set forth by Otto Fenichel in his chapter on perversion in his standard work on psychoanalytic theory: patients with the perversions tend to be infantile; they have unreconciled Oedipal problems, and they all display castration anxiety. Indeed, Fenichel concludes that 'castration anxiety (and guilt feelings that are derivatives of castration anxiety) must be *the* decisive factor.'[28] If the clinical literature is correct in concluding that sado-masochism, Oedipal problems, infantilism, anal fixation, and castration anxiety are the marks of perversion, then Adolf Hitler certainly had the symptomology.

But there is a more specific reason why his symptoms were particularly intense and why a sexual perversion of the kind described was, psychologically, an appropriate response to sexual problems from his earliest years. Hitler viewed genital sexual intercourse with abhorrence, something that he personally wanted to avoid.[29] He could do so by redirecting his sexual energies in deviant ways.[30]

We cannot be certain that Hitler practised this sexual perversion. Those who reject this hypothesis can find evidence to support their assertions that he was sexually normal. But that conclusion, too, is based on fragmentary evidence of uncertain reliability. And it simply does not fit the psychological data.

I conclude that Adolf Hitler may have ordered young women to urinate or defecate on his head. This assertion is made not because direct evidence is convincing, but because it is reinforced by persuasive psychological data and is consistent with what we know about Hitler's private life and public performance. Such a repulsive perversion would help explain why this person whose public image was one of grandiosity, austerity, and moral rectitude, might have harbored subliminal feelings of guilt and an impulse for self-punishment.

Addendum 6: Hitler and Incest

What evidence we have about Hitler's physical relationship with his mother is suggestive rather than conclusive. Dr Eduard Bloch, the family doctor, reported that many neighbours in Linz believed it 'verged on the pathological.' While the doctor himself did not think it was abnormal, he asserted that never in his long practice 'have I witnessed a closer attachment between mother and son.'[1]

It is possible that a searing infantile memory of seeing his hated father rape his loving mother[2] influenced Hitler's thinking about incest, for analysts tell us that infantile exposure to the sex act of parents may awaken incestuous fantasies and fears. The male child is both repelled and attracted by the thought of incest, of replacing his father as his mother's sexual partner.

Hitler expressed both fears, and obsession, with incest in oblique ways. After demonstrating his concern in the number of times he used the word, he then vehemently denied that he himself had any such desires, insisting that it was not he but the Jews who were guilty of incest. Or he would say that Vienna was the very 'personification of incest (*die Verkörperung der Blutschande*).'[3]

The specific accusations he projected onto the Jews are revealing. Hitler made them directly responsible for almost every crime in the book, but his chief charge against them was that they were guilty of dark and evil sexual practices. 'Never did he become so emotional, so arbitrary and so absurd' as when he fulminated against Jewish sexual perversions. To Hitler, Jews were the kind of people, for example, who had sex with their mothers.[4] In an early letter he asserted that Jews were guilty of 'a thousand years of incest.'[5] Incest among Jews was one of the standard themes of Hitler's favourite magazine, Julius Streicher's unspeakable *Stürmer.*

It is also noteworthy that in all Hitler's bedrooms – in his Munich apartment on the Prinzregentenstrasse, in the Berlin chancellery, and on the Obersalzberg – his mother's picture hung over the head of his bed.[6]

Hitler told Putzi Hanfstaengl that when his terrifying father was away from home his mother often asked him to sleep with her in the big bed 'for company.'[7] A passage in Hitler's memoirs may be more revealing than the author intended. Hitler is expressing gratitude that he had been driven from his mother's 'downy bed' and transformed from a soft 'Mother's boy (*Muttersöhnchen*)' into a hard and ruthless fighter. For this transformation he thanks 'Dame Misery, my new mother.'[8]

It may be significant that several of the women with whom Hitler had sexual relations of one sort or another were mother substitutes who played the role of Klara Hitler to Adolf's role of his father. Each of these women was as young in relation to Hitler as Klara had been to her husband.[9] Hitler also seems to have been attracted to the young women because some physical or personal trait reminded him of his mother. With each he apparently manifested the cruelty that, to his mind, characterized his parents' relationship with each other.

After young Hitler's vicarious love affair with 'Stefanie' in Linz, and perhaps with a young woman named Emilie during his Vienna years,[10] there is no reliable evidence showing Hitler's interest in a woman until 1926, when he was thirty-seven years old. Then, while staying in the lovely Alpine village of Berchtesgaden, he was attracted by a pretty blonde girl who clerked in her mother's dress shop on the ground floor of Hitler's hotel. She was sixteen. Her name was Maria Reiter, though Hitler, who preferred Austrian diminutives, called her 'Mizerl.' He asked her to call him 'Wolf.' He talked to her a great deal about his mother's death, took her to visit graveyards, and gave her a wristwatch for her birthday, 23 December – the day his mother had been buried. Ms Reiter later told an interviewer that sexually 'I let him do whatever he wanted with me (*Ich liess alles mit mir geschehen*).'[11] In 1927 she almost succeeded in taking her own life.

Hitler often told intimates that the only woman he really loved or could possibly have married was his niece, Geli Raubal. After moving into his spacious Munich apartment during the autumn of 1929, Hitler had asked his half-sister Angela, who years before had been his little substitute mother, to come and be his housekeeper. She arrived with her daughter, also named Angela but called 'Geli' by everyone. Hitler was immediately attracted to her. She was much younger than he – at eighteen about as young as his mother had been when she married Alois. Just as his own parents had called each other 'uncle' and 'niece,' Hitler asked Geli to call him 'Uncle Alfi.' He referred to her as 'my niece Geli.' He was pleased to notice that her hair and eyes were the same colour as his mother's and that, like his mother, she was deeply religious and attended Mass regularly. She committed suicide in 1931.[12]

One day, some time after Geli's death, Hitler wandered into the Schwabing photography studio of Heinrich Hoffmann, an avid Nazi who had joined the party in 1919 and was rapidly becoming wealthy, thanks to the monopoly he enjoyed on all official photography done for the movement. Hitler struck up a conversation with Hoffmann's new employee, Eva Braun, who served as a receptionist and photographer's model. It was the beginning of Hitler's most publicized love affair.

Eva had a kind of 'impersonal chocolate-box type of prettiness' and an attractive, if slightly plump, figure that occupied her daily attention. At eighteen she was twenty-three years younger than Hitler, and her eyes were exactly the colour he always found compelling. They were, a contemporary recalled, 'limpid, porcelain blue'[13] – exactly like his mother's.

The Führer showed only intermittent interest in Eva until she tried to commit suicide. On 11 August 1932 she had shot herself over the heart – as Geli Raubal had done almost a year earlier. At first Hitler suspected she was faking suicide to gain his attention, but when the surgeon, a Dr Platte, assured him that she had come, literally, within an inch of her life, Hitler was favourably impressed, and he began to see a good deal of her. To him she seemed to be a living doll, the embodiment of the ideal woman: cute, cuddly, naive, tender, sweet, and stupid,[14] a pleasantly undemanding companion on picnics and at motion-picture shows. Totally ignorant of politics, she listened avidly to her Führer's ideas and agreed with all of them. He saw to it that she was kept out of the public eye and was excluded from party functions. Albert Speer told an interviewer, 'Hitler kept his Eva like a puppet in a doll's house. She was a part of the ambience, like the canary cage, the rubber tree ... and the kitschy wooden clocks.'[15]

Over the years, Hitler became really fond of her, addressing her, both in private letters and within the intimate circle at the Berghof, with tender Austrian diminutives. But he chose curious terms of endearment – *Tschapperl*, *Hascherl*, *Patscherl*. The words are asexual and neuter-gendered, as well as virtually untranslatable. To the Austrian or south German ear, however, they have a condescending tone, with a slight echo of derogation that sounds inappropriate for adult lovers. They express intimacy and endearment, but in the way a mother would talk to her infant child. *Patscherl*, for example, is derived from the Austrian equivalent of the baby game 'Pat-a-cake, pat-a-cake, baker's man.'[16]

Why did the adult Hitler use these words to express affection for a woman? Was it because they stirred unconscious memories of the words his loving mother had murmured to him as an infant? A remark made by one of his secretaries during the war lends support to this suggestion. In a post-war interview, Frau Junge remembered vividly that the Führer called Eva Braun by that diminutive in urging her to eat food – much as Adolf's mother had forced food upon her sickly little boy. 'He would pat her hand,' the secretary recalled, 'calling her "my *Patscherl*" ... He always urged her to eat this or that, saying, "Now, my dear *Patscherl*, do eat this little bit, it is good for you."[17] Eva, who enjoyed being treated like a child, responded with loyalty, love, and compliance to Hitler's peculiar sexual demands. She married Hitler in April 1945 and joined him next day in fulfilling a suicide pact.[18]

The question of Hitler's possible sexual relations with his own mother illustrates one way in which a historian's approach to a problem may differ from that of a clinical psychologist. All the training and professional instincts of the historian focus on the question: Did it actually happen? Did this incest really take place? Psychologists try to establish the objective truth about what actually happened, but they are also interested in a different question: Whether it happened or not, did the patient actually have this fantasy – did he *believe* that it happened? For analysts know from clinical experience that psychic reality may be as determinant of human behaviour as 'what actually took place.' As one psychoanalyst has put it, 'Historically it may be important to decide whether Hitler actually behaved in a certain way ... But psychologically people feel just as guilty for the thought as they do for the deed. Thus if Hitler "only" had the fantasy of [incest], he would feel as guilty as if he had actually acted it out.'[19]

The kind of evidence I have presented here is not sufficient to warrant the flat assertion that Adolf Hitler had incestuous relations with his mother. But I believe the evidence is strong enough to suggest that Hitler's feelings of guilt may have been associated either with the actual memory or with the fantasy of such a relationship.

Addendum 7: Dr Bloch and the Genesis of Hitler's Anti-Semitism

The following theory about the origins of Hitler's anti-Semitism was formulated in an article by Gertrud Kurth, 'The Jew and Adolf Hitler,' which appeared in the *Psychoanalytic Quarterly* in 1947. Dr Kurth's assumption that Hitler had a troubling Oedipal problem seems warranted. As we have noted, Adolf showed a deep ambivalence towards his father. Publicly he spoke well of the 'old gentleman.' But he also hated him for battering him and for being a half-Jew who 'poisoned' his own blood.

Alois had died, but now the Jewish family doctor arrived and reactivated Adolf's bitter conflict with his father. Kurth suggested that through the process of 'displacement,' Dr Bloch became a substitute for Adolf's own father. Adolf was ambivalent towards Dr Bloch, as he was towards his real father: he was both consciously appreciative and unconsciously resentful. (Other evidence supports Dr Kurth here. Adolf's gratitude is attested by hand-painted postcards sent from Vienna before his mother's death with the inscription, 'From your ever-grateful patient, Adolf Hitler.') Unconsciously, according to Kurth, Adolf resented Bloch for doing many of the things he had seen his father do in reality or in fantasy: he too had entered his mother's bedroom; he too had undressed her and had examined her breasts. Other medical intimacies were associated in Adolf's mind with his image of his father as the lecherous attacker of his mother. Brutality and mutilation were now represented by the ablation of the breast; the poisoning of the blood, for which he blamed his father, was now represented by the Jewish doctor's almost daily hypodermic injections of morphine into Klara's bloodstream to alleviate her suffering. Thus, though Hitler consciously expressed his gratitude to the kindly family doctor, he unconsciously perceived this Jew as the brutal attacker who had mutilated and murdered his beloved mother.[1]

Something else about Klara Hitler's medical treatment may have contributed to Adolf Hitler's hatred of the Jewish doctor and hence to his rapidly developing anti-Semitism. Rudolph Binion discovered that, as a dressing for the postoperative wound, Dr Bloch applied iodoform, an iodine derivative. Although it is unlikely that the iodoform was either excessively painful or lethally toxic,[2] Hitler may have *believed* that it was. He believed (erroneously) that a Jew had tortured and killed his mother. Once again, his beliefs were as determinant as actuality.

I am suggesting the possibility that the obsessive anti-Semitism that dominated Hitler's private life and determined so much of his public policy originated in his childhood and was associated with both of his parents; the German Motherland became a substitute, through displacement, for his own mother; the Jews became a father substitute – a substitute made more real by his suspicions about his father's blood; that in Hitler's psychopathology, not only was the Jewish Dr Bloch the torturer and murderer of this mother but, by Hitler's identification of his mother with the Motherland, 'the Jew' became the poisoner of the entire nation.

Addendum 8: Hitler and Psychiatrists

In May 1945 the *Basler Nachrichten* of Switzerland reported that in the 1920s Hitler had been treated for hysteria in a Heidelberg clinic, and in January 1967 the *New York Times* reported that a German psychiatrist named Friedrich Panse had treated Hitler in 1918 for 'blindness induced by hysteria.' But Dr Panse stated in a personal letter that he 'never treated Hitler and only saw him once from a distance.' He too had heard that Hitler had been treated in Heidelberg by a certain Dr Wilmanns.

The director of the Psychiatric and Neurological Clinic of Heidelberg, however, Dr Ritter von Baeyer, asserted that Hitler had never been a patient at his clinic. It is true, Baeyer wrote, that his predecessor and teacher, Dr Karl Wilmanns, had called Hitler a 'hysteric' during a lecture, but he had never actually examined him. (As soon as Hitler came to power Dr Wilmanns was examined by the Gestapo and relieved of his duties.) Other doctors in the Heidelberg clinic had heard that 'in the twenties' Hitler was treated for mental disorders in a Linz hospital. But a letter from the director of mental health of the Upper Austrian Health Institute states that Hitler had never been a patient at the institute nor at any other mental facility in Linz.[1]

It is likely that Hitler was given medical examinations in connection with temporary blindness associated with gassing in 1918, again in 1924, when he was imprisoned in Landsberg am Lech after the Beer Hall Putsch, and once again during the Second World War on the occasion of the Bomb Plot of June 1944. To my knowledge, however, there is no record of any of these examinations. It is also possible that in 1918 Hitler was seen briefly at the Pasewalk military hospital by a psychiatrist named Edmund Forster. But the records of this examination, if it ever took place, were apparently destroyed, perhaps at Hitler's order. In 1933 Forster either committed suicide or was murdered.[2]

There does exist a brief 'Report of the Mental Condition of Prisoner Adolf

Hitler,' dated 8 January 1924 and signed by Dr Brinsteiner, the prison doctor at Landsberg. This report was not the result of psychological examination. The doctor, a general practitioner who was clearly impressed with his famous prisoner, wrote a few general comments that simply repeated what everyone knew: Hitler was a man of high intelligence, broad general knowledge, and great oratorical ability. Brinsteiner did add, however, that Hitler was depressed and suffering from 'a very painful neurosis (*sehr schmerzhaften Neurose*)' at the time of his arrest. No details were given, and the doctor emphasized that the prisoner soon recovered and was 'now in excellent spirits.' A few months later, on 2 April 1924, Brinsteiner filled out a standard medical form for the prisoner, Hitler, Adolf:

Physical condition and general health: healthy; moderately strong condition

Evidence of mental illness and psychopathic feelings of inferiority (*Minderwertigkeit*): [no entry]

Work capacity: adequate

Special remarks: [no entry][3]

During the Second World War a remarkable book appeared purporting to be the memoirs of an emigré psychiatrist who claimed to have had Hitler under analysis for a protracted period from August 1919 to July 1934. Relying on this account, reputable psychiatrists and psychologists reached a general diagnosis of 'schizoid-hysteria.' This diagnosis, however, suffers from the fact that 'Dr Krueger' was a fraud.[4]

Hitler may actually have had a brief encounter with a genuine psychiatrist. One of his secretaries, usually a reliable witness, recalled that in 1943 'a well-known psychiatrist ... whose name I have forgotten' was called to Hitler's headquarters. He concluded that Hitler needed a long period of complete rest in a mental sanatorium. Instead, shortly after the consultation, the doctor was committed to the care of Heinrich Himmler, who apparently prescribed a much longer rest: 'No trace of him was ever found.'[5]

Notes

Preface

1 Alan Bullock as interviewed in the *Observer* (London, 16 June 1991).
2 In an important article, John Röhl has shown that the published version of the valuable diary of Admiral Georg Alexander von Müller, Chief of the Kaiser's Naval Cabinet, omits crucial passages that appear in the original handwritten manuscript. See John C.G. Röhl, 'Admiral von Müller and the Approach of the War, 1911–1914,' *Historical Journal* 12 (1969), 651–73. Similarly, the huge collection of German documents relating to the origins of the Great War, *Die Grosse Politik der europäischen Kabinette* (*GPEK*), 40 volumes (Berlin, 1923–7) were carefully selected to put Germany and the Kaiser in the most favourable light. See Addendum 2. Hitler's speeches, which were usually delivered extemporaneously, were altered before being published in the party newspaper, *Völkischer Beobachter*. We have no written record of many of his most important orders which were given verbally, his usual way of issuing commands.
3 See Robert G.L. Waite, *The Psychopathic God: Adolf Hitler* (New York, 1977, 1993), Appendix: 'A Note on Spurious Sources.' Historians who accepted Greiner's memoirs include Alan Bullock, Joachim Fest, Bradford Smith, John Toland, Hugh Trevor-Roper, and, alas, Robert Waite.
4 Of the many scholarly works on Bismarck, see especially those of the American historian Otto Pflanze. This paragraph draws from his illuminating article, 'Toward a Psychoanalytical Interpretation of Bismarck,' *American Historical Review* 77/1 (April 1972), 437.

Chapter 1: Two Profiles

1 That is probably Thomas Carlyle's Victorian euphemism; more likely the word

Friedrich Wilhelm actually used was *Arschloch*. For the monarch's colourful vocabulary, see Addendum 1.

2 Marc Raeff, 'The Well-ordered Police State,' *American Historical Review* 80 (Dec. 1975), 1226–9; Otto Hintze, *Die Hohenzollern und Ihr Werk: Fünfhundert Jahre vaterländischer Geschichte* (Berlin, 1915), 319–20; Carl Heinrichs, *Friedrich Wilhelm I: König von Preussen – Eine Biographie* (Darmstadt, 1968); and Robert Ergang, *The Potsdam Führer: Frederick William I, Father of Prussian Militarism* (New York, 1941), 8–10.

3 O. Spengler, 'Preussentum und Sozialismus,' *Politische Schriften* (Munich, 1933), 31.

4 S. Fischer-Fabian, *Herrliche Zeiten: Die Deutschen und ihr Kaiserreich* (Munich, 1986), 180; and see Chapter 2.

5 Huis Doorn in Holland is now a national Dutch museum; I am grateful to the curator for permitting me to visit the exiled Kaiser's private rooms.

6 *Hitlers Tischgespräche, im Führerhauptquartier, 1941–1942*, Percy Ernst Schramm, ed. 2nd ed. (Stuttgart, 1965) 11 May 1942. See also entries 11 Nov. 1941. Hereafter cited as *Tischgespräche*.

7 When Frederick the Great's armies were surrounded by Austrian and Russian forces during the Seven Years' War, and the military situation seemed hopeless, he was saved by the death of Elizabeth of Russia (5 Jan. 1762), who was succeeded by Peter III, an admirer of Frederick, who immediately concluded peace. On 12 April 1945, when news came to the bunker that President Roosevelt had died in Warm Springs, there was great jubilation. Hitler saw it as a sure sign from heaven that he would yet conquer. Goebbels congratulated him and broke out champagne to toast 'inevitable victory.'

8 Wilhelm's enthusiasm for chopping down trees, cutting them up, and personally stacking the wood, increased in exile. He kept a careful account of his accomplishments. By 5 Dec. 1919 Wilhelm had disposed of 1300 trees. He cut slivers of wood which he signed and gave to guests as mementoes. Captain Sigurd von Ilsemann, *Der Kaiser in Holland*, 2 vols. (Munich, 1967, 1969) I, 204, 208; Lady Norah Bentinck, *The Ex-Kaiser in Exile* (London, 1921), 48. One can still see samples in Huis Doorn (June 1990).

9 The British journalist and historian Donald Mackenzie Wallace, in a letter to Valentine Chirol, 28 Aug. 1894, as quoted in *The History of the Times: The Twentieth Century Test, 1884–1912* (London, 1947), 154. I am indebted to Jonathan Steinberg for this reference.

10 *The Private Lives of William II and His Consort: A Secret History of the Court of Berlin, From the Papers and Diaries of Ursula Countess von Eppinghoven, Dame du Palais to Her Majesty the Empress Queen*, ed. Henry W. Fischer, 3 vols. (New York, 1909) vol. 2, 426. The Battle of Rossbach, fought 5 Nov. 1757 against

French and Imperial forces, was one of Frederic the Great's most spectacular victories.

11 Bentinck, *Kaiser in Exile*, 115, and Stanley Shaw, *William of Germany* (London and New York, 1913), 345.

12 *Countess von Eppinghoven*, vol. 2, 500.

13 Walther Rathenau, *Der Kaiser: Eine Betrachtung* (Berlin, 1923, first published in 1919), 17. Rathenau was a cultured gentleman and a German patriot who had served his country well during both the Empire and the Republic. He was gunned down by Free Corps extremists who rejoiced in murdering 'that Jewish son of a bitch.' See Robert G.L. Waite, *Vanguard of Nazism: The German Free Corps Movement in Post-war Germany, 1918–1923* (Cambridge, MA, 1954).

14 Reinhold Niebuhr, America's greatest theologian–philosopher, noted our dichotomies and found in them hope for democracy. As he looked about him at the siren calls for dictatorship in the world of the 1930s, he sounded a warning while setting forth a classic argument in favour of democratic governance: 'Man's capacity for goodness makes democracy *possible*; man's inclination for evil makes democracy *essential*.'

15 For 'ego splitting,' see, among many others, Otto Kernberg, 'Structural Derivatives of Object Relationships,' *International Journal of Psycho-Analysis*, 47 (1966), 236–53.

16 See the extensive papers and books of Heinz Kohut, most notably, *The Analysis of the Self: A Systematic Approach to the Psychoanalytic Treatment of Narcissistic Personality Disorders* (New York, 1971) and *The Restoration of the Self* (New York, 1977).

17 See Chapter 2.

18 Letter 5 April 1897, *Briefe an Georg Friedländer*, ed. Kurt Schreimert (Heidelberg, 1954), 309, quoted in Modris Eksteins, *Rites of Spring: The Great War and the Birth of the Modern Age* (Boston, 1989), 89.

19 See Chapter 6.

20 Anne Topham, *Memories of the Fatherland* (London, 1916), 298.

21 Eulenburg, as quoted in Lemar Cecil, 'History as Family Chronicle,' in John C.G. Röhl and Nicolaus Sombart, eds., *Kaiser Wilhelm II: New Interpretations* (Cambridge, 1982), 101.

22 Theodore Roosevelt, *The Autobiography of Theodore Roosevelt*, condensed ed. (New York, 1958), 313.

23 Cecil, 'History,' 106.

24 Sir John Wheeler-Bennett, *Knaves, Fools and Heroes* (London, 1974), 181.

25 Karl Alexander von Müller, *Mars und Venus: Erinnerungen, 1914–1919* (Stuttgart, 1954), 102.

26 Georg Alexander von Müller, *The Kaiser and His Court: The Diaries, Notebooks*

and Letters of Admiral Georg Alexander von Müller, Chief of the Naval Secretariat, 1914–1918, ed. Walter Goerlitz, transl. Mervyn Savell (London, 1961), 26.

27 *Grosse Politik der Europäischen Kabinette (GPEK),* Document 4517, quoted in Ernst Johan, ed., *Reden des Kaisers: Ansprachen, Predigten und Trinksprüche Wilhelms II.* (Munich, 1966), 140.

28 See Chapter 3; Röhl and Sombart, *Kaiser,* 31, and Johan, *Reden,* 140.

29 Johan, *Reden,* 56.

30 See below, Two Profiles: 'The Führer.'

31 Michael Balfour, *The Kaiser and His Times* (London, 1972), 159. Recall that Wm expressed a desire to *behead* the Socialists.

32 These morbid reminders of death, she recalled, '[must] be set up in every imperial residence where the Court stops for any length of time. [They are] carted from Potsdam to Berlin, from there to ... the yacht *Hohenzollern.*' *Countess von Eppinghoven,* vol. 1, 35. The English ed. of these papers was confiscated throughout Prussia. According to the publishers, the U.S. edition contains the entire original manuscript. The shrouded portraits are no longer in the ex-Kaiser's bedroom in Huis Doorn (June 1990).

33 Ibid., vol. 2, 491.

34 Paul Liman, *Der Kaiser, 1888–1909: Ein Charakterbild Kaiser Wilhelms II.* (Leipzig, 1909), 23.

35 G.A. Müller, *Kaiser,* diary entry 15 Sept. 1916.

36 Copy of letter, Wilhelm (Wm) to Queen Victoria (QV) 21 Dec. 1899 and 6 Dec. 1899, in Politisches Archiv, Bonn, Auswärtiges Amt, 78 (Thomas A. Kohut notes).

37 Sir Sidney Lee, *King Edward VII,* 2 vols. (London, 1925–7), vol. 1, 754–5. Thomas Kohut has suggested that there is a touch of sadism in these letters to his uncle. While expressing sorrow, Wilhelm seems to have enjoyed, indeed revelled, in the English dead (personal communication, March, 1993).

38 Isaac Don Levine, ed., *Letters from the Kaiser to the Czar* (New York, 1920), 191–2.

39 *GPEK,* Document 4320, p. 306. Marginal comment of 21 June 1899. The German reads, '*nur auf Gott und mein scharfes Schwert verlassen und berufen! Und sch----auf die ganzen Beschlüsse!* (ellipses are the editors').

40 Alfred von Kiderlin-Wächter, letter to Holstein, 16 July 1888, *Holstein Papers,* vol. 3, 281.

41 In Germany there is a long-standing infatuation with faeces. Masters of German literature from Luther and Goethe to Thomas Mann, Günter Grass, and Heinrich Böll, as well as ancient folklore and modern commercial advertising, all manifest a remarkable fascination with excrement and anality. Indeed, a respected anthropologist has made the remarkable assertion that this preoccupation is *the* most distinguishing characteristic of Germans. For commentary on this assertion and further discussion of this issue, see Addendum 1.

384 Notes to pages 9–12

42 Her Highness Princess Marie Louise, *My Memories of Six Reigns* (London, 1936 and 1937), 86.
43 G.A. Müller, *Kaiser*, diary entry 29 May 1918.
44 Ibid., diary entry 23 Feb. 1916.
45 Johan, *Reden*, 121–2.
46 Among Wilhelm's personal papers is a ledger he kept of the people to whom he sent letters of congratulation on their birthdays, e.g.: '8 February: cloakroom attendant Kasper Joseph ... 19 February: Major von Ilsemann ... 27 February: King Ferdinand of Bulgaria' (Papers of ex-Keizer Wilhelm II, Rijksarchief, Utrecht, folder 364.)
47 See, for example, Wilhelm's kindly notes to Albert Ballin, in Berhard Huldermann, *Albert Ballin* (London, 1922), 198.
48 Mary Theresa Olivia, *Daisy Princess of Pless by Herself*, ed. Desmond Chapman-Huston (London, 1928), 436.
49 Joachim von Kürenberg, *A Life of Wilhelm II: Last Emperor of Germany*, transl. by Russell and Herta Hagen (New York, 1955), 100, 113.
50 Hatzfeldt's dispatch of 2 Dec. 1899. Auswärtiges Amt, Preussen Nr. 1, Nr. 40 (TAK notes).
51 Viscount John Morley, *Recollections*, 2 vols. (London, 1921) vol. 2, 99.
52 Geneviève Tanbouis, *The Life of Jules Cambon*, trans. C.F. Atkinson (London, 1938), 174–5.
53 Count Robert Zedlitz-Trütschler, *Twelve Years at the Imperial German Court*, trans. Alfred Kalisch (London, 1924). See also n85.
54 Topham, *Memories*, 154.
55 Lee, *Edward VII* vol. 1, 646.
56 Graf Ernst Reventlow, *Von Potsdam nach Doorn*, (Berlin, 1940), 368. See also the same writer's *Kaiser Wilhelm II. und die Byzantiner*, 5th ed. (Munich, 1906).
57 See Chapter 3.
58 Quoted in Fürst Philipp zu Eulenburg, *Mit dem Kaiser als Staatsmann und Freund auf Nordlandsreisen*, ed. Fürstin zu Eulenburg-Hertefeld, 2 vols. (Dresden, 1931), vol. 1, 38.
59 Arthur N. Davis, *The Kaiser I Knew: My Fourteen Years with the Kaiser* (London, 1918), 23.
60 The only time I can recall was when he wrote to Bülow urging him to remain in office. See Wilhelm Schüssler, *Kaiser Wilhelm II: Schicksal und Schuld* (Gottingen, 1962), 140.
61 Thomas A. Kohut, *Wilhelm II and the Germans: A Study in Leadership* (New York, 1991), 44.
62 *Countess von Eppinghoven*, vol. 1, 133.
63 Friedrich Zipfel, 'Kritik der deutschen Oeffentlichkeit an der Person und an der

Monarchie Wilhelm II Bis zum Ausbruch des Weltkrieges,' PhD dissertation, Free University of Berlin, 1952, 157.

64 In 1914 there was a tiny hamlet southeast of Ypres named Amerika. Near this hamlet, during the first battle of Ypres, Lance Corporal Adolf Hitler, as *Meldegänger* (courier) won the Iron Cross for the first time. It is possible that when Hitler again went to war, not as runner between command posts, but as supreme commander with a post of his own, that he named his travelling command post after the Belgian hamlet where he had first won military distinction.

65 Quoted in Balfour, *Kaiser*, 147.

66 See Chapter 3.

67 G.A. Müller, *Kaiser*, 237 and *passim*.

68 Rathenau, *Kaiser*, 17.

69 Henri de Noussanne, *The Kaiser, as He Is or the Real William II (Le véritable Guilliame II)*, trans. Robert Littlefield (New York, 1905), 118. For many years Noussanne was a French newsman in Germany.

70 *Daisy Princess of Pless*, 259.

71 Letter Eulenburg to Bülow, 29 July 1903, in *Philipp Eulenburgs Politische Korrespondenz*, ed. John C.G. Röhl, 3 vols. (Boppard am Rhein, 1983), vol. 3, 295.

72 Quoted by J.C.G. Röhl, *Kaiser, Hof und Staat: Wilhelm II und die deutsche Politik* (Munich, 1988), 24.

73 Letter Kiderlin-Wächter to Holstein, 3 Aug. 1891, *Holstein Papers*, vol. 3, 383. Eight exclamation marks are in the original. Kiderlin Wächter added, 'Comment unnecessary.'

74 G.A. Müller, *Kaiser*, 159.

75 Wheeler-Bennett, *Knaves*, 186.

76 Hildegard Freifrau Hugo von Spitzemberg, *Das Tagebuch der Baronin Spitzemberg*, ed. R. Vierhaus (Göttingen, 1960), 469.

77 Generaloberst Helmuth von Moltke, *Erinnerungen, Briefe, Dokumente, 1877–1916*, ed. Eliza von Moltke (Stuttgart, 1922), 347.

78 Ilsemann, *Kaiser in Holland*, vol. 2, 160.

79 Waldersee, *Denkwürdigkeiten*, 167; Graf Carl von Wedel, *Zwischen Kaiser und Kanzler: Aufzeichnungen des Generaladjutanten Carl von Wedels Aus den Jahren 1890–1894* (Leipzig, 1943), 168.

80 Bentinck, *Kaiser*, 53.

81 Lydia Franke, *Randbemerkungen Wilhelms II. in den Akten der Auswärtigen Politik als historische und psychologische Quelle* (Leipzig, 1934), 99.

82 Davis, *Kaiser*, 219–20.

83 Ilsemann, *Kaiser in Holland*, vol. 1, 60.

84 Isabel V. Hull, *The Entourage of Kaiser Wilhelm II, 1888–1918* (Cambridge, 1982), 201.

85 Zedlitz-Trüschler, *Twelve Years*, 62, 68, 236. Zedlitz-Trüschler had been controller of the household and court marshall from 1903 to 1910. See also Reventlow, *Potsdam nach Doorn*, 378, and Sir James Rennell Rodd, *Social and Diplomatic Memories*, 3 vols. (London, 1902–14), vol. 1, 50. A picture of the Kaiser sitting on the Duke of Saxe-Coburg-Gotha's stomach is reproduced in Röhl and Sombart, *Kaiser*, 34.

86 M.J. Bonn, *Wandering Scholar* (London, 1949), 146.

87 See Chapter 3.

88 Anne Topham, *Chronicles of the Prussian Court* (London, 1926 [?]), 15; E.F. Benson, *The Kaiser and His English Relations* (London, 1936), 243. When Wm was 80 in 1939, his right hand was still powerful from years of wood chopping. Wilhelm greeted an English historian with his heavy rings turned inward and a grip that caused excruciating pain. 'I hung on and just managed not to wince.' Wheeler-Bennett, *Knaves*, 179.

89 Balfour, *Kaiser*, 140.

90 A memoir of Spencer Leigh Hughes, M.P., *The Times* (London, 13 Dec. 1917).

91 *Countess von Eppinghoven*, vol. 1, 69.

92 Wilhelm may also have known that his hero, Frederick the Great, also sat at his desk in a saddle.

93 Frances Donaldson, *Edward VIII* (New York, 1980), 65.

94 Lawrence Wilson, *The Incredible Kaiser: A Portrait of William II* (New York, 1963), 91; see also Johannes Haller, *Philipp Eulenburg: The Kaiser's Friend*, trans. Ethel Colburn Mayne (London, n.d.) vol. 2, 61, 160.

95 See Chapter 3.

96 Letter of 1898 to Wilhelm's mother, quoted in Schüsler, *Kaiser*, Appendix. In a response to a toast given by Prince Rupprecht of Bavaria on 3 July 1900 Wilhelm expressed similar sentiments, saying that throughout the world 'without the German Kaiser no great decision may be made.' Johan, *Reden*, 89.

97 Topham, *Memories*, 121–2. For seven years (1902–9), Miss Topham had been English tutor to the Princess Victoria Louise.

98 Ilsemann, *Kaiser in Holland*, vol. 1, 17 and 208.

99 Balfour, *Kaiser*, 165.

100 Maurice V. Brett, ed., *Journals and Letters of Reginald Viscount Esher* (Reginald Baliol Brett), 4 vols. (London, 1934–8), vol. 1, 295.

101 Davis, *Kaiser*, 57.

102 Letter 31 Dec. 1901, Houston Stewart Chamberlain, *Briefe: 1882–1924 und Briefwechsel mit Kaiser Wilhelm II*, ed. Paul Pretzsch, 2 vols. (Munich, 1928).

103 Spitzemburg, diary entry 19 Dec. 1897.

104 The opinion of the Belgium ambassador to Germany. See his memoirs, Baron

Beyens, *Deux Années à Berlin: 1912–1914*, 2 vols. (Paris, 1931), and English ed., *Germany before the War* (London, 1916), 13–14.

105 Bülow, as quoted by Wilson, *Kaiser*, 91.
106 'Kaiserliche Indiskretion,' Eulenburg Papers, Bundesarchiv, Koblenz, vol. 74. (TAK).
107 Johan, *Reden*, 32.
108 Letter Vicky (V) to Queen Victoria (QV), 26 Sep. 1863; Roger Fulford, ed., *Dearest Mama: Letters between Queen Victoria and the Crown Princess of Prussia, 1861–1864* (London, 1971), 272.
109 In 1987 when I complimented Michael Balfour on this felicitous phrase, he said that he had not originated it and could not remember who had.
110 Letter W to QV, 21 Dec. 1879, RA Z80/48. He sent Queen Victoria another painted photograph of himself for Christmas in 1882.
111 Letter Wm to QV, 29 Jan. 1879, RA Z 80/15.
112 *Memoirs of Prince von Bülow*, 3 vols. trans. F.A. Voigt (Boston, 1931), vol. 2, 405 and 415.
113 Valentine Chirol, *50 Years in a Changing World* (London, 1927), 276.
114 For a psychological interpretation of Wilhelm's acting, see Chapter 5.
115 Henry Wickham Steed, *Through Thirty Years*, 2 vols. (London, 1924), vol. 1, 20–4.
116 Ilsemann, *Kaiser in Holland*, vol. 2, 115–16.
117 See Chapter 6.
118 *Daisy Princess of Pless*, 282–3.
119 Herbert Eulenberg, *The Hohenzollerns*, transl. M.M. Bozman (London, 1929), 291.
120 Isaiah Berlin, 'Benjamin Disraeli, Karl Marx and the Search for Identity,' in *Against the Current* (New York, 1980).
121 Reventlow, *Potsdam nach Doorn*, 366.
122 Quoted by Harold Nicolson, *Diplomacy* (London, 1939), 44.
123 To take only one or two examples: In Jan. 1900, Wilhelm told his grandmother QV that Russia was plotting against England, while at the same time he was telling the Russian ambassador that England was about to strike Russia and urged Russia to attack first. Neither assertion was true. See dispatches and letters reprinted in Lee, *Edward VII*, vol. 1, 761–4.
124 Balfour, *Kaiser*, 297.
125 Ralph R. Menning and Carol Bresnahan Menning, '"Baseless Allegations": Wilhelm II and the Hale Interview of 1908,' *Central European History* 16/4 (Dec. 1983). See Chapter 3.
126 See Chapter 3.
127 Letter Wm to QV, 27 March 1890, RA I 58/32; also in Daphne Bennett, *Vicky: Princess Royal and German Empress*, 296.
128 Wilhelm's conversation with Col. Stuart Wortley is recorded in Wortley's unpub-

388   Notes to pages 21–3

lished letter to 'My Darling,' 2 Dec. 1907, Bodleian Library, mss division, English history, d-256.

129 Conversation with Wilhelm's childhood friend. Poultney Bigelow, *Prussian Memoirs, 1864–1914* (New York, 1915), 47.

130 The diary entry of the Archbishop of Canterbury, who performed Queen Victoria's last rites, makes it clear that 'at the very moment she quietly drew her last breath, the whole Family [was] present in the room.' George K.A. Bell, Bishop of Chichester, *Randall Davidson, Archbishop of Canterbury*, 3rd ed. (London, 1925), 354–5.

131 Eulenburg, undated memorandum, in John C.G. Röhl, *Germany Without Bismarck: The Crisis in Government in the Second Reich, 1890–1900* (London, 1967), 222; original emphasis.

132 G.A Müller, *Kaiser*, 57; see also Reventlow, *Kaiser*, 26.

133 '*Ich muss mich ihr gegenüber ebenso verstellen wie für allen anderen Menschen.*' Ilsemann's diary entry, 20 Sept. 1935.

134 Speech reported in *Münchener Nachrichten*, in Johan, *Reden*, 121–2.

135 Interview with Col. Stuart Wortley, as quoted in Johannes Hohlfeld, ed., *Dokumente der deutschen Politik und Geschichte: von 1848 bis zur Gegenwart*, 2 vols. (Berlin, 1951), vol. 2, 190. For Hitler's similar insistance, see below.

136 Letter Wm to his mother, 1 June 1898, AA Preussen 1, Nr ld (TAK notes); letter 24 April 1928 in Brig.-Gen. W.H.-H. Waters, *Potsdam and Doorn* (London, 1935), 96–7. Waters had been British military attaché in Berlin.

137 Letter to Waters, *Potsdam*, 266. Sir Sidney Lee (1859–1926), in addition to his Shakespearean studies, was co-founder and editor of the *Dictionary of National Biography*. His name had indeed been Solomon Lazarus Lee, and early in 1890 he adopted the name Sidney Lee. The Kaiser does not make clear why Sir Sidney's Jewish background should disqualify him from telling the truth (see *DNB*, 2140).

138 Otto Hammann, *Um den Kaiser* (Berlin, 1919), 92.

139 Ilsemann, *Kaiser in Holland*, vol. 1, 223. On another occasion, however, Wilhelm said that it was the 'politicians,' and not the German people who had betrayed him. Bentinck, *Kaiser*, 397.

140 Bentinck, *Kaiser*, 53.

141 Letter 27 June 1886 to Wilhelm's paternal grandmother, Kaiserin Augusta, reprinted in Appendix, William II, *My Early Life* (New York, 1926), 314.

142 The court chamberlain reported that Wilhelm told him about all the plots his uncle kept planning against him: 'He closed these revelations with the remark, 'He is a Devil! You can't believe what a Devil he is!'

143 Kaiser's marginalia to report 5 Sept. 1905 from Oberndorff to Bülow, AA England 78, A 15610 (TAK notes).

144 Conversation 9 Aug. 1914, reported in Evelyn, Princess Blücher, *An English Wife in Berlin: A Private Memoir* (London, 1920), 14.

145 Ilsemann, *Kaiser in Holland*, vol. 2, 287.
146 See below, Chapter 2, 'The Kaiser and the Jews.'
147 Müller, *Kaiser*, 274.
148 Ilsemann, *Kaiser in Holland*, vol. 2, 287.
149 Bülow, *Memoirs*, vol. 1, 100.
150 Letter Eulenburg to Bülow, Bundesarchiv Koblenz, quoted in Hull, *Kaiser*, 112; original emphasis.
151 Bülow, *Memoirs*, vol. 1, 527.
152 Diary entry 31 Oct. 1896, in G.A. Müller, *Kaiser* xxi. See also Wedel, *Kaiser*, 130.
153 Waldersee, *Denkwürdigkeiten*, vol. 2, 181.
154 Asa Don Dickinson, ed., *The Kaiser: A Book about the Most Interesting Man in Europe* (New York, 1914), 143.
155 Victoria to Frau von Bülow, 3 Jan. 1899, Bundesarchiv Koblenz, BN 110 (TAK notes); original emphasis.
156 Dickinson, *Kaiser*, 165.
157 Ibid., 165–6.
158 Liman, *Kaiser*, 112–13.
159 Ilsemann, *Kaiser in Holland*, vol. 2, 140.
160 Moltke, *Erinnerungen*, 311–12, 341, 350, 352.
161 Sir Frank Lascelles, *British Documents on the Origins of the War: 1898–1914*, ed. G.P. Gooch and Harold Temperley (London, 1928), vol. 3, 436.
162 Ilsemann, *Kaiser in Holland*, vol. 2, 323.
163 Isolde Rieger, *Die Wilhleminische Presse im Ueberblick: 1888–1918* (Munich, 1957), 12.
164 Marginal comment 4 April 1902, Bundesarchiv BAF/RM 2 1594 (TAK notes).
165 Spitzemberg, 386. The book, written by a Professor Quidde, *Caligula: Eine Studie über römischen Cäsarenwahnsinn*, first appeared in 1894 and went through 32 editions by 1926. The Kaiser's defenders wrote a less successful rejoinder, *Cäsarenwahn oder Professorwahn?* (Mad Emperors or Mad Professor?).
166 Ilsemann, *Kaiser in Holland*, vol. 1, 154. On one occasion, however, Wilhelm did admit to a mistake. The British ambassador reported, 'The Emperor admitted to a friend of mine that he had made a great mistake in going to Tangiers.' Lascelles, *British Documents*, vol. 3. It should be noted, however, that the idea of going to Tangiers was not Wilhelm's, it was Bülow's. The Kaiser's mistake was not so much his going to Morocco as in making an inflammatory speech that alarmed both France and England.
167 Reventlow, *Kaiser*, 26.
168 Letter V to QV, 29 Jan. 1887, RA 66/53.
169 Letter V to QV, 27 Dec. 1890 (TAK notes).
170 Letter 25 Nov. 1912, quoted in Röhl, *Kaiser, Hof und Staat*, 27. Wilhelm had

expressed the same idea in a public speech 10 Aug. 1910 in Königsberg, 'The chief duty of German women consists in ... placid work in the house and family.'

171 *Daisy Princess of Pless*, 160.

172 G.A. Müller, *Kaiser*, 57, and Reventlow, *Kaiser*, 26.

173 Röhl, *Kaiser Hof und Staat*, 24–6, and Seminar paper, St Antony's College, Oxford, 26 Jan. 1982.

174 Wilhelmine Emilie Elisabeth Gräfin von Wedel, *Meine Beziehungen zu S.M. Kaiser Wilhelm II*, 2nd ed. (Zurich, 1900).

175 Noussanne, *Kaiser*, 133.

176 Letter Wm to Eulenburg, 28 Aug. 1888, in Röhl, *Eulenburgs Korrespondenz*, vol. 1, 310.

177 For a sensitive discussion of their relationship, see T.A. Kohut's biography, *Wilhelm II*.

178 Eulenburg destroyed many letters which were, he said, 'intimate personal matters.' Röhl's Introduction to his 3-vol. ed. of Eulenburg's correspondence, 32–6.

179 Letter Eulenburg to Wm, quoted. Kohut, ms p. 24.

180 *Der Prozess musste fortgehen, auch wenn E. im Feuer blieb!* Letter Wm to Bülow, 18 July 1908, cited in Helmuth Rogge, *Holstein und Harden* (Munich, 1959), 314, quoted by Röhl, *Eulenburgs Korrespondenz*, vol. 1, 46.

181 The group may well have included Chancellor von Bülow, who, like Eulenburg, was probably bisexual. See Röhl, *Eulenburg's Korrespondenz*, vol. 1, 46. Joachim von Kürenberg claimed that Holstein was blackmailing Bülow with evidence that Bülow and Eulenburg had frequented homosexual dives under assumed names. *His Excellency the Spectre: The Life of Fritz von Holstein*, trans. E.O. Lorimer (London, 1933), 58, 187, 215.

182 Letter Wm, 8 Sept. 1927, in Marburg, Staatsarchiv, Nl, quoted by Röhl, *Eulenburg's Korrespondenz*, vol. 1, 46.

183 Wilson, *Kaiser*, 75 and 77.

184 Kohut, *Wilhelm II*, 279.

185 Princess Marie Radziwill, *This Was Germany! An Observer at the Court of Berlin: Letters of Princess Marie Radziwill to General De Robilant*, trans. Cyril Spencer Fox (London, 1937), 90.

186 Moltke, *Erinnerungen*, 24.

187 Hull, *Kaiser*, 69–70.

188 Ibid., 64. The Kaiser's inclination to paranoia – his suspicions of plots against him, his conviction of persecution, and so forth – may also have a bearing on the question of latent homosexuality. In psychoanalytic theory and practice, paranoia has long been associated with homosexuality.

189 A fuller discussion of issues raised here, and in the chapter on Hitler's childhood, is given in my biography, *The Psychopathic God: Adolf Hitler* (New York, 1977, 1993).

190 William L. Shirer, *Berlin Diary: The Journal of a Foreign Correspondent, 1934–1941* (New York, 1941), 16–18.

191 Lloyd George's article in *Daily Express* (London), quoted in Joachim Remak, ed., *The Nazi Years: A Documentary History* (Englewood Cliffs, NJ, 1969), 82.

192 Winston S. Churchill, *Great Contemporaries* (New York, 1937), 226.

193 Helmut Heiber, *Adolf Hitler: Eine Biographie* (Berlin, 1960), 116.

194 During both the Second and the Third Reichs, it became popular to copy the moustache-style of the ruler. The Kaiser's barber, Hof Friseur François Haby, patented the special wax and slinglike apparatus called a '*Kaiser Binde*' which he used with such success on the royal moustache. Haby claimed that any man could achieve the same results if he would wear the contraption overnight for a week. (See advertisement reprinted in S. Fischer-Fabian, *Herrliche Zeiten*, 252. The popularity of the more easily achievable 'Führer-Schnurrbart' is attested by the pictures of Nazis in *Das Deutsche Führer-Lexikon* (a sort of Who's Who of the Nazi Party) (Munich, 1934).

195 Friedrich Oechsner, *This Is the Enemy* (New York, 1942), 77. For a physical description of Hitler, in addition to published memoirs, see 'Hitler as Seen by His Doctors,' Military Intelligence, Consolidated Interrogation Report, 29 May 1945, National Archives, Washington, DC (NA). Hereafter cited as 'Hitler's Doctors, MIR.'

196 Robert Coulondre, *Von Moskau nach Berlin, 1936–1939: Erinnerungen des französischen Botschafters* (Bonn, 1950), 307; René Juvet, *Ich war dabei: 20 Jahre Nationalsozialismus, 1923–1943 – Ein Tatsachenbericht* (Zurich, 1944), 13.

197 Joseph O. Baylen and Ralph F. Munster, 'Adolf Hitler as seen by Houston Stewart Chamberlain: A Forgotten Letter,' *Duquesne Review* (Fall 1967), 83.

198 August Kubizeck, *The Young Hitler I Knew*, trans. E.V. Anderson (Boston, 1955), 17–18.

199 Martha Dodd in 'Hitler Source Book,' ed. Walter C. Langer from documents collected by the OSS in 1942–3, NA, 58. Hereafter cited as 'OSS Source Book.'

200 Albert Speer, *Inside the Third Reich: Memoirs*, trans. Richard and Clara Winston (New York, 1970), 100.

201 Testimony of Christa Schroeder, one of Hitler's secretaries, in Albert Zoller ed., *Hitler Privat: Erlebnissbericht seiner Geheimsekretärin* (Düsseldorf, 1949), 69; Oechsner, *Enemy*, 113–14. Oechsner was Central European Manager of the United Press, 1933–42.

202 Gordon W. Prange, ed., *Hitler's Words* (Washington, DC, 1944), 11; Dietrich Bracher, *The German Dictatorship: The Origins, Structure and Effects of National Socialism*, trans. Jean Steinberg (New York, 1970), 151.

203 *Zerschmettern* (smash), it may be recalled, was a favourite word of the Kaiser.

204 Carl J. Burckhardt, *Meine Danziger Mission: 1937–1939* (Munich, 1960), 344; *Tischgespräche*, 168.

205 Speer in interview with Thomas P. O'Connell, 'The Devil's Architect,' *New York Times Magazine*, 26 Oct. 1969, 48.

206 Dr Hans Frank, *Im Angesicht des Galgens: Deutung Hitlers und seiner Zeit auf Grund eigener Erlebnisse und Erkenntnisse*, ed. Oswald Schloffer (Munich, 1953), 312; Bracher, *Dictatorship*, 347.

207 Willie Schneider, 'Aus nächster Nähe,' *Die 7. Tage: Illustrierte Wochenschrift aus dem Zeitgeschehen* (Baden-Baden, 17 Oct. 1952). Schneider was a member of the Waffen SS, who served for a time as the Führer's valet.

208 Oran J. Hale, 'Adolf Hitler: Taxpayer,' *American Historical Review* 609 (July 1955), 830–42.

209 Speer interview in *New York Times Magazine*, Oct. 26, 1969.

210 *The Testament of Adolf Hitler*, ed. R.H. Stevens (London, 1961), 13 Feb. 1945.

211 Hitler's 'Table Talk' as recorded in *Tischgespräche*, previously cited, and in *Hitler's Secret Conversations, 1941–1944*, trans. Norman Cameron and R. Stevens (New York, 1953). Hereafter cited as *Secret Conversations*.

212 Oberösterreische Landes Archiv, Politische Akten (Linz), Kubizek's affidavit, folder 63.

213 Kubizek, *Young Hitler*, 24.

214 Baldur von Schirach, *Ich glaubte an Hitler* (Hamburg, 1967), 122.

215 See Chapter 5.

216 Werner Maser, *Hitlers Mein Kampf: Entstehung, Aufbau, Stil, Aenderungen, Quellen, Quellenwert, Kommentierte Auszüge*, 2nd ed. (Munich, 1966), 112.

217 See Chapter 2.

218 Heinrich Hoffmann, *Hitler Was My Friend*, trans. R.H. Stevens (London, 1955), 204–5. This order was never carried out.

219 For Hitler's affection for ravens, see affidavit of Percy Schramm on Hitler, Bundesarchiv Bestand, 441; for regulations on lobsters and other animals, *Deutsches Tierschutzrecht* in *Reichsgesetzblatt*, nos. 39 and 132. I am grateful to the late Jan Stephan, Reference Librarian of Harvard Law School Library, for sending me copies of these documents.

220 Hoffmann, *Hitler My Friend*, 88, 197. Hoffmann became a millionaire after becoming Hitler's official photographer. See, as an example of his wares, *100 Bild-Dokumente aus dem Leben des Führers* (Berlin, n.d. [1934?].

221 Peter Hoffmann, *Widerstand, Staatsstreich, Attentat: Der Kampf der Opposition gegen Hitler* (Munich, 1969), 476.

222 Speer, *Third Reich*, 99–100.

223 'Hitler's Doctors, MIR.' Psychoanalysts have found a clear connection between anality and sadism. 'Anal compulsive' patients are also noted for rigidity, stubbornness, and refusal to yield, for a tendency towards compulsive repetition, and for being meticulously and compulsively clean. Adolf Hitler fit this pattern.

224 There are several versions of Hitler's 'Table Conversations' at his headquarters during the war. All legitimate accounts are based on the original *Bormann Vermerke*
(Bormann Notes). Martin Bormann, the sinister, immensely powerful, and fanatically loyal secretary to Hitler, wanted to preserve the Führer's 'imperishable
thoughts' for posterity. But Hitler would allow no recording apparatus or secretary
taking full notes of his conversations. Finally, Bormann persuaded him to permit a
trustworthy assistant to jot down inconspicuous notes that served as the basis for
extensive dictations which secretaries immediately transcribed. The notes were
taken largely by two trusted adjutants, Heinrich Heim and Dr Henry Picker. Bormann himself went over the typescript which he edited and 'corrected' in order to
enhance the Führer's image. Some 1,200 typed pages came into the hands of a
Swiss, M. François Genoud, who published a portion under the title, *Libres Propos
sur la Guerre et la Paix* (Paris, 1952). Heim's original notes were edited by Werner
Jochmann and published as *Adolf Hitler Monologe im Hauptquartier 1941–1944:
Die Aufzeichnungen Heinrich Heims* (Hamburg 1980). Picker's version, which
incorporates much of Heim's text, appeared as *Tischgespräche*, previously cited.
Picker's account comprises slightly over one-half of the matter contained in the
Bormann Vermerke, the fullest version of which is given in the English editon, with
an Introduction by H.R. Trevor-Roper. These editions will be cited here as *Secret
Conversations*, or *Monologe*, or *Tischgespräche*.

225 Albert Speer, *Spandau: The Secret Diaries*, trans. Richard and Clara Winston (New
York, 1976), 346. For other examples of Hitler's preoccupation with faeces, see
Waite, *Psychopathic God*, 148–9.

226 Max Planck, radio script for RIAS, Berlin, 24 Nov. 1966. A military aide wrote
about the Führer: 'The strong nerves which he so often praised, he himself did not
possess.' Friedrich Hossbach, *Zwischen Wehrmacht und Hitler: 1934–1938*
(Wolfenbüttel, 1949), 23.

227 Max Domarus, ed., *Hitler: Reden und Proklamationen, 1932–1945*, 4 vols.
(Würzburg, 1962), 1629; pagination is given serially throughout the four volumes,
my emphasis.

228 Schroeder, *Hitler Privat,* 56; Otto Dietrich, *12 Jahre mit Hitler* (Munich, 1955), 16;
Paul Schmidt, *Hitler's Interpreter: The Secret History of German Diplomacy,
1935–1945* (London, 1951), 266.

229 See *Hitler's Testament*, 14 Feb. 1945.

230 See Chapter 6.

231 Kubizek, *Young Hitler*, 176.

232 General Karl Koller, *Der letzte Monat: die Tagebuchaufzeichnungen des ehemaligen Chefs des Generalstabes der deutschen Luftwaffe vom 14. April bis 27. Mai
1945* (Mannheim, 1949), 31; Domarus, *Reden,* 2186; *Tischgespräche* and *Hitler's
Testament*.

233 Dr Förster, former Chargé d'Affaires, German embassy in Paris, letter to the editor, *Wiener Bulletin* (London), 10, nos. 5/6 (1956), 46.

234 Heinz Linge was a member of the SS and Hitler's valet and confidant of the last years. See his articles, 'Kronzeuge Linge' (State's Witness Linge) in *Revue* (Munich), 28 Jan. 1956 and 3 March 1956.

235 Linge, 'Kronzeuge,' 3 March 1956; Kurt von Schuschnigg, *Austrian Requiem*, trans. Franz von Hildebrand (New York, 1946), 15, and Miscellaneous OSS File, NA. For Hitler's 'Monumental History,' see Waite, *Psychopathic God*, Chapter 2, p. 56.

236 Domarus, *Reden*, 1424.

237 Ibid., 1842.

238 Nerin E. Gun, *Eva Braun-Hitler: Leben und Schicksal, Mit 108 Aufnahmen, Urkunden und Dokumenten* (New York, 1968), 202, and *Secret Conversations*, 278.

239 *Mein Kampf* (New York, 1939), unless otherwise noted, this is the edition that will be cited here. 65, 511; Joachim C. Fest, *The Face of the Third Reich: Portraits of the Nazi Leadership*, trans. Michael Bullock (New York, 1970), 51; Speer, 101; italics are mine.

240 'OSS Source Book,' 935; Linge, 'Kronzeuge' *Revue*, 26 Dec. 1955; Ernst Hanfstaengl, *The Missing Years* (London, 1957), 238, and in personal interview in Munich, June 1967; Schirach, *Hitler*, 268.

241 Richard M. Hunt, 'Joseph Goebbels: A Study of the Formation of his National-Socialist Conscience (1897–1929),' PhD dissertation, Harvard University, 1960.

242 Schroeder, *Hitler Privat*, 23; Schneider, *Aus nächster Nähe*; and Linge, 'Kronzeuge,' 3 March 1956.

243 Waite, *Psychopathic God*, 10.

244 H. Hoffmann, *Hitler My Friend*, 83–4, 102; Schneider, *Aus nächster Nähe*, 17.

245 As reported in the German government's *News of the Week*, 3 July 1992.

246 *Secret Conversations*, 257, and Linge, 'Kronzeuge,' 26 Dec. 1955.

247 Gun, *Eva Braun*, 14.

248 Kubizek, *Young Hitler*, 26; Ernst von Weizsäcker, *Erinnerungen* (Munich, 1950), 200; Schroeder, *Hitler Privat*, 84; Schneider, *Aus nächster Nähe*.

249 *Tischgespräche*, passim. See also *Secret Conversations*; *Hitler's Testament*; and Hitler Papers, Library of Congreses, Manuscript Division.

250 Schroeder, *Hitler Privat*, 50.

251 *Mein Kampf*, 30, 84, 161–2. *Secret Conversations*, 211.

252 Schramm, 'Erläuterung' to *Tischgespräche*, 31; Nathan Eck, 'Were Hitler's Political Actions Planned or Merely Improvised?' *Yad Vasham* 5 (1963), 368–9.

253 Herman Hammer, 'Die deutschen Ausgaben von Hitlers *Mein Kampf*,' *Vierteljahreshefte für Zeitgeschichte* 4 (1956), 178 and *passim*. Hereafter this periodical will be cited as *VfZ*.

254 Dietrich, *Hitler*, 216.
255 See Karl Wilhelm Krause, *Zehn Jahre Kammerdiener bei Hitler* (Hamburg, n.d.), as well as the memoirs of Krause, Kubizek, Linge, Schroeder, previously cited, and the affidavit of Dr Hans Karl Hasselbach, in Bundesarchiv, Bestand, 441–3b.
256 Dr Hugo Blaschke, in 'Hitler's Doctors, MIR.' Blaschke graduated in 1911 from the University of Pennsylvania School of Dentistry.
257 Schirach, *Hitler*, 115, 130, Dr Erwin Giesing, in 'Hitler's Doctors, MIR'; Schroeder, ed., *Hitler Privat*, 91; *Tischgespräche*, 451.
258 Hanfstaengl recalled that Hitler occasionally took rum in his tea when he had a cold and that when, on returning from England in 1934, he took him a gift of a bottle of rare rum, Hitler had said that he would drink it 'only for colds.' 'Adolf Hitler,' General Services Administration, National Archives and Records Services, Dec., 1942. This report, prepared privately for President F.D. Roosevelt, was based largely on the testimony of a 'Dr Sedgewick,' who was actually Hanfstaengl, as he told me in a personal interview of June 1967. The report is available in the Roosevelt Library, Hyde Park. (Hereafter cited as 'AH' in FDR)
259 *Der Hitler Prozess vor dem Volksgericht in München* (Munich, 1924); personal interview with Ernst Hanfstaengl, Munich, June 1967.
260 Kubizek, *Young Hitler*, 160–1; Schramm, affidavit in Bundesarchiv, Bestand 441–B; 'AH' in FDR; Dr Karl Brandt, in 'Hitler's Doctors, MIR.'
261 *Mein Kampf*, 38, 39, 43–4, 65, 75, 116–8, 416; my emphasis.
262 Ibid., 748. Memoirs of Linge, Reiter, Hoffmann, Schirach, and Schroeder. The 'wolf has been born' is quoted in Reginald H. Phelps, 'Hitler and the Deutsche Arbeiterpartei,' *American Historical Review* 68 (July 1963), 983. Information about Wolfhardt from S. Lane Faison, Jr, 'Linz, Hitler's Museum and Library,' Consolidated Interrogation Report No. 40 (15 Dec. 1945), War Department, Art Looting Investigation Unit. Interview with Frau Wolf, cited in Robert M.W. Kampner, *Das Dritte Reich im Kreuzverhör: Aus den unveröffentlichten Vernehmungsprotokollen des Anklägers* (Munich, 1969), 33, 43. About Winnifred Wagner, see Nicolaus Sombart, 'Zum dokumentation über Winnifred Wagner,' *Merkur* (Munich, Dec., 1975), 331.
263 The swastika banner which, allegedly, had been blood stained by SA 'martyrs' during Hitler's abortive attempt to seize power.
264 The process of acquiescing to atrocity through participation in it is well illustrated in the experience of Prof. D. Hans Herman Kramer, who had had a distinguished medical career and was chairman of the medical faculty of the University of Münster before joining the SS. One of Kramer's first assignments as an SS doctor at Auschwitz was to attend what was euphemistically called a *Sonderaktion* ('special action'), which was an early method of mass execution. Prisoners, especially mothers and their babies, were thrown alive into pits measuring some 20 by 40 metres

onto piles of wood soaked in kerosene. The piles were then ignited. When Kramer witnessed his first *Sonderaktion*, he found the experience totally shattering: 'Awful ... Dante's Inferno ... I cannot stand it.' But Kramer's diary indicates that, after repeated exposure to these actions, he was able to take them in stride and indeed could discuss them with equanimity: '6 September [1942]: Today, Sunday, excellent lunch of tomato soup, half a chicken with potatoes and red cabbage ... sweets and marvelous vanilla ice ... In the evening at 20.00 hours, outside for a *Sonderaktion* ... 23 September [1942]: Sixth and seventh *Sonderaktion* ... In the evening at 20.00, a real banquet. We had pike ... good coffee, excellent beer and rolls.' Elie A. Cohen, *Human Behavior in the Concentration Camp* (New York, 1953), 236 and *passim*.

265 *Mein Kampf*, passim.

266 Schroeder, *Hitler Privat*, 232.

267 *Hitlers Lagebesprechungen: die Protokollfragmente seiner Militärkonferenzen, 1942–45*, ed. Helmut Heiber (Stuttgart, 1962), 18; Karl Wilhelm Krause, *Zehn Jahre Kammerdiener bei Hitler* (Hamburg, n.d.), 41; Zoller, 44, 74.

268 Domarus, *Reden*, 2291; see also Schroeder, *Hitler Privat*.

269 Linge, 'Kronzeuge,' 3 March 1956.

270 *Testament politique de Hitler*, quoted in Joachim C. Fest, *Hitler: Eine Biographie*, 5th ed. (Frankfurt/Main and Berlin, 1973), 1012; my emphasis.

271 Domarus, *Reden* 226, 1423. See also interviews conducted during De Witt Poole Mission, microfilm, roll 3. General Records of the Department of State, Record Group (RG) 59, Special Interrogation Mission to Germany 1945–6, 3 microfilm rolls, NA, 1946.

272 Birger Dahlerus, *Der Letzer Versuch: London–Berlin, Sommer 1939* (Munich, 1948), 71.

273 See text of the speeches at Ludwigshaven, 25 March 1934; Nuremburg, 16 Sept. 1935; Koenigsberg, 18 March 1936; Breslau, 22 March 1936; and Berlin, 21 May 1935, 7 March 1936, and 26 Sept. 1938.

274 Domarus, *Reden*, 2035.

275 Schroeder, *Hitler Privat*, 48; 'AH' in FDR.

276 *Secret Conversations*, 292.

277 Domarus, *Reden*, 214; Lascelles, *British Documents*, vol. 2, 499.

278 Quoted in Harold C. Deutsch, *The Conspiracy against Hitler in the Twilight War* (Minneapolis, 1968), 32.

279 Linge, 'Kronzeuge,' 3 March 1956.

280 See Chapter 3.

281 Col. Gen. a.D. Franz Halder, 'The Diary of Franz Halder.' Photocopy of German typescript, copyright 1946 U.S. Attorney General, Archives of Institut für Zeitgeschichte (IfZ), Munich.

282 Konrad Heiden, *Der Fuehrer: Hitler's Rise to Power* (Boston, 1944), 360.

283 Lutz Graf Schwerin von Krosigk, *Es geschah in Deutschland: Menschenbilder unseres Jahrhunderts* (Stuttgart, 1951), 220.

284 Weizsäcker, *Erinnerungen*, 252.

285 Staff Conferences, Folder 16; *Hitlers Lagebesprechungen: Die Protocolls fragmente seiner militarischen Konferenze, 1942–45*, ed. Helmut Heiber (Stuttgart, 1962), 24.

286 Karl Wahl, '... *es ist das deutsche Herz': Erlebnisse und Erkenntnisse eines ehemaligen Gauleiters* (Augsburg, 1954), 204, 340; Gerhard Herrgesell, interview in *Time*, 21 May 1945; Sir Ivone Kirkpatrick, *The Inner Circle* (London, 1959), 96.

287 The incident is reported by David Irving, and cited by Alan Bullock, *Hitler and Stalin* (New York, 1992), 579.

288 Dahlerus, *Der letzte Versuch*, 65–7.

289 Personal conversation with Lane Faison, Williamstown, MA, Oct. 1991. Schroeder, *Hitler Privat*, 52; Friedrich Heer, *Der Glaube des Adolf Hitler: Anatomie einer politischen Religiosität* (Munich, 1968), 293.

290 Erich Czech-Jochberg, *Hitler: Reichskanzler* (Oldenburg, n.d.), 160.

291 Fest, *Biographie*, 404–6.

292 Frank, *Deutung Hitlers*; Dietrich Orlow, *The History of the Nazi Party*, 2 vols. (Pittsburgh, 1969 and 1973); vol. 1, 272; 'OSS Source Book,' 936.

293 *Documents in German Foreign Policy*, Series D (Washington, DC, 1956), vol. 5, 201–2. Baldur von Schirach, quoted in *Stern*, 3 Sept. 1967.

294 Reginald Phelps, 'Dokumentation: Hitler als Parteiredner im Jahre 1920,' *VfZ* 11 (1963), 309.

295 'OSS Source Book,' 410; 'Hitler's Doctors, MIR.'

296 Linge, 'Kronzeuge,' 26 Nov. 1955.

297 See below, p. 148.

298 Joseph Goebbels, *The Early Goebbels Diaries*, 1925–26, ed. Helmut Heiber, trans. Oliver Watson (New York, 1963), 100.

299 A copy of the promissary note may be seen in the NA, Washington, prints division.

300 Ernst Hanfstaengl, *Unheard Witness* (New York, 1957), 69; and 'AH' in FDR.

301 Personal letter from Jan Stepan, Director, Harvard Law School Library, 4 Dec. 1974; Albert Speer, as interviewed in *Playboy*, June 1971, 193.

302 Interview with E. Hanfstaengl, Munich, June 1967. A photograph of the desk may be seen in *Die Kunst im Dritten Reich* 3 (1939), 413. See also Frank, *Deutung Hitlers*, 179.

303 Sigmund Freud, 'Medusa's Head,' *International Journal of Psycho-Analysis* (London, 1941); Coulondre, *Moskau nach Berlin*, 422; Burckhardt, *Mission*, 345; my emphasis.

304 Quoted in Richard Hanser, *Putsch! How Hitler Made Revolution* (New York, 1970), 194.
305 *Mein Kampf*, 2 vols. in 1 unabridged ed. (Munich, 1941), 235.
306 Heiden, *Der Fuehrer*, 377.
307 Otto Strasser, *Hitler and I*, trans. Gwenda David and Eric Mosbacher (Boston, 1940), 64–5.
308 'OSS Source Book,' 627.
309 Erik Erikson first called my attention to Hitler's ambivalent treatment of the feminine goddesses and urged me to reread the German edition of *Mein Kampf* for examples.
310 Personal communication from Karl Menninger, 10 Oct. 1966.
311 *Mein Kampf, passim*; Munich speech in Phelps, 'Dokumentation,' 68; Berlin speech in Prange, *Hitler's Words*, 19–20.
312 Kubizek, *Young Hitler*, 233; *Secret Conversations*, 305.
313 *Secret Conversations*, 305.
314 Kubizek, *Young Hitler*, 59–60; 63–4.
315 See above, 'Kaiser Wilhelm II.'
316 Quoted in *Quick* (Munich), 3 May 1964, 104.
317 Quoted in Douglas M. Kelly, *22 Cells in Nuremberg: A Psychiatrist Examines the Nazi Criminals* (New York, 1947), 211. When a reporter commented on the number of beautiful women in Hitler's company at tea or at the opera, Hitler explained, 'To the greatest warrior belong the most beautiful women.'
318 H. Hoffmann, *Hitler My Friend*, 145; Paula Hitler, interviewed in *New York Times*, 5 March 1945.
319 *Secret Conversations*, 37.
320 Friedelind Wagner, *The Royal Family of Bayreuth* (London, 1948), 91.
321 Goebbels, *Diary*, 367 and *passim*.
322 *Tischgespräche*, 188 and *passim*; Speer, *Third Reich*, 92; *Secret Conversations*, 206; 'AH' in FDR.
323 *Mein Kampf*, 56.
324 *Secret Conversations*, 391; 'OSS Source Book,' 902–3.
325 'AH' in FDR; Schirach, *Hitler*, 67.
326 Mimi Reiter tried, and almost succeeded, in hanging herself in 1928. Geli Raubal shot herself in 1931. Eva Braun attempted suicide in 1932 and again in 1935 and succeeded in doing so, together with Hitler, in 1945. Frau Inge Ley was a successful suicide, as were Renate Mueller and Suzi Liptauer. Unity Mitford's attempted suicide in 1939 seems clearly to have been prompted by political reasons.
327 For a critical discussion of this assertion, see Addendum 5.
328 James P. O'Donnell, *The Bunker: The History of the Reich Chancellory Group* (Boston, 1978), 246.

329 Helmut Ulshöfer, ed., *Liebesbriefe an Adolf Hitler: Briefe in den Tod. Unveröffentlichte Dokumente aus der Reichskanzlei* (Frankfurt/Main, 1994). This edition contains 43 of the original letters, some in facsimile.

330 Harold Nicolson, *Diaries and Letters*, 2 vols. (New York, 1967), vol. 2, 39; 'AH' in FDR; Shirer, *Berlin Diary*, 137; Werner Maser, *Adolf Hitler: Legende, Mythos, Wirklichkeit* (Munich, 1971), 309.

331 Hanfstaengl interview and 'OSS Source Book,' 894.

332 Schneider, 'Kronzeuge,' 28 Nov. 1952. Another valet, Karl Wilhelm Krause, agreed that the relationship with Hess was very close indeed – but that was all he said about it. Krause, *Zehn Jahre*, 47. Finally, there is the inconclusive but interesting fact that one of the Führer's prized possessions was a handwritten love letter that King Ludwig II of Bavaria had written to a manservant.

333 *Rudolph Hess, Briefe: 1908–1933*, eds. Wolf Rüdiger Hess and Dirk Bavendamm (Munich, 1987).

334 Interview cited by Peter Padfield in his biography of Hess. My thanks to him for letting me read his book in manuscript prior to publication. Padfield, *Hess: Flight for the Führer* (London, 1991).

335 Handwritten letters Rudolf Hess (RH) to Ilse Pröhl, Munich, 29 June and 23 July 1924.

336 Typed letter RH to Ilse Pröhl, 23 July 1924.

337 Gitta Serenyi, *Albert Speer: His Battle for the Truth* (New York, 1995), 137, 157, 237, 614.

338 Ibid., 428, 497.

339 Wolfgang Harthauser, *Die Verfolgung der Homosexualen im Dritten Reich*, quoted in Richard Grunberger, *The Twelve-Year Reich: A Social History of Nazi Germany, 1933–1945* (New York, 1971), 121.

340 Domarus, *Reden*, 1843. For further discussion of homosexuality under Hitler, see U.S. government document, 'Homosexuals: Victims of the Nazi Era,' Holocaust Memorial Museum, n.d., Washington, DC, and Richard Plant, *The Pink Triangle: The Nazi War against Homosexuals* (New York, 1986).

341 Mann writing in foreword to an edition of Hitler's conversations, *Unmasked: Two Confidential Interviews with Hitler in 1931*, ed. Edouard Calic (London, 1971), 7.

Chapter 2: Weltanshauugen

1 Count Robert Zedlitz-Trütschler, *Twelve Years at the Imperial German Court*, trans. Alfred Kalisch (London, 1924), xiv, xv.

2 Wilhelm Schüsler, *Kaiser Wilhelm II. Schicksal und Schuld* (Göttingen, 1972), 41, and Graf Ernst Reventlow, *Von Potsdam nach Doorn* (Berlin, 1940), 368.

3 Sir Frank Lascelles, 'General Report on Germany: 1906–The Emperor,' *British Doc-*

uments on the Origins of the War: 1898–1914, ed. G.P. Gooch and Harold Temperley (London, 1928), vol. 3, 434.

4 *This Was Germany! An Observer at the Court of Berlin: Letters of Princess Marie Radziwill to General Di Robilant, One Time Italian Military Attaché at Berlin,* ed. and trans. Cyril Spencer Fox (London, 1937), 100.

5 *Das Königtum im alten Mesopotamien* (Berlin, 1938), and his study of the yin-yang monad and its relationship to the swastika: *Die chinesische Monade: Ihre Geschichte und Ihre Deutung* (Leipzig, 1934). In addition to the monographs, see Kaiser Wilhelm II, *Erinnerungen an Korfu* (Berlin and Leipzig, 1924); Hans Helfritz, *Wilhelm II als Kaiser und König: eine historische Studie* (Zurich, 1954), 181 ff; and Rudolf von Valentini, *Kaiser und Kabinettschef: nach eigenen Aufzeichnungen und dem Briefwechsel des wirklichen geheimen Rats,* ed. Bernhard Schwertfeger (Oldenburg, 1931), 113–14. The first drafts of several of the Kaiser's manuscripts may be found among his papers in the Rijksarchief (RA), Utrecht.

6 'The Diaries of Admiral Philip W. Dumas, CB, CVO, Microfilm No. PP/mer/96 (Imperial War Museum, London). Philip was British naval attaché to Germany, 1906–8.

7 AA Preussen, Nr. ld (Dumas TAK).

8 Wilhelm's papers are now deposited in the RA, Utrecht. All scholars are indebted to D.T. Coen for his indispensable guide to the Kaiser's papers: *Inventaria van het Archief van ex-Keiser Wilhelm II. tÿdjensÿn verblÿt in Nederland, 1918–1941* (Utrecht, 1977). I am also indebted to Henk Ooft for his kindness and cooperation in providing me with the document folders I requested.

9 Among memoirs, see esp. Albert Zoller, ed., *Hitler Privat: Erlebnisbericht seiner Geheimsekretärin* (Christa Schroeder) (Dusseldorf, 1949); Otto Dietrich, *12 Jahre mit Hitler* (Munich, 1955); Heinrich Hoffmann, *Hitler Was My Friend,* trans. R.H. Stevens (London, 1955); Albert Speer, *Inside the Third Reich: Memoirs,* trans. Richard and Clara Winston (New York, 1970); personal conversations with Ernst Hanfstaengl, Munich, April–June 1967; depositions of Percy Schramm, Karl Brandt, and Hans Karl Hasselbach in Bundesarchiv, Koblenz, Bestand 441; 'Hitler as Seen by His Doctors,' Military Intelligence Consolidated Interrogation Reports, National Archives, Washington, DC (NA), hereafter 'Hitler's Doctors, MIR'; and the testimony given to OSS agents in 1942–3 and ed. Walter C. Langer, 'Hitler Source Book,' (hereafter cited as 'OSS Source Book'), 3 vols., mimeographed, N.A.

10 Heinz Assmann, 'Some Personal Recollections of Adolf Hitler,' *United States Naval Institute Proceedings* 79 (July 1953), 1293.

11 A German physician in Hitler's entourage said that the Führer's knowledge of medicine and biology 'went far beyond that of the average informed layman ... In ten years I was not able to catch him in a single factual error.' Hasselbach deposition, Bundesarchiv; Brandt in 'Hitler's Doctors, MIR.'

12 Erich von Manstein, *Verlorene Siege* (Frankfurt/Main, 1963), 305, 315.

13 John Kenneth Galbraith, *New York Times Book Review*, 22 April 1973; see also John Heyl, 'Hitler's Economic Thought: A Reappraisal,' *Central European History* 6 (March 1973), 85.

14 Notes were dutifully taken by members of his entourage who had been told to preserve the pronouncements of their leader for the enlightenment of posterity. For the various eds. of the *Tischgespräche*, see Chapter 1, note 224.

15 Interestingly, Hitler made exactly the same comment in an interview he gave in 1931. (See Edouard Calic, ed., *Unmasked: Two Confidential Interviews with Hitler in 1931* Foreword by Golo Mann, trans. Richard Bury (London, 1971), 80. Hitler's interviews were with Richard Breiting, editor of the influential *Leipziger Neuste Nachrichten*. In point of fact, there was virtually no Irish immigration to America in 1641. The *total* population, including whites and blacks, in all colonies in America was about 26,600 in the year 1640. Ten years later the total population was 50,400. *Historical Statistics of the United States: Colonial Times to the Present* (Washington, DC: US Dept. of Commerce, Bureau of the Census 1975), 756. The great wave of Irish immigrants came in the late nineteenth century.

16 This comment was reported by Dorothy Thompson, *New York Post*, 3 Jan. 1944. Hitler gave one of his very few private interviews to Miss Thompson. Other citations in the above pages are from *Tischgespräche*.

17 Schroeder, *Hitler Privat*, 49, 115. Other quotations are from the 'Table Conversations.'

18 I am indebted to Th. L.J. Verroen, archivist and curator of Huis Doorn, for graciously permitting me in June 1990 to spend several hours in the Kaiser's private library, study, and bedroom. (There is also a card file of his books.)

19 Typically, Wilhelm used Goethe to show his scorn for the British decision to neglect its army in favour of the Royal Navy. Wilhelm, who believed that a choice between two indispensables was irrational, commented, 'To that [decision] one can say ... what Mephistopheles said to Faust: "Verachte nur Vernunft und Wissenschaft / Des Menschen allerhöchste Kraft / Lass nur in Blend- und Zauberwerken / Dich von dem Lügengeist bestärken (Have but contempt for reason and for science / Man's noblest force spurn with defiance / And cling to magic and illusion)' (AA England, 81. Nr. 2 (TAK).

20 See below, 'Their Mentor in Racism.'

21 Willi Schneider, 'Aus nächster Nähe,' *Die 7 Tage: Illlustrierte Wochenschrift aus dem Zeitgeschehen* (Baden-Baden), Oct. 1952. Karl Wilhelm Krause, also in *7 Tage*. Heinz Linge, 'Kronzeuge Linge,' *Revue* (Munich), Dec. 1955. Schneider, Krause, and Linge had all been, at various times, Hitler's valets.

22 See Kubizek's 14-page memorandum, 'Erinnerungen an mit dem Führer gemeinsam verlebten Jünglingsjahre: 1904–1908 in Linz und Wien' (n.d., possibly 1938),

Oberoesterreichisches Landesarchiv, Politische Akten no. 64 (hereafter cited as OLA). I am indebted to the Linz archivist, the late Franz Jetzinger, for showing me this document.

23 Heinrich Hoffmann, *Hitler My Friend*, xiv.

24 Colic, *Hitler Unmasked*, 78.

25 Schroeder, *Hitler Privat*, 50. My own investigation of the library confirms Fräulein Schroeder's judgment, as do Reginald H. Phelps, 'Die Hitler-Bibliothek,' *Deutsche Rundschau* 80 (1954), 929, and Arnold Jacobus, Staff Librarian, Library of Congress, 'The Books Hitler Owned' (unpublished manuscript). One exception might perhaps be made. Hitler lauded *Robinson Crusoe* for 'gathering together in one man the history of all mankind.' Conversation 17 Feb. 1942, *Secret Conversations*, 256–7.

26 Hitler as quoted by Albert Speer, *Spandau, The Secret Diaries*, trans. Richard and Clara Winston (New York, 1976), 313.

27 Handwritten and typescript drafts of his letters, sermons, and scholarly papers show thoughtful revision and careful selection of words. See Papers of the Ex-Keiser, Rijksarchief, Utrecht, folders 289–90.

28 The last paragraph in German reads: 'Denn tapfer und heldenmutig für ihren Kaiser und ihr Vaterland sind auch die französischen Soldaten in ihr ruhmvolles Grab gesunken, und wenn unsere Fahnen sich grüszend vor dem erzenen Standbilde neigen werden und wehmutsvoll über den Gräbern unserer lieben Kameraden rauschen, so mögen sie auch über den Gräbern unserer Gegner wehen, ihnen raunen, dass wir der tapfern Toten in wehmutsvoller Achtung gedenken. A. Oscar Klaussmann, ed., *Kaiserreden, Reden, and Erlasse, Briefe und Telegramme Kaisers Wilhelm II: Ein Charakturcelt des Deutschen Kaisers* (Leipzig, 1902), 59.

29 There is some question whether Wilhelm actually composed all his sermons himself. He probably drew ideas from his large collection of homilies written by chaplains and favourite preachers. Yet the consistency of the prose and the many alterations he made in manuscript versions clearly put his personal stamp on them.

30 Henri de Noussanne, *The Kaiser as He Is (Le Véritable Guillaume II)*, trans. Walter Littlefield (New York, 1905), 166–7. Wm also penned an ode in blank verse to honour the artist Adolf Menzel (1815–1905), who had painted a portrait of the Kaiser and his court, dressed in Fredrickian costume, for the Neues Palais at Sans Souci (built by Frederick the Great). At the age of 20, he had also written an ode to Pallas Athena. See Lamar Cecil, *Wilhelm II, Prince and Emperor, 1859–1900* (Chapel Hill, 1989), 39.

31 Alex Hall, *Scandal, Sensation and Social Democracy: The SPD Press and Wilhelmine Germany, 1890–1914* (Cambridge, 1977), 158. Interestingly, the verb *aegiren* means to act, as in a play – to play-act.

32 We do have the prospectus of one of his unfinished dramas about mountain men and

a sacrificial bull; see Robert G.L. Waite, *Psychopathic God: Adolf Hitler* (New York, 1977, 1993), 69.

33 Hitler could never forgive or forget the low grade in German and insisted it was entirely his teacher's fault. Years later he remembered that 'congenital idiot,' that 'repellent creature.' This 'disgusting teacher had succeeded in giving me an intense dislike for my mother-tongue! He asserted that I would never be capable of writing a decent letter! If this blundering little twerp (*dieser Stümpfer, dieser kleine Knirps*) ...'

34 For other examples of Hitler's prose, see Adolf Hitler, *Sämtliche Aufzeichnungen, 1905–1924*, ed. Eberhard Jäckel and Axel Kuhn (Stuttgart, 1980), and Waite, *Psychopathic God*, 70ff.

35 Otto Lurker, who was imprisoned with Hitler in Landsberg in 1924, recalled him dictating to his friend Rudolph Hess, as did Ernst Hanfstaengl. Lurker, *Hitler hinter Festungmauren* (Munich, 1933), 56, and personal interview with Hanfstaengl, Munich, June 1967. But in his published letters Hess does not mention taking dictation from Hitler, and Hess's wife asserted that Hitler typed the manuscript himself.

36 Milton, Goethe, Henry James, Napoleon, and Frederick Schuman, among many other writers, dictated their works to stenographers.

37 As late as 1976 *Mein Kampf* still appeared on a publisher's list of 'the best sellers of all time' in Germany. Classified grotesquely as belles-lettres, it easily won class honours with total sales in excess of 9 million copies. (*Die Zeit*, 25 June 1976). See also Hermann Hammer, 'Die deutschen Ausgaben von Hitlers *Mein Kampf*,' *Vierteljahr-shefte, für Zeitgeschichte* (VfZ) (1956), 163, and *Wiener Bulletin*, nos. 5/6, (1952).

38 Hammer, 'Hitler's *Mein Kampf.*'

39 One example: 'Protestantism in itself represents the considerations of Germanism better, as far as this lies based in its birth and later tradition altogether, but it fails at the moment when this defence of national interests must take place in territory which in general lines is either lacking in its conceptual world or is simply rejected for one reason or another.'

40 The point is made in D.C. Watt's Introduction to Ralph Manheim's translation of *Mein Kampf* (London, 1969).

41 *Secret Conversations*, 205 (see Chapter 1, n224).

42 See Chapter 6.

43 The translation is Helm Stierlin's, who first published the poem in his monograph, *Adolf Hitler: A Family Perspective* (New York, 1976).

44 Entry into the guest book at Schoiber's Inn. The poem was first discovered by Professor Eberhard Jäckel, who called it to Stierlin's attention. Stierlin, *Family Perspective*, nn.18, 19, and 20. It is now reprinted in entirety in the valuable collection, *Hitler: Aufzeichnungen*.

45 *Secret Conversations*, 159.

46 See Chapter 6.

47 Stierlin, *Family Perspective*, 69.
48 The poems appear as documents nos. 36 and 38 along with three other quite prosaic poems in *Hitler: Aufzeichnungen*. As the editors point out, we cannot be absolutely certain that Hitler wrote these poems. But the fact that he signed them and associated himself with their sentiments persuaded the editors to accept them as Hitler's poetry. The style is consistent with his other verse. My translation with an assist from Harlan Hanson.
49 The French and the Russian diplomats who, according to German patriots, were responsible for setting up the hostile coalition that encircled the Fatherland.
50 The last couplet poses problems.

> *Wenn's der [...] später nicht zerstörte,*
> *Stü[n]de noch heut[e] der Wöchnerin!*

The editors suggest that the missing word may be 'Tocko,' a German soldier's slang for a Frenchmen, derived, presumably, from 'toque,' a type of knitted hat associated with Frenchman. Other slang terms used during the war were 'Frogs' for the French; 'Heinies,' 'Huns,' and 'Boche' for the Germans; 'Limeys' for the British; 'Yanks' and 'Amis' for Americans, and so forth. My translation, with thanks to Geoffrey Waite for the Tocko.
51 *Sonntag-Morgenpost*, 14 May 1933. My translation. The German reads:

> Denk' es!

> Wenn deine Mutter alt geworden
> Und älter du geworden bist,
> Wenn ihr, was früher leicht und mühlos,
> Nunmehr zur Last geworden ist,
> Wenn ihre lieben, treuen Augen
> Nicht mehr, wie einst, in's Leben seh'n
> Wenn ihr müd' geword'nen Füsse
> Sie nicht mehr tragen woll'n beim Geh'n –
> Dann reiche ihr den Arm zu Stütze
> Geleite sie mit froher Lust –
> Die Stunde kommt, da du sie weinend
> Zum letzten Gang begleiten musst!
> Und fragt sie dich, so gib ihr Antwort,
> Und fragt sie wieder, sprich auch du!
> Und fragt sie nochmals, steh' ihr Rede,
> Nicht ungestüm, in sanfter Ruh!
> Und kann sie dich nicht recht verstehen,
> Erklär' ihr alles frohbewegt,
> Die Stunde kommt, die bitt're Stunde
> Da dich ihr Mund nach nichts mehr frägt.

52 Personal communication, F.H. Stocking, Dec. 1989.

53 *New York Mail and Express*, cited by Naussanne, *Kaiser*, 147.

54 'Eine Kunst, die sich über die von mir bezeichneten Gesetze und Schranken, hinweg-setzt ist keine Kunst mehr.' Ernst Rohan, ed., *Reden des Kaisers: Ansprachen, Predigten und Trinksprüche Wilhelms II.* (Munich, 1966), 102.

55 Peter Paret, *The Berlin Secession: Modernism and Its Enemies in Imperial Germany* (Cambridge, MA, 1980), 25.

56 Ibid., 26.

57 Peter Paret, 'Art and the National Image: The Conflict over Germany's Partici-pation in the St Louis Exposition,' *Central European History* 11/2 (June 1978), 183.

58 A German cultural historian has suggested that Wilhelm appealed to the masses because he shared their artistic taste. Hermann Glaser, *Die Kultur der Wilhelminis-chen Zeit: Typographie einer Epoche* (Frankfurt/Main, 1984).

59 Paret, *Berlin Secession*, 160. Isabella Stewart Gardner, who became Zorn's patroness in America and whose portrait he painted, would have been surprised by the Kaiser's characterization of one of her favourite artists. See the collection of Zorns in the Gardner Museum, Boston.

60 *Memoirs of Prince von Bülow*, 3 vols., trans. F.A. Voigt (Boston, 1931), vol. 2, 421.

61 Speech 18 Dec. 1901, Rohan, *Reden*. An English version is given in Wolf von Schierbrand, ed. and trans., *The Kaiser's Speeches, forming a Character Portrait of Emperor William II* (New York and London, 1930), 234–6.

62 On a report from London saying that paintings by German artists in an exhibit of modern art were not well received, Wm wrote in the margin: 'The English are show-ing their good taste and don't bother with these filthy things (*diese Schmutzich-keiten*).' AA England, 78/A 100 (TAK).

63 Marion F. Deshmukh, 'Art and Politics in Turn-of-the-Century Berlin: The Berlin Secession and Kaiser Wilhelm II,' *Turn of the Century: German Literature and Art, 1890–1915* (Bonn, 1981), 466. Yet in April 1895 the mercurial Wm had invited a number of French artists to participate in an exhibition he was sponsoring in Berlin. Many artists refused on patriotic grounds – the French defeat of 1870–1 was still rankling. Those academic painters who accepted were roundly castigated by the patriotic French press. See Paul Hayes Tucker, *Monet in the '90s: The Series Paint-ings* (Museum of Fine Arts Catalogue, Boston, 1989), 183. My thanks to John H. Brooks for this reference.

64 Paret, *Berlin Secession*, 160.

65 Lovis Corinth, *Das Leben Walter Leistikows: Ein Stück Berliner Kulturgeschichte* (Berlin, 1910), 29, cited by Deschmukh, 'Art as Politics,' 466.

66 Ibid., 471.

67 He subsequently became director of the Bavarian State Gallery in Munich.

68 Quoted by Barbara Tuchman, *The Proud Tower* (New York, 1966), 303.
69 Paret, *Berlin Secession*, 92–3.
70 Ibid., 143, and Deschmukh, 'Art and Politics,' 473.
71 Paret, *Berlin Secession*, 142.
72 Letter Queen Victoria (QV) to Vicky (V), 11 July 1883 (TAK).
73 Deshmukh, 'Art and Politics,' 464.
74 See below.
75 In June 1990 neither the curator nor I could find the following paintings listed in the House catalogue: no. 3366, 'Warship at Sea in a Storm,' and no. 3899, 'An Enemy Sighted: *HMS Devastation*.'
76 Helfritz, *Kaiser und König*, 357.
77 Bülow, *Memoirs*, vol. 1, 79.
78 Joachim von Kürenberg, *The Kaiser: A Life of Wilhelm II, Last Emperor of Germany*, trans. H.T. Russell and Herta Hagen (New York, 1955), 220. The Kaiser's title was actually 'German Emperor,' not 'Emperor of Germany' – the German princes having insisted on the former formulation in 1871.
79 *Simplicissimus*, 24 April 1911.
80 Bülow, *Memoirs*, vol. 1, 79. Bülow reported that in this instance the Kaiser was not at all angered by the criticism. Indeed he shook with laughter. Wilhelm could take criticism if it were done with humour and not publicized.
81 Modris Eksteins, *Rites of Spring* (Boston, 1989), 88, and Georg Alexander von Müller, *The Kaiser and His Court: The Diaries, Notebooks and Letters of Admiral Georg von Müller, Chief of the Naval Secretariat, 1914–1918*, ed. Walter Goerlitz (London, 1961), 303.
82 See Waite, *Psychopathic God*, 102–3.
83 *Daily Telegraph* article of 22 June 1894, AA Preussen I, Nr ld (TAK); for his 'Ode to Aegir,' see above.
84 See picture in Waite, *Psychopathic God*.
85 Geoffrey G. Field, *Evangelist of Race: The Germanic Vision of Houston Stewart Chamberlain* (New York, 1981), 167.
86 Alfred Rosenberg, *Letzte Aufzeichnungen* (Göttingen, 1955), 320, 342.
87 Karl Menninger, *Man against Himself* (New York, 1961), 386.
88 August Kubizek, *The Young Hitler I Knew*, trans. E.V. Anderson (Boston, 1955), 188; and 'AH' in FDR (see Chapter 1, n258).
89 Quoted by Peter Viereck, *Metapolitics: From the Romantics to Hitler* (New York, 1941), 132; Hitler, *Mein Kampf*, 23; Kubizek, *Young Hitler*, 191–2; and Frederick C. Oechsner, *This Is the Enemy* (Boston, 1942), 87. Oechsner was Central European manager of the UP until 1941; he interviewed Hitler several times in 1941. For further discussion of Wagner's influence on Hitler, see Waite, *Psychopathic God*, 99–113.

90 Kubizek, *Young Hitler*, 205; Friedrich Heer, *Der Glaube des Adolf Hitler: Anatomie einer politischen Religiosität* (Munich, 1968), 37; 'AH' in FDR.

91 For Hitler's method of suicide, see Waite, *Psychopathic God*, 414–6.

92 *Tischgespräche*, 27.

93 Several sketches of the heads have been preserved in the Library of Congress Manuscript Division, 'A. Hitler Collection.' Other sketches appear in Baldur von Schirach, *Ich glaubte an Hitler* (Hamburg, 1967), in an anonymous volume, *Katalog der privaten Galerie Adolf Hitlers* (n.p., n.d.). Hitler's sketches also form the endpapers of Hoffmann's *Hitler Was My Friend*. The masturbation cartoon is now in the German National Archives in Koblenz. Werner Maser, a German biographer who reprinted it, thought that the teacher is depicted as 'overbearing,' 'suspicious,' and 'arrogant,' and that he is holding an ice-cream cone in his hand. I do not find the teacher arrogant and that is no ice-cream cone in his hand. Cones made their first appearance at the St Louis World's Fair of 1904 – four years *after* Adolf drew this caricature of his teacher. See Werner Maser, *Hitlers Briefe und Notizen: Sein Weltbild in handschriflichen Dokumenten* (Vienna, 1973), 38. In this drawing done at the age of 11 or 12 of a frightened *Realschule* teacher apparently caught in the act of masturbation, young Hitler may possibly have been expressing anxiety about his undescended testicle by projecting his own fears onto the teacher. Or, more plausibly, he was simply trying to diminish an authoritarian figure by showing him in an embarrassing position. See Chapter 6.

94 Speer, *Third Reich*, 75 and 532; see also his 'Playboy Interview: Albert Speer,' *Playboy* magazine (June 1971), 80.

95 Oechsner, *Enemy*, 84, and testimony of Percy E. Schramm, Bundesarchiv, Bestand 441.

96 Speer, *Third Reich*, 159. It took Albert Speer a long time to reach that conclusion.

97 Conversation with Lane Faison, September 1979.

98 See George Mosse's fine chapter, 'Hitler's Tastes,' in his *The Nationalization of the Masses: Political Symbolism and Mass Movements in Germany from the Napoleonic Wars through the Third Reich* (New York, 1975).

99 Adolf Hitler, 'Skizzenbuch' (unpublished ms which Albert Speer deposited in the Kunstgeschichtliches Seminar, Göttingen, cited by Mosse, *Masses*, 189–90.

100 S. Lane Faison, Jr, 'Linz: Hitler Museum and Library,' Consolidated Interrogation Report no. 4, 15 Dec. 1945, Office of Strategic Services (OSS), War Department, Washington, DC, mimeographed. Used through the courtesy of the author.

101 Conversations with Hanfstaengl, April 1967.

102 The leading authority on von Stuck has catalogued the following themes: Women as the personification of sin, evil, or depravity, 23 paintings (with 10 different portrayals of 'Sin'); pursuit and possession of women, 14 paintings; men duelling over women, 15; centaurs chasing women, 29; sensuality, temptation, or women as

seducers of men, 39. See Heinrich Voss, *Franz von Stuck, 1863–1928: Werkkatalog der Gemälde* ... (Munich, n.d.).

103 See Cornelia Berning, *Vom 'Abstammiungsnachweis' zum 'Zuchtwart': Vokabular des Nationalsozialismus* (Berlin, 1964).

104 See Gordon A. Craig's review of Peter Adams, *Art of the Third Reich*, in *New York Times Book Review* (21 June 1992).

105 The chancel Bible, which he also presented, bears an inscription in the words of Jesus, but the Kaiser seems to have given himself credit for the saying, since it appeared over his usual signature and without quotation or attribution: 'Apart from me ye can do nothing. Wilhelm I[mperator] R[ex].' Alex Hall, *Scandal*, 155. According to one of his disciples, Jesus said, 'I am the vine, you are the branches. He who abides in me, and I in him, he it is that bears much fruit; for apart from me you can do nothing.' John 15:5 (RSV).

106 Karl Wippermann, ed., *Deutscher Geschichtskalendar* (Leipzig, 1885–1944), vol. for 1910, 90. Wm made a similar statement in a speech Feb. 1892, saying that he went on his way 'in the direction Heaven has laid out for me.' Hildegard Freifrau Hugo von Sitzemberg, *Das Tagebuch der Baronin Spitzemberg*, ed. R. Vierhaus (Göttingen, 1960), 298.

107 Max Domarus, ed., *Hitler: Reden und Proklamationen, 1932–1945*, 3 vols. with continuous pagination (Munich, 1965), 606.

108 *Spitzemberg*, 368.

109 Lady Norah Bentinck, *The Kaiser in Exile* (London, 1921).

110 The Prussian dynasty, since the time of Elector John Sigismund, tended to be Calvinist. But since the majority of their Prussian subjects were Lutheran, King Friedrich Wilhelm III (1770–1840) sought to bridge the denominational gap between rulers and people by uniting the two churches. On 31 Oct. 1817, the tercentenary of Martin Luther's posting of his Ninety-Five Theses, Friedrich Wilhelm announced the formation of the 'Evangelical State Church of Prussia' – a union of the Lutheran and the Reformed (Calvinist) denominations. The present Evangelical Church of Germany (EKD) continues that tradition.

111 Wm in conversation with Dr Hadern, as reported in AA Preussen 1, Nr. 1d. Doc. A 16987 (TAK), and G. Hinzpeter, *Kaiser Wilhelm II. Eine Skizze*, 8th ed. (Bielefeld, 1888).

112 Letter Wm to QV, 2 Sept. 1874. Royal Archives, Windsor (RA), Z64/58.

113 Letter from Doorn, dated 12 March 1923, in Houston Stewart Chamberlain, *Briefe: 1882–1924 und Briefwechsel mit Kaiser Wilhelm II*, ed. Paul Pretzsch, 2 vols. (Munich, 1928), vol. 2.

114 The Archbishop of Canterbury recorded in his diary that the Kaiser told him he had been preaching that morning on board the royal yacht, *Hohenzollern*. The sermon, Wm had said, had been largely written by his chaplain-general, but he had altered it,

in his own words, '*"leaving out all dogmatic trash."*' Diary entry 30 July 1893, quoted in George K.A. Bell, *Randall Davidson, Archbishop of Canterbury*, 3rd ed. (London, 1952), 239–40. Emphasis in original.

115 Papers of Ex-Keizer Wilhelm II, Rijksarchief, Utrecht, folders 256–7 and 598–600, and Schierband, *Speeches*, 325–30.

116 The German reads: 'Herr wir lassen Dich nicht, du segnest uns denn! Amen!' Klaussmann, *Kaiserreden*, 437.

117 Rijksarchief, folder 598.

118 Bruce Lockhardt, *Retreat from Glory* (New York, 1934), 327, and Sir John Wheeler-Bennett, *Knaves, Fools and Heroes* (London 1974), 191. Lockhardt was a British journalist who visited the Kaiser in 1929; Wheeler-Bennett was a historian who interviewed the ex-Kaiser extensively in 1939 in preparation for a biography which he never completed.

119 See below.

120 Rijksarchief, folder 256. The same folder contains a sermon preached in Doorn House by Hofprediger Joehring on 27 Jan. 1940, to honour the ex-Kaiser's 81st birthday. The preacher extolled Wilhelm for his faith which was 'a shining example to us all.' On his bedside table in the room where he died may still be seen the Kaiser's New Testament and books of daily devotion. On the bedroom wall is a calligraphed quotation: 'Thou shalt know that the Lord thy God is a true God.'

121 Kaiser Wilhelm II, *Erinnerungen an Korfu* (Berlin and Leipzig, 1924), 36.

122 Typescript of interviews with Frau Rosalia Hörl and with Zollobersekretär Hebenstreit, Hauptarchiv der Nationalsozialistichen Deutschen Arbeiter Partei, Microfilm, Reel XVII-A, NA. Hereafter cited as HAP with appropriate folder and reel number.

123 *Secret Conversations* 155 (night of 8–9 Jan. 1942).

124 *Mein Kampf*, unabridged German ed., 635th ed. (Munich, 1941), 4 (hereafter cited as *MK*). English ed. (New York: Reynal and Hitchcock, 1939), 7.

125 Conference with party leaders in Berlin Chancellory, 29 Oct. 1937, Domarus, *Reden*, 745.

126 Night of 1–2 Jan. 1942, *Secret Conversations*, 135.

127 *MK*, 70. Hitler had a penchant for raising personal prejudices into cosmic principles.

128 Domarus, *Reden*, 817.

129 Ibid., 850.

130 *Völkischer Beobachter*, 1 Jan. 1943.

131 Linge as interviewed in *Revue*, no. 12 (24 March 1956).

132 Schroeder, *Hitler Privat*, 181 and 185–6.

133 Hans-Jochen Gamm, *Der braune Kult* (Hamburg, 1962), 139.

134 Ibid., 213–14. 'Führer, mein Führer, von Gott mir gegeben / Beschütz und erhalte noch lange mein Leben! / Du hast Deutschland gerettet aus tiefster Not / Dir danke ich heute mein täglich Brot. / Bleib lang noch bei mir, verlass mich nicht / Führer, mein Führer, mein Glaube, mein Licht! / Heil, mein Führer!'

135 Hasselbach Papers, Bundesarchiv, Koblenz, Bestand, 441–2.

136 Hildegard Brenner, *Die Kunstpolitik des Nationalsozialismus* (Hamburg, 1963), 155. The architectural plans are given in an unpublished ms, Armand Dehlinger, 'Architektur der Superlative: Eine kritische Betrachtung der Nationalsozialistischen Bauprogramme von München und Nürnberg.' Typescript in Institut für Zeitgeschichte (IfZ), Munich.

137 *Mein Kampf*, 84; see also speech 23 Nov. 1939, Domarus, *Reden*, 1421. (The day before their joint suicide, Hitler had married Eva Braun.)

138 Speech 12 April 1922, quoted by Detlev Grieswelle, *Propaganda der Friedlosigkeit: Eine Studie zu Hitlers Rhetorik, 1920–1933* (Stuttgart, 1972), 56.

139 Domarus, *Hitler Reden*, 214. Speech 24 Feb. 1933.

140 *Völkischer Beobachter*, 17 Dec. 1925, quoted in Grieswelle, *Propaganda*, 57. The last quoted sentence comes from an earlier speech, that of 28 July 1922.

141 Speech 26 Aug. 1934 following the 'Blood Purge.' Domarus, *Reden*, 446.

142 In a speech of 7 May 1933 to the SA in Kiel Hitler said, 'Thou art in me and I in thee.' Again in addressing the SA on 20 Jan. 1936: 'I have come to know thee. Everything that thou art, thou art through me, and everything that I am I am only and alone through thee.' On another occasion he said, 'Behold, I make all things new!' He sounded the millennial note from the Revelation of John whenever he spoke of his Thousand Year Reich and proclaimed that it would be 'a Reich of power and glory forever' – using the adjectives from Luther's version of the Lord's Prayer: [Thine is] *das Reich, die Kraft und die Herrlichkeit in Ewigkeit. Amen.* In a speech to a few party members he quoted the words of Jesus as recorded in John's Gospel, 'Much more could I have said unto you but ye could not have borne or understood it.' In Graz on 3 April 1938 Hitler used the words of Jesus that have been taken over for wedding ceremonies in the Christian Church. Having said that it was God who had created the German nation, the Führer concluded: 'What the Lord has joined together, let no man put asunder!'

143 Otto Wagener, *Hitler aus nächster Nähe: Aufzeichnungen eines Vertrauten: 1919–1932*, ed. H.A. Turner, Jr. (Frankfurt/Main, 1978), 359. There is now a fine English translation by Ruth Hein, *Hitler: Memoirs of a Confidant*, ed. H.A. Turner Jr. (New Haven, 1985).

144 Grieswelle, *Propaganda*, 57.

145 Wagener, *Nächste Nähe*.

146 Conversation of 25 April 1991 with Dr E.F. Proelss, a theologian and student of the German classics.

147 Actually Goethe has Faust play with several translations: Word (*Wort*); Mind
      (*Sinn*); Power (*Kraft*), before choosing Deed. *Faust*, Part I, 'Faust's Study.'
148 The quotations in this section come from Wagener, *Nächste Nähe* 134–6, 147,
      257–8, 481.
149 For a convenient discussion of the authorship of the two books, see entries for Saint
      John's Gospel and for the Revelation to John in *Harper's Bible Dictionary* (New
      York, 1985).
150 See the excellent review article, Claus E. Bärsch, 'Goebbels und die Apokalypse:
      Die Offenbarung des Johannes als Quelle für eines der furchtbarsten Verbrechen
      der Geschichte?,' *Die Zeit* no. 36 (8 Sept. 1988).
151 See Chapter 5.
152 John reports Jesus saying that the Jews are not the children of God; they are the
      spawn of Satan: 'Why do you not understand what I say? It is because you cannot
      bear to hear my word. You are of your father the devil, and your will is to do your
      father's desires. He was a murderer from the beginning and has nothing to do with
      the truth; because there is no truth in him. When he lies, he speaks according to his
      own nature, for he is a liar and the father of lies ... He who is of God hears the
      words of God; the reason why you do not hear them is that you are not of God'
      (John 8: 43–7).
153 The Nazis, like the Catholics, used the word 'propaganda' positively. The Nazis
      insisted that it not be applied to baser things. Thus, in 1937 instructions were given
      to journalists admonishing them never to speak of 'Bolshevist propaganda'; they
      should use the term 'Bolshevist *Greuelhetze*' (literally: incitation to outrage). The
      Instruction to the Press concluded, 'Propaganda is [used] only when it applies to us;
      Hetze when it is against us.' Berning, *Vokabular*, 150–1.
154 Quoted by Bärsch in 'Goebbels.'
155 The following paragraphs are drawn from R.G.L. Waite, 'The Holocaust and His-
      torical Explanation,' *Genocide and the Modern Age: Etiology and Case Studies of
      Mass Death*, ed. Isidor Wallimann and Michael N. Dobkowski (New York, 1987),
      163–84.
156 Quoted in Michael Balfour, *The Kaiser and His Times* (London, 1972), 164–5.
157 Captain Sigurd von Ilsemann, *Der Kaiser in Holland*, 2 vols. (Munich, 1967 and
      1969), vol. 1, 175.
158 Hitler, *Adolf Hitler an Seine Jugend* (Munich, 1938). In the Preface to this edition
      of his speeches to the Hitler Youth, Hitler urged young people to 'hold these eternal
      words in your brave hearts.'
159 1 Corinthians 13:2. (Jesus also spoke about moving mountains: Mathew 17:20;
      21:21).
160 Speer, *Spandau*, 353.
161 H.R. Ellis Davidson, *Gods and Myths of Northern Europe* (London, 1964), 61, 149.

162 A specialist on Nordic gods has said that the best interpretation of his name is 'the one who makes Mad (*Wut*).' Adam of Bremen, a 10th-century chronicler, wrote of him, '*Wodan id est furor.*' Ibid., 66.

163 See above.

164 Elisabeth Fehrenbach, *Wandlungen des deutschen Kaisergedankens, 1871–1918* (Munich and Vienna, 1969), 228.

165 Kubizek, *Young Hitler,* 187.

166 Waite, *Psychopathic God,* 102.

167 Night of 25–6 June 1942, *Tischgespräche,* 168, and *Secret Conversations,* 205.

168 Testimony of Percy E. Schram, 'Originalnotizen von P.E. Schramm über Hitler, gemacht während der Befragungen von Hitlers Leibärtzen,' Summer, 1945, Bundesarchiv, Koblenz.

169 See *The Center of the Web,* Time–Life Series on the Third Reich (New York, 1990).

170 See Chapter 1.

171 Schroeder, *Hitler Privat,* 150–1.

172 Thomas Wunder, ed. *Das Reichsparteigelände in Nürnberg* (Nuremburg, 1984), 31.

173 Waite, *Psychopathic God,* 68.

174 *Tischgespräche,* 186, and *Secret Conversations,* 278. He must also have been fantasizing when he said during the same monologue, 'I have a horror of people who enjoy inflicting suffering on others' bodies and tyranny upon their souls ... I shall never believe that lies can endure forever. I believe in the truth; I am sure that in the long run truth must be victorious.'

175 See Waite, *Psychopathic God,* 409–10.

176 Quoted in Johnnes Haller, *Philipp Eulenburg: The Kaiser's Friend,* trans. Ethel Colburn Mayne (London, n.d.), 48–9.

177 The editor of the extensive Eulenburg corrrespondence has written, 'We must conclude that a common interest in spiritualism ... was an important element in the friendship ... and that this interest was deliberately stirred up by Eulenburg to strengthen their friendship and that this theme ... played a not unimportant role in the correspondence between the two friends.' John C.G. Röhl, *Philipp Eulenburgs Politische Korrespondenz,* 2 vols. (Boppard am Rhein, 1976), vol. 1, 50.

178 Haller, *Eulenburg,* 50.

179 Ibid., 47.

180 Sir F. Lascelle, 'General Report on Germany for 1906,' *British Documents,* vol. 3, 435.

181 Henry Wickham Steed, *Through Thirty Years,* 2 vols. (London, 1924), vol. 1, 193–4. Steed had been a student in Germany as a youth and subsequently served as the London *Times* correspondent in Germany, Austria-Hungary, France, and Italy.

182 Wagener, *Nächste Nähe,* 466–7. Goldzier was a writer of pseudo-scientific tracts that appeared from 1905 until 1911 under the title *Einige Weltprobleme.*

183 Ibid., 101–2. Karl Freiherr von Reichenbach, *Odisch-Magnetische Briefe* (Leipzig, 1921), which originally appeared in 1845 as *Untersuchungen über den Magnetismus and damit verw.* Editor's note in Wagener, *Nächste Nähe*, 489. Hitler was also much taken with the pseudo-scientific theories of one Hans Hörbiger.

184 *Mein Kampf*, 137.

185 He also affected other names and titles: Adolf Lanz, Dr Jörg Lanz, Schurl Lanz, Georg Lancz von Liebenfels, Lancz von Liebens. The name on his birth certificate is given as Adolf Josef Lanz. He confided to an intimate that he took various names because he did not wish to be looked up in hostile horoscopes, hence these 'astrological pseudonyms.' On his life and career see Wilfried Daim, *Der Mann, der Hitler die Ideen gab: von den religiösen Verwirrungen eines Sektierers zum Rassenwahn des Diktators* (Munich, 1958).

186 Dozens of his pamphlets have been preserved. They are available in the National Library of Austria, Vienna.

187 See Daim, *Rassenwahn*, and Waite, *Psychopathic God*, 93.

188 The word *Schrättling* needs explanation. In German mythology, a *Schrat* or *Waldschrat* was a repulsive forest demon with animal fur, wolves' teeth, obnoxious odour, and eyebrows that joined over a flat nose. A *Schrättling* was a particularly degenerate form of a *Schrat*. He was a creature given to stealing infants and replacing them with hideous changelings (*Wechselbälge*). He was also known for waylaying young women in dark woods and raping them. The resulting offspring were thus 'the children of Schrättling.' See the extensive entries under *Schrat* and *Schrättel* under *Wechselbalg* in Hanns Bächtold-Stäbli, *Handwörterbuch des deutschen Aberglaubens*, 10 vols. (Berlin, 1927–1942).

189 Lanz's letter is quoted in Joachim Riedl, 'Hitlers Lehrmeister,' *Die Zeit* (13 June 1986).

190 See Addendum 2.

191 Lydia Franke, *Die Randbemerkungen Wilhelms II. in den Akten der Auswärtigen Politik als historische und psychologische Quelle* (Leipzig, 1934), 86.

192 Ibid., 87–9.

193 Bülow, *Memoirs*, vol. 1, 506. Among the ex-Kaiser's papers in Huis Doorn are several pencil sketches of the poster.

194 The fullest treatment of the speech is given by Bernd Sösemann, 'Die Sog[enannte] Hunnenrede Wilhelms II. Textkritische und interpretatorische Bemerkungen zur Ansprache des Kaisers vom 27 Juli 1900 in Bremerhaven,' *Historische Zeitschrift*, 222 (1976), 242–58. The full text may also be found in Johannes Hohlfeld, ed., *Dokumente der deutschen Politik und Geschichte von 1848 bis zur Gegenwart*, vol. 2, *Das Zeitalter Wilhelms II. 1890–1918* (Berlin, 1951), 114–15. Portions of the speech are quoted by Ludwig Reiners, *The Lamps Went Out in Europe*, trans. Richard and Clara Winston (New York, 1955), 30. It is noteworthy that a sympa-

thetic collection of the Kaiser's speeches, 'based on the official German sources,' omits the Kaiser's reference to the Huns. Klaussmann, ed., *Kaiserreden*, 358.

195 Fischer-Fabian, *Herrliche Zeiten*, 315.

196 Schierband, *Speeches*, 262–3, and Kraussmann, *Kaisserreden*, 359, 360–1.

197 Kaiser Wilhelm II, *Die chinesische Monade*.

198 *The Kaiser's Letters to the Tsar*, ed. N.F. Grant (London, 1920 [?]), 10, 19, 45. On 26 Sept. Wilhelm sent 'Nicky' one version of his 'Yellow Peril' cartoon depicting Europe united against the evil darkness of Asiatic hordes; on 4 Jan. 1898 Wilhelm sent another drawing which showed Russia and Germany proclaiming 'The Gospel of Truth and Light to the East.'

199 Bülow, *Memoirs*, vol. 2, 72.

200 *Die Grosse Politik der Europäischen Kabinette* (hereafter cited as GPEK), 19(I), 210–12. Emphasis in original. I am indebted to Thomas A. Kohut for this reference.

201 *Kaiser's Letters to the Tsar*, 239.

202 John C.G. Röhl, *Kaiser, Hof und Staat: Wilhelm II und die deutsche Politik* (Munich, 1988), 21.

203 Lockhardt, *Retreat*, 322.

204 Ilsemann, *Kaiser in Holland*, vol. 2, 26.

205 Bundesmilitärarchiv, Freiburg, RM 2 (TAK).

206 The German foreign office got wind of its contents and put immediate pressure on President Theodore Roosevelt to urge the periodical not to publish the incendiary interview for fear of precipitating an international crisis. For further commentary on Hale's interview, see Chapter 3.

207 This account, drawn from Hale's papers, was published by his son in the *Atlantic Monthly* (June 1934), 523.

208 B. Huldermann, *Albert Ballin* (Oldenburg, 1922), 273, quoted by Röhl, *Deutsche Politik*, 189.

209 Röhl, *Deutsche Politik*, 22.

210 Even though it appeared in rather expensive editions – several in half-leather, heavily embossed – it ran through eight editions in German and English and had sold over 100,000 copies by 1914. Hitler would give it even wider circulation.

211 *Grundlagen des Neunzehnten Jahrhunderts*, 2 vols., 2nd ed. (Munich, 1900), vol. 1, 310.

212 Ibid., 14.

213 The Kaiser's letter to Chamberlain as quoted by Field, *Evangelist*, 252–3.

214 Bülow, *Memoirs*, vol. 1, 200.

215 Ibid., 25.

216 See Chamberlain, *Briefe*, vol. 2, letter 31 Dec. 1901.

217 His confidant in exile reported on 22 Sept. 1921 that 'for three weeks the Kaiser has been reading aloud the latest book by Chamberlain, *Gott und Menschen*. He is

absolutely of the author's opinion and finds no points of difference. This book is an important support for the Kaiser's beliefs. "Chamberlain is a new prophet, a second Luther," he told me the other day.' Ilsemann, *Kaiser in Holland*, vol. 1, 191.

218 Johan, *Reden*, 60.

219 AA Preussen, telegram 3 June 1900, Wm to QV (TAK).

220 Joseph O. Baylen and Ralph F. Munster, 'Adolf Hitler as Seen by Houston Stewart Chamberlain,' *Duquesne Review* (Fall 1967), 183. See also Heiden, *Der Fuehrer*, 245–6, and memoirs of Friedelind Wagner, *The Royal Family of Bayreuth* (London, 1948).

221 Isabel V. Hull, *The Entourage of Kaiser Wilhelm II, 1888–1918* (Cambridge, 1982), 74–5.

222 In Lydia Franke's methodical study of the Kaiser's marginalia, in which she devotes one chapter specifically to 'Racial Political Ideas,' she makes no mention of Wm's attitude towards Jews. Surely if she had found any anti-Jewish comments during his reign she would have included them in her book which was published in both Germany and Switzerland during the Nazi period. Franke, *Randbemerkungen*.

223 John C.G. Röhl, 'Wilhelm II: "'Das Beste wäre Gas,'" *Die Zeit*, no. 48 (2 Dec. 1994).

224 For his relationship to his parents, see Chapter 6.

225 Röhl, 'Das Beste.'

226 Marginal comment by Kaiser on a report of Bernstorf, GPEK, 21 (1) 16 Jan. 1895, Nr. 6851 (TAK).

227 Röhl, 'Das Beste.'

228 See, e.g., a letter of Feb. 1899 Chancellor Prinz von Hohenlohe, who, though saying he was '"no admirer of Jews," he was emphatically not anti-Semitic nor was His Majesty.' Admiral Georg Alexander von Müller made a similar declaration. Fürst Chlodwig zu Hohenlohe-Schellingsfürst, *Denkwürdigkeiten der Reichskanzlerzeit*, ed. Karl Alexander von Müller (Berlin, 1931), 481 (TAK).

229 'I am myself *kein Judenfreund* and neither is Your Majesty. We have occasionally exchanged opinions about that. But the character of this anti-Semitism ... presents an immediate danger.' Eulenburg to Kaiser, 17 Dec. 1892, J.C. Röhl, *Eulenburgs Korrespondenz*, vol. 2, 997.

230 E. Zechlin, *Die deutsche Politik und die Juden im ersten Weltkrieg* (Göttingen, 1969), 48–9 as cited by Field, *Evangelist*, 254.

231 Letter 26 April 1900, AA Preussen, i (TAK).

232 Lamar Cecil, *Albert Ballin* (Princeton, 1967), 101.

233 Letter Oct. 1898 written during the Kaiser's trip to Jerusalem, quoted in Balfour, *Kaiser*, 216.

234 Lamar Cecil, 'Wilhelm II. und die Juden,' *Juden im Wilhelminischen Deutschland, 1890–1914*, eds. Werner Mosse and Arnold Paucker (Tübingen, 1976), 332.

416   Notes to pages 121–3

235 *Journals and Letters of Reginald Viscount Esher*, ed. Maurice V. Brett, 4 vols. (London, 1934–8), vol. 2, 255.
236 Röhl, 'Wm II.'
237 Papers of the Ex-Keizer, Rijksarchief, Utrecht, folder 265.
238 Cecil, *Juden*, 346–7, and G.A. Müller, *Kaiser*, 334, 339.
239 Letter 2 Dec. 1919 to Field Marshal August von Mackensen, Bundesarchiv, MA Nachlasse Mackensen, as quoted by Röhl, *Deutsche Politik*, 22.
240 Letter to the American fascist John Sylvester Viereck, quoted in Cecil, *Juden*, 346–7.
241 RA Utrecht, the ex-Kaiser's sermons, folder 255, 6 June 1926.
242 RA Utrecht, folder 5, 'Wilhelm II, Bericht über Philipp zu Eulenburg, 2 Sept. 1927, with marginalia by Wilhelm II as cited by Willibald Gutsche, *Ein Kaiser im Exil: Der letzte deutsche Kaiser Wilhelm II. in Holland. Eine kritische Biographie* (Marburg, 1991), 239.
243 RA Utrecht, folder 243, Wilhelm II, 'Vatikan und Völkerbund,' June 1926.
244 Röhl, 'Wm II.'
245 See Chapter 3.
246 Letter to Alwina, Gräfin von der Goltz, 28 July 1940. RA Utrecht, quoted by Gutsche, *Kaiser im Exil*, 208.
247 Baronin Vera von der Heydt, 'Wilhelm II. und die Juden' (London, 8 Oct. 1959), unpublished ms, typescript, Wiener Library London PID No. 1142. The author's father, Paul von Schwabach, a senior member of Bleichröder's banking firm, 'enjoyed the especial confidence of Wilhelm II.' The Baroness had visited Wm in Doorn 'on several occasions.'
248 Gutsche, *Kaiser im Exil*, 208.
249 Affidavit of Joseph Hall, IfZ Archives, Document ZS 640, Folio 6, as quoted by John Toland, *Adolf Hitler* (New York, 1976), 118.

Chapter 3: Kaiser and Führer as Rulers in Peacetime

1 Hitler never won the support of a majority of Germans in a free election. Even after virtually banning the Communist party and mounting a campaign of propaganda, intimidation, and terror, the best he could do in the spring of 1933 was to win 43.9% of the popular vote.
2 At his coronation, Wilhelm put the crown on his own head.
3 G. Hinzpeter, *Kaiser Wilhelm II. Eine Skizze*, 8th ed. (Bielefeld, 1888). See also Koppel Pinson, *Modern Germany: Its History and Civilization* (New York, 1954), 281.
4 The testimony of his tutor in French: Franz Ayme, *Kaiser Wilhelm II. und seine Erziehung: Aus den Erinnerungen seines französischen Lehrers* (Leipzig, 1898), 62. The tutor's high regard seems warranted. The Kaiser's school exercise books show

an impressive command of the French language. (Papers of ex-Keizer Wilhelm II, Rijksarchief [RA], Utrecht).

5 See Chapter 6.

6 S. Fischer-Fabian, *Herrliche Zeiten: Die Deutschen und ihr Kaiserreich* (Munich, 1968), 186. After Prince Wilhelm's first diplomatic mission in 1884, when he charmed the difficult Russian Tsar, Alexander III, Bismarck expressed delight with his protégé's performance. Lamar Cecil, *Wilhelm II, Prince and Emperor, 1859–1900* (Chapel Hill, NC, 1989), 81.

7 Elisabeth Fehrenbach, *Wandlungen des deutschen Kaisergedankens, 1871–1918* (Munich and Vienna, 1969), 120. After his dismissal, however, Bismarck bitterly opposed the Kaiser's 'personal regime.'

8 Wilhelm Ziegler, *Volk ohne Führung* (Hamburg, 1941), 296.

9 Joachim von Kürenburg, *The Kaiser: A Life of Wilhelm II, Last Emperor of Germany*, trans. H.T. Russell and Herta Hagen (New York, 1955), 138.

10 Poultney Bigelow, *The German Emperor and His Eastern Neighbors* (New York, 1892), 30. See also Bigelow's *Prussian Memories, 1864–1914* (New York, 1915). Bigelow was the son of an American foreign service officer.

11 Walther Rathenau, *Der Kaiser, eine Betrachtung* (Berlin, 1923), 27. This pamphlet, first published in 1919, went through 57 printings. It has been reprinted as an essay in Rathenau's works, 'Der Kaiser,' *Schriften und Reden*, ed. Hans Werner Richter (Frankfurt/Main, 1964).

12 Lady Norah Bentinck, *The Ex-Kaiser in Exile* (London, 1921), 80.

13 Martin Luther, 'Treatise on Good Works,' in *Luther's Works*, 54 vols., ed. Jaraslav Pelikan (St Louis, 1955–75), vol. 44, 92, 105, 113. Luther demanded something more than mere obedience to those in authority; he demanded *Staatsfrömmigkeit*, literally 'piety towards the state.' See also George Sabine, *A History of Political Theory* (New York, 1937), 261.

14 Wilhelm was a staunch Lutheran who believed deeply in a tradition that buttressed so strongly his own convictions about a ruler's authority and his subjects' obligations. He also sought spiritual guidance and sustenance from Luther's sermons and prayers. The dominant portrait in his crowded bedroom in Doorn was a fine reproduction of Cranach's *Martin Luther*, and his private library contained, in addition to Luther's more political tracts, such volumes as *Selected Thoughts of Martin Luther* and *Luther's Spiritual Songs*. On the ex-Kaiser's bedside table in the death room are little books of Luther's prayers and meditations.

15 During Wilhelm II's reign, none but Hegelians occupied chairs of philosophy and political economy in every Prussian university. Hegel remained Germany's favourite philosopher during the Third Reich. Gordon Craig recalled that as an undergraduate studying at the University of Munich in 1935, he took a course in German culture in which 'the argument seemed to be that Hegel invented the State.' See Craig's fine

book, *The Germans* (New York, 1983). The Kaiser's private library in Doorn contains many works of Hegel.

16 G.W.F. Hegel, 'Philosophy of Right and Law,' in *The Philosophy of Hegel*, ed. Carl Friedrich (New York, 1963), 283, 309, 323–4. Emphasis in original.

17 This brief discussion of the constitution is based on the definitive treatment, by Ernst Rudolf Huber, *Deutsche Verfassungsgeschichte seit 1789*, 4 vols. (Stuttgart, 1963), vol. 3, *Bismarck und das Reich*.

18 Ibid., 815. Another writer has underscored the importance of this assumption: 'In the German constitution, the only item falling into the category of "things untouchable" was the Emperor, serving as the symbol of the unity of the nation. As that unity was not to be impeached, the Emperor had to be inviolable and accountable to no one.' Ed. Reiner C. Baum, *Holocaust and German Elites, Genocide and National Suicide in Germany, 1871–1945* (Totowa, NJ, 1981), 815–17.

19 Gordon A. Craig, *The Politics of the Prussian Army: 1640–1945* (New York, 1955), 123.

20 Gerhard Ritter, *Staatskunst und Kriegshandwerk: Das Problem des 'Militarismus' in Deutschland*, 4 vols. (Munich, 1965), vol. 2, 117.

21 Sombart as quoted in *Die Zeit*, 24 Aug. 1984, in a feature article on the 70th anniversary of Germany's invasion of Belgium, drawing its title from the statement of General von Moltke justifying the shooting of Belgium civilians: 'Wer sich uns in den Weg stellt ... (Whoever stands in our way ...).'

22 Dieter Düding, 'Die Kriegervereine im Wilhelminischen Reich und ihr Beitrag zur Militärisierung der deutschen Gesellschaft,' *Bereit zum Krieg: Kriegsmentalität im Wilhelminischen Deutschland, 1890–1914* (Göttingen, 1986).

23 Quoted in Düding, 'Kriegervereine,' 119.

24 As cited by Golo Mann, *Wilhelm II*, in series, *Archiv der Weltgeschichte*, ed. Karl Dietrich Bracher (Munich, 1964), 5.

25 Friedrich Zipfel, 'Kritik der deutschen Oeffentlichkeit der Person und an der Monarchie Wilhelm II. bis zum Ausbruch des Weltkrieges,' PhD dissertation, Free University of Berlin, 1952. Zipfel was citing Otto Mittelstädt, *Vor der Fluth: Sechs Briefe zur Politik der Gegenwart* (Leipzig, 1897).

26 Karl Buchheim, *Ultramontanismus und Demokratie* (Munich, 1963), 345, quoted in Fehrenbach, *Kaisergedankens*, 194.

27 Fehrenbach, *Kaisergedankens*, 194.

28 Wolfgang J. Mommsen, *Max Weber und die Politik, 1890–1920* (Tubingen, 1959), 53, 80, 87, and see Imanuel Geiss, ed., *July 1914: The Outbreak of the First World War, Selected Documents* (New York, 1967), 21.

29 Ibid., 91. This speech may have been one of the reasons the Nazis included Meinecke's name and picture in the *Führer-Lexikon* of their party. Meinecke does not seem to have objected to his inclusion – nor did Martin Heidegger, Germany's most influential living philosopher. *Das Deutsche Führer-Lexikon* (Munich and Berlin,

1934). Another famous historian, Otto Hintze, was equally supportive of royal power. In 1913 he gazed into a clouded crystal ball and predicted 'the dawn of a new world epoch' in which Germany would fulfil its 'world political purposes' because it enjoyed 'strong monarchical leadership.' Fehrenbach, *Kaisergedankens*, 158.

30 Karl Dietrich Bracher, *The German Dictatorship: The Origins, Structure and Effects of National Socialism*, trans. Jean Steinberg, with Introduction by Peter Gay (New York, 1970), 199.

31 Hitler's *Mein Kampf*, and speeches as cited by Svend Ranulf, *Hitlers Kampf gegen die Objektivität* (Copenhagen, 1946).

32 Helmut Heiber, quoted with approval by Eberhard Jäckel, *Hitler's Weltanschauung: A Blueprint for Power*, trans. Herbert Arnold (Middleton, CT, 1972), 19.

33 *Deutsche Justiz*, 97/28, 998, quoted by Cornelia Berning, *Vom 'Abstammungsnachweis' zum 'Zuchtwart': Vokabular des Nationalsozialismus* (Berlin, 1964), 83.

34 Quoted in Berning, *Vokabular*, 89.

35 Speeches of 7 March 1936 and 8 Nov. 1938, as quoted in Fritz Nova, *The National Socialist Führerprinzip and Its Background in German Thought* (Philadelphia, 1943), 4; and *Secret Conversations*, 143 (see Chapter 1, n224).

36 Hans Buchheim, 'The SS: Instrument of Domination,' in *Anatomy of the SS State*, ed. Helmut Krausnick (New York, 1968), 133.

37 Alan Bullock, 'The Political Ideas of Adolf Hitler,' ed. Maurice Beaumont, John H.E. Fried, Edmond Vermeil, in *The Third Reich* (New York, 1955), 368.

38 Dr Hans Frank, as quoted by Bullock, ibid.

39 Fritz Stern, *The Führer and the People* (London, 1975), 111, as cited by Ian Kershaw in *Führerstaat*, 131. See also Kershaw's essay, 'The "Hitler Myth,"' *Image and Reality in the Third Reich* (New York, 1994).

40 Berning, *Vokabular*, 50.

41 Birthday editions of Nazi publications, as cited in Gertrud M. Kurth, 'The Image of the Fuehrer: A Contribution to the Role of Imagery in Hero-Worship,' *New School for Social Research Library* (New York, n.d.), 53, 68–9, 74, 97, 100.

42 The fullest edition of Hitler's speeches is Max Domarus, ed., *Hitler: Reden und Proklamationen, 1932–1945* (Munich, 1965). In English his speeches can be found conveniently in, Norman H. Baynes, ed. *The Speeches of Adolf Hitler* (London, 1942).

43 Domarus, *Reden*, 1423.

44 *Mein Kampf*, 74 and *passim*. A monograph devoted to Hitler's vocabulary notes that 'blood ... [was] one of the central mystical concepts of his ideology.' Indeed the number of times and the peculiar ways he used the word are extraordinary. A few examples: He spoke of 'blood-conscience,' 'blood-soul,' 'blood of honour,' the 'blood-right of dreamers,' the 'Blood-Fate Community,' and 'blood-sin.' See Berning, *Vokabular*, 42–6.

45 Hitler in conversation with Otto Strasser, in Strasser, *Aufbau des deutschen Sozialismus – Als Anlage das historische Gespräch mit Dr Strasser* (Prague, 1936), 124, 118. Other quotations are from *Mein Kampf.*

46 *Mein Kampf*, 397–8; Gordon W. Prange, ed., *Hitler's Words* (Washington, DC, 1944), 5.

47 Ernst Deuerlein, 'Dokumentation: Hitlers Eintritt in die Politik und die Reichswehr,' *Vieteljahreshefte für Zeitgeschicte* (VfZ) 7 (1959).

48 Domarus, *Reden*, 2329.

49 For the genesis of Hitler's personal anti-Semitism, see Chapter 6.

50 See Detlev J.K., Peukert's article, 'The Genesis of the "Final Solution" from the Spirit of Science,' in Thomas Childers and Jane Caplan, eds., *Reevaluating the Third Reich* (New York and London, 1993).

51 *Mein Kampf*, 947, 950–1. Emphasis in original.

52 See esp. Hitler's comments of 5–6 July; 8–10, 13–14 Aug.; 17 Oct. 1941, and 11 April 1942 as recorded in *Tischgespräche* and in *Secret Conversations*.

53 See Chapter 5.

54 Speech of 12 April 1922 in Munich, as quoted by Hans Müller, 'Der pseudoreligiöse Charakter der nationalsozialistischen Weltanschauung,' *Geschichte in Wissenschaft und Unterricht (GWU)* 6 (1961), 349.

55 *Mein Kampf*, 124, as quoted in Frederich Heer, *Der Glaube des Adolf Hitler: Anatomie einer politischen Religiosität* (Munich, 1968), 118.

56 Müller, 'Weltanschauung,' 349. My emphasis.

57 Berning, *Vokabular*, 92–3. See also Detlev Grieswelle, *Propaganda der Friedlosigkeit: Eine studie zu Hitlers Rhetoric, 1920–1933* (Stuttgart, 1972).

58 Grieswelle, *Friedlosigkeit*, 82.

59 Uriel Tal, 'Nazism as a "Political Faith,"' *Jerusalem Quarterly*, 15 (Spring 1980), 82. My emphasis.

60 '... and this must be thy creed: *My will is thy Faith!* (*mein Wille ist eurer Glaube!*), Domarus, *Reden*, 503.

61 Hans-Jochen Gamm, *Der braune Kult* (Hamburg, 1962), 184–6.

62 Müller, 'Weltanschauung,' 339.

63 Personal communication from a former member of the SS.

64 *Westdeutscher Beobachter*, as quoted in J.S. Conway, *The Nazi Persecution of the Churches, 1933–1945* (New York, 1968), 146.

65 There were several versions; this one is given by Conway, *Persecution*, 155.

66 Neues Lied der Hitlerjugend

Wir sind die fröhliche Hitlerjugend
Wir brauchen keine christliche Tugend;
Denn unser Führer ist Adolf Hitler.

Er ist unser Erlöser und Mittler;
Kein Pfaff, kein Böser kann uns hindern
Dass wir fühlen als Hitlerkindern.
Nicht Christus folgen wir, sondern Horst Wessel;
Fort mit Weihrauch und Weihwasserkessel,
Ich bin kein Christ, kein Katholik,
Ich geh' mit der SA durch dünn und dick.
Deine kirche kann uns gestohlen werden
Das Hakenkreuz macht uns selig auf Erden.

Reprinted in Müller, 'Weltanschauung,' 340. Horst Wessel was a leader of the Berlin SA who was killed in a street brawl. He had written the song which Hitler and Goebbels raised to the status of a national anthem: 'Die Fahnen hoch! Die Reihen fest geshlossen! / SA, marchiert ... (Unfurl the flags, our ranks stand fast together / SA is marching ...'). ·

67 Albert Speer interview, *New York Times*, 7 April 1969.
68 *Secret Conversations*, 167, night of 20–1 Jan. 1942.
69 Among the many excellent political studies of his reign, see Michael Balfour, *The Kaiser and His Times* (London, 1975); Cecil, *Kaiser*, Erich Eyck, *Das persönliche Regiment Wilhelm II. Politische Geschichte des deutschen Kaiserreiches von 1890 bis 1914* (Zürich,1948); John C.G. Röhl, *Germany without Bismarck: The Crisis in Government in the Second Reich, 1890–1900* (London, 1967), and *Kaiser, Hof und Staat: Wilhelm II and die deutsche Politik* (Munich, 1988), as well as the volume of valuable essays, ed. by John C.G. Röhl and Nicholas Sombart, *Kaiser Wilhelm II: New Interpretations* (Cambridge, 1982). The first volume of Röhl's massive biography of the Kaiser has appeared: *Wilhelm II Die Jugend des Kaisers, 1859–1888* (Munich, 1993). Thomas A. Kohut, *Kaiser Wilhelm II and the Germans: A Study in Political Leadership* (New York, 1991); and Johannes Ziekursch, *Politische Geschichte des neuen deutschen Kaiserreiches*, 3 vols. (Frankfurt/Main, 1925), an early but still useful study.

There are now many thousands of books and articles on Hitler and the government of Nazi Germany. Of particular value are: Karl Dietrich Bracher, *Die deutsche Diktatur: Entstehung, Struktur, Folgen des Nationalsozialismus* (Köln, 1969), in English, *Dictatorship*. Martin Broszat, *Der Staat Hitlers* (Munich, 1969), in English, *The Hitler State: The Foundation and Development of the Internal Structure of the Third Reich*, trans. John W. Hiden (New York, 1981). Klaus Hildebrand, *Das Dritte Reich* (Munich, 1979), in English, *The Third Reich*, trans. P.S. Falla (London, 1984). Hans Mommsen, *Beamtentum im Dritten Reich* (Stuttgart, 1966). Wolfgange Runge, *Politik und Beamtentum im Parteienstaat* (Stuttgart, 1965). The best single volume on the Nazi period is Klaus B. Fischer, *Nazi Germany: A New History* (New York, 1995).

70 Otto Pflanze, *Bismarck and the Development of Germany*, vol. 3, *The Period of Fortification, 1880–1898* (Princeton, NJ, 1990), 327.

71 Quotations from the memoranda given here are taken from *Dokumente der deutschen Politik und Geschichte von 1848 bis zur Gegenwart*, vol. 2, *Das Zeitalter Wilhelms II, 1890–1918*, ed. Johannes Hohlfeld (Berlin, 1951).

72 One of his proposals was a remarkable anticipation of the Bonn government's *Mitbestimmungsrecht* (Right of Co-determination) for the coal and steel industries. This law established councils in which representatives of labour and management meet to discuss and determine a company's labour, wage, and investment policies, a practice that contributed significantly to industrial harmony and productivity in Germany. Wm's memorandum of 22 Jan. 1890 similarly called for cooperation between labour and management, saying that 'rancour and distrust' could be mitigated if both sides met to work out their differences. The state would offer its services as arbiter, and workers should feel that they could get a 'sympathetic response' from Wilhelm's government.

73 Pflanze, *Bismarck*, vol. 3, 401.

74 Ibid., 233, and Cecil, *Kaiser*, 226.

75 Wm as quoted in Zipfel, 'Kritik.'

76 Speech 26 Feb. 1897, in Johan, *Reden*, 70, and Zipfel, 'Kritik,' 60.

77 'The Kaiser and the Socialists,' in Asa Don Dickinson, ed., *The Kaiser: A Book about the Most Interesting Man in Europe* (New York, 1914), 175, and Paul Liman, *Der Kaiser: Ein Charakterbild* (Leipzig, 1909), 253–5. Georg Alexander von Müller, *The Kaiser and His Court: The Diaries, Notebooks and Letters of Admiral Georg Alexander Von Müller, Chief of the Naval Secretariat, 1914–1918*, ed. Walter Goerlitz, trans. Mervyn Savill (London, 1961). Johan, *Reden*, 15, and Zipfel, 'Kritik.'

78 The incident is reported in Fischer-Fabian, *Herrliche Zeiten*, 188–9.

79 Quoted by Kohut, *Wilhelm II*, 228–9.

80 Pflanze, *Bismarck*, vol. 3, 305.

81 Röhl, *Germany without Bismarck.*

82 Ibid., 43.

83 Gagliardi, *Entlassung*, vol. 1, 153, 170–1, as cited by Pflanze, *Bismarck*, vol. 3, 373.

84 Balfour, *Kaiser*, 132.

85 See Röhl, 'Staatsstreichplan oder Staatsstreichbereitschaft,' *Historische Zeitschrift (HZ)*, 203 (1966).

86 After his dismissal, Bismarck's triumphant processions throughout Germany produced the kind of 'frenzied delirium' Count Harry Kessler observed in one reception of 1891 when, 'for the first time since 1870, possibly for the first time in his life,' Bismarck became genuinely popular. See Harry Graf Kessler, *Gesichter und Zeiten: Erinnerungen, gesammelter Schriften in drei Bänden*, ed. Cornelia Blasberg and

Gerhard Schuster (Frankfurt/Main, 1988), 217. On his 85th birthday in 1895, 35 special trains took thousands of admirers to Friedrichsruhe to pay tribute to the national hero. It is noteworthy, however, that the Reichstag failed to pass a resolution sending their congratulations. In private, the embittered Bismarck referred to Wm II as 'that dumb kid,' and spoke his animosity from the grave. Carved deeply in the simple marble sarcophagus, his epitaph reads, 'Bismarck: A Loyal German Servant of Kaiser Wilhelm I.' The roman numeral was carefully chosen. See Pflanze, *Bismarck*, vol. 3, 410–13; 426–8.

87 One of the Kaiser's typical designs for a cruiser serves as the frontispiece in Volker Berghahn's *Der Tirpitz-Plan: Genesis und Verfall einer innenpolitischen Krisenstrategie unter Wilhelm II* (Düsseldorf, 1971). Photographs of these designs are preserved in Huis Doorn.

88 It seems pointless to debate whether the Kaiser or Tirpitz was 'the real founder' of the German navy. Both were essential. As Jürg Meyer noted. 'The whole issue of the navy entering German politics with such intensity must be ascribed, above all, to the Kaiser's driving force.' Tirpitz himself – no one to hide his own light under a bushel – agreed. 'Germany's estrangement from the sea,' he wrote, 'would never have been overcome without the Kaiser: that is his historic service.' The Kaiser supported Tirpitz fully and enthusiastically for 19 years. Wilhelm supplied flair, inspiration, and some bright ideas; Tirpitz the hard work, organizational genius, constancy, and drive without which the Kaiser's dream could never have been realized. See Jürg Meyer, *Die Propaganda der deutschen Flottenbewegung*, 1899–1900 (Bern, 1967), 15–16; Grand Admiral von Tirpitz, *My Memoirs*, 2 vols. (New York, 1919), vol. 1, 203–4; and Berghahn, *Tirpitz-Plan*, 23, 30.

89 Röhl, *Germany without Bismarck*, 258.

90 Pogge von Strandmann, 'Nationale Verbände zwischen Weltpolitik und Kontinentalpolitik,' *Marine und Marinepolitik im kaiserlichen Deutschland, 1871–1914*, eds. Herbert Schottelius and Wilhelm Deist (Düsseldorf, 1972), 307.

91 See Meyer, *Flottenbewegung*, which quotes extensively from the pamphlet literature.

92 Wolf von Schierbrand, *The Kaiser's Speeches, Being a Character Portrait of Emperor Wilhelm II* (New York, 1903) 190–1.

93 Meyer, *Flottenbewegung*, 26.

94 The hundreds of thousands of propaganda pamphlets that were issued by the government and naval pressure groups were read eagerly by the German population. Strandmann, 'Nationale Verbände,' 307.

95 It might be noted, however, that Germany's enormous investment of time, resources, money, and energy did not bring the rewards Wilhelm had expected. The Imperial Navy failed to play a major role during the war since it was effectively bottled up in the North Sea by the British fleet. Moreover, by increasing the relentless pressures

of the arms race, the Kaiser's navy 'contributed more than any other German organization to the disruption of peace.' Jonathan Steinberg, 'The Kaiser's Navy and German Society,' *Past & Present*, 28 (July 1964), 103, 110.

96 The following paragraphs draw on Helmuth Pogge von Strandmann's article, 'Staatsstreichpläne, Alldeutsche und Bethmann Hollweg,' in *Die Erforderlichkeit des Unmöglichen: Deutschland am Vorabend des ersten Weltkrieges*, eds. Pogge von Strandmann and Imanuel Geiss (Frankfurt/Main, 1965).

97 The earliest, and still valuable, account of Bismarck's putsch plan may be found in Johannes Ziekursch, *Politische Geschichte des neuen Deutschen Kaiserreiches*, 3 vols. (Frankfurt/Main, 1925).

98 Born in 1882, the Crown prince was christened Friedrich Wilhelm after the Kaiser's father, but unlike him, was called Wilhelm. Both he and his brother August Wilhelm, or 'Auwi,' were to join the Nazi party.

99 Wm II. an den Kronprinz, DZA Merseburg, Kgl Hausarchiv, Rep. 53 J, Lit P. Nr 16. Reprinted as Anhang II in Strandmann, 'Staatsstreichpläne,' 37–9.

100 'Unsere dämliche Presse ... diese Saupresse soll den Schnabel halten,' quoted by Isolde Rieger, *Die Wilhelminische Presse im Ueberblick: 1888–1918* (Munich, 1957), 10.

101 Geheimes Staatsarchiv Preussischer Kulturbesetz, Berlin, quoted by Willibald Gutsche, *Wilhelm II, Der letzte Kaiser des Deutschen Reiches* (Berlin, 1991), 106–7.

102 Generaladjutant Graf Carl von Wedel, *Zwischen Kaiser und Kanzler: Aufzeichnungen ... aus den Jahren 1890–1894*, ed. Graf Erhard von Wedel (Leipzig, 1943), 183–4; G.A. Müller, *Kaiser*, 81 and 118; Röhl, *Germany without Bismarck*, 71, 86.

103 Wm, speech 26 Feb. 1897, quoted in Röhl, *Germany without Bismarck*, 212.

104 *Denkwürdigkeiten des General-Feldmarschalls Alfred von Waldersee*, ed. H.O. Meisner, 3 vols. (Stuttgart and Berlin, 1923), vol. 2, 179.

105 Quoted by Craig, *Politics of the Army*, 239.

106 Cecil, *Kaiser*, 129–30.

107 'The Kaiser and His Army,' in Dickinson, 173.

108 Ibid., vol. 2, 125; Hildegard Freifrau Hugo von Spizemberg, *Das Tagebuch der Baronin Spitzemberg*, ed. R. Vierhaus (Göttingen, 1960), 402; and Wedel, *Zwischen*, 183–4; G.A. Müller, *Kaiser*, 118; General Waldersee, quoted by Bülow, *Memoirs of Prince von Bülow*, 3 vols., trans. F.A. Voigt (Boston, 1931), vol. 1, *I*, 423, and *Memoiren*, 260–1. My thanks to TAK for this latter reference.

109 Quoted in Röhl, 'Admiral von Müller and the Approach of War, 1911–1914,' *Historical Journal* 12/4 (1969), 667.

110 See Holstein's letter 26 Nov. 1904 to his cousin Ida von Stülpnagel, in *Friedrich von Holstein: Lebensbekenntnis in Briefen an eine Frau*, ed. Helmuth Rogge (Berlin, 1932), 236, and Walter Goetz, 'Kaiser Wilhelm II, und die deutsche Geschichtsschreibung,' *Historische Zeitschrift*, 179 (1955), 28.

111 Lamar Cecil, 'William II and his Russian "Colleagues,"' in *German Nationalism and the European Response, 1890–1945*, ed. Carole Fink, Isabel V. Hull, and MacGregor Knox (Norman, OK, 1985), 96.

112 Röhl, 'Müller and War,' 657.

113 'Metternich soll einen Schwärmer in den H-------kriegen; er ist zu schlapp.' Marginalia to Dispatch no.756, 1 Aug. 1908, Metternich to Chancellor Prinz von Bülow, *G Politik, EK*, vol. 24, 116.

114 Quoted in Balfour, *Kaiser*, 232.

115 Letter 21 Feb. 1905, 13 pages, handwritten in English, *The Kaiser's Letters to the Tsar*, ed. NF Grant (London, 1920), 168–81. To tell Nicholas II that he should 'electrify' his people is not unlike casting Casper Milquetoast in the role of King Lear.

116 Henri de Noussanne, *The Kaiser as He Is or The Real William II (Le Véritable Guillaume II*, trans. Robert Littlefield (New York, 1905), 18. Noussanne was a French journalist who had covered Wm's Italian reception; Balfour, *Kaiser*, 146.

117 Cecil, 'Russian Colleague.' Princess Marie Radziwill, *This Was Germany! An Observer at the Court of Berlin*, trans. Cyril Spencer Fox (London, 1937), 109–ll; *Spitzemberg* 517.

118 For examples of such interference, see Graf Ernst Reventlow, *Von Potsdam nach Doorn* (Berlin, 1940), 239–40; Prince Gebhard Lebrecht Blücher, *Memoirs of Prince Blücher*, ed. Evelyn Princess Blücher (London, 1932), 76–7, and Noussanne, *Kaiser*, 96.

119 Zipfel, 'Kritik,' 50–1.

120 Wilhelm II, *The Kaiser's Memoirs*, trans. Thoma R. Ybarra (New York, 1922), 41.

121 Letter 20 July 1892 from Wm to Leo von Caprivi, *The Holstein Papers*, ed. Norman Reich and M.H. Fisher, 5 vols. (Cambridge, 1964), 420, and Röhl, *Germany Without Bismarck*, 93.

122 Quoted in Röhl, *Germany without Bismarck*, 208.

123 Reventlow, *Potsdam nach Doorn*, 398. He expressed the same sentiment in prose, writing in the margin of a diplomatic document, 'I remain serene and look down from my horse on the (rabble) *Gesindel* beneath me.' Lydia Franke, *Randbemerkungen Wilhelms II. in den Akten der Auswärtigen Politik als historische und psychologische Quelle* (Leipzing, 1934), 81.

124 Count Robert Zedlitz-Taüschler, *Twelve Years at the Imperial German Court* (London, 1924), 280.

125 *Bülow Memoirs*, vol. 1, 47.

126 Zipfel, 'Kritik,' 158.

127 Alex Hall, 'Youth in Rebellion: The Beginnings of the Socialist Youth Movement, 1904–1914,' in Richard J.W. Evans, ed., *Society and Politics in Wilhelmine Germany* (London, 1978), 257–8.

128 See Chapter 5.

129 Wilhelm Schüssler, *Wilhelm II. Schicksal und Schuld* (Göttingen, 1962), 43.

130 *Spitzemberg*, 368; in Johan, *Reden*, 15; and Röhl, *Germany without Bismarck*, 223.

131 Speech 3 July 1900 at Wilhelmshaven, in Johan, *Reden*, 131. Chancellor Bülow repeatedly warned the Kaiser that calling himself 'Admiral of the Atlantic' was highly provocative and would alarm England, but Wm kept repeating it. See, e.g., *GPEK*, vol. 9, Document 6037 .

132 Bülow, *Memoirs*, vol. 2, 420.

133 An original letter 16 Feb. 1908, written in the Kaiser's beautiful script on his light-blue stationery with gold-embossed Imperial crest, and red wax seal, may be found in the Manuscript Division of the Bodleian Library, Oxford. The letter is signed, 'Wilhelm, I.R. Admiral of the Fleet.' The letter is published in *GPEK*, vol. 24, Document 8181.

134 Some of these 'Gedankensplittern über den Krieg in Transvaal' are reprinted in *GPEK*, vol. 15, Document 4507.

135 The account given here is based on the text of the interview as given in *GPEK*, vol. 24, Anlage to Document 8251, and a manuscript copy in the Wortley papers, Manuscript Division, Bodleian Library, Oxford. The German version, as printed in contemporary newspapers, may be found in Hohlfeld, *Dokumente*.

136 Neither this plan nor his letter to Queen Victoria can be found in the Royal Archives (RA) at Windsor Castle; members of the German general staff asserted that they had never been consulted on the Kaiser's alleged military plan for the Boer War.

137 Reventlow, *Potsdam nach Doorn*, 400.

138 Cited in Roger Chickering, *We Men Who Feel Most German, A Cultural Study of the Pan-German League, 1886–1914* (Boston, 1984), 232.

139 Dispatch from Berlin, *The World* (New York), 1 Nov. 1908.

140 *Stenographische Berichte des Deutschen Reichstags*, vol. 233, p. 5394, Quoted in Anton Drewes, *Die 'Daily Telegraph' Affäre vom Herbst 1908 und ihre Wirkungen*, PhD dissertation, University of Münster, 1933, 33.

141 *Regierung und Volkswille: eine akademische Vorlesung* (Berlin, 1914), 186.

142 Quoted by Drewes, *Affaire*, 73. The 'Humiliation of Olmütz' was a bitterly remembered historical moment in 1851 when Prussia was forced to yield to Austria.

143 Spitzemberg, *Tagebuch*, 513.

144 *Simplicissimus*, 13 (28 Dec. 1908).

145 Original letter from Kaiser to Wortley, Neues Palais, Oct. (no day given) 1908, may be found in the Wortley correspondence, 'Papers Concerning the Daily Telegraph Incident,' Manuscript Division, English History, d. 256, Bodleian Library, Oxford.

146 See the memoirs of Valentini, the chief of the Kaiser's cabinet and those of Zedlitz-Trützschler, Controller of the household and court marshal, in Rudolf von Valentini, *Kaiser und Kabinettschef nach eigenen Aufzeichnungen ...*, ed. Bernhard Schwert-

feger (Oldenburg, 1931), 101, and Zedlitz-Trützschler, *Twelve Years*, 224–5. For the skits, see Chapter 1.

147 Politishes Archiv des Auswärtiges Amtes, Bonn, quoted by Gutsche, *Der Letzte Kaiser*, 128.

148 Bülow's own version of the incident is given in his memoirs.

149 After visiting the Kaiser and receiving an extensive correspondence from him, Roosevelt (TR) wrote in 1899 that 'the Kaiser ... is by far the most impressive man among the crowned heads of our time.' In 1901 TR added, 'The more I hear about the Kaiser, the more my respect for him grows,' and in 1907, 'He is a great man and I admire him with my whole heart.' Quoted by Howard Beale, 'Theodor Roosevelt, Wilhelm II und die deutsch-amerikanischen Beziehungen,' *Die Welt als Geschichte: eine Zeitschrift für Universalgeschichte* 15 (1955), 182. See also TR's letters 3 July 1901 to British diplomat Spring Rice and to Andrew Carnegie, letter 15 July in *The Letters of Theodore Roosevelt*, 6 vols., selected and ed. Elting E. Morison, with the assistance of John M. Blum, Alfred D. Chandler Jr, and Sylvia Rice (Cambridge, Mass, 1952).

150 The version of the interview given here draws on William Harlan Hale, 'Thus Spoke the Kaiser: The Lost interview which Solves an International Mystery,' *Atlantic Monthly*, 153/5 (May 1934), 513–23, and continued in the June issue, 695– 705. The author of these articles was the son of William Bayard Hale. See also Ralph R. Menning and Carol Bresnahan Menning, 'Wilhelm II and the Hale Interview of 1908,' *Central European History* 16/4 (Dec. 1983), which shows that the Hale interview was known to the German, British, French, and Japanese and had far greater consequence than had previously been thought. See also *The World* (New York) issues 22–30 (Nov. 1908).TR's own version of the incident, which supports these accounts, was given in a long letter to Elihu Root, his Secretary of State (1905–9). Roosevelt ms. 4838, in *Roosevelt Letters*, vol. 6.

151 Beale, 'Theodor Roosevelt,' 18.

152 Roosevelt ms, letter 22 Nov. 1908, quoted in ibid., 184.

153 Walter Goerlitz, Introduction, G.A. Müller, *Kaiser*, xxvii.

154 Radziwill, 77.

155 Hohlfeld, *Dokumente*, vol. 2, 226.

156 Quoted in Röhl, *Germany without Bismarck*, 260.

157 Zedlitz-Trützschler, diary entry 19 March 1910, quoted by Erich Eyck, *Die Monarchie Wilhelms II nach seinen Briefen, seinen Randbemerkungen und den Zeugnissen seiner Freunde* (Berlin, 1924), 20.

158 Ibid., 17.

159 The Kaiser's yearly schedule looked something like this: Jan.–Feb. in Berlin for height of the court season, balls, and celebration of His Majesty's birthday on 27 Jan.; April–May: his home on the island of Corfu; early May: Wiesbaden for

operatic festival, then to spring parades of Potsdam and Berlin garrisons; June: yachting at Kiel and the Cowes Regattas; June until Sept. (!): cruise of the *Hohen-zollern* in Norwegian waters; Sept.–early Oct.: Army manoeuvres; Oct.–Nov.: hunting in various lodges; Dec.: Potsdam for Christmas. Compiled by an anonymous court official, in Dickinson, *Kaiser*, 5. For a similar schedule see Balfour, *Kaiser*, 147.

160 Zipfel, 'Kritik,' 157.

161 Entry 16 Jan. 1902, in Spitzemberg's *Tagebuch.*

162 The phrase is Thomas Kohut's, *Kaiser Wilhelm II*, 133.

163 As quoted in Röhl, *Deutsche Politik*, 134.

164 Letter is reprinted in Bülow, *Memoirs*, vol. 2, 160–2, and in Schüssler, *Schicksal*, 140–1.

165 Bülow, *Memoirs*, vol. 2, 424.

166 Isabel V. Hull, 'Kaiser Wilhelm and the "Liebenberg Circle,"' in Röhl and Sombart, *Kaiser*, 204.

167 Ernst Jäkh, ed., *Kiderlen-Wächter: Der Staatsmann und Mensch, Briefwechsel und Nachlass*, 2 vols. (Berlin and Leipzig, 1925), vol. 1, 143.

168 According to a close friend, General von Caprivi had one obsession: the dread of a two-front war which, he kept saying, would happen 'next year.' See Tirpitz, *Memoirs*, vol. 1, 37. Caprivi surprised the progressives (and everyone else), however, by supporting a progressive income tax in Prussia, lowering the tariff, and reducing military service from 3 to 2 years. In so doing, he ran afoul of the Junkers who forced him out of office.

169 The phrase was Theodore Roosevelt's.

170 Moltke refused to accept his new post until the Kaiser promised not to win all the war games; and on 1 August 1914 he flatly refused to carry out the Kaiser's sudden orders to scrap the Schlieffen Plan and move solely against Russia. Barbara Tuchman, *The Guns of August* (New York, 1962), 78–9.

171 Quoted in Correlli Barnett, *The Swordbearers: Studies in Supreme Command in the First World War* (London, 1963), 16.

172 Herbert Rosinski, *The German Army* (Washington, 1944), 91, quoted with approval by Craig, *Prussian Army*, 301.

173 Ian Kershaw, 'Hitler and the Germans,' in Richard Bessel, ed., *Life in the Third Reich* (New York, 1987).

174 See the indispensable study by Thomas Childers, *The Nazi Voter: The Social Foundations of Fascism in Germany 1919–1933* (Chapel Hill, NC, 1983).

175 Michael H. Kater, *The Nazi Party: A Social Profile of Members and Leaders, 1919–1945* (Cambridge, MA, 1983), 236.

176 Lothar Kettenacher, 'Sozial-psychologische Aspecte, der Führer-Herrschaft' in *Führerstaat: Mythos und Realität.'* Gerhard Huichfeld und Lothar Kettenacher, eds. (Stuttgart, 1981), 103.

177 Konrad Heiden, *Der Fuehrer: Hitler's Rise to Power*, trans. Ralph Manheim (Boston, 1944), 419.

178 See the valuable collection of documents ed. by Jeremy Noakes and Geoffrey Pridham, *Nazism, 1919–1945*, vol. 2, *State, Economy and Society, 1933–1939* (University of Exeter, 1984), 266.

179 Dieter Pezina, 'Germany and the Great Depression,' *Journal of Contemporary History* 4 (Oct. 1969), 124.

180 Else Frenkel-Brunswick, 'The Role of Psychology in the Study of Totalitarianism,' *Totalitarianism*, ed. Carl J. Friedrich (Cambridge, MA, 1954), 173.

181 *Escape from Freedom* (New York, 1941).

182 Hitler in an interview with George Sylvester Viereck, an American admirer, as reported in the *American Monthly* (New York), Oct. 1923. Reprinted in *Hitler Aufzeichnungen, Sämtliche 1905–1924*, ed. Eberhard Jäckel (Stuttgart, 1980) as Document 578, 1023.

183 Quoted in Berning,*Vokabular*, 137.

184 Naumann called for a powerful national-socialist leader and asked rhetorically, 'What is Nationalism?' His answer: 'It is the drive of the German *Volk* to impose its influence over the globe'; and socialism, he asserted, could come only through a nationalist state under the Kaiser's leadership. He had no confidence in democracy. 'Who will conduct our grand politics?' he asked in a pamphlet entitled *Demokratie und Kaisertum*, and concluded briskly: 'Not the Parliament, only the Kaiser!' Quotations from *National-Sozial Katechismus* and from *Demokratie und Kaisertum* in Fehrenbach, *Kaisergedankens*, 200, 201, 206.

185 One of the reasons Hitler chose Nuremberg as the site of his enormous party rallies was to dramatize the continuity of Nazism with past glories. The medieval town of the *Meistersinger* had been a sort of capital for the First Reich, the Holy Roman Empire, and Emperor Wilhelm II liked to call it an imperial city, 'mein Nürnberger Kaiserberg' of his Second Reich. See Thomas Wunder, ed., *Das Reichsparteitagsgelände in Nürnberg: Entstehung, Kennzeichen, Wirkung* (Nürnberg, 1984), 27.

186 Berning, *Vokabular*, 55–6.

187 Conversation with Harold Nicolson as recorded in his *Diaries and Letters: The War Years, 1939–1945*, 3 vols. (New York, 1967), vol. 2, 39.

188 Theodore Abel, *Why Hitler Came into Power: An Answer Based on the Original Life Stories of 600 of His Followers* (New York, 1938), 149–50.

189 Hermann Glaser, 'Adolf Hitlers *Mein Kampf* als Spiesserspiegel,' *Aus Politik und Zeitgeschichte*, 9 (24 July 1963), 13–22. The word is difficult to translate. It can also be rendered 'Philistine's code.'

190 See Hans Kohn's perceptive early essay, 'The Mass-Man: Hitler,' *Atlantic Monthy*, 173 (April 1944), 100–4.

191 Heiden, *Der Fuehrer*, Ralph Mannheim, trans. (Boston, 1944), 377–8.

192 Dorothy Thompson, *I Saw Hitler!* (New York, 1932). Thompson misspelled his first name.

193 (*lasse mich in Stücke schlagen*) Speech of 20 Oct. 1932, in Domarus, *Reden*, 140.

194 As the journalist Paule Sethe observed at the time: one can govern tyranically against the will of the people, but one cannot govern democratically against the will of the people. See Hans-Jürgen Eitner, *Hitlers Deutsche: Das Ende eines Tabus* (Berlin, 1991), 41.

195 David Schoenbaum, *Hitler's Social Revolution: Class and Status in Nazi Germany, 1933–1939* (New York, 1966), 270–1.

196 Ibid., 310–11.

197 The economic recovery of Germany under Hitler was much more spectacular than the 'economic miracle' associated with Konrad Adenauer and Ludwig Erhard. Between 1933 and 1938 the annual rate of economic growth in Nazi Germany was an astonishing 8.2% – far exceeding the *Wirtschaftswunder* of 1949–59.

198 Hermann Rauschning, *Gespräche mit Hitler* (Zurich and New York, 1940). There is some doubt about Rauschning's reliability as a historical source. A review article of his books in *Historische Zeitschrift* 220 (1975) finds Rauschning 'generally reliable.' But a Swiss historian doubts that Rauschning ever in fact had all the 'Conversations with Hitler' that he reported and thinks that the 'Conversations' were reconstructed from *Mein Kampf*, Hitler's speeches – and from Rauschning's imagination. See Karl-Heinz Janssen's review article, 'Kümmerliche Notizen: Rauschnings "Gespräche mit Hitler" – wie ein Schweizer Lehrer nach 45 Jahren einen Schwindel auffliegen liess,' *Die Zeit* 30 (26 July 1985). English translation: *The Voice of Destruction* (New York, 1940) where the quotation appears on page 83.

199 See Samir-al Khalel's insightful book, *Republic of Fear: The Inside Story of Saddam's Iraq* (New York, 1990).

200 Michael Balfour, *Propaganda in War, 1939–1945* (London, 1979), 48. Quoted by Eksteins, *Rites of Spring*, 315.

201 *Völkischer Beobachter*, 15 Sept. 1936, as quoted by Areh L. Unger, *The Totalitarian Party: Party and People in Nazi Germany and Soviet Russia* (Cambridge, 1974), 34.

202 Albert Speer, *Third Reich* (New York, 1970), 265–6. It was only when it was much too late – well after the bomb plot of 1944 – that Hitler finally and reluctantly gave orders for fuller mobilization, prompting Goebbels to write in his diary on 23 July 1944, 'It takes a bomb under his arse to make Hitler see reason.' (Quoted in Eleanor Hancock, *The National Socialist Leadership and Total War* (New York, 1991), 137.

203 The only day of national celebration attempted by the republic was 'Constitution Day.' Held during August – when school was out anyway – it was a drab affair of lethargic, ill-organized parades and dull speeches.

204 Barrington Moore, *Injustice: Social Origins of Democracy and Dictatorship* (New York, 1978).

205 James H. McRandle, *Track of the Wolf: Essays on National Socialism and Its Leader, Adolf Hitler* (Evansville, IL, 1965), 225.

206 Quoted by Andreas Dorpalen, 'Hitler – Twelve Years After,' *Review of Politics* 19 (1967), 501. My emphasis.

207 Harold J Gordon, Jr, *Hitler and the Beer Hall Putsch* (Princeton, NJ, 1972), 264.

208 Ibid., 256–7, 286.

209 Peter Heydebreck's memoirs, *Wir Wehrwölfe*, quoted by Gordon, *Putsch*, 385–6. For similar complaints, see Albert Krebs, *Tendenzen und Gestalten der NSDAP: Erinnerungen* (Stuttgart, 1959), 124.

210 Richard Hansser, *Putsch! How Hitler Made Revolution* (New York, 1970), 327, 342, 359, 365; Ernst Hanfstaengl, *Unheard Witness* (New York, 1957), 98, 108.

211 Gordon, *Putsch*, 401, 332. My emphasis.

212 Captain Ernst Röhm, it is true, had taken the district army headquarters across the city, but had neglected to seize its telephone switchboard. He did not communicate with Hitler. The next morning (9 Nov., the day of the march) he surrendered the building upon orders from General Ludendorff.

213 Testimony at International Military Tribunal (Nuremberg, 1949), vol. 12, 313.

214 Gordon, *Putsch*, 332.

215 Hanser, *Putsch;* see also Gordon, *Putsch*, 352.

216 This suggestion is examined in Chapter 5.

217 Interview with Ernst Hanfstaengl, Munich, July 1967.

218 Truman Smith, 'Hitler and the National Socialists,' typescript ms now in Yale University Library, Manuscript Division.

219 *Der Hitler-Prozess vor dem Volksgericht in München* (Munich, 1924), 224 and *passim*. A full account of the trial is also available in English: *The Hitler Trial before the People's Court in Munich*, trans. H. Francis Freniere, Lucie Garcic, and Frank Fandek, with introduction by Harold J. Gordon Jr, 3 vols.

220 For other benevolent – and malign – mother-figures see Chapter 1.

221 *Hitler-Prozess*, as quoted by Hanser, *Putsch*, 393.

222 Papers of Ex-Keizer Wilhelm II, RA, Utrecht, folder 647.

223 Hitler's sentence was about what could have been expected from the sympathetic court system of the Weimar Republic, which was still dominated by the Kaiser's appointees. He was not deported to Austria, as the law for treason clearly required, the judge ruling that although technically he might be an Austrian, he certainly *'thought* like a German.' Formally he was sentenced to serve five years of 'honourable fortress confinement' at Landsberg am Lech, southwest of Munich. He actually served less than nine months, from 1 April to 20 Dec. 1924. With the approval of indulgent guards, Hitler's comfortable suite in the Landsberg fortress was

adorned with party emblems, pictures, and a huge swastika. It was laconically called the 'first Brown House' (the name of party headquarters in the Königsplatz, Munich). The state's attorney made a special concession on 3 Dec. 1924, allowing Hitler's shepherd dog to live with him. He was permitted to read or talk until midnight and to sleep late in the morning. His breakfast was served in bed by prison guards who were assigned to him, in effect, as servants. Here he wrote or dictated the memoirs that were to make him wealthy. He also dictated editorials and drew anti-government cartoons for the prison newspaper the *Landsberger Ehrenbürger* (Landsberg Honorary-Citizen). Regrettably, these issues have been lost. On his 35th birthday, 20 April 1924, military airplanes circled the fortress and dipped their wings in salute to the Führer. Hanfstaengl, who called to congratulate him on that day, found that 'the place looked like a delicatessen. You could have opened up a flower and fruit and wine shop with all the stuff stacked there. People were sending presents from all over Germany and Hitler was growing visibly fatter as a result.' When it was suggested that he really ought to participate in prison games to take off some excess weight, Hitler replied, 'No ... It would be bad for discipline if I took part in physical training. A leader cannot afford to be beaten at games.' Interview with Hanfstaengl of June 1967, which substantially repeated what he had written in *Witness*. See also Otto Lurker, *Hitler hinter Festungsmauern* (Berlin, 1933), 52–6.

224 Alan Bullock, *Hitler and Stalin* (New York, 1992), 138.

225 The Enabling Act made him dictator. The Nuremberg Laws of 1935 codified Jewish persecution. The Law for the Restoration of a Professional Civil Service barred Jews from government. A law of 1935 on the Formation of Parties made the Nazis the only legal party in Germany. A law of March 1939 made it obligatory for every boy and girl in Germany to join the Hitler Youth. The law on 'Withdrawal of Products of Decadent Art' determined the artistic canons of the land. And so it went – all of it completely legal.

226 'The worst kind of corruption is the corruption of the best.' I am indebted to Detlev Grieswelle for this quotation.

227 Speech 27 Oct. 1928 in Passau, quoted in Klaus Scholder, *Die Kirchen und das dritte Reich* (Berlin, 1977), 123.

228 For an analysis of the elections, see Richard F. Hamilton, *Who Voted for Hitler?* (Princeton, NJ, 1982).

229 Radio address 1 Feb. 1933, in Domarus, *Reden*, 192–3.

230 The editor of Hitler's speeches writes in a footnote, 'The Evangelical Lord's Prayer drawn from Matthew contains the sentence: *Denn dein ist das Reich und die Kraft und die Herrlichkeit in Ewigkeit. Amen.*' Domarus, *Hitler Reden*, 208.

231 Quoted in Scholder, *Kirchen*, 282.

232 The hymn, 'We Gather Together,' appears in most English-language hymnbooks. It

is sung to the tune of a Netherlands folk song and is a favourite at Thanksgiving services: 'We gather together to ask the Lord's blessing / He chastens and hastens his will to make known / The Wicked oppressing now cease from distressing / Sing praises to His name; He forgets not his own / Beside us to guide us, our God with us joining / Ordaining, maintaining his kingdom divine / So from the beginning the fight we are winning / Thou, Lord wast at our side, the vict'ry is thine.' The Nazis later changed the wording in one of the lines to delete 'freedom.'

233 Scholder, *Kirchen*, 284–5.

234 Ibid., 230.

235 The Nazi party was a young party. Between 1930 and 1933 the average age of party members was 25. Among the Social Democrats, by contrast, fewer than 8% were under 25 years of age.

236 Scholder, *Kirchen*, 165.

237 Editorial in *Allgemeine Evangelisch-Lutherischen Kirchenzeitung*, quoted in ibid., 174.

238 Ibid., 307.

239 See Chapter 2.

240 Hitler, disdaining the title of President, took that title immediately following the death of President Hindenburg the next year. At the outset of the war in 1939 he dropped the chancellor part of his title to be called simply 'Der Führer.'

241 Splendid descriptions of the ceremony are given by Alan Bullock, *Hitler: A Study in Tyranny*, rev. ed. (New York, 1961), 267–8; and by Hans-Jürgen Eitner, *Hitlers Deutsche: Das Ende eines Tabus*, 2nd ed. (Gernsbach, 1991), 88–90.

242 Domarus, *Reden*, 226–8. The Garrison Church lay in ruins after a RAF bombing raid of 14/15 April 1945. What remained was levelled by the Communist regime of East Germany.

243 Eitner, *Deutsche*.

244 Machiavelli, *The Prince*, trans. W.K. Marriott (London, 1908), Chapter 18, 'Concerning the Way in which Princes Should Keep Faith.'

245 Fydor Dostoyevsky, *The Brothers Karamazov*, trans. Constance Garnett (New York, 1933), 266. See also the translation by David Magarshack (New York, 1987), 301. Original emphasis.

246 See Chapter 2.

247 Dostoyevsky, *Brothers*. This rendering combines two translations: Magarshack, 297, and Garnett, 263.

248 The numbers killed during the Blood Purge will probably never be known. The figure chosen by Hitler, 77, is meaningless. The official who's who of the party, *Das deutsche Führerlexikon*, was printed before the purge and, as the editors say, 'rectified' after it took place. The book contains over 100 names that have been deleted by pasting strips of paper over them. The *Führerlexikon*, of course, contains

only those men whom the party hierarchy endorsed as leaders of the movement. Former Chancellor Brüning, who escaped the purge only because he was warned by a telephone call from a friend, told me that he had personally seen a list of over 5,000 names of people to be killed at Hitler's order. That figure, however, seems unlikely. (Interview with Heinrich Brüning, 1947.)

249 Robert G.L. Waite, *Vanguard of Nazism: The German Free Corps Movement in Postwar Germany, 1918–1923* (Cambridge, MA, 1952).

250 John W. Wheeler-Bennett, *The Nemesis of Power: The German Army in Politics, 1918–1945* (London, 1943), 310.

251 See Röhm's memoirs defiantly titled, *Die Geschichte eines Hochverräters* (The Story of an Arch-traitor), 7th ed. (Munich, 1934).

252 In this they reminded Alan Bullock of the 'Young Lady of Niger' who, it will be recalled,

'... once smiled as she rode on a tiger
But they returned from the ride
With the lady inside,
And the smile on the face of the tiger.'

253 Wheeler-Bennett, *Nemesis*, 309, and Craig, *Prussian Army*, 474.

254 Wheeler-Bennett, *Nemesis*, 312–13; and Alan Bullock, *Hitler, a Study in Tyranny*, rev. ed. (New York, 1962), 300.

255 Craig, *Prussian Army*, 477.

256 Waite, *Free Corps,* 279–81; Joseph Nyomarchy, *Charisma and Factionalism in the Nazi Party* (Minneapolis, MN, 1967), 133–5; and Domarus, *Reden*, 503. All Nazi accounts of the purge are based on Hitler's version as he gave it in press releases and in his Reichstag speech 13 July, as printed in the *Völkischer Beobachter*, 14 July. Reliable accounts are given in the standard biographies of Hitler, in Domarus, and in an anonymous contemporary book entitled, *Hitler Rast: Die Blut-tragödie des 30. Juni 1934: Ablauf, Vorgeschichte und Hintergründe*, 3rd ed. (Saar-brücken, 1934). This book was placed in the closed archives of the NSDAP and stamped with a large 'V,' for *Verboten* – a sign attesting to the book's validity. See also the anonymous pamphlet *Weissbuch über die Erschiessungen des 30. Juni 1934: Authentische Darstellung der deutschen Bartholomäusnacht*, 3rd ed. (Paris, 1935) and Otto Strasser's *Die deutsche Bartholomäusnacht*, 7th ed. (Prague, 1938). These last two accounts, however, must be used with caution.

257 Heiden, *Der Fuehrer*, 385–6.

258 See Addendum 5.

259 Personal interviews with Brüning in 1947 and Hanfstaengl in 1967.

260 Domarus, *Reden*, 396–8.

261 The text is given in Domarus. A briefer English version can be found in Norman H. Baynes, *The Speeches of Adolf Hitler, 1922–1939*, 2 vols. (Oxford, 1942).

262 For Hess's sexual tastes, see Peter Padfield's biography, *Hess: Flight for the Führer* (London, 1991).

263 Domarus, *Reden*, 398.

264 Dietrich Orlow, *The History of the Nazi Party 1919–1945*, 2 vols. (Pittsburgh, 1967 and 1973), vol. 1, 124.

265 Domarus, *Reden*, 406.

266 Robert Tucker, *Stalin in Power* (New York, 1990), as quoted in *New York Times Book Review*, 18 Nov. 1990.

267 Domarus, *Reden*, 403.

268 Craig, *Prussian Army*, 477.

269 The terms 'personalists' and 'structuralists' were first suggested in a seminal essay by Tim Mason, 'Intention and Explanation: A Current Controversy about the Interpretation of National Socialism,' reprinted in *Der Führerstaat: Mythos und Realität*, ed. Gerhard Hirschfeld and Lothar Kettenacher (Stuttgart, 1981). In the same volume, on the same subject, see also Klaus Hildebrand, 'Monokratie oder Polykratie? Hitlers Herrschaft und das Dritte Reich.' See also Ian Kershaw's valuable discussion and the essays in his, *The Nazi Dictatorship, Problems and Perspectives of Interpretation*, rev. and expanded edition (London, 1989); R. Piper, ed. *'Historikerstreit': Die Documentation der Kontroverse um die Einzigartigkeit der nationalistischen Judenvernichtung* (Munich, 1987), and Thomas Childers and Jane Caplan, eds., *Reevaluating the Third Reich* (New York, 1993). Mommsen writes, 'In all questions which needed the adoption of a fundamental and definitive position [Hitler was] a weak dictator.' *Beamten im Dritten Reich* (Stuttgart, 1966), 98. Wilhelm repeated that assertion in several valuable, if combative essays: 'Hitlers Stellung im nationalsozialistischen Herrschaftssystem,' in Hirshfeld and Kennacher, *Führerstaat*, and 'Die Realisierung des Utopischen: die Endlösung der Judenfrage im Dritten Reich,' in *Geschichte und Gesellschaft* 9 (1983).

270 T.W. Mason, 'Some Origins of the Second World War,' *Past & Present*, 29 (Dec. 1964).

271 Volker R. Berghahn in *New York Times Book Review*, 19 Feb. 1989.

272 Uwe D. Adam, *Judenpolitik im Dritten Reich* (Düsseldorf, 1972), 15, 360.

273 Jeremy Noakes and Geoffrey Pridham, *Nazism, 1919–1945*, vol. 3, *Foreign Policy, War and Racial Extermination: A Documentary Reader* (Exeter, 1988), 906.

274 Ibid., 434–5.

275 As a youth in Vienna Hitler had lectured his roommate on ways to control the masses; his chapter on propaganda in *Mein Kampf* is, by all odds, the most impressive in the book.

276 See the monograph by Peter Longerich, *Propagandisten im Krieg: Die Pressabteilung des Auswärtigen Amtes unter Ribbentrop* (Munich, 1987).

277 Goebbels had great influence over German education as well as propaganda: Robert

Ley was given immense discretion over the vast Labour Front. Göring for a time was permitted to control the economy of the Four-Year Plan. Himmler controlled the police and the concentration camp system and during the war pushed his Waffen SS into competition with the regular army. See Kershaw, *Nazi Dictatorship*, 72–3.

278 Speer, *Third Reich*, 131.

279 See Chapter 2.

280 Kershaw, *Nazi Dictatorship*, 72–3, as quoted by Bullock, *Hitler and Stalin*, 379–80. See also Speer's memoirs.

281 Quoted in *Center of the Web* (New York, 1990).

282 He had written the language badly ever since his school days when he had received low grades in German – perhaps because he may have been dyslexic. *Mein Kampf* required a great deal of editing before it was publishable; his second *Secret Book* was a collection of his speeches; he never kept a diary.

283 I follow here the conclusion reached by Kershaw, *Nazi Dictatorship*, 76.

284 Christopher R. Browning, *The Path to Genocide: Essays on Launching the Final Solution* (New York, 1992), 120.

285 Martin Broszat, 'Hitler und die Genesis der "Endlösung," Aus Anlass der Thesen von David Irving,' *Vierteljahrshefte für Zeitgeschichte* 25 (1977), 739–75. Broszat was on the editorial board of the *VfZ*. Hans Mommsen agrees with Broszat's interpretation and argues that major actions against the Jews were not ordered directly by Hitler, though he subsequently endorsed them. The boycott of Jewish businesses of April 1933 and the Nov. pogrom of 1938 were inspired by Goebbels. The 'aryanization program' of confiscating Jewish property was initiated by Göring and Ley (Mommsen, 'Realisierung des Utopischen,' in *Geschichte und Gemeinschaft* (1983), 388–9. There is one notable exception. Hitler supervised the wording of the Nuremberg racial laws with their peculiar proviso that no 'Aryan' woman under the age of 45 was to work (as he believed his own grandmother had done) in a Jewish household.

286 Arno J. Mayer, *Why Did the Heavens Not Darken? The 'Final Solution' in History* (New York, 1988), 234. For a devastating criticism of Mayer's thesis, see Christopher Browning's review-essay, 'The Holocaust as By-product: A Critique of Arno Mayer,' in *Path to Genocide*.

287 Christopher R. Browning, 'Beyond "Intentionalism" and "Functionalism": A Reassessment of Jewish Policy, 1939–1941,' in Childers and Caplan, eds., *Reevaluating*, and *Hitler's Secret Conversations, 1941–1944* (New York, 1953), 212.

288 Mayer, *Heavens Not Darken*, 332, 367.

289 See the definitive study by Christian Streit, *Keine Kameraden: Die Wehrmacht und die sowjetischen Kriegsgefangenen, 1941–1945* (Stuttgart, 1978), and the monumental work on the German army at war ed. by Wilhelm Deist, Manfred Messerschmidt, Hans-Erich Volkmann, Wolfram Wette, *Das deutsche Reich und der*

Zweite Weltkrieg, produced by the Militärgeschichtliche Forschungsamt, Freiburg/ Breisgau (1980–). For the army's cooperation with the SS in massacring Jews, see also Helmut Krausnick and Hans-Heinrich Wilhelm, *Die Truppe des Weltanschauungskrieges: Die Einsatzgruppen der Sicherheitspolizei und des SD: 1938–1942* (Stuttgart, 1981). Plans for massacring more than 33,000 Kievan Jews at Babi-Yar, e.g., were worked out jointly by the SS and the XXIXth Corps of the 6th German Army.

290 See the devastating study by Joseph Borkin, *The Crime and Punishment of I.G. Farben* (New York, 1978). Fritz Meer, one of the directors of IGF, was given a small fine at Nuremberg and in 1956 was elected chairman of the board of Bayer, one of the largest IGF companies. Daimler-Benz, in addition to manufacturing heavy trucks and military vehicles, made airplane motors and large components for V-2 rockets. Hitler held a large portfolio of D-B stocks. See Berard P. Bellou, *Mercedes in Peace and War: German Automobile Workers, 1903–1945* (New York, 1990).

291 Robert Proctor, *Racial Hygiene: Medicine under the Nazis* (Cambridge, MA, 1988), 3, 185–7, 193–4.

292 Christopher R. Browning, 'Genocide and Public Health: German Doctors and Polish Jews, 1939–1941,' *Path to Genocide.*

293 Daniel Jonah Goldhagen, *Hitler's Willing Executioners: Ordinary Germans and the Holocaust* (New York, 1996). Goldhagen's explanation for the causes of the Holocaust is simplistic, but his evidence for widespread participation in the genocide is overwhelming.

294 Christopher Browning, 'One Day in Józefów: Initiation in Mass Murder,' *Path to Genocide.*

295 Paul Webster, *Pétain's Crime: The Full Story of French Collaboration in the Holocaust* (London, 1990), as reviewed. Frederick Raphael, *Sunday Times* (London), 1 July 1990, 3.

296 See the deeply disturbing book by Judith Miller, *One by One, by One: Facing the Holocaust* (New York, 1990).

297 David S. Wyman, *The Abandonment of Jews: America and the Holocaust* (New York, 1984), gives an authoritative account.

298 See, above all, the definitive studies by Raul Hilberg, *The Destruction of the European Jews* (Chicago, 1961), 122–5, 297, 316, 343, 662–9, now revised and expanded in 3 vols. (New York, 1985), and other essays by Hilberg, including 'The *Judenrat:* Conscious or Unconscious "Tool,"' *Proceedings of the Third Yad Vashem International Historical Conference*, 4–7 April 1977 (Jerusalem, 1979); 'The Ghetto as a Form of Government,' *Annals of the American Academy of Political and Social Sciences* 450 (July 1980), and his introductory essay in Joel Dimsdale, ed., *Survivors, Victims and Perpetrators: Essays on the Nazi Holocaust* (Washington, DC,

1980). Hannah Arendt, *Eichmann in Jerusalem: Report on the Banality of Evil*, rev. ed. (New York, 1964), 18, 284. Isaiah Trunk, '*Judenräte:* The Jewish Councils of Eastern Europe,' *Proceedings of the Third Yad Vashem International Historical Conference* (Jerusalem, 1979), 29. Yehuda Bauer disputes the conclusions reached by Hilberg, Arendt, and Trunk. See his valuable collection of essays, *The Holocaust as Historical Experience: Essays and Discussion* (New York, 1981), a volume that reprints comments made orally at a conference of scholars of the Holocaust. During the heated debate on the role of the *Judenräte*, Hilberg reached a conclusion that I share: 'That the Councils [were] pained we are convinced. That in desperation Council members committed suicide is a matter of record. But that notwithstanding ... they went on doing what they were asked – that is a matter of record too' (ibid., 254–5).

299 Hilberg, *Destruction*, 343. See also Yisrael Gutman and Livia Rothkirchen, eds., *The Catastrophe of European Jewry: Antecedents, History, Reflections* (Jerusalem, 1976), 423–32, and Trunk, 'Judenräte,' 29.

300 Arendt, *Eichmann*, 118.

301 Emmanuel Ringelblum, *Notes from the Warsaw Ghetto: The Journal of Emmanuel Ringelblum*, ed. and trans. Jacob Sloan (New York, 1958), 331–2.

302 See Reuben Ainzstein, *Jewish Resistance in Nazi-Occupied Eastern Europe: With a Historical Survey of the Jew as Fighter and Soldier in the Diaspora* (New York, 1974); Miriam Novitch, *Sobibor: Martyrdom and Revolt* (New York, 1980); and, for a brief account, Yisrael Gutman, 'Rebellion in the Camps: Three Revolts in Face of Death,' *Critical Issues of the Holocaust*, ed. Alex Grobman and Daniel Landes (Los Angeles, 1983).

303 Ringelblum, *Notes*, 332–3.

304 Karl Dietrich Bracher, quoted by Christopher Browning, *Fateful Months: Studies in the Emergence of the Final Solution* (New York and London, 1985), 9. For a similar view, see Lucy S. Dawidowicz, *The War Against the Jews, 1933–1945* (New York, 1975).

305 For a strong statement of this position, see the article by the Dutch historian L.J. Hartog, 'Als Hitler den Massenmord prophezeite,' *Die Zeit*, 5 (3 Feb. 1989).

306 Archives of Institut für Zeitgeschichte (IfZ), Sammlung Irving, cited. Broszat, 'Endlosung' (1977), 749.

307 Interestingly, Broszat himself quotes that conversation of 27 Jan. 1942. 'Endlosung,' 758.

308 'Sehe ich keinen anderen Weg als die Vernichtung.' Ibid., 758.

309 For many examples, see Berning, *Vokabular*, and Robert G.L. Waite, *The Psychopathic God: Adolf Hitler* (New York, 1977 and 1993), 371.

310 Hitler actually made the prophecy to which he refers in a Reichstag speech of the previous Jan.

311 The speeches 30 Jan., 30 Sept., and 8 Nov. 1942 are given in Domarus, *Reden*. My emphasis.

312 The closest Hitler seems to have come to a written order was a note to Himmler dated 7 Oct. 1939, which gave the Reichsführer SS *carte blanche*. It reads in part, 'In accordance with my directive, the Reichsführer has the duty ... of eliminating the harmful influence of those alien sections of the population that constitute a danger to the Reich and to the German *Volksgemeinschaft* ... The Reichsführer SS is authorized to issue such general regulations and to take such measures as may be necessary to carry out these directives.' See Noakes and Pridham, eds., *Nazism*, vol. 3, Document 649. In 1966 Eichmann testified, during his Israeli trial, that '[sometime in August or Sept. 1941] Heydrich ordered me to come and see him ... He said to me, *"The Führer has ordered the physical extermination of the Jews."* He said this sentence to me and then ... paused for a long time as if he wanted to test the effect of his words on me. At first I could not grasp the implication ... But then I understood and said nothing further because there was nothing more I could say.' Ibid., Document 826. My emphasis. Hoess, the commandant at Auschwitz, testified, 'In the summer of 1941, I cannot remember the exact date, I was suddenly summoned to see the Reichsführer SS. Contrary to his usual custom, Himmler received me without his adjutant being present and said to me in effect: "The Führer has ordered that the Jewish Question be solved once and for all and we, the SS, are to implement that order. The existing extermination centres in the East are not in a position to carry out large actions that are anticipated. I have therefore earmarked Auschwitz for this purpose,"' (ibid., Document 827).

313 Broszat, 'Endlosung,' 747.

314 Late in 1940 he told his Gauleiters and SS that he wanted from them one simple, single announcement: that the Reich was entirely *Judenrein* (purified of Jews). He did not care how they did it. Kershaw, *Nazi Dictatorship*, 101–2.

315 Browning, *VfZ* (1981), 105. My emphasis. Eberhard Jäckel has argued persuasively that Reinhold Heydrich, rather than his rival in the SS, Heinrich Himmler, 'was the actual architect of the Final Solution. He took the initiative because he knew that Hitler wanted him to.' See his article, 'Die Conference am Wannsee,' *Die Zeit*, 4 (17 Jan. 1992).

316 Kershaw, *Dictatorship*, 90.

317 David Irving, *Hitler's War* (New York, 1977), xiv, 326–7, 330–1, and *passim*. Irving now seems to have revised his opinion as the result of discovering Adolf Eichmann's private diary. He claims that he found this typed manuscript of some 1,000 pages in Argentina and that it is undoubtedly genuine. It may be recalled, however, that Irving initially accepted the forged Hitler diaries. If Eichmann's diaries, which have been sent to the German NA in Koblenz, do indeed prove genuine, they will add additional testimony that the decision to murder the Jews of Europe came from

a direct, personal order of Adolf Hitler. Irving told an interviewer in Jan. 1992 that his new discovery caused him 'considerable anguish' and that 'I now may have to revise my views' – that the Holocaust took place 'without Hitler's knowledge or approval.' (Irving as interviewed by Martin Bosley, *Observer* (London, 12 Jan. 1992).

318 The Bullock-Speer conversation was printed in *Die Zeit* (9 Nov. 1979). See also the testimony given by Speer and others during the Nuremberg Trials, *International Military Tribunal*, notably vol. 10, 532; and vol. 11, 41, 230, 275, 335, 337; and vol. 17, 181.

319 Albert Zoller, ed., *Hitler Privat Erlebnisbericht seiner Geheimsekretärin* (Christa Schroeder) (Düsseldorf, 1949), 194–5.

320 Conversation with Gitta Sereny, London, June 1977. Sereny had just returned from interviewing Schroeder in Germany. See also Sereny and Lewis Chester, 'Mr Irving's Hitler: The $1000 Question,' *Sunday Times* (London, 10 July 1977).

321 Transcript of Hitler's speech to generals and officers of the Wehrmacht, 22 June 1944 at the Platterhof, Document LC-50, Special Collections Department, Brandeis University Library. Used with permission.

322 I agree with Elie Wiesel. See his review of Goldhagen's *Hitler's Willing Executioners*, in *the Observer* (London, 31 March, 1996).

323 Golo Mann, 'Wilhelm II' in *Archiv der Weltgeschichte*, ed. Karl Dietrich Bracher (Munich, 1964); Wheeler-Bennett, *Knaves, Fools and Heroes* (London, 1974). Balfour wrote, 'The simple truth about the Kaiser is that for all his undoubted gifts, he was not up to the outsize job which destiny assigned to him.' *Kaiser*, 434.

324 Thomas A. Kohut, 'Mirror Image of the Nation: A Psychohistorical Investigation of Kaiser Wilhelm II's Leadership of the Germans,' *Psychoanalytic Study of Leadership*, ed. Charles B. Strozier and Daniel Offer (New York, 1984). The thesis is developed further in Kohut's fine biography of the Kaiser.

325 Quoted by Karl-Heinz Janssen, 'Dem Vergängnis entgegen ... Preussen im Dreikaiserjahr 1888,' *Die Zeit* 25 (24 June 1988). We have noted the scornful sobriquets that Berliners bestowed on their 'Travelling Emperor.'

326 Other patriotic songs popular in Wilhelmian Germany were *Die Wacht am Rhein* and *Heil dir im Siegerskranz*. Interestingly, *Deutschland über Alles* was not officially adopted as the national anthem of Germany until 1922, well after the Kaiser had abdicated. It remained official under Hitler, as it does today, the Bonn Government in 1950 having proclaimed the third verse ('Unity and Law and Freedom for the German Fatherland') the national anthem. It was adopted by the newly united Germany in Oct. 1990. 'The Star Spangled Banner' was also late in becoming official, waiting until 1931. 'God Save the King/Queen' was first sung during the Stuart uprising in 1745 but, apparently, has never been officially adopted as *the*

national anthem of Great Britain. The 'Marseillaise,' widely sung since the French Revolution, waited 100 years until it was made official on 14 Feb. 1879. 'O, Canada' did not become official until 1980. The Russian Imperial Anthem was adopted in 1833. Prior to that time patriotic Russians sang a song entitled 'The Thunder of Victory Resounding.'

327 Isabel V. Hull, *The Entourage of Kaiser Wilhelm II 1888–1918* (Cambridge, 1982). Photographs of typical flag-nailing ceremonies may be seen in Doorn House.

328 Moltke, *Erinnerungen*, 337–8. I am indebted to Isabel Hull for this reference. The always insightful and candid Baroness Hildegard von Spitzemberg attended the unveiling of yet another 'national' monument on 24 Jan. 1912 (this time of Friedrich II, King of Prussia) and reflected sadly on the misplaced priorities of a monarch who offered the masses flag-waving ceremonies and noisy parades instead of meaningful reforms to cope with the rising social unrest that was making the Marxian Social Democrats the largest party in the Reichstag. Spitzemberg, *Tagebuch* entry 25 Jan. 1912.

329 See Isabel Hull's perceptive article, 'Prussian Dynastic Ritual and the End of Monarchy,' in *German Nationalism and the European Response, 1890–1945*, ed. Carol Fink, Isabel V. Hull, and Magregor Knox (Norman, OK, 1985), 13–42.

330 See Chapter 1.

331 Werner Jochmann, ed., *Adolf Hitler Monologe im Führer-Hauptquartier, 1941–1944* (Hamburg, 1980), conversation of 20 Aug. 1942.

332 He added that Wilhelm II had ruined his chances by running away like a coward. Conversation of Nov. 1922 with Captain Truman Smith, Assistant Military Attaché in Berlin, as reported in *Hitler Aufzeichnungen*, Document 427, p. 733.

333 See Willibald Gutsche's article, 'Man Rufe Mir! Ich Komme! Amen,' *Die Zeit* (10 July 1992).

334 Ibid.

335 The memorandum is reprinted in Willibald Gutsche, 'Dokumentation: Zur Rolle von Nationalismus und Revanchismus in der Restaurationsstrategie der Hohenzollern, 1919 bis 1933,' *Zeitschrift für Geschichtswissenschaft*, 34/1 (1986), 629–30.

336 Sigurd von Ilsemann, *Der Kaiser in Holland, Aufzeichnungen aus den Jahren 1924–1941: Monarchie und Nationalsozialismus* (Munich, 1961), vol. 2, 175–6. See also Willibald Gutsche, *Ein Kaiser im Exil: Der letzte deutsche Kaiser Wilhelm II. In Holland. Eine Kritische Biographie* (Marburg, 1991).

337 Ilsemann, *Kaiser in Holland*, vol. 2, 194–5.

338 Gutsche, *Kaiser im Exil*, 168, and Gutsche, 'Restaurationsstrategie.'

339 Gutsche, *Kaiser im Exil*, 138, 168.

340 Ilsemann, *Kaiser in Holland*, vol. 2, 251–2. The Kaiser was mistaken about Hitler's house-painting. Nor was he ever a paper-hanger.

341 Ibid., 257. In pleading the cause of Hohenzollern restoration with Göring, Crown
     Prince Friedrich Wilhelm let Göring know that he had himself, and not his father, in
     mind, telling the Reichsmarschall that his father was 'incapable of ruling.' The
     Crown prince subsequently gave Göring one of Wilhelm II's personal letters critical
     of Hitler (ibid., 240, 249, 283).
342 Letter 28 July 1940 Wm II to Alma Gräfin von der Goltz, RA Utrecht, folder 53.
343 Letter 24 Dec. 1940 Wm II to Nieman RA Utrecht, folder 53, cited by Gutsche, *Wil-
     helm II*, 222.
344 See Chapter 5.
345 Gutsche, *Kaiser im Exil*, 200–1.
346 Ilsemann reprints the texts of the telegrams, in *Kaiser in Holland*, vol. 2, 315.
347 Gutsche, *Kaiser im Exil*, 214–16.

Chapter 4: Kaiser and Führer as Rulers in War

1 The following estimates of total casualties (dead and seriously wounded) for all
   major combatants have been given: Austria-Hungary, perhaps 2.5 million; Britain
   (including the Empire), more than 3 million; France, 4 million; Germany, 6 million;
   Italy, 1 million; Russia, 5 million; USA, 300,000. See William L. Langer, ed., *An
   Encyclopedia of World History*, rev. ed. (New York, 1948).
2 Jack J. Roth, ed., *World War I: A Turning Point in Modern History* (New York,
   1967), 109.
3 Gustav Stolper, Karl Häuser, and Knut Borchardt, *The German Economy: 1870 to
   the Present*, trans. Toni Stolper (New York, 1967), 110. Hitler's economic system
   would draw heavily on Germany's experience in the First World War.
4 Alan Bullock, *Hitler and Stalin* (New York, 1992), 726. Bullock gives a breakdown
   of the civilians killed by countries. See his Appendix II, 986–7.
5 See Louis L. Snyder, *The War: A Concise History, 1939–1945* (New York, 1960).
   The Germans and Japanese were not the only nations to massacre innocent people.
   British and American bombs killed 50,000 civilians during a single raid on Dort-
   mund in May 1943 and 40,000 in a raid on Hamburg in July 1943. One American
   firebombing of Tokyo in March 1945 killed 80,000 Japanese. America's use of the
   atomic bomb killed 138,890 civilians in Hiroshima and 48,857 in Nagasaki in Aug.
   and left thousands more maimed for life. Watching films of the firestorm of a German city in June 1943, Winston Churchill turned to an aide and asked 'Are we
   beasts? Are we taking this too far?' Yet in Feb. 1945, with the war virtually won, he
   gave the orders for firebombing Dresden.
6 Dirk Stegmann, *Die Erben Bismarcks: Parteien und Verbände in der Spätphase des
   Wilhelminischen Deutschlands, 1897–1918* (Köln, 1970), 105ff, 277ff, as cited in

Imanuel Geiss and Bernd Jürgen Wendt, eds., *Deutschland in der Weltpolitik des 19. und 20. Jahrhunderts* (Düsseldorf, 1974), 323. See also Wilhelm Deist's essay, in Michael Stürmer, ed., *Das Kaiserliche Deutschland: Politik und Gesellschaft: 1870–1918* (Düsseldorf, 1970).

7 Volker R. Berghahn, 'Flottenrüstung und Machtgefüge,' in Stürmer, *Deutschland*, 393. Berghahn notes that in 1933 the same people, fearing the rise of social democracy, saw in Hitler a tool for maintaining their dominant position in society (p. 363).

8 *Germany and the Next War*, trans. Allen H. Powles (New York, 1914), 18.

9 Theodor Heuss, who in 1949 was to become the first president of the Bonn Government, wrote an essay in 1914 agreeing with Bernhardi and asserting that Germany's 'moral superiority' over other nations gave it the 'moral right' to go to war. Theodor Heuss, 'Der Weltkrieg,' *März* (5 Aug. 1914), 221–5, as quoted by Eksteins, *Rites of Spring* (Boston, 1989), 91.

10 This outpouring of support prompted a respected German historian to conclude (and to weaken his point by overstatement): 'There is not a single document in the world which could refute the central truth that in July 1914 a desire for war existed solely and alone on the German side.' Fritz Fischer, 'Vom Zaun gebrochen – Nicht hineingeschlittert (Picking a Quarrel – Not Sliding into One),' *Die Zeit* 36 (7 Sept. 1965). Another leading authority on the causes of war agrees with Fischer. In an essay, 'Germany and the Coming of the War,' Pogge von Strandmann concluded: 'The evidence makes the view that Germany fought a defensive war untenable and the interpretation that all nations "slithered over the brink ... into war" untenable.' R.J.W. Evans and Hartmut von Strandmann, *Coming of the First World War* (Oxford, 1988), 98.

11 See Fritz Fischer, *Germany's Aims in the First World War* (New York), 1967, and the same author's *The War of Illusions: German Policies from 1911 to 1914* (New York, 1975); Imanuel Geiss, ed., *July 1914: The Outbreak of the First World War, Selected Documents* (New York, 1967), and his earlier *Julikrise und Kriegsausbruch, 1914*, 2 vols. (Hannover, 1963).

12 Adolf Gasser, 'Der Deutsche Hegemonialkrieg von 1914,' in Imanuel Geiss and Bernd Jürgen Wendt, eds., *Deutschland in der Weltpolitik des 19. und 20. Jahrhunderts* (Düsseldorf, 1974), 336.

13 Russia was struggling to recover from the national trauma of its defeat by Japan and its subsequent revolution of 1905. England too was ill-prepared for war and beset by both labour unrest and the threat of civil war in Ireland. In contrast to Germany, where a victorious war was touted as a means of 'cleansing internal ills,' the British feared that war would increase domestic problems. British business circles wanted no part of war. France was torn between the political right and left, with the right trying to blunt leftist criticism by an openly non-belligerent stance. On 1 Aug. 1914, the

French actually *pulled back* their troops 10 km from the German frontier, thereby dangerously exposing the important Briey basin to German attack. See Arno J. Mayer, 'Domestic Causes of the First World War,' *The Responsibility of Power: Historical Essays in Honor of Hajo Holborn*, ed. Leonard Krieger and Fritz Stern (New York, 1968), 297.

14 Schlieffen's memoranda of 1909 and 1912 are reprinted in Gerhard Ritter, *The Schlieffen Plan: Critique of a Myth* (New York, 1958), 101–2.

15 Generaloberst Helmuth von Moltke, *Erinnerungen, Briefe, Dokumente, 1877–1916*, ed. Eliza von Moltke (Stuttgart, 1922), 14.

16 Gerhard Ritter, *Staatskunst und Kriegshandwerk: Das Problem des 'Militarismus' in Deutschland*, 3 vols. (Munich, 1960), vol. 2, 270–1.

17 Elisabeth Fehrenbach, *Wandlungen der deutschen Kaisergedankens, 1871–1918* (Munich, 1969), 91.

18 A reproduction of the heroic figure astride a warhorse is reproduced in Asa Don Dickinson, ed., *The Kaiser: A Book about the Most Interesting Man in Europe* (New York, 1914), 19.

19 Michael Balfour, *The Kaiser and His Times* (London, 1975), 83–5.

20 Lamar Cecil, 'History as Family Chronicle: Wilhelm II and the Dynastic Roots of the Anglo-German Antagonism,' in John C.G. Röhl and Nicolaus Sombart, eds., *Kaiser Wilhelm II: New Interpretations* (Cambridge, 1982), 101. Wilhelm was so taken with the remarkably popular 'Song of Hatred' (*Hassgesang*) that he bestowed the Order of the Red Eagle on its Jewish author. On several occasions the Kaiser joined his guests in singing the best-known stanza:
> Hate by water and hate by land
> Hate of the heart and hate of the hand
> We love as one, we hate as one,
> We have but one foe alone, England!

21 See Paul Kennedy, 'The Kaiser and German Weltpolitik: Reflections on Wilhelm II's place in the Making of Foreign Policy,' in Röhl and Sombart, *Kaiser*, 158.

22 See Chapter 5 and Chapter 6.

23 See Chapter 3.

24 The public also learned that one of Wilhelm's intimates, Count Hülsen-Haesler, died of a heart attack under embarrassing circumstances. The count had tried to cheer up the Kaiser on 14 Nov. by dressing in a tutu and lumbering about the room as a ballerina. His death was 'an especial loss to the Kaiser.' Georg Alexander von Müller, *The Kaiser and His Court: The Diaries, Notebooks and Letters of Admiral Georg Alexander von Müller, Chief of the Naval Secretariat, 1914–1918*, ed. Walter Goerlitz (London, 1961), 71.

25 As Fritz Stern has suggested, his use of this word may well be 'an unconscious allusion ... to frequent charges of ... effeminacy.' See Stern's essay, 'Bethmann Hollweg

and the War: The Limits of Responsibility,' *Responsibility of Power*, ed. Leonard Krieger and Fritz Stern (London, 1968), 267.

26 The text of Ambassador Lichnowsky's report 3 Dec. 1912, along with the Kaiser's marginalia 8 Dec. is given in *GPEK*, vol. 29, Document 15612.

27 The fullest documentary account of the Dec. meeting is given in Röhl's article, 'An der Schwelle zum Weltkrieg: Eine Dokumentation über den "Kriegsrat" von 8. Dezember 1912,' *Militärgeschichtliche Mitteilungen* (1977), 77–134. The letter is reprinted as Document 8.

28 The complex relationship between mother and son will be explored in Chapter 6.

29 Precise knowledge of what took place during this 'War Council' (*Kriegsrat*) was first revealed in 1969 when John Röhl published extensive excerpts from the private diaries of Admiral Georg Alexander von Müller, Chief of the Kaiser's Naval Council from 1906 to 1918, who took extensive notes on what was said at the conference. Admiral Müller's diaries had been edited and published by the German historian Walter Görlitz in 1965, as *Der Kaiser ... Aufzeichnungen des Chefs des Marinekabinetts Admiral Georg Alexander von Müller über die Aera Wilhelm II* (Berlin and Zurich, 1965), but Görlitz had allowed Müller to delete passages from the printed version. See Röhl's indispensable article, 'Admiral von Müller and the Approach of War, 1911–1914,' *Historical Journal* 12/4 (1969).

30 The term was first used by Chancellor Bethman Holweg.

31 Admiral von Müller's unpublished diary, as cited by Röhl, 'Dokumentation,' 77 and in 'Admiral von Müller,' 662.

32 'Ich halte einen Krieg für unvermeidbar und je eher je besser.' Müller's diary, as cited by Gasser, 'Hegemonialkrieg,' 312; and Röhl, 'Admiral von Müller,' 662. My emphasis.

33 Röhl, 'Admiral von Müller,' 662; and Gasser, 'Hegemonialkrieg,' 320.

34 See below.

35 Quoted in Fischer, *War of Illusions*, 192–3.

36 See Chapter 2.

37 The letter is published as document 23 in Röhl, 'Dokumentation.' Emphasis is the Kaiser's.

38 See Baron Beyens, *Deux Anneés à Berlin, 1912–1914* (Paris, 1931), vol. 1, 38–40.

39 Fischer, *War of Illusions*, 168.

40 See especially Gasser's essay, 'Hegemonialkrieg,' in *Deutschland in der Weltpolitik*, 315–17.

41 'Sobald das Prestige Oesterreich-Ungarn es erheische, müsse energisch gegen Serbien vorgehen. Deutschland würde "unter allen Umständen" Oesterreich unterstützen, auch wenn es darüber einen Weltkriege "mit dem drei Entente-Mächten käme."' See Franz Ferdinand's report of his conversation with Wm in Berlin, 22 Nov. 1912. *Oesterreich-Ungarns Aussenpolitgik von Bosnischen Krise 1908 bis zum*

Kriegsausbruch 1914: Diplomatische Aktenstücke des Oesterreichisch-ungarischen Ministeriums des Aeusseren, vol. 4 (Vienna, 1930), no. 4571, 4590, which is reprinted as Document 29 in Röhl, 'Dokumentation.'

42 The Bavarian military attaché in Berlin reported, 'At the Kaiser's orders an invasion in the grand style of England is being worked out.' Dispatch 15 Dec. 1912. Document 22 in Röhl, 'Dokumentation.'

43 Szögenyi-Marich, as quoted by Isabel V. Hull, *The Entourage of Kaiser Wilhelm II, 1888–1918* (Cambridge, 1982), 264.

44 Ibid., 83.

45 Ibid., 262–5.

46 Otto Hammann, *Um den Kaiser* (Berlin, 1919), 93–4.

47 Imanuel Geiss, 'The Crisis of July 1914,' *Journal of Contemporary History*, 1 (1966), 86. See below.

48 After the death of Alfred Krupp, founder of the famous munitions factory at Essen, the firm was inherited by his daughter Bertha, who married a man who received special dispensation from the Kaiser to adopt the family name and style himself 'Gustav Krupp von Bohlen und Halbach.' Gustav was indicted for war crimes after the First World War; his son, Alfred, would be charged with similar crimes after the Second World War.

49 Volker Berghahn, who reports the incident, translates the phrase, 'This time I won't chicken out!' But that rendering, while certainly catching Wilhelm's meaning in contemporary slang, seems anachronistc for 1914. *Germany and the Approach to War* (London, 1973), 193. The Kaiser's exclamation can also be rendered, 'This time I won't give in!' or 'This time I won't collapse' or 'This time I'll stand firm!'

50 Bernadotte W. Schmidt and Harold Wedeler, *The World in Crucible, 1914–1919* (New York, 1984), 8. Of the vast literature on the 'July Crisis,' see especially Luigi Albertini's magisterial work, *The Origins of the War of 1914*, trans. and ed. Isabella M. Massey, 3 vols. (London, 1953). Vol. 2 is devoted entirely to 'The Crisis of July 1914.' For recent German views, see the works of Fritz Fischer and Imanuel Geiss, particularly the latter's *July 1914: the Outbreak of the First World War* (New York, 1967), which reprints important documents.

51 The following account is based on the research of Albertini, Geiss, Fischer, and Gasser. I am particularly grateful to Geiss for calling my attention to the Kautsky edition of documents, *Die Deutschen Dokumente zum Kriegsausbruch, 1914: Vollständige Sammlung der von Karl Kautsky Zusammengestellten amtlichen Aktenstücke ... im Auftrage des Auswärtigen Amtes ... herausgegeben von Graf Max Montgelas und Prof. Walter Schücking*, 4 vols. (Berlin, 1922). Hereafter cited as *DD*.

52 'Jetzt oder nie! ... den Serben muss aufgeräumt werden und zwar bald!' See *DD* document 7, '*Der Botschafter in Wien an den Reichskanzler*,' Vienna, 30 June 1914.

53 Geiss, *July 1914*, 62–3.

54 After another private conversation with the Kaiser, the Austro-Hungarian ambassador reasssured his government of German support in a war against Serbia and added, 'The German government considers the present moment to be "politically optimal" from the German standpoint as well [as our own].' Imanuel Geiss, ed., *Julikrise und Kriegsausbruch, 1914*, Document 75. Quote by Fritz Fischer, *From Kaiserreich to Third Reich: Elements of Continuity in German History, 1871–1945*, trans. and with an introduction by Roger Fletcher (London, 1968), 51.

55 Geiss, *July 1914*, 73, who concurs with Hermann Kantorowicz: 'In this most important decision ever confronted by the nation the Kaiser said, "I order" and his advisers responded obediently, "As you command!" [*"Ich befehl! ... Zu Befehl!"*] Kantorowicz, *Gutachten zur Kriegsschuldfrage, 1914 aus dem Nachlass herausgegeben und eingeleitet von Imanuel Geiss* (Frankfurt/Main, 1967). For comments on Kantorowicz, see Addendum 2.

56 *DD* document 74, 'Der Oberquartiermeister im Grossen Generalstabe an den Staatssekretär des Auswärtigen (Privatbrief).'

57 *DD* document 271, 'Antwortnote der serbischen Regierung auf das oesterreischisch-ungarische Ultimatum,' which appends the Kaiser's marginalia. This document becomes document 72 in the Geiss collection, which does not, however, give the Kaiser's marginal comment.

58 Wilhelm II to Jagow, 28 July 1914, Geiss, *July 1914,* 575. Quoted in Fischer, *War of Illusions*, 487.

59 Moltke's reply to the Kaiser, as Geiss notes dryly, was 'another of those key documents for which no place could be found in *Grosse Politik* [*GPEK*].' Geiss, *July Crisis*, 43. My emphasis. For Moltke's despair at the Kaiser's meddling into affairs he did not understand, see his memoirs, *Erinnerungen*, 19–20.

60 For accounts of 'Operation Himmler,' as this bogus attack was called, see testimonials given at *Trial of the Major War Criminals at Nuremburg*, vol. 2, 450; vol. 3, 235; vol. 4, 242; and vol. 5, 33. A brief account may be found in William Shirer, *The Rise and Fall of the Third Reich* (New York, 1959), 518–20.

61 *DD* document 790, 'Der Reichskanzler an den Botschafter in London,' Telegram 223.

62 *DD* document 664, 'Der Staatssekretär des Auswärtigen an den Botschafter in Rom,' Telegram 162.

63 *DD* document 710, 'Der Staatssekretär des Auswärtigen an den Botschafter in London,' Telegram 214.

64 This paragraph is based on Richard M. Hunt's perceptive article, 'Myths, Guilt and Shame in Pre-Nazi Germany,' *Virginia Quarterly Review* 34 (Summer 1958), 355–71.

65 For a discussion of the ways the war-guilt question affected historical research, see Addendum 2.

66 A fuller discussion of this issue is given in Robert G.L. Waite, *The Psychopathic God: Adolf Hitler* (New York, 1977 and 1993), 310–11.

67 There is particular poignancy in the copy of the Kaiser's postcard in my possession. It was sent in 1915 by a Jewish volunteer in the Imperial Army to his mother in Brooklyn. The soldier writes that he is absolutely convinced of the rectitude of Germany's cause and of a 'magnificent victory of German arms.' He mailed the postcard from Theresienstadt – the future site of a Nazi concentration camp that, for tens of thousands of Jews, was a way-station on the road to Auschwitz.

68 See above, p. 9.

69 See Lamar Cecil's essay, 'Wilhelm II and his Russian Colleagues,' in *German Nationalism and the European Response, 1890–1945*, ed. Carole Fink, Isabel Hull, and Mac Gregor Knox (Norman, OK, 1985), 132.

70 Cited in Fischer, *Kaiserreich*, 375–7.

71 Ibid., 382.

72 Paul Kennedy, *The Rise of Anglo-German Antagonism, 1860–1914* (London, 1980), 458–9.

73 Geiss, *July 1914*, 367.

74 I follow Kantorowicz here. See his *Gutachten*, 255–6.

75 Fritz Stern, 'Bethmann Hollweg,' 265.

76 Quoted by Golo Mann, 'Wilhelm II.,' in the series *Archiv der Weltgeschichte*, ed. Karl Dietrich Bracher (Munich, Bern, Vienna, 1964), 6.

77 One version of the famous line, written in Wilhelm's hand, was used as the caption of his portrait on postcards which were printed by the thousands at the outbreak of war.

78 Wilhelm could never really trust his people. The distrust and suspicion he had learned as a little child plagued him throughout his life. Now, at the very time he was talking glowingly about trust and domestic harmony, he was taking the precaution of invoking a Prussian law of 1851 that gave the army supreme authority over the civilians with power to abrogate civil rights. When the *Frankfurter Allgemeine Zeitung* wrote that his action showed a distressing lack of confidence in the loyalty and patriotism of the German people, Wilhelm's comment was brusque: 'In war, Politics keeps Her mouth shut until Strategy [that is the Army] permits Her to speak again.' Otto Hammann, *Bilder aus der letzten Kaiserzeit* (Berlin, 1922), 128–9. My thanks to Gerhard Masur for this reference.

79 See Chapter 3.

80 G.A. Müller, *Kaiser* diary entry 30 April 1917.

81 Ibid., entry 19 Sept. 1918.

82 Quoted in Balfour, *Kaiser*, 391.

83 The Kaiser's personal physician, Dr Nieder, in a private letter of 1 March 1927 to Müller, reported the incident and said that the plan to depose the Kaiser was suggested by Admiral von Tirpitz, who had sought his professional advice. The physi-

cian strongly opposed such a move because it showed 'unpardonable disloyalty to the Kaiser.' G.A. Müller, *Kaiser*, 74.

84 Wilhelm Deist, 'Kaiser Wilhelm II in the Context of His Military and Naval Entourage,' in Röhl and Sombart, *Kaiser*, 185.

85 See Chapter 1 and Chapter 6.

86 Walter Goetz, 'Kaiser Wilhelm II und die deutsche Geschichtsschreibung,' *Historische Zeitschrift* 179 (1955), 37.

87 Steiner's conversation as quoted by Gasser, 'Hegemonialkrieg,' 319.

88 Admiral Georg Alexander von Müller, *Der Kaiser: Aufzeichnungen des Chefs des Marinekabinetts ... über die Aera Wilhelms II*, Walter Görlitz, ed. (Berlin, 1965), 42. Wilhelm repeated this complaint on 16 Aug. 1917. Fehrenbach, *Kaisergedankens*, 116.

89 Gordon A. Craig, *The Politics of the Prussian Army, 1600–1945* (New York, 1955), 327.

90 Diary entries 18 June, 8 Aug., and 4 Nov. 1916.

91 John W. Wheeler-Bennett, *Hindenburg: The Wooden Titan* (London, 1936).

92 Wheeler-Bennett, *Knaves, Fools and Heroes*, 97. For a thorough discussion of the generals' power, see Martin Kitchen, *The Silent Dictatorship: The Politics of the German High Command under Hindenburg and Ludendorff, 1916–1918* (London, 1976).

93 Quoted by Golo Mann, 'Wilhelm II.,' 16.

94 Craig, *Politics of the Prussian Army*, 346.

95 Henry, Graf Kessler, *Tagebücher: 1918–1937* (Frankfurt/Main, 1961).

96 Evelyn Princess Blücher, *An English Wife in Berlin: A Private Memoir of Events and Politics and Daily Life in Germany ...* (London, 1920).

97 For a brief description of the Kaiser's life in exile, see Addendum 3.

98 'Warum hat Deutschland den Krieg begrüsst und sich zu ihm bekannt als er hereinbrach? Weil er den Bringer seines dritten Reiches in ihm erkannte ... die Synthese von Macht und Geist.' Letter to the editor of *Swenska Dagbladet* (Stockholm, April 1915). Reprinted in Thomas Mann, *Gesammelte Werke*, 13 vols. (Frankfurt/Main, 1974), vol. 13, 551. My thanks to Adolf Gasser and Edson Chick for directing me to this quotation.

99 For a brief discussion of the lively and instructive debate among historians between those who argue that change has been the dominant characteristic of recent German history and those who insist on the primacy of continuity, see Addendum 4.

100 See the comprehensive study by Thomas Childers, *The Nazi Voter: The Social Foundations of Fascism in Germany: 1919–1933* (Chapel Hill, NC, 1983), and Richard F. Hamilton, *Who Voted for Hitler?* (Princeton, NJ, 1962).

101 In 1940, of the nine division chiefs in the foreign office all but one (Herr Gaus) were career officers who had served Kaiser and Republic and Third Reich

with equal devotion. See Paul Seabury, *The Wilhelmstrasse* (New York, 1954), 103.

102 See Wilhelm Deist, 'Die Aufrüstung der Wehrmacht: Hitler und die operative Planning der Wehrmacht,' in *Ursachen und Voraussetzungen der deutschen Kriegspolitik*, vol. 1. Andreas Hillgruber, 'Militarismus am Ende der Weimarer Republik und im Dritten Reich,' in *Grossmachtspolitik und Militarismus im 20. Jahrhundert* (Dusseldorf, 1974), 41.

103 The full text of this important memorandum was first published in Nov. 1948: 'Der Seeckt-Plan aus unveröffenltichten Dokumenten. Neues Tatsachenmaterial über die geheime Zusammenarbeit zwischen Reichswehr und Sowjet-Armee,' *Der Monat* (Nov. 1948). Translated excerpts of this memorandum are given in John Wheeler-Bennett, *Nemesis of Power: The German Army 1918–1945* (London, 1953), 136–8.

104 'Der Seeckt-Plan,' *Monat* (Nov. 1948).

105 Imanuel Geiss, *Der polnische Grenzstreifen, 1914–1918: Ein Beitrag zu deutschen Kriegszielpolitik im Ersten Weltkrieg* (Hamburg, 1960), 5, 105, 108, 149, and Fischer, *Kaiserreich*, 56–60.

106 Fischer, *Kaiserreich*, 84.

107 Rolf-Dieter Müller, 'Der andere Holocaust: Der Krieg gegen die Soviet Union,' *Die Zeit*, Jg. 27 (8 July 1988).

108 This discussion is based on the documents found in government archives by Carl Dirks, a former Wehrmacht official who has spent years ferreting out facts about German rearmament in the 1920s. See the important article by Denis Staunton, 'Secret Army Was Ready to Follow Hitler,' *The Observer* (London), 9 March 1977.

109 Geoff Eley, *Reshaping the German Right: Radical Nationalism and Political Change after Bismarck* (New Haven, 1980), and see above.

110 The Stahlhelm was actually one of the more moderate of the many veterans' associations of the 1920s. For more radical groups, see Robert G.L. Waite, *Vanguard of Nazism, the German Free Corps Movement in Postwar Germany, 1918–1923* (Cambridge, MA, 1952).

111 Fischer, *Kaiserreich*, 110–11.

112 See John A. Moses, *The Politics of Illusion: The Fischer Controversy in German Historiography* (London, 1975), 18.

113 See H. Alberts and I. Thomsen, eds., *Christen in der Demokratie* (Wüppertal, 1978).

114 Guenther Lewey, *Catholic Church and Nazi Germany* (New York, 1964), 221. It is true that many courageous German priests spoke out against Hitler's tyranny and the persecution of Jews. But they got little support from their superiors in the Church. Indeed prison chaplains were instructed to deny Holy Communion and the last rites of the Church to priests who had been imprisoned for resisting Hitler. Heinrich Himmler had good reason for praising Pope Pius XII (1939–58) for his 'discretion' in remaining silent about the Holocaust.

115 T.W. Mason, 'Some Origins of the Second World War,' *Past and Present* (Dec. 1964), reprinted in Esmonde M. Robertson, ed., *The Origins of the Second World War* (London, 1971), 124–5. Other specialists in Germany's economy on the eve of war agreed: 'Hitler's economic policies could not possibly have been fulfilled without war.' Wolfgang Sauer and Gerhard Schulz, eds., *Die Nationalsozialistische Machtergreifung: Studien zur Einrichtung des totalitären Herrschaftssystems in Deutschland* (Cologne, 1960), 751–2.

116 David Cameron Watt, *How War Came: The Immediate Origins of the Second World War, 1938–1939* (London, 1989), 610.

117 James P. O'Donnell, *The Bunker: A History of the Reich Chancellery Group* (Boston, 1978), 383.

118 Gerhard Weinberg, *The Foreign Policy of Hitler's Germany: Starting World War II* (Atlantic Highland, NJ, 1994), 463, 466.

119 Paul Kennedy, *Rise and Fall of the Great Powers* (New York, 1989), 305.

120 Welle, 'Die Rolle der Wehrmacht bei den psychologisch-propandistischen Kriegsvorbereitung,' *Zweite Weltkrieg in Bildern und Dokumenten*, ed. Hans Adolf Jacobsen and Hans Dolliger (Munich, 1963), 121–3.

121 Not even Dr Schacht, the finance minister, was given a copy. He saw it for the first time during the Nuremberg Trials, when Speer showed him his copy. Bullock, *Hitler and Stalin*, 445.

122 Jeremy Noakes and Geoffrey Pridham, eds., *Nazism, 1919–1945*, vol. 2, *State, Economy and Society, 1933–1939* (Exeter University, 1984), 1009.

123 For the text of the speech and critical comment, see Wilhelm Treue, 'Rede vor der deutschen Presse, 10 November 1938,' *VfZ* 5/2 (April 1958), 175–91. An English translation of the speech is given by Noakes and Pridham, vol. 3, *Foreign Policy War and Racial Extermination: A Documentary Reader* (Exeter, 1988).

124 Speech 21 May 1935, in Max Domarus, *Hitler: Reden und Proklamationen 1932–1945*, 4 vols. (Würzburg, 1962), 506–7. My emphasis.

125 On Saturday, 16 March 1935, also in defiance of the Versailles Treaty, Hitler had announced the re-introduction of general conscription and on Saturday, 7 March 1936 he announced the rearmament of Germany. He had planned to invade Poland on Saturday, 25 August 1939, at 0430 hours, but had postponed the date when Mussolini's support was problematical.

126 Domarus, *Reden*, 1422–3. See also Waite, *Psychopathic God*, 386–8.

127 Peter Bor, *Gespräche mit Halder* (Wiesbaden, 1959), 23.

128 General Hans Halder, *Tagebuch*, as cited in Harold C. Deutsch, *Hitler and His Generals: the Hidden Crisis, January–June 1938* (Minneapolis, MN, 1938), 190.

129 Deist, 'Die Aufrüstung der Wehrmacht,' 526, 528, 529, 709–12. The same conclusion was reached by Hartmut Schustereit, *Vabanque: Hitlers Angriff auf die Sovietunion* (Hereford, 1988).

130 Albert Speer, *Inside the Third Reich: Memoirs*, trans. Robert and Clara Winston (New York, 1970), 213; and, among many other studies, Alan S. Milward, *The German Economy at War* (London, 1965), 43–6, 88–9; Bernice A. Carroll, *Design for Total War: Arms and Economics in the Third Reich* (The Hague, 1968), 232, 239, 249; and Eleanor Hancock, *The National Socialist Leadership and Total War* (New York, 1991).

131 Ernst Hanfstaengl recalled that during a campaign trip in Sept. 1931, Hitler, in referring to the Maginot Line, said, 'Whenever a nation is so afraid to fight the "barbarians" that it builds a wall around itself to keep them out, that nation is decadent – look at ... the great wall of China ... This constructional feat marked the beginning of the downfall of a great Empire.' He went on to say that after gaining power, he would smash France and that he was confident France would fall without a fight. 'Recollections of Adolf Hitler,' OSS interview, 1943, Miscellaneous Declassified and Sterilized OSS Documents, National Archives (NA), Washington, DC.

132 Sir Basil Liddell-Hart, 'Hitler as War Lord,' *Encounter* (1968), 30–1.

133 Bullock, *Hitler and Stalin*, 673.

134 Ibid., 667–70.

135 See Chapter 6.

136 On 26 Feb. 1945, Hitler complained that Churchill stupidly refused to cooperate with him: 'He was quite unable to appreciate the sporting spirit of which I had given proof by refraining from annihilating them at Dunkirk.' *The Testament of Hitler*, trans. R.H. Stevens (London, 1956), 96.

137 Among many discussions of Hitler's decision at Dunkirk, see Hans-Adolf Jacobsen, *Dunkirchen: Ein Beitrag zur Geschichte des Westfeldzuges, 1940* (Neckargemünd, 1958), 96–8; Hans Meier-Welcker, 'Der Entschluss zum Anhalten der deutschen Panzer-Truppen in Flandern, 1940,' *VfZ* 2 (1954), 274–90; Halder, *Tagebuch*, 302; Walter Warlimont, *Inside Hitler's Headquarters, 1939–1945* (New York, 1964), 97–9; Bor, *Gespräche*, 170; Feldmarschall Heinz Guderian, *Erinnerungen eines Soldaten* (Heidelberg, 1951), 105–6; and Hans-Adolf Jacobsen's essay, 'Dunkirk, 1940,' in J. Rohwer, *Decisive Battles of World War II: The German View*, ed. H.A. Jacobsen and J. Rohwer, trans. Edward Fitzgerald (New York, 1965).

138 For the connection between Hitler's decision to invade the Soviet Union and his attendance at the Bayreuth Festival, see Walter Ansel, *Hitler Confronts England* (Durham, NC, 1960), 178, and Joachim Fest's report of an interview with Speer. Joachim C. Fest, *Hitler: Eine Biographie*, 5th ed. (Frankfurt/Main and Berlin, 1973), 712; Speer, who sat on the other side of Frau Wagner, had observed the scene.

139 See Norman Rich, *Hitler's War Aims*, vol. 1, *Ideology of the Nazi State and the Course of Expansion* (New York, 1973), 207, 190.

140 *Secret Conversations*, 276.

141 Rich, *Hitler's War Aims*, vol. 1, 228–9.

142 Carroll, *Total War*, 159.

143 Buchheit, 'Hitler als Soldat,' in *Führer ins Nichts*, 53–5; Milward, *German Economy*, 43; and Schustereit, *Vabanque*.

144 Robert Cecil, *Hitler's Decision to Invade Russia, 1941* (London, 1975), 142.

145 Bullock, *Hitler and Stalin*, 697.

146 Otto Dietrich, *Hitler*, trans. Richard and Clara Winston (Chicago, 1955), 67; Albert Zoller, ed., *Hitler Privat: Erlebnisberichte seiner Geheimsekretärin* (Christa Schroeder) (Dusseldorf, 1949), 160; Andreas Hillgruber, *Hitlers Strategie: Politik und Kriegsführung, 1940–1941* (Frankfurt/Main, 1965), 511; Bor, *Gespräche*, 203.

147 Barton Whaley, *Codeword Barbarossa* (Cambridge, MA, 1973), 18.

148 Institut für Zeitgeschichte (IfZ), Munich, Document 7 S89, Archives.

149 For Hitler's breath-holding, see Waite, *Psychopathic God*.

150 Night of 17–18 Oct. 1941, *Secret Conversations*.

151 Fest, *Biographie*, 827, and nn294, 295.

152 Bullock, *Hitler and Stalin*, 697. For an example of a typical order demanding the starvation of Ukrainians, see B.H. Liddell-Hart, *The Other Side of the Hill*, 3rd ed. (London, 1951), 289, as quoted by Bullock, *Hitler and Stalin*, 697.

153 Percy Schramm, Introduction to Picker's version of the *Tischgespräche*, 105.

154 See Alan Bullock's essay, 'Hitler and the Origins of the Second World War,' *British Academy for the Promotion of Historical, Philosophical and Philological Studies: Proceedings* (London, 1963), vol. 53, 259–87.

155 The Poole Mission interviews with German officials may be found on microfilm: NA, Department of State, General Records of the Department of State, Record Group 59. Special Interrogation Mission to Germany, 1945–1956.

156 James B. Compton, *The Swastica and the Eagle: Hitler, the United States, and the Origins of World War II* (Boston, 1967), xiii, 236.

157 Albert Seaton, *Russo-German War, 1941–1945* (New York, 1971), 211.

158 Quoted in Compton, *Swastica and Eagle*, 31, 60, 17.

159 Hanfstaengl interview, Munich, June 1967.

160 Johanna Menzel Meskill, *Hitler and Japan: The Hollow Alliance* (New York, 1966), 30–1, 51. See also Paul Schroeder, *The Axis Alliance and Japanese–American Relations, 1941* (Ithaca, NY, 1958); Hans Trefouse, 'Germany and Pearl Harbor,' *Far Eastern Quarterly* 2 (1951), 50.

161 It is true that during the first week of Dec. 1941 (at the time Barbarossa was in serious trouble), Hitler made verbal promises to join Japan in a future war against the United States, and he drew up a draft treaty to that effect. It is said that he did so because he desperately needed Japan to attack the Soviet Union from the rear. But the wording of this draft treaty of 5 Dec. 1941 *makes no mention whatsoever* of

Japanese help in fighting Russia, nor did the Japanese give verbal assurance of such an attack. As Norman Rich has noted, 'Once Japan had committed itself to war with the United States ... Hitler might surely have found excuses to procrastinate about fulfilling his pledge to join Japan in that war. At the very least he might have demanded Japanese support against Russia in return for German support against America, if only a promise to stop American shipments to Russia via Vladivostok.' But Hitler made no such request. *Documents of German Foreign Policy*, Series D, vol. 12, 958–9; Rich, *Hitler's War Aims*, vol. 1, 230–5, 237; testimony given at Nuremberg, IMT X, 297–8; and *Nazi Conspiracy and Aggression*, Supplement B, 2 vols., vol. 1, *Warenberg War Crimes* (Washington, DC, 1947–8), 1199–1201.

162 *Testament of Adolf Hitler*, 76.

163 Warlimont, *Inside Hitler's Headquarters*, 203. It might also be noted that at the same time Hitler had also received bad news from North Africa. The Allies had mounted a serious threat to encircle Rommel, who was forced to withdraw from Tobruk (which he later recaptured in June 1942).

164 Jodl's Testimony at Nuremberg, *Trial of the Major War Criminals*, IMT, vol. 15, 398. For interviews with other Nazi generals and with Reichsmarschall Göring, see Poole Mission, Microfilm, NA. Jodl also testified that the German high command had no plans whatsoever for war against the United States.

165 Galbraith in interview with Gitta Sereny, quoted in *Albert Speer: His Battle for the Truth* (New York, 1995), 268.

166 Congresswoman Jeannette Rankin, a pacifist, was the only person who demurred. She voted 'present.' All others voted a resounding 'aye.' 77 Congress, 1st Session. Congressional Record (House), 11 Dec. 1941, vol. 87, part 9, 966–7.

167 Trefouse, 'Germany and Pearl Harbor,' 50.

168 Walter L. Langer and S. Everett Gleason, *The Undeclared War, 1940–1941* (New York, n.d.), 941.

169 *Testament of Hitler*, 87. Hitler convinced himself that Pearl Harbor was a diabolic plot by Roosevelt to get America involved in war, just as the sinking of the *Lusitania* in 1914 had been designed by the 'diabolical' President Wilson.

170 For a discussion of Hitler's personal role in the 'Final Solution,' see above.

171 The victors at Versailles had hoped to thwart future German aggression by building 'buffer states' in the east and by demilitarizing the Rhineland in the west. But the new countries of Czechoslovakia, Poland, and the Baltic republics served as no eastern buffer; their very weakness invited Hitler to fulfil his version of Germany's historic *Drang nach Osten*. When Hitler's troops marched into the Rhineland in 1936, France was too paralyzed by domestic turmoil to respond. Hitler had gambled and won; the western barrier was broken.

Although the Russia of 1939 – despite Stalin's purge of Red Army officers – was far stronger militarily and industrially than it had been in 1914, that strength was nullified by Hitler's pact with Stalin removing the spectre of a two-front war that had haunted the Kaiser. Moreover, mutual distrust between Soviet Russia and the Western powers was so bitter that they did not form a pre-war alliance against Germany, as they had in 1914.

172 Bullock, *Hitler and Stalin*, 648, 665, 671.

173 See Hans-Jürgen Eitner, *Hitlers Deutsche: Das Ende eines Tabus*, 2nd ed. (Gernsbach, 1991), 427–9.

174 Ibid.

175 Hitler's own 'Security Office' (*Reichssicherheitshauptamt*) reported 'anti-war psychosis.' Welle, 'Kriegsfurcht,' *Zweite Krieg*, 139–40.

176 'Jetzt ist eine Lust zu leben!' Bülow's memoirs, German ed., vol. 2, 358; English, 417.

177 Balfour, *Kaiser*, 158.

178 Hitler had originally signed orders for war on 23 Aug., a Friday, for starting the war Saturday at 0430 hours to increase the element of surprise and shock. But he was forced to postpone implementing his orders when Mussolini suddenly backed away and proclaimed Italian neutrality. Hitler signed the orders on Thursday, 31 Aug. The war began on Friday at 0430 hours. See Watt, *How War Came*, 474, 479, 532.

179 William L. Shirer, *20th Century Journey: The Nightmare Years; 1930–1940* (New York, 1984), 440.

Chapter 5: Psychological Dimensions

1 In a personal letter commenting on my interest in Hitler's psychopathology, Taylor wrote, 'I am in total disagreement with it. Once given Hitler's desire to make Germany a World Power, all his acts were rational.'

2 Lecture, 9 Feb. 1982. My notes.

3 Dan Diner, 'Between Aphoria and Apology: On the Limits of Historicizing National Socialism,' in Peter Baldwin, ed., *Reworking the Past: Hitler, the Holocaust and the Historians' Debate* (Boston, 1990), 142.

4 Address to the Chicago Conference on Psychoanalysis and Biography, as reported in the *Chronicle of Higher Education* 25 (2 Nov. 1982), 24.

5 The story is 'Louisa Pallant,' published in 1888.

6 The necessity of psychological understanding has recently been denied by the admirable journalist Robert W. Apple Jr. In a laudatory review of Stephen Ambrose's biography of Richard Nixon (*Nixon: The Triumph of a Politician; 1962–1972* (New York, 1989), Apple commends the author for eschewing psychology and quotes with approval Ambrose's disarming confession: 'As to questions of motive, of why he did what he did, I confess that I do not understand this complex man.' Apple is grateful that the author does not ask for help from psychology: 'Some will regret the absence

of psychohistorical techniques in this book. I do not – not only because I have little confidence in them, but also because I wonder whether any technique can fully explain [!] the crippling lack of self-confidence, the hatreds, the self-obsession, the sheer awfulness of Richard Nixon's personality.' I disagree with Apple. I do have some confidence in 'psychohistorical techniques' – not because they can perform a miracle and 'fully explain' a personality, but because they can deepen our understanding of what without them remains inexplicable. Perhaps their absence in Ambrose's book is one of the reasons Apple finds that, despite the great merit of the book, 'the reader does long for more.' *New York Times Book Review*, 12 Nov. 1989.

7 Isaiah Berlin, *Against the Current: Essays in the History of Ideas* (London, 1975), 114.

8 Marginal comments in English to the *Strand Magazine* (March 1912), PAB, Prussia 1, Nr. id., vol. 22, quoted by Thomas A. Kohut, 'Kaiser Wilhelm II and His Parents,' *Kaiser Wilhelm II: New Interpretations*, ed. John C.G. Röhl and Nicolaus Sombart (Cambridge, 1982), 87. Original emphasis.

9 John Röhl points to two reasons why he believes Wilhelm's brain may have been injured at birth: First, he notes a statistically high percentage of brain damage among infants who suffer loss of oxygen if, like Wilhelm, they had experienced protracted, frank-breach (rump first) deliveries because the umbilical cord is often contracted by being pressed against the side of the head or wrapped around the throat. Second, he notes that during the excruciatingly painful and protracted delivery of some 10 hours, his mother inhaled chloroform for 'several hours.' John C.G. Röhl, 'Kaiser Wilhelm II. Eine Charakterskizze,' *Kaiser, Hof und Staat: Wilhelm II und die deutsche Politik* (Munich, 1988), 32–3.

10 Emil Ludwig, *The Kaiser* (London and New York, 1926), and Joachim von Kürenburg, *The Kaiser: A Life of Wilhelm II, Last Emperor of Germany*, trans. by H.T. Russell and Herta Hagen (New York, 1955).

11 'The Kaiser's Background: A Biologist's View,' anonymous essay in *The Kaiser: A Book about the Most Interesting Man in Europe*, ed. Asa Don Dickinson (New York, 1914). For an extension of the heredity argument, see Wilhelm Schüssler, *Kaiser Wilhelm II. Schicksal und Schuld* (Göttingen, 1962).

12 Empress Hermine, *Days in Doorn* (London, 1928), 272.

13 Michael Balfour, *The Kaiser and His Times* (London, 1975), 83–5.

14 Schüssler, *Kaiser*, 128.

15 *Three Episodes in the Life of Kaiser Wilhelm.* The Leslie Stephen Lecture of 1955 (Cambridge, 1956), 12.

16 John Röhl lists these books in his footnotes and agrees with their conclusions. 'Eine Charakterskizze,' 32, 210.

17 Walther Rathenau, *Der Kaiser, eine Betrachtung* (Berlin, 1923), 27.

18 It is more accurate to speak of 'narcissistically disturbed personalities.' But for

brevity, these patients are sometimes referred to simply as 'narcissists.' We should also note that narcissism may be healthy. I describe here only those who have pathological problems.

19 Of course not every patient's symptomology fits the composite picture given here. For a presentation of case studies of narcissistic personality disorders and a discussion of their treatment, see Arnold Goldberg, ed., *The Psychology of the Self: A Casebook Written with the Collaboration of Heinz Kohut, MD* (New York, 1978). Of Kohut's major work, see esp. *The Analysis of the Self: A Systematic Approach to the Psychoanalytic Treatment of Narcissistic Personality Disorders* (New York, 1971), *The Restoration of the Self* (New York, 1977), and *The Search for the Self: Selected Writings of Heinz Kohut*, ed. Paul H. Ornstein, 4 vols. (New York, 1978–1991). A resume of Kohut's work is given in *The Kohut Seminars on Self Psychology and Psychotherapy with Adolescents and Young Adults*, ed. Miriam Elson (New York and London, 1987). Other approaches are also useful, e.g., Margaret Mahler with Fred Pine and Anni Bergman, *The Psychological Birth of the Human Infant: Symbiosis and Individuation* (New York, 1975); M. Mahler, *On Human Symbiosis and the Vicissitudes of Individuation* (New York, 1968); D.W. Winnicott, *Through Paediatrics to Psycho-Analysis*, Collected Papers of D.W. Winnicott, Introduction by K. Masud and R. Khan (London, 1978); E. James Anthony, ed., *The Child and His Family: Vulnerable Children* (New York, 1978); and Alice Miller, *Prisoners of Childhood: The Drama of the Gifted Child and the Search for the True Self*, trans. Ruth Ward (New York), 1981. I am grateful to Elizabeth Kohut for her critical reading of this chapter.

20 Miller, *Prisoners of Childhood*, 440.

21 Anthony Storr in conversation, Oxford, June 1982.

22 Conversation with Robert F. Savadove, MD, 28 Sept. 1991. For Wm's relationships with his brothers, see Chapter 6.

23 Prinz Bernhard von Bülow, *Denkwürdigkeiten*, 2 vols. (Berlin, 1930), vol. 2, 149. Original emphasis.

24 Eulenberg to Holstein, 17 Jan. 1890, *Philipp Eulenbergs Politische Korrespondenz*, ed. John C.G. Röhl (Bopard am Rhein, 1976), cited by Judith M. Hughes, *Emotion in High Politics, Personal Relations at the Summit in Late Nineteenth-Century Britain and Germany* (London), 135.

25 Wilhelm (Wm) to Queen Victoria (QV), RA I 60/45.

26 Lamar Cecil, *Wilhelm II: Prince and Emperor* (Chapel Hill, NC, 1989), 223.

27 Quoted by Elisabeth Fehrenbach, *Wandlungen des deutschen Kaisergedenkens, 1871–1918* (Munich, 1969), 89ff.

28 Erich Eyck, *Die Monarchie Wilhelms II. nach seinen Briefen, seinen Rankbemerkungen und den Zeugnissen seiner Freunde* (Berlin, 1924), 56.

29 Georg Alexander von Müller, *The Kaiser and His Court: The Diaries, Notebooks*

and *Letters of Admiral Georg Alexander von Müller, Chief of the Naval Secretariat, 1914–1918*, ed. Walter Görlitz, trans. Mervyn Savell (London, 1961), 153, 202, and Captain Sigurd von Ilsemann, *Der Kaiser in Holland*, 2 vols. (Munich, 1967 and 1969), vol. 1, 228.

30 Several of Wm's maxims are quoted in J.L. Bashford's article on Wilhelm in the *Westminister Gazette* (11 Nov. 1907). Wilhelm had allowed Bashford to copy some of the maxims over his desk in Rominten and assured him that they also appeared in his home in Berlin. AA Preussen, Nr ld/A 17330 (Thomas A. Kohut notes, TAK).

31 *Memoirs of Prince von Bülow*, trans. F.A. Voigt, 3 vols. (Boston, 1931), vol. 1, 70, 412.

32 Eyck quotes the German translation, 'Doch ich bin standhaft wie der Norden Stern,' *Monarchie*, 54.

33 Yet they may be highly sensitive to the weaknesses of those to whom they feel antagonistic and know exactly how to hurt them. Conversation with Elizabeth Kohut, Jan. 1992.

34 See the case of 'Mr E,' in Goldberg, *Psychology of Self*, 265.

35 G.A. Müller, *Kaiser*, 23.

36 Kürenberg, *Kaiser*, 91.

37 Ilsemann, *Kaiser in Holland*, vol. 1, 190.

38 Wilhelm II to Eitel Friedrich, 9 Feb. 1941, Papers of Ex-Keizer, Rijksarchief (RA) Utrecht, folder 169.

39 Letter 14 Sept. 1940 Wm to Poultney Bigelow, Papers of Ex-Keizer Wilhelm, RA Utrecht, folder 39, quoted by Willibald Gutsche, *Ein Kaiser um Exil der letzte deutsche Kaiser Wilhelm II. in Holland, Eine Kritische Biographie* (Marburg, 1991), 205, 212.

40 Once, in complaining that a journalist talked entirely too much, Wilhelm stopped himself, smiled ruefully, and said, 'I could hardly get a word in – and with me, as you know, that doesn't happen very often!' Isolde Reiger, *Die Wilhelminische Presse im Ueberblick, 1888–1918* (Munich, 1957), 12.

41 Quoted in Dickinson, *Kaiser*, 143.

42 Empress Frederick's letter 3 Jan. 1899 is quoted in BAK-B N, 110 (TAK).

43 Quoted in Dickinson, *Kaiser*, 165–6. Original emphasis.

44 Gerald Adler, MD, on the other hand, reports that he has treated both narcissistic and borderline patients who have deep-seated feelings of guilt. One borderline patient saw herself 'as malevolent and totally bad' and exhibited self-destructive impulses. Gerald Adler, 'Uses and Limitations of Kohut's Self Psychology in the Treatment of Borderline Patients,' *Journal of the American Psychoanalytic Association*, 37/3 (1989), 771, 781.

45 Count Ernst Reventlow, *Kaiser Wilhelm II und die Byzantiner*, 5th ed. (Munich, 1906), 26.

46 Cecil, *Wilhelm II*, 289.

47 Quoted in Koppe Pinson, *Modern Germany, Its History and Civilization*, (New York, 1954), 307.

48 See Chapter 1.

49 Evelyn Princess Blücher, *An English Wife in Berlin: A Private Memoir of Events, Politics and Daily Life in Germany Throughout the War and the Social Revolution of 1918* (London, 1920), 217–18, 319.

50 Lawrence Wilson, *The Incredible Kaiser: A Portrait of William II* (New York, 1963), 179.

51 H. Kohut, *The Restoration of Self*, 114–15.

52 Typical is the diary entry 3 Jan. 1896 of one of Wilhelm's chancellors: 'Yesterday Hahnke [a military aide to the Kaiser] came in, very excited and said that a very agitated scene had taken place between S.M. [His Majesty] and the war Minister [Walther Bronsart von Schellendorf, 1893–6] ... Hanke was greatly disturbed and told me that the K had gone much too far and lost all control over himself ... Bronsart came to me this morning and told me the details of the scene ... He said that if anyone else had acted that way he would have drawn his sword ... The minister is of the opinion that the Kaiser is not completely normal and has great concern for the future.' Fürst Chlodwig zu Hohenlohe-Schellingsfürst, *Denkwürdigkeiten der Reichskanzlerzeit*, ed. Karl Alexander von Müller (Berlin, 1931), 151.

53 Graf Erhard von Wedel, ed., *Zwischen Kaiser und Kanzler: Aufzeichungen des Generaladjutanten Grafen Carl von Wedel aus den Jahren 1890–1894* (Leipzig, 1943), 130.

54 See Lydia Franke, *Die Randbemerkungen Wilhelms II. in den Akten der Auswärtigen Politik als historische und psychologische Quelle* (Leipzig and Zurich, 1934), esp. 27, 155, 161, 163.

55 Ilsemann, *Kaiser in Holland*, vol. 2, 115.

56 See Chapter 1.

57 Oberstleutnant Alfred Niemann, a.D., *Kaiser und Revolution: Die Entscheidenden Ereignisse im grossen Hauptquartier im Herbst 1918* (Berlin, 1922), 43, 45. Admiral Müller reports substantially the same remarks. G.A. Müller, *Kaiser*, 379.

58 Ilsemann, *Kaiser in Holland*, vol. 2, 18.

59 G.A. Müller, *Kaiser*, 417.

60 Ilsemann, *Kaiser in Holland*, vol. 2, 35–6.

61 Ibid., 346.

62 Bülow's memoirs, as quoted by Röhl, *Germany Without Bismarck: The Crisis in Government in the Second Reich, 1890–1900* (London, 1967).

63 The son of the Archbishop of Canterbury recalled that during a luncheon at the British embassy, Wilhelm's mother turned to him, a total stranger, and burst out with this extraordinary comment. E.F. Benson, *As We Were: A Victorian Peep-Show* (London, 1930), 161. She repeated the remark to others. See Dickinson, *Kaiser*, 27.

64 See Hohenlohe-Schillingsfürst, *Denkwürdigkeiten*, 151, and Eulenburg who worried about his friend's sanity. Röhl in seminar discussion, St Antony's College, Oxford, 26 Jan. 1982.

65 Lady Norah Bentinck, *The Ex-Kaiser in Exile* (London, 1921), 81.

66 See Chapter 6.

67 Harold D. Lasswell, *Psychopathology and Politics*, rev. ed. (New York, 1960), 261–2. The noted political scientist David Barber has made a similar argument in his studies of presidential style.

68 Quoted in Eyck, *Monarchie*, 32.

69 Friedrich Naumann in speech to Reichstag, 1908, as quoted by Hermann Glaser, *Die Kultur der Wilhelminischen Zeit: Typographic einer Epoche* (Frankfurt/Main, 1984), 158. Naumann was a Lutheran pastor and founder of the National-Social Association. He was often critical of the Kaiser.

70 This is the persuasive thesis of Thomas A. Kohut, 'Mirror Image of the Nation: A Pychohistorical Investigation of Kaiser Wilhelm II's Leadership of the Germans' *Psychoanalytic Study of Leadership* ed. Charles B. Stozier and Daniel Offer (New York, 1991). Kohut expanded his thesis in his volume, *Kaiser Wilhelm II and the Germans* (New York, 1991).

71 T.A. Kohut, *Kaiser* 10–13, 119.

72 Elisabeth Fehrenbach, 'Images of Kaiserdom: German Attitudes to Kaiser Wilhelm II,' in *Kaiser*, Röhl and Sombart, 278. Fehrenbach draws here from her comprehensive study, *Kaisergedankens*.

73 Ibid.

74 Ibid., 279.

75 See Chapter 3.

76 Marginal comment on a dispatch from London of 1904, as quoted by T.A. Kohut, *Kaiser*, 212. My emphasis.

77 Ibid., 210.

78 See Chapter 3.

79 Ibid.

80 For his mother, see Chapter 6.

81 Interview with Charles Brenner, MD, 2 Aug. 1989. See also Brenner's article, 'Masochistic Character,' *Journal of the American Psychoanalytic Association*, 2 (1959).

82 Conversation with Dr Storr at St Antony's College, Oxford, 21 May 1982.

83 See *Philipp Eulenburgs politische Korrespondenz*, ed. John C.G. Röhl, 3 vols. (Bopard am Rhein, 1976), vol. 1, 739, and Johannes Haller, *Philipp Eulenburg, the Kaiser's Friend*, trans. Ethel Colburn Mayne (London, n.d.), 63–4.

84 Mary Theresia Olivia, *Daisy, Princess of Pless by Herself*, ed. Desmond Chapman-Huston (London, 1928), 265.

85 Lamar Cecil, *Albert Ballin: Business and Politics in Imperial Germany, 1890–1945* (Princeton, NJ, 1967), 173. My thanks to Isabel Hull for this reference.

86 Sir Frank Lascelles, *British Documents on the Origins of the War: 1898–1914*, ed. G.P. Gooch and Harold Temperley (London, 1928), vol. 3, 436.

87 Princess Marie Radziwill, *This Was Germany: An Observer at the Court of Berlin – Letters of Princess Marie Radziwill to General Di Robilant*, ed. and trans. Cyril Spencer Fox (London, 1937), 197.

88 See Röhl, *Deutsche Politik*, 108.

89 See Eulenberg's diary entries July 1899, as reported by Haller, *Eulenburg*, vol. 2; see also Graf Ernst Reventlow, *Von Potsdam nach Doorn* (Berlin, 1940), 358.

90 See Chapter 6.

91 'Ein Zweigespräch,' Bundesarchiv, Koblenz, Eulenburg Papers, vol. 74, as quoted by TAK, *Kaiser*, 176. Original emphasis.

92 Ibid.

93 See Chapter 3.

94 Quoted by Pinson, *Modern Germany*, 306–7

95 Imanuel Geiss, *July 1914: The Outbreak of the First World War* (New York, 1967), 369.

96 The phrase is Thomas Kohut's.

97 Quoted. Cecil, *Wilhelm II*, 330.

98 Quoted. John C.G. Röhl, 'The Emperor's New Clothes,' in Röhl and Sombart, *Kaiser*, 31.

99 The wife of one of them, Prince Blücher (the great-great-grandson of old 'Marshal Forward' of the Napoleonic Wars) remembered Wilhelm as a lonely man amidst his fawning entourage: 'My husband yesterday had a private audience with the E[mperor] at the Bellevue Palace ... He came away with a feeling of pity in his heart for the loneliness of the monarch. The Kaiser struck him as being so helpless and alone, though at the same time surrounded by cringing, obsequious courtiers.' (Prince Gebhard Lebrecht Blücher, *The Memoirs of Prince Blücher*, ed. by his wife, Evelyn Princess Blücher and Major Desmond Chapman-Huston (London, 1932), 168–9.

100 The phrases are Imanuel Geiss's. See his *July 1914*, 365–7.

101 Jonathan Steinberg, 'Copenhagen Complex,' *The Journal of Contemporary History*, vol. 1, no. 3 (July 1966), 41, quoted by Geiss, *July 1914*, 367–8.

102 Telegram with the Kaiser's marginalia, is given as Document 368, *Deutsche Dokumenten [DD] zum Kriegsausbruck, 1914*, ed. Karl Kautsky. It is translated and published as Document 178 in Geiss's collection of documents on the outbreak of war, *July 1914*, 288–9. See also Hughes, *Emotion in High Politics*, 218.

103 Marginalia to telegram from Pourtales, German ambassador to St Petersburg, dated 30 July 1914 and received at 7:10. Published in *DD* as no. 401 and reprinted in Geiss's documents as no.135, 293–5. Emphasis and exclamation marks in both marginalia are in original.

104 See Addendum 8.

105 'Hitler as Seen by His Doctors,' Military Intelligence, Consolidated Interrogation Report, 29 May 1945, National Archives, Washington, DC (NA). Hereafter cited as 'Hitler's Doctors, MIR.'

106 Walther C. Langer, 'Psychological Analysis of Adolph [sic] Hitler: His Life and Legend,' mimeographed report, Office of Strategic Services (OSS) Report, NA (1943), 247. Hereafter cited as 'OSS Report.' A printed version of this report was published as The Mind of Adolf Hitler, Foreword by William L. Langer, Afterword by Robert G.L. Waite (New York, 1972), 212.

107 Douglas M. Kelley, Twenty-Two Cells in Nuremberg: A Psychiatrist Examines the Nazi Criminals (New York, 1972), 235–6.

108 Heinz Guderian, Erinnerungen eines Soldaten (Heidelberg, 1957), 402–3; Dietrich von Choltitz, Soldat unter Soldaten (Zurich, 1951), 222; Percy Ernst Schramm, Hitler: The Man and the Military Leader, trans. Donald S. Detwiler (Chicago, 1971); Gerhard Boldt, Hitler: The Last Ten Days – An Eyewitness Account (New York, 1973), 15, 63–4. Karl Wahl, '. . . es ist das deutsche Herz': Erlebnisse und Erkentnisse eines ehemaligen Gauleiters (Augsburg, 1954), 391; and 'Adolf Hitler: A Composite Picture,' NA. Hereafter cited as 'Hitler: Composite, MIR.'

109 Harrison's Principles of Internal Medicine, 12th ed. (New York, 1991), 2065–7, and Israel Wechsler, A Textbook of Clinical Neurology (London, 1943), 597–600.

110 Reported by Willi Frischhauer, Himmler: The Evil Genius of the Third Reich (London, 1953), 242–3.

111 Hans Berger-Prinz, interviewed in the New York Times (21 Nov. 1968). Another German specialist concluded, 'Not only with probability but with certainty,' that Hitler suffered from Parkinsonism. This disease, this specialist insisted, was responsible for remarkable changes in Hitler's personality and explains the atrocities and the military defeats that occurred after 1942.

112 Johann Recktenwald, Woran hat Adolf Hitler gelitten? Eine neuropsychiatrishe Deutung (Munich, 1963), 24, 42–64.

113 John H. Waters, 'Hitler's Encephalitis: A Footnote to History,' Journal of Operational Psychiatry 6 (1975), 99–111.

114 See Abraham Lieberman's important article, 'Hitler, Parkinson's Disease,' Barrow Neurological Institute Quarterly (Phoenix, AZ) 2/3 (1995).

115 Matthew A. Mensa, Lawrence I. Golbe, Ronald A. Cody, and Nancy E. Forman, 'Dopamine-related Personality Traits in Parkinson's Disease,' Neurology (March 1993), 506–8.

116 H.D. Röhrs, Hitler: Die Zerstörung einer Persönlichkeit (Neckargemünd, 1965), 49–51, 71–2, 118. Morell's prescriptions are given in 'Hitler's Doctors, MIR'; Röhrs, Zerstörung, 93–6; Der Spiegel 18 (1969); and Werner Maser, Adolf Hitler: Legende, Mythos, Wirklichkeit (Munich, 1971), 326–8. See esp. the careful study of

Hitler's medications in Leonard L. Heston and Renate Heston, *Hitler's Medical Casebook* (New York, 1980), which gives a long list of prescriptions and dosages in Appendix C.

117 Heston and Heston, *Casebook*, 113, 136.

118 Ibid., 71–2.

119 The ECGS were first interpreted in 1944 by Karl Weber, Director of the Bad Nauheim Heart Institute. An American cardiologist, Collier Wright, confirmed the diagnosis on 28 Nov. 1968. The Hestons reprinted the ECGs in *Casebook*, Appendix B.

120 Wechsler, *Textbook*, 364–5.

121 For a summary of Redlich's findings, see his article, 'A New Medical Diagnosis of Adolf Hitler: Giant Cell Arteritis – Temporal Arteritis,' *Archives of Internal Medicine*, 153 (22 March 1993). Oxford University Press will publish his forthcoming book.

122 Felix Kersten, Heinrich Himmler's Swedish masseur and father-confessor, reported that one day in 1942 a distraught Himmler summoned him to his office. After demanding a pledge of absolute secrecy, he asked Kersten to interpret a 'blue manuscript of 26 pages' which Himmler had removed from a secret Gestapo file. Purportedly, it contained Adolf Hitler's medical record dating from his hospitalization at Pasewalk in Nov. 1918. The records convinced Kersten 'beyond any shadow of doubt' that Hitler was suffering from progressive paralysis associated with neurosyphilis. Felix Kersten, *The Kersten Memoirs, 1940–1945*, trans. Constantine Fitzgibbon and James Oliver (New York, 1957), 165–6. The rather curious fact that Hitler chose as his personal physician a specialist in venereal disease, 'Professor' Theodor Morell, might give some credence to the theory that he had once contracted syphilis; and Hitler's fascination with syphilis, manifested in page after page of his memoirs, may also be pertinent. Then, too, rumours were rife in German medical circles that in 1932 Hitler had been treated in a Jena clinic by a Dr Bodo Spiethoff for mental disorders associated with syphilis. Certainly the symptoms of advanced neurosyphilis correspond to descriptions we have of Hitler during the last months of his life. The disease in its last stages can produce tremours, insomnia, difficulty in walking, and personality changes. Patients may become irritable, their conscience dulled, their memory weakened. They may feel depressed and, alternately, exuberant with grandiose fantasies; paranoid tendencies are not uncommon. Wechlser, *Textbook*, 445–6.

It is conceivable that Hitler, at one time or another, contracted syphilis, but it is unlikely. The mysterious blue pages which Kersten insists prove the case have never appeared, and Kersten was neither a medical doctor nor an unimpeachable witness. It is also possible that Hitler was treated for syphilis in a Jena clinic in 1932. But Jena medical authorities have assured me they can find no evidence that Hitler was ever admitted to their clinic. Letter 10 Nov. 1969 from Dr Dieter Fricke, chairman of School of Medicine, Jena University. Further, the fact that Hitler's medical records show a negative Wassermann test for 15 Jan. 1940 does not argue in support of the syphilis theory. 'Hitler's Doctors, MIR,' Annex 13, NA, and discussion with Robert K. Davis, MD, 28 April 1975.

123 See the invaluable collection of Hitler's early statements, speeches, and jottings carefully collected and expertly ed. by Eberhard Jäckel and Axel Kuhn, *Hitler: Sämtliche Aufzeichnungen, 1905–1924* (Stuttgart, 1980) which show clearly that his essential ideas and attitudes did not change from his teens until his death.

124 Hitler exhibited neither the deep-seated sense of moral guilt nor the feelings of 'panicky aloneness' that Gerald Adler finds 'at the core of borderline psychopathology.' *Journal of the American Psychoanalytic Association* (1989), 77, 781.

125 See esp. the work of Heinz Kohut, Paul Tolpin, Otto Kernberg, Norbert Bromberg, and J.C. Perry. Knight's seminal article, 'Borderline States and the Management and Psychotherapy of the Borderline Schizophrenic,' appeared in *Psychoanalytic Psychiatry and Psychology* (New York, 1954). See esp. Tolpin's article, 'The Borderline Personality: Its Makeup and Analyzability,' *Advances in Self Psychology, with Summarizing Reflections by Heinz Kohut,* ed. Arnold Goldberg (New York, 1980); Kernberg's articles, 'Borderline Personality Organization,' *Journal of the American Psychoanalytic Association* 15 (July 1967), 'Structural Derivatives of Object Relationships,' *International Journal of Psycho-Analysis,* 47 (1966), 236–53, and his volume, *Borderline Conditions and Pathological Narcissism* (New York, 1975). Eric Pfeiffer, 'Borderline States,' *Diseases of the Nervous System* (May 1974); J.C. Perry and G.L. Klerman, 'Clinical Features of the Borderline Personality Disorder,' *American Journal of Psychiatry* 137 (1980); R. Grinker and B. Weble, eds., *The Borderline Patient* (New York, 1977), esp. the article by F. Walsh, 'The Family of the Borderline Patient'; and Adler, 'The Borderline Personality Disorder: Continuum,' *American Journal of Psychiatry* 138 (1981). The late Norbert Bromberg, who was adjunct professor of clinical psychiatry at the Albert Einstein College of Medicine, where he conducted seminars on borderline personalities, made a valuable contribution in a volume he wrote with Verna Volz Small, *Hitler's Psychopathology* (New York, 1983). I am grateful to Dr Bromberg for the critical reading he gave this chapter in an earlier form.

126 Bromberg believed that Hitler was a borderline who manifested extreme narcissistic impairment. He diagnosed him as 'a narcissistic-borderline,' but emphasized that he was 'shaped to a greater degree by the borderline personality disorder.' *Hitler's Psychopathology,* 8 and 23.

127 Heinz Kohut described their condition as 'a milder or disguised form of psychosis.' *Analysis of Self,* 1–3. Other psychoanalysts, however, find less contrast between narcissists and borderlines and believe that there is a continuum in which the latter simply manifest more extreme symptomology than the former. For this position, see

Adler's article, 'Uses and Limitations of Kohut's Self Psychology in the Treatment of Borderline Patients,' *Journal of American Psychoanalytic Association* (1989).

128 See Chapter 1.

129 There is disagreement about the degree of difficulty. Kernberg tends to differ from Kohut and Tolpin in suggesting that borderlines can be psychoanalysed, but even he notes the 'extreme difficulty' and the 'therapeutic stalemate' that often occurs. Kernberg, *Borderline Conditions and Pathological Narcissism*, 71–3. Gerald Adler, who sees a continuum between narcissists and borderlines, reports a borderline patient whose condition improved under therapy to the point that she exhibited the symptomology of a disturbed narcissist. He writes that she 'gradually shows increasing evidence of greater self coherence ... [which] marks the end of the time the patient can be called a borderline. The patient is [now] in the sector ... belonging to the narcissistic personality disorder.' Adler, 'Treatment of Borderline Cases,' *Journal of the American Psychoanalytic Association*, 773. For a fuller treatment of his thesis, see his chapter, 'The Borderline-Narcissistic Personality Disorder Continuum,' in *Borderline Psychopathology and Its Treatment* (New York, 1985).

130 Tolpin, 'Borderline,' 301–3.

131 H. Kohut, *Analysis of Self*, 2.

132 Albert Speer, *Inside the Third Reich: Memoirs*, trans. Richard and Clara Winston (New York, 1971), 100.

133 See Chapter 1.

134 See Chapter 2.

135 See Chapter 6, and for the problem of the missing testicle, see Robert G.L. Waite, *The Psychopathic God: Adolf Hitler* (New York, 1977 and 1993).

136 Kernberg, 'Borderline Personality Organization,' 652, 671–4.

137 R. Grinker and B. Werble, *The Borderline Patient* (New York, 1977), 42. In this study, see especially the article by F. Walsh, 'The Family of the Borderline Patient.'

138 Ibid., 47.

139 Ibid., 123.

140 H. Kohut, *Analysis of Self*, 8.

141 Bromberg, *Psychopathology*, 11.

142 Kernberg, 'Borderline Personality Organization,' 649.

143 See Addendum 2.

144 Albert Speer, *Spandau: The Secret Diaries*, as quoted in *New York Times Book Review* (22 Feb. 1976). For examples of conflicts and contrasts in Hitler's personality, see Chapter 1.

145 André François-Poncet, *The Fateful Years: Memoirs of a French Ambassador in Berlin, 1931–1938*, trans. Jacques LeClercq (New York, 1949), 286.

146 See Hitler's poems, 'An Idyll of Wartime' and 'Once in a Thicket,' in Chapter 2.

147 Letter from Munich, 16 Oct. 1923, reprinted as Document 585 in Jäckel and Kuhn.

148 See Chapter 2.
149 Luncheon meeting 27 Feb. 1942, *Tischgespräche*, 186, and *Secret Conversations*, 279. (See Chapter 1, note 300.)
150 Statements 6 and 13 Feb. 1945, *The Testament of Adolf Hitler*, ed. R.H. Stevens (London, 1961), 40, 54–5.
151 Kernberg, 'Structural Derivatives,' 238, and discussions with Bromberg.
152 Writing in the *Frankfurter Allgemeine Zeitung* (25 April 1977). My thanks to Fritz Epstein for sending me this clipping from the *FAZ*.
153 John Toland was mistaken when he wrote that Hitler could not have been influenced by Le Bon because his work had 'not been translated into German.' *Adolf Hitler* (New York, 1976), 221. In addition to the 1908 translation, a second German ed. appeared in 1912, a third in 1919, and a fourth in 1922. Later editions appeared in 1932, 1938, and 1939.
154 Gustav Le Bon, *The Crowd: A Study of the Popular Mind* (London, 1913).
155 *Mein Kampf* and *Secret Conversations*, 391, as quoted by Bromberg, 313.
156 Personal Conversation, Munich, 1957. See also Ernst Hanfstaengl, *The Missing Years* (London, 1957), 69.
157 Joachim C. Fest, *Hitler Eine Biographie*, 5th ed. (Frankfurt/Main and Berlin, 1973), 452–3; and Fest, *The Face of the Third Reich: Portraits of the Nazi Leadership*, trans. Michael Bullock (New York, 1970), 36–7.
158 *Mein Kampf*, German ed., 116–7. My emphasis.
159 Eva G. Reichmann, *Hostages of Civilization* (London, 1950), and conversations with Ms. Reichmann, Wiener Library, London, Sept. 1953.
160 Georges Sorel, *Reflections on Violence* (New York, 1961), 17; Rollo May, interviewed in *New York Times* (25 Nov. 1968).
161 Speer, *Third Reich*, 446.
162 See Harold Lasswell's early but still valuable essay, 'The Psychology of Hitlerism,' *Political Quarterly* 4 (1933), 378.
163 Waite, *Psychopathic God*, 369.
164 See Chapter 6.
165 Peter Kleist, *Die Europäische Tragödie*, quoted in Percy Ernst Schramm, *Hitler: the Man and the Military Leader*, trans. and ed. Donald S. Detirler (Carbondale, IL, 1971), 30–1.
166 Kernberg, 'Borderline Personality Organization,' 677.
167 Heinrich Hoffmann, *Hitler Was My Friend*, trans. R.H. Stevens (London, 1955), 41–2. Hoffmann became a millionaire as Hitler's court photographer.
168 There was one notable exception. Hitler's dramatic talents were wasted on Generalissimo Franco of Spain. Hitler later admitted his inability to impress Franco and said that rather than meet with him again he would rather have a tooth pulled – and that was a terrifying prospect for him. To the Spaniard, Hitler was 'an affected

man with nothing sincere about him ... an actor on a stage and one could see the mechanics of his acting!' George Hills, *Franco: The Man and His Nation* (New York, 1967), 363.

169 See Chapter 1.

170 François-Poncet, *The Fateful Years*, 286; Douglas Hamilton, *Motive for a Mission: The Story Behind Hess's Flight to Britain* (London, 1971), 63; *Wiener Bulletin* (London) 10 (1956); Fest, *Hitler*, 609.

171 See Joseph Goebbels, *The Early Goebbels Diaries, 1925–26*, ed. Helmut Heiber, trans. Oliver Watson (New York, 1962), *passim*.

172 Speer, *Third Reich*, 16, 60, and diary entry 20 Nov. 1952.

173 Fest, *Third Reich*, 75.

174 Nuremberg Documents, quoted by Alan Bullock, *Hitler, a Study in Tyranny*, rev. ed. (New York, 1962), 409.

175 Speer, *Third Reich*, 431, 455, 480, 487.

176 Schramm, *Hitler*, 35.

177 T.A. Kohut, *Kaiser*, 143.

178 Colonel General, a.D., Franz Halder, 'The Diary of Franz Halder' (photocopy of German typescript, copyright 1946 by the Attorney General of the United States, Archives of Institut für Zeitgeschichte, Munich).

179 Bromberg and Volz Small, *Hitler's Psychopathology*, 185.

180 Hans Buchheim, 'Hitler als Soldat,' *Führer ins Nichts: Eine Diagnose Adolf Hitlers*, ed. Gert Buchheit (Cologne, 1960), 63.

181 Adolf Hitler, *Hitler's Secret Book*, trans. Salvatore Attanasio (New York, 1961), 63.

182 De Witt Clinton Poole Mission, NA, microfilm roll no. 2.

183 Max Domarus, ed., *Hitler Reden und Proklamationen, 1932–1945*, 4 vols. (Würzburg, 1962), 1695. My emphasis.

184 New Year's Proclamation, 1 Jan. 1945, Domarus, *Reden*, 2186.

185 New Year's Proclamation, 1 Jan. 1944, Domarus, *Reden*, 2076.

186 See Addendum 5.

187 In a conversation at field headquarters on 25 Jan. 1942, Hitler observed that one of his dogs was plagued *mit schlechtem Gewissen*. Henry Picker, ed., *Hitlers Tischgespräche im Führerhauptquartier, 1941–1942* (Stuttgart, 1963), 165.

188 Italics are mine. These quotations were collected by the psychoanalysts and clinical psychologists who drew up a report on Hitler's personality for the OSS during the Second World War, 'A Psychological Analysis of Adolph [*sic*] Hitler,' Typescript, Declassified Historical OSS Records, National Archives, Washington, DC, n.d. This report is accompanied by a three-volume 'Source Book' of mimeographed material. One version of the original report was published under the title, *The Mind of Adolf Hitler: The Secret Wartime Report*.

189 G.M. Trevelyan, *Clio, A Muse and Other Essays Literary and Pedestrian* (London, 1913), 9. Trevelyan was responding to J.R. Bury's confident assertion in a lecture of 1903 that 'history is science, nothing more and nothing less.'

190 See Chapter 6.

191 See Addendum 5.

192 See Chapter 6.

193 See Addendum 6.

194 This discussion is based on Klaus Dörner, 'Nationalsozialismus und Lebensvernichtung,' *Vierteljahrshefte für Zeitgeschichte* 15 (1967), 120–52.

195 Ibid., 148–9.

196 There are several versions of this statement made on 18 April 1945. See Schramm, *Hitler*, 176.

197 Dörner, 'Nationalsozialismus,' 149.

198 Bradley F. Smith, *Adolf Hitler: His Family, Childhood and Youth* (Stanford, 1967), 113–14, and see August Kubizek, *The Young Hitler I Knew*, trans. E.V. Anderson (Boston, 1955), 143–225.

199 Werner Maser, *Hitler*, 84.

200 Kubizek, *Young Hitler*, 143–245.

201 Richard Hanser, *Putsch! How Hitler Made Revolution* (New York, 1970) Harold J. Gordon, Jr, *Hitler and the Beer Hall Putsch* (Princeton, NJ, 1972), James H. McRandle, *Track of the Wolf: Essays on National Socialism and Its Leader, Adolf Hitler* (Evanston, IL, 1965).

202 Conversation 22 April 1992.

203 Robert Cecil, *Hitler's Decision to Invade Russia* (London, 1975), 2, 119.

204 The clinical literature on suicide is extensive. Reference is made here, specifically, to the following studies: Sigmund Freud, 'Mourning and Melancholia' (1917) in *Collected Papers* (London, 1949), vol. 4; Kate Friedlander, 'On the "Longing to Die,"' *International Journal of Psycho-Analysis* 21 (1940); Herbert Hendin, 'Suicide,' *Psychiatric Quarterly*, 30 (1956); Ives Hendrick, 'Suicide as Wish-Fulfillment,' *Psychiatric Quarterly* 14 (1940); Donald D. Jackson, 'Theories of Suicide,' *Clues to Suicide*, ed. Edwin S. Schneidman (New York, 1957); Lewis Siegal and Jacob Friedman, 'The Threat of Suicide,' *Diseases of the Nervous System* 16 (Feb. 1955); Charles Wahl, 'Suicide as a Magical Act,' *Bulletin of the Menninger Clinic* (May 1957); Karl Menninger, 'Psychoanalytic Aspects of Suicide,' *International Journal of Psycho-Analysis* 14 (1933), also *Man against Himself* (New York, 1961); Gregory Zilboorg, ' Considerations on Suicide,' *American Journal of Orthopsychiatry* 3 (1937). I am indebted to James M. Randle for first suggesting this approach to Hitler's death.

205 Theodor Reik, *Masochism in Sex and Society*, trans. Margaret Beigel and Gertrud Kurth (New York, 1962), 429. Original emphasis.

206 Siegel and Friedman, 'Threat of Suicide,' 38.
207 Interrogation of Hanna Reitsch, 8 Oct. 1945, Nuremberg Document 3734 PS, NCA, 6: 554–5.
208 Menninger, *Man against Himself*, 63. Another psychoanalyst agrees: 'Through the primitive act of suicide, man achieves a fantasied immortality ... It is a method of restating and reasserting one's own immortality.' Such fantasy, according to the same observer, is a reversion to childhood.
209 Conversation with the archivist Franz Jetzinger, Linz, Spring 1954. See his volume *Hitlers Jugend: Phantasien, Lügen – und die Wahrheit* (Vienna, 1956). There is a slightly abridged English translation, *Hitler's Youth*, trans. Lawrence Wilson, Foreword by Alan Bullock (London, 1958). Jetzinger had spoken with several of young Hitler's playmates, including the later Abbot of the Cistercian monastery at Wilhering.
210 Kubizek, *Young Hitler*, and Jetzinger, *Hitlers Jugend*.
211 See Chapter 2.
212 The two had much in common. In German mythology Wotan is seen as a deeply divided deity, the god of both creation and destruction. A magic worker who – like the Führer – appeared in different forms to different people. He was the all-knowing god, source of inspiration, inventor of the runes. But he was also the god of desolation and death, insatiable in his demands for human sacrifice. Wotan was also the Wild Huntsman who at the end of the world rode forth leading his Furious Host (*wütendes Heer*). Hitler, we have suggested, saw himself in precisely that role as depicted in the painting *Die wilde Jagd*, by his favourite artist, Franz von Stuck. Indeed, he may have seen in Stuck's painting of 1889 a miraculous portrait of himself: Hitler as Wotan, the Wild Huntsman, painted in the very year of his own birth. Hitler also shared with Wotan similar tastes in animals. He too was fond of ravens and wolves. Two ravens, Hugin and Munin, perched on the god's shoulders; the great grey wolf Fenrir, symbol of chaos and destruction, crouched fettered at his feet, eating food from his hand alone. By order of the Führer, ravens were protected throughout the Reich. In his last days, Hitler permitted no one but himself to touch or feed Blondi's pup. A secretary recalled 'He stroked the animal interminably, all the while sweetly repeating his name, "Wolf, Wolf, Wolf."' Wotan's pet wolf Fenrir – according to the legend – will play a key role when Wotan orders the time of Ragnarok, the end of the world. Then will occur a cataclysmic battle and 'appalling deeds of murder and incest ... Fenrir advances, his great gaping jaws filling the gap between earth and sky ... Relentlessly, hideously, he devours gods and men.' Hilda Roderick Davidson, *Gods and Myths of Northern Europe* (Baltimore, 1964), 31, 37, 205; Wolfgang Golther, *Handbuch der Germanischen Mythologies* (Leipzig, 1895), 284, 303, 313, 347; Edith Hamilton, *Mythology* (New York, 1942), 444.
213 Kubizek, *Young Hitler*, 55.

214 See Hamilton, *Mythology*, 444.
215 It did not work out that way. Hitler had given orders that his body was to be utterly consumed by flames, but the sandy soil of Berlin rapidly absorbed much of the precious petrol that had been collected for the funeral pyre. Moreover, it was a windy day, and the pallbearers had trouble relighting the Führer and his new bride. Their badly burned but not completely consumed bodies were found in a shallow grave next to a cement-mixer by Red Army soldiers. An autopsy performed by Soviet pathologists, after identification had been made by a careful examination of the Führer's rotting teeth, showed that cyanide poisoning was the primary cause of death. The finale had not been as Wagnerian as Hitler would have wished. It was not, however, an inappropriate ending to his monstrous career. Waite, *Psychopathic God*, 421–2, and notes. In an article in the French medical journal, *Semaine des Hopitaux*, four French physicians dispute Waite's findings and suggest that the Soviet pathologists examined the wrong cadaver. They hope to substantiate their hypothesis by examining the skull that the director of the Russian National Archives, Sergei Mironenko, claims is that of Adolf Hitler. See *Guardian Weekly* (28 March 1993).
216 Wahl, 'Suicide as a Magical Act,' 23. My emphasis.
217 Ibid., 30.
218 The words Hitler had used in excoriating Field Marshal Friedrich Paulus for not committing suicide rather than surrendering at Stalingrad may be relevant here: 'He could have freed himself from all sorrow and have *ascended into eternity and national immortality.*' Felix Gilbert, ed., *Hitler Directs His War: The Secret Records of His Daily Military Conferences* (London, 1950), 22. My emphasis. The Führer's death could have been inspired by Wagner, who, after complaining bitterly of disloyalty, ingratitude, and treachery, had concluded, 'Someone will be sorry one day ... Yes I would fain perish in the flames of Valhalla.' See Wilhelm Altmann, ed., *Letters of Richard Wagner*, trans. M.N. Bozman (New York, 1968), vol. 2, 35, 243. The description I have given here of Hitler's suicide is drawn from Waite, *Psychopathic God*.
219 In reviewing W.W. Meisner's biography, *Ignatius of Loyola: The Psychology of a Saint* (New Haven, CT, 1992), in the *Sunday Observer* (London, 17 Jan. 1993).
220 Diary entry 20 Nov. 1952.
221 See Gitta Sereny's superb biography, *Albert Speer: His Struggle for the Truth* (New York, 1995), 137.
222 For example, it is not listed in any of the following works: *The Encyclopedia of Human Behavior: Psychology, Psychiatry and Mental Health*, ed. Robert M. Goldenson (New York, 1975), rev. ed.; *Encyclopedia of Adult Development*, ed. Robert Kastenbaum (Phoenix, AZ, 1993); or in the comprehensive work, *The Encyclopedia of Mental Health*, 6 vols., general ed. Albert Deutsch (New York, 1963).
223 Eric Fromm, *The Heart of Man: Its Genius for Good and Evil* (New York, 1973), 77.

224 These patients usually have had at least one evil parent. (As we shall see, Adolf Hitler's father was a sadist who abused him physically and mentally.) Denial and projection are dominant characteristics. Patients insist that they personally are beyond reproach, other people are vicious and evil. (Hitler said that he was a decent and honourable man. Priests were immoral liars, Jews were evil incarnate.) The most salient characteristic of these patients is that they – like Hitler – are unable to tell the truth either about themselves or about others – hence the title of his book: *People of the Lie: The Hope for Healing Human Evil* (New York, 1983).

225 For a compelling description of the process of exorcism, see Malachi Martin, *Hostage to the Devil: The Possession and Exorcism of Five Americans*, new ed. (New York, 1992). Martin is a former Jesuit and professor at the Vatican's Pontifical Biblical Institute.

Chapter 6: Kaiser and Führer: The Childhood Experience

1 Communication from Elizabeth Kohut, July 1992, to whom I am greatly indebted for a critical reading of this and the previous chapter.

2 Alden Nichols, *The Year of the Three Kaisers: Bismarck and the German Succession, 1878–1888* (Urbana and Chicago, 1987), 23.

3 Werner Richter, *Kaiser Friedrich III* (Zurich, 1938), 214.

4 G.P. Gooch in Foreword to Richard Berkeley, The *Empress Frederick: Daughter of Queen Victoria* (London, 1956).

5 Quoted by Nichols, *Year*, 183.

6 In reviewing Friedrich's chances of fulfilling the reformers' hopes for a 'Liberal era,' a student of his brief career concluded, 'For Friedrich's posthumous fame, it may indeed have been fortunate that his reign was as short-lived as it was.' Andreas Dorpalen, 'Frederick and the German Liberal Movement,' *American Historical Review*, 55/1 (1948), 51, 31.

7 *Das Tagebuch der Baronin Spitzemberg*, ed. R. Vierhaus (Göttingen, 1960), 247. Baron von Holstein, the powerful 'grey eminence' of the foreign office, reported that Victoria had said, 'Now Bismarck governs not only the German Reich, but also the 88 year-old-Kaiser [Wilhelm I]. But how will it be when Bismarck is faced with a real Kaiser?' Holstein's comment is withering: 'Her words sound like a jest when one thinks of the Crown Prince's [Friedrich's] personality. She is the only possible "real Kaiser."' *The Holstein Papers*, 4 vols., ed. Norman Rich and M.H. Fischer (Cambridge, 1951), vol. 2. *The Diaries*, 174. My thanks to Thomas A. Kohut (TAK) for this reference.

8 Vicky (V) to Queen Victoria (QV), 3 July 1863, in Roger Fulford, ed., *Dearest Mama: Letters between Queen Victoria and Crown Princess of Prussia, 1861–1864* (London, 1971), 242–3. Quoted in Judith Hughes, *Emotion in High Politics:*

Personal Relations at the Summit in Late Nineteenth-Century Britain and Germany (Berkeley, 1983), 126.

9 Letter 9/10 March 1864, Cronberg Archives, quoted by Egon Caesar Corti, *The English Empress: A Study of the Relations Between Queen Victoria and her Eldest Daughter, the Empress Fredrick of Germany*, trans. E.M. Hodgson (London, 1957), 125.

10 Frederick III, *The War Diary of the Emperor Frederick III (1870–1871)*, trans. and ed. A.R. Allinson, reprint (New York, 1988), 285.

11 William II, *My Early Life* (New York,1926), 19.

12 Friedrich to Queen Victoria (QV), Royal Archives, Windsor Castle (RA) Z71, 75.

13 Vicky (V) to QV, 3 Sept. 1859, as quoted in Roger Fulford, ed., *Dearest Child: Letters Between Queen Victoria and the Princess Royal of Prussia, 1858–1861* (London, 1964), 209; she repeated the same complaint in subsequent letters.

14 V to QV, 18 June 1859, RA, Z-8.

15 William II, *My Early Life*, 16–18.

16 Lord Ampthill (Odo Russell) British ambassador in Berlin, as quoted by Friedrich von Holstein, *Holstein Papers: Diaries*, vol. 2, entry 17 March 1882 (Thomas A. Kohut notes, TAK).

17 Herbert Bismarck to his father, letter 4 Oct. 1886, in Walter Bussmann, ed., *Staatssekretär Herbert von Bismarck, aus seinen politischen Privatkorrespondenzen* (Göttingen, 1946), 86 (TAK). Much later, however, during his long exile in Doorn after the First World War the ex-Kaiser's opinion of his father rose considerably. Indeed Friedrich III became glorified in Wilhelm's eyes as the real founder of the Second Reich. 'I must make it clear to the German people,' Wilhelm said on 16 June 1928, 'that it was my father who established the German Reich and not, as others say, Bismarck. The deeds of my Father are far too insufficiently recognized.' Captain Sigurd von Ilsemann, *Der Kaiser in Holland*, 2 vols. (Munich 1967 and 1969), vol. 2, 100.

18 Her husband reported that she had 'acted several times as wet-nurse' for his sister-in-law. Frederick III *War Diary*, 167, entry 22 Oct. [1870].

19 Fulford, *Dearest Mama*, nn. 1, 25. Since the pope in question was Pius IX (1846–1878), who had become an arch-conservative after the revolutions of 1848, he could not have been favourably impressed with Victoria's political opinions.

20 Sir James Rennell Rodd, *Social and Diplomatic Memoirs*, 3 vols. (London, 1922–5), vol. 1, 49.

21 George W. Smalley, *Anglo-American Memories* (London, 1911), 357–8.

22 Letter V to QV, 30 Jan. 1871, in Roger Fulford, ed., *Your Dear Letter: Private Correspondence of Queen Victoria and the Crown Princess of Prussia, 1865–1871* (London, 1971), 316.

23 S.F. Benson, *The Kaiser and His English Relations* (London, 1936), 18, quoting Sir Frederick Ponsonby, ed., *The Letters of Empress Frederick* (London, 1929), 41–2.

24 Letter 30 Jan. 1878, as quoted in Berkeley, *Empress Frederick*, 169.

25 The question, notorious for its diplomatic complexity, produced Lord Palmerston's memorable *mot*: 'Only three people ever really understood the Schleswig-Holstein Question: Prince Albert, and he is dead; a German professor, and he went mad; myself, and I have forgotten.'

26 Charles Greville, *The Greville Memoirs, 1814–1860*, ed. Lytton Strachey and Roger Fulford, 7 vols. (London, 1938), vol. 7, 305.

27 Roger Fulford, *The Prince Consort* (New York, 1966), 98.

28 Ibid., 99.

29 Mary Ponsonby, Queen Victoria's maid of honour, knew him well and admired him greatly, but found that he had no sense of fun – except at the expense of others: 'He went into immediate fits of laughter if anyone ... nearly fell into the fire or smashed his finger in a door ... his mirth knew no bounds.' Magdalen Ponsonby, ed., *Mary Ponsonby: A Memoir, Some Letters and a Journal* (London, 1927), 2–6.

30 Quoted by Fulford, *Consort*, 104.

31 Ibid., 105.

32 Ponsonby, *Empress Frederick*, 35.

33 Princess Catherine Radziwill, *The Empress Frederick* (London, 1934), 72.

34 David Duff, *Victoria and Albert* (New York, 1972), 231.

35 Fulford, *Consort*, 252.

36 V to Prince Albert (PA), 26 Jan. 1858, RA, Zi/2.

37 V to PA on board *Victoria and Albert*, n.d., RA Z1/3.

38 V to PA, Berlin, 25 Dec. 1858, RA Z3/5.

39 V to PA, 27 Jan. 1860, RA Z3/5.

40 V to QV, 16 Dec. 1861, RA Z12/50. Emphasis in original.

41 V to Albert Edward, 16 Dec. 1861, RA M64/1.

42 V to QV, 23 Dec. 1861, RA Z/12; also 1 Jan. 1862, 21 Jan. 1862, and 25 Jan. 1862.

43 V to QV, 4/?? Jan. 1862, RA Z12/64.

44 V to QV, 11 Jan. 1862, RA Zi2/63.

45 V to Sophie, 1893, in Arthur Gould Lee, ed., *The Empress Frederick Writes to Sophie: Letters, 1889–1901* (London, 1955), 136–7. The last sentence is from another letter to Sophie dated 26 Aug. 1895.

46 V to QV, in Fulford, *Consort*, 272–3.

47 V to PA, 10 Feb. 1858, RA Z1/4.

48 V to QV, 20 Aug. 1861, Corti, *English Empress*, 71.

49 V to QV, 1887, quoted in Radziwill, *Empress Frederick*, 174.

50 V (through lady-in-waiting) to PA, 29 Jan. 1859, RA 7/2. Emphasis in original.

51 V to QV, 16 Dec. 1861 in Fulford, *Dearest Child*, 375; and 26 Dec. 1861, Fulford, *Dearest Mama*, 29; and 17 Dec. 1861, RA Z12/51.

52 V to QV, 30 Jan. 1871, in Fulford, *Your Dear Letter*, 316–7.

53 Wm to QV, 2 Sept. 1874, RA Z64/58. When Queen Victoria sent him the five-volume official biography of Prince Albert she had commissioned, Wilhelm wrote her an effusive thank-you letter saying it was now his favourite bedtime reading. Scarcely. A visitor to Doorn in 1939 found the volumes in the guest house. The dedication reads, 'To darling Willy with love from Grandmother.' The pages remain uncut. See Sir John Wheeler-Bennett, *Knaves, Fools and Heroes* (London, 1974), 180. Wilhelm actually felt contempt for his maternal grandfather, referring to him in a letter of Oct. 1886 as a 'petty anglomaniac.' Letter from Herbert von Bismarck to Otto von Bismarck; my thanks to Thomas A. Kohut for this citation.

54 Robert Graf von Zedlitz-Trützschler, *Twelve Years at the Imperial German Court*, trans. Alfred Kalisch (New York, 1924), xii-xiii.

55 V to QV, 27 Feb. 1892, in Ponsonby, *Empress Frederick*, 434.

56 The attending obstetrician's report of the birth, 'Bericht über die Entbindung Ihrer Königlichen Hoheit der Frau Prinzessin Friedrich Wilhelm Princes [*sic*] Royal von Grossbrittanien,' dated Berlin 9 Feb. 1859, and signed by Dr Eduard Martin, may be found in the RA, Windsor Castle, addl mss U-34. See also Lamar Cecil, *Wilhelm II: Prince and Emperor, 1859–1900* (Chapel Hill, 1989), 12; and John C.G. Röhl, *Kaiser Hof und Staat: Wilhelm II. und die deutsche Politik* (Munich, 1988), 33.

57 V to QV, 30 June 1876, RA Z29/89; V to QV, 3 Jan. 1877, RA Z/31; V to QV, 7 Aug. 1872, in Fulford, *Darling Child*, 57; V to QV, 23 May 1873, ibid., 139.

58 V to PA, 16 July 1859, RA Z2/28. Emphasis in original.

59 V to PA, 16 July 1869, RA Z72/20.

60 V to QV, 31 Jan. 1872, RA Z26/46.

61 V to QV, 12 Dec. 1859, in Fulford, *Dearest Child*, 224.

62 V to QV, 11 Aug. 1859, RA Z/29.

63 V to PA, Berlin, RA 74/20 (TAK). Victoria had wanted to let the boy out or at least to open a window but the doctors, fearing he might catch a cold, forbade it. John J. Martin, MD, an oculist, on the basis of Victoria's letter suggested the diagnosis given here and said that without modern medicine the pain and the treatment would probably have lasted from five to eight weeks. Conversation of 18 March 1989.

64 Margaret S. Mahler, with Fred Pine and Anni Bergman, *The Psychological Birth of the Human Infant: Symbiosis and Individuation* (New York, 1975), 71–2, 99; see also Louise J. Kaplan, *Oneness and Separateness: From Infant to Individual* (New York, 1978), 34, 215.

65 V to QV, 27 Jan. 1860, RA Z3/5.

66 V to QV, 7 April 1860, RA Z9/50, and V to Mary (a cousin), 31 March 1860, RA additional mss A/8/1326.

67 V to QV, 14 May 1861, RA Z/11.

68 I must admit, however, that in neither the Royal Archives at Windsor nor the published collections of her letters, was I able to find a letter written by Victoria stating explicitly that she had read Schreber's books. And the archivists have informed me that among the thousands of her letters, they, too, were unable to find one such explicit statement. Nevertheless, for the reasons given here, I believe she must have been familiar with Schreber's books.

69 Not all of Schreber's ideas were pernicious. A firm believer in 'returning to the soil,' he popularized the *Schrebergarten*, which still bears his name – small plots of land where citizens could enjoy the benefits of exercise, fresh air, and sunshine. Generations of Germans belonged to the Schreber societies which he established to popularize his ideas about health, exercise, and the proper methods of raising children. A hundred years after his death, over 2 million West Germans were members of various *Schrebervereine*. He also championed balanced diet, exercise, and sanitation, opposed the widespread contemporary practice of indiscriminate bloodletting, led a campaign against restrictive infantile swaddling, and inveighed against frightening children by threatening them with ghosts and bogeymen.

70 William G. Niederland, 'Schreber's Father,' *American Psychoanalytic Association Journal* 8 (1960), 492; see also Morton Schatzman, *Soul Murder: Persecution in the Family* (New York, 1974), 151; Daniel Gottlieb Moritz Schreber, *Das Buch der Gesundheit oder Lebenskunst*, 2nd enlarged ed. (Leipzig, 1861); *Kallipadie oder Erziehung zur Schönheit durch naturgetreue und gleichmässige Forderung ...* (Leipzig, 1858); and *Die Eigenthumlichkeiten des kindlichen Organismus ...* (Leipzig, 1852).

71 Niederland, 'Schreber's Father,' 495.

72 Schatzman, *Soul Murder*, 26–7; William G. Niederland, 'The "Miracled-Up" World of Schreber's Childhood,' *Psychoanalytic Study of the Child* 14 (1959), 387.

73 Ibid.

74 Niederland, 'Schreber's Childhood,' 159.

75 Ibid.

76 V to QV, 13 Feb. 1866, RA Z18/25.

77 V to QV, 16 May 1863, RA Z 15, 210 (TAK).

78 Schreber, *Gesundheit oder Lebenskunst*, 60.

79 V to QV, 21 April 1863, RA Z15/13, and 28 April, Z15/15.

80 V to QV, 28 April 1863, Z15/15.

81 V to QV 23 May 1863, RA Z15/25.

82 V to QV, 26 Dec. 1863, Z16/3. My emphasis.

83 Friedrich III, *War Diaries*, Nov. 1865. RA contain a letter from One J----- Clark to Dr Wegener, apparently written at Victoria's request, endorsing the use of 'galvanistic treatment.' RA, additional mss, J/1600.

84 Joachim Kürenberg, *The Kaiser: A Life of Wilhelm II, Last Emperor of Germany*, trans. H.T. Russell and Herta Hagen (New York, 1955), 13–14.

85 Wm II, *My Early Life*, 36.

86 Bennett-Wheeler, *Knaves*, 187.

87 Serge Sazonov, *Fateful Years, 1909–1916: The Reminiscences of Serge Sazonov, Russian Minister for Foreign Affairs* (New York, 1928), 45.

88 Nina Epton, *Victoria and Her Daughters* (New York, 1971), 179, and Ponsonby, *Recollections of Three Reigns* (London, 1951), 233.

89 Ponsonby, *Empress Frederick*, 285.

90 V to QV, 7 March 1887, RA Z/3914 (TAK).

91 Epton, *Queen Victoria*, 179.

92 V to QV, 20 Feb. 1888, in Ponsonby, *Empress Frederick*, 248, 270

93 Years later Vicky still insisted that she had been right all along in the dispute with Wilhelm. She wrote to her daughter Sophie in 1896 that she was glad 'that we listened to the excellent Sir Morell and that dear Papa was not murdered [by German surgeons].' Lee, *Empress Frederick*, 218.

94 Wm to Eulenburg, 12 April 1888, in *Philipp Eulenburg's Politische Korrespondenz*, ed. John C.G. Röhl, 3 vols. (Boppard am Rhein, 1976), vol. 1, 284.

95 *Holstein Papers: Diaries*, vol. 2, 348, 351.

96 Radziwill, *Empress Frederick*, 222; Count Corti, *English Empress*, 282–303; and S. Fischer-Fabian, *Herrliche Zeiten: Die Deutschen und ihr Kaiserreich* (Munich, 1986), 176–7.

97 Conversation with Kürenberg, quoted in Kürenberg, *Kaiser*, 81. In discussing his father's death in his memoirs Wm does not mention the incident. Was he ashamed of his behaviour?

98 See Sir Frederick Ponsonby's fascinating account in the Introduction to his edition of Victoria's letters. A similar thing happened to Friedrich's war diary: it had to be smuggled out of Germany to Windsor in order to get around Bismarck's agents who were searching for it.

99 Philipp zu Eulenburg-Hertefeld, *Aus 50 Jahren: Aus Erinnerungen, Tagebücher und Briefe aus dem Nachlass*, ed. Johannes Haller, 2nd ed. (Berlin, 1925), 184 and 264.

100 Benson, *Kaiser and English Relations*, 34–5.

101 V to QV, 28 Jan. 1871, quoted in Ponsonby, *Empress Frederick*, 119.

102 QV to V, 11 Feb. 1871, RA Z25/53.

103 V to QV, 7 Dec. 1866, Fulford, *Your Dear Letter*, 111.

104 V to QV, 17 May 1865, ibid., 25–6.

105 V to QV, 19 June 1866, and 19 June 1866, RA Z18/60 and Z18/62. Emphasis in original.

106 V to QV, 30 June 1866, Z18/63.

107 V to QV, 12 Dec. 1866, RA 19/31.

108 V to QV, 10 Dec. 1866, RA 19/30.

109 Daphne Bennett, *Vicky: Princess Royal of England and German Empress* (London, 1971), 163. Friedrichshof, as Vicky had renamed the New Palace in honour of her husband; Wm restored its old name.

110 Lady Anne Macdonell, *Reminiscences of Diplomatic Life* (London, 1913), 158. There is disagreement whether the statue of the child was done in wax (Macdonell) or in marble (Bennett). Since Victoria had carved her father in marble, and associated Siggy so closely with him, and wanted to keep the memory of both alive in perpetuity, it seems not unlikely that she would have used marble for her beloved son.

111 Anne Topham, *Memories of the Fatherland* (London, 1916), 290. Miss Topham knew the German royal family well. For many years she had been governess to Princess Viktoria Louise.

112 V to QV, 1 Sept. 1874, RA Z28/56.

113 Wilhelm, *My Early Life*, 44.

114 Ibid., 30.

115 V to QV, 10 Dec. 1866, RA 19/30.

116 Ibid., and 20 June 1876, RA Z29/86.

117 Radziwill, *Empress Frederick*, 131.

118 Wilhelm, *My Early Life*, 34; Admiral Müller, who was told the same thing, comments laconically, 'This seemed somewhat ironical to people who are well acquainted with the type of life the Kaiser lives.' *The Kaiser and His Court, The Diaries, Notebooks and Letters of Admiral Georg von Müller, Chief of the Naval Cabinet 1914–1918*, ed. Walter Görlitz, trans. Mervyn Savell (London, 1961), 380.

119 Telegram Wm to Prinz von Eulenburg, 21 Jan. 1890, reprinted in Röhl, *Eulenburgs Korrespondenz*.

120 Wheeler-Bennett, *Knaves*, 187.

121 V to QV, 10 Dec. 1866, RA 19/30.

122 Hinzpeter's memoir on Wilhelm's education apparently has been lost. This fragment is quoted by Wilhelm, *My Early Life*, 37.

123 Kürenberg, *Kaiser*, 114 and 29.

124 Fischer-Fabian, *Herrliche Zeiten*, 77.

125 Wm to QV, 20 May 1869, 278/3.

126 V to QV, 16 Jan. 1869, in Fulford, *Your Dear Letter*, 218.

127 Victoria and Friedrich had eight children: Wilhelm, Sigismund, Waldemar, Henry, Charlotte, Victoria, Sophia, and Margareta.

128 V to QV, 27 March 1879, Z65/85, and V to QV, 28 March 1879, Z65/98.

129 V to Duchess of Connaught, 2 Jan. 1885, RA, additional mss A15/4374.

130 Robert Jay Lifton, *History and Human Survival: Essays on the Young and Old, Survivors and the Dead, Peace and War* (New York, 1970), 169–71, and the same author's essay, 'On Death and Death Symbolism' in the same volume.

131 Emil Ludwig, *The Kaiser* (London and New York, 1915), 6.

132 An American psychiatrist who has read these pages disagrees with my interpretation. He writes, 'I do not see compassion here.' He also notes that it misses the
point to defend or criticize Vicky for her conduct: 'She acted according to her own
inner needs. Her good intentions served her, but not her child.' Personal communication, David Beres, 21 Aug. 1989.

133 Bennett, *Vicky*, 87.

134 V to QV, 25 March 1865, RA Z17/51, and 7 April 1865, RA Z17/53.

135 V to QV, 5 Nov. 1863, in Fulford, *Dearest Mama*, 278.

136 QV to V letter, quoted in Bennett, *Vicky*, 87.

137 V to QV, quoted in Egon Caesar Corti, *Wenn ... Sendung und Schicksal Einer
Kaiserin* (Vienna, 1954), 259, and in Fulford, *Your Dear Letter*, 112.

138 See above.

139 V to QV, 28 Jan. 1871 in Ponsonby, *Empress Frederick*, 119–20, and letters of 27
March 1875 and 28 Nov. 1876.

140 D.W. Winnicott, 'Ego Distortion in Terms of the True and False Self,' *The Matura-
tional Processes and the Facilitating Environment* (New York, 1965–80), 140–52.

141 Ibid., 147.

142 Anita Bell and William Niederland, who have written monographs on the psychological consequences of infantile pain, have concluded that infants experience pain
as coming from *outside* themselves, inflicted upon them by others. And to the
infant, the most important 'other' is his mother. This was clearly true of Wilhelm
whose mother boasted that she stood over Willy every day, supervising all his painful 'treatments.' (Bell in *Psychoanalytic Quarterly*, vol. 34 (1966); Niederland in
Psychoanalytic Study of the Child, vol. 20 (1965).

143 Many of Victoria's original letters were deposited in the royal archives, Windsor
Castle, in 56 folio volumes. An archivist's note in the first volume alone (for 1858)
reads: 'The number of letters in this series from the Princess Royal [is] ... 4,161.'
(RA/Z1).

144 The correspondence about her widow's pension was written by a clerk in the parish
council of Leonding.

145 Fragmentary Gestapo Berichte (Gestapo Reports) dealing with Hitler's childhood
and family background may be found in NA, Washington, Hauptarchiv der [Nation-
alsozialistischen] Partei (also on microfilm). See also Library of Congress, Prints
and Photographs, 'Hitler materials.'

146 The reports of OSS agents during the Second World War are collected in 'Hitler
Source Book,' 3 mimeographed vols., continuous pagination. (OSS Files, NA,
Washington.) Both these and the Gestapo Reports must be treated with caution.

147 Joachim C. Fest, *Hitler: Eine Biographie*, 5th ed. (Frankfurt/Main, Berlin, 1973),
30–1.

148 After the Anschluss with Austria in 1938, local party officials took the initiative to erect two rather handsome stones for Hitler's mother and father in the little grave-yard in Leonding. He paid a perfunctory, pro forma visit, took one look at the graves, turned on his heel and departed. He never returned.

149 Fest, *Hitler: Eine Biographie*, 30–1.

150 Because he was so closely related to Klara, Alois needed a special papal dispensation before he could be married in a Catholic church.

151 Robert G.L. Waite, *The Psychopathic God: Adolf Hitler* (New York, 1977 and 1993), 138ff.

152 The adult Adolf Hitler's fear of strangulation may have had its inception by hearing his mother talk about the way his little brother and sister died.

153 Joseph Mayrhofer, interviewed in *Revue* (Munich, 27 Sept. 1952).

154 Helm Stierlin, 'Hitler as Delegate of His Mother,' *History of Childhood Quarterly*, 3/1 (Spring 1976), 484.

155 Testimony of William Patrick Hitler, the son of Alois Hitler Jr, 'OSS Source Book,' 925.

156 August Kubizek, letter of 28 June 1949, Oberoesterreischishe Landes-Archiv, Politische Akten, Hitler Akten, folder 63.

157 Mayrhofer interviewed by the Linz Archivist, Franz Jetzinger, Linz Provincial Archives, Folder 159, and personal interview with Jetzinger, in Linz, Summer, 1960. See also affidavits of Alois Hitler Jr and his wife, Bridget, in OSS 'Source Book' (mimeographed, NA, Washington, DC) and Mayrhofer interview in *Revue*, previously cited.

158 John Toland interview with Paula Hitler, The John Toland Collection, quoted by Helm Stierlin, *Adolf Hitler: A Family Perspective* (New York, 1976), 25.

159 'Hitler Source Book,' 925.

160 Albert Zoller, ed., *Hitler Privat: Erlebnisbericht seiner Privatsekretärin* [Fräulein Christa Schroeder] (Düsseldorf, 1949), 46. It is unlikely that Hitler underestimated the number.

161 Frau Hanfstaengl as quoted by Alice Miller, MD, *For Your Own Good: Hidden Cruelty in Child Rearing and the Roots of Violence* (New York, 1984), 156.

162 Judith Herman, MD, J. Christopher Perry, M.D., and Bessel A. van der Kok, MD, 'Childhood Trauma in Borderline Personality Disorder,' *American Journal of Psychiatry* 146 (April 1989).

163 Dr Hans Frank, *Im Angesicht des Galgens: Deutung Hitlers und seiner Zeit auf Grund eigner Erlebnisse und Erkenntnisse* (Munich, 1953), 320–1. Frank would be given special privileges and power in the Third Reich. He became president of the Academy of German Law, leader of the National Socialist Lawyers' Association, SS Obergruppenführer, and Governor-General of Poland. He wrote his memoirs before being hanged at Nuremberg as a war criminal.

164 There are serious doubts on this score. See Waite, *Psychopathic God*, note, p. 127.

165 In Hitler's death camps, thousands of Jewish skulls of all ages were collected and carefully calibrated in an effort to prove the intrinsic inferiority of the Jewish people.

166 Hitler considered Stalin a rival worthy of his steel. He spoke admiringly of 'the cunning Caucasian,' who commanded 'unconditional respect,' and who was 'in his own way, just one hell of a fellow! He knows his models Genghis Khan and the others very well.' The reason for the Führer's admiration is revealing: 'For him [Stalin], Bolshevism is only a means, a disguise designed to trick the Germanic and Latin people.' Hitler, as quoted by Solomon F. Bloom, 'The Peasant Caesar: Hitler's Union of German Imperialism and Eastern Reaction,' *Commentary* 23 (May 1957), 406–18. Joseph Stalin returned the compliment – and helped Hitler into power by ordering German Communists to attack the moderate Social Democrats and not the Nazis. Stalin's respect for Hitler seems to have started with his approval of Hitler's murder of opponents during the Röhm Purge: 'Have you heard what happened in Germany?' he asked a meeting of the Politburo, 'Some fellow that Hitler! He knows how to treat his political opponents.' Stalin, as quoted by David K. Shipley in review of Robert C. Tucker, *Stalin in Power: The Revolution from Above, 1921–1941* (New York, 1990), *New York Times Book Review* (18 Nov. 1990).

167 Shipley review. Allan Bullock reports the same incident, *Hitler and Stalin* (New York, 1992).

168 Conversation 22 Feb. 1942, *Secret Conversations*, 269 (see Chapter 1, n224).

169 For a discussion of the Gestapo Reports on these investigations into the Führer's background, see footnote at page 129, Waite, *Psychopathic God*.

170 'OSS Source Book,' 73, and Gordon W. Prange, ed., *Hitler's Words* (Washington, DC, 1944), 79. President Richard Nixon made a similar comment about Italians. '"They're [the Italians] not like us. They smell different, they look different, they act different. The trouble is, you can't find one that's honest."' Nixon tapes, quoted by Tip O'Neill, with William Novak, *Man of the House: The Life and Political Memoirs of Speaker Tip O'Neill* (New York, 1987), 256.

171 *The Testament of Adolf Hitler*, trans. R.H. Stevens (London, 1961), 56. My emphasis.

172 For a discussion of this aspect of their relationship, see Chapter 5 and Addendum 6.

173 See Chapter 1.

174 Karl Menninger, *Love against Hate* (New York,1942), 118–19.

175 Personal communication, David Beres, MD, Aug. 1989.

176 Although the autopsy was performed on 8 May 1945, the report was not released until 1968, in a book published in both German and English. See Lev Bezymenski, *The Death of Adolf Hitler: Unknown Documents from Soviet Archives* (New York,

1968). Identification of the corpse had been made by a careful examination of the Führer's teeth. The assertion of the Russian pathologists that this was indeed Hitler's body has been independently verified by American and Norwegian specialists in dental medicine. Writing in professional journals, they set forth the evidence, showing conclusively that the teeth in question in identifying the corpse were indubitably those of Adolf Hitler, for they matched precisely the X-rays and plaster casts found in the office of the Führer's private dentist, Otto Blaschke, who had received his training at the University of Pennsylvania. See Waite, *Psychopathic God*, 150 and notes.

177 Peter Blos, 'Comments on the Psychological Consequences of Cryptorchism,' *Psychoanalytic Study of the Child* 15 (1960), 408–20. See also Bell, 'Pre-puberty Male,' 192.

178 Quoted in *Hitler's Testament*, 64; my emphasis. See also Chapter 1.

179 Hitler told Hanfstaengl that one of his earliest and most pleasant memories was when he slept with his mother 'in the big bed.' See Addendum 6.

180 One of the greatest contributions psychologists have made to biographers is the insight that pathological symptoms may not be related to any actual event. They may be derived from what is often dismissed as 'pure fantasy.' But psychic reality is more formative in human life than is objective reality. What a person *imagines* to have happened must therefore be taken seriously. His fantasies, the words and turns of phrase used to describe them, the intensity of his imagery, the number of times he recounts them – none of these should be written off as coincidental or accidental. Of a thousand other events in his childhood, Hitler in dictating his memoirs chose to dwell on this particular incident and he described it with certain specific words rather than many alternative figures of speech that he might have used.

181 This passage was first called to my attention in the OSS psychological profile of Hitler drawn by Dr Walter Langer and his colleagues and published in a restricted edition in 1943. For a later, edited version of this report, see Walter C. Langer, *The Mind of Adolf Hitler*, with Foreword by William L. Langer and Afterword by Robert G.L. Waite (New York, 1972).

182 '... prügelt zur Abwechslung auch noch selber das zusammengerissene Wesen das einst seine Mutter war.' *Mein Kampf*, German ed., unabridged, 2 vols. in one (Munich, 1941), 32–4; English ed., 42–4; Langer, *Mind of Hitler*, 142–3.

183 See Appendix 5.

184 *Mein Kampf*, German ed., 28; English ed., 38. My emphasis.

185 Psychotherapists know from clinical experience that when a patient constantly repeats an image or an association, or has the same dream again and again, it is an 'indication of the depth an impression has made and the intensity of what he wishes to communicate.' Peter Loewenberg, review article, *Central European History* (Sept. 1974), 265.

186 Schroeder, *Hitler Privat*, 46.
187 For interviews with the villagers of Leonding, see Thomas Orr, 'Das war Hitler, das Ende eines Mythos,' *Revue* (Munich, 4 Oct. 1952), which confirms my interviews with Dr Franz Jetzinger, the Linz archivist.
188 Menninger, *Love against Hate*, 35.
189 Miller, *For Your Own Good*, 193.
190 Stierlin, *Hitler* 65, and 'Hitler as Delegate.'
191 Stierlin, 'Hitler as Delegate,' 484–5.
192 See August Kubizek, *The Young Hitler I Knew*, trans. E.V. Anderson (Boston, 1955), 82–97, 98–104.
193 Miller, *For Your Own Good*, 189.
194 Stierlin, *Hitler*, 64–5.
195 *Mein Kampf*, German ed., 135–6. Actually, there was a more prosaic and pressing reason behind this smokescreen of rhetoric: he left Austria because he was being sought as a draft-dodger from the Austro-Hungarian Army. See Franz Jetzinger, *Hitlers Jugend, Phantasien, Lügen – und die Wahrheit* (Vienna, 1956), 144–54.
196 Quoted by Stierlin, 'Hitler as Delegate,' 494. My emphasis.
197 Norman Cohn, *Warrant for Genocide: The Myths of the Jewish World Conspiracy and the Protocols of the Elders of Zion* (London, 1967).
198 See 15th-century woodcuts from Liber Cronicarum, British Museum, reproduced in ibid., 145.
199 Personal communication, Richard Q. Ford, Sept. 1989.
200 Erik H. Erikson, 'The Problem of Ego Identity,' *Psychological Issues* 1 (1959), 131, and oral communication during Daedalus Leadership Conference, Cape Cod, 20 Oct. 1967.
201 Michael Musmanno, *Ten Days to Die* (New York, 1950), 100.
202 See Hitler's own account, *Mein Kampf*, Chapter 2; 'Wiener Lehr- und Leidens-jahre,' esp. 88, and 155, 470, 610.
203 *Mein Kampf*, 83; Hauptarchiv der Partei, folder 172; conversation with Chamber-lain at the Berghof, 15 Sept. 1938, *Documents of German Foreign Policy*, Series D (Washington, DC, 1956), vol. 2, 787.
204 For a psychoanalyst's interpretation of the part Dr Bloch inadvertently played in Hitler's anti-Semitism, see Addendum 7.
205 Photocopies of his disability record are given in Central Information Office for War Casualties, HAP, folder 12, reel 1a. See also the fine article by Ernst Deuerlein, 'Dokumentation: Hitlers Eintritt in die Politik und die Reichswehr,' *Viertel-jahrshefte für Zeitgeschichte* 7 (1959).
206 *Mein Kampf*, German ed., 223.
207 'Mit den Juden gibt es kein Paktieren, sondern nur das harte Entweder/Oder. Ich aber bechloss, Politiker zu werden.' ibid., 225.

208 Cecil, *Wilhelm II*, 13; Leonard L. Heston and Renate Heston, *Hitler's Medical Casebook* (New York, 1980), 65.

Reflections

1 'If you require a monument, look around you.' Wren's epitaph of 1723, St Paul's Cathedral, London.
2 Adolf Hitler, *Adolf Hitler an seine Jugend* (Munich, 1938).
3 See Michael Geyer's perceptive essay, 'The Nazi State Reconsidered,' *Life in the Third Reich*, ed. Richard Bessel (New York, 1987), and the fine collection of essays ed. by David F. Crew, *Nazism and German Society* (New York, 1994).
4 *Hitler an seine Jugend.*
5 He was lucky he was not deported to Austria as an undesirable alien after trying to overthrow the German government in 1923. He was lucky that he was appointed chancellor in Jan. 1933, even though his party had lost heavily in the elections of the previous Nov. As Thomas Childers has noted, 'It ... remains one of history's tragic ironies that at precisely the moment when the party's electoral support had begun to falter, Hitler was installed as chancellor by representatives of those traditional elites who had done so much to undermine the parliamentary system in Germany.' *The Nazi Voter: The Social Foundations of Fascism in Germany, 1918–1993* (Chapel Hill, NC, 1983), 269.
6 George F. Kennan, 'America and the Russian Future,' *Foreign Affairs*, 3 (April 1951), 366.
7 Addendum 4.
8 Weizsäcker's speech entitled 'The Dignity of Man Is Inviolable,' was reprinted and distributed by the German Information Center, New York, in *Statements and Speeches*, 15/17 (Nov. 1992). The title comes from Article I of the Federal Constitution of 1949, which, as the president reminded his audience, 'does not state that the "dignity of Germans shall be inviolable," but rather that the "dignity of *man* shall be inviolable." It must remain so.'
9 *New York Times* News Service, 7 Dec. 1992. A week later more than 400,000 Germans bearing candles and lanterns and carrying signs with such slogans as 'Stop Hatred' and 'A Light for Reason against Violence and Racism,' gathered in Hamburg and Frankfurt to protest neo-Nazi violence. And again the following Sunday, in Karlsruhe, Stuttgart, Hanover, and Bremen, hundreds of thousands gathered in silence to protest neo-Nazi terror. Associated Press reports, 14 Dec. and 21 Dec. 1992.
10 *New York Times* (31 Jan. 1933). Martin Kinzer, dispatch from Berlin, 30 Jan.
11 Quoted by Friedrich Heer, *Der Glaube des Adolf Hitler: Anatomie einer politischen Religiosität* (Munich, 1968). According to Saint Matthew's Gospel, Jesus said,

'Ye shall know them by their fruits. Do men gather grapes of thorns, or figs from thistles'? (7:16, King James Version).

Addendum 1: Scatology in German Life and Letters

1 Alan Dundes, *Life Is Like a Chicken-Coop Ladder: Portrait of German Culture through Folklore* (New York, 1984).

2 Ibid., 10–12. I have slightly altered Dundes's translations.

3 It should be noted, however, that until the 20th century, Rabelais is almost unique in French letters in his preoccuption with anality. Realists such as Zola certainly write about excrement, but not shit (*merde*). Nor does the great Spanish realist, Cervantes, use that term. In the whole of *Don Quixote*, there is only one reference to defecation and that is expressed discreetly when, in a moment of fear, Sancho Panza 'soils his pants.' A distinguished authority on romanic languages has noted, 'In France, *merde* is used by actors as the equivalent of our "break a leg" ... But there is certainly no recurring use of excremental vocabulary in French, Spanish or Portuguese to remotely approach German usage.' Personal communication, Anson C. Piper, March 1990. The same comment can be made about Russian letters. Personal Communications, Nicholas Fersen and Dara Goldstein, April 1990. In Italian, there are scattered references to *merda* in Dante's *Inferno* and in Boccaccio, who uses euphemisms for the word, but generally speaking 'Italians are more concerned with their sex organs than with their faeces.' Personal communication, Dario Delpuppo, May 1990.

4 Mark Twain, however, was unable to find a commercial publisher for his most explicit scatological satire, *1601: or Conversation as It Was by the Fireside in the Time of the Tudors* (privately printed, 1880 and 1882 editions. No publisher given, no place, no date).

5 Chaucer is of course notorious for scatological language such as 'Filthe,' 'Fartes,' 'Ordure,' 'Buttoks,' 'Erse,' 'Tuel' (anus). It is interesting, however, that in the whole of *The Canterbury Tales*, Chaucer used the word 'shit' or a variant thereof only once. In line 504 of the General Prologue to the Tales, we hear the contrast between 'A shiten sheperde and a clene sheep.' *The Canterbury Tales*, in *The Riverside Chaucer*, 3rd ed., ed. F.N. Robinson (Boston, 1978), 31.

6 For a brilliant discussion of Swift's concern with faeces, see the chapter, 'The Excremental Vision,' in Norman O. Brown's classic work, *Life versus Death: The Psychoanalytic Meaning of History* (Middleton, CT, 1959, and many subsequent printings). Brown makes two points of interest to this discussion: First, although there are many scatological references in Swift, he prefers euphemisms such as 'Filth,' 'Nastiness and Dirt,' or 'Stinking Ooze.' Only once, in his poem 'Cassinus and Peter,' is the word specifically used and then with ellipses: 'Nor wonder why I lost my wits / Oh, Caelia, Caelia, Caelia sh ---.' Second, Swift's English critics are so embarrassed by

his scatology that they try 'to domesticate and housebreak this tiger of English literature' by attempting to bury what they call Swift's 'noxious compositions.' Or else, like Middleton Murry, they use amateur analysis in an effort to 'lobotomize Swift's scatology' (ibid., 180–1). German critics make no such effort to bowdlerize Luther or Goethe; see below.

7 James Joyce expressed his infatuation with anality and faeces explicitly in his fiction and in his letters. See esp. his letters to Nora Barnacle Joyce of 2, 6, 8, 9, 13 [?], 20 Dec. 1909, in *Selected Letters of James Joyce*, ed. Richard Ellmann (New York, 1975). My thanks to Steven Wright for these references. Joyce's compulsion to have Nora squat over him while he watched her defecate on his head seems to have been shared by Adolf Hitler. See Addendum 5.

8 See note 7.

9 Dundes, *Chicken-Coop Ladder*, 108.

10 Ibid. My thanks to the late Harlan P. Hanson for the licorice.

11 *Verbatim: The Language Quarterly* 18/2 (Autumn 1991).

12 Martin Luther's *Tischgespräche*, as quoted by Erik Erikson, *Young Man Luther: A Study in Psychoanalysis and History* (New York, 1958), 244, 206.

13 Johann Wolfgang Goethe, *Sämtliche Werke: Der junge Goethe, 1757–1775*, ed. Gerhard Sauder (Munich, 1985), vol. 1, 615.

14 Personal communication, Edson Chick, Professor of German Literature, Williams College, March 1990.

15 Page references are to the English translation of the original German ed. of 1669, prepared by Hellmuth Weissenborn and Lesley MacDonald, *Simplicius Simplicissimus* (London, 1961).

16 Peter Gay, *The Bourgeois Experience: Victoria to Freud*, vol. 3 (New York, 1993), 419.

17 Students of humour have detected national patterns in bawdy jokes. In France such jokes tend to involve seduction, adultery, and sexual techniques; in the U.S. and England, oral-genital themes and homosexuality. It has been argued that the Germans are 'champions of scatology,' with the word *Scheisse* appearing in virtually all their jokes. See the serious 2-vol. study by Gershon Legman, *Rationale of the Dirty Joke: An Analysis of Sexual Humor* (New York, 1968 and 1975), cited by Dieter Rollfinke and Jaqueline Rollfinke, *The Call of Human Nature: The Role of Scatology in Modern German Literature* (Amherst, MA, 1986), 9–10.

18 Rollfinke and Rollfinke, *Scatology*, 12. For pictures of these advertisements, see ibid., 12–16.

Addendum 2: The 'Kriegsschuldfrage'and Historical Evidence

1 For a discussion of the *Kriegsschuldreferat*, see Imanuel Geiss, 'The Outbreak of the

First World War and German War Aims,' *Journal of Contemporary History*, I/3 (July 1966).

2 See Isabella M. Massey's important letter to the editor, *Times Literary Supplement* (11 Sept. 1953).

3 Geiss, 'Outbreak,' 75.

4 See Introduction by Imanuel Geiss to Hermann Kantorowicz, *Gutachten zur Kriegsschuldfrage, 1914 aus dem Nachlass herausgegeben und eingeleitet von Imanuel Geiss* (Frankfurt/Main, 1967).

5 Luigi Albertini, *The Origins of the War of 1914*, ed. and trans. Isabella M. Massey, 2 vols. (Oxford, London, and New York, 1952).

6 For a critical evaluation of the edition of these diaries, see esp. the devastating article by Bernd Sösemann, 'Die Tagebücher der Kurt Riezlers: Untersuchungen zu ihrer Echtheit und Edition,' *Historische Zeitschrift* 236 (1983), 327–69. See also the comments of John C.G. Röhl, *Kaiser, Hof, und Staat: Wilhelm II und die deutsche Politik* (Munich, 1988), 233.

7 See Adolf Gasser's article, 'Der deutsche Hegemonialkrieg von 1914,' in *Deutschland in der Weltpolitik des 19. und 20. Jahrhuderts*, ed. Imanuel Geiss and Bernd Jürgen Wendt (Dusseldorf, 1974.)

8 For a discussion of comparative national self-justification for the Great War, see Kantorowicz.

Addendum 3: The Kaiser in Exile

1 Rijksarchief (RA), Utrecht, folder 647.

2 Ibid., folders 668–9; 670–1.

3 In addition to the records preserved in either Doorn House or the Rijksarchief in Utrecht and the memoirs of the Countess Bentinck and Captain Ilsemann, I have drawn on personal observations and conversations with Th. L.J. Verreon, the curator of Huis Doorn. See also Sally Marks, '"My Name Is Ozymandias": The Kaiser in Exile,' *Central European History* 16/2 (1983), 122–70; and Willibald Gutsche, *Ein Kaiser im Exil: Der letzte deutsche Kaiser Wilhelm II. in Holland, Eine kritische Biographie* (Marburg, 1991).

Addendum 4: Historical Continuity versus Change

1 William L. Shirer, *The Rise and Fall of the Third Reich* (New York, 1959), 90, 95.

2 Fritz Fischer, *From Kaiserreich to Third Reich: Elements of Continuity in German History, 1871–1945*, trans. and with an Introduction Roger Fletcher (London, 1986), 98.

3 This thesis is set forth in two influential books: *Griff nach der Weltmacht* (Dussel-

dorf, 1961), English ed., *Germany's Aims in the First World War*, with Introductions by Hajo Holborn and James Joll (New York, 1967), and *Krieg der Illusionen* (Düsseldorf, 1969), English ed., *War of Illusions: German Policies from 1911 to 1914*, trans. Marion Jackson, Foreword by Sir Alan Bullock (New York, 1975). See also two critical commentaries by John A. Moses, *The Politics of Illusion: The Fischer Controversy in German Historiography* (London, 1975), as well as *The War Aims of Imperial Germany: Professor Fritz Fischer and His Critics* (Brisbane, 1968), as well as the important article by Imanuel Geiss, 'Die Fischer-Kontroverse: Ein kritischer Beitrag zum Verhältnis zwischen Historiographie und Politik in der Bundesrepublik,' *Studien über Geschichte und Geschichtswissenschaft* (Frankfurt/Main, 1972).

4 G. Ritter, 'Eine neue Kriegsschuldthese?' *Historische Zeitschrift* 194 (1962), 657–758; I am indebted to D.E. Lee for this reference.

5 T.W. Mommsen, 'Zur Kriegsschuldfrage, 1914,' *Historische Zeitschrift* 212 (1971), 606–14, and his essay, 'The Typos of Inevitable War in Germany in the Decade before 1914,' in *Germany in the Age of Total War*, eds. Volker Berghahn and Martin Kitchen (London, 1981).

6 See Roger Fleming's Introduction to Fischer, *Kaiserreich*.

7 Martin Luther had joined Catholic saints and bishops in denouncing Jews as 'a depraved and despicable race.' Fichte had demanded the expulsion of Jews from Germany. Kant believed that Jews 'lacked the necessary qualities for true humanity.' Schopenhauer, who asserted that Jesus was not Jewish, had called Jews a 'sneaking, dirty race of parasites who should be utterly destroyed.' Paul de Lagarde had expressed his hatred of Jews in words and metaphors later apppropriated by Hitler: 'With trichinae and bacilli one does not negotiate, nor are they subject to education. They are to be exterminated as quickly and as thoroughly as possible.' Heinrich Treitstchke, Germany's most influential historian of the 19th century, had coined the expression that would be taken over by the Nazis, 'Perish the Jew!' Richard Wagner had deplored the 'Jewishization' (*Verjudung*) of Germany and demanded 'national purification.' In 1899 the Hamburg Program of United Anti-Semites, proclaimed the need for a 'Final Solution to the Jewish Problem' that could take place with 'the complete destruction of the Jewish people (*schliessliche Vernichtung des Judenvolkes*).'

8 E. Fehrenbach, 'Images of Kaiserdom: German Attitudes to Kaiser Wilhelm II,' *Kaiser Wilhelm II, New Interpretations*, ed. John C.G. Röhl and Nicolaus Sombart (Cambridge, 1982), 280.

9 The scope and quality of the achievement is suggested by great names in every field. In physics: Max Planck and Albert Einstein, whose Quantum Theory and the General Theory of Relativity were formulated in Berlin; in medicine: Robert Koch, Paul Ehrlich, and Wilhelm Konrad Röntgen; in philosophy and theology, Adolph von Harnack, Ernst Troeltsch, and Wilhelm Dilthey, whom Ortega y Gasset called 'the

most important thinker in the second half of the nineteenth century'; in history and the social sciences: Theodor Mommsen, Friedrich Meinecke, and Max Weber; in art: Paul Cassirer and Max Liebermann and the secessionists – who thwarted the Kaiser's efforts to repress modern art; in architecture: Peter Behrens and the youthful Walter Gropius and Le Corbusier ; in the theatre: Gerhart Hauptmann, Max Reinhardt, and the 'Free Stage' movement; in music: new directions of Richard Wagner and Richard Strauss; in journalism: wide-ranging opinion from the conservative *Kreuzzeitung* on the right to the Marxist *Vorwärts* on the left, in the satire and lampoons of *Simplicissimus*, and the scathing exposés of Maximilian Harden's weekly, *Die Zukunft*.

Addendum 5: Coprophilic Perversion?

1 Robert G.L. Waite, 'Adolf Hitler's Anti-Semitism: A Study in History and Psychoanalysis,' *The Psychoanalytic Interpretation of History*, ed. Benjamin B. Wolman (New York, 1971), 225.

2 Walter C. Langer, *The Mind of Adolf Hitler: The Secret Wartime Report*, Foreword by William L. Langer, Afterword by Robert G.L.Waite (New York, 1972.)

3 Ibid., 134.

4 H.R. Trevor Roper, *Book World* (10 Sept. 1972).

5 Otto Strasser in 'Hitler Source Book,' ed. Walter C. Langer from documents collected by the Office of Strategic Services (OSS) in 1942–3, National Archives, Washington, DC (NA), 919. Hereafter 'OSS Source Book.'

6 Langer, *Mind of Hitler*, 134.

7 Konrad Heiden, *Der Fuehrer: Hitler's Rise to Power*, trans. Ralph Mannheim (Boston, 1944), 385–9.

8 See Chapter 1.

9 Felix Gilbert, ed., *Hitler Directs His War: The Secret Records of His Daily Military Conferences* (New York, 1950), 18.

10 See among other studies, *Sexual Variants*, ed. George W. Henry (New York, 1948); George W. Henry, L.S. London, and F.S. Caprio, *Sexual Deviations* (Washington, DC, 1959); Harold Greenweld, *The Elegant Prostitute: A Social and Psychoanalytic Study* (New York, 1973); Richard Krafft-Ebbing, *Psychopathia Sexualia*, trans. F.J. Rebinan, rev. ed. (New York, 1937); Havelock Ellis, *Studies in the Psychology of Sex*, 3 vols. (New York, 1936); and testimony of Raymond de Saussure, 'OSS Source Book,' 932.

11 Phyllis Greenacre, 'Perversions: General Considerations Regarding Their Genetic and Dynamic Background,' *Psychoanalytic Study of the Child* 23 (1968), 58. My emphasis.

12 August Kubizeck, as quoted in Norbert Bromberg, 'The Psychotic Character as Political Leader: A Psychoanalytic Study of Adolf Hitler' (unpublished paper).

13 Langer, OSS Report, 222. My emphasis.

14 Henriette Schirach, *Price of Glory*, trans. Willi Freischauer (London, 1960), 73.

15 'AH' in FDR, Hyde Park, Roosevelt Archives (See Chapter 1, n300).

16 Hans Baur, *Hitler's Pilot*, trans. Edward Gerald (London, 1958), 64.

17 Heinz Linge, 'The Private Life of Adolf Hitler,' *News of the World* (20 Nov. 1955).

18 Testimony of the cinema director, A. Zeissler, 'OSS Source Book,' 922.

19 *Mein Kampf*, 38, 39, 43–4, 65, 75, 116–8, 416. My emphasis.

20 Bormann Papers, 'Hitler Privat Gespräche,' Berlin Document Center, microfilm group 7, reel 2. See also, *Secret Conversations*, 160, and Bradley F. Smith, *Adolf Hitler: His Family, Childhood and Youth* (Stanford, 1967), 99.

21 *Hitler Privat: Erlebnisbericht seiner Geheimsekretärin* (Christa Schroeder), ed. Albert Zoller (Düsseldorf, 1949), 231.

22 Letter Kubizeck to Jetzinger, 6 May 1949, Oberösterreichische Landesarchiv, Linz, Hitler Files, folder 64.

23 *Mein Kampf*, 58.

24 *Secret Conversations*, 409.

25 Sigmund Freud, *General Introduction to Psycho-Analysis*, 320. See also Otto Fenichel, *Psychoanalytic Theory of Neurosis* (New York, 1945), 68.

26 Greenacre, 'Perversions,' 57–8.

27 Fenichel, *Theory*, 332.

28 Ibid., 326. My emphasis.

29 See Chapter 1.

30 Norbert Bromberg, 'Hitler's Childhood,' *International Review of Psycho-Analysis*, 1 (1974), 239. Conversations with Dr Bromberg, Williamstown, Mass, Aug. 1976.

Addendum 6: Hitler and Incest

1 Eduard Bloch, 'My Patient Adolf Hitler,' *Collier's Magazine*, 15 March 1941, 36.

2 See Chapter 6.

3 *Mein Kampf*, German ed., 135.

4 Gertrude M. Kurth, 'The Jew and Adolf Hitler,' *Psychoanalytic Quarterly* 16 (1947), 11–32. Private conversations with Dr Kurth.

5 Hitler's letter to Adolf Gemlich, 16 Sept. 1919, is preserved in the Ernst Deuerlein Documents, document 10, cited by Joachim Fest, *The Face of the Third Reich*, trans. by Michael Bullock (New York, 1970), 16.

6 Interview Friedlinde Wagner, 'OSS Source Book,' 940; Carl Wilhelm Krause, *Zehn Jahre Kammerdiener bei Hitler* (Hamburg, n.d. [early 1950s]), 52; conversations with Hanfstaengl, Munich, May 1967.

7 Hanfstaengl Interview, Munich, May 1967.

8 *Mein Kampf*, German ed., 20.

9 A psychotherapist in reading this passage commented, 'My own clinical experience with such patients is that they choose women so much younger than themselves because of their fear of intimacy, of being close to anyone who might have the capacity to know and understand the patient's inner life.' Communication from Richard Q. Ford, 14 June 1992.

10 Anton Joachimstahler, *Hitler in München, 1908–1910* (Frankfurt/Main, 1992), 16.

11 Details of their relationship may be found in a taped interview she gave to Günther Peis, reprinted in the sensationalistic magazine, *Stern* 24 (1959). Eugen Kogon, a responsible German writer, verified the story after checking names, dates, places, and the handwritten letter she received from 'A. Hitler.' See also, Domarus, *Reden*, 2220; *Time* magazine (9 Jan. 1959), and Waite, *Psychopathic God*, 223–5.

12 For fuller discussion of Hitler's relations with Geli Raubal and with Eva Braun, see Waite, *Psychopathic God*.

13 Conversations with Ernst Hanfstaengl, Munich, 1967.

14 See Chapter 1.

15 Speer interview with James P. O'Donnel, *New York Times Magazine* (26 Oct. 1969), 100–2.

16 *Tschapperl* may loosely be rendered 'my cutie-pie.' *Hascherl* is more condescending, something like 'my poor little thing.' I am indebted to my former colleague Professor Kurt Tauber for these translations.

17 Interview with Frau Traudl Junge, Munich, 7 Feb. 1948, Musmanno Archives, quoted in Glenn B. Infield, *Eva and Adolf* (New York, 1974), 315.

18 Eva's diary entries and letters to Adolf reveal an immature and limited young woman whose love for Hitler is unmistakably sincere. In the end she flew to crumbling Berlin to die with the man she loved. Amid the bedlam of the last days in the Führer's air-raid shelter, while others faced death with varying degrees of panic and histrionics, Eva Braun grew in stature and achieved a quiet inner strength. Even someone who had cordially disliked her said that at the end 'she attained heights which more than atoned for the vanities and frivolities of the past.' Nerin E. Gun, *Eva Braun-Hitler: Leben und Schicksal* (New York, 1968), 164–5; Heinrich Hoffmann, *Hitler Was My Friend*, trans. R.H. Stevens (London, 1955), 163–4.

19 Conversation with Lawrence Mamlet, MD, Austen Riggs Center, Stockbridge, MA, April 1968.

Addendum 7: Dr Bloch and the Genesis of Hitler's Anti-Semitism

1 Gertrude M. Kurth, 'The Jew and Adolf Hitler,' *Psychoanalytic Quarterly* 16 (1947), 11–32.
2 Binion has attempted to demonstrate that the treatment was excruciatingly painful, that it produced psychosis in Klara, and that it was iodoform, rather than cancer, which was the actual cause of her death. For my disagreement with these conclusions, see Waite, *Psychopathic God*, 189.

Addendum 8: Hitler and Psychiatrists

1 Personal correspondence with Drs Friedrich Panse, 25 Feb. 1967, Ritter von Baeyer, 3 March 1967, and C. Weiser, 12 May 1967.
2 Two biographers of Hitler, John Toland and Rudolph Binion, have contended that Doctor Forster not only examined Hitler in 1918, but actually gave him psychiatric treatment. Toland calls Forster 'the first psychiatrist to treat Hitler.' There is no record to substantiate that claim. One may well ask if it is credible that in the hectic last weeks of the war the distinguished and overworked director of a German university clinic would have taken the time to give special psychiatric treatment to an unknown common soldier who, like hundreds of his comrades, was suffering 'shell shock.' To support their thesis, Binion and Toland relied on an inconsequential and factually inaccurate report on Hitler submitted to U.S. Naval Intelligence in 1943 by Karl Kronor, a Viennese 'nerve specialist.' Kronor, they claimed, was present during Hitler's examination at Pasewalk in 1918. Binion stated flatly that Kronor was Forster's 'psychiatric assistant.' Kronor himself made no such claim. Had he actually been in attendance at the purported examination, he certainly would have stated so in his report which concluded that Hitler's blindness in 1918 was caused by hysteria. Instead, Kronor did not even claim that he had ever seen Hitler, much less served as a 'psychiatric assistant' in treating him. See Dr Karl Kronor, 'Adolf Hitler's Blindness,' OSS Document 31963, NA, Washington, DC; Binion, 'Hitler's Concept of Lebensraum: The Psychological Basis,' *Childhood Quarterly* (Fall 1973), 203–6 and *Hitler among the Germans* (New York, 1976), 6–14. John Toland, *Adolf Hitler* (New York, 1976), 925.
3 'Gutachten über den Geisteszustand des Untersuchungsgefangenen Adolf Hitler,' signed by Obermedizinalrat Dr Brinsteiner, Landsberg a.L., 8 Jan. 1924, reprinted in 'OSS Source Book,' 19–20. See also Otto Lurker, *Hitler Hinter Festungsmauren* (Berlin, 1933), 35.
4 See Waite, *Psychopathic God*, Appendix, 'A Note on Spurious Sources.'
5 Albert Zoller, ed., *Hitler Privat*, 69.

Index

Abdul Hammid II, 121
Absolutism of Wilhelm II, 125–9
Abuse, Hitler's by father, 328–9; Hitler's mother by husband, 327; Wilhelm II's by mother, 305–12. *See also* Childhood, Hitler's and Wilhelm II's compared
Administration, Hitler's, 161–202
Aegir, Wilhelm II, identification with, 87, 106
Angriff, Der, anti-Reichstag editorial, 163
Albert, King (of Belgium), misled by Wilhelm II, 211
Albert, Prince Consort (of Britain), 124, 299–307; death of, 299; Victoria (daughter), Princess, relationship with, 302–7; Wilhelm II, as surrogate of, 303–8; women, attitude towards, 299
Alexander III, correspondence with Bismarck, 142
Anal fixation, of Hitler, 37, 46; of Wilhelm II, 28–9. *See also* Coprophilia and Scatology
Anschluss, 229
Anti-Semitic, legislation, 276–7; literature, Hitler's interest in, 74, 111–12
Anti-Semitism, 99, 113–17, 117–24,

275–8; of August Wilhelm, 147; of Catholic Church, 103; of Goebbels, 103; of Luther, 103; of St John, 103; of Wilhelm II, 22, 94, 120–3. *See also* Jews and Holocaust
Arendt, Hannah, on collaboration of Jewish leaders, 192
Army. *See* Germany, army of
Art, political use of, 92
Artists and Wilhelm II, 84–6
August Wilhelm, Crown Prince, 121; involvement with Nazis, 201
Auguste Viktoria, Empress (first wife of Wilhelm II), death of, 360; relationship with Wilhelm II, 21, 26–7
Auschwitz, I.G. Farben factory at, 190
Austria-Hungary, blank cheque of Wilhelm II, 211, 213; German occupation of, 229; Serbian question, 211; Serbian reply to ultimatum of, 214

Balance of power, 209
Ballin, Albert, 68, 121; correspondence with Wilhelm II, 210–11; inability to criticize Wilhelm II, 257
Barbarossa, Friedrich, Hitler's identification with, 235

Barbarossa, Operation, 135, 190, 233–4,
    236, 238–9; Hitler's self-defeating
    behaviour during, 238–9. *See also*
    Russia
Beefsteak Nazis, 183
Beer Hall Putsch, 59, 161, 170–5,
    285
Belgium, invasion of, Wilhelm II's reac-
    tion to, 7
Bentinck, Count Godard van, Wilhelm
    II's host, 223
Berger-Prinz, Hans, Hitler's probable
    Parkinsonism confirmed by, 263. *See
    also* Hitler, health of
Bernhardt, Sarah, on Wilhelm II as actor,
    18
Bethmann Hollweg, Theobald von (Ger-
    man chancellor), 146
Bismarck, Otto von (German chancellor),
    10
    Alexander III, correspondence with,
        142
    coup d'état, participation in, 146
    dismissal of, 21–2, 142–4
    socialism, reaction to, 140
    Wilhelm II: dependence upon chancel-
        lor, 248; tutor for, 125, 158
Björko agreement, 9
Black Shirts. *See Schutz-Staffel*
Bloch, Eduard, Klara Hitler's physician,
    341–2, 376–7
Blomberg, Werner von (field marshal;
    German defence minister), ultimatum
    to Hitler by, 183
Blood Purge. *See* Night of the Long Knives
Blutkitt, 47
Boer War, Wilhelm II's meddling with,
    152
Bonn, University of, 125
Borderline personality disorder, Hitler's,

266–72; similarity to narcissistic
    impairment, 266–7
Bormann, Martin, 175, 185
Bormann Vermerke. *See* 'Table Conversa-
    tions'
Bound delegate, Hitler, of mother,
    338–43, 345; Victoria, Princess
    (Empress Frederick), of father, 302–7;
    Wilhelm II, of mother, 303–18, 323–4,
    345
Boxer Rebellion, Wilhelm II's reaction
    to, 7, 24, 114
Brandenburg, 3
Braun, Eva, Hitler's mistress and wife,
    61, 98, 374
Broszat, Martin, Holocaust as result of
    defeat in Russia, 189–90
Brown Shirts. *See Sturmabteilung*
Bullock, Alan, Ardennes Offensive
    success, 232; Speer interviewed by,
    195
Bülow, Bernhard von (German chancel-
    lor), 17, 114
    Wilhelm II: accusation of treachery by,
        156; denigration by, 150; depen-
        dence of, 247
Burden of Freedom, The, 163
Bürgerbraükeller. *See* Beer Hall Putsch

Casalis, Georges, on Speer and Hitler, 65
Catholic Church
    anti-Semitism of, 103–4
    Hitler as member of, 94–105
    model for *Schutz-Staffel*, 137
    Nazism: endorsed by, 226; resisted by,
        178
    See also Christian Church
Chamberlain, Houston Stewart, 73,
    117–24
    anti-Semitism of, 118–24

Chamberlain, Houston Stewart, (*cont.*)
Foundations of the Nineteenth Century, 17
Hitler, influence on, 118, 210
Wagner: connection to, 119; correspondence with, 16, 94, 118; influence on, 118–19, 210
Wilhelm II, influence on, 117–24
Childhood, Hitler's, 324–43; Hitler's and Wilhelm II's compared, 343–5; Wilhelm II's, 213, 297, 323
Christian Church, Hitler's relationship with
adherence to, 94–105
destruction planned by, 105
National Socialism endorsed by, 226
response to, 175–6
Wilhelm II, belief in tenets of, 92–6
See also Catholic Church
Christian, Gerda Daranowski, 63
Churchill, Winston, on Hitler, 31, 278
Communist party, Reichstag elections, gains in, 163
Concentration camps, started, 168
Coprophilia, Hitler's, 37–8, 269, 352, 365–71. *See also* Anal fixation and Scatology
Corfu, archaeological excavation at, by Wilhelm II, 69
Coup d'état. See Royal *coup d'état*
Crensis, Max de, Hitler's probable Parkinsonism confirmed by, 263
Cryptorchism, behaviour in, 334

Daily Telegraph, Wilhelm II's interview in, 151–6, 208
Daisy of Pless, Princess: Wilhelm II described as actor by, 20; Wilhelm II's newspaper cutting service described by, 257

Danzig, bombing of, 229
Delbrück, Hans, Wilhelm II criticized by, 154–5
Depression, Great, opportunity for Hitler provided by, 162
Dibelius, Bishop Otto, supports Hitler, 226
Dietrich, Otto, propaganda responsibilities of, 188
Displaced Persons, 204
Divine missions, Hitler's, 345; Wilhelm II's, 208, 345
Doorn House, Wilhelm II's exile in, 86, 122, 359
Dual personality, 6; Hitler's, 6, 33–5, 269; Wilhelm II's, 6–7
Dumas, Philip (British admiral), on Wilhelm II, 69
Dunkirk, 231–2
Dutch people, Holocaust supported by, 191

Eden, Anthony, Hitler described by, 278
Edward VII, King (of Great Britain)
Entente Cordiale as plot of, 208
Wilhelm II: correspondence with, 8, 152; mistrusted by, 156
Eichmann, Adolf
diaries of, legitimacy of, 439n317
Holocaust: directed by, 192, 195; Hitler's responsibility for, 194–5; Jewish cooperation in, 191, 192
Enabling Act, 176, 178
England. *See* Great Britain
Eulenburg-Hertefeld, Count Philipp zu, 7, 109–10, 122
anti-Semitism of, 121
homosexuality of, 26–7
Liebenberg Circle of, 27
Wilhelm II: personality of described

Eulenburg-Hertefeld, Count Philipp zu
(*cont.*)
by, 253; relationship with, 21, 26–7,
208
Evil, 291–2
Exhibitionism, Wilhelm II's, 248
Exile, of Wilhelm II, 5, 359–61

Faeces. *See* Coprophilia
Falkenhayn, Erich von (General; Wil-
helm II's chief of staff), ineptness of,
160–1
Fehrenbach, Elisabeth, 363–4
Fenichel, Otto, on sexual perversion, 370
Ferdinand, King (of Bulgaria), denigrated
by Wilhelm II, 149
Fest, Joachim, Hitler's sexual rapport
with audience described by, 273
Final Solution. *See* Holocaust
First World War
causes of, according to Wilhelm II, 14
declaration of, by Wilhelm II, 214–15
foreign office support of, 214–15
Hitler's poetry about, 80–1
inevitability of, for Germany, 210, 218
Jews as cause of, 121, 122
justification of, 215–16
military leadership in, 220–2
political legacy of, 203–4
preparations for, 209–10
War Guilt Review Office, published
documents from, 356–8
Wilhelm II: causes of war analysed by,
14; declaration of, 210–12, 219–20;
loss of power in, 220–2; military
leadership in, 220–2; mixed emotions about, 212–15; reaction to beginning of, 240–1; responsibility for,
207–19, 251; role in, 205; Second
World War, as result of, 244, 362–4

Fischer, Fritz, 362
Flag-nailing, by Wilhelm II, 197
*Foundations of the Nineteenth Century,
The. See Grundlagen des neunzehnten
Jahrhunderts*
France, Wilhelm II's attitude towards,
116, 122, 208
Frank, Hans, Holocaust involvement of,
195; on German Constitution, 131
Franke, Lydia, 113
Franz Ferdinand, Crown Prince (of Aus-
tria), Wilhelm II's meeting with, 211
Franz-Joseph, Emperor (of Austria), Wil-
helm II's correspondence with, 22
Frederick, Empress. *See* Victoria, Prin-
cess
Frederick the Great, King (of Prussia),
Hitler and Wilhelm II's identification
with, 4, 130
Freikorps, 182
French people, Holocaust supported by,
191
Freud, Anna, on intimidation, 168
Friedrich II, King (of Prussia). *See* Fred-
erick the Great
Friedrich III, King (of Prussia) and Kai-
ser, 4, 293–4; cancer, treatment of,
313–14
Friedrich Wilhelm, Crown Prince (of
Germany), correspondence with Wil-
helm II, 147; involvement with Nazis,
201; regency proposed, 221
Fromm, Erich, on 'Escape from Freedom,'
163–4; on malignant narcissism, 291
Führer. *See* Hitler, Adolf
Führer*prinzip*, 130–2

Galbraith, John Kenneth, on Roosevelt's
reaction to Hitler's declaration of war,
238

Geheime-Staatspolizei. See Gestapo
Genocide, detrimental to war effort,
  239–40
German Democratic Republic, censorship by, 357–8
Germany
  army of: attempted coup by, 146–7;
    constitutional position of, 127;
    expansion of, 225–6; Hitler, rela-
    tions with, 183; Holocaust, role in,
    190; influence of, 206; Night of the
    Long Knives condoned by, 185;
    Regulations of 1726, 3; *Sturmabtei-
    lung*, relations with, 183; Wilhelm
    II, relations with, 127, 147–8
  constitution of, 126–7
  democracy's failures in, 167
  economy, not mobilized by Hitler,
    234–5
  Hitler's mother symbol of, 339–40
  Japan treaty obligations of, 237
  psychological condition of: at Hitler's
    rise, 272–4; despair of, 163; group
    agoramania of, 259–60; paranoia of,
    208; war guilt denied by, 216–17;
    Wilhelm II as mirror of, 255–6
  remilitarization of, 224
  Rhineland occupied by, 229
  war guilt of, 216–17
  Wilhelm II: psychological mirror of,
    255–6; vision for, 6
Gestapo, public opinion surveys by, 169
Gods, identification with, Hitler, 60, 103,
  107–8, 131, 136–7, 180, 279, 287,
  469n121; Wilhelm II, 87, 106, 208
Goebbels, Joseph (minister of propaganda and enlightenment), 61; anti-
  democracy editorial of, 163; anti-
  Semitism of, 103; educational responsibilities of, 187; Hitler's psychological

manipulation of, 278; Nazism as religion described by, 102; propaganda,
  169, 188; responsibilities of, 188; sexual licence of, 185; speeches of, 73
Goldhagen, Daniel, on German support
  of Holocaust, 191
Goldzier, Hans, 111
Göring, Hermann *(Reichsmarschall)*, 52,
  121, 183; economic responsibilities of,
  187, 228; German royal family curries
  favour with, 201; Hitler as object of
  devotion, 279; speeches of, 73
Grand Council of Fascism, in Italy, 130
Grandiosity, Hitler's, 39–40, 268, 285–7;
  Wilhelm II's, 15, 39–40, 248
Great Britain: Holocaust escapees turned
  back by, 192; Wilhelm II, outrage of,
  caused by, 151–6; Wilhelm II's attitude
  towards, 7, 152, 208–9, 251–60
Great Strike, May 1889, 140
*Grundlagen des neunzehnten Jahrhun-
  derts,* 118
Guderian, Heinz (German general), on
  Dunkirk, 232

Hague Peace Conference, the, and Wilhelm II, 9
Halder, Franz von (German general),
  Dunkirk described by, 232; Hitler's
  lack of war plan, 230
Hale, William Bayard, Wilhelm II interviewed by, 156
Hanfstaengl, Ernst (Putzi), Hitler's
  behaviour described by, 56, 77, 91,
  173, 273
Hauptmann, Gerhart, despair with
  democracy of, 163
Haushofer, Karl, Professor, 77
Hegel, Georg Wilhelm Friedrich, influence on Wilhelm II, 126

Heidegger, Martin (German philosopher), pro-Nazi speech, 226

Heines, Edmund, homosexuality of, 182

Henderson, Nevil, Sir, 52

Henry, Prince (of Germany), 318–19

Hermine, Empress (Wilhelm II's second wife), banned from Doorn, 360; relations with Nazis, 201; relationship with Wilhelm II, 26

Herzl, Theodor, as National Socialist, 164; supported by Wilhelm II, 121

Hess, Rudolph, Hitler's charisma described by, 290–1; Hitler's homoerotic relationship with, 51, 64–5; imprisonment of, 53; sexuality of, 64–5, 185

Heston, Leonard, Hitler's amphetamine toxicity diagnosed by, 264

Heydrich, Heinrich, Hitler's responsibility for Holocaust described by, 194–5; Holocaust involvement of, 194–5

Hilberg, Raul, on collaboration of Jewish leaders, 192

Himmler, Heinrich (*Reichsführer* SS), 75, 175; educational responsibilities of, 187; Holocaust, Hitler's responsibility for, 194–5; Holocaust, involvement in, 194–5; Night of Long Knives, commanded by, 183–4; *Schutz-Staffel*, commanded by, 183–4

Hindenburg, Paul von (field marshal; president), *de facto* dictator, 222–3; Night of the Long Knives condoned by, 185–6; *Reichspräsident* (1932), 178; Reichstag, 1933 opening of, 179

Hinzpeter, Georg, Wilhelm II's tutor, 124–5, 140, 319–20

Historiography, continuity and change in history, 362–4

Hitler, Adolf, 161–202
    abused by father, 328–9
    agent of change, 348–9

Hitler, Adolf (*cont.*)
    anal fixation of, 37
    anti-Semitism, roots of, 340–3, 376
    autopsy of, 265, 470n215, 480–1n176
    Barbarossa, identification with, 235
    Beer Hall Putsch, 59, 161, 170–5, 288
    biographical information, quality of, 325
    Bloch, perceived as mother's attacker, 376–8
    borderline personality disorder of, 243, 266–72
    Braun, Eva, relationship with, 61, 98, 374–5
    brutality of, 268
    Catholic Church: adherence to, 94–105; destruction planned by, 105; Pius XI's endorsement of him, 178; religion of, 96; resistance to, 178; response to, 175–6; support sought by, 179
    charisma of, 290–1
    childhood of, 293, 322–4
    Churchill's description of, 31, 278
    compassion of, 35–6
    coprophilia of, 37–8, 269, 352, 365–71 (*see also* Scatology and Anal fixation)
    courage of, 38
    criticism of, inability to accept, 38–9
    cult of personality, 130
    description of: by Burckhard, 34; by Churchill, 31, 278; by Lloyd George, 31; by Speer, 33
    divine mission of, 97–100, 233, 267
    dual nature of, 33–5, 173, 269–70
    Dunkirk unfinished by, 231–2
    Edmund, funeral of, 337–8
    electrocardiograms of, 264–5
    evil in, 291, 347
    failures of, 198–9, 284–5

Hitler, Adolf (*cont.*)
    father of (Alois): childhood abuse by,
        328–9; 'Jewishness' of, 339–40;
        memory of, 325; rape of mother by,
        335–7, 372
    fears of, 43, 168–70, 235
    games of, 41
    Göring's devotion to, 279
    government powers of, 13, 186
    grandiosity of, 39–40, 268, 285–7
    health of, 26, 48, 246, 262–6, 333–4,
        342–3
    Hitler, Alois (*see* Hitler, Adolf, father
        of)
    Hitler, Klara (*see* Hitler, Adolf, mother
        of)
    Holocaust, 101–2, 189–96, 239–40,
        272; therapeutic for, 272
    homoerotic relationships of, 64–6
    homosexuality, attitude towards, 66,
        182
    humour of, 43, 267
    hysterical blindness of, 342–3
    identification: with Barbarossa, 235;
        with Friedrich II, 4; with Messiah,
        279; with Wotan, 103, 287, 469n121
    ideology of, 129–34
    imprisonment of, 53, 77, 431–2n223
    incest: with mother, 335, 372–3; with
        niece, 372
    infantilism in, 40–3, 277, 370
    Jewish grandfather of, 325–6, 329–31
    Jews: as disease, 46, 193–4, 277; early
        opinions about, 54; obsession with,
        275–8, 330–2, 372; symbolic of
        father, 339–40; wars caused by,
        121–2 (*see also* Holocaust)
    Last Political Testament of, 40, 44,
        143, 195
    Lebensraum, attitude towards, 134–5
    legacy of, 349–50

Hitler, Adolf (*cont.*)
    library of, 74, 111–12
    Liebenfels, influence of, 111–13
    Lohengrin painting, 87
    marriage, attitude towards, 59–60
    medical records of, 463–4n122 (*see
        also* Hitler, Adolf, health of)
    megalomania of, 286
    Mein Kampf, 43, 44, 58, 65, 73, 77–8,
        135, 137, 165, 169, 325, 337; Hit-
        ler's childhood memories in, 325;
        holy writ, substitute for, 137; primal
        scene in, 337; propaganda discussed
        in, 169
    Messiah, identification with, 136, 279;
        mistrust in, 50–1
    Monumental History of Humanity, The,
        39, 77
    Morell, Theodor: treatment by, 48, 265
        (*see also* Hitler, Adolf, health of)
    mother of (Klara): abused by husband,
        327, 335–7, 372; conflicted feelings
        towards, 283, 332–8; Germany as,
        339–40; remembered as icon by,
        325
    Night of the Long Knives instigated
        by, 77, 182–3
    Norse mythology, interest in, 74, 87,
        107–9
    obsessions: coprophilic, 37–8, 269,
        352, 365–71; with blood, 47, 276–8;
        with castration, 56; with cleanliness,
        45, 283; with contamination, 45–6,
        269, 283–4; with death, 27–8, 53–6,
        82–3, 235, 268; with eyes, 32–3;
        with hands, 32–3, 55, 89; with Jews,
        275–8, 330–2, 372; with mothers,
        174; with sado-masochism, 79; with
        space, 233–4; with time, 48–54,
        334; with wolves, 46, 108
    occult beliefs of, 111–13

Hitler, Adolf (*cont.*)
  Od-Ray Theory, belief in, 111
  Operation Barbarossa, as self-
    defeating behaviour, 238–9
  oralism of, 41
  paganism of, 103, 107–9, 269n121, 287
  painting of, Viennese Academy of Art
    rejects as student, 284–5
  paranoia of, 280–1
  personality of, 227–30, 279–82
  photographs, refusal to allow, 278
  poetry of, 78–82
  Poland, on invasion of, 51
  policies of, affected by personality,
    229, 279–82
  political: appeal of, 161–8; failures of,
    171; skills of, 170–5
  Political Testament of (*see* Hitler,
    Adolf, Last Political Testament of)
  prudishness of, 37
  pseudonyms of, 278, 413n185
  psychiatric examinations of, possible,
    262, 378–9, 491n2
  psychological continuity of, 265
  psychological manipulation of: audi-
    ence, 273–4; Goebbels, 278; Speer,
    278
  Psychologie der Massen used by, 272–3
  psychology inadequate to explain,
    289–90
  psychoneurosis of, 262
  racial purity, attitude towards, 132 (*see
    also Volksgemeinschaft*)
  Raubal, Geli, Hitler's niece, 60, 184,
    265, 366
  reading habits of, 73–5
  relationships of, quality, 267, 269–70
  religion of, 92, 96–105 (*see also* Hitler,
    paganism of)
  rigidity of, 43–4, 281

Hitler, Adolf (*cont.*)
  role-playing by, 278, 280
  Roosevelt, suspicions about, 238
  sado-masochism of, 62, 184, 284, 328–
    9, 366–8
  Schlieffen Plan changed by, 231–2
  Second World War: desired by, 227;
    first official act of, 227; no planning
    for, 230; reaction to beginning of,
    240–1; responsibility for, 227–30
  self-defeating behaviour of, 172, 230,
    232–3, 236, 238–41, 284–5
  self-doubt of, 39–40, 51
  self-image of, 35
  sermons of, 101–2
  sex partners: audience as, 273–4;
    Braun, Eva as, 374; mother figures,
    373; Reiter, Maria as, 373; suicides
    of, 373–4, 398n326; youth of, 373
  sexual practices of, 62, 269, 283,
    365–71, 373; coprophilia, 365–71
  siblings, deaths of, 326
  Stefanie, imaginary relationship to, 60
  suicide of, 88, 286–7, 470n215
  supernatural beliefs of, 111–13
  syphilitic infection, possible, 265,
    463–4n122
  'Table Conversations,' 37–8, 43, 344,
    393n224
  terror, as tool of, 168–70
  testicle missing in, 333–4
  Thompson interview of, 166
  trial of, 59, 173–4
  unworthy feelings of, 283–4
  U.S., opinions about, 237
  U.S., war against self-defeating, 237
  veracity of, 50–1
  Viennese Academy of Art rejects,
    284–5
  Wagner family, relationship with, 233

Hitler, Adolf (*cont.*)
  Wilhelm II: attitude towards, 122,
    199–200; comparison with, 347–51
  women: political supporters of, 176;
    appeal to, 62–4
  work habits of, 188–9
  World War II (*see* Second World War)
  Wotan, identification with, 103, 287,
    469n121
  writings of, 40, 44, 77–83, 133, 137,
    143, 169, 195, 228, 269, 325, 337
  written orders, aversion to, 188–9,
    194–5
  youth attracted to, 177–8
Hitler, Alois (Schickelgruber), 326–31;
  abuse of Adolf, 328–9; abuse of wife,
  327–8; children of, 326–7; Hitler's
  memories of, 325; illegitimacy of,
  329–31; Jewishness of, alleged,
  329–31
Hitler, Klara Pölzl, abuse by husband,
  327, 335–7, 372; as symbol for Germany, 339; children of, 326–7; Hitler's
  conflicted feelings towards, 283,
  332–8; Hitler's memories of, 325;
  mothering by, 326–8, 333
Hoffmann, Heinrich, 91
Holland, Wilhelm II's abdication to, 5
Holocaust, 102–3, 189–96, 239–40, 272;
  backers of, 190–1; British Foreign
  office's refusal to accept escapees
  from, 192; European support of, 191;
  Goldhagen on, 191; Hitler responsible
  for, 193–5; Hitler, therapeutic for, 272;
  Jewish police cooperation in, 192–3;
  Jewish resistance to, 193; planning of,
  189–90; refugees from, rejection of,
  192; religious foundations in favour of,
  102–3; Russian defeat cause of, 190;
  support for, European, 191; U.S. State

Department's refusal to accept escap-
  ees from, 192
Homosexuality
  Eulenburg's, 26–7
  Heines's, 182;
  Hitler's advisers', 182
  Hitler's ambiguous relationships with
    Hess and Speer, 64–5
  Krupp's, 27–8
  Moltke's, 27–8
  persecution of, 66
  Röhm's, 182
  Sturmabteilung's, 66, 182
  Wilhelm II: ambiguousness of sexual
    orientation, 27; homosexual friends
    of, 208–9
Honour Cross. *See* Mother's Award
Horst Wessel, 420–1n66
Hülsen-Haesseler, Dietrich von (German
  count), anal fixation of, 28–9
Humour, German, anality of, 254;
  Hitler's, 43, 267; Wilhelm II's, 250

I.G. Farben, Auschwitz labour camp of,
  190–1
Ilsemann, Sigurd von, on Wilhelm II,
  inflexibility of, 14; political hopes of,
  200–1; role-playing of, 19
Iron Cross, Hitler's, 342
Irving, David, on Hitler's ignorance of
  Holocaust, 195

Japan, German treaty obligations
  towards, 237; Operation Barbarossa
  unknown by, 234; Wilhelm II, attitude
  towards, 114, 156
Jewish police, cooperation of, in Holocaust, 192–3
Jews, 102–3, as dirt, 46; as disease,
  193–4, 277–8; Hitler's obsession with,

275–8; Holocaust of, 102–3, 189–96, 239–40, 272; Wilhelm II, attitude towards, 120–3; World Wars caused by, 121–2. *See also* Anti-Semitism and Holocaust

July Crisis (1914), Wilhelm II's role in, 213–26

Junge, Gertrude Humps (Traudl), 40, 63

Kahr, Gustav von, murder of, 184

KdF. *See* Strength through Joy Organization

Keitel, Wilhelm (German field marshal), 238

Kershaw, Ian, on German people's support of Holocaust, 195

King, William Lyon Mackenzie, spiritualism of, 244

Knight, Robert K., borderline personality disorder, definition of, 266–7

Kohut, Elizabeth, on Hitler's narcissistic grandiosity, 285–6

Kohut, Heinz, on acting as a defence mechanism, 252; on narcissistic personality disorder, 246

Kohut, Thomas
on Eulenburg, 27–8
Wilhelm II: failures analysed by, 196–7; need to be heard identified by, 258

Konzentrationslager. See Concentration camps

Kraft durch Freude. See Strength through Joy Organization

Kriegervereine, 127–8

Kriegsschuldfrage. See War Guilt Question

Krüger Telegram, English reaction to, 152; Wilhelm II's disowning of, 251

Krupp von Bohlen und Halbach, Gustav,

correspondence with Wilhelm II, 212–13

Krupp, Friedrich Alfred, homosexuality of, 27–8

Kubizek, August, on Hitler's reading, 74

Kurth, Gertrud, 'The Jew and Adolf Hitler,' 376–7

Labour camps, I.G. Farben's use of, 190–1

Labour Front, 98, 187

Labour movement, Wilhelm II's reaction to, 140–2

Landsberg am Lech prison, 53, 77, 431–2n223

Lasswell, Harold, policy-personality theories of, 254

Last Political Testament, Hitler's, on Holocaust, 40, 44, 143, 195

Le Bon, Gustav, Hitler's use of theories of crowd, 272–3

Lebensraum, Hitler on, 134–5

Ley, Robert, 98, 185, 187

Liebenberg Circle, 27, 28

Liebenfels, Lanz von, 112–13

Lieberman, Max, 85

Linge, Heinz, 98

Lloyd George, David, Hitler described by, 31, 278

Locarno Pact, 225

Lohengrin, Hitler as, 87

Ludendorff, Eric (German general), dictator, 222–3; ignored by Hitler, 171; Munich march ordered by, 171–2; paganism of, 222

Luther, Martin, anti-Semitism of, 103; doctrine of two realms of, 126

Mackenzie, Donald, Sir, 120

Majestätsbeleidigung, 250. *See also* Wilhelm II, criticism of

Manic-depression, Wilhelm II's, 246
Mann, Thomas, characterization of Nazism, 226; on the coming of the Great War, 24
Marineschwärmerei, 145–6
Mars, Wilhelm II as, 208
Mason, Tim, on economy of Germany, 224, 227
May, Karl, 74
Mayer, Arno, on Holocaust as result of defeat in Russia, 190
Medusa, Hitler's mother as, 333; Wilhelm II's archaeological find of, 69
megalomania, collective, of Germans, 206
Mein Kampf, 43, 44, 58, 65, 73, 77–8, 135, 137, 165, 169, 325, 337; Hitler's childhood memories in, 325; holy writ, substitute for, 137; primal scene in, 337; propaganda discussed in, 169
Meinecke, Friedrich, demanding a Führer, 128
Mendelssohn, Franz von, 68, 121
Menninger, Karl, on betrayals by mothers, 333; on music, 88; on suicide, 287
Menzel, Adolf von, 4
Messiah, Hitler as, 60, 99–100, 131, 136–7, 180, 279; Wilhelm II on, 94
Militarism, 127–8
Mischerlisch, Alexander, 65
Moltke, Helmuth von (Prussian field marshal), popularity of, 127
Moltke, Helmuth von (the younger; German general)
  Chief of Staff, unsuitability for position of, 160
  War Council, 210
  Wilhelm II: criticized by, 25, 148; Schlieffen Plan not divulged to, 222
Moltke, Kuno von, homosexuality of, 27–8

Mommsen, Hans, 186, 363
Mommsen, Wolfgang, 363
Montague, Mary, 26
Monumental History of Humanity, The, 39, 77
Moore, Barrington, on outrage as revolutionary, 170
Morell, Theodor, Hitler's medical treatment by, 48, 264–5
Morley, John, Wilhelm II's charm, 10
Motherhood, Hitler on, 59; Hitler's poetry about, 82
Motherland, Germany as, 339–40
Mother's Award, 59
Müller, Georg Alexander von (German admiral), on Wilhelm II's mental condition, 7, 220–1
Munich, as holy city, 136
Mussolini, Benito, 130, 237
Myth, Hitler's use of, 274–5

Narcissism, borderline personality disorder, similarity to, 266–7; description of, 246–8; malevolent or malignant, 291–2; therapeutic value of, 253; Victoria, Princess, 324; Wilhelm II's, 243, 246–54, 261
National Socialism, as religion, 131, 135–6, 138–9, 180–1; creation of, by Naumann, 164; Friedrich Wilhelm I as first adherent of, 4; ideology of, 129–40; Munich as holy city of, 136; roots of, 112–13; use of term, 164; youth attracted to, 177–8. See also Nazi party
Naumann, Friedrich, established first National Socialist party, 164
Naval League, 145
Nazi ideology. See National Socialism
Nazi party, Church endorsement of, 226; establishment of power by, 163, 182–8;

Stahlhelm as precursor of, 226;
Wilhelm II, attitudes towards, 200–2.
See also National Socialism
Neuert, Th. *See* Goldzier, Hans
New Order, 112–13, 133, 164
New Temple, 112
Nicholas II, Tsar (of Russia) and Wilhelm
II, Björko agreement with, 9; corre-
spondence with, 114, 149; Nicholas II
denigrated by Wilhelm II, 149
Nicolson, Harold, on Hitler's sexuality,
64
Night of the Long Knives, 77, 161,
182–4
Nordic mythology, Hitler's interest in, 74,
87, 107–9; Wagner's interest in, 87;
Wilhelm II's interest in, 87, 106–7. *See
also* Paganism
Numerology, Wilhelm II's belief in,
110–11
Nuremberg, Racial Laws, 277, 331; ral-
lies, 181, 130; stadium, 89

'Observations on Workers' Problems,'
140
Od-Ray Theory (*Od-Strahlentheorie*),
111
Oedipal problems, in borderline personal-
ity disorder, 267
Old Fighters, 174
Operation Barbarossa, 234, 236, 238–9
Ostara, 112
Oxford Union debate, anti-war, 228

Paganism, 175; Hitler's interest in,
107–9; Ludendorff's practice of, 222;
Wilhelm II's interest in, 106–7
Pan-German League, 121, 145, 154
Paranoia, German, 208, 210
Parkinsonism, Hitler's possible, 262–4

Pasewalk Hospital, Hitler's vocation
resolved at, 343
Patriotic societies, 145
Peck, Scott, on evil and malevolent nar-
cissism, 291–2
Picker, Henry, 37
Pius XI (Pope), Hitler endorsed by, 178
Plague in Florence, 53
Pless, Daisy of. *See* Daisy of Pless
poetry, Hitler's, 78–82; Wilhelm II's,
76–7
Poland, invasion of, 51, 53, 225
Politics and art, 92
'Potsdam Council,' non-existence of, 214
Prague, threatened destruction of, 53
Propaganda, Dietrich's responsibilities
for, 188; First World War, preceding,
210; Goebbels on, 168–9; Hitler's
mastery of, 169–70; Ministry of, film
of Reichstag opening distributed by,
179–80; pro-war, 228; terrorism, form
of, 169
'Proposals for Improving the Conditions
of Workers,' 140
Protestants, Hitler's supporters, 176
Prudishness, of Hitler, 37; of Wilhelm II,
9, 84
Psychologie der Massen, Hitler's use of,
272–3
Psychology, inability to explain Hitler,
289–90. *See also* Germany, psychological condition of; Hitler, psychological;
and Wilhelm II, psychological

Queiroz, Eca de, Wilhelm II, as actor,
18–19

Racial purity, Hitler on, 132. *See also*
Volksgemeinschaft
Racism, 113–24. *See also* Anti-Semitism

Radziwill, Marie, on Wilhelm II, 69, 157
Rathenau, Walther, on dual personality of Wilhelm II, 6
Raubal, Geli, 60, 184, 265, 366
Redlich, Fritz C., Hitler's arteritis diagnosed by, 265
Reich, use of term, 164–5
Reichmann, Eva, Hitler's sexual rapport with audience described by, 274
Reichstag, 23, 25, 129
  election of 1930, 163
  Enabling Act passed by, 176, 178
  Hitler's opening of, 178
  legislation of, 144–6, 176, 178
  Night of the Long Knives condoned by, 186
  Wilhelm II: alienation of, 151; criticized by, 154
Reiter, Maria, Hitler sex partner, 373
Religion, divine missions of Hitler and Wilhelm II, 208, 345; Hitler as Messiah, 136, 279; Nazism as, 135–9; paganism, 106–9, 175; Wilhelm II's, 92–6. See also Catholic Church and Christian Church
Revolutions, Barrington Moore's concepts of causes of, 170; labour's role in, 140–1; Wilhelm II's concepts of causes of, 140–1
Rhineland, German occupation of, 229; remilitarization of, 23
Ribbentrop, Joachim von (German foreign minister), 53; propaganda responsibilities of, 188
Riefenstahl, Leni, Nuremberg rally filmed by, 181
Ringelblum, Emmanuel, diary of, 193
Ritter, Gerhard, 127, 262–3
Röhm, Ernst, 99; homosexuality of, 64, 182, 185

Röhm Purge. See Night of the Long Knives
Roosevelt, Franklin (U.S. president), Barbarossa as good news for, 238; death as sign to Hitler, 4; Hitler's suspicions of, 238
Roosevelt, Theodore (U.S. president), Wilhelm II interview alarms, 156–7
Rosenberg, Alfred, educational responsibilities of, 187; on Führerprinzip, 131
Royal coup d'état, Wilhelm II's reaction to, 146–7
Rundstedt, Gerd von (German general), on Dunkirk, 232
Russia, German defeat in, as causing Holocaust, 190; invasion by Hitler, 135, 233–4, 236, 238–9; prisoners of war, extermination of, 190, 194; Wilhelm II, attitude towards, 208, 260

SA. See Sturmabteilung
sado-masochism, of Germany, 164; of Hitler, 62, 79, 184, 284, 366–8
Saint John, anti-Semitism of, 103
Scatology, comparative international interest in, 484n3–7; German preoccupation with, 352–5. See also Coprophilia and Anal fixation
Schacht, Horace Greely Hjalmer, 52, 187
Scheidemann, Philip (German chancellor), 163
Schirach, Baldur von, Hitler youth director, 187
Schleicher, Kurt von (German general and chancellor), murder of, 184
Schlieffen Plan, 160, 215; changed by Hitler, 231–2; Wilhelm II's ignorance of, 211, 222
Schreber, Daniel Moritz, Princess Victoria influenced by, 306–10, 475n69

Schroeder, Christa (Hitler's secretary), 63, 97, 195

Schüssler, Wilhelm, character assessment of Wilhelm II, 245

Schutz-Staffel (SS), 47, 49, 54; death camps staffed by, 194; Himmler commander of, 183; homosexuality in, 66; Jesuits model for, 137; Night of the Long Knives executed by, 183–4; Stempfle, Father Bernhard, murdered by, 77; stud farms of, 59

Scientists, Holocaust, support of, 191

Second World War
   beginning of: continuity with First World War, 224, 362–4; first moves, 229; Hitler's reaction to, 240–1; in 1933, 227
   economic results of, 204–5
   end of, 281
   First World War continuation, 224, 362–4
   German troops undersupplied, 230–1
   Hitler: euphoria at beginning of, 240–1; lack of plan for, 230; responsibility for, 227–30
   Jews as cause of, 122
   plans ready by 1940, 228
   U.S., war declared against, 237–8
   Wilhelm II, leadership of, 250
   See also Holocaust

'Secret Conversations.' See 'Table Conversations'

Seekt, Hans von (German general), Versailles Treaty defiance, 224–5

Serbia, Austrian problems with, 211; reply to Austrian ultimatum, Wilhlem II's reaction to, 214

Seven Years' War, 4

Shirer, William I, on German continuity, 362; on Hitler's femininity, 64

Siegesallee, 84

Sigismund (German prince), birth and death of, 316–18

Sobibor death camp uprising, 193

Social Democrats, growth of, 151

Socialism, Bismarck's reaction to, 140; coup d'état and threat of, 146; forbidden to youth, 151; Wilhelm II, reaction to, 140

Society for the Expansion of Germanism Abroad, 145

Sombart, Werner, on German militarism, 127

Speer, Albert (German economic minister; Hitler's architect)
   economic responsibilities of, 187, 231, 278
   Hitler: described by, 33, 105; drawings of, 89, 227; dual personality of, 269; relationship with, homoerotic, 65–6, 267; responsibility for Holocaust described, 195; scatology of, 37–8

SS. See Schutz-Staffel

Stahlhelm, Nazi precursor, 226

Stalingrad, 98

Steinberg, Jonathan, on paranoia of Germany, 259–60

Stempfle, Father Bernhard, murder by SS, 77, 184; on Hitler's coprophilia, 366–7

Stern, J.P., on Führerprinzip, 131

Storm troops. See Sturmabteilung

Strasser, Otto, on Hitler, 57

Streicher, Julius, sexual licence of, 175, 185

Strength through Joy Organization, 167

Stresemann, Gustav (German chancellor): German expansion planned by, 225; Locarno Pact, 225; Nobel peace prize, 225

Strike of 1918, Wilhelm II's reaction to, 17

Stuck, Franz von, 56, 91, 108

Sturmabteilung, Beefsteak Nazis, 183; early history, 182–4; German army, threatened by, 183; German royal family membership in, 201; homosexuality in, 182; political agents, 176

Suicide, Hitler's, 287–8

'Table Conversations,' 37–8, 43, 334; editions of, 393n224

Terrorism, Hitler's use of, 168–70

Third Reich, administration of, 187–9

Thompson, Dorothy, Hitler interviewed by, 166

Tischgespräche. See 'Table Conversations'

Totalitarianism, 203–4

Toynbee, Arnold J., Hitler described by, 278

Transvestism, Wilhelm II, attitude towards, 29

Trieb, Hitler's search for, 111

Tripartite Pact, validity of, 237–8

Trunk, Isaiah, on collaboration of Jewish leaders, 192

Tschudi, Hugo von, 85

United States, Hitler's opinions about racial mix of, 237; Holocaust escapees turned back by, 192; war declared against, 237

Versailles Treaty, German resentment of, 224–5; War Guilt Clause, 216–17

Veteran's societies. *See Kriegervereine*

Victor Emmanuel II, King (of Italy), denigrated by Wilhelm II, 149

Victoria, Princess Royal (of Great Britain) and Empress Frederick, 294–6, 297–324

Albert, Prince (father of): death, effect of, 301–7; partner of, 302–7; relationship with, 299–307

as mother, 307–23

death of, 315

Friedrich III's cancer denied by, 313–14

husband of (*see* Friedrich III)

imperiousness of, 298

narcissistic impairment of, 324

sacred mission of, 302–4

Schreber's influence on, 307–10

sons mourned by, 317–21

Wilhelm II: abuse of, 310–12, 315–16; birth of, 304–5; criticism of, 247; hostile relationship with, 312–14; insanity of, 253; volubility of, 17; withered arm appalls, 305

Victoria, Princess Royal (of England; Empress Frederick)

correspondence on Prince Albert's death, 301–2

Wilhelm II, correspondence with, 8, 18, 86, 93, 153–4

Victoria, Queen (of Great Britain), 3, 27; death of, 21

Viennese Academy of Art, Hitler rejected by, 284

Volksgemeinschaft, 134. *See also* Racial purity

Wagener, Otto, on Hitler's identification with Jesus Christ, 101–2

Wagner family, 61; Hitler's friendship with, 61, 119, 233; Wilhelm II's friendship with, 68

Wagner, Richard, Hitler inspired by, 87–8, 233; Wilhelm II inspired by, 73, 87

Waldemar, Prince (of Germany), Princess Victoria's mourning of, 320–1

War, as social force, 205–6; Germany fated to, 208

War Council, of Wilhelm II, 209–10
War Guilt Question, in Germany, 216–17, 356–8
War Guilt Review Office, First World War documents obtained from, reliability of, 356–8
Warlimont, Walter (German general), on Dunkirk, 232
Warsaw Ghetto Uprising, 193
Weber, Max, on German expansion, 128
Weimar Republic, Versailles Treaty, non-compliance with, 225
Wessel, Horst, song, 420–1n66
Wheeler-Bennett, John, Wilhelm II, character assessment of, 245
Wilhelm I, King (of Prussia) and German Kaiser, 4; Wilhelm II's exaltation of, 110–11
Wilhelm II, King (of Prussia) and German Kaiser, 1–29
  abdication of, 223
  absolutist tendencies of, 125–9
  administration of, 157–61
  advisers intimidated by, 257
  advisers of, 160–1
  Aegir identified with, 106
  agent of change, 348–9
  Albert, King (of Belgium) misled by, 211
  Alexander III, Tsar (of Russia), as prospective host of, 142
  anality of, 28–9
  anti-Semitism of, 22, 28, 113–17, 120–3
  appearance of, 5, 7
  arm deformation of, 244
  army, relations with, 127, 146–7
  art of, 86–7
  artistic taste of, 83–6, 92
  Auguste Viktoria (Dona; wife of), relationship with, 21, 26–7, 360

Wilhelm II (cont.)
  Austria, blank cheque for, 211, 213
  Balfour's character assessment of, 245
  Belgian invasion, reaction to, 7
  birth problems of, 244, 304–5, 456n9
  Bismarck: dependence on, 248; disagreement with, over labour, 140; resignation of, 21–2, 142–4
  blank cheque, 211, 213
  bloodthirstiness of, 7, 9
  Boxer Rebellion, reaction to, 7, 114
  brain damage, possible, 456n9
  British navy, reaction to, 152
  brothers' deaths, effect on, 317–18, 320–1
  Bülow, dependence on, 247
  Chamberlain, influence of, 16, 94, 118–19, 210
  character of, 6, 8–12, 15, 18–21, 119, 125–9, 158, 245–54, 250–1, 252, 255–6, 347, 350
  charm of, 10, 11
  childhood of, 293–7: painful memories, 312
  compared with Hitler, 347–51
  compassion of, 8–10, 119
  correspondence of: with Chamberlain, 16, 94, 118; with Edward, Prince of Wales, 8, 152; with Emperor Franz-Joseph, 22; with Krupp, on determination to declare war, 212–13; with Mary Montague, 26; with Nicholas II, 114, 149; with Victoria, Queen (of Great Britain), 8, 18, 86, 93, 153–4
  coup d'état, response to, 146–7; courage of, 11
  criticism of: by Germans, 154–5; inability to accept, 23–6, 250–1
  Daily Telegraph interview, 152–6, 208

Wilhelm II (*cont.*)

death, fascination with, 8

death of, 360–1

defeats, avoidance strategies for, 257

delegate of mother, 303–8

delusions of, 252–3

denigration of notables by, 149–50

destiny of, 4–5, 104, 125–7, 208, 304

diplomatic corps, relations with, 148–9

domination by, 14–15

dual personality of, 211

education of, 124–5

Edward VII, King (of England): correspondence with, 8; distrusted by, 156

electric shock treatments of, 311–12

Entente Cordiale, attitude towards, 208

Eulenburg, relationship with, 21, 26–7

evil absent in, 347, 350

exhibitionism of, 15, 248

exile of, 5, 359–61

failures of, 11, 196–8, 208–9

father of (*see* Friedrich III)

First World War: analysis of causes of, 14; declared by, 214–15; loss of power during, 220–2; mixed emotions about, 212, 215; reaction to beginning of, 240–1; responsibility for, 217–19, 251; role in, 205; speech declaring, 219–20

Franz Ferdinand, Crown Prince (of Austria), meeting with, 211

Franz-Joseph, Emperor (of Austria), correspondence with, 22

Friedrich III, Kaiser (father of), relationship with, 296–7

funeral of, 202

Germany: vision of, 6; mirror of his psychology, 255–6

Wilhelm II (*cont.*)

Göring, guest of, 201

grandiosity of, 15, 248

Great Britain: dual attitude towards, 7; frustration by, 251–2; perceived as enemy by, 156; unpopularity in, 151–6

habits of, 5–6

Hague Peace Conference, attitude towards, 9

health of, 244–5, 304–6, 311–12, 456n9

Hermine, relationship with, 21, 26–7

Herzl supported by, 121

Hinzpeter, tutor of, 319–20

Hitler: attitude towards, 199–200; comparison with, 347–51; Final Solution of, reaction to, 122; trial of, reaction to, 174

homosexuality: attitude towards, 26–9, 208–9; repressed, 27–9

humour of, 250

Hun Speech, 7

immaturity of, 12–14

infidelities of, 27

inflexibility of, 12

insecurity of, 248

instability of, 208–10

intelligence of, 68–9

interviews with, 151–7, 208

Japanese, attitude towards, 114 (*see also* 'Yellow Peril')

Jews: attitude towards, 120–3; parents positive towards, 120

July Crisis, role in, 213

Krüger Telegram, disowning of, 251

labour relations of, 140–2

languages spoken by, 68

legacy of, 348

legislation of, 144–6

Wilhelm II (*cont.*)
  library contents of, 73
  lying of, 20–1
  Majestätsbeleidigung, 250
  manic-depressive diagnosis of, 246
  marriages of, 26–7
  Mars, as, 208
  masochism of, 256
  Medusa, monograph on, 69
  mental ability of, 220–2
  military: leadership of, 245; relations
    with, 147–8
  mistrust by, 21–2
  musical taste of, 87
  narcissism of, 243, 246–54: policy
    effects, 261; therapeutic value of,
    253; Victoria (Empress Frederick),
    324
  National Socialists: attitude towards,
    200–2; connections in family of,
    201, 360–1
  navy: build-up of sponsored by, 144–6;
    competition with Britain, 255
  Nicholas II, Tsar (of Russia), Björko
    agreement with, 9
  Night of the Long Knives condoned
    by, 185
  Norse mythology, interest in, 87,
    106–7
  occult beliefs of, 109–11
  Pan-German League's criticism of, 154
  personality: dualism of, 6; effect of on
    policy, 254–61
  poetry of, 76–7
  policy, personality reflected in, 254–61
  political hopes of, 200–1
  popularity of, 5, 147–57
  projection of blame by, 251
  prudishness of, 9, 84
  pseudonyms of, 24

Wilhelm II (*cont.*)
  psychological condition of, during
    First World War, 221
  reading habits of, 72–3
  Reichstag, relationship to, 129, 151,
    154
  relationships of, quality, 21
  religion of, 92–6
  role-playing of, 18–20, 252
  scatology of, 9
  Schlieffen Plan: ignorance of, 211;
    unknown by, 222
  Schüssler's character assessment of,
    245
  Second World War: German victories
    his own, 250; observations on, 202
  self-defeating behaviour of, 241, 255–7
  self-esteem of, 306
  sensitivity of, 10, 249
  Serbian reply, reaction to, 214
  sermons of, 94–5
  speeches of, 16, 76, 114, 219–20
  supernatural beliefs of, 109–11
  Supreme War Lord, 207–8, 219–23
  suspicion of other countries by, 260–2
  transvestism, attitude towards, 29
  treatments for deformities of, 310–12
  Victoria, Princess (Empress Frederick;
    mother of): abused by, 310–12,
    315–16; correspondence with, 8,
    18, 93, 153–4; criticism by, 17, 247,
    253; narcissism of, 324; relation-
    ship with, 299–307, 312–13, 315
  Victoria, Queen (of Great Britain): cor-
    respondence with, 8, 18, 86, 93,
    153–4; death of, 21
  vindictiveness of, 10
  volubility of, 16–17
  Wagner, Richard: family, friendship
    with, 68–9; influence of, 73, 87

Wilhelm II (*cont.*)
  War Council (1912), 209–10
  war criminal, 359
  war guilt denied by, 217
  Wheeler-Bennett's character assessment of, 245
  women, attitude towards, 26–7, 60, 150–1
  working habits of, 158
  World War I (*see* First World War)
  World War II (*see* Second World War)
  Wotan, as, 106
  writings of, 75–6, 140
  Zeppelin, reaction to, 18
Wolf, Johanna (Hitler's secretary), 63
Women, Hitler's political relations with, 57–63, 176; Prince Albert's attitude

towards, 229; Wilhelm II's attitude towards, 26–7, 60, 150–1
World War I (*see* First World War)
World War II (*see* Second World War)
Wortley, Edward Stuart, Wilhelm II's reported conversation with, 152–6
Wotan, identification with, Hitler's, 103, 107–8, 287, 469n212; Wilhelm II's, 106
'Yellow Peril,' 86, 114–17

Zeppelin, Graf Ferdinand von, Wilhelm II, reaction to, 18
Zhukov, Georgi (Russian marshal), counteroffensive by, 238
Zorn, Anders, 84